Imperatives and Commands

OXFORD STUDIES IN TYPOLOGY AND LINGUISTIC THEORY

General Editors: Ronnie Cann, *University of Edinburgh*; William Croft, *University of New Mexico*; Martin Haspelmath, *Max Planck Institute for Evolutionary Anthropology*; Nicholas Evans, *University of Melbourne*; Anna Siewierska, *University of Lancaster*

PUBLISHED

Classifiers: A Typology of Noun Categorization Devices
Alexandra Y. Aikhenvald

Imperatives and Commands
Alexandra Y. Aikhenvald

Auxiliary Verb Constructions
Gregory D. S. Anderson

Pronouns
D. N. S. Bhat

Subordination
Sonia Cristofaro

The Paradigmatic Structure of Person Marking
Michael Cysouw

Adpositions: Function marking in languages
Claude Hagège

Indefinite Pronouns
Martin Haspelmath

Anaphora
Yan Huang

Reference in Discourse
Andrej A. Kibrik

The Emergence of Distinctive Features
Jeff Mielke

Applicative Constructions
David A. Peterson

Copulas
Regina Pustet

The Noun Phrase
Jan Rijkhoff

Intransitive Predication
Leon Stassen

Predicative Possession
Leon Stassen

Co-Compounds and Natural Coordination
Bernhard Wälchli

PUBLISHED IN ASSOCIATION WITH THE SERIES

The World Atlas of Language Structures
edited by Martin Haspelmath, Matthew Dryer, Bernard Comrie, and David Gil

IN PREPARATION

Reciprocals
Nicholas Evans

Imperatives and Commands

ALEXANDRA Y. AIKHENVALD

The Cairns Institute
James Cook University

OXFORD

UNIVERSITY PRESS

OXFORD
UNIVERSITY PRESS

Great Clarendon Street, Oxford, OX2 6DP,
United Kingdom

Oxford University Press is a department of the University of Oxford.
It furthers the University's objective of excellence in research, scholarship,
and education by publishing worldwide. Oxford is a registered trade mark of
Oxford University Press in the UK and in certain other countries

© Alexandra Y. Aikhenvald 2010

British Library Cataloguing in Publication Data
Data available

Library of Congress Cataloging in Publication Data
Data available

ISBN 978–0–19–920790–9 (hbk.)
ISBN 978–0–19–966555–6 (pbk.)

Printed in Great Britain by
MPG Books Group, Bodmin and King's Lynn

For Yobate, Ropate, Nyaywi, and Serewhali,
the inspiration behind this work

Contents

Plea

This book is not the last word on imperatives or on commands. I welcome reactions, counterexamples, new facts, new ideas, to further develop, refine, and perhaps redefine the hypotheses and generalizations put forward here. Please send them to me at the Cairns Institute, James Cook University, Cairns, North Queensland, 4870, Australia, or, in a quicker way, to Alexandra. Aikhenvald@jcu.edu.au or nyamamayratakw@gmail.com.

Preface and acknowledgements

My first encounter with dauntingly complex imperatives was through field-work on Tariana, an Arawak language in the Vaupés River Basin in Brazil, and the neighbouring East Tucanoan languages. When I ran across several prohibitives in Manambu, my field language in the Papuan area, with only one positive imperative, I was astounded. As a way of coming to grips with these new facts, I decided to undertake a typological study of imperatives and command.

In January 2003, I wrote a 100-page typological essay, 'Imperatives and other commands', accompanied by a list of suggestions for fieldworkers on how to describe commands. The text, based on data collected from about 300 languages, was a 'position paper' for a Local Workshop on 'Imperatives and Other Commands' which ran throughout 2003 at the old Research Centre for Linguistic Typology in Melbourne. The workshop featured presentations on forty languages, spanning Europe, Asia, Africa, the Americas, Oceania, and Australia. The position paper remained available on the website for two years, and was viewed by over 300 visitors. That preliminary draft manuscript—which was not intended for reference or quoting—came to be a precursor of this book.

I am indebted to many people, of different continents and backgrounds.

My gratitude goes to all those native speakers who taught me their languages and how to command in them: Cândido, José, Jovino, Olívia, Rafael, Leo, and the late Gracialiano and Ismael Brito (speakers of Tariana of Santa Rosa); Marino, Domingo, Ismael, Jorge, and Batista Muniz (Tariana of Periquitos); Humberto Baltazar and Pedro Ângelo Tomas (Warekena); Afonso, Albino; and João Fontes, Celestino da Silva, Cecília and Laureano da Silva, and the late Marcília Rodrigues (Baniwa); the late Tiago Cardoso (Desano, Piratapuya), the late Candelário da Silva (Bare) and Alfredo Fontes (Tucano). I am forever indebted to Pauline Agnes Yuaneng Luma Laki, James Sesu Laki, David Takendu, Jacklyn Yuamali Benji Ala, Katie Teketay, Jenny Kudapa:kw, and Gemaj, and to so many others who revealed the beauty of their native Manambu (Papua New Guinea).

Indefatigable support came from those who gave me comments on earlier versions, patiently answered my questions on imperatives, provided me with references and additional sources, and commented on earlier versions of this book—Anvita Abbi, Willem Adelaar, Emma Aikhenvald (Breger), Janet Barnes, Ellen Basso, Edith Bavin, Gavan Breen, Kate Burridge, Eithne Carlin, Éva Csató, Mark Collins, Tim Curnow, Josephine Daguman, Stefan Dienst, Anthony Diller, Gerrit Dimmendaal, Carola Emkow, Pattie Epps, Franck Floricic, Bronwen Forster, Zygmunt Frajzyngier, Alice Gaby, Carol Genetti, Valeria Gerlin, Antoine Guillaume, Bernd Heine, Ken Hill, Jane Hill, Hans Henrich Hock, Lars Johanson, Brian Joseph, Christa König-Heine, Ago Künnap, Yolanda Lastra, Mary Laughren, Aet and Boris Lees, Yongxian Luo, Helle Metslang, Marianne Mithun, Ongaye Oda, Knut Olawsky, Tom Payne, Mark Post, Bob [Baːb] Rankin, Lucy Seki, Matt Shibatani, Elena Shmeleva, the late Margarethe Sparing-Chavez, Kristine Stenzel, Anne Storch, Andrew Swearingen, René van den Berg, Johan van der Auwera, the late David Watters, Nigel Vincent, Defen Yu, Ulrike Zeshan, and Ghil'ad Zuckermann.

The conference 'Omotic Utterance Type, Mood and Attitude Markers, and Linguistic Typology', organized by Azeb Amha and Maarten Mous in Leiden University (23–5 October 2008), opened new perspectives on imperatives in Omotic and Cushitic languages. I am deeply grateful to Azeb and to Maarten, and also to many fine experts in Omotic and Cushitic—Haro Hirut, Binyam Sisay, Ongaye Oda, Christian Rapold, to name just a few.

Lise Menn was instrumental in providing information on imperatives in language dissolution. Shmuel Bolozky and Ghil'ad Zuckermann provided me with fascinating materials on the newly emerging imperative paradigm in Modern Hebrew.

Invaluable comments on just about every page came from R. M. W. Dixon, without whose incisive criticism and constant encouragement and support this book would not have appeared. My son, Michael, and my many true friends were a source of constant support. Brigitta Flick carefully read through the drafts of this book and corrected it with her usual skill, perspicacity, dedication, and good humour. Thanks are equally due to her.

This volume would have never been brought to fruition without John Davey, the Linguistics Editor of Oxford University Press, with his enthusiasm and indomitable support which makes the author, and the book, feel wanted.

The stimulating atmosphere and warm support of colleagues and friends at James Cook University is what finally made it all possible.

Abbreviations

=	clitic boundary
-	morpheme boundary
1, 2, 3	1st, 2nd, 3rd person
A	transitive subject
ABL	ablative
ABS	absolutive
ACC	accusative
ACT.FOC	action focus
ADD.HON	addressee honorific
ADV	adverbializer
AFF	affix
ALL	allative
Anp	anaphoric pronoun
ANT	anticipatory
AOR	aorist
APPR	apprehensive
ART	article
ASP	aspect
ATTR	attributive
AUX	auxiliary
BAS.NP	basic non-past
BAS.VT	basic versatile tense
BEN	benefactive
CAN	canonical imperative
CAUS	causative
CESS_MOD	cessative modal
CL	classifier
COMIT	comitative
COMPL	completive
CON.IMPV	conative imperative 'try and do'
COND	conditional
CONJ	conjunction
CONT.IMPV	continuous imperative
CONV	converb
COP	copula
COREF	coreferential
CTEMP	cotemporaneous

DAT	dative
DECL	declarative
DEF	definite
DEM.F	demonstrative feminine
DEM:LOC	demonstrative locative
DEP	dependent
DEP.INTRANS	dependent intransitive
DESID	desiderative
DIM	diminutive
DIR	directional
DS	different subject
du, DU	dual
DUB	dubitative
EMPH	emphatic
ERG	ergative
excl	exclusive
F	factative tense/aspect/modality
fem, FEM	feminine
FOC	focus
FUT	future
GEN	genitive
GO.TEMP	go temporally
HON	honorific
HORT	hortative
HPL	plural of animate class
IM	imperative sentence-type suffix in Korean
IMM	immediate
IMPF	imperfective
IMPV	imperative
INC	inceptive
INCH	inchoative
incl	inclusive
IND	indicative
INDEF	indefinite
INDIV	individuation particle
INF	infinitive
INSTR	instrumental
INTENS	intensifier
INTER	interrogative
INTR, intr	intransitive
IRR	irrealis
JUSS	jussive
LIG	ligature

LIM	limiter
LK	linker
LOC	locative
MALEF	malefactive
MASC, masc	masculine
min	minimal-augmented
MOT	motion
n	neuter
NCL	noun class
NEG	negative
nf	nonfeminine
NFEM	nonfeminine
NFUT	non-future
NOM	nominative
NOMZ	nominalizer
NONACC	non-accomplished
NONCAN	non-canonical
NONDECL	non-declarative
NON.PROX	non-proximate
NPS	nonpast
nsg, NSG	nonsingular
O	object of a transitive verb
OBJ	object
OBL	oblique
OBLIG	obligation; obligative
OM	object marker
OPT	optative
p	person
PART	particle
PASS	passive
PAUS	pausal
PERF	perfect, perfective
PERI	peripheral
PERM	permissive
pl, PL	plural
PN	personal name
POL	polite speech level suffix or particle
POSS, poss	possessive
POT	potential
PRED	predicate marker
PREP	preposition
PRES	present
PRES.REP	present reported

PRF	perfective
PRIV	privative
PROH	prohibitive
PROH.GEN	prohibitive general
PROPOS	propositive
PROX	proximate
PURP	purposive
Q	question
QUOT	quotative
REC.PAST	recent past
REC.P.VIS	recent past visual
REFL	reflexive
REITR	reiterative
REL	relator
REP	reported
REQUEST	requestive
S	intransitive subject
SEC.IMPV	secondhand imperative
SEQ	sequential
sg, SG	singular
SH	subject honorific suffix
SJ	subjunctive
SS	same subject
ST.PAT.IRR	stative patient irrealis
SUB	subordinator
SUBJ	subject
SUBJ.HON	subject honorific
SUBJUNC	subjunctive
SUP.LAT	superlative 'on top'
TAM	tense, aspect, mood
TEMP	temporal
THEM	thematic
T.LNK	temporal link
TOP	topic
TOP.NON.A/S	topical non-subject
TR	transitive form
TRANS	transitivizer
UNCERT	uncertainty
VIS	visual
VOC	vocative
VOLUNT.POT	voluntative potential

Tables, diagram, figures, and schemes

Tables

Diagram

Figures

Schemes

1

Imperatives and commands: setting the scene

1.1 Imperatives and commands

In every language one can make a statement, ask a question, or tell someone else what to do. An imperative gets an addressee to act. The form of a statement is declarative, and that of a question is interrogative. Declarative, interrogative and imperative are known as grammatical moods.[1]

This book is about imperatives, their grammar and their meanings. The idea of an 'imperative' is a command.[2] In day-to-day usage, the adjective, and the noun, 'imperative', have a similar meaning, to do with 'commanding'. A bossy woman talks 'in a quick imperative tone'. It is 'imperative' that a scholar 'check their quotations'. Being imperative implies demanding 'obedience, execution, action, obligatory'—*The condition of our sick men made it imperative that I should return at once* and *The work is quite imperative, and its result will be most beneficial.* The opposite—negative imperative or prohibitive—implies trying to make someone not do something, having the effect of forbidding, preventing, or excluding; preventative or restrictive of something. Prices may be prohibitive, if they are too high.

Do 'imperative' and 'command' always refer to the same thing? Not really. *Go away!* is a command, and is imperative in form. But one can command without using an imperative. A question *Why don't you go away?*, or a stern statement *You will go away*, or just one word *Away!* serve the same purpose. And imperatives themselves do not have to 'command'.

Imperatives are good for

- entreaties and requests: *Let me back on the computer!* and *Try and behave!*
- advice and instructions: *Don't repeat other people's mistakes!* or *Mix two spoonfuls of water with flour.*

Imperatives can also express invitations: *Meet the Joneses!* Or principles and life mottos: *Publish or perish!* Or they may have an 'anti-command' meaning. For example, a 'recipe for disaster' may be cast in an imperative. An example is in 1.1, a spoofy passage on how to destroy your festive season (from Börjars and Burridge 2001: 130; see example 7.33 in Chapter 7):

1.1   Yule be sorry!
        <u>Be</u> well on the way to going completely insane weeks beforehand. <u>Act</u> like
        an idiot at the Christmas party. <u>Try</u> to reassure yourself that one day,
        some of the people you work with might consider speaking to you again.
            <u>Go</u> beserk on your credit card(s). <u>Get</u> yourself ridiculously in debt. <u>Take</u>
        every available opportunity to eat like a pig. <u>Put</u> on five kilos you will never lose.

These imperatives are mock commands, warnings, and, importantly, instructions as to what you might want to avoid at Christmas time.

Imperatives may refer to conditions, threats and ultimatums: *Buy from that shop and you will regret it,* or *Be quiet or I'll send you to bed.* Saying *Take care!* or *Fare thee well!* are not commands; these are conventional speech formulae, part of our linguistic repertoire.

How do imperatives relate to the world of commands?[3] Imperative is a category in the language, and command is a parameter in the real world. It is not uncommon for a linguistic term to have such a counterpart in the real world. The idea of 'time' in the real world translates into 'tense' when expressed in a language. 'Time' is what our watch shows and what often passes so quickly; 'tense' is a grammaticalized set of forms we have to use in a language we speak. Not every time distinction acquires grammatical expression in the language: the possibilities for time are infinite, and for tense they are rather limited.[4]

It is the same for imperative: languages of the world have limited means of expressing imperatives. The possibilities for commands are immense, and open-ended.[5]

Imperative mood is the commonest way of expressing commands in languages of the world—covering directive speech acts with their multiple meanings. As Bolinger (1974: 4) puts it, 'trying to distinguish command imperatives from other imperatives is a vain attempt to catch metaphors in a bag of grammar'. What are imperatives good for, and why should they be of interest? Depending on a language, they may give the impression of simplicity in form. But they can also be dauntingly complex.

1.2 What imperatives are good for

Imperative structures are commands par excellence. In their meanings, they often go beyond commands. In their form, they stand apart from statements, and from questions. Imperatives tend to be short and may have no marking at all. Negating an imperative may involve a subjunctive, or an infinitive. These weird traits have led some to ask: Are imperatives defective? Or are they parasitic upon other forms? Do they exist at all? Do they constitute propositions in the same way declaratives do?[6]

Those with a fondness for truth value and truth tests for declarative sentences will find themselves at a loss. '*Be quiet!*—is it true or false?' is a meaningless question. As Jakobson (1971: 34) puts it, 'it is precisely the inapplicability of such a test that sharply delimits genuine imperative constructions from all their transpositions into the language of declarative sentences'. Imperative sentences can hardly be transformed 'directly into interrogative sentences'. As a consequence, 'the pairs *You should do it—Shall you?* and *You should do it—Should you?* beside such pairs as *You have done it— Have you?* sharply contrast with the single *Do it!*'.[7]

Imperatives are special in more than one way. They often have their own intonation contour, ways of marking subject and object, and of expressing tense and aspect. The subject of an imperative is invariably the addressee. The most common and prototypical imperative is a command directed at the second person, and often just a singular 'you'.

As Kuryłowicz (1964: 137) put it, 'the status of the second person of the imperative differs from that of the rest of its paradigm (if there is one). It is in fact the second person singular that is fundamental in the imperative.'

Commands directed at 'me' or 'us', or a third person—her, him, them, or it—often stand apart from the addressee-oriented ones. For some scholars—including Lyons (1977)—these are not imperatives at all: in the Indo-European linguistic tradition their form is very different from an imperative addressed at 'you'. In many languages of the world their overtones may vary. Ordering myself to do something may be tantamount to asking for a permission, and ordering 'him' is often interpretable as a wish rather than manipulating 'him' directly. However, the divide between the basic addressee-oriented—or 'canonical'—imperatives and those addressed to first or third person—'non-canonical' imperatives—is not cross-linguistically uniform. Uncovering the principles and tendencies behind these is one of the aims of this book.

Scholars of many traditions, and of varied theoretical persuasions, have been trying to come to grips with the fact that, in a given language, 'imperative' may cover just commands to 'you', something which never happens with other moods. If one wants to command 'us' or 'me', or a third person, another form, from another mood, may well be co-opted. The status of different persons in the imperative is not the same as in statements and in questions. Some rather confusing terminological conventions reflect this.

Individual grammars and individual linguistic traditions are at variance with each other in describing commands with a first and a third person addressee. 'Hortative' (also called 'exhortative' and 'adhortative') is a frequent label for first person imperative. Alternatively, this term may describe an extra meaning of an imperative, to do with counselling, or warning, or 'exhorting'. 'Jussive' and 'injunctive' often refer to commands directed at a third person. But in the Semitologist tradition, 'jussive' covers all non-second person imperative marking.[8]

Scholars of languages where all person values in imperative form one paradigmatic set simply stick to one term, 'imperative'. The same mood suffix on the verb is used for second, first and third person addressee. We will see in the following chapter that for languages like Evenki, from the Tungusic family, or Una, from the Papuan area, treating imperative as one paradigm for all the persons is the most appropriate decision.[9]

Imperatives are centred on speech-act participants—commander and addressee. But this is different from the expression of speech-act participant (first and second person) in questions and statements. Among the systems which group together speech-act participants is so-called conjunct-disjunct marking. The first person subject in a statement is expressed in the same way as the second person in questions, with a form called 'conjunct'. The form called 'disjunct' is used for second and third person in statements, and first and third person in questions.[10] No language described to date has conjunct-disjunct in the imperative constructions. Imperatives are different—and often more daunting than any other set of verbal forms.

The purpose of this cross-linguistic study is to find common ground and tendencies for imperatives shared by languages of different type, location and affiliation. I retain 'imperative' as a cover term for all persons. However, for a particular description setting a third person apart from the rest—and thus using the term 'jussive', provided one defines it (rather than taking it for granted)—can be justified on language-internal principles. Imperatives with a second person addressee are the core of the imperative mood. This is why they are referred to as 'CANONICAL' imperatives. Imperatives with first and third person addressees are the 'fringe' imperatives—and are called 'NON-CANONICAL'.

The special status of imperatives has indeed been a puzzle for scholars. Calvert Watkins, a major Indo-Europeanist, has made an attempt to capture the special status of second person imperative in his classic paper on the Old Irish verb (1963: 44):

> The imperative is by its nature an extragrammatical, extrasyntactical form, a quasi-interjection . . . incapable of combination with grammatical categories such as person and number, or syntactic categories such as negation.

This statement is not watertight. Imperatives in many languages do distinguish person and number, they can combine with aspects, have their own tense systems or can be negated. But the intuition behind this statement reflects the fact that imperatives are different and hard to cope with.

And different they are. No one has ever said that commands are 'primitive'. Yet one often hears it said that imperatives are. This is a common myth about imperatives. The imperative forms in many familiar Indo-European languages are short, and have no formal marking. From *amāre* 'to love' one forms the second person singular imperative *amā*! 'love' in Latin. Imperatives appear to lack the subtle distinctions of tense, aspect, and modality so richly attested in statements, and in questions. However, the simplicity of imperatives is nothing but an illusion. Debunking the 'myth' of 'the primitive' imperatives is one of my aims here.

In many familiar European languages, imperatives have fewer categories than other moods. But elsewhere in the world, imperatives have what other words do not have. In a number of languages outside Europe imperatives have a category specific just to them. Distance in space 'do here', 'do there' appears marked on imperatives and can also extend to distance in time 'do now', 'do later'. A distal imperative in Jarawara, an Arawá language from Southern Amazonia, may refer to a distant time or place (Dixon 2004a: 397):

1.2 otara   noki   ti-jahi
    1excl.o   wait   2sgA-DISTAL.POSITIVE.IMPV.fem
    'You (sg) wait for us (in some distant time or place)'

1.3 otara   noki   ti-na-hi
    1excl.o   wait   2sgA-AUX-IMMEDIATE.POSITIVE.IMPV.fem
    'You (sg) wait for us (here and now)'

Other languages distinguish distance in time, and distance in space. In Tariana, from northwest Amazonia, saying *pi-ñha!* (2sg-eat) implies 'eat!', with an expectation that the command be performed immediately. An alternative is to say *pi-hña-wa* (2sg-eat-POSTPONED.IMPERATIVE) 'eat later!', or to say *pi-hña-si!* (2sg-eat-PROXIMAL.IMPERATIVE) 'eat here!', or *pi-hña-kada!* (2sg-eat-DISTAL.IMPERATIVE) 'eat there!'. Declarative clauses, and imperatives, in both Jarawara and Tariana, are each complex in their own right.

Every verb, and every predicate, can be used in a statement. This may not be the case in an imperative. Imperatives can typically be formed on any transitive verb, and a good portion of intransitive verbs. Intransitive verbs which encode potentially uncontrollable actions are dispreferred in imperatives.

A command *Melt!* is pragmatically odd. 'With special contexts, however, such imperatives are possible. For instance, one could imagine an impatient cook standing over a pot of hard chocolate saying *Melt!* Of course, this would be a case of an indirect speech act. The cook is not really trying to alter the behaviour of the chocolate. He is expressing a desire, *I wish this chocolate would melt quickly*' (Whaley 1997: 237). However, in some languages—such as Seneca, an Iroquoian language, or Tariana, from north-west Amazonia—such commands are not acceptable at all.

How to use an overt subject with imperatives is a much-debated issue for many languages, including English. The English imperative is perhaps the simplest form in the language. It consists of the base form of the verb without any tense inflection, whose subject—typically, the addressee—is often omitted, quite unlike statements or questions where it has to be there:

1.4   Close the window!

But this curt and short way of putting things does not exhaust the options of framing directive speech acts. A command can be made more forceful, if the pronoun is added:

1.5   You close the window!

This 'force' of command is not the only overtone of an overt subject to the English imperative. In Huddleston's (2002: 926) words, 'very often it contributes to a somewhat impatient, irritated, aggressive, or hectoring effect'—as in *You mind your own business!* But it can also have 'very much the opposite effect of soothing reassurance, encouragement, support', as in *You sit down and have a nice cup of tea; everything is going to be all right.*

The actual effect depends on the tone of voice, the context and the content. In each case, including *you* presupposes that the speaker, that is, the 'commander', has authority—in an 'aggressive case', to tell you what to do, and in the 'reassuring' case to be in the position of the one who can offer reassurance and advice, the one who knows best. One other reason is to mark contrast between several addressees: *you* (pointing at one addressee) *close the window and you* (pointing at another addressee) *wash the dishes!*

Non-canonical imperatives in English have to include a subject: *Let us go* and *Let them stay* behave differently from an addressee-oriented *Stay!* or *You stay!*

A language may have more than one imperative form. Tucanoan languages, and their neighbours, from the remote Vaupés River Basin boast up to eleven imperatives. Facts of familiar languages make us believe that, for instance, an imperative cannot be used in a subordinate clause. One can say, in English, *After you run, shower!*, but not *After run! you will shower* nor *After run! shower!* (see Whaley 1997: 237). But in a few languages in the Highlands of Papua New Guinea—Hua and Yagaria among them—imperatives can occur in dependent clauses (see §3.4, in particular example 3.46). This is where 'out-of-the-way' 'exotic' languages come in handy: languages from different parts of the world help us understand the intricacies of similar categories in more familiar varieties.

Every language has ways of expressing commands, and many types of directives, permissives and so on. Not every language has a dedicated imperative paradigm. A form from some other paradigm can be co-opted to function as a primary port of call for directive meanings. This can be a future form, as in Rembarnga and Ngalakan, two Australian languages, and in Western Apache, an Athapascan language. Which forms are used in lieu of imperatives is an interesting one for a typologist.

In many languages an imperative is not the only way of telling people what to do. It may not even be the preferred way. In his classical grammar of Japanese, Samuel Martin (1975: 959) notes that

Requests in Japanese are made either by a direct command that uses an IMPERATIVE form or—more commonly—by various circumlocutions, typically, by asking as a favour.

Imperatives may sound too imperious, or too harsh. Then, other forms come into play. Shouting 'Charles!' may be the equivalent of 'Charles, come here' or 'Charles, don't do it'—and the exact interpretation would depend on the tone of voice and the situation' (Löfstedt 1966: 7). Once again, inference plays a role.

The linguistic form labelled 'imperative' tends to be the shortest in a language, and may be just too abrupt—as the principles of iconicity teach us. One word commands—like *Silence!*—or short elliptical expressions—like

Hands off, you bastard!—have overtones of abruptness, military discipline, and urgency: do it immediately!

Choosing a way of framing a command may be a matter of courtesy. An eye-doctor could just say to a patient: *Keep your eyes open. Tuck your chin in and hold your breath. Sit back now.* What she may want to say to sound nicer would rather be *Your eyes are open. Tucking in your chin. Holding your breath. If you could sit back now.* If I want to be brusque, I will say *Open the window!* But if my intention is to sound nice, I may cast my command as a question: *Could you open the window?* Or just hint of what I want the person to do by saying, *Mmm, it's stuffy in here . . .* Or cast the commanding question in a negative form, making it sound as a suggestion: *Why don't you open the window?* This does not even sound as a question: this is effectively telling a person what to do rather than asking them if they are willing to do this.

To be especially polite, I could use a statement in lieu of a request—*If you could close the window, I would be very grateful.* And a free-standing *if*-clause can nowadays be used as a polite command or a request in some varieties of English: *if you could close the window* (Stirling 1998). Even a statement *I am cold* can be interpreted as a suggestion that the addressee should close the window (especially if this statement is accompanied by a look in the direction of an open window). It is however not true that 'anything goes' as a command strategy; languages vary as to what structures can be used in lieu of an imperative.

Beware of cross-linguistic variation: a question can express a command more imperious than the imperative itself. In Amharic 'an emphatic order is expressed by interrogative forms' (Amha 2001: 127). The imperative, *Go!*, expresses simple order, while a negative interrogative form, *Why aren't you going?*, is understood as 'entailing punishment if the order is not complied with'.

The imperative forms, their usage—and the potential interpretation of non-exclusively imperative forms as commands—can only be understood though the broad prism of other ways of framing directives, related meanings, and social conventions. Imperatives are a window to social structures and the ethnography of communication—the unwritten rules we abide by.

1.3 The plan of this book

The title of this book is self-explanatory. It is a study of cross-linguistic patterns of imperatives, and of non-imperative ways of phrasing commands, that is, of directives in general. In the first place, the focus is on the meanings expressed in imperative forms. Other ways of phrasing commands—and non-command meanings of imperatives themselves—come into play as much as they are relevant. This is why the study is not limited to just commands: rather, it is focused on imperatives and any functional substitutes and variants they may have.

What is the nature of imperatives, their semantics, and usage? How do they relate to other forms and categories in the languages of the world? What are the parameters of their formal and semantic variation, within a cross-linguistic perspective? And what is the place imperatives occupy among an array of directive speech acts? Do imperatives always command? And what alternatives to imperatives do languages offer? How are imperatives used in the different linguistic communities around us? How are imperatives acquired by children? And what happens to them under tragic circumstances known as language dissolution, in aphasia and suchlike? Where do imperatives come from? How do they fare in language contact situations? These are the questions we attempt to answer.

There have, of course, been a number of earlier studies of imperative constructions, but no general cross-linguistic account. To do even partial justice to the history of studies of imperatives and commands of all sorts would require another, and a different, book. Some of the previous work is mentioned in endnotes.[11]

I start with an overview of kinds of imperative constructions we encounter across the world's languages. Chapter 2, 'Imperatives worldwide', is the longest in the book. It offers a glimpse into the diverse means of expressing canonical imperatives with second person addressee, and other person-oriented, non-canonical, imperatives. We also discuss forms used as commands in those languages which lack imperative mood as a separate mood. The problem of imperative and person, and which person distinctions we expect an imperative to have, is addressed next. Person-specific meanings of imperative forms, iconicity and markedness are also discussed. Special attention is accorded to the English imperative—not least because this category has been the subject of so many incisive studies, but also because English is the common ground I share with my readers.

Are imperatives a special clause type, and in what ways? This is what Chapter 3, 'How imperatives are special?' is about. It provides a brief survey of means by which imperative clauses are set apart from clauses of other types.

Imperative clauses differ from both declarative and interrogative clauses. Sometimes they appear impoverished in that the grammatical categories they may express are fewer than those of statements and questions. In other instances, they may be just as rich, simply expressing different categories from declaratives. Among such categories are distance in place (as in examples from

Jarawara given above), illocutionary force which allows us to distinguish strong and weak imperatives, and politeness which correlates with social status and stance. Or the same category can appear in imperative and declarative clauses, but with somewhat different meaning overtones. Imperfective aspect in Yankutjatjara, an Australian language, is used as a politeness strategy in commands. Imperatives may have a pattern of argument marking distinct from other types, as in Uto-Aztecan, Balto-Finnic, and a few Australian languages. Imperative-specific categories and the ways in which grammatical categories of other clause types are realized within imperatives are discussed in Chapter 4, 'Imperatives and other grammatical categories'.

We then turn to the way negative commands can be framed. Negative imperatives (or prohibitives) may differ from negative declaratives, and from positive imperatives. Chapter 5 'Don't do it: a vista of negative imperatives' addresses their formal marking, grammatical categories expressed, and the ways in which they correlate with grammatical categories.

The meanings of imperative forms are manifold. They cover more than just directives. Imperatives can differ in strength, or sternness: some are stronger, some are milder. Imperatives correlate with politeness and honorifics. These are the topic of Chapter 6, 'Imperatives and their meanings'.

In Chapter 7, we turn to 'Imperatives which do not command', starting with conditional and concessive overtones of imperatives in complex sentences, such as English *Open your mouth and I will shoot you*, but going well beyond just this. We then turn to other imperatives which do not require having to do what is being 'commanded'. These cover imprecatives and conventional swearing formulae, farewells, blessings, and so on.

Questions, statements, ellipsed clauses, and just plain nouns can be used as commands, in lieu of imperatives. The meanings and the conditions of use of these 'imperative strategies' vary from language to language. A command strategy may be pictorial: a cigarette with a red line through it is a conventional way of informing smokers that they are not welcome—without having to say 'don't smoke'. Chapter 8 discusses these 'Imperatives in disguise', in the context of the versatility of speech acts.

How do people use imperatives and other commanding forms? Chapter 9, 'Imperatives we live by', addresses correlations between imperatives and speech genres, existing social hierarchies and interactional stereotypes, in a variety of linguistic communities. Imperatives are often among the first forms acquired by children—which is, no doubt, related to their frequency in the carers' language.

The question 'Where do imperatives come from?' is addressed in Chapter 10. Canonical imperative forms tend to be archaic. Non-canonical forms may result from reanalysis or grammaticalization of other forms. And if a command strategy, an imperative 'in disguise', becomes the main way of framing command, it may replace the imperative, giving rise to a new set of forms. Some ways of issuing commands and of using imperatives, both negative and positive, appear highly borrowable. We discuss this in Chapter 11, 'Imperatives in contact'.

The last chapter summarizes our findings about 'The ubiquitous imperative', pulling together the conclusions and tentative generalizations from the previous chapters.

What is a typological study good for, if not for providing new analytic options and suggestions for the major business of linguistics—writing grammars and analysing previously unknown or poorly understood languages? This book is meant to alert scholars to out-of-the way patterns in imperatives and commands, and to encourage them to undertake fieldwork-based in-depth investigations of commands all over the world—rather than focussing on 'garden-variety' Standard Average European ways of saying things.

The Appendix 'Imperatives and commands: how to know more' contains a brief checklist of points to be addressed, and suggestions to fieldworkers working on imperatives and commands. This checklist, and the questions raised, aim at helping fieldworkers and grammar analysts disentangle the ways in which the language they work on handles directives in general, and how these are embedded within the grammar, and cultural conventions of the speech community. This is followed by a glossary of linguistic terms used throughout the book, within the context of imperatives, commands, and directives.

Throughout the volume, only a selection of examples are given in the text. Additional examples illustrating the same point, and also references, are given in the endnotes to each chapter.[12]

1.4 The empirical basis, and conventions

My aim here is to present a typological, empirically based account of imperatives and other ways of expressing manipulative speech acts across the world's languages. The categories and their properties are explained inductively—based on facts, not assumptions. As Leonard Bloomfield (1933: 20) put it:

The only useful generalizations about language are inductive generalizations. Features which we think ought to be universal may be absent from the very next language that becomes accessible [....] The fact that some features are, at any rate, widespread, is worthy of notice and calls for an explanation; when we have adequate data about many languages, we shall have to return to the problem of general grammar and to explain these similarities and divergences, but this study, when it comes, will not be speculative but inductive.[13]

Any inductive study—if it aims at achieving significant cross-linguistic generalizations and hypotheses—needs to account for as many linguistic systems as possible. This book is based on examination of about 700 grammars of languages from various language families, linguistic areas, and regions of the world. Special attention has been paid to data from languages on which I have first-hand expertise, and to those languages which may not have been given enough prominence as yet, simply because good descriptions have only recently become available. Among these are many languages from South America and from New Guinea.

Following the footsteps of classical typologists, I have made it my task to look at every language on which I could find reliable information, making sure I cover all the areas, and as many families as possible. This approach allows me to make the study as comprehensive as possible in our present level of knowledge of the languages themselves. My conclusions are truly empirically based.

There is a tendency for some typologists to work with just a sample of languages. The ways in which such samples are selected vary a good deal. Many of them include few or no languages from the two linguistically most diverse areas, New Guinea and Amazonia (see Dixon 2010, Volume 1: 257–61, for the criticism of sampling methodology). This work is not restricted to any artificially selected sample.

How do I choose examples? I could not cite all the examples of every particular phenomenon—otherwise the book would have been immense. I usually provide a particularly illustrative example, and mention other similar ones (in an endnote). If a certain phenomenon is found in more than half of the languages under consideration I call it 'relatively frequent'; if it is found in a restricted number of languages (one to ten), I cite all of them and indicate its rarity. Note, however, that what appears rare to us at the present stage of knowledge may turn out to be frequent when we start learning more about hitherto little-known languages and areas. This is the reason why I chose at this stage not to give any statistical counts. Only about one-tenth of all human languages have been documented so far—it therefore seems most judicious to follow a qualitative approach, postponing a professional quantitative analysis until some time in the future, when more data is available and can be assessed.

A word on conventions. This book contains many examples from—and many mentions of—languages from various areas and genetic groupings. When the language is introduced for the first time, its affiliation and where it is spoken is given in brackets—for instance, 'Kwami, Bole-Tangale group of Chadic, Afroasiatic, spoken in Northeast Nigeria'. Later mentions of the same language do not include this information—which is summarized in the Index of languages at the end of the book.

It is incumbent upon a typologist—or any linguist with any sense—to separate fact from unsubstantiated hypothesis. Highly speculative entities like Indo-Pacific, Amerind, Macro-Equatorial or Nostratic have no place in a piece of scholarly writing. In fact, any genetic unit with the label 'Macro' is highly suspicious. (The only exception is the Macro-Jê family in South America: Ribeiro 2006; Rodrigues 2006).

Along similar lines, I eschew unsubstantiated hypothetical groupings such as Pama-Nyungan in Australia (see the criticism of this hypothesis in Dixon 2002: 44–54), or the 'Trans-New Guinea phylum' for non-Austronesian languages of the New Guinea region (interested readers are referred to Aikhenvald and Stebbins 2007, for an appraisal of a current classification of the languages of the Papuan area). That is, Aboriginal languages of Australia are referred to as belonging to the Australian area; for Papuan languages a family is given if established, e.g. Alamblak (Sepik Hill, Papuan area), or Manambu (Ndu, Papuan area).

Language names and languages examples are quoted as they are given in the sources (I have made no attempt to respell any of the examples). So are examples emanating from my own fieldwork. There is a fashion among some English-speaking linguists to add a suffix *-an* to names of language families spoken in South America. Some say Carib, others say Cariban. Some say Tupí, few say Tupian. Very few—if any—say 'Tupí-Guaraníian': the majority sticks to Tupí-Guaraní. But hardly anyone says Jê-an—the name of the Jê branch of the Macro-Jê family is Jê. This is a matter of personal choice. In some cases, adding *-an* is a way of distinguishing a language from the family named after it. This is why most people refer to the family which was named after the language called Tucano as Tucanoan.

In just one case, using *-an* with the name of a family is totally unacceptable in scholarly work. The largest family in South America and Central America is Arawak, also known—especially among North American scholars—as Maipure or Maipuran. The family got its name 'Arawak' from the language known as Lokono Arawak, Arawak, or Lokono Dian (still spoken in Guiana). Its second name is based on Maipure, formerly spoken in Venezuela. South American scholars refer to the family as aruak or arouaque. The genetic unity of this family was first demonstrated as far back as 1793. Then, as part of Greenbergian attempts to lump languages into speculative units. 'Arawakan' was postulated (see Aikhenvald 2006e)—putting together Arawak or Maipuran with Arawá, Chapacura, Uru-Chipaya, and umpteen other families and languages with which no relationship can be proved. The term 'Arawakan' is improper, and should be avoided.

This book is not an encyclopaedia of imperatives, nor can it be the last word on imperatives, commands and related issues. As Bolinger (1991: 319) puts it, 'no matter how wide the net is cast, a fish or two always escapes'. My apologies to the fish which got accidentally left out. Let upcoming ichthyologists cast their nets wider.

Notes

1. Mood, as grammatical category expressing a speech act, has been discussed by Palmer (1986), Jakobson (1995), Chung and Timberlake (1985: 241), and many more. Mood should not be confused with modality, understood as a grammatical category covering the degree of certainty of a statement (epistemic), obligation (deontic), and permission (see Palmer 1986; and also Narrog 2005 and Nuyts 2006, among others). Here and throughout the book, ! is used as a orthographic symbol marking imperatives in language examples, ? is used for interrogatives, and a full stop (or a period) indicates declaratives.

    Mood is linked to a speech act. Any utterance can be conceived of as an act, by which the speaker does something. Saying 'Gregory is my brother' involves the act of making a statement. Saying 'Is Gregory my brother?' involves asking a question. 'Go away!' is a command, and a directive speech act, by which a speaker attempts to make the addressee do something, directing them. Directive speech acts are the prototypical domain of the imperative mood, in the same way as the declarative is the domain for assertive speech acts, stating something. For the theory of speech acts as developed by Searle see, in the first place, Searle (1969, 1975, 1976, 1979, 1999) and brief surveys in Cruse (2006: 167–9), and also Matthews (1997: 348).

2. This is how the 1999-edition of the Oxford English Dictionary defines imperative as a grammatical term: 'Expressing command: applied to the verbal mood (or any form belonging to it) which expresses a command, a request, or exhortation'.

3. Jakobson (1984: 33); also see Whitney (1924: 571) quoted in Chapter 6.

4. See Comrie (1976). Along similar lines, the term 'evidential' primarily relates to information source as a closed grammatical system whose use is obligatory. The term 'information source' relates to the corresponding conceptual category. This is akin to the distinction between the category of 'tense', as grammaticalized location in time, and the concept of 'time' as a real world category (Aikhenvald 2008d).

5. The term 'command' covers a large semantic range. It may be extended to include requests, entreaties, advice, recommendation, wishes, obligations, and commands in a narrower sense of 'order'. The term 'mand' has been suggested, to cover some of the directives (Lyons 1977: 745–6). While 'mand' is a useful semantic and pragmatic notion, the realm of imperatives goes beyond that.

6. Some of these issues have been summarized in an appropriately entitled paper 'Untangling the imperative puzzle', by Alcázar and Saltarelli (forthcoming). For further discussion of imperatives and logic, the readers may wish to consult Hamblin (1987), Moutafakis (1975), Schmerling (1980, 1982), Davies (1986), to name a few.

7. The discussion of imperatives and directives in English, by Huddleston (2002: 929–30) and Quirk et al. (1985) are particularly relevant here, highlighting the issues of truth value and the restrictions on the use of judgement words, such as *unfortunately* in imperatives.

8. As a result of this terminological confusion Matthews (1997: 192) doubts whether the term 'jussive' is needed at all.

9. See van Marle (2003), for a summary of the notion of paradigm; also Xrakovskij and Birjulin (2001).

10. This is an approximate description. Such systems have been described for Barbacoan languages in South America, and for Tibeto-Burman. See Dixon (2010, Volume 1), for a summary; also see Siewierska (2004); and Aikhenvald (2004: 123–8).

11. Hamblin (1987) is a study of the logical structure and use of imperative, with a focus on English rather than on cross-linguistically attested patterns. Various aspects of imperatives and commands have been fruitfully discussed by van der Auwera, and his co-authors (e.g. van der Auwera 2006a, b; van der Auwera et al. 2005a, b, 2004; Miestamo and van der Auwera 2007; and other work mentioned in the references). While all analysts seem to agree as to the existence of special syntactic forms for expressing commands in every language, they assign these forms a different place with respect to other parts of the grammar. Sadock and Zwicky (1985: 170–1) consider imperatives a separate speech act. Palmer (1986: 29–30) includes it among 'directives', as an 'unmarked or neutral form within the deontic system, or at least within the subsystem of directives'. Chung and Timberlake (1985: 247–9) treat imperatives as a subtype of the 'deontic' mode (that is, a mode that characterizes an event as non-actual), on a par with desiderative, optative, jussive and so on. Further issues related to imperatives covering a wide range of functionally related manipulative speech acts and varying in their grammatical expression include Givón (1993), Sadock and Zwicky (1985), and also Bhat (1999). Important—albeit short—studies of imperatives include discussions in Sadock and Zwicky (1985: 172–8), Schmerling (1980, 1982), Palmer (1986: 29–30), Chung and Timberlake (1985: 247–9), and König and Siemund (2007). Imperatives and commands are typically assigned a shortish section in more general books on non-declarative sentences (e.g. Zuber 1983), or on speech acts. A number of

book-length investigations of imperative in individual languages deserve special mention. Davies (1986) is a comprehensive study of English imperative. Some of the conclusions are extended by insightful discussion by Huddleston (2002). Old English imperatives are discussed by Millward (1971). Löfstedt (1966) is an inspiring study of imperatives in Latin. Russian imperative has been the object of many monographs, among them Xrakovskij and Volodin (2001), and Fortuin (2004). Cross-linguistic data were assembled in Birjulin, Bondarko and Xrakovskij (1988), and Xrakovskij (1992a, and its English version 2001). Van der Wurff (2007a) contains numerous articles on imperatives, from a formal perspective. Recently produced typological studies, based on samples, include Schalley (2008) and Goussev (2005)—the latter showing a substantial overlap with Aikhenvald (MS), a manuscript position paper for a workshop on imperatives and commands (written in 2003) which became a trigger for this book.

12. Language examples are numbered separately for each chapter, with the first number referring to the chapter number, e.g. 2.1 is the first language example in Chapter 2, 2.2 is the second example in Chapter 2 and so on.

13. The analysis is cast in terms of basic linguistic theory, the fundamental typological theoretical apparatus 'that underlies all work in describing languages and formulating universals about the nature of human language', where 'justification must be given for every piece of analysis, with a full train of argumentation' (Dixon 2010, 1997: 132; see also Dixon 1994: xvi).

2

Imperatives worldwide

For many linguists and language learners alike, 'imperative' implies a command to a second person—such as English *Get out!* And indeed, in many languages a set of special imperative forms is restricted to commands directed at 'you'. Addressee-directed imperatives are always central to the imperative paradigms. This follows the well-established traditional approach—in Lyons' (1977: 747) words, 'it is implicit in the very notion of commanding and requesting that the command or request is addressed to the person who is expected to carry it out'. These canonical imperatives, or imperatives in a narrow sense, are the topic of §2.1.

If a language has no dedicated form used just for imperative, another form of the verb could be regularly redeployed for canonical commands. Present, future, or irrealis forms—in declarative mood—are often used this way.

However, commanding expressions do not have to be restricted to just the addressee. Command forms addressed to persons other than the addressee may or may not form one grammatical system and one paradigm with canonical imperatives. Alternatively, they may be co-opted from a different set of forms—such as subjunctive. 'Non-canonical imperatives', or 'imperatives in a broad sense' covering commands with non-second person reference, are addressed in §2.2. These include commands directed to first person—'me', or 'us' (often labelled 'hortatives')—and commands to third person (referred to as 'jussives').

If the canonical and the non-canonical imperatives form one paradigm, it is sensible to employ a general term 'imperatives' for all person values. If they belong to different grammatical systems and paradigms, separate terms would be appropriate for distinct person values, and the term 'imperative' would be kept just for second person-oriented commands. In §2.3 we discuss the problem of 'person' in English imperative, as a case study.

Then, in §2.4, we turn to the meanings of imperatives depending on the person of the addressee. The final section of this chapter offers conclusions, and tentative generalizations.

Imperatives—both canonical and non-canonical ones—are special in many ways.[1] Clauses containing imperatives—and commands in general—often differ from other types in their constituent order, intonation patterns, meanings of persons, and various other language-specific ways. The special features of imperatives which confirm their status as distinct clause types are the topic of the next chapter.

2.1 Canonical imperatives

Second person imperatives—the prototypical commands—can be expressed with a variety of means. These include affixes, clitics, particles, special forms of pronouns, and even periphrastic constructions. Quite frequently, a bare root or stem of a verb marks a command. Synthetic languages tend to mark imperatives with inflectional means. And isolating and highly analytic languages will employ particles (short independent function words) as command markers.[2]

We start with canonical imperatives with a singular addressee (§2.1.1). This section also includes forms which do not distinguish number. We then look at canonical imperatives addressed to two or more participants (§2.1.2). In §2.1.3, we turn to further issues in marking canonical imperatives—suppletive imperatives, and imperatives in Sign Languages.

If a language has no special set of forms for canonical imperatives, another form of the verb is recruited in the prototypical command function. §2.1.4 provides an overview of the kind of stand-in forms in languages without a dedicated imperative.

Correlations between form and meaning in imperatives, and the issue of iconicity are discussed in §2.1.5.

2.1.1 *Imperatives with a singular addressee*

In Kuryłowicz's words, 'it is in fact the second person singular that is fundamental in the imperative' (Kuryłowicz 1964: 137). In about one-third of the languages of the world, the second person singular imperative coincides with either the verb root or the stem. It is thus the shortest, and the simplest verb form in the language. We discuss this in (A). Many languages, discussed under (B), have an overt indicator of imperative: this can be a segmental affix, a special set of pronominal markers, a tone contour, or a particle. We then turn to imperatives expressed with analytic constructions (C).

A. Bare root or stem of the verb can be used as singular canonical imperative.

We find this in a wide variety of languages, Classical Latin among them. One of the shortest words in Latin is a canonical imperative *i!* 'go!', from the verb *īre* 'to go'. The second person singular imperative regularly coincides with the stem of the verb. So, from *amāre* 'to love' one forms the second person singular imperative *amā!* 'love!', and from *audīre* 'to listen', *audī!* 'listen!'. For a handful of often-used verbs, the second person imperative is shorter than the stem itself: *dīcere* means 'to say', and its second person imperative is *dīc!*, *facere* 'to do, make' forms *fac!* 'do, make!', *dūcere* 'to lead' forms *dūc!*, and *ferre* 'bear' forms *fer!*

Compared to second person indicative *amās* 'you (sg) love' and *dīcis* 'you (sg) say', imperatives appear impoverished—they bear no overt expression of person or tense. This is similar to English imperatives. They appear stripped of markers of person or tense, and are seemingly primitive compared to other forms. (But see §2.3 for analytic problems associated with them.[3])

Using the simplest and often the shortest form for the second person singular command goes beyond the domain of European languages. Tinrin, an Austronesian language spoken in New Caledonia, employs a subjectless form of the verb as a command. The verb bears no marking of person, tense, or aspect.

Tinrin (Osumi 1995: 236)
2.1 <u>tôbwerrî</u> nrîfò-nrü
     shut   mouth-2sg
     'Shut your mouth!'

Similar examples abound. Khalkha-Mongolian (Poppe 1951: 76) also employs the verb stem to mark commands, e.g. *bos* 'stand up!' (sg and pl), *bitši* 'write!'. In Kannada, a Dravidian language (Sridhar 1990: 31), the singular form of the canonical imperative is 'the only instance where the tenseless verb root, without any suffix, functions as a finite verb . . . It is therefore treated as the canonical (dictionary citation) form.'[4]

If a canonical imperative is unmarked for person, how do we know that its subject is the second person singular addressee? Syntactic tests help us demonstrate this. In Koyra Chini, a zero-marked subject of imperative forms is second person because it controls a second person reflexive—see §4.1.[5]

As noted by Sadock and Zwicky (1985: 173), the lack of special marking on a canonical imperative is 'reflective of the inherent semantics of the imperative . . . the subject naturally refers to the addressee, so second person inflection becomes redundant.' That is, lack of formal marking reflects the functionally unmarked status of the most prototypical of commands. We return to this in §2.1.5.

B. OVERT MARKERS OF IMPERATIVES can be of various sorts.

A SPECIAL SUFFIX OR A CLITIC marks the verb as imperative in many Australian languages.[6] In Yidiñ, the verb appears marked with *-n* (its allomorphs are ø or *r*)—see 2.2.

Yidiñ (Dixon 1977: 370)
2.2   ɲanda   wiwi-n   waŋal
      I+DAT   give-IMPV   boomerang+ABS
      '(You) give me (your) boomerang!'

A similar example comes from Panyjima, another Australian language. The imperative marker is *-ma*:

Panyjima (Dench 1991: 174)
2.3   minyma   panti-ma
      still   sit-IMPV
      'Sit still!'

Dâw, a Makú language from Northwest Amazonia, Brazil, is almost isolating in its profile; there are just a few suffixes, and one of these is the imperative *-ɔh* attached to the verb root.

Dâw (Martins 1994, 2005)
2.4   ham-ɔh   mẽɲ   jód
      go-IMPV   1sg.poss   ELATIVE
      'Go away from me!'

A segmental marker of an imperative can be a clitic, that is, a bound morpheme distinct from an affix in terms of its prosodic properties.[7] An example comes from Semelai, an Aslian language from Malaysia.

Semelai (Kruspe 2004a: 331–3)
2.5   ʔot=cəʔ!   bapaʔ   khləŋ
      return=IMPV   father   QUOTE
      ' "Come (home)!", the father said'

Or an imperative marker can be a particle—a prosodically independent word. Imperative particles are particularly common in languages of isolating profile—such as Thai and Lao:

Lao (Enfield 2007: 67; numbers indicate tones)
2.6   peet5   patuu3   haj5   dèèl
      open   door   give   IMPV.SOFT
      'Please open the door'

An imperative can be shorter than the verbal stem if it is formed via SUBTRACTION, similarly to the examples from Latin mentioned at (A). Forming an imperative in Dyirbal, an Australian language from North Queensland, involves deleting the final stem consonant.[8] The imperative of *baniy* 'to come' is *bani* as in 2.7, and of *balgal* 'to hit'—*balga* as in 2.8. The singular personal pronoun is optional (and is in brackets):

Dyirbal

2.7　(ŋinda)　bani!
　　 you　　 come:IMPV
　　 'You come!'

2.8　(ŋinda)　bayi　　　　　yaṟa　　　balga
　　 you.sg　 one:NCL:MASC　man.ABS　 hit:IMPV
　　 'You hit the man!'

Imperatives are marked with subtraction in a few other languages. In Dumi, a Tibeto-Burman language from eastern Nepal, forming an imperative involves deleting a person prefix *a-* from second person preterite forms.[9] The second person imperative in Hebrew involves the omission of personal prefixes (see Table 2.4). The reason why a canonical command is often shorter than the corresponding declarative partly lies in its illocutionary force—see §2.1.5.

Subtraction can be accompanied by a segmental marker. The canonical imperative in Manambu, a Ndu language from the Sepik area in Papua New Guinea, is formed by attaching a prefix and deleting the verb-final vowel, e.g. *wa-* 'to speak', *aw* 'speak!'. Imperative stands apart from all other verbal forms in Manambu, since it is the only form in the language with a fully productive prefix.

An imperative form may contain an overt indicator of second person. In Tauya, from the Brahman family in Papua New Guinea, imperative is formed by adding an *-e* suffix to the second person future marker on the verb:

Tauya (MacDonald 1990: 212)

2.9　ni-a-e
　　 eat-2sg.FUT-IMPV
　　 'Eat (singular addressee)!'

In addition, imperatives can distinguish person and gender of the addressee (see 4.6, an example from Chipaya, an Uru-Chipaya language from Bolivia). In Lakhota, a Siouan language (Boas and Deloria 1941: 111–12), the imperative is marked by particles postposed to the verb which vary according to the sex and number of the speaker: *kaška 'yo'* (tie:stem IMPV.masc.sg) 'tie it!' (man ordering or permitting), *kaška' na* (tie:stem IMPV.fem.sg) 'tie it!' (woman ordering). These particles together with interjections and a few other markers are among the few instances in the Lakhota grammar where gender—masculine and feminine—is differentiated depending on the speaker's sex. This makes imperatives in Lakhota somewhat semantically and formally more complex than straightforward declaratives—we return to this in Chapters 3 and 4. In the vast majority of cases, imperatives distinguish genders if declaratives also do so.

A TONE PATTERN can be the sole mark of an imperative on a verb. In Mina, a Chadic language, imperative is marked by lowering the tone on the verb. So a monosyllabic high tone verb—such as *ɓám* 'eat'—acquires a low tone. 2.10a is a declarative sentence with this verb. Its imperative form with a low tone is illustrated in 2.10b.

Mina (Frajzyngier and Johnston 2005: 231)

2.10a kə̀   ɓám   ɬì   zà
     INF   eat   meat   END.OF.EVENT.MARKER
     'He ate the meat'

2.10b ɓàm   ɬì
     eat:IMPV   meat
     'Eat the meat!'

Along similar lines, in Kisi, an Atlantic language (Childs 1995: 229), imperatives are marked just by the high tone on the verb, e.g. *yó* 'dance!'. In Kiowa, spoken in Oklahoma, imperatives are marked by falling tone if a root ends in a nasal or a liquid *l*. The imperative of *t'á•l* 'to sever (one object)' will be *t'âl*, with a falling tone. But for all other verbs, the imperative will be unmarked, as in *hâ•pè* 'to pick up', *hâ•pè* 'pick up!' (Watkins 1984: 167–8).[10] Note that here the differences between verbal conjugations are not neutralized in imperatives, in contrast to Dyirbal (2.7–8).

Imperative forms may require A SPECIAL SET OF PRONOMINAL CROSS-REFERENCING AFFIXES different from that used in statements. This is the case in many Indo-European languages (including Slavic and Romance), in Balto-Finnic and Samoyedic languages, and in a few languages from the New Guinea area (e.g. Anamuxra, from the Papuan area: Ingram 2005). The morphological distinction between imperatives and non-imperatives in Modern Greek lies in the inflectional person ending on the verb: compare the indicative *gráf-is* 'you (sg) are writing' and *gráf-e* 'you (sg) be/get writing!' (Joseph and Philippaki-Warburton 1987: 183).

Quechua languages from Peru[11] have a second person suffix used only in imperatives, e.g. Ayacucho Quechua *wata-y* (tie-2sg) 'tie!'. This form is in paradigmatic opposition with declarative forms and other person–number combinations on the imperative itself (see §2.1.2). Aymara varieties have a special person paradigm just for imperatives with more than one form involving the second person addressee: forms vary depending on whether the object or the recipient of a verb like 'give' is first person (as in 2.11), or third person (2.12):

Aymara (Adelaar 2004: 285)

2.11   čura-m

       give-2SUBJ+3OBJ

       'Give it to him/her!'

2.12   čura-ita

       give-2SUBJ+1OBJ

       'Give it to me!'

Forming an imperative may involve vowel alternation. The second singular imperative of a number of strong verbs in German is formally marked with a vowel change and no person inflection, e.g. *sprechen* 'to speak', *sprich*! 'speak!' (you sg). (But note that there is no vowel change in plural forms: 2pl familiar *sprech-t*, 2pl polite *sprechen*—see §2.1.2, and Table 2.2 below).

C. Having a special ANALYTIC CONSTRUCTION for a canonical imperative is a rather rare option across the world's languages. In Ika, a Chibchan language from Colombia, imperative is expressed by a combination of a verb root and an auxiliary. An example of the immediate imperative is in 2.13.[12]

Ika

2.13   amase   ú

       get.up   AUX

       'Get up!' or 'Stand up!'

Ika has three imperatives, all of which are marked with an auxiliary, whose choice depends on distance in time (see note 25 to Chapter 4).

An imperative may involve an analytic construction of a different kind. Boumaa Fijian (Dixon 1988: 286–94) has a number of clause relators; one of these, *me*, introduces complement clauses, similarly to English *that . . . should* in *I told Nana Maa that Eroni should go to Vidawa*, and also means *in order to* as in *I eat a lot in order to be healthy*. It is also used in imperatives. The structure of the Boumaa Fijian imperative construction is given in Scheme 2.1:

SCHEME 2.1 The structure of imperative construction in Boumaa Fijian
1. Relator *me*
2. Subject pronoun
3. Optional tense-aspect markers
4. Optional discourse markers
5. Verb
6. Optional adverb, post-head modifiers etc.

A command in 2.14 contains the relator, the subject pronoun (fused with it), and the transitive verb 'look':

Boumaa Fijian
2.14 mo   rai-ca
      REL+2sg   look-TR
      'Look!'

The relator-cum-second singular pronoun combination can be omitted. Then the imperative equals the verb root on its own with the meaning of 'look!'. This agrees with a very widespread tendency for the second person imperative to coincide with the verb root—see (A) above, and §2.1.5:

2.15 rai-ca
      look-TR
      'Look!'

This omission is a property of just the imperatives with a singular addressee (see §2.1.2).

A similar construction is found in Nigerian Pidgin, an English-based Creole (Faraclas 1996: 24–5). Here, imperative sentences are formally almost identical to declaratives. The major difference is that the 'subjunctive clause introducer' *mek* appears before the subject:

Nigerian Pidgin
2.16 Mek   yù   go   fam
      SUBJ   2sg   go.SJ   farm
      'Go to the farm!'

A corresponding declarative clause is:

2.17 Yù   go   fam
      2sg   go.F   farm
      'You went to the farm'

Unlike *me* in Boumaa Fijian, *mek* is not a subordinator; this form only appears in canonical (second person) and non-canonical (first person) imperatives. It comes from the verb *make* 'make' and is also used in causative serial verb constructions, as in *im gò mek mì go* ((s)he IRR make+ me go+) 'She or he will make me go'.[13]

There is one additional, and instructive, similarity between Nigerian Pidgin and Boumaa Fijian. If the addressee is second person singular, both the linker *mek* and the pronoun can be omitted. That is, an alternative to 2.16 is 2.18. This is reminiscent of omitting the combination of relator-cum-pronoun in 2.15, from Boumaa Fijian.

2.18a Go   fam!
       go.SUBJUNC   farm
       'Go to the farm!'

If the pronoun is omitted, so is *mek*. The ungrammatical alternatives are at 2.18b–c:

2.18b   *Mek go fam!
2.18c   *Yu go fam!

In these instances an imperative form is hardly more 'primitive' than a declarative, in terms of its formal complexity. In fact, the imperative in 2.16 can be said to be more complex than its declarative counterpart in 2.17. Following a cross-linguistically recurrent tendency, there is an additional option for a second person singular imperative. The bare root, which is the simplest possible form, can be used—similarly to the most frequent and straightforward option in (A) above.

2.1.2 *Addressing more than one person*

The canonical imperatives addressing more than one person offer three options. We return to number and imperatives in §4.2.

1. A language may employ the SAME FORM FOR SINGULAR AND NON-SINGULAR ADDRESSEE with a preferred or optional mechanism of disambiguation for non-singular addressee. This is typical for non-prefixing Australian languages, for instance, Dyirbal and Mbarbaram.[14] But if the addressee is non-singular, the personal pronoun is likelier to be included. Otherwise, the pronoun is optional (as we can recall from 2.7 and 2.8 above). In 2.19 and 2.20, also from Dyirbal, the dual and the plural pronouns are included in the command, for the purpose of disambiguation:

Dyirbal
2.19   ñubala   bani
        you.dual   come:IMPV
        'You two come!'

2.20   ñura   bani
        you.pl   come:IMPV
        'You (three or more) come!'

In Vitu, an Oceanic language spoken in West New Britain,[15] an imperative clause typically consists of a verb root which can be accompanied by an object, as in 2.21.

Vitu
2.21   taba-ri-a   hatama
        close-TR-3sg.OBJECT   door
        'Close the door (singular addressee)!'

The main function of subject pronouns in imperative clauses is to make explicit that the command is addressed to more than one person by the use of the non-singular pronouns *moro/mo* 'you two' and *miu* 'you plural', as in 2.22:

2.22   Mo   guri-a
        you.du   wait-3sg. OBJECT
        'Wait for him (the two of you)!'

In Manambu, a subject pronoun is typically omitted in canonical imperatives which make no distinction between feminine and masculine singular, and plural and dual addressees. This is in contrast to declarative clauses which distinguish two genders and three numbers in bound pronouns on the verb. A subject pronoun—singular, dual or plural—can be supplied for disambiguation in canonical imperatives.[16] Compare:

Manambu

2.23   a-war!
      IMPV-go.up!
      'Go up (you woman, you man, you dual, you plural)!'

2.24   mən   a-war   gur-abaːb   a-war
        you.masc IMPV-go.up! you.pl-ALL IMPV-go.up!
        'You (man) go up! You all go up!'

2. A language may have NO SEGMENTAL MARKER FOR SINGULAR ADDRESSEE, AND A SEGMENTAL MARKER FOR NON-SINGULAR ADDRESSEE.
In Latin, the suffix -*te* is only used for plural addressees in imperative—*amā!* '(you one person) love!', *amā-te!* '(you many) love!', *audī!* '(you one person) listen!', *audī-te!* '(you many) listen!'. The marker of the imperative with a plural addressee in Arapaho (an Algonquian language from Oklahoma and Wyoming) is a glottal stop while the singular imperative is formally unmarked: it lacks subject person markers on the verb, and has no initial change in the verb stem (Cowell 2007: 45–6).

Comanche, a Uto-Aztecan language from Oklahoma, has three numbers—singular, dual, and plural. The second person singular imperative is the simple verb stem (Robinson and Armagost 1990: 261–3):

Comanche

2.25   ihka   buni   tʉi-h
        this   see   friend-VOC
        'Look at this, friend!'

If the command is addressed to two people, a special dual marker is used:

2.26a   ʉhkooi bʉhʉ̠
         sleep   COREF.DUAL
         'You two sleep!'

If the command is addressed to more than two people, the verb takes a plural marker -*ka*. It is a clitic which has to attach to the first word in the sentence:[17]

2.26b   ohka-ka   kwasinabooʔa wʉhkupa̠
         that-IMPV.PL snake   kill
         'All of you, kill that snake!'

These examples illustrate a general principle: that a canonical imperative with a singular addressee is shorter and often morphologically simpler than a corresponding form addressed to more than one person.

3. A language may have SEGMENTAL MARKERS FOR BOTH SINGULAR AND NON-SINGULAR ADDRESSEES. In Kwami (from the Bole-Tangale subgroup of Chadic), second person singular imperative is marked with a suffix -*ú*, and the plural imperative with the suffix -*á*:

Kwami (Leger 1994: 236–7, 77; the accents on vowels indicate high tone)
2.27 ɗín-ú   'cook!' (singular)
      ɗín-á   'cook!' (plural)

In Modern Welsh, the singular imperative is marked with the suffix -*a* attached to the verb stem; the plural imperative involves the suffix -*wch*:[18]

Modern Welsh (King 1993: 224)
2.28 verb stem *tafl-*   sg imperative *tafl-a*   pl imperative *tafl-wch* 'throw!'
      verb stem *arhos*   sg imperative *arhos-a*   pl imperative *arhos-wch* 'wait!'

In Dolakha Newar (Genetti 2007: 179–82), singular non-honorific imperatives may have an explicit marker or not, depending on the type of stem. Plural imperatives have a suffix -*n*, -*un*, or -*dun* (the exact form also depends on the verb stem), e.g. *so-u* (look-impv.sg) 'look (sg)!', *so-n* (look-impv.pl) 'look (pl)!', *hat* 'say (sg)!', *hat-un* 'say (pl)!'.

A canonical imperative with a singular addressee can require segmental marking, as in Northern Embera, a Choco language from Colombia, with a plural marker attaching to it if the addressee is plural. Compare 2.29a and 2.29b. An imperative with a plural addressee requires the suffix -*da-*.

Northern Embera (Mortensen 1999: 85)
2.29a pɨ-ra   ɨbɨa   sʼe-tua
       2sg-ABS   strong   come-IMPV
       'Hurry up!'

2.29b hūmaẽnã   ẽsʼoa-da-tua
       everyone   disperse-PL-IMPV
       'Everyone get off the bus!'

The markers of a canonical imperative can partially OVERLAP with declarative forms. The regular imperative with a singular addressee in Italian is the same as third person indicative for verbs of the first declension, such as *canta* 'sing (you sg)!, he/she sings'. For verbs of other declensions, it is the same as second singular present indicative, as in *temi* 'fear!, you fear'. An imperative of a verb of any conjugation if addressed to more than one person is identical to second person plural indicative—e.g. *cantate* '(you many) sing!, you sing' (also see Table 2.18 below) (Maiden and Robustelli 2007: 246–8).

That the imperative shares its form with other categories should not make us think that Italian has no imperative as such. The patterns of overlapping forms are specific for the imperative.[19] In addition, some verbs have their own somewhat irregular imperative forms: we return to these in §2.1.3 below.

Paumarí, an Arawá language from Brazil, has special imperative person prefixes, listed in Table 2.1. The choice of a prefix depends on the verb's transitivity (see §4.4, for further discussion of transitivity and the expression of imperatives).

TABLE 2.1 Person prefixes in imperatives and declaratives in Paumarí

	IMPERATIVE	DECLARATIVE
2sg.Intransitive	ø	*i-*
2sg.Transitive	*i-*	*i-*
2pl.Intransitive/Transitive	*va-/vi-*	*ava-/avi-*

An intransitive second person singular imperative is illustrated in 2.30a.

Paumarí
2.30a ø-vithi-ø   hida
      2sg-sit-IMPV   DEM:LOC
      'Sit here!'

An intransitive second person declarative form is given in 2.30b, for comparison.

2.30b i-naba'daha-ni
      2sg-fish-DEP.INTRANS
      'You are fishing'

Transitive singular and plural imperatives are given in 2.31a and b (Chapman and Derbyshire 1991: 217; Shirley Chapman, p.c.):

2.31a i-vi-kha-ra-foni-ø
      2sg-COMITATIVE-MOTION-down-port-IMPV
      'You (sg) bring it down to the port!'

2.31b va-vi-kha-ra-foni-ø
      2pl-COMITATIVE-MOTION-down-port-IMPV
      'You (pl) bring it down to the port!'

Transitive second person imperative is formally identical to a declarative: 2.31a could be understood as a statement as well as a command (they can be differentiated by their intonation).

A similar example comes from German. The plural imperative—both familiar and polite—is formally identical with the present tense of the verb. The second person familiar form is the shortest: it has no overt personal markers. This form is the least polite and the most direct. Table 2.2 features a paradigm of the German verb *sagen* 'say', compared with its present and past forms:

TABLE 2.2 Imperative, present, and past in German: 'to say'

	IMPERATIVE	PRESENT	PAST
2sg familiar	*sag*	*sagst*	*sagtest*
2pl familiar	*sagt*	*sagt*	*sagtet*
2sg/pl polite	*sagen*	*sagen*	*sagten*

The second person familiar singular imperative is formally the simplest. However, this is not the only way imperatives can be formed in German. We can recall, from §2.1.1 above, that the imperatives of some strong (that is, irregular) verbs addressed to one person involve vowel alternation. For the verb *sprechen* 'speak, talk', the formal second person plural form is *sprechen* and the second person plural familiar *sprecht*, while the second singular is marked with vowel change: *sprich!*

Formation of a canonical imperative may involve further complexities. In Arabic, the imperative prefix *ʔi-* is attached to the verb stem also used for the indicative imperfect. An extract from the paradigm of the verb *ktb* 'write' is in Table 2.3, from Cairene Egyptian Colloquial Arabic (Gary and Gamal-Eldin 1982: 97–8, 100). Imperfect and perfect forms are included for comparison.

TABLE 2.3 Canonical imperative in Cairene Egyptian Colloquial Arabic: 'to write'

PERSON/GENDER/NUMBER	IMPERATIVE	IMPERFECT INDICATIVE	PERFECT INDICATIVE
2 masc sg	*ʔi-ktib*	*ti-ktib*	*katab-t*
2 fem sg	*ʔi-ktib-i*	*ti-ktib-i*	*katab-ti*
2 masc/fem pl	*ʔi-ktib-u*	*ji-ktib-u*	*katab-u*

Forming imperatives may involve subtraction. In Hebrew, canonical imperatives are the same as future forms, but without personal prefixes. Table 2.4 shows a paradigm of the verb 'go' in future and in the imperative. Past tense forms are given in the last column, for comparison.

TABLE 2.4 Imperative in comparison with future and past in Hebrew:[20] 'to go'

PERSON/GENDER/NUMBER	IMPERATIVE	FUTURE INDICATIVE	PAST INDICATIVE
2 masc sg	*lex*	*te-lex*	*halax-ta*
2 fem sg	*lx-i*	*te-lxi*	*halax-t*
2 masc pl	*lx-u*	*te-lxu*	
2 fem pl	*(lex-na)*	*(te-lex-na)*	*halx-u*

The second person masculine imperative is the shortest verbal form in the language, and the least formally marked. However, this does not make it the least complex. As Table 2.4 shows, tense and mood in Hebrew are expressed with a combination of internal vowel change, suffixes, and prefixes. Forming an imperative does not involve just stripping the verb of all inflections. Short command forms like *lex!* 'go (you man)' only appear to be simplistic. In fact, their formation can only be understood as part of a complex verbal paradigm.

Bound morphemes marking singular and non-singular second person on imperatives are cross-linguistically common. In contrast, having special free pronouns used just in commands appears to be a rarity. Examples come from Yawelmani and Gashowu, two dialects of Yokuts, a now extinct isolate from California (Newman 1944: 118–19, 232). Two special forms of non-singular pronouns were used to accompany the verb marked for imperative mood (whereby a special suffix is attached to a truncated stem). These pronouns are used exclusively in this function and not inflected for case; they cover second person non-singular, that is, dual and plural: Yawelmani dual *wik̃*, plural *wil*, Gashowu dual *dil*, plural *dul*. There is no pronoun for singular imperative, which is, not unexpectedly (§2.1.5), the least formally marked of all:

Yawelmani
2.32a la[·]n/k̃a   nim   wiya
      hear:IMPV   my   words
      'Hear my words!' (*la·na* 'hear')

2.32b wa'aṣgi   t'ɔyix/k̃a   wik̃
      well   doctor:IMPV(him)   you.dual
      'Well, doctor him, you dual' (*t'ɔyɔx* 'doctor, give medicine to')

The number distinctions in canonical imperatives addressing more than one person can be the same as the number in corresponding declaratives. A similar example comes from Boumaa Fijian—see Table 2.5 and further discussion in §4.2.

This paradigm shows that the canonical imperative with a singular addressee is the least formally marked of all. Similarly to 2.29a–b (from Northern Embera), non-singular imperatives build upon singular imperatives.

TABLE 2.5 Number in canonical imperatives in Boumaa Fijian (Dixon 1988: 293, 55)

2sg	*mo* REL+2sg	*rai-ca* see-TR		'look (at someone)!'
2du	*mo* REL+2	*mudrau* 2du	*rai-ca!* see-TR	'you two look (at someone)!'
2 paucal	*mo* REL+2	*mudou* 2paucal	*rai-ca!* see-TR	'you few look (at someone)!'
2pl	*mo* REL+2	*munuu* 2pl	*rai-ca!* see-TR	'you (many) look (at someone)!'

Imperatives may express fewer number distinctions than do declaratives. Canonical imperatives in Manambu do not distinguish number—it can be disambiguated with personal pronouns (see 2.23–4). In contrast, declaratives obligatorily distinguish three numbers. Hardly any languages have more number distinctions in imperatives than in declaratives.

If a language has several imperatives, some of these may have different forms for different number of addressees. In Maale, an Omotic language from Ethiopia (Amha 2001: 157), the regular imperative distinguishes singular addressee and plural addressee, and so does the polite imperative. The impolite imperative has no number distinctions. We return to correlations between imperatives and number in §4.1. The expression of gender in non-singular imperatives is also discussed in §4.1.

Non-singular imperatives are never marked just with a special tone contour, unless the tone is also used for singular imperatives. However, in some cases different contours are involved. We recall that marking imperative on the verb in Mina involves a tone change. Singular pronouns can be used to accompany an imperative. Plural pronouns are obligatory for commands directed at more than one person. Both plural and singular pronouns accompanying imperatives have to have high tone. In statements, plural pronouns always have high tone, while singular pronouns have low tone (Frajzyngier and Johnston 2005: 81–3, 233–4).

In summary: canonical imperatives with non-singular addressees are always more formally marked than their singular counterparts. This is partly due to the relative markedness of non-singular as opposed to singular—also see §2.1.5. No language has been found (so far) which would employ an analytic construction to form a canonical imperative with a non-singular addressee, but not for one with a singular addressee.[21]

We now turn to some further issues of marking canonical imperatives.

2.1.3 *Further issues in imperative formation*

A reduplicated verb can form an imperative, but reduplication is never the sole marker of an imperative.[22] A marker of imperatives can occasionally be reduplicated: in Kambaata, a Cushitic language from Ethiopia, the plural marker on a canonical imperative may be reduplicated to indicate an extra degree of politeness (Treis MS). This agrees with the principles of iconicity an the more polite and elaborate the form, the longer and the more morphologically complex it is.

An additional device involved in marking canonical imperatives is SUPPLETION. This device involves using a stem different from that of the verb in statements or questions.[23]

In Manambu, a Ndu language from New Guinea, the otherwise regular verb *yi-* 'go' has a suppletive imperative *ma:y!* 'go (singular, plural, or dual addressee)', and the verb *ya-* 'come', also regular, has an imperative *mæy!* 'come (singular, plural, or dual addressee)'. Table 2.6 contains a full list of verbs with suppletive canonical imperatives in Manambu. This is a fairly typical situation. Suppletive imperatives are typically a minority restricted to a few semantic groups: these often include motion verbs 'come' and 'go', and positional verbs 'sit', 'stand', and 'lie'.

TABLE 2.6 Verbs with suppletive canonical imperatives in Manambu

VERB ROOT	CANONICAL IMPERATIVE
rə- 'sit, stay, copula'	*ada*
tə- 'stand, be, have, copula'	
kwa- 'stay, lie, copula'	*adakw*
yi- 'go'	*ma:y*
ya- 'come'	*mæy*
da- 'go down'	*adi:d*

Verbs 'eat', 'give', 'say', 'do', and 'let, leave' may also have suppletive imperatives.[24] Chrau, an Austronesian language from Vietnam (Thomas 1971: 207), distinguishes three (suppletive) forms of imperative 'eat!' depending on the 'emotional mood' of the speaker: *sa* 'eat!', *dro'* 'eat! (getting impatient)', *taplĭh tapli* 'eat! (angry)'. In Chalcatongo Mixtec, an Otomanguean language from Mexico, only one verb of motion *kii* 'come' has a suppletive imperative form *nǎʔā*. Additional verbs with suppletive imperatives are 'bring' and 'take' (Macaulay 1996: 135–6).

Suppletive imperatives may distinguish special forms depending on the number and gender of addressee. A suppletive imperative form can have all the same gender and number options as a regular one. The suppletive imperative form of a motion verb *geh, yíigi* 'to come' in Egyptian Arabic (Mitchell 1962: 97) distinguishes two genders in the singular and a plural form, just like any other imperative. The second person indicative forms of perfective and of imperfective aspect are contrasted with the corresponding imperative formed using a stem different from either of these:

Egyptian Arabic

2.33		Perfect Indicative	Imperfect Indicative	Imperative
	2masc.sg	*geet*	*tíigi*	*taʔáala*
	2fem.sg	*géeti*	*tíigi*	*taʔáali*
	3pl	*gum*	*yíigu*	*taʔáalu*

A similar example from Figuig, a North Berber language of Morocco (Kossmann 1997: 126), is discussed in §2.2.1 (2.62).

Canonical imperatives in Harar Oromo, a Cushitic language from Ethiopia, appear marked with the suffix -*i* if the addressee is singular, and -*aa* if plural. Another singular marker, -*uu*, appears with non-suppletive imperatives of verbs meaning 'do for yourself' (its plural counterpart is -*aa* everywhere). The suppletive imperative of the verb *d'uf* 'come' in Harar Oromo involves the unrelated stem *xóot*, accompanied by person and number markers otherwise used in reflexive verbs: -*uu* for singular, and -*aa* for plural:

Harar Oromo

2.34 xóot-uu
      come:IMPV-2sg
      'come (you singular)!'

2.35 xóot-aa
      come:IMPV-2pl
      'come (you plural)!'

TABLE 2.7 Marking canonical imperatives in Harar Oromo

NUMBER	SUBJECT-REFLEXIVE VERBS	SUPPLETIVE VERB	ALL OTHER VERBS
	bit-at 'buy for self'	*d'uf* 'come'	*déem* 'go'
singular	*bitádd'-uu* 'buy for yourself!'	*xóot-uu* (2.34) 'come (sg)!'	*déem-i* 'go (sg)!'
plural	*bitádd'-aa* 'buy for yourselves!'	*xóot-aa* (2.35) 'come (pl)'	*déem-aa* 'go (pl)!'

Regular and suppletive canonical imperatives in Harar Oromo are contrasted in Table 2.7 (Owens 1985: 67, 259).

A suppletive imperative with a singular addressee may be shorter and formally less marked than a regular imperative. Imperatives in Modern Greek have their own inflectional endings, different from non-imperatives (Mackridge 1985: 87). The suppletive imperative of the verb *erxo-* 'to come' is *ela*. This form has no special imperative ending. Its plural counterpart is marked with the suffix *-te* (*ela-te* 'come (you pl)!'), just like regular plural active imperfective imperatives, cf. *líne* 'unloosen!' (singular), *líne-te* 'unloosen!' (plural) (Joseph and Philippaki-Warburton 1987: 192, 183).

Alternatively, suppletive imperatives may have fewer distinctions than their regular counterparts. The verb 'give' in Eastern Pomo has an anomalous imperative form *déʔ* which does not distinguish singular and plural, while imperatives of all other verbs do (McLendon 1996: 529).[25]

Or suppletive imperatives may express more number and gender categories than non-suppletive ones. Hausa does not mark gender or number on regular imperatives. The singular addressee form equals the root (Newman 2000: 262–9):

Hausa

2.36a tàfi   àbinkà!
      go   thing.of.2masc
      'You (masc) go on your way!'

2.36b tàfi   àbinkì!
      go   thing.of.2fem
      'You (fem) go on your way!'

A command to a plural addressee involves a combination of special 'subjunctive' pronouns and the unmarked verb:

2.37 kù   tàfi   àbinkù!
     you.pl.SUBJUNC go   thing.of.3pl
     'You (many) go on your way'

Verbs 'go' and 'come' have special imperative forms which distinguish masculine and feminine in the singular, and a distinct plural form:[26]

2.38 jè-ka 'go (masc.sg)!'
     jè-ki 'go (fem.sg)!'
     jè-ku 'go (pl)!'

2.39 yā-kà 'come (masc.sg)!'
     yā-kì 'come (fem.sg)!'
     yā-kù 'come (pl)!'

In contrast to imperatives with a singular addressee, suppletion alone is hardly ever used to mark a non-singular imperative. Modern Welsh offers a rare example of suppletive pairs of singular and plural imperatives. Neither is derived from the other—suppletion is the only way of indicating number (King 1993: 224–6):[27]

TABLE 2.8 Suppletive singular and plural imperatives in Modern Welsh

CITATION FORM	SINGULAR IMPERATIVE		PLURAL IMPERATIVE	
	Northern Welsh	Southern Welsh	Northern Welsh	Southern Welsh
dod 'to come'	*tyrd*	*dere*	*dewch*	
mynd 'to go'	*dos*	*cer*	*ewch*	*cerwch*

Only languages with a suppletive singular canonical imperative also have a suppletive non-singular one, never the other way round. Table 2.9 summarizes the expression of number in suppletive canonical imperatives, and how this compares to number in their non-suppletive counterparts.

TABLE 2.9 Number in suppletive and regular canonical imperatives

NUMBER ON VERB	REGULAR IMPERATIVES	SUPPLETIVE IMPERATIVES	EXAMPLE LANGUAGE
Number distinction	no		Manambu
Non-singular addressee marked on verb	yes		Modern Greek, Modern Welsh
	yes	no	Eastern Pomo
	no	yes	Hausa

Frequently used verbs may form irregular, but not suppletive, imperatives using the same stem as in declaratives. In Modern Welsh (King 1993: 225–6), the singular imperative is formed by attaching *-a* to the verb's stem, as in *tafl-* 'throw', *tafla!* 'throw!' (second person singular addressee). In addition to this, a few forms are irregular. These include *bod* 'be', 2nd singular imperative *bydd!*, *gadael* 'let, leave', 2nd singular imperative *gad!*, *cael* 'have, get', 2nd singular imperative *cei!* We recall, from (A) at §2.1.1, that a handful of frequently used verbs in Latin form imperatives via subtraction—as in *dīc!* 'say!', from *dīcere* 'to say'.

Italian has special imperative forms for the singular addressee of the following high frequency verbs:

Infinitive or 'citation form'	Imperative with singular addressee[28]
andare 'go'	*vai, va'*
dare 'give'	*dai, da'*
dire 'say'	*di'*
fare 'do'	*fai, fa'*
stare 'stand'	*stai, sta'*

The verbs *avere* 'have', *essere* 'be', *sapere* 'know', and *volere* 'want' have special imperative forms in the second person singular and plural: 2sg impv *abbi, sii, sappi, vogli*, 2pl impv *abbiate, siate, sappiate, vogliate*. (These special forms are almost identical to the present subjunctive.)

A language may have imperative-only lexemes whose only function is to command the addressee (see §9.3). Alternatively, such forms can be considered as suppletive forms of canonical imperatives. Such imperative-only forms of motion verbs have been documented for Berber languages of Morocco, and for numerous Cushitic languages.[29] We will see, in §9.3, how imperative formation can provide additional criteria for distinguishing lexical subclasses of verbs.

COMMANDS IN SIGN LANGUAGES are marked in a way different in nature from the devices employed in spoken languages. In Indo-Pakistani Sign Language (Zeshan 2000: 83), commands with immediate force involve the sign for the desired action, or object, and an eye-gaze directed at the addressee. Users of Indo-Pakistani Sign Language sometimes add a mouth pattern to the verb of the command: that is, they make a silent sign with their mouth, mimicking the marker of an imperative in Hindi/Urdu spoken in the area, *-o*. This is the only inflectional marker borrowed from Urdu, the dominant spoken language, into the Sign Language—perhaps due to its salience and frequency in Urdu. Indo-Pakistani Sign Language also has special, 'suppletive' imperative handshapes for 'get up' and 'sit down'.

In American Sign Language (Baker-Shenk and Cokely 2002: 139), a command involves 'stress' on the verb—which involves making a sign faster and sharper—and direct eye-gaze on the addressee. 'Eye-gaze' is one of the non-manual signs in Sign Languages (Zeshan 2004: 18), and is an integral feature of various clause types, including questions and commands. Since it has scope over the whole clause, it is considered a suprasegmental feature, often compared to the use of intonation in spoken languages (Sandler 1999).[30] Having a distinctive intonation contour is a recurrent property of commands as a special clause type. We return to this in §3.1.

2.1.4 *Non-imperative forms in commands*

Commands and directive speech acts are universal: every language has a way of urging someone to do something. But some languages lack dedicated imperative forms. Another verbal category could then be 'co-opted' to express a command.[31] A command and a non-command meaning of the same form have to be distinguished by relying on the context, or through additional means, such as intonation (see §3.1 on intonation as a feature of imperative clauses). In languages lacking dedicated canonical imperatives, commands are regularly expressed using (i) present tense forms of verb, or forms unmarked for tense; (ii) future forms; (iii) potential and intentional modalities; or (iv) irrealis.[32]

Further, less widely attested, options are considered at (v). In (vi) we turn to languages which co-opt non-imperative forms for just the commands addressed to more than one person. At the end of this section we offer some tentative generalizations.

(i) Present tense forms of verb, or forms unmarked for tense in command function. Simplest examples include verb forms unmarked for tense. The simplest form of the verb consisting of a person-marking prefix and a root in Bare (a now extinct North Arawak language formerly spoken in Brazil and the adjacent areas of Venezuela) can be used in statements and in commands, if it is cast in second person. 2.40 has two meanings.

Bare

2.40   bi-hiwa   phaní-ute
       2sg-go   house-DIR
       (a) 'Go home!'
       (b) 'You go/are going home'

The conventional meaning of an unmarked verb in a declarative clause is present or progressive; it can also have a past reference, depending on the context. Tense and aspect markers on the declarative verb are optional: they can be added to the declarative verb, if this is necessary for disambiguation:

2.41a   bi-hiwa-ni
        2sg-go-IMPF
        'You are going home'

In contrast, no such markers can occur together with the verb in its command meaning: 2.41b is ungrammatical:

2.41b *bi-hiwa-ni
'?be going home?'

The formally unmarked *bi-hiwa* is versatile. But this form behaves differently depending on whether it is used as a command or as a statement. A command is usually pronounced with rising intonation, and accompanied by eye-gaze (Aikhenvald 1995a).[33]

Present declarative is consistently used in commands in Ngalakan, from the Australian area, another language with no dedicated imperative form (Merlan 1983: 101–2):

Ngalakan
2.42 ŋiñ-waken   ṛere-kaʔ
      2sg-return.PRES camp-ALL
      (a) 'Go home!'
      (b) 'You are going home'

A verb marked for imperfective aspect is a conventional way of expressing commands addressed to second person in Athabascan languages, including Slave and Western Apache (Rice 1989: 1109; de Reuse 2003, 2006: 343). 2.43–4 come from the Hare and Bearlake dialects of Slave:[34]

Hare dialect of Slave
2.43 ʔáradiḷa
      you.sg.IMPF.go.home
      'You (sg) go home!'
      'You (sg) are going home'

Bearlake dialect of Slave
2.44 kágodawhi
      you.pl.IMPF.go.outside
      'You (pl) go outside!'
      'You (pl) are going outside'

These examples are consistent with a cross-linguistic tendency to use declarative clauses as an additional option for directive speech acts. In many languages, including English, saying *You are going home now* can be understood as a stern command.[35] In languages like English, which do have a specialized imperative, this directive use of a non-directive verb form is part of a plethora of imperative strategies. As we will see in Chapter 8, command strategies can be used as a way of avoiding an imperative form because of its stylistic overtones. A command strategy can also convey extra meanings which conventional imperatives lack.

The use of a primarily non-directive form as a conventionalized command—if no other dedicated command form is available—is parallel to the ways in which non-command forms can be used as command strategies. In many cases, they may undergo further reinterpretation and gradually become command forms par excellence. This is reminiscent of how evidentiality strategies develop over time into bona fide evidentials.[36] We return to this in Chapter 8.

(*ii*) *Future forms of verbs used as commands.* This comes as no surprise: semantically, commands are often associated with future projection. Future is a standard way of marking commands and a multiplicity of other directive speech acts, e.g. obligation and prediction in Bunuba, an Australian language (Rumsey 2000: 91):[37]

Bunuba

2.45   ngangga'wu-in-yha
        give.FUT-1sg.to.2sg-VERB.YHA:TELIC.TRANSFER
        (a) 'Give it to me'
        (b) 'You will/must give it to me'

Using future forms to express commands is not a uniquely Australian phenomenon. In Yagua, from Peru, canonical imperatives are expressed by an analytic construction containing an irrealis auxiliary, just like the future (Payne and Payne 1990: 314–15). The sentence in 2.46 is ambiguous—it can be understood as a command or as a statement.

Yagua

2.46   jiryey-ą   murrą́ą́y
        2pl-IRR.AUX   sing

        'You all sing!' or
        'You all will sing'

(*iii*) *Modal forms with the meanings of possibility and intention* frequently express commands in the absence of a dedicated imperative paradigm. Djapu, an Australian language of the Yolngu group (Morphy 1983: 141–2), has no separate imperative form of a verb. Example 2.47 contains a command marked with potential modality.

Djapu

2.47   ma'   wa<u>d</u>utja   dharpa   gäyu   gulkthu-rr
       come.on   quickly   tree+ABS   tree+ABS   cut-POT
       'Come on, quickly cut a tree down!'

In Djapu, it is 'common to preface or end a command' with an interjection *ma'* 'come on, get on with it!', as in 2.47, or with *gatjuy* 'go on!'. The presence of an interjection is an overt mark of a command, and serves to disambiguate them from a potential form. The addressee can be omitted (as in 2.47) or included.[38]

The second person form of the intentional mood is the standard way of framing a command in Chukchi, a Chukotka-Kamchatkan language spoken in Siberia (Dunn 1999: 188–9, 90). Only the second person intentional form in Chukchi has a command meaning as its primary sense. First and third person forms have hypothetical, future, and desiderative meanings (and do not express commands). This is in line with the second person as the prototypical addressee of a command.

Future forms are often used for getting somebody to do something even if there is a dedicated imperative paradigm—such is the case in Chemehuevi (Uto-Aztecan) or Nishnaambewin (or Ojibwe, Algonquian) (Press 1979: 80–81, Valentine 2001: 994–5). In Modern Hebrew, future is consistently used in lieu of imperatives to express commands: commands cast in future are perceived as less brusque and more polite (Coffin and Bolotzky 2005: 44; Malygina 2001: 270–1). This is in line with the generally abrupt and brusque nature of a prototypical imperative—see §2.1.5.

A form with a potential meaning refers to a possibility of something happening. A command can be viewed as the presentation of a possibility (Davies 1986: 57), something yet unrealized. This provides an intuitively plausible justification for using the same form as a potential, as a future, as intentional modality, and as a command. Another common feature of these four is their 'reality' status. This takes us to the next point.

(iv) Irrealis forms can express commands in languages with the grammatical category of reality status. Realis forms refer to the location of an event or state in the real world, while irrealis places an event in some hypothetical world.[39]

In Manam, an Oceanic language (Lichtenberk 1983: 188), the irrealis expresses commands, as in 2.48, and also events which are likely to take place in near future, as in 2.49.

Manam

2.48   go-moanáʔo
        2sg.IRR-eat
        'Eat!'

2.49   sariŋa-túʔa   go-palála
        near-INTENS   2sg.IRR-be.bald
        'You'll be bald very soon'

Counterfactual events, which could have taken place but did not, are also cast in irrealis. The irrealis form in 2.50 appears in the counterfactual conditional clause:

2.50   ʔáiʔo   nóra-be   go-ra-yá-be   n-duma-íʔo
        2sg.   yesterday-FOC   2sg.IRR-talk.to-1sg.OBJ-and   1sg.IRR-help-2sg.OBJ
        'If you had told me yesterday, I would have helped you'

Irrealis in Manam has additional, language-specific meanings: it is also used to express sequences of customary, habitual activities. This is the essence of what Marianne Mithun (1995) called 'the relativity of irreality': the exact semantic content of irrealis varies from one language to the next, and can sometimes be explained by the historical development of the category and its place within the language's system.[40] We return to the correlations between imperatives and reality status in §4.2.5.

(v) Other options include employing a non-future tense form in lieu of an imperative. In Amele, imperative forms are the same as second person singular, dual, and plural today-past forms (Roberts 1987: 39, 227). The subject has to be marked on the verb; the overt pronominal or a nominal subject is optional:

Amele

2.51   (hina)   h-og-al
        2sg   come-2sg-IMPV/TODAY.PAST
        (a) 'Come!' (2sg)
        (b) 'You came (today)'

The past tense forms of numerous verbs in perfective aspect in Russian can be used as abrupt and familiar commands. Past tense forms distinguish gender and number (but not person) of the subject, and—when used in commands—that of the addressee. So, for instance, the past tense form *po-šel* (PREVERB-go.past.masc.sg) means 'I(masc)/you(masc)/he went'. Combined with an imperative intonation, the same form means 'you:masc go!'.

The past tense form *nacha-li* (begin-past.pl) meaning 'we/you(pl)/they began', if pronounced with an imperative intonation means 'we(inclusive)/ you(pl) start!'. This has rude overtones; the speaker is in the position of authority and the command is to be carried out straightaway.[41] This 'imperative of authority' (a term introduced by Belikov 2001) coexists with a dedicated imperative paradigm.[42]

A marker of imperative may be homonymous with another morpheme. A small subset of verbs in Mara, an Australian language, have a single form for the imperative and the future punctual positive (Heath 1981: 189).[43]

(vi) Using a non-imperative form in lieu of some canonical imperatives. Part of the paradigm for a canonical imperative may overlap with another paradigm. In Rumanian (Mallinson 1986: 24–5), the plural form of canonical imperative is always identical with the second person plural indicative, while the singular form can be different from the indicative. In German, the second person plural form (also used as a polite imperative for second person singular addressee) coincides with present indicative form (see Table 2.2). Similar examples come from Italian, and also Nuer, a Nilotic language (Crazzolàra 1933: 140).

A rather complex example comes from Supyire, a Gur language from Mali (Carlson 1994: 523). Here, the subjunctive marks canonical imperatives with plural addressee, since the dedicated imperative which consists of the verb root without a subject marker or auxiliary can only be used to command one person. As we saw in Table 2.1, second person singular imperative of transitive verbs in Paumarí coincides with the declarative marking.[44]

Such homonymy between an imperative and a non-imperative form can be further resolved, by way of additional phonological processes typical of imperatives. The plural of the imperfective active imperative for all verbs in Modern Greek is the same as second person plural of imperfective active non-past form (Mackridge 1985: 187). But, unlike the corresponding declarative forms, plural imperatives are often subject to vowel syncope, not found with declarative forms: *γrápsete* means 'you (pl) are writing' and a plural imperative 'you write!'. A shortened form *γrápste!* can only be a second person plural imperative. Imperatives do tend to be shorter than forms used in statements—see §2.1.5 for discussion of this.

Languages without a dedicated set of imperative forms may use more than one other form to express command. A command in Ngalakan can be cast in the present—see 2.42 above. Or a future form may be used (Merlan 1983: 101–2):[45]

Ngalakan
2.52   ju-wulup-ga-na
2sg/3sg-bathe-CAUS-FUT
'Bathe him!' or 'Make him bathe!'

As we expect, different 'non-imperative' command forms have different semantic overtones. This is how Young and Morgan (1969: 53–4), the senior scholars of Athabascan studies, summarize it for Navajo: 'imperative has no special form, but is rendered by the future tense forms (which are obligatory in force), the imperfective or progressive mode (when the act is to be carried out at once), and by the optative (when the act is to be carried out in the proximate future, and in a negative sense).'

To conclude: verbal forms used as conventionalized commands in languages which do not have a dedicated imperative paradigm overlap with forms used as command 'strategies' (see Chapter 8). These strategies have additional overtones of politeness, familiarity, authority, strength, and so on, and are available as an extra option. Over time, they can undergo reinterpretation and gradually turn into a de facto main choice for marking commands. In Chapter 10, we look at how erstwhile non-imperative forms can be reinterpreted as a new imperative paradigm.[46]

If a language does not have a dedicated canonical imperative, what do we expect? We can now make tentative GENERALIZATIONS:

GENERALIZATION 1. If a language uses a form from another, non-imperative category, for a canonical imperative with a non-singular addressee, it may or may not also use one for singular imperative. No language has been found to employ a non-imperative form for singular addressee, and have a special imperative paradigm just for a non-singular. This agrees with the basic character of second singular canonical imperative. In other words, if a language has a special imperative form, it must exist at least for second singular addressee.

GENERALIZATION 2. No known language employs forms from different paradigms for singular and non-singular canonical imperative (e.g. a subjunctive form for singular and a declarative for non-singular).

2.1.5 *Markedness and iconicity in canonical imperatives*

There is a fundamental distinction between two kinds of markedness—formal and functional. A formally unmarked term will be the only one in its system to have zero realization (or a zero allomorph). Functional markedness relates to the context of use—the marked term(s) may be used in a restricted, specifiable context, with the unmarked term being used in all other circumstances. Formal and functional markedness do not necessarily coincide—a functionally unmarked term in a system need not be formally unmarked, and vice versa.[47]

A canonical imperative addressed to one person is often the shortest verbal form in a language, and also the least formally marked: it can be just the bare root, or the stem (exemplified in A at §2.1.1). However, not every short form is inflectionally simple: Table 2.4 shows that the imperatives of some verbs in Modern Hebrew are segmentally short, but their formation involves complex morphological rules.

A formally marked canonical singular imperative form may optionally 'lose' its marking. We can recall, from 2.15, that imperatives in Boumaa Fijian are marked with a combination of the relator *me* plus a personal pronoun; this marker can be omitted in the singular canonical imperative. This abbreviated form coincides with the verb root. Along similar lines, just the verb root can be used as a singular canonical imperative in Nigerian Pidgin (see 2.18a).

Similar examples abound. Both singular and plural canonical imperatives in Kwami are marked with a special suffix (2.27). In addition, the most frequently used singular canonical imperative forms lose their final vowel, e.g. *móy* from *móy-ú* 'see, look!', *ɗáw* from *ɗáw-ú* 'go back!'. These abbreviated imperatives have overtones of abruptness, and are considered impolite.

Consider another example. The canonical imperative in Lango, a Nilotic language from Uganda (Noonan 1992: 143), is marked with special suffixes (one for singular, one for plural), the omission of personal prefixes, change of vowel, and a tonal contour. The singular imperative of the verb *dàccò* 'drop' is shown in 2.53a, and the plural imperative in 2.53b:

Lango

2.53a dàcí
       2sg.drop+IMPV
       'Drop it (you sg)!'

2.53b dàcú
       2pl.drop+IMPV
       'Drop it (you pl)!'

In the singular imperative, the final vowel can be dropped. A variant of 2.53a is *dǎc* 'Drop it (you sg)!'.

A similar tendency appears in the historical development of imperative forms throughout Slavic languages: 'one observes in Ukrainian, just as in the other offshoots of proto-Slavic, a definite tendency toward reducing the imperative singular form to the bare stem' (Jakobson 1965: 37–8).[48]

That is, a command to a second person addressee displays a strong tendency towards being, or becoming, the shortest and often the simplest, confirming the basic character of this most 'fundamental' of commands.[49] More often than not, a non-singular canonical imperative will be derived from a singular one—never the other way round. And we saw that a language is expected to have suppletive non-singular imperatives only if there are also suppletive singular counterparts (see e.g. forms in Table 2.8, from Modern Welsh).

The second person singular commands tend to be less formally marked than a command to more than one person for yet another reason. It has often been claimed that, in terms of form, a singular number tends to be less marked than any of the non-singular numbers. It is often the case that the singular has no special marker, and the plural, or any other non-singular number, has one.[50]

The tendency towards formal brevity of a canonical imperative also has a functional motivation. Directives 'conveyed by means of an imperative tend to be perceived as more abrupt and authoritative, and less deferent and polite' than commands phrased using other mechanisms (Davies 1986: 64).[51] Imperatives tend to require immediate reaction. The brusqueness and abruptness of an imperative is a corollary of its formal brevity, as in Kwami (see 2.27 and earlier in this section).

This correlation between form and function can be accounted for by the principle of 'ICONIC MOTIVATION'—whereby semantic relations are reflected in the formal realization: longer utterances and circumlocutions tend to give an impression of higher deference and politeness. As Haiman puts it, 'the greater the politeness, the longer the message' (Haiman 2003: 59).[52] For instance, the periphrastic imperative in Maidu has connotations of mildness and respect, in agreement with the principle of iconicity (Shipley 1964: 54). We return to the politeness distinctions in commands in Chapter 6.

We conclude that if a language has several imperative forms, the shortest one is likely to be an abrupt order, not infrequently perceived as rude, or as having overtones of urgency and immediacy. In contrast, imperatives with further specifications—such as delayed or future ('do later on'), distal ('do elsewhere'), reported ('do following someone else's order'), and others—will always be segmentally longer and more formally marked.

Examples 1.2–3, from Jarawara, illustrate this: the marker of immediate imperative is *-hi* or *-ho* depending on whether the addressee is feminine or masculine, and the marker of a distant imperative—meaning 'do in some distant time or place'—is *-ja-hi* and *-ja-ho*. Mbabaram, a now extinct

Australian language formerly spoken in North Queensland, had two imperatives. A simple imperative indicating a command to do something was
marked by *-g* on the verb root (Dixon 1991: 383–5).

Mbabaram
2.54   nda-g
        shoot-IMPV
        'Shoot (him)!'

The continuative imperative—'an invitation to someone to continue with
what they were doing'—was marked by a longer morpheme, either *-nu-g* or
-ṭu-g (depending on the conjugation the verb belongs to):

2.55   nda-ṭu-g
        shoot-CONT-IMPV
        'Carry on shooting!'

Similar examples abound. The more formally marked the imperative, the
more likely it is to refer to a polite request rather than an order (see further
discussion in Chapter 6, and Aikhenvald 2008b).[53] At present, we can safely
predict that a canonical imperative with a non-immediate meaning or
overtones of polite request will never be less formally marked than a
corresponding immediate or less polite form.

Certain devices are more iconic in their meanings than others. Full reduplication and repetition of the verb often have iconic meanings—to do with
plurality, iterativity, duration, and suchlike. That these devices are hardly ever
used to mark canonical imperatives may be the consequence of the basic
meaning of the prototypical imperative—that of a short command which
requires immediate action.[54]

2.2 Expressing non-canonical imperatives

Commands can be directed at persons other than the addressee—that is, at
first person ('me' or 'us') and third person ('her', 'him', 'them'). The Indo-
European-based linguistic tradition sets these apart from canonical, addressee-oriented imperatives. In Lyons's (1977: 747) words, since only second
person imperatives are addressed 'to those who are to carry them out',
'what are traditionally described as first-person and third person imperatives
[...], in the Indo-European languages at least, are not true imperatives', as
'the subject of these so-called imperatives does not refer to the addressee'.

Commands addressed to first person are often referred to with the term 'hortatives' or 'exhortatives'.[55] This term reflects their function—to incite or urge the speaker, with or without the addressee, to perform a required activity. The latter can be exclusive (without the addressee) or inclusive (with the addressee).[56] Commands addressed to third person, singular or non-singular, are referred to as indirect commands, 'jussive', or as 'injunctive'.

This analysis of commands is at variance with that of other clause types. No grammar would use one term for first person declarative, another one for second person, and yet another one for third. The reasons why different person values for commands tend not to be subsumed under one term, 'imperative', are both formal and semantic (see §2.4).

Setting commands addressed to second person apart from all other commands is justified for some languages. This has been captured by Weinreich (1963: 151):

the indication of the imperative seems typically to intersect with deictic categories ... and to be more highly developed for second person than for first or third, for future/ present tense than for past. The equivalents of the imperative for non-second person are often grammatically more analytic and are asymmetrical with the second-person expression (cf. Yiddish *gejn* 'to go': 2. *gejt*, 1. *lomir gejn*, 3. *zoln zej gejn*).

Lyons (1977: 747) stresses:

the imperative is intimately connected with the second person (or vocative). It is implicit in the very notion of commanding and requesting that the command or request is addressed to the person who is expected to carry it out. In so far as the imperative is the mood whose function is that of being regularly and characteristically used in mands, the subject of an imperative sentence will necessarily refer to the addressee.

But this definition appears to be too narrow for those languages where imperative forms addressed to second person, and to a non-second person, can be justified as parts of one paradigmatic set—as is the case, for instance, in Sanskrit.[57]

We start with languages where commands directed at any person form one paradigm (§2.2.1). Non-canonical imperatives may form one paradigm, which sets them apart from canonical imperatives (§2.2.2). An addressee-directed imperative can overlap in form with a non-canonical imperative: see §2.2.3. Or first person and third person non-canonical imperatives can each differ from imperatives directed at the addressee: this is the topic of §2.2.4. In §2.3 we turn to the much-debated issue of person in the English imperative.

How are non-canonical and canonical imperatives similar in their meanings, and how are they different? We turn to person-specific meanings of imperatives, and further correlations between imperatives and person, in §2.4.

2.2.1 *Canonical and non-canonical imperatives as part of one paradigm*

Command forms covering all person–number combinations may constitute one paradigmatic set.[58] In Kobon, a language from Karam family in New Guinea (Davies 1981: 23–4), all person and number combinations are available for marking the subjects of imperatives, just as in declaratives. The imperative paradigm is shown in Table 2.10.

TABLE 2.10 Subject markers in imperatives in Kobon

PERSON	SINGULAR	DUAL	PLURAL
1	*-ɨn/-in*	*-ul*	*-un*
2	*-ø*	*-il*	*-im*
3	*-aŋ*	*-il*	*-laŋ*

As expected, the second person singular imperative forms are the least formally marked: 2.56 illustrates a command to a singular second person addressee, and 2.57 to a third person plural.

Kobon
2.56   Arɨk-ø
       leave-2sg.IMPV
       'Leave it! (you sg)'

2.57   Kale   mab   ud   ar-laŋ
       3pl   tree   take   go-3pl.IMPV
       'They must take the timber and go'[59]

The imperative in Boumaa Fijian (see Scheme 2.1 and 2.14–15) can be used to address any person. A command to third person plural is at 2.58 (Dixon 1988: 326, T4.197; p.c.):

2.58   me-ra   la'i   la'o   mai
       REL-3pl   GO   go   here
       'Let them come here'

Non-canonical and canonical imperatives tend to form one paradigmatic set in many Uralic languages. Table 2.11 contains a paradigm of the verb *vár* 'wait, expect' in Hungarian (Ugric: Kenesei et al. 1998: 310–12). The imperative is formed with the suffix -*j*- attached to the verb stem before personal suffixes (in bold face in the table). The imperative distinguishes indefinite conjugation (employed when the object is omitted or is indefinite), and definite conjugation (used when the object is definite):

TABLE 2.11 Imperative in Hungarian: the verb *vár* 'wait, expect'

PERSON/ NUMBER	INDEFINITE CONJUGATION	DEFINITE CONJUGATION
1sg	*vár-jak*	*várjam*
2sg	*vár-j(al)*	*vár(ja)d*
3sg	*vár-jon*	*várja*
1pl	*várjunk*	*várjuk*
2pl	*várjatok*	*várjátok*
3pl	*várjanak*	*várják*

Individual forms may have other, non-command meanings. In Hungarian, imperatives are used in purposive complement clauses, and they can also occur in questions—see §2.4.[60]

TABLE 2.12 Imperatives in Evenki: the verb *baka-* 'find'

PERSON/ NUMBER	NEAR FUTURE IMPERATIVE	TRANSLATION	REMOTE FUTURE IMPERATIVE	TRANSLATION
1sg	*baka-kta*	let me find	*baka-ngna:-m*	let me find afterwards
2sg	*baka-kal*	find!	*baka-da:-vi*	find afterwards!
3sg	*baka-gin*	let him/her find	*baka-ngna:-n*	let him/her find then
1pl excl	*baka-kta-vun/ baka-vvun*	let us find ('you' excluded)	*baka-ngna:-v*	let us find then ('you' excluded)
1pl incl	*baka-gat*	let us find ('you' included)	*baka-ngna:-p*	let us find then ('you' included)
2pl	*baka-kallu*	(you pl) find	*baka-da:-ver*	(you pl) find afterwards/then
3pl	*baka-ktyn*	let them find	*baka-ngna:-tyn*	let them find then

A more complex paradigm comes from Evenki, a Tungisic language spoken in Siberia, (see Table 2.12). There are two imperative paradigms—'near future' imperatives and 'remote future' imperatives. Each of these has forms for all person–number combinations (see §4.3) (see Nedjalkov 1997: 262).[61] Note that Evenki distinguishes first person plural inclusive ('us including you') and first person plural exclusive ('us without you').

A language with a full set of person–number distinctions in imperatives can have a suppletive imperative-only stem used throughout the paradigm. In Krongo (Kadugli, Nilo-Saharan: Reh 1985: 198) the verb *-yààw-* 'go' has a full suppletive paradigm, for all the forms. Table 2.13 contrasts a full imperative paradigm for a regular verb *-òmúnóoní* 'call (someone)', with that for the verb *-yààw-* 'go' with its suppletive imperative-only stem *-ín-*:

This full parallelism of regular and suppletive forms can be used as an argument in favour of a one-paradigm analysis.

TABLE 2.13 Regular and suppletive imperative forms in Krongo: a sample

PERSON/NUMBER	*-òmúnóoní* 'call'	*-yààw-* 'go'
1sg	*ómúnón-tí*	*t-ín-tí*
2sg	*ómúnón-tú*	*t-ún-tú*
3sg	*ómúnón-tíní*	*t-ín-tíní*
1pl exclusive	*ómúnón-tíŋ*	*t-ín-tiŋ*
1pl inclusive	*ómúnón-ca*	*t-ín-cá; ón-cá*
2pl	*ómúnón-túkwà*	*t-ún-túkwà*
3pl	*ómúnón-tàày*	*t-ín-tàày*

In a language with no dedicated imperative, the same, essentially non-imperative, form can be employed to express commands addressed to any person. In Gooniyandi (McGregor 1990: 521, 425), 'the unmarked mode of expressing a command to do something is by a clause with a future tense' (cf. Dixon 2002: 79):

Gooniyandi
2.59 mangaddi nyamnyamginggira-woo   thiddirli jagma
     not   you:whisper-DEFINITE.MODE   loud   you:will:speak
     'Don't whisper, speak loudly'

Commands addressed to any person use the future form of the verb. A command to a third person is illustrated in 2.60:

2.60 wamba   bagiwi
     later   he:will:lie
     'Let him lie' (don't get him up)

With a first person plural inclusive actor, the future form also has the effect of a first person command. This sense is said to usually occur in conjunction with the interjection *ba* 'come on, let's go', following the principle of non-canonical commands being more formally marked than canonical ones (see §2.5 below).

2.61   ba   wardbadda
       come:on   we:will:go
       'Come on, let's go'

Not all person–number combinations are equally represented in each language. Which options are attested? The 'missing' person values include (A) first person singular; (B) third person; and (C) first person non-singular.

A. Canonical and non-canonical imperatives without first person singular.
Finnish (Balto-Finnic: Karlsson 1999: 165–7) has a full person paradigm for imperatives, except for the first person singular.[62] The imperative paradigm of the verb *sanoa* 'to say' is given in Table 2.14.

TABLE 2.14 Imperative in Finnish: the verb *sanoa* 'to say'

PERSON/NUMBER	
1sg	–
2sg	*sano*
3sg	*sano-koon*
1pl	*sano-kaamme*
2pl	*sano-kaa*
3pl	*sano-koot*

The first person plural often has an inclusive reading, that is, 'us including you', and is rarely used in the spoken language, 'its function being assumed by the passive indicative' (Sulkala and Karjalainen 1992: 23).

It is indeed often the case that the first person non-singular imperative form has an inclusive reference—whereby the addressee is included in the command. First person imperative in English has a distinctly inclusive meaning: *let's go* implies the participation of the addressee (see §2.3). Along similar lines, a command addressed to first non-singular in Russian has an inclusive meaning.[63] In both instances, the inclusive meaning of non-singular is found just in imperatives. In Huallaga Quechua (Weber 1989: 102), a first person inclusive (you and me) imperative is a polite alternative to a second person imperative.

This takes us to the next item—languages which have no specialized form for third person command, but have one for first person non-singular with inclusive reference.

B. Canonical and non-canonical imperatives without specialized form for third person commands.

In a number of languages, the first person inclusive commands—which include the speaker and the addressee—form one paradigm with the canonical imperative. Passamaquoddy (Sherwood 1986: 142–3), like many other Algonquian languages, has a special imperative 'order' which has forms for second person and first person inclusive subjects. (A different mode, 'injunctive', is employed for third person commands.)

In Figuig, a North Berber language of Morocco, canonical imperatives with a singular and plural addressee are grouped into one paradigm with the command addressed to first and second person (Kossmann 1997: 126).[64]

Figuig

2.62		Imperative person markers	Example:	
	2sg	-ø	ɣres	'slit the throat!'
	1incl	-axdd	ɣers-axdd	'let's (you and me) slit the throat!'
	2pl masc	-et	ɣers-et	'you pl (masculine) slit the throat!'
	2pl fem	-emt	ɣers-emt	'you pl (feminine) slit the throat!'

No languages have been found which would have first person singular imperatives—but not non-singular or inclusive first person imperatives—as part of the same paradigm with canonical imperatives. This is no doubt due to a predilection for including the addressee in an imperative. It will normally be subsumed under non-singular or inclusive first person form.

C. Canonical and non-canonical imperatives without a form for first person.

Second person and third person imperatives form one paradigm in Gahuku (Gorokan family, Papua New Guinea: Deibler 1976: 34–5). Table 2.15 shows that all number combinations for these persons are available. The same form is used for singular, dual, and plural third person. Second person imperative forms are illustrated in 2.63a–b, and a third person form is shown in 2.64.[65]

TABLE 2.15 Markers of person, number, and mood in the Gahuku imperative paradigm

	PERSON		NUMBER		IMPERATIVE MARKER	
NUMBER	2ND	3RD	2ND	3RD	2ND	3RD
SINGULAR	*-o*	*-i*	∅ marker		*-zo*	*-no*
PLURAL	*-a*				*-lo*	
DUAL			*-li*	*-si*	*-zo*	

2.63a   v-o-zo
         go-2p-IMPV.2p
         'Go (sg)!'

2.63b   v-i-li-zo
         go-2p-du-IMPV.2p
         'Go (du)!'

2.64   v-am-i-no
         go-NEG-3sg-IMPV
         'Let him not go!'

The maximum number of distinctions are made in second-person, addressee-directed imperative. This goes together with the basic character of the addressee-directed command.

If a language has several imperatives, different person distinctions may be available for each. Standard Estonian is similar to Finnish in the person–number combinations available in the imperative. Unlike Finnish, number distinctions are partly neutralized in third person imperative (as they are in Gahuku: Table 2.15). This form 'has been generalized' to all persons 'to render an indirect order or a forced action' (Viitso 1998b: 137).[66] The paradigm of the direct imperative and of the 'mediated', or 'indirect', imperative is shown in Table 2.16. Personal pronouns are optional, and are in brackets.

TABLE 2.16 Direct imperative and 'mediated imperative' in Estonian: *kirjutama* 'to write'

PERSON/NUMBER	DIRECT IMPERATIVE	MEDIATED IMPERATIVE
1sg	—	*(ma) kirjuta-gu*
2sg	*(sa) kirjuta*	*(sa) kirjuta-gu*
3sg	*(ta) kirjuta-gu*	*(ta) kirjuta-gu*
1pl	*(me) kirjuta-gem*	*(me) kirjuta-gu*
2pl	*(te) kirjuta-ge*	*(te) kirjuta-gu*
3pl	*(nad) kirjuta-gu*	*(nad) kirjuta-gu*

The direct imperative has no form for first person singular, while the 'mediated' imperative can be used with any person. These forms have additional overtones of wish, obligation, and also of indirect information source. In addition, in the informal style the first person plural form of the present indicative is used instead of the imperative mood: one hears *kirjuta-me* (write-1pl.IND) 'let's write!' (lit. we write) instead of rarer *kirjuta-gem* (write-1pl.IMPV) 'let's write!'.

Along similar lines, Koromfe, a Gur language from Nigeria (Rennison 1997: 38–9), has direct imperative only for second person singular and plural addressees. An alternative imperative construction which allows any person–number value contains the conjunction *ke* accompanied by an indicative verb and has the meaning of an indirect command.

This is congruent with the basic character of second person oriented imperative which has a meaning of direct command—see §2.4 for further person distinctions in systems with multiple imperatives (and also §2.1.5 above).

An additional issue arises with further potential person values in imperative forms. Algonquian languages have two values for third person: 'proximate', referring to an established topic, the centre of attention, and 'obviative' for someone or something less central in that part of the discourse ('obviative' has been labelled as '4th person', with the term 'third person' being reserved for proximate: Anderson and Keenan 1985: 262). However, no such distinctions are made in the imperative paradigm (called 'imperative order' in the Algonquianist tradition).

A number of languages of the world distinguish an additional term in their person system. This term may have an impersonal value, as in numerous Arawak languages. This can be roughly translated by German *man* or French *on*, and English *one* and the impersonal sense of *you*, as in 'One does not have sex before hunting'.[67] In none of the Arawak languages does an impersonal form have a corresponding imperative. Since these are often used in prescriptive statements outlining 'what to do and what not to do', their function overlaps with 'command strategies'—the topic of our Chapter 8.

Impersonal referents may require special command forms. In Italian, 'the infinitive is extensively used as an imperative in what might be termed "generic instructions"—those directed at anyone who might happen to read or hear them' (Maiden and Robustelli 2007: 248). These constructions are found in public notices, recipes, and instructions:

Spingere (sign on a door) 'Push'
Tirare (sign on a door) 'Pull'
Lavare prima di tagliare 'Wash before cutting'

The reflexive pronoun in this construction is third person: *Mettersi nella corsia di destra* 'Get in right-hand lane'. That is, 'impersonal' commands can be considered a subtype of non-canonical imperatives, partly overlapping with third person. We return to the person values within imperatives in Chapter 3.

The 'infinitive' form is used in a similar way in many European languages—in many cases, in negative instructions with a formal, threatening overtone—see §8.4.

2.2.2 *Canonical versus non-canonical imperatives*

Canonical, addressee-oriented imperatives may form one paradigmatic set, with non-canonical imperatives set apart and marked in a different fashion. Consider Paumarí.[68] Markers for canonical imperatives are listed in Table 2.1 (repeated here for easy reference).

TABLE 2.1 Person prefixes in imperatives and declaratives in Paumarí

	IMPERATIVE	DECLARATIVE
2sg.Intransitive	∅	*i-*
2sg.Transitive	*i-*	*i-*
2pl.Intransitive/Transitive	*va-/vi-*	*ava-/avi-*

In contrast to these, non-canonical—first and third person-oriented—imperatives are marked with a verb-final suffix *-va*. Commands to first person, singular and plural, are illustrated in 2.65–6. A command to a third person is in 2.67.

Paumarí

2.65 a-'bai-'a-va
      1pl-eat-ASP-IMPV.NONCAN
      'Let us eat'

2.66 hana-ja   o-vithi-va
      where-DIR   1sg-sit-IMPV.NONCAN
      'Where may I sit?'

2.67 vadi-va   oni   isai
      sleep-IMPV.NONCAN   DEM.F   child
      'Let the child sleep'

We can recall, from Table 2.1 and 2.30a–b, that canonical imperatives in Paumarí differ from corresponding declaratives in that the choice of their person markers depends on whether the verb is transitive or not. The choice of marker on first and third person imperatives does not show such dependency.[69]

Another, similar example comes from Alamblak, a language from the Sepik Hill family in New Guinea. The canonical imperative is marked with a prefix *wa-*, while non-canonical imperatives take the prefix *a-*. The imperatives take the same person marking for subject and for object (or a second argument) as do all other inflected verb forms, but no exponents of tense or other categories (Bruce 1984: 136–7, 184–8, 216–30). An overt pronoun can be optionally included. A canonical imperative with a singular addressee is in 2.68. Examples 2.69–70 illustrate non-canonical imperatives.

Alamblak

2.68 (ni)   nuat   wa-ya-n-t
       (you)   sago.patty   IMPV.CAN-eat-2sg-3sgf
       'You (sg) eat the sago patty!'

2.69 (nëm)   nuat   a-ya-nëm-t
       (we (pl)) sago.patty   IMPV.NONCAN-eat-2sg-3sgf
       'Let us eat the sago patty!'

2.70 (rër)   nuat   a-ya-r-t
       (he)   sago.patty   IMPV.NONCAN-eat-3sgm-3sgf
       'He should eat the sago patty!'

A somewhat more complex situation obtains in Sare (or Kapriman: Sumbuk 1999: 197–8), from the same family as Alamblak: non-canonical imperatives share similarities and contrast with canonical imperatives, but are not fully identical. Canonical imperatives differ from non-canonical ones in two ways:

- Canonical imperatives take the prefix *wa-* and personal suffixes, while non-canonical imperatives take the prefix *Φa-* (except for first person dual, where the marker is *da-*), and subject-marking prefixes in all forms;
- Canonical imperatives have no subject marking in singular, and take subject marking suffixes in dual and plural, while non-canonical imperatives always take subject markers.

Non-canonical imperatives in first and third person share similarities in their morphological form. But, unlike in Alamblak, they are not fully identical. Table 2.17 summarizes the principles of marking canonical and non-canonical imperatives in Sare.

TABLE 2.17 Canonical and non-canonical imperatives in Sare

PERSON	SINGULAR	DUAL	PLURAL
1		prefix *da-* preceded by personal prefixes: 2.74	prefix *Φa-* preceded by personal prefixes: 2.75
2	prefix *wa-* with no person markers on verb: 2.71	prefix *wa-* and personal suffixes on verb: 2.72–3	
3	prefix *Φa-* preceded by personal prefixes: 2.76		

Sare: canonical imperatives

2.71 (nɨ)   wa-sedsa   sagi-m
      2sg   IMPV.CAN-drink   water-PL
      'You (sg) drink (some) water!'

2.72 (Φɨn)   wa-sedsa-Φɨn   sagi-m
      (2du)   IMPV.CAN-drink-2DU   water-PL
      'You two drink some water!'

2.73 (mɨ)   wa-ki-m   wunɨ-r
      (2pl)   IMPV.PL-build-PL house-sgm
      'You (pl) build a house!'

Sare: non-canonical imperatives

2.74 (nənd)   nan-da-sedsa   sagi-m
      (1du)   1du-IMPV.NONCAN-drink   water-PL
      'Let us two drink some water!'

2.75 (nəm)   na-Φa-ki   wunɨ-r
      (1pl)   1pl-IMPV.NONCAN-build.house   house-sgm
      'Let us (pl) build a house!'

2.76 Φɨ   Φɨ-Φa-ki   wunɨ-r
      (3du)   3du-IMPV.NONCAN-build   house-sgm
      'Let them two build a house!'

In terms of their syntactic properties, canonical and non-canonical imperative clauses in Sare appear to be fairly similar, and distinct from declaratives.[70] We turn to these differences in Chapter 3.

Canonical imperatives may be set apart from non-canonical ones in yet another way. Only canonical imperatives may have a dedicated marking, while imperatives addressed to first or third person employ a form of a different category. In Latin, first and third person commands are expressed through subjunctive, e.g. *vivamus et amemus* 'let's live and love', *fiat lux* 'let it be light', and second person commands are expressed through imperative. Along similar lines, subjunctive is used for non-canonical imperatives in Rumanian (Mallinson 1986: 24–5),[71] as is the case in many other Romance languages (Harris and Vincent 1988; Posner 1996).

2.2.3 *Overlap in forms of canonical and non-canonical imperatives*

Forms of some non-canonical imperatives can partly overlap with canonical ones. First person imperatives may form one paradigm with second person imperatives, and third person may be marked quite differently. In Fox (Algonquian: Dahlstrom MS: 138–9), the immediate imperative is used for positive commands with second person or first person inclusive plural subjects. The injunctive paradigm is employed for third person imperatives. In Italian, the second person singular imperative is identical to the third person singular present indicative or second person singular present indicative, depending on the verb's conjugation. First person plural imperative is always identical to the first person plural present indicative, and second person plural imperative to second person plural present indicative. In contrast, third person imperative (singular and plural) is expressed by using subjunctive form—see Table 2.18 (Maiden and Robustelli 2007: 247–8).

TABLE 2.18 Canonical and non-canonical imperatives in Italian

2sg imperative = 3 sg present indicative: Verbs of first conjugation: *canta!* 'sing!' *canta* 'he/she sings'
2sg imperative = 2 sg present indicative: Verbs of other conjugations: *dormi!* 'sleep!' *dormi* 'you sleep'
2pl imperative = 2 plural present indicative: Verbs of all conjugations: *cantate!* 'you pl sing!' *cantate* 'you sing'
1pl imperative = 1pl present indicative: Verbs of all conjugations: *cantiamo!* 'let's sing!' *cantiamo* 'we sing'
3sg and pl imperative = 3 sg and pl subjunctive: Verbs of all conjugations: *canti!* 'May she sing! Sing (singular polite)!'
cantino! 'May they sing! Sing (plural polite)!'

Third person imperative forms are more often than not used in a canonical imperative function—with *Lei* and *Loro*, polite equivalents of 'you singular' and 'you plural' respectively. The iconicity principle is at work again – the more polite, the longer and the more elaborate the form. We return to politeness in imperatives in Chapter 6.

Just one of the canonical imperatives may show an overlap with another category. We can recall, from §2.1.4, that Supyire employs subjunctive for non-canonical imperatives with plural addressee, since its dedicated imperative can only be used to command one person. The dedicated form, called 'bare imperative' by Carlson (1994: 520–6), is shown in 2.77.

Supyire

2.77 Lwɔhɔ   kan   náhá
     water   give   here
     'Give me some water!' (lit. Give water here)

The subjunctive construction for plural addressees is shown in 2.78:

2.78 Yìi   í   ú   kán   na   à!
     you.PL SUBJUNC   her   give   me.NONDECL   to
     'Give her to me!'

The subjunctive is also used to mark non-canonical commands, addressed to first plural, and to third person—an example is in 2.79:

2.79 Pi   í   tí   lyî
     they   SUBJUNC   it   eat
     'Let them eat it!'

Canonical and non-canonical imperatives display further complexities: subjunctive with second person singular addressee may be used for a particularly strong command—see Chapter 6. And, in addition, special non-declarative pronouns can be considered a feature of commands—compare examples from Yawelmani (2.32a–b), and also subjunctive pronouns in Hausa (2.37).

Mekens, a Tuparí language from Brazil, has two kinds of non-canonical imperative addressed to first person plural. One of these is marked in the same way as a regular canonical imperative in intransitive constructions.

Mekens

2.80 e-er-a
     2sg-sleep-THEMATIC
     'Sleep!'

2.81 ki-er-a
     1pl.incl-sleep-THEMATIC
     'Let's sleep!'

Transitive non-canonical imperatives are analytic: they involve a special 'hortative' verb *-ot* 'go, let's':[72]

2.82 ki-or-a   i-at
      1pl.incl-go-THEMATIC   OBJECT.MARKER-get
      'Let's go get it!'

Forms of canonical and non-canonical imperatives overlap—but the most basic imperative, the one addressed to singular 'you', remains separate.

2.2.4 *Different forms for canonical and for each of the non-canonical imperatives*

Canonical imperatives may have a dedicated marking, and each of first and third person be expressed in a different way.

A prime example comes from Cavineña, a Tacana language from Bolivia (Guillaume 2004: 179–87). Each of the person values in imperatives is expressed with a separate paradigm. Table 2.19 contains the second person imperative inflection.

TABLE 2.19 Second person imperative inflection in Cavineña

Singular	-kwe
Non-singular	ne-...-kwe

A command to a singular addressee is illustrated in 2.83:

Cavineña
2.83 bute-kwe
      go.down-IMPV.SG
      'You (sg) go down!'

Cavineña has dual and plural pronouns—however, in the imperative, one non-singular form is used for dual and plural addressees. In 2.84, a dual pronoun 'us dual' shows that the non-singular command is addressed to two people:

2.84 Tudya=yatse   señora=ra   a-tsa-chine:
      then=1dual   woman=ERG   affect-COME-REC.PAST
      Ne-je-nuka-kwe   lasiete   chine=ju
      IMPV.NSG-come-REITR-IMPV.NSG   at.seven   evening=LOC
      'Then the lady told (lit. affected) us (dual): "(you dual) come again at seven in the evening"'

And in 2.85, the command is addressed to several people:

2.85 Ne-kwinana-wisha-kwe
      IMPV.NSG-go.out-FAST-IMPV.NSG
      'You (pl) go out (of the plane)!'

First person imperatives distinguish singular, dual (or inclusive: you and me), and plural:

TABLE 2.20 First person imperative inflection in Cavineña

Singular	pa-
Dual	ne-
Plural	ne-...-ra

The three forms are illustrated in 2.86–8:

2.86 Ikwene   e-ra   e-kwe   rimu   pa-keti
      first   1sg-ERG   1sg-DAT   lemon   HORT.SG-fetch
      'Let me first fetch a lemon for myself'

2.87 Ne-iye   chai=kwana!
      HORT.DU-kill   bird=PL
      'Let us (dual) hunt (lit. kill) birds!'

2.88 Jutakiju   gobierno   ne-baka-ra   ekwana   tsawa=ishu
      therefore   government   HORT.PL-ask-HORT.PL   1PL   help-PURP
      'Therefore, let's (pl) ask the government to help us'

To mark a command to a third person, the verb acquires the prefix *pa-* (homonymous with the first person singular command marker). No number distinctions are made. The three number values—singular, dual, and plural—are illustrated in 2.89–91. In each case, number is not marked on the verb (it can be optionally marked on the noun phrase outside the verb):

2.89 Esiri-ke   pa-diru
      old-LIG   JUSS-go
      'Let the old one (man) leave!'

2.90 Pa-kastere=jari   ekatse
      JUSS-become.tired=STILL   3DU
      'Let these (two monkeys) get tired (quarrelling) (and then I will kill them easily)'

2.91 Tuna-ra   pa-isara-ti
      3pl-ERG   JUSS-talk.to-GO.TEMP
      'Let them go and talk to them (the Araona people)'

All three person values in Cavineña are negated in different ways—see Chapter 5.

A language may have a special construction for first person, and employ a form of another different category for third person command. In Dolakha Newar, from the Tibeto-Burman family (Genetti 2007: 337–41, 179–86), imperative mood is restricted to canonical addressee-oriented imperative. The canonical imperatives distinguish singular and plural forms of the second person addressee. Forms of number marking correlate with the verb's transitivity value and its stem form (see §4.4.1).

Dolakha Newar

2.92 jana   mica   ya-ŋ
     1sg.GEN   daughter   take-IMPV.SG:TRANS
     'Take my daughter!'

2.93 chipe   thau   thau   chē   o-n
     2sg.GEN   REFL   REFL   house   go-IMPV.PL:INTRANS
     'Go each to your own house!'

A dedicated hortative construction is used for first person inclusive commands: the marker *-lau* attaches to the infinitive form of the verb, as in 2.94:

2.94 u=ri   thijin   kā-i-lau
     this=IND   1incl.ERG   take-INF-HORT
     'Let's take this one!'

To command a third person, optative is used—as in 2.95:

2.95 tha-hat
     OPT-speak
     'May he speak!'

The major meaning of the optative is expressing a wish that something should happen. Optative can only occur with first and second person if the action is not volitional—we return to this in §4.4. Just like the canonical imperative, the optative distinguishes different forms for transitive and intransitive verbs—a feature absent from first person commands, the 'hortative'.

In Komi (Permic subgroup of Finno-Ugric), canonical imperatives are expressed with suffixed forms. As expected, the second person singular form is zero-marked. Commands addressed to first and third persons acquire additional marking with particles (Mikushev 1988: 82)—which vary depending on the person: the particle *vaj* is used for first person commands, and *med* for third person.[73]

TABLE 2.21 Canonical and non-canonical imperatives in Komi

PERSON/NUMBER	*kor* 'invite'
1sg	*vaj kor-a*
2sg	*kor-ø*
3sg	*med kor-as* or *med-korę*
1pl inclusive: singular addressee	*kor-am* or *vaj kor-am*
1pl inclusive: plural addressee	*kor-amęj* or *vaj kor-amęj*
2pl	*kor-ęj* or *kor-ę*
3pl	*med kor-asnį* or *med kor-ąnį*

Another option is to employ non-imperative categories for the expression of first, and third person commands, keeping the special imperative forms for just the canonical imperatives. In Spanish,[74] first person plural imperatives are formed using the present subjunctive, e.g. *empecemos* 'Let's get started!' (Butt and Benjamin 2004: 291–2), while third person imperatives are commonly formed with *que* 'that' and a subjunctive, e.g. *Que nos cuente qué política económica querría que hiciéramos* 'Let him tell us what economic policy he'd like us to follow'. The subjunctive in Spanish has a variety of meanings and uses in main and subordinate clauses (including wish, desire, and so on). A second person subjunctive can also be preceded by *que*, and appear in commands, 'this makes the order more emphatic or presents it as a reminder', e.g. *¡Que se diviertan!* 'Have a good time!' (you many).

In languages with multiple imperatives—which distinguish parameters outlined in Chapters 4 and 6—it is common to have a special form for first person non-singular command, and make the maximum distinctions for second person (see Aikhenvald 2008b, on multiple imperatives in the languages of the Vaupés area).

The special status of a non-canonical imperative may be corroborated by the existence of irregular, suppletive forms.[75] Many such examples include verbs of motion. Dolakha Newar has a suppletive form *ŋā* 'let's go' (the verb 'go' is *ū*).[76] Tariana and Baniwa (both Arawak) have suppletive forms *wasá* and *ahʃa* 'let's go' respectively, and Tucano (Tucanoan) has *te'a*, with the same meaning. Neither of these languages has suppletion in the formation of canonical imperatives.[77] Note, however, that instances of third person suppletive imperative forms have not been attested so far.

We saw above that Rembarnga, an Australian language, utilizes future forms as commands (also see 2.60, from Gooniyandi).[78] An 'anomalous' invariant verb *maɲ*—whose meaning on its own is 'went' (past punctual)—can be used with first person pronominal prefixes in the hortative meaning:

Rembarnga

2.96 ya-maɲ
     1/2min.S-'went'
     'Let's go!'

Suppletive forms of non-canonical imperatives may offer further complexities.

Figuig, a North Berber language from Morocco (see 2.62 above), has three 'imperative-only' suppletive verbs. The imperative-only verb 'come' uses the suffix *-it* instead of *-et* in second plural masculine imperative. It has all the gender and number combinations of a regular imperative, except for the first person plural:

Figuig

2.97	2sg	*(a)rwaḥ*	'come!'
	1du	*(a)rwaḥ-axdd*	'let's come!'
	2pl masc	*(a)rwaḥ-it*	'come (masculine pl)!'
	2pl fem	*(a)rwaḥ-emt*	'come (feminine pl)!'

The verb *yaḷḷeh/yaḷḷah* 'let's go!' has three first person forms: inclusive (with no gender distinction), first plural masculine, and first plural feminine:

2.98	1incl	*yaḷḷh-axdd*	'let's go (you and me)!'
	1pl.masc	*yaḷḷah-ut*	'let's go (masculine plural)!'
	1pl.fem	*yaḷḷah-emt*	'let's go (feminine plural)!'

An additional regular non-canonical first person plural imperative is formed somewhat differently, and requires a 'hortative' particle *ad/an/a*. Note two different gender forms:

2.99			Example	
	1pl masc	*n-...-(e)t*	*an ne-ẕwa-t*	'let's go away!' (masculine)
	1pl fem	*n-...-(e)mt*	*an ne-ẕwa-mt*	'let's go away!' (feminine)

The special suppletive forms set first person-addressed commands apart from the rest—thus confirming the existence of an opposition between some, or all, canonical and non-canonical imperatives.

Expressing and interpreting different person values of an imperative can be fraught with analytical problems. Imperatives in English are a case in point.

2.3 Imperative and person in English

2.3.1 *The canonical imperative and its addressees*

The canonical second person imperative in English 'has no particular ending' (Jespersen 1924: 314). Or, in Sweet's (1891: 112) words, 'the inflection of the imperative is, then, a purely negative one, being merely the common form of the verb used as a sentence-word in the second person'.[79] Canonical imperatives in English have three defining properties.

Firstly, as Börjars and Burridge (2001: 127) put it, 'the most striking structural characteristic of an imperative is that it need not have an overt subject'. The subject is understood as being second person, the prototypical addressee,[80] as in:

2.100   Close the window!

An overt subject—'you'—can be added, as in

2.101   You close the window!

Sure enough, the subject in English can also be omitted in declarative clauses—statements, as in 2.102a and 2.102b—and interrogatives—questions, as in 2.103:

2.102a   Have to go now (cf. I have to go now)
2.102b   Looks like not a very good idea (cf. It looks like not a very good idea)
2.103   Fancy a drink? (Do you fancy a drink?)

However, such examples are restricted to a highly colloquial register, are often idiomatic, are felt by native speakers to be elliptical, and would hardly ever be used in formal or written genres. And supplying an overt subject to (2.102a–c) would not produce the same effect as adding the overt subject in 2.101. In Davies's (1986: 131) words, 'intuitively, we are perhaps more likely to feel that those imperatives which do contain a subject possess some extra specification than to feel that there is something missing from those which do not have a subject'. In other words, the subject of an imperative is 'something supplementary'.[81]

The pragmatic functions of an overt subject—second or third person—in imperatives in English have been a bone of contention in linguistics for many decades. A *you* subject in (2.101) has been seen as a marker of impatience (Levenston 1969), of irritation (Quirk et al. 1972: 403), or, as Schmerling (1975: 502) puts it, the presence of *you* may correlate with 'an attitude of impatient hearer-directed anger on the part of the speaker'. While 2.101 does invoke what Huddleston (1984: 360) calls 'bullying or aggressive tone', one can think of many examples which sound rather friendly and encouraging, if perhaps a trifle patronising—such as, for instance, 2.104–5:

2.104   You just take your time

2.105   You help yourself

What most instances of the overt second person pronoun *you* in English imperatives appear to have in common is 'that in each case the speaker is laying claim to a certain authority over his addressee'.[82]

Secondly, the imperative in English has 'either a main verb in the base form or (less commonly) an auxiliary in the base form followed by the appropriate form of the main verb' (Quirk et al. 1985: 827). And **thirdly**, it also requires the presence of *do* with negation, or when the imperative is 'emphatically affirmative' (Davies 1986: 7).

2.106a   Don't hurry

2.106b   Do hurry up

Do appears even with *be* and *have* as an auxiliary. This is in contrast to non-imperatives—(2.107a) and (2.108a) are grammatical, and (2.107b) and (2.108b) are not:

2.107a   Do be ready on time

2.107b   *He does be ready on time

2.108a   Do have eaten your breakfast by the time I get home[83]

2.108b   *He does have eaten his breakfast by the time I get home

In addition to this, the verb in imperative lacks tense inflection, and does not allow modal auxiliaries.[84] Progressive forms can be used, as in 2.109, and so can perfective forms, as in 2.110.

2.109   Be listening to this station this time tomorrow night

2.110   Start the book and have it finished before you go to bed

However, these are judged rare and are not easily acceptable by all speakers.[85] Imperative stands apart from declarative and interrogative in yet another way. Any noun phrase can be used as a subject of declarative and interrogative clauses. Not so with imperatives. The English imperative is often described as 'virtually in the second person, even if seemingly addressed to a "third person", as in *Oh, please, someone go in and tell her*'. The addition of *somebody,*

one, and *someone* may mean 'one of you present' (Jespersen 1933/1972: 148).[86]
That is, a noun or a pronoun with a seemingly third person referent can be understood as second person. A tag question cast in second person sounds felicitous while a third person does not:[87]

2.111   Somebody strike a light!
2.112   Somebody strike a light, will you?
2.113   ???Somebody strike a light, ???*will they?

However, if a reflexive is inserted, it has to be third person; a second person reflexive sounds questionable:

2.114   Somebody strike a light for himself/herself/themself!
2.115   ??? Somebody strike a light for yourself???

A possessive is usually co-referential with third person, as in:

2.116   Somebody lend me his coat

Note that a subject-less canonical imperative requires second person possessive:

2.117   Lend me your coat (*Lend me his coat)

To say *Lend me his coat* as a variant of 2.117 is impossible, which is why this sentence is starred. It will have a different meaning—referring to someone else's coat.

The subjects of imperatives may include indefinite and negative pronouns and full noun phrases, as in:

2.118   Parents with children go to the front.
2.119   The man with the list come up here.

Second person and indefinite pronouns are common as imperative subjects, but first and third person pronouns are hardly acceptable: one can say *someone close the window* or *everybody stay inside* but hardly *I/we/he/she/they close the window*.[88]

Most examples which involve overt third person subject appear to involve contexts where an order to a third person is conjoined with another command which does have a subject referring to the second person addressee, as in:

2.120   You make the dinner and John do the washing up. No? All right then, John cook and you wash up.

Outside such conjoined structures where a third person in a command role accompanies a second person—which sets the scene for the command reading of the whole sentence—'subjects with entirely third person referents are rare' (Davies 1986: 168), but possible. In examples like 2.121, 'the motivation for addressing an order to someone other than the intended agent seems to be to get the addressee to report the directive to the third persons addressed':

2.121   These children of yours keep out of my garden, or I'll set the dog on them

That is, the addressee is still covertly present; in other words, the non-canonical reference of a canonical imperative still bears the trace of the canonical person reference. That is, a condition for non-addressee subject in a canonical imperative structure is the presence of an addressee, in the background.

Subjects can be confused with vocatives. But, as Quirk et al. (1985: 829) point out, the subject of the imperative always precedes the verb, and vocative—which is essentially external to the verb's argument structure—can occupy initial, medial, or final position in the clause. When placed sentence-initially, the vocative 'has a separate tone unit (typically fall-rise); the subject merely receives ordinary word stress':

2.122a   Màry, play on mỳ side
2.122b   Play, Mary, on mỳ side
2.122c   Play on mỳ side, Màry

In contrast, 2.122d does not contain a vocative:

2.122d   Mary play on my side, and Peter play on yours

A vocative and an imperative subject can occur together—this is an additional indicator of how distinct they are: *Mary, you listen to me!*

This is how Davies (1986: 145) summarizes the motivation for including a subject in an English imperative construction:

Where a speaker wishes to indicate that [their] intended agents do not include all the addressees, or that they include some non-addressees, [they] must signal this by providing an overt subject.[89]

We conclude at this point that canonical imperative in English can be extended beyond commands to just the addressee, albeit in a limited and context-dependent way.

Just as in many other languages, an analytic alternative exists for expressing other persons in imperatives.

2.3.2 *Analytic non-canonical imperatives*

First and third person imperatives in English can be formed by preposing the verb *let* to the subject (a pronominal subject takes then the 'objective' case'):[90]

2.123   Let me think what to do next
2.124   Let us all work hard
2.125   Let each man decide for himself

These—except for the *let me*—are judged to be 'generally archaic and elevated in style'.[91] A more common, and more colloquial alternative to *let us* is the abbreviated contraction *let's*, as in

2.126   Let's enjoy ourselves!

The form *let's* is used as first person inclusive imperative, with addressee included.[92] In Davies (1986: 234)'s words, 'the first person examples [with *let's*] do seem to constitute some sort of directive to an addressee, whereas the third person examples [...] need not be understood to involve any kind of appeal to an addressee'.

2.127   Let's go!

The first person inclusive subject of *let's* (you and I) can be understood from the context, as in 2.128. Here, the two policemen are checking each other's identification. One is saying to the other:

2.128   Now let's check our identifications (Tony Hillerman, *The Ghostway*)

Or this can be reinforced by overt pronouns *you* and *I*, as in:

2.129   Let's you and me (or you and us) do something (OED *let* 14).

The *let* constructions share the following properties with canonical imperatives:

I. *Let* constructions are in complementary distribution with canonical imperatives: the ordinary subjectless imperative is understood to have a second person addressee, the *let* imperative is used in other contexts, where the intended subject is third or first person. Interestingly, an indefinite like *someone* or *everyone* is possible both with a canonical imperative and in a *let*-construction, the referential possibilities are different.

In 2.130, *somebody* is understood as referring to one of the speaker's addressees—and this is confirmed by the form of the tag question which has to be second person.

2.130   Somebody try explaining that to them, will you?

In 2.131 *someone* refers to a third person who may not be present at all at the time of the utterance:

2.131   Let someone try explaining that to them

II. The *let* construction can be used in a parallel fashion to canonical imperatives in their conditional-like use (this not-quite-commanding function of English imperative forms is discussed in Chapter 7). The following examples come from Davies (1986: 242). In 2.133, a *let*-construction with third person reference parallels the canonical imperative form in 2.132:

2.132   Make them an offer and they won't refuse
2.133   Let her make them an offer and they won't refuse

III. *Let* constructions can be negated using *don't*, just like canonical imperatives:

2.134a   Don't let's make a mistake
2.134b   Let's not make a mistake[93]

Similarly to other languages, in which canonical imperatives stand apart from non-canonical ones, the *let*-imperative in English is 'an imperative of a rather special kind, which complements the ordinary imperative in allowing the specification of types of subject which cannot occur in other imperatives' (Davies 1986: 250).[94]

2.3.3 *Additional options for third person commands*

Formulaic expressions—called optative subjunctives (Quirk et al. 1985: 839)—are used to express a wish directed to someone else. As is expected in a fixed expression, the nature of the subject is limited to just a few conventionalized options. In some, the subject has to occur after the verb:

2.135   Far be it from me to spoil the fun
2.136   So be it
2.137   Suffice it to say that we lost
2.138   Long live the King!

In others, the subject occurs before the verb:

2.139   God save the Queen!
2.140   God forbid!

And for some, both orders are acceptable:

2.141a   God help you if you are late!
2.141b   So help me God!

According to Quirk et al. (1985), these expressions have an archaic feel to them. They cannot be negated. An additional—less archaic—formula for wishes directed at any person, singular or non-singular, involves *may*—subject—verb. This is used for expressing wishes, blessings and also curses:

2.142   May you break your neck!
2.143   May all your troubles be small!
2.144   May the best man win!

The productivity and the range of these expressions is too limited to call them regular third person commands. However, they represent an additional option for a non-canonical person value in English.

2.3.4 *Canonical and non-canonical imperatives in English: a summary*
The summary in Table 2.22 of the forms of canonical and non-canonical imperatives comes from Quirk et al. (1985: 830).

TABLE 2.22 Imperatives and person in English

		1ST PERSON	2ND PERSON	3RD PERSON
without subject		–	(i) Open the door	–
with subject	without *let*	–	(ii) You open the door	(iii) Someone open the door
	with *let*	(iv) Let me open the door. Let's open the door	–	(v) Let someone open the door

In addition to this, an imperative without *let* and with a subject can have first person reference, as in *You take the low node and I'll take the high node*, and third person reference, as in *John wash the dishes and Mary clean the floor* (in agreement with Davies 1986: 241)—all given the command context already established.[95]

In summary, the English imperative is not as simple as it may appear. We are faced with a rather unusual system with multiple overlaps between addressee-oriented imperatives, and imperatives involving other persons.

2.4 Person-specific meanings of imperatives

Commands to the addressee, to the speaker, and the 'third person' tend to have different meaning overtones. Person-specific meanings of imperatives in Manambu, a Ndu language from the Sepik area of New Guinea, are a case in point. This language has synthetic forms for first, second, and third person commands. Second person command forms do not distinguish gender or number (in contrast to second person pronouns and second person forms of declarative verbs). The first and third person commands distinguish three numbers (singular, dual, and plural). Throughout the Manambu grammar, third person singular forms distinguish two genders, masculine and feminine. Table 2.23 contains a set of sample forms of the verb 'listen'. We recall, from Table 2.6, that Manambu also has suppletive second person imperative forms. There are no suppletive forms for other person values.

In terms of their form and the categories expressed, the second person imperatives stand apart from other person forms. There are additional semantic differences between the three sets of person values. Second person forms are used for straightforward commands and are highly frequent in discourse.

TABLE 2.23 Imperative cross-referencing in Manambu: the verb *wuk(ə)* 'listen'

PERSON/ GENDER	SG	DU	PL
1	*wukə-u* 'let me listen, may I listen?'	*wukə-tək* 'let us two listen!'	*wukə-nak* 'let us listen!'
2	*a-wuk* 'you (sg, du, pl) listen!'		
3masc	*wukə-kwa-d* 'let him listen!'	*wukə-kwa-bər* 'let them two listen!'	*wukə-kwa-di* 'let them listen!'
3fem	*wukə-kwa* 'let her listen!'		

First person singular imperative has a permissive meaning, and is often used for mild requests, as in 2.145:

2.145   kwasa   wiya:r   <u>yau</u>
        small+fem.sg   house+LK+ALL   go+1sg.IMPV
        'May I go to the toilet; let me go to the toilet'

It is also used as a turn-taking device, as in *wa-u?* (talk-1sg.IMPV) 'may I talk?' First person non-singular (dual and plural) forms of imperative are usually employed as invitations to do something, with an inclusive meaning—that is, the addressee is within the scope of command, e.g. *yi-tək* (go-1du.IMPV) 'let's (two of us) go!'. The inclusive meaning is not distinguished anywhere else in the Manambu grammar.

Third person imperative is used for commands and instructions with reference to a third person. It often has permissive overtones, and may imply letting something happen by itself, as in 2.146—an instruction on how to take sore throat lozenges.

2.146   kəmarki-tukwa   dayim   kurə-n   kwa:n
        swallow-PROH.GEN   mouth+LOC   get-SEQ   stay+SEQ
        yi-kəta-kəta-kwa
        go-AROUND?-AROUND?-IMPV.3p+fem.sg
        'Do not swallow (it), having got (it in your mouth) with it staying (there) let it dissolve'

Third person imperative is also used with a generic meaning, in instructions and prescriptive statements (where English would use a generic *you* or *one*). In 2.149, a speaker tells her audience that, traditionally, only initiated men were allowed to sit on a bench. This is cast in third person imperative.

2.147   də-kə-dəka   təkər-əm   <u>rə-yi-kwa-d</u>
        he-OBL-ONLY   bench-LK+LOC   sit-go-IMPV.3p-masc.sg
        'Only he (the initiated man) could sit on the bench'

The person-specific meanings of forms for different person of imperatives in Manambu reflect the following common linguistic principles.

FIRSTLY, a command to oneself, that is, first person singular, implies suggestion, proposition, or seeking permission. A first person command in Hungarian has permissive overtones, and is often used in questions, as in *Ide hozzam?* 'Shall I bring (it) here?' Such an imperative may be understood as an offer to do something, as in *Lemasoljak edy kulcsot?* 'Shall I copy a key?'[96]

The first person singular 'hortative' in Cavineña is used when 'the speaker expresses his will/intention to himself'.[97] An alternative is to use the imperfective declarative form with future reading, to communicate one's desires to an addressee: this shows how restricted the use of first person singular command is in the language (Guillaume 2004). First person plural imperatives marked with *let's* in English are often interpreted as invitations or asking for permission, rather than straightforward commands (Davies 1986; Hopper and Traugott 1993: 11–12).

Secondly, third person imperatives have strong overtones of indirect commands, and wishes. This agrees with the principle of iconicity in those languages where third person commands are formed analytically: the longer the form, the less direct the meaning. Third person commands in Romance languages are typically referred to as 'optatives', e.g. Italian, Spanish (¡)*venga!* 'Let him come!' (Posner 1996: 142). This is reminiscent of the so-called 'optative subjunctives' in English and modal forms used to express wishes and blessings involving third person (see 2.138–41).

Third person commands are used as polite alternatives to second person commands in Romance languages, such as Italian (see above) and in Spanish. This is consistent with third person as a means of establishing a distance between the speaker and the addressee, thus making the command into a less abrupt—or less prototypical, and more mediated—order.

We thus arrive at a not unexpected conclusion. While the canonical addressee-oriented imperative is expected to imply a straightforward command, orders directed at other people tend to develop meaning overtones which set them apart from canonical imperatives: first person commands may imply seeking a permission, while third person commands refer to wishes and indirect ways of inciting people to do things.

2.5 Imperatives and their addressees: conclusions and generalizations

Marking an imperative may involve a variety of means:

- verbal inflection (frequent in synthetic languages);
- particles (frequent in isolating and highly agglutinating languages);
- a special set of pronouns.

An imperative directed at a singular addressee—the most prototypical of all—often coincides with the bare stem of the verb. Imperatives addressed to first or to third person (called here 'non-canonical' imperatives) tend to be more formally marked. And not infrequently, they are expressed analytically, while a one-word, synthetic expression is used for a straightforward command to the addressee.

In agreement with the principle of iconicity in grammar, the least formally marked imperative in a language is likely to refer to a single action to be performed by a single person immediately. That is, we expect continuative or durative imperatives, and delayed ('future') imperatives, to be formally marked. We return to this in Chapter 4.

The traditional analysis of commands is at variance with that of other clause types. No grammar would use one label for first person declarative, another one for second person, and yet another one for third. The reasons why different person values for commands tend not to be subsumed under one term, 'imperative', are both formal and semantic. First and third person imperatives are often formed using different means than second-person imperatives, and do not form a single paradigm with them. Second person imperatives are primarily commands. In contrast, first person imperatives may develop overtones of suggestion or permission, and third person commands shade into the expression of indirect, mediated wishes.

The most common non-canonical imperative is a first person plural inclusive—that is, the one involving the addressee plus the speaker. A special form for first person singular is absent from a number of languages which have first person plural (with an inclusive reading) and third person imperative, in addition to the canonical values. Diagram 2.1 summarizes our expectations as to which person distinctions are likelier than others, in imperative forms.

DIAGRAM 2.1 Person distinctions in imperatives: what we expect

Non-canonical values			Canonical values
1sg and/or 1p exclusive	> 3 sg or pl	>1p inclusive; non-singular	>2p (sg, pl, or non-singular)
(a)	(b)	(c)	(d)

That is, if a language has (b) third person imperatives, we also expect it to have (c) an imperative form expressing first person non-singular, with an inclusive reading. And if a language has (a) an imperative for first person singular or exclusive, we expect it to have (b) a third person imperative, and consequently, (c) a first person non-singular one. These expectations are borne out by the facts of languages discussed in §2.2.

Part of the motivation behind the principle reflected in this diagram is intuitively clear—the most likely imperative forms involve the addressee.

They are thus expected to be directed at the addressee, or have an inclusive meaning—that is, be addressed to 'you' and 'me'.

Numerous languages have no dedicated imperative form. We saw, in §2.1.4, that a form of another category—irrealis, present, imperfective, future, intentional, and some others—can be adopted in a regular command function. All such forms can be used as command strategies in languages which do have a dedicated imperative paradigm. We will see in Chapter 10 how command strategies can be reinterpreted as command-only forms, during the course of linguistic history.

If a language has a special imperative form, it will cover at least the second singular addressee. No language employs a non-imperative form for singular addressee, and has a special paradigm just for non-singular. This agrees with the basic character of the second singular canonical imperative. And no known language employs forms from different paradigms for singular and non-singular canonical imperative (for instance, a subjunctive form for singular and a declarative for non-singular). This is the essence of the generalizations stated in §2.1.4.

Canonical imperatives can have irregular or suppletive forms. Typical candidates include verbs of motion and stance (but the range of possibilities extends beyond these). The same applies to suppletive first person imperatives. In a number of languages, suppletive imperatives have a full paradigm of forms. Only languages with a suppletive singular canonical imperative also have a suppletive non-singular one, never the other way round.

Special person values and marking in imperatives constitute part of the argument in favour of the imperative as a distinct clause type—this is the topic of our next chapter.

Notes

1. See Schmerling (1975), for the first statement of this.
2. For typological parameters of classification of languages, see Aikhenvald (2006) and references there, including Sapir (1921).
3. Along similar lines, the second person imperative is the simplest form of the verb in Danish: it is identical with the verb stem. So, for the verb *læse* 'to read' the imperative form is *læs!*, and for *køre* 'drive' it is *kør!* No tense or aspects are distinguished. Danish verbs fall into several conjugation classes, depending on whether a vowel intervenes between the root and some of the suffixes or not. So, the verb *købe* 'to buy' forms the past tense *købte*, and the verb *hoppe* 'to hop' forms *hoppede*. In the imperative, this difference disappears: *køb* 'buy!', *hop* 'hop!'. That is, the difference between verbal conjugations is neutralized in the imperative. In the closely related Swedish, the difference in conjugation class is preserved in the imperative: *köp* 'buy!', *hoppa* 'hop!'. (See Allan et al. 1995: 243, 301–3; Sadock and Zwicky 1985: 173.) The distinction between conjugation classes is also neutralized in Dyirbal in the imperative (2.7–8).

4. A bare verbal root marks a second person singular command in Kugu Ngannhcara, and Margany and Gunya. Imperative in these languages is not the citation form of the verb—despite it being essentially just the verb root. (See Smith and Johnson 2000: 409–10; Breen 1981: 337; an overview is in Dixon 2002: 213.)

5. See Heath (1999: 165). Kawachi (2007) provides similar tests for Sidaamo, an East Cushitic language from Ethiopia.

6. See Dixon (1977: 213, 370). In his exhaustive overview of Australian languages, Dixon (2002: 213) recognizes a recurrent imperative affix -*ga* (sometimes reduced to -*g*) in numerous language groups, among them the Wik group, Kukatj, Kuku-Yalanji, Mbabaram, and Wirangu, and another suffix -*a* in languages of South-East Cape York peninsula, Nyangumarta, Karatjarri, Yanyuwa, and Wagaya.

7. See Aikhenvald (2002) and references there for cross-linguistic properties of clitics as distinguished from affixes and prosodically independent morphemes. On clitics in Semelai see Kruspe (2004a: 87). The sign = indicates a clitic boundary. Also see Glossary.

8. See Dixon (1972: 110–11). Verbs divide into conjugations depending on the type of final consonant. Since final consonants are deleted in the imperative, verbal conjugations are no longer differentiated. We return to this in Chapter 4.

9. Van Driem (1993: 250–51). This refers to second person subject with first person object, and second person subject and third person object.

10. Further examples of tone as a marker of imperatives include Babungo, a Bantu language (Schaub 1985: 22), where imperative is marked by the absence of the overt subject and by floating high tone. In Aghem, also Bantu (Anderson 1979: 108–11), imperatives are marked by floating tone. Along similar lines, the imperative in Hausa (Newman 2000: 263–9, 601) has a distinctive tone pattern (usually Low-High); its other distinctive feature is the absence of weak subject pronouns before the verb and no overt TAM markers. A similar example is Bora, a Bora-Witotoan language from Peru (Thiesen 1996: 67, 119). In Kana, a Benue-Congo language from Cross River subgroup (Ikoro 1996: 188–9), one of the morphologically determined imperative types is marked exclusively by tone. Tonal change also plays a role in the formation of imperatives of motion verbs in Chalcatongo Mixtec (Macaulay 1996: 134–5). A tone pattern may be just one of the properties of an imperative. In Somali, a Cushitic language, second person singular imperative is marked with zero and with a special tone pattern. The form *súg!* with high tone means 'wait!' (compare this with the simple past form *sug-tay* 'you waited', or present general *sug-taa* 'you are waiting', with low tone) (Saeed 1993, 1999: 86; Tosco 1999a). Saeed (1999: 20–24) provides an overview of grammatical functions of tone in Somali.

11. Adelaar (2004: 219); see also Cole (1982); Parker 1969; Weber (1989).

12. Frank (1990: 86–9). Negative imperatives are more often formed with auxiliary constructions than are positive imperatives (see Chapter 5).

13. Faraclas (1996: 194). Faraclas offers no synchronic explanation for this curious polysemy. Causatives in Nigerian Pidgin imply control of the subject. And as we

will see in Chapter 6 and in §4.4, the semantic core of imperative involves the commander's control over the addressee. The feature of 'control' is what the two instances of *mek* share, synchronically.

14. Dixon (1991); see also Dench (1991) on Panyjima, Patz (1991) on Djabugay, and Dixon (2002: 173). The same form covers singular and non-singular addressee in a few other languages mentioned in §2.1.1—Manambu, Semelai, Dâw, and Khalkha Mongolian (where it is the shortest form in the language: Poppe 1951: 76).

15. Van den Berg and Bachet (2006: 192–3). Along similar lines, in Mina, a Chadic language from Cameroon, the second person plural pronoun 'must be used', 'if the order is given to more than one addressee' (Frajzyngier and Johnston 2005: 233–4). The singular addressee is optional (but can be obligatory under some circumstances—such as a sequence of commands).

16. Using non-singular subject pronouns with any kind of canonical imperative is a tendency rather than a steadfast rule in Mussau, an Oceanic language spoken in the New Ireland Province of Papua New Guinea. Here, a singular subject is usually omitted in imperative constructions, whereas a non-singular subject can be omitted if clear from the context. See Brownie and Brownie (2007: 177–8).

17. Along similar lines, canonical imperatives with a singular addressee in Tukang Besi (an Austronesian language from Sulawesi, Indonesia: Donohue 1999b: 452–3) coincide with a verbal root without subject prefixes. Subject prefixes are used if the addressee is plural (or if the speaker wants to show respect to the addressee: cf. §2.1.5), e.g. *wila-tinti* (go-run) 'Go away' (singular addressee); *i-sumbere-waliako* (2pl.real-immediate-return) 'Go back home this instant, you lot!' (plural addressee). Also, in Ute, a Uto-Aztecan language from Colorado (Givón 1980: 117), the simplest verb form in the language is the most direct and least polite imperative which is also used if 'the speaker wishes to be *rude* to the hearer'. This coincides with the bare stem of the verb and can be addressed to one or two people. The plural addressee is marked with a suffix, e.g. *káa* 'sing! (you singular or dual)'; *ká-x̂a* 'sing! (you, three or more)'.

18. Languages in which singular and non-singular canonical imperatives are equally formally marked include Epena Pedee (a Choco language from Colombia: Harms 1994: 115–16) (to be also mentioned in §4.6).

19. Cf. Harris (1997), for an attempt at such an approach to Spanish, another language in which imperative forms have lookalikes among other categories.

20. These Modern Hebrew forms are quoted from Malygina (2001: 270), in her transliteration. The forms in brackets are considered archaic and hardly ever used in the modern language (see Coffin and Bolozky 2005: 60; Aikhenvald 1990).

21. Also see Schalley and van der Auwera (2005) for a discussion of analytic and synthetic imperatives in Slavic.

22. Partial reduplication as a component in marking imperatives has been described for Sidaama (Kawachi 2007: 425–6): the singular addressee canonical imperative is formed by adding suffix -*i*, and the plural addressee imperative is formed by repeating the stem-final consonant and adding -*e* to it: *sagalé it-i* (food(ACC)

eat-IMPV.2sg) 'Eat the food!' (to a singular addressee), *sagalé it-te* (food(ACC) eat-IMPV.2pl) 'Eat the food!' (to plural addressees).

23. Commonly accepted criteria for suppletion are discussed in Mel'čuk (1994, 2000); also see Corbett (2007). Tosco (2000) summarizes the suppletive imperatives for motion verbs as an areal feature of languages in Ethiopia (also see Ferguson 1976). Further examples are found in Kambaata (Treis MS), Alaaba (Schneider-Blum 2007), and Sidaama (Kawachi 2007), East Cushitic languages from Ethiopia. These languages differ in whether suppletive forms are also used in prohibitives (as in Kambaata) or not (as in Sidaama; see Chapter 5).

Veselinova (2003: 153–66) discusses suppletion in imperatives, based on a limited 'sample' of languages. The reader must be warned that her discussion suffers from lack of faithful adherence to the sources, and of distinction between imperative-only words and suppletive forms.

24. Such frequently used verbs may have suppletive forms throughout the paradigm. The verb 'go' in Acoma (Maring 1967: 101–2) is a case in point: it has 'six shapes which regularly appear, three in singular number, two in dual and plural number, and one hortative form' (note that Maring uses hortative in lieu of imperative and command of any sort). The 'hortative' stem /-ʔiima/, translated as 'you go', appears to contain the same stem as -*ma* used for third person declarative. The suppletive paradigm of 'go' is as follows:

	Singular	Dual and plural	'Hortative' (command)
1.	-*yu*	-*eyU*	
2.	-*cuʔu* ~ *ceʔe*	-*cuun*	-*ʔiima*
3.	-*ma*		

25. See also Oswalt (1961: 255), on the same verb, in closely related Kashaya.

26. Newman (2000: 269) notes that the forms in 2.38 'are easily analysable synchronically as the verb *jē* 'go' + an ICP (intransitive copy pronoun), with the imposition of the regular L-H imperative tone pattern'. The forms in 2.39 'with H-L tone [. . .] are anomalous archaisms whose structure and etymology are still unknown'.

27. Other Celtic languages also have suppletive imperatives (see Ball and Fife 1993).

28. But note that at least some derivatives of *dire* have regular imperative forms. See Maiden and Robustelli (2007: 248–9).

29. Laoust (1928: 51); Kossmann (1997: 126); Treis (MS). Nunggubuyu (Australian area: Heath 1984: 343) has a defective verb 'come' which occurs only in imperative (also see Dixon 1972: 116).

30. Similar marking of commands has been described for the Australian Sign Language by Johnston and Schembri (2007: 201).

31. In her treatment of future in command functions in Chemehuevi, a Uto-Aztecan language, Press (1979: 80) calls such uses 'semantic imperatives'.

32. Lacking a dedicated imperative does not have to be considered a 'gap' in a verbal paradigm. Dixon (2002: 79) notes that, in a minority of Australian Aboriginal

languages, 'imperative is one sense of an inflection with more general meaning. For example, imperative falls together with future in [. . .] Rembarnga, [. . .] Ngandi, and [. . .] Mirning; with non-past irrealis in [. . .] Uwinjmil; and with potential in [. . .] Djapu.'

33. A similar situation obtains in other North Arawak languages, e.g. Warekena of Xié (3.1) and Achagua, a North Arawak language from Colombia (Wilson 1992). !Xun, a Khoisan language from Namibia (König and Heine forthcoming), employs the same unmarked verb form for both imperatives and declaratives; also see Rubino (1998) for Ilocano.

34. Some Athabascan languages do have a special imperative suffix (see, for instance, Hargus 2007: 338–9 on Witsuwit'en).

35. See e.g. discussion by Ervin-Tripp (1976) and references there.

36. See Aikhenvald (2004) and further discussion and references there.

37. Similar examples are found in prefixing languages spoken in northern parts of Australia, e.g. Rembarnga (McKay 1975: 169) (see also Dixon 2002: 79, 211):

    (i)   ta-pəttəʔ-ma-ŋaṛa
          3min.O+2min.A-carry.in.arms-get-FUT
          'Carry (pick up) the baby!'

    Nungubbuyu, another prefixing Australian language (Heath 1984: 343), has no differences in inflectional form between verbs which function as commands and ordinary future forms. So, /ba=bura:-/ can mean either 'sit!' or 'you will sit'. We can recall, however (from §2.1.1) that Nungubbuyu has one imperative-only lexeme—a defective verb 'to come' used just in imperative sense.

38. Another option is using the unmarked form of the verb; this is preferred for a different conjugation class (p. 142). It can be argued that the paradigmatic distribution of forms creates a special imperative subset.

39. For the cross-linguistic validity of reality status, with a basic distinction between realis and irrealis, see Elliott (2000). Irrealis forms are typically used in constructions with negative, potential, and conditional meanings, and not infrequently in commands (also see Elliott 2000: 69, 75–7).

40. Irrealis forms are indeed used in commands, and in statements with potential meaning, in Maung, an Australian language (Capell and Hinch 1970: 67), Terêna, a South Arawak language from Brazil (Ekdahl and Grimes 1964; Ekdahl and Butler 1979), and Pilagá and Toba, Guaicuruan languages from Argentina (Vidal and Klein 1998: 188). However, in Jamul Tiipay and Maricopa, two Yuman languages from North America, and in Caddo, a Caddoan language (Mithun 1999: 179), commands are cast as realis, and irrealis forms are employed in other instances of future projection. Alternatively, different kinds of imperatives can be cast in realis or irrealis depending on the imperative's semantics. In a few Papuan languages, an irrealis form is used for polite imperatives (see Roberts 1990: 390; Mithun 1995: 378), while more abrupt ones are realis.

41. Contrary to Xrakovskij and Volodin (2001: 292), these forms are not restricted to motion verbs with the preverb *po-*. Examples of other verbs in past tense, including 'give' and 'finish eating', used as familiar abrupt commands, are discussed by Belikov (2001). That perfective aspect forms should be employed in these rude and familiar commands goes together with the correlations between politeness and aspect choice in imperatives in Russian (see §3.4, and Shmelev 2002: 272ff.). The constructions involving 'imperative of authority' differ from corresponding declarative constructions in intonation, and in the placement of the personal pronouns: while the unmarked order in a declarative clause involves pronoun preceding the past tense verb, in an 'imperative of authority' construction a pronoun (optionally included for person disambiguation or emphasis) follows the verb: declarative *ty po-šel* 'you(masc) went'; 'imperative of authority' *po-šel ty!* 'may you go (e.g. to hell)'. The latter construction has strong imprecative overtones.

42. This arose as a result of reinterpretation of the old optative: see Jakobson (1965: 34–5).

43. This is the case just for those verbs which have *-mi* in both indicative and imperative. For all other verbs, these forms are different. See also §3.3.2 on the second person meaning of third person marking in Mara imperatives.

44. Imperatives may share their stem with another category. In Arabic or Hebrew, imperfective stems are employed to form imperatives; however, imperatives do have their own set of markers. The choice of a verbal form used to mark commands—whose markers in each case partially overlap with another paradigm—may depend on the transitivity of the verb. In Worora, an Australian language (Clendon 2000: 255–6), imperatives of intransitive verbs are constructed using the subjunctive prefix, as in *ba=ya* (SUBJ=go) 'Get out of it'. Transitive imperatives contain optative markers (p. 256: see tables 8.4 and 6.1 there).

45. Cf. Dixon (2002: 79): in Ngalakan, 'either a future or a present suffix is used in an imperative clause'.

46. See, for instance, Jakobson (1965) for Slavic.

47. See Aikhenvald (2004), Aikhenvald and Dixon (1998: 60), and Dixon (1994: 56–7).

48. This tendency is attested in the history of Polish and Czech.

49. This is, however, a tendency rather than a universal rule. Marking person and gender in canonical singular imperatives may involve complexities. Sadock and Zwicky (1985: 174) observe that 'if only some of the forms of an imperative paradigm are devoid of explicit personal markers, it appears that these will always include the second person singular, and—provided the language has such categories—masculine familiar'. As a categorical statement, this is not borne out by the facts (see Chapter 4, on the expression of various grammatical categories in commands). For instance, the bare verb stem in Abkhaz is used only for second singular imperatives of transitive verbs. Intransitive verbs and second

person plural forms of transitive verbs retain the subject prefixes (which explicitly mark genders).

Vowel reduction itself may be a property of both singular and plural canonical imperatives, as is the case in Modern Greek (Joseph and Philippaki-Warburton 1987: 250). For instance, *fére to* 'bring (2sg) it' can be shortened to *fér to*; and *fére-té to* (bring-2pl it) 'you (pl) bring it' to *fér-te to*. This 'syncopated' form is 'the more common one in the plural for most verbs'. The shortened singular imperatives are common with verbs of high frequency, such as *féro* 'bring', *káno* 'make, do', etc. We can recall, from (vi) at §2.1.4, that this vowel loss often differentiates plural imperatives in Modern Greek from homophonous non-imperative forms (Joseph and Philippaki-Warburton 1987: 183). According to Jakobson (1965: 37–8), as a result of analogy, vowel shortening spread from second person singular to plural imperative, and then to first person imperative forms in the history of Ukranian.

50. In other words, 'it is common for the singular to have zero expression; it is less usual for the plural to be marked in this way, even for a smaller group of lexical items' (Corbett 2000: 151, 154). This ties in with the Universal 35 formulated by Joseph Greenberg (1963) : 'There is no language in which the plural does not have some non-zero allomorphs, whereas there are languages in which the singular is expressed only by zero. The dual and the trial are almost never expressed only by zero.'

51. See also Leech and Svartvik (1975: 145–6).

52. Along similar lines, the canonical imperative in Dutch coincides with the stem of the verb—cf. *kijken* 'to look', *kijk* 'look!' But, to make it sound more polite, the marker *-t* is added to the verb and the pronoun *u* is used (Shetter 1994: 49).

53. Hup, a Makú language from Northwest Amazonia, is another prime example of the same principle: direct imperative consists of a bare stem (Epps 2005: 958–64), e.g. *nǽn* 'come!'. Imperatives with other overtones—those of motion, special urgency, or impatience—carry additional suffixes. In Koromfe, a Gur language spoken in Mali and Burkina Faso (Rennison 1997: 37–8), a 'normal', non-durative, imperative consists of a bare verb stem, e.g. *pa!* 'give!' A durative imperative has a special marking. Similar examples come from Kiowa, Yidiñ, Igbo, and Eskimo.

54. Along similar lines, vowel lengthening does not seem to mark imperatives. I have no explanation as to why no examples have been found in which serial verbs mark commands (Aikhenvald 2006a shows that they can express intentional meanings). It remains important to remember that what we have just described represents pervasive tendencies rather than steadfast rules. In a few languages, imperatives with different meanings are equally formally marked. An additional example comes from Lavukaleve (Papuan, Solomons: Terrill 2003: 340–43).

55. As pointed out in Chapter 1, individual grammars are not averse to using these and other terms in fairly idiosyncratic ways to refer to first person commands. One finds 'hortative' as a cover term for first and second person commands (Bruce 1984: 137, for Alamblak); or as a cover term for all commands (Maring

1967, for Acoma). We recall, from Chapter 1, that Lyons (1977) suggested a term 'mand' as a cover.

56. Sadock and Zwicky's (1985) suggestion that hortative is used to 'urge or suggest a course of action to be followed by the [speaker] and the addressee' is only partially correct. Examples of first person exclusive hortative have been described in this chapter.

57. See Whitney (1924 (1891): 208, 215). Baum (2006: 11–20) provides an incisive analysis of the place of the imperative in the verbal system of the Rigvedic Sanskrit.

58. A broad definition of paradigm is given by Matthews (1997: 263–4) as 'forms of a given noun, verb, etc, arranged systematically according to their grammatical features'; see also van Marle (2003: 239) and Plank (1991).

   The existence of paradigmatic rather than syntagmatic relationships between the different forms of canonical and non-canonical imperatives may be corroborated by formal analogies between different person values. Jakobson (1965: 37–40) describes a tendency towards vowel shortening in the Ukrainian imperative which spread from second singular to second plural imperative, and then to first person imperative forms. In Chapter 3 we turn to special properties of imperative clauses, which include intonation, constituent order, and others. Once again, clauses with non-canonical imperatives may be set apart from canonical ones.

59. The English translation involves 'must'. As pointed out by Hardman (2000: 65) in her discussion of a full imperative paradigm in Jaqaru (Aymara family), 'the imperatives from other than the second person are very difficult to translate since English requires the introduction of some second person. I use "let" or "may" but, of course, there is nothing like that in the Jaqaru, they are genuinely third, first, or fourth person (= first person plural: A.A.) imperatives.' As pointed out in Chapter 1, the reader should not be guided (or misguided) by the translation.

60. In Saami (Balto-Finnic: Sammallahti 1998: 73–4) and in Nganasan (Helimski 1998a: 505), imperatives are available for three persons in three numbers (singular, dual, and plural). Other languages with the same set of person distinctions available in imperatives and in declaratives include Nigerian Pidgin, Maori, Sanskrit (Whitney 1924 (1891): 208, 215), Jaqaru, Apalaí, Hixkaryana (both North Carib, from South America), West Greenlandic, Koasati (Muskogean), and Motuna (Papuan, from Bougainville), and also Livonian (Balto-Finnic: Laanest 1975: 180–81).

61. A similar example from Una, a Papuan language (Louwerse 1988: 36) is mentioned in §4.2.2.

62. First singular imperative is absent from Quechua languages (see Cole 1982: 31, on Imbabura Quechua; Crapo and Aitken 1986: 9, on Bolivian Quechua; and Weber 1989: 101–2, for Huallaga Quechua). First person imperative is not attested in Veps (Laanest 1975: 170) and Standard Estonian (Laanest 1975: 177); but see below and Erelt (2002a) and Viitso (1998b).

63. See Davies (1986: 239–42). This is how Sweet (1891: 112 (§310)) formulates it: 'there can be an imperative of the first person plural when it is equivalent to *I* or *we+you*.' Inclusive overtones of first person non-singular imperatives in Russian are discussed in Xrakovskij and Volodin (2001).

64. This command has an inclusive meaning (me and you); Kossmann terms it 'dual'. Two genders—masculine and feminine—are distinguished in plural, but not in singular. This feature, typical for most Berber languages, will be looked at in §4.1.

65. Negative and positive imperatives are formed in a similar way (see Chapter 5 on other possibilities). Only second and third person imperatives have also been documented in Ingric, Karelian, Votic, and Võru dialect of Estonian (all from Balto-Finnic subgroup of Fennic: Laanest 1975: 172, 174, 179), Selkup (Helimski 1998b: 568) and Enets (Künnap 1999: 24–5) (from the Samoyedic group of Uralic), Udmurt (Permic subgroup of Finno-Ugric: Csúcs 1998: 291–2), and Mari (Mari subgroup of Finno-Ugric: Kangasmaa-Minn 1998: 230).

66. This form is also known as 'jussive' (Erelt 2002a: 112; de Sivers 1969: 60–61).

67. The label '4th person' has been used for such impersonal terms; for instance, Aikhenvald (2003) for Tariana, Ramirez (1992: 41) writing on Bahuana, and Rowan and Burgess (1979: 18) on Parecis.

68. Non-canonical imperatives form one paradigm which is distinct from that of canonical imperatives in Dhasanaac (Tosco 2001: 278–80).

69. This also makes non-canonical imperatives more similar to declaratives than the imperatives oriented towards addressee (see Chapman and Derbyshire 1991: 217–18).

70. A similar example comes from Dogon (Plungian 1995: 27), where non-canonical imperatives partly overlap in their marking, and canonical imperatives are marked distinctly from both. See Table 3.2. Afar (Cushitic, Ethiopia: Bliese 1981: 139ff.) is another example of the same principle. English *let's* marks both first person and third person commands: see discussion in §2.3.

71. Subjunctive can also be used with second person, with different illocutionary force and politeness overtones (Mallinson 1986: 25–6). On comparable use of subjunctive in Hausa, see Newman (2000: 591–3). In Somali and Ilocano, optative is used for non-second person imperatives (see Tosco 1999a; Rubino 1998).

72. There is an additional hortative-permissive construction used for both second and first commands (Galúcio 2001: 157–9).

73. Other descriptions of Komi adopt a different approach—Lytkin (1966: 309) includes only canonical singular and plural imperatives in the paradigm, as do Tepljashina and Lytkin (1976: 180). Apart from the pressure of the traditional grammar, an additional reason for this could lie in the inherent semantic differences between different persons in commands.

74. Although traditionally not called 'imperatives', these forms fall into the realm of 'non-canonical' imperatives as presented here.

75. Just as in the case of canonical imperatives, suppletion is never the only way of marking a non-canonical imperative—see §2.1.3.

76. Genetti (2007: 341) notes that this verb can also occur with the first person imperative suffix: *ū-i-lau* 'let's go!'.

77. A similar example, also for suppletive hortative of 'go', comes from Chalcatongo Mixtec (Macaulay 1992: 417).

78. McKay (1975: 141). Using a past tense form in a command is reminiscent of Amele (see (v) in §2.1.4 above).

79. The formally unmarked verb base has other functions; see Bolinger (1967, 1977: ch. 8, 'Is the imperative an infinitive?').

80. See Davies (1986: 5–7, 131–2); Darbyshire (1967).

81. Bolinger (1977: 8) suggests that '*Shut up* does not delete *you*; rather, *You shut up* adds it. The subjectless imperative has become a structure in its own right.' In Jespersen's words (1928: 222), a subject can be added to an imperative 'chiefly to give an emotional colouring to the imperative'; also see discussion in Chapter 3.

82. See Davies (1986: 147), and further discussion there. She points out that the difference in the 'tone' of imperative clauses with *you* in examples like 2.100 and 2.104–5 may be attributed to the different purposes: while 2.100 is a straightforward command, 2.104 and 2.105 are likely to be interpreted as expressing advice, or invitations, the speaker being concerned for the addressee's well-being. See further discussion of the effects of including an overt subject in English imperatives in Davies (1986: ch. 5).

83. See Dixon (2005: 50, 224) on *have* as a marker of past tense within complement clause constructions and in 'back-shifting' in English.

84. Chapter 1 of Davies (1986: ch. 1) contains a detailed and fascinating discussion of other possible definitional properties of imperatives. Some scholars (e.g. Stockwell et al. 1973) claimed that the restriction on forming imperatives on stative verbs could be another of their definitional properties. However, Davies shows that this restriction—rather loose, especially given the potential use of such forms in ironic, sarcastic and 'imprecative' contexts—is a corollary of the semantic overtone of 'control' implicit in English imperatives. We return to this in §4.4.

85. The issue of 'perfective' in imperative is closely linked with the contentious problem of whether a command can refer to past—see further discussion in §4.2.2, and Bolinger (1967: 348–50).

86. See Schmerling (1982: 202), and Davies (1986: 132–51) on the range of subjects for canonical imperatives in English.

87. The ambiguity between second and third person in English extends to command strategies. Questions in English can be used as polite alternatives to imperatives. And even in these questions third person may in fact have a second person reference marked in pronouns, as in the announcement in a Medical Centre in Melbourne *Would all patients please present your medicare card.*

In numerous languages of the world, third person forms are used in lieu of second person as exponents of politeness. The use of what can be seen as 'generic third person' with addressee in view in English can be seen as a variation on that.

88. In a sequence of commands, the formally unmarked verb can be used with third person and with first person reference, as a kind of 'echo-effect', e.g. *You strike a light and all the others follow suit* or *You strike a light and I follow you*. A proper name can also appear as the subject, especially in a sequence of commands: *John scatter the files, Bill ransack the desk, and I'll watch the door*.

89. Some speakers lament that Modern English is somewhat 'deficient' in that no distinction is made between singular and non-singular second person. This gap is being filled in colloquial varieties of English: *yous*, *you guys*, and *you all* are effectively used as emergent second person plural forms. I hypothesize that, if singular and plural reference in canonical imperatives has to be disambiguated, such as second plural pronoun is inserted for disambiguation (similarly to other languages, such as Manambu in examples 2.23–4 above, where the imperative form itself does not differentiate number). However, more corpus studies need to be conducted before this impressionistic observation can be taken as a fact.

90. The link between first and third person *let* commands is incisively summarized by Davies (1986: 234): 'it seems intuitively quite unsatisfactory to treat the first and third person *let*-constructions as entirely unrelated and only coincidentally similar, particularly when we recognise the possibility of examples like (i) and (ii):

(i) Let the boys stay here and us go and fetch help
(ii) Let us take the Daimler and Fred take the MG.'

91. See Quirk et al. (1985: 830). Davies (1986: 229ff.) discusses the differences between *let* 'allow' and *let* in the imperative construction, and presents convincing arguments in favour of treating the *let* constructions on a par with canonical imperatives, with a different person value. In particular, constructions with *let* as a main verb 'allow' and the *let*-commands are negated differently, e.g. *He let us not pay*, *He didn't let us pay*, and *Let's not pay* or *Don't let's pay*.

92. Some grammarians treat it as an imperative particle (e.g. Börjars and Burridge 2001).

93. A variant *Let's don't make a mistake* appears to be highly colloquial.

94. In different varieties of English, the range of possible subjects of *let's* appears to be extending from first person inclusive to first person singular, and also to second person. In very colloquial English, *let's* can be used for a first person singular imperative, thus extending from first person inclusive to first person singular (Quirk et al. 1985: 830), e.g. *Let's give you a hand*. (Historically, such development of person value is rather unusual. In some languages, e.g. Terêna, an Arawak language from Brazil, an erstwhile first person singular developed into first exclusive.)

Hopper and Traugott (1993: 11) report that some Midwestern American speakers extend *lets* to include second person, e.g. *Lets you and him fight*. This is said to be 'perhaps jocular'. Another example, *Lets you go first, then if we have any money left I'll go*, was produced in a neutral context. In *Lets wash your hands*, *lets* does not imply speaker's participation—it is interpreted as a sign of 'the speaker's condescending encouragement' in addressing a child. These extensions of *let's* (whose meanings cover a variety of directive speech acts, including suggestion, invitation, permission and direct command) are indicative of gradual semantic change—whereby the *lets* construction tends to expand to cover further person values.

95. Further discussion of English *let's* is in van der Auwera and Taeymans (2004).

96. See Kenesei et al. (1998: 21–2), on non-command meanings of first person imperative.

97. Along similar lines, first person singular imperative ('hortative') in Awa Pit is used to state that the speaker is about to carry out an action (Curnow 1997a: 243–50).

3

How imperatives are special

What is special about imperatives as a clause type?[1] The recurrent properties which set the imperatives apart from other major clause types include

- intonation and other phonological features (§3.1);
- order of constituents (§3.2);
- meaning and expression of verbal categories (§3.3).

Then, in §3.4, we look at how imperatives correlate with other clause types. §3.5 contains a brief conclusion.

3.1 The phonology of imperatives

Intonation has been a 'stepchild' of grammar writers for a long time—few grammars pay any attention to it. Dwight Bolinger, in his general paper on intonation (1972), talks about it as being 'around the edge of language'. This 'edge' is particularly significant for describing an imperative.

Morphologically speaking, imperatives are often the simplest and the most straightforward forms in a language. A typical situation is found in Lote, an Oceanic language spoken in the province of New Britain in Papua New Guinea (Pearson and van den Berg 2008: 121). The imperative clauses have no special marking, apart from the absence of noun phrase subjects. The only way of differentiating a second-person command from a second person statement is by intonation. The imperative-specific intonation patterns are then the sole marker of an imperative. In Warekena of Xié, from the Arawak language family,[2] second person verb forms are used in the function of a positive imperative; the clause has a falling intonation on the last word.

Warekena of Xié (Aikhenvald 1998)
3.1 piya-hã   nu-yaɾitua   pi-ʃa   pi-teɾuka   a:tapi
     you-PAUS   1sg-brother 2sg-go   2sg-cut   tree
     'You, brother, go and cut the tree!'

This is in contrast to a declarative clause which would have a flat intonation. A special intonational contour distinguishes the imperative sense from the future sense of the same forms in Ngandi and Patjtjamalh, both Australian (Dixon 2002: 79).

Motuna (Onishi 1994; 1996), spoken in the Bougainville area of Papua New Guinea, has a special affix for imperative. In addition, there is a sharp falling intonation after the stressed syllable of the imperative verb.[3]

In a language where a form of another category is consistently used in lieu of an imperative, intonation can be decisive in differentiating the meanings of a form. In Toba, a Guaicuruan language from Argentina, irrealis forms express commands (see §2.1.4 for other similar examples). But while 'a statement can be identified by a long level contour or several short contours with falling pitch at the end of each', an imperative 'is indicated by a long level pitch which ends abruptly with a rapidly rising pitch which drops on the stressed syllable' (Klein 1986: 217–18).[4]

The exact intonation contour may depend on the force of the command and the control and authority of the one issuing the command. In English, 'an imperative used to convey an authoritative command is likely to be uttered with a low fall':

3.2   Stop it

'The sequence of high fall followed by low rise seems more likely to be used with 'a plea or earnest request' (Davies 1986: 59–60):

3.3   Please help me

'A rise-fall seems appropriate for an imperative used to express indifference or defiance' (Davies 1986: 59–60).[5] In Japanese, the falling intonation 'would range from a frank informal request to even a brusque command; while the rising intonation would sound less informal, or would often afford a feeling of courteous request' (Abe 1972: 342–3). A typology of intonation contours which differentiate commands from statements, and also from questions, is a task for the future.

Having a special intonation contour is not a universal property of imperatives. Languages with an imperative-specific verbal marking may not have any particular intonation distinguishing imperatives and other clause types. In Urarina, an isolate from Peru (Olawsky 2006: 569), intonation plays no role in distinguishing imperatives from other clause types: this is done by verbal morphological markers.[6]

We can recall, from §2.1.3, that eye-gaze is an integral component of marking imperatives in the American Sign Language. This is considered a suprasegmental marker, similar to intonation in spoken languages.

Eye-gaze may accompany imperatives in spoken languages. Eye-gaze in Boumaa Fijian is used as a way of singling out a particular addressee, supposed to perform the intended task. An imperative sentence, 'Let these empty drums be stacked here!', 'might be said by the chief, looking at a particular youth, who would thus indirectly be told that it was his job to stack the drums'.[7]

An imperative can display segmental idiosyncrasies not found with declarative or interrogative forms. The imperative in Dagbani, a Gur language from Ghana (Olawsky 1999: 101), has a different realization depending on the position of the verb in a command. The singular imperative is marked with the suffix -*ma* if it is not followed by any other word. If it is, the suffix is -*mi* (and the final *i* is often omitted, so the resulting form is just -*m*). The imperative suffix attaches straight to the verbal root unmarked for any aspect.

Dagbani

3.4   nyu-ma
        drink-IMPV.FINAL
        'Drink!'

3.5   nyu-m(i)   kom!
        drink-IMPV.NONFINAL   water
        'Drink water!'

Imperatives may differ from declaratives and other verbal forms in the application of clause-level phonological rules. In Welsh, positive imperatives differ from declarative verbs in that they do not have initial consonant mutation.[8] In Italian, a number of monosyllabic second person singular imperatives do not trigger consonant lengthening at the beginning of the subsequent word. This process of *rafforzamento fonosintattico* (Maiden and Robustelli 2007: 10–11),[9] also known as 'syntactic doubling', is described as 'phenomenon whereby a consonant at the beginning of a word receives a "double", or a little more accurately a "lengthened", pronunciation when preceded by certain other words within the same phrase'. An example is ['va 'sotto] 'go under!', and not [*'va s'sotto]. (Compare 'ki s'sɛi'] 'who are you', where this process takes place after a monosyllabic word.) But when the imperative is followed by a clitic pronoun, the consonant of the immediately following clitic is doubled, e.g. *Vai a casa* 'Go home!' and *Vallo a sotterare* (go+him to bury) 'Go and bury him!' (Maiden and Robustelli 2007: 249).

The order of clitics in clauses containing imperatives may also differ from that in other clause types—see the next section.

3.2 Order of constituents

In the vast majority of the world's languages the subject of canonical imperatives—especially ones with a singular addressee—does not have to be overtly expressed (see Chapter 2). This follows from the semantics of canonical, addressee-oriented imperatives: the addressee (i.e. the subject) is implicit in the form itself. However, it can be added for a variety of reasons—including disambiguation, force of command, and emphasis. In many languages, English among them, the absence of the overt subject is a distinguishing property of an imperative clause. Order of clausal constituents is another feature that may differentiate imperatives from other clause types. This concerns the order of full noun phrases, and of clitics.

Languages with pragmatically determined constituent order in statements may have a fixed order in imperative constructions. Constituent order in Tariana depends on topicality and focality of constituents. The verb in declarative clauses tends to be placed at the end of the clause, but does not have to be. Not so in imperative clauses. The subject of the imperative (which could be a pronoun, if contrastive, or the vocative form of a noun) is always postposed to the verb:

Tariana (Aikhenvald 2003, 2008b)
3.6a wasã   wa-ka   wha!
      come.on 1pl-see we
      'Let us go and see!'

The unmarked order in a declarative clause would have been the subject NP followed by the verb:

3.6b wha   wa: wa-ka-mhade
      we   1pl+go 1pl-see-FUTURE
      'We will go and see'

In addition, imperatives have a falling intonation, and may take a variety of enclitics with imperative-specific meanings (see Chapter 6). Along similar lines, the imperatives in Semelai, an Aslian language spoken in Malaysia, have a verb-initial order. In 3.7, the addressee—which does not have to be expressed – and the locative complement follow the verb:

Semelai

3.7 pʔɔt=cəʔ kɒ haʔ nɔʔ!
    stay=IMPV_intr you AT this
    'You stay here!'

In contrast, constituent order at the clause level is fluid in declarative and interrogative clauses, 'with variation driven by pragmatic factors'. In an intransitive clause the subject may wither precede or follow the verb:[10]

3.8a kəhn swak
      3sg go
      'He went'

3.8b swak kəhn
      go 3sg
      'He went'

In Catalan (Romance), the subject of an imperative is typically omitted. If it is included, it appears in postverbal position:

Catalan (Hualde 1992: 25)

3.9 canta l'himne tu
     sing.IMPV.2sg the'hymn you
     'Sing the hymn!'[11]

The order of constituents in declarative clauses is Subject-Verb-Object. The subject can also appear in a postverbal position, given the right discourse context.[12]

Since imperatives are about giving instructions to perform an action, and the action is encoded in the verb, the 'verb-first' principle in imperatives intuitively makes sense: the action should be more important than the identity of those who are to perform it.

But this tendency is far from universal. A verb-final order is characteristic of imperatives and not of declaratives in Siberian Yupik Eskimo (Vaxtin 1992: 92).[13]

In languages with fixed constituent order, imperatives may offer additional ordering options not available in declarative clauses. In Dogon, a Dogonic language spoken in Mali, canonical and non-canonical imperatives form one paradigm, and allow an object-initial order:

Dogon (Plungian 1995: 27–8)

3.10a [wo ŋ]_O yaba-mɔ
       he OBJ take-IMPV.1du
       'Let's (us two) take him!'

An OAV order is not attested in clauses of other types—compare 3.10b:

3.10b   wo_A   [wo   ŋ]_O   yab-e-Ø
        he   he   OBJ   take-AOR-3sg
        'He took him'[14]

In Lele, a Chadic language spoken in the Republic of Chad, 'the syntax of giving orders differs from the syntax of the indicative' in the constituent order. While the subject pronoun for the second person plural precedes the verb in a statement, it follows it in a command. Any complements—such as the direct object in 3.12—follow. Constituent order is fixed for both clause types.

Lele (Frajzyngier 2001: 100–101, 270–71)
3.11   pàmà   ngú
       search.IMPV   2pl
       'Search!'

3.12   kùlù   ngú   kùlbá
       buy.IMPV   2pl   cow
       'Buy a cow!'[15]

A second person pronoun in a declarative clause precedes the verb:

3.13   me   me   è
       you.fem   2fem   go
       'You (woman) go'

The constituent order in non-canonical imperatives is also a mirror image of that in declaratives. A third person pronoun in a statement is placed after the verb:

3.14   càgdí   dú
       spread   3fem
       'She spread (something)'

And in a command the pronoun has to precede the verb:

3.15   dú   ìrà   kàsúgú
       3fem   go:IMPV   market
       'Let her go to the market'

Imperatives and declaratives may also differ in the possibilities for placement of adverbs. Sentential temporal adverbs in English can occupy initial or final position in declarative and interrogative clauses; some can also occur between the verb and the auxiliary. In contrast, most of these can only occur sentence-finally when used with imperatives—both canonical and non-canonical ones (see §2.3). This is summarized in Table 3.1 (based on Dixon 2005: 406, and p.c.).

TABLE 3.1 Placement of some temporal adverbs in English depending on clause type

ADVERB	IN DECLARATIVE AND INTERROGATIVE CLAUSES	IN IMPERATIVE CLAUSE
today, tomorrow	Final; Initial (3.16a–b)	Final (3.16c)
now	Final; Initial; After auxiliary (3.17a–c)	Final and Initial (3.17d–e)
presently, eventually, soon, later	Final; Initial; After auxiliary	Final

The orders illustrated in 3.16a–b are acceptable:

3.16a Today he will paint the wall
3.16b He will paint the wall today

But in an imperative, *today* can only occur in final position:

3.16c Paint the wall today!
3.16d *Today paint the wall!

An example like 3.16d could only be acceptable if there was a pause between *today* and the rest of the clause—that is, if *today* were dislocated to the left and treated as a separate topic.

The temporal adverb *now* appears to have fewer restrictions on its placement in the imperative. 3.17a–c are acceptable:

3.17a Now he will paint the wall
3.17b He will paint the wall now
3.17c He will now paint the wall

And so are 3.17d–e:

3.17d Paint the wall now!
3.17e Now paint the wall!

The reason why *now* behaves differently from other temporal adverbs—including *soon, later, presently*—is because it has immediate pragmatic force correlating with that of an imperative.

English sentential adverbs are unique in the grammar of the language: other constituents do not have such freedom of placement within declarative clauses. But this freedom is greatly reduced in imperative clauses.

We have seen that imperative clauses tend to allow less freedom in ordering constituents than do declarative clauses. This is especially apparent in those languages where constituent order in declarative clauses is 'free'—that is, determined by pragmatic factors rather than by syntactic rules. Since the person of the imperative subject is implicitly known, fixing the constituent order may serve to assign fixed positions to other arguments. Another reason may be that the focus of imperatives is on an action of the verb, which creates a pragmatic restriction on the surface positions of other constituents. A full explanation awaits future debate.

Clitic pronouns may occur in a different order in imperative clauses, and in statements, across the Romance languages. In Rumanian and Catalan, clitic pronouns (including locationals) immediately follow the imperative, and precede all other forms.[16] In addition, French has a different order of clitics depending on the person value. Compare 3.18a and 3.18b. The order of clitics is different in an imperative and in a declarative:

French

3.18a Je   te   le   donne
       I   to.you   it.masc.OBJECT   give.1sg.PRES
       'I give it to you'

3.18b Donne   le   moi
       give.IMPV.2sg   it.masc. OBJECT   to.me
       'Give it to me!'

But note that for two third person arguments, the order remains the same:

3.18c Je   le   lui   donne
       I   it.masc.OBJECT   to.him/her   give.1sg.PRES
       'I give it to him/her'

3.18d Donne   le   lui!
       give.IMPV.2sg   it.masc.OBJECT   to.him/her
       'Give it to him/her!'

In Italian, pronominal clitics precede all first person, second person and third person forms of the declarative verb:

Italian

3.19 Mi   alzo   alle   sette
      Me   get.up   at+ARTICLE.DEFINITE.PLURAL   seven
      'I get up (lit. get myself up) at seven'

With imperative forms, the clitics follow the verb forms which formally correspond to second person and first person (*tu*, *voi*, and *noi*), but precede the forms with third person polite imperative forms (*Lei*, polite singular, and *Loro*, polite plural):

3.20a Alza-ti   subito
       get.up.IMPV.2sg-you   immediately
       'Get up immediately' (lit. get yourself up)

3.20b Si   alzi   subito (Lei)
       'Get up immediately' (third person polite form *Lei*)[17]

Synchronically speaking, these rules are idiosyncratic. They illustrate a general principle: that imperatives as a special clause type are markedly different from clauses of other types.

Having an imperative-specific constituent order is far from universal: in many languages—which include Paumarí, Urarina, and many more—the order of core arguments within imperative clauses is no different from that in statements. Then other distinguishing factors may come into play—see §3.3.

3.3 Meaning and expression of verbal categories

A form, or a category, may have different meanings depending on whether it is used in an imperative or in a non-imperative clause. We start with some examples of how particles and affixes can have different meanings in statements and in commands (§3.3.1). The grammatical categories which tend to have different meanings in imperative clauses, and in other clause types, are number and person (§3.3.2), aspect, and (more rarely) tense (§3.3.3). In §3.3.4, we turn to examples of imperative-specific uses and meanings in other categories.

3.3.1 *Imperative-specific meanings of particles and suffixes: some examples*

Let's start with some relatively simple examples. Meanings of sentential particles in isolating languages may vary depending on whether they are used in commands or not. The particle *dèèl* in Lao is an imperative marker which 'softens or plays down the burden of the request'. It then occurs at the end of a clause, as in 2.6 and 3.21a.

Lao (Enfield 2007: 67; numbers indicate tones)
3.21a   qaw3   kùa3   haj5   khòòj5   **dèèl**
      take   salt   give   1SG.POLITE   IMPV.SOFT
      'Please give me the salt'

When used in a statement, *dèèl* has a slightly different meaning—what it does is 'attenuate the strength of the proposition, along the lines of "a little", "partly"'. In this function, the particle occurs after the verb, but before the aspectual and modal markers. In 3.21b, it occurs before the aspectual particle:

3.21b   jaak5   kham1   mùùt4   **dèèl**   lèèw4
      tend   evening   dark   a.little   PRF
      'It was already getting a little dark'

In another example, this particle described Western hippies living in Vientiane as speaking Lao 'a little bit':

3.21c   mii2   khon2   man2 vaw4   khuan2 laaw2 kaø   daj4   **dèèl**
      there.is person   3   speak sense   Lao   T.LNK CAN   a.little
      'Some people, they could speak Lao a little'

A complex construction X *dèèl*, Y *dèèl*—also used in statements—means 'some X, some Y' (as in 'Some were crying, some were hungry').

Along similar lines, in Chrau, the final particle *vô* (variant *vôh*) marks a very mild imperative or exhortation in a command; in a declarative clause it is a 'mild attention-getter' (Thomas 1971: 182).

Having particles whose meanings vary with clause types, and having different semantic overtones within a command, is not restricted to isolating languages. In German, *mal* 'time, once' is used to make a command sound milder, as in 3.22:

German
3.22   Gib   mir   mal   eine   Zigarette
      give:IMPV   I:DAT   once   INDEF.ART.ACC.SG.FEM   cigarette
      'Could you give me a cigarette'

Similarly, in Sochiapan Chinantec, the verificational $dá^M$ means 'truth, indeed' in declarative clauses, and in imperative clauses it marks a plea (Foris 2001). In Cantonese, the expression *tùhhng ngóh* means 'for me'. But when used to 'reinforce' imperatives, the meaning is 'for me, on my orders' and the overtones are rather impolite:

Cantonese

3.23   Léih   faai dī   **tùhng   ngóh**   ché!
       you   fast-ish   for   me   leave
       'Do me a favour and get out of here'[18]

An affix may also have special meaning overtones within an imperative clause. The suffix -*uri* (and its allomorphs; in bold in the examples below) in Urarina means 'quickly':

Urarina

3.24   aresiɲe   mɨkɨ-**ɨri**-ɨ̃
       mojara.fish   catch-RAPIDLY-PARTICIPLE
       'He quickly caught a mojara fish and...'[19]

Its salient meaning in imperative clauses is that of a politeness marker, as in 3.25:

3.25   ka=iri   aua-**ri**-ɨ-tɕe=ra
       1sg=pet   taste-RAPIDLY-IMPV-PL=EMPH
       'Please try [to eat] my pet!' (an invitation to a meal)

This same form may also have a diminutive meaning, 'do a little bit'. The exact interpretation depends on the context:

3.26   basihĩĩ   kuak-**uri**-ɨ
       a.while   wait-RAPIDLY-IMPV
       'Please wait a little while!'

This same suffix in an imperative construction can also have a meaning 'do quickly'; but this appears to be exceptional. The following example is polysemous:

3.27   kukwa-**ri**-ɨ
       give.to.drink-RAPIDLY-IMPV
       'Please give him to drink'/'Give him a little to drink!'/'Quickly give him to drink!'

We can see that this form in Urarina has a wider variety of meanings in imperatives than in declaratives.[20]

The imperative-specific overtones of particles or affixes parallel the major semantic distinctions in imperatives themselves. These include politeness and degree of command (making it softer or more abrupt: see Chapter 6). For instance, in Upper Necaxa Totonac, from Mexico, the reciprocal morpheme *la:-* is used to soften commands with first person, 'by effectively turning them into reciprocal expressions (i.e. changing 'do X to/for me!' to 'let's X to/for each other'.[21] This highlights another imperative-specific meaning of grammatical categories: explicitly marking the addressee's involvement. This takes us to the next section.

3.3.2 *Imperative-specific overtones of person and number*

We can recall, from Diagram 2.1, that first person singular is often 'missing' from a paradigm of imperative forms. Imperatives then have fewer PERSON–NUMBER distinctions than do declarative forms or personal pronouns—see examples in Table 2.14, from Finnish; Table 2.15, from Gahuku; and 2.16, from Estonian.

This is not unexpected—imperative forms have a strong tendency to contain a reference to the addressee. And, not surprisingly, if imperatives have more person–number combinations than declaratives, the additional form has 'inclusive' reference—covering 'you' and 'me', that is, the addressee and the speaker. For instance, in Dogon, the inclusive 'dual' form is distinguished only in imperatives. The imperative markers are shown in Table 3.2.

The 'dual' referring to 'you and me' is illustrated in 3.28:

Dogon
3.28 wo   ŋ   yaba-mɔ
      he   OBJ   take-IMPV.1du
      'Let's take him (the two of us)'

In Awa Pit, a Barbacoan language from Colombia and Ecuador, dual with inclusive reference ('you and me') occurs exclusively in the imperative system. 'Dual hortative' exemplified in 3.29a refers to the speaker plus one addressee. First person plural pronouns do not differentiate inclusive and exclusive reference. But the plural 'hortative' is interpreted as inclusive—this form refers to the speaker plus more than one addressee (3.29b).

TABLE 3.2 Imperative markers in Dogon (Plungian 1995: 27–8)

	SG	DUAL = 1ST+2SG	PL
1	—	*-mɔ*	*-mɛŋ*
2	*-ø*	*-ŋ*	
3	Subject *V-mɔ*	Subject *V-mɛŋ*	

Awa Pit (Curnow 1997a: 243–50)

3.29a   ku-pay
        eat-HORT.DUAL
        'Let's eat!' (the two of us)

3.29b   ɨ-shaɥŋ
        go-HORT.PL
        'Let's go!' (the three or more of us)

The first person 'hortative', which forms part of the same paradigm as other command forms, has a special meaning—it is used to state that the speaker is about to carry out an action. This is part of the issue of person-specific meanings of commands—see §2.4.

An imperative can distinguish the same persons, but fewer numbers than declarative—we saw in 2.84–5, from Cavineña, that one non-singular imperative form covers dual and plural referents, which are distinguished in declaratives. Alternatively, number in imperatives may be expressed using a declarative form with a different meaning. In Tunen, a Bantu language, the reciprocal is used for plural addressees in commands (Mous 2003: 290).

The meaning of the same person–number form in imperative and in declarative may be different. We saw that in English, first person commands usually have inclusive reference (§2.3.2): *let's* involves the speaker, or speakers, and the addressee. Along similar lines, the first person plural imperative in Russian has a dual (rarely, plural) inclusive meaning. The form itself is homophonous with first person plural declarative present. But the declarative lookalike can have either inclusive or exclusive reference. For instance, the first person declarative present *idëm* means 'we (plural) go'; the same form, *idëm!*, when used as a command means 'let's go (you.sg and me)'. A plural imperative marker *-te* can be added to the first person inclusive imperative to mark plural (*idëm-te* means 'let's go (you.plural and me)') but not to the declarative.[22]

Person–number values other than first non-singular may develop imperative-specific overtones. The second person singular imperative in Russian has a collective meaning, absent from the singular declarative. In 3.30, the hussars are addressed as a group; this explains why a singular form *pytaj* 'try' is used instead of the plural *pytaj-te*. Throughout the remainder of the poem (cast in declarative),[23] they are referred to with plural.

Russian

3.30   siniye   gusar-y   pytaj   sudjb-u
        blue:NOM.PL   hussar-NOM.PL   try:IMPV.SG.IMPF   fate-ACC.SG
        'Blue hussars, try (sg) fate'

In a number of northern Australian languages, canonical imperatives—directed at the second person addressee—take third person subject agreement affixes. A command in 3.31, from Nyangumarta, is directed at several addresses. But the subject agreement affixes are the same as those for third person plural in a declarative clause:[24]

Nyangumarta

3.31   Mirtawa   karrama-rna   janaku
        woman   say-NFUT   3pl.DAT
        Mima-li-ji-yi   ngaju-ku
        wait.for-IMPV-1sg.DAT-2pl.SUBJ   1sg-DAT
        'The girl called out to them:"Wait for me!"'

In his grammar of Mara, Heath (1981: 189) offers a functional explanation for this 'anomaly'. The third person is the least marked in the declarative clauses: in Heath's words, 'the "non-person", the residual category left behind when the participants in the speech event are excluded'. In contrast, the second person is the least semantically marked in imperatives. And the functionally unmarked third person declarative marker extends to cover another functionally unmarked term – the second person.

The reference of second person and third person in commands may show overlaps. We saw in §2.3.1 that in English, commands directed at a third person may arguably have a second person reference, as is the case in addressee-oriented usage of third person imperatives in English discussed by Jespersen (1933: 148), e.g. *Oh, please, someone go in and tell her.*[25] In Bagwalal, a Northeast Caucasian language, a third person imperative is used if one addressee is singled out of a group. An example is in 3.32a.

Bagwalal (Dobrushina 2001: 323)

3.32a   o-šu-r   b=ah-a
         this-OBLIQUE.MASCULINE-ERGATIVE   NEUTER.CLASS=take-POT.IMPV
         (The speaker says, addressing several people, 'You take my money!'
         The addressees answer: 'Who?' The speaker answers, 'He (one of the
         addressees) take (it)!'

If one gives orders to several groups of people, the first order is given in second person, and subsequent orders are in third person, as in 3.32b:

3.32b   bišdi tukan-lā   b=eɬi,   o=ba   ešaX   b=uk'-ē
       you   store-SUP.LAT HPL=go.IMPV this=HPL at.home HPL-be-IMPV
       'You go to the store, let them stay at home'

Changing the person of an imperative can be a way of making it sound more polite. In Huallaga Quechua, commands are made more polite by avoiding the second person imperative, which is perceived as too 'straightforward'. They can be rephrased with the first person inclusive (you and me), or third person imperative. The latter is reminiscent of familiar Indo-European languages such as German or Italian where third person forms are uniformly used as politeness strategies (Weber 1989: 440). Along similar lines, using the third person plural marker increases the politeness of an imperative in Haya, a Bantu language from Tanzania.[26]

Person marking in imperatives may have additional, idiosyncratic features. Awa Pit has a special pronominal form for the first person object in imperatives, which replaces the imperative markers. The resulting form does not distinguish number of the addressee:

Awa Pit (Curnow 1997b: 244–5)

3.33a   pihshka-tɨ
       sweep-IMPV.SG
       'Sweep!'

3.33b   i-tayŋ
       go-IMPV.PL
       'Go away!'

3.33c   titizh-zha
       wait.for-1SG.OBJ.IMPV
       'Wait for me' (singular or plural addressee)

Imperatives and declaratives often use different person marking paradigms (see numerous examples in §2.1.1). Some, more exotic, person values are never expressed in imperatives. Conjunct-disjunct systems—also known as locutor/non-locutor—have been described for Awa Pit and a number of other Barbacoan languages, and in numerous languages of the Tibeto-Burman family.[27] These are restricted to statements and questions, and never occur in imperatives. Imperatives have no logophoric distinctions, or proximate/obviative marking (found in Algonquian languages, for instance, Fox, and Menomini: (Bloomfield 1962: 187; also see §2.2.1).[28]

3.3.3 *Imperative-specific overtones of aspect and tense*

Imperatives and non-imperatives may have the same aspectual distinctions, employing the same marking, but with somewhat different meanings. These imperative-specific meanings often involve politeness.

In Russian, positive imperatives have perfective and imperfective aspect forms. The imperfective imperative sounds politer than the perfective imperative:

3.34a   Sadite-sj!
       sit.IMPF+2pl.IMPV-REFLEXIVE
       'Sit down (imperfective, considered more polite)'

3.34b   Sjadjte!
       sit.PERF+2pl.IMPV
       'Sit down (perfective, considered less polite)'[29]

In Yankunytjatjara, an Australian language, the imperfective imperative has a 'less pressing, more polite effect, presumably because it implies less attention to the result or completion of the action in question' (Goddard 1983: 190).[30]

The imperfective in Supyire frequently has the same meaning in commands as it has in statements and questions: it indicates that the event is expected to be durative, or incomplete. In addition to this, imperfective can be used as a politeness strategy: in the imperative contexts it is more deferential than the perfective.

Supyire (Carlson 1994: 521)
3.35   Ta   ma   náhá
       IMPV.IMPF come.IMPV here
       'Come here, please!'

Other aspects may also have different meanings in commands, and in other clause types. The inceptive aspect in Awa Pit refers to 'starting' an action when used in statements, and conveys a meaning of 'immediacy' in command context. In Warekena of Xié, the aspect marker *-wa* describes an unaccomplished or continuative action in statements and in questions. In commands it has an inchoative meaning:

Warekena of Xié (Aikhenvald 1998; own field data)
3.36   pi-teɾuka-wa!
       2sg-cut-NONACC
       'Cut (start cutting)!'

The negative perfective imperative has an apprehensive meaning ('warning') in Lithuanian and in Russian—see Chapters 5 and 6 (Geniušenė 1988; Xrakovskij 2001).

We will see, in §4.4, that imperatives can have their own aspect marking, distinct from that in declaratives and other clause types. These include punctual and continuative meanings (e.g. 2.54–5, from Mbabaram, an Australian language). And, in accordance with these preferred aspectual meanings in commands, the same aspect marker can express continuative action in imperatives and elsewhere.

A continuous imperative in Yidiñ can include the derivational suffix -:ɖ i-n 'continuous action', as an 'exhortation to continue an action that is already in progress':[31]

Yidiñ (Dixon 1977: 371, 291)

3.37 mandi: galabuɖun   galiŋa:ɖin   ɖaba:ngu
      hand+LOC   spear+ABS+STILL   go+COMIT+CONT+IMPV   eel+PURP
      'Keep going, with your spear still in your hand, for eels!'

Future forms are frequently used as polite ways of expressing commands—as is the case in Modern Hebrew. Future in imperatives in Huallaga Quechua has two meanings—it can indicate that the ordered action has to be performed in the future, as in 3.38.

Huallaga Quechua (Weber 1989: 103)

3.38 Chaka-y   oora   kuti-mu-nki
      be:dark-INF   time   return-afar-2FUT
      'Come back when it gets dark'

This use is consistent with a cross-linguistically well-attested category of delayed imperatives—see §4.2.3. Alternatively, future can be used as a way of making a command sound more polite.

Past tense forms of verbs are used as imperatives of 'authority' in Russian (with reference to first person non-singular and second person singular and plural).[32] These forms have no overtones of past tense—see §2.1.4.[33]

We conclude that the imperative-specific overtones of aspects—and, more rarely, of tenses—are congruent with the frequently expressed aspectual meanings in imperatives. They are often extended beyond their aspectual meanings to express politeness, another semantic dimension prominent in commands. Then, we expect the imperfective aspect—with its inherent lack of endpoint and reference to incomplete or prolonged activity—to refer to more tentative, and more polite, suggestions, invitations, and directive speech acts of other sorts, in the imperative contexts.

3.3.4 *Imperative-specific meanings of other categories*

Imperative-specific meanings of other verbal categories relate to degrees of commands and politeness. In Indonesian, an imperative of a transitive verb can be expressed with the passive. The resulting form is 'more indirect and consequently less forceful than an imperative with an active verb'.[34]

Modal words in Western Apache can have the effect of command softeners. For instance, the epistemic *shįh* 'maybe' makes a request more tentative and thus more polite (de Reuse 2003). In Northern Subanen, the mirative marker *masiʔ* indicates 'delayed remembrance' in imperative clauses (Daguman 2004). The reportative evidential *quiha* in Amahuaca is used as an attention-getter in imperatives (Sparing-Chavez 2008, and see §4.2.4 for imperative-specific meanings of evidentials).

Marking grammatical relations in imperatives may differ from that in other clauses. In Indonesian, imperatives of intransitive verbs coincide with the bare stem. Transitive verbs drop the transitivity marker, prefix *meN-*, if they describe an action performed on a specific object. If the action involves a generic referent or the verb is used intransitively, the prefix is retained. This correlation between the occurrence of *meN-*, the transitivity of the verb, and the specificity of the object is only found in imperative constructions. The use of *meN-* on an imperative reduces the force of the command, and produces 'a milder imperative'. In contrast, omission of *meN-* in declaratives is a feature of colloquial speech and has nothing to do with the properties of an object or assertiveness of the statement (Sneddon 1996: 324–5; 67–8; 4.58–60 in §4.4.1).

Grammatical relations in imperatives and in declaratives are often marked differently. The direct object of an imperative is not marked for the accusative case in a number of Northern Uto-Aztecan languages (Cahuilla, some dialects of Hopi, Southern Paiute, and Serrano: Langacker 1977)—that is, it takes the formally unmarked shape of a nominative. Similar examples are found in Finnish and Estonian.[35]

A direct object in a declarative clause is marked with the accusative case:

Finnish
3.39   Pekkä   söi   kala-n
       Pekka   ate   fish-ACCUSATIVE
       'Pekka ate the fish'

In contrast, the object of first and second person commands appears unmarked for case:

3.40   Syö   kala!
        eat.2sg fish+NOMINATIVE
        'Eat the fish!'

3.41   Syökäämme kala
        eat.1pl   fish+NOMINATIVE
        'Let's eat the fish!'[36]

This feature is shared with the impersonal construction:

3.42   Syötiin   kala
        eat.IMPERSONAL.PAST   fish+NOMINATIVE
        'They ate the fish; the fish was eaten'

In both Finnish and Estonian, nominative case is the least formally marked. The motivation behind having such an unmarked noun as the object of a canonical imperative and of impersonal is intuitively clear: the functionally unmarked subject of an imperative is second person, and so any other form in a transitive clause can only be an object. The same principle applies to the impersonal—whose subject is the impersonal generic referent, 'they'.

There may be further imperative-specific constructions and usages. In statements and in commands in English, the *do*-support reinforces the positive sense of the imperative (*do have some more tea*). As we saw in 2.106a–b, *do* support is obligatory in negative imperatives. And in imperatives, but not in statements, it can be used with *have* and *be* as auxiliaries—see 2.107–8. One can say *Do be ready on time*, but not *He does be ready on time* (also see Quirk et al. 1985: 833).

A reduplicated adjective is used as an adverb in Cantonese canonical imperatives, in preference to an adverbial construction with *dāk*:

Cantonese (Matthews and Yip 1994: 360, 184).

3.43a   Léih   lóuh-lóuh-saht-saht   tùhng   ngóh   góng   a   há!
         you   honest-honest   with   me   say   PART   PART
         'Tell me honestly, will you?'

Adverbial constructions with *dāk* occur in declarative and interrogative clauses (Matthews and Yip 1994: 179):

3.43b   Gó   dī   sīnsāang   gaau   dāk   géi   hóu   wo
         those   CL   teacher   teach   ADVERB   quite   well   PART
         'Those teachers teach pretty well'

In Diyari, an Australian language, the copula *ngana-* is 'only rarely used in the present tense' in non-imperative sentences, but 'when the attribute, equation or possession is not located in the present, *ngana-* must be used to carry the tense or mood inflection' (Austin 1981: 104). An imperative involving an adjective as copula complement requires a copula to host the imperative suffixes:

Diyari (Austin 1978: 240)
3.44 ŋuma   ngana-a-ø-mayi
      good   be-IMPV-NUMBER.MARKER-EMPH
      'Be good!'

Imperative clauses have a further, almost universal, property. If a language has a dedicated focus construction, or focus markers, these are likely not to be used in imperatives. In Urarina, focus markers do not occur in canonical imperatives. This makes them similar to dependent clauses which also do not take focus markers; however, unlike imperatives, focus in dependent clauses can be expressed by the change in constituent order.[37]

Focus markers can occur in first person plural imperatives, which sets them apart from canonical imperatives:

Urarina (Olawsky 2006: 703–5)
3.45 kwane=te   kana+kwaaʉn-era   baha-akatçe
      let's=FOC   [our.creator]   ask-1pl.incl
      'Let's pray'

Along similar lines, no constituent can be focused in imperative clauses in Manambu and in Aghem (Hyman 1979: 61), two languages with special grammatical configurations for focus.[38] Cleft constructions never occur in imperatives. In contrast, they do occur in statements, and are often used in interrogative clauses.[39]

Grammatical categories linked to the discourse-pragmatic properties of a constituent are hardly ever expressed in imperatives. The 'indefinite' person prefixes in Baniwa, Bare, and Warekena are employed when the subject (A/S) argument is fronted and topicalized, as in Baniwa *pi-aku* (2sg-talk) 'you talk' and *phia i-aku* (you INDEF-talk) 'it is you who talks' (Aikhenvald 1995b). This topicalization is not compatible with imperatives; consequently, indefinite person is not used in imperative constructions. Warekena does not employ focus forms in imperatives at all. In Tagalog, focus forms other than agent and patient focus are not used in imperatives (Schachter and Otanes 1972).

This restriction is intuitively plausible. Imperatives constitute prima facie directive acts to which the verb is central. This centrality of the verb is what makes the imperative mutually exclusive with grammatical focus marking of a nominal constituent within the clause (in Hyman's 1979: 61 words, 'imperatives have an overriding intrinsic focus' which is mutually exclusive with focus marking of individual constituents).

Many other grammatical categories are expressed differently in imperatives, and in clauses of other types. These include negation patterns—we return to these in Chapter 5. Grammatical categories specific to imperatives will be further discussed in Chapter 4.

3.4 Imperatives and other clause types

How do imperatives interact with other clause types? In their directive—that is, command—meanings they appear to be restricted to main clauses. We will see in Chapter 7 that imperative forms do appear in conditionals and concessive dependent clauses—but then they are not commands.[40]

Just occasionally imperatives can be used in bona fide dependent clauses. Hua, from Papua New Guinea Highlands (Haiman 1980: 61–3, 162–3), has a special set of markers for imperatives used in medial dependent clauses, with a sequential meaning. Imperatives may be followed by a verb with a different subject. Then, the medial imperative takes the marking of A/S of the following verb—that is, the predicate of the final declarative clause,[41] *o-kati* (come-non. dual+1nonsg.subject.of.final verb) 'come, and then we ...' In Yagaria, closely related to Hua, a medial clause can be cast in imperative, and the final clause may also contain an imperative, or be cast in future. The subject of an imperative medial clause can be the same as that of the final clause, or it can be different. Example 3.46 illustrates an imperative in a medial clause whose subject is different from that of the main clause.

Yagaria (Renck 1975: 121)

3.46   eli-ga-ta'a-o   elemi-s-u'-agi
        take-DS-1du-IMPV   go.down-1FUT-1du-EMPH
        'Take it, and let us two go down!' (lit. 'After you take! it, let us two go down')

A medial clause cannot be used on its own, just as expected of a dependent clause. The existence of cases like Hua, Yagaria, and a few others goes against the 'conventional wisdom'—that imperatives do not occur in non-main clauses (cf. Whaley 1997: 237).[42]

Imperative clauses show similarities with other clause types, especially questions. In Ainu, questions and commands share rising intonation (Onishi 1997a; also Tamura 2000: 247–8). In Indo-Pakistani Sign Language, content questions and imperatives have similar constituent orders. In Mao Naga, a Tibeto-Burman language (Giridhar 1994: 451), the unmarked constituent order for declarative sentences is AOV, SV, while interrogatives and imperatives commonly have OVA and VS orders. And we will see in §7.3 that imperatives can occur in questions, in not-quite-command meanings.

The exact correlations may depend on the type of question and on the type of imperative. One of the nine imperatives in Tariana, 'polite suggestion', is marked with the visual interrogative enclitic. In Jacaltec (Mayan), polar questions and negative imperatives have a similar intonation pattern. In Kana, echo questions and negative imperatives have the same tone pattern (commands and questions are distinguished by their context).[43] An extensive study of intonation for a corpus of spoken Modern Greek (Arvaniti and Baltazani 2005) shows similarities between imperatives, negative declaratives, and *wh*-questions. 'Requesting' imperatives (which have the same structure and form as other imperatives) share a somewhat different intonation contour with 'involved' *wh*-questions and negative declaratives showing 'reservation'.[44]

Imperatives can have surface similarities to subordinate clauses. The polite imperative in Awa Pit appears to have arisen from a complement clause (or an indirect question complement). In Boumaa Fijian, the canonical structure for an imperative involves the relator *me* which is also used as complement clause introducer, 'should', and a clause linker 'in order to' or 'as a result that'.[45]

Complementizers and other subordinate clause markers may participate in forming non-second person imperatives. In some Romance languages, subordinators mark third person imperatives, while in Kurmanjî, an Iranian language (Haig 1997a), a multiclausal construction with a subordinator expresses commands to first and third person. The ways in which non-imperative forms and clauses may be used to express polite and indirect commands are considered in Chapter 8.

A further question arises. Do canonical—that is, addressee-oriented—and non-canonical imperatives form the same clause type? For languages in which imperatives addressed to all the persons form one paradigm, the answer is 'yes'. Even if canonical imperatives are marked in one way and non-canonical ones in another, they may share syntactic properties. Canonical imperatives differ from non-canonical imperatives in Sare in terms of their morphological structure (see Table 2.17 in §2.2.2, and discussion there). But all clauses containing imperatives share the AVO constituent order, different from the AOV order in declarative clauses (Sumbuk 1999: 198–9).

In languages where different persons of imperatives do not form one paradigm, an argument can be made in favour of several distinct imperative clause types. In Dogon, the subject of third person commands has to be obligatorily expressed: this is not the case for commands directed to other persons—compare 3.10a, 3.28 (repeated here as 3.47a) and 3.47b:

Dogon (Plungian 1995: 27)
3.47a wo   ŋ   yaba-mɔ
      he   OBJ   take-IMPV.1du
      'Let's take him (the two of us)'

3.47b wo   ŋ   wo   yaba-mɔ
      he   OBJ   HE   take-IMPV.3sg
      'May he take him!'

In Finnish, the nominal object of first person plural and second person imperatives is unmarked for case (see 3.40–41). But third person imperatives require accusative marking on their objects, just like declaratives (in 3.39):

Finnish (Comrie 1975a)
3.48 Pekkä   syökköön   kala-n
     Pekka   eat.3sg.IMPV   fish-ACC
     'Let Pekka eat the fish!'

This could be considered a reason for distinguishing non-canonical third person imperative as a special clause type. In Lavukaleve, continuative aspect is distinguished only for canonical second person imperative, and not for hortative or prohibitive (Terrill 2003). This alerts us to the fact that negative imperatives can also be considered a special clause type—see Chapter 5. Such decisions have to be made on language-specific grounds.

An additional feature of imperative clauses can be the use of special vocative forms. Siberian Yupik Eskimo (Vaxtin 1992: 90) has a special vocative pronoun 'hey you' which accompanies imperative verb forms.[46]

A number of languages have special morphological marking for addressees of imperatives, known as vocative forms. In Aleut, these coincide with absolutive forms. In Siberian Yupik Eskimo, and in numerous Omotic and Indo-European languages, such as Old Church Slavonic and Latin, they take special affixes.[47] In Tariana and Tucano, only personal names, kinship terms, and a handful of other nouns with human reference have vocative forms. In Nivkh, vocative forms distinguish distance from speaker and also number: the absolutive (formally unmarked) case is used when the addressee is close to the speaker; if the addressee is far away, a suffix is added (Gruzdeva 1992: 63). Vocative forms of nouns have so far only been found in languages either with a special verb form or with pronominal cross-referencing as the main methods for marking imperatives. In other words, they are never the only way of expressing imperatives. And they do not have to be restricted to commands—not infrequently, they occur as attention-getting devices in 'calling' clauses and in statements.

A final word on one further aspect of the form of commands. The occurrence of IMPERATIVE is likely to be restricted to direct speech and main clauses in general, and an alternative construction used in indirect speech: an imperative *Go and clear up that mess* can be reported as *He told me to go and clear up that mess*, with a *to*-infinitive, or with *He told me that I should go and clear up that mess*, with a *that* + *should* construction (see Huddleston 2002: 943–4; McGregor 1994: 73). Languages vary in the ways imperatives appear in speech reports.

In Hdi (Frajzyngier 2002 :451), a simple verb form in the indirect speech report corresponds to the imperative in the direct speech report; and in Finnish, conditional is used in reported commands. In Taba (Western Austronesian: Bowden 2001: 390–1), the equivalent of an imperative in direct speech reports is a resultative form of the verb. It is not uncommon to employ a different construction type for an indirect speech report of a statement and of a command, as is the case in English and in Gulf Arabic (here a complementizer marks indirect speech report unless it is a reported command—then it is omitted: Holes 1990: 2). Reported commands may share certain features with imperatives (as in Tuvaluan, where the same politeness markers occur in both: Besnier 2000: 61). Or they may be completely different in structure and marking (as in Maori: Bauer et al. 1993: 47). We will see in Chapter 8 that reported commands can be used in lieu of a straightforward imperative, to 'tune down' its force.[48]

3.5 Summary

Numerous features demonstrate that imperative clauses are a type of their own, distinct from other clause types. First, they often have specific intonation patterns which set them apart from clauses of other types. Some languages have phonological processes setting imperatives apart from other clause structures.

Table 3.3 summarizes some of the general features which set imperatives apart from statements and from questions (with reference to sections where these are discussed).

Secondly, imperative clauses may have constituent order configurations different from those in declarative or interrogative clauses. In many cases— but not everywhere—this involves putting the verb first. In languages with

TABLE 3.3 How imperatives are special

FEATURES	IMPERATIVES AS DISTINCT FROM OTHER CLAUSE TYPES	RELEVANT SECTIONS
Phonological properties	Distinctive intonation contour; occasionally, special phonological processes	§3.1
Order of constituents	Special order configurations (often verb first); likely to have a fixed order in languages with pragmatic-based order	§3.2
Meanings of verbal categories	• Verbal particles may add overtones of politeness and pragmatic force to imperatives • Different number of person distinctions • Tendency to have inclusive overtones ('you and me') of first person imperative	§3.3

'free' constituent order—determined by the pragmatics of the constituents—imperatives are likely to have a fixed order. A striking feature of Romance languages is the difference in the placement of clitics in declaratives and in imperative clauses.

Thirdly, various markers—be they particles or affixes—may have different meanings in imperatives and in other clause types. Imperative specific meanings consistently involve politeness overtones and pragmatic force.

Imperatives may have more or fewer number and person distinctions than do other clause types. Imperatives tend to have inclusive forms. In numerous instances, first person in imperatives has inclusive overtones, and thus refers to 'you and me'.

Imperatives can be used in non-main clauses. They can appear in questions—and if they do, their function is somewhat different from that of a straightforward command. We take this up again in §7.3.

The same aspectual (and, more rarely, tense) and other forms of verbs can have different implications in imperatives and in other clause types. These meanings tend to fit into the mould of semantic features of politeness and degree of command which are characteristic of imperatives. They also correlate with the preferred aspectual meanings expressed by imperatives. This takes us to the next chapter.

Notes

1. This chapter owes its title to Susan Schmerling's (1982) paper, which is among the first attempts at outlining some specific properties of imperatives as a clause type (mostly based on English). However, her basic thesis about imperatives as a 'primitive' and 'poorly elaborated' clause type is fundamentally unsound. Numerous scholars pointed out the special status of imperatives—see e.g. Jakobson (1965: 34), and Trubetzkoy's letter to Jakobson (first week of November 1931) (Trubetzkoy 1975: 223).

2. Also see 2.40, from Bare, of the same language family.

3. Further examples of specific intonation contours for imperatives include Tibeto-Burman languages Lahu (Matisoff 1973: 353), Mulao (Wang Jun and Zheng Guoqiao 1993: 100–101), and Tai languages Nung (Saul and Wilson 1980: 120) and Dong (Long and Guiqiao 1998: 179). The descriptions differ in the level of detail and in the terminology employed: the imperative intonation is characterized as 'short and sharp' in the grammar of Nung, while the grammar of Mulao distinguishes 'short and abrupt' imperative sentences with 'falling intonation' used to express commands or prohibitions, and sentences which express request or advice pronounced with 'a relatively relaxing intonation'. Delattre (1972: 172–4) describes the specific intonation contour in French commands. Arvaniti and Baltazani (2005) offer a detailed corpus-based study of intonation in Modern Greek sentences, including imperatives. Mackridge (1985: 39) mentions the rising intonation in some imperative types in Modern Greek. In Vurës and in Tamambo, two Oceanic languages spoken in Vanuatu (Hyslop forthcoming; Dorothy Jauncey p.c.), an imperative starts with a higher pitch followed by a sharp fall. In Chrau (Thomas 1971: 182), imperative sentences are 'marked by a forceful intonation drop on the last word'. And so on.

4. Pilagá, from the same family, appears to have similar intonation patterns for irrealis forms used as commands (Vidal and Klein 1998: 189).

5. See also Bolinger (1982: 13–14; 1972: 141). An incisive analysis of a variety of intonation contours in British English is in Halliday (1970: 28–9). We will see in Chapter 8 that a command does not have to involve an imperative. In many languages, including English, questions and statements can be employed in directive speech acts. They may or may not share intonational properties with imperatives—see the discussion in Bolinger (1972: 141–4).

6. Imperatives also have the same intonation contour as declaratives in Koasati, a Muskogean language (Amberber 1997b, based on Geoffrey Kimball, p.c.), Irakw, Southern Cushitic (Mous 1993: 164; and p.c.), and Anamuxra, a Pomoikan language from New Guinea (Ingram 2003). Different imperative types may share their intonation contours with different other clause types. In West Greenlandic (Fortescue 1984: 24–5), 'the intonational contour in all forms of imperative sentence is of the declarative fall-rise type, with a marked final rise, as also for exclamatory utterances'; the yes-no question intonation appears in command forms cast in the optative mood with the semantics of 'offer'. An additional, as yet unsolved, question concerns intonation contours in commands expressed with forms other than imperatives. We return to this in Chapter 8.

7. Dixon (1988: 295). Rather than using a transitive sentence, 'Stack these empty drums here', the chief chose to use the corresponding intransitive.

8. Watkins (1993: 338); King (1993: 225). Special phonological processes can also be part of imperative formation, as is, for instance, consonant deletion in the imperatives in Kana (Ikoro 1996: 191–3). This is entirely different from phonological processes resulting from the position of imperatives in a clause.

9. This process is also known as *radoppiamento sintattico* and *rafforzamento sintattico*.

10. See Kruspe (2004a: 333) on imperatives, and pp. 5, 254–8 on constituent order in other clause types. Toratán (Austronesian, Sulawesi) also has a verb-initial constituent order just in imperatives (Himmelmann and Wolff 1999: 24).

11. A similar principle of verb-initial order in imperatives applies in Galician (Freixeiro Mato 2000: 702).

12. Hualde (1992: 96–8) discusses principles of ordering constituents in declarative clauses.

13. Wai Wai, from the Carib family (Hawkins 1998: 61), has a free—that is, pragmatically determined—constituent order in most clause types; but in imperatives 'the order of the object preceding the transitive verb seems to be more fixed, with less variation than in other sentences'. In Koromfe, imperatives are the only construction to allow subject–verb inversion (Rennison 1997: 37).

14. In Sare, a Sepik Hill language from Papua New Guinea (Sumbuk 1999: 198), an AVO order in imperatives is contrasted to AOV order in declarative clauses.

15. Subject pronouns preceding the verb have mid tone, and those following the verb have high tone. Mid tone is unmarked (e.g. *ngu* 'you.plural') (Frajzyngier 2001: 100).

16. See Mallinson (1986), on Rumanian, Hualde (1992: 25) on Catalan, e.g. *dóna-me* (give.IMPV.2s -1sg 3pl.masc.ACC) 'Give them to me!', and Freixeiro Mato (2000: 702), on Galician.

17. Maiden and Robustelli (2007). Note that in negative imperatives, clitics tend to precede rather than follow the verb. This may alert us to the possibility of prohibitives displaying different clause-type properties.

18. Matthews and Yip (1994: 360). The form *tùhng* is morphologically a 'coverb', or a 'preposition' (p. 60).

19. Examples of the suffix *-uri* and its allomorphs are in Olawsky (2006: 471, 546–7, 571).

20. Along similar lines, numerous Russian discourse particles have different meanings in imperatives and non-imperatives; for instance, the particle *nu* in declarative clauses usually means 'not up to a certain point in time'. In commands, it conveys the meaning of insistence, repeated request or plea (then it is usually repeated: *nu daj, nu pozhalujsta* (*nu* 'give', *nu* 'please') 'please, give me!'), or of disinterested permission (*hochesh idti—nu idi* (you.want to.go—you may well go) 'you want to go—then do go, I don't really care') (Borisova 1988).

21. Beck (2004: 47). In Huallaga Quechua, the suffix *-ycU* /-ykU/ has as its basic meaning 'impact' and intensity of affect; it also takes part in the formation of perfective (§§9.1.4, 9.4.3 of Weber 1989). When used with imperative, it functions as a politeness marker (Weber 1989: 103, 440).

22. The inclusive person reference of the Russian first person plural imperative was noted and argued for by Trubetzkoy (1931) in Jakobson (1975); also see Xrakovskij (2001) and Vinogradov (1947). Vinogradov (1947: 593) notes the overtone of familiarity in second person singular imperatives with collective reference.

23. From the poem 'Blue hussars', by Nikolaj Aseev.

24. Sharp (2004: 185, 255–6). Similarly, in Nakkara (Eather 1990: 201), imperatives with a second person addressee always take third person prefixes. In Mara (Heath 1981: 189), imperatives of intransitive verbs take third person prefixes. In imperatives of transitive verbs the marking is more complex: 3rdA to 3rdO prefixes are used for semantic 2ndA to 3rdO, and for 2ndA to 1stO the same forms are used in the imperative and in the indicative (and there are no 3rdA to 1stO forms).

25. Here, a second person can be supplied, as in *And bring out my hat somebody, will you*. A personal name can be used in such a third person addressee-imperative, if the addressee is conceived as 'one of you present' (Jespersen 1933: 149); cf. also *John scatter the files, Bill ransack the desk, and I'll watch the door*. Instances of this kind led Jespersen to state that 'any imperative is virtually in the second person' (p. 148). In contrast, Quirk et al. (1985: 829) accept the interpretation of sentences like *Nobody move* and *Parents with children go to the front* as having a third person subject. (This ambiguity of interpretation is corroborated by the grammaticality of both third and second person reflexive pronouns as in *Everyone behave themselves* and *Everyone behave yourselves*.) Vocative forms can be distinguished from third person imperatives by intonation breaks (Quirk et al. 1985: 829).

26. According to Lehman (1977: 147), such a form 'could be used with visitors, by a prospective son-in-law to the father, to one's in-laws, and so on'.

27. This type of system is also known as 'locutor' versus 'non-locutor': 'locutor' refers to first person in statements and to second person in questions, and 'non-locutor' covers second or third person in a statement, and first or third person in a question. Classical examples come from Tibeto-Burman languages—these were described by Hale (1980) for Newari and Schöttelndryer (1980) for Sherpa (also see Woodbury 1986: 192). They are also found in a few Barbacoan languages from South America (an overview is in Curnow 2002). See the summary and further references in Aikhenvald (2004).

28. See Siewierska (2004) for a typological overview of person systems; and especially Dixon (2010). Fleck (2008: 281) provides an overview of different uses of the term 'fourth person', with a special attention to clause combining. Systems which distinguish first person from other persons, or third person as opposed to other persons (as in Tucanoan languages: Aikhenvald 2002) are not attested in the imperatives. This is no doubt due to the salience of the second person in

imperatives, which has to acquire an independent expression. It can be said that imperatives always contain some indication of person, no matter whether person is overtly marked in the indicative or not (Birjulin and Xrakovskij 1992; especially their examples from Nivkh or Lezgian).

29. We return to this in §6.4.2; also see discussion of aspect in Slavic imperatives in van der Auwera et al. (2009), Kučera (1985), Bogusławski (1985), and Benacchio (2002).

30. Russian imperative and the varied overtones of its aspectual forms are discussed by Shmelev (2002: 272ff.); see references therein; also see Vinogradov (1947: 597ff.). For Yankunytjatjara, see Goddard (1983: 190). In Tukang Besi, the perfective *-mo* with a drop in pitch is used to 'soften' the imperative (Donohue 1999b: 59).

31. Other Australian languages with continuative imperatives are Western Desert and Watjarri; a similar distinction is also found in Igbo, Lavukaleve, and Eskimo (see §4.2.1).

32. In non-standard language, the past tense of 'go' used as imperative takes on the imperative plural marker *-te*, thus creating double marking of plural, e.g. *poshli-te* 'let's go'. This past tense lookalike used as an imperative distinguishes three genders in the singular, e.g. *poshel!* (go:PAST+MASC.SG) 'you (man) go, come on!'; *poshla* (go:PAST+FEM.SG) 'you (woman) go, come on!'; *poshlo* (go: PAST+NEUTER.SG) 'you (animal) go, come on'.

33. There may be further, less frequent, imperative-specific overtones of tense markers. In Vurës, an Oceanic language from Vanuatu, the delayed imperative uses the marking employed for 'unspecified time reference' in declaratives (Hyslop 2003). See §2.1.4 for a number of other examples.

34. The passive is marked with the prefix *di-*. See Sneddon (1996: 326).

35. Comrie (1975a); also see Laanest (1975) for a wider Balto-Finnic perspective. Further similar examples are discussed in §4.2. Historically speaking, this marking may reflect archaic patterns—see discussion of Australian languages in Chapter 10 (and Dixon 1972: 135–7).

36. Personal pronouns occur in the accusative case with imperatives and with impersonal passives. Also see Sulkala and Karjalainen (1992: 23–5). An object marked with partitive case retains its case marking in an imperative.

37. To focalize a constituent within an imperative clause, one can use emphatic particles, which are different from focus markers.

38. Further languages with grammatical focus in declarative clauses, but not in imperatives, include numerous Chadic languages, e.g. Mina (Frajzyngier and Johnston 2005) and Lele (Frajzyngier 2001). The whole imperative clause can be focused in Urarina if followed by another clause; this has a sequential meaning. Note that in many languages, including English, a noun phrase can undergo left-dislocation within an imperative construction, for contrastive effect, as in *This book, take it away, that book, leave it here!*

39. See e.g. Lambrecht (1994) on cleft and focus in interrogative and declarative clauses.
40. See also Whaley (1997: 235–7) and Lakoff (1984) on incompatibility of imperatives with 'because'-clauses. Takahashi (2008) discusses some examples of imperative forms in reason and concessive clauses in English, e.g. *I only make US $6000 in the whole year, and even like the next two years, I was just like getting by, because don't forget our expenses are very high* (see the discussion in Verstraete 2005: 621). Further examples of imperative forms in non-main clauses in English are in Takahashi (2005).

    In his grammar of Sanskrit, Whitney (1891: 215) remarks that 'the imperative also sometimes signifies an assumption or concession; and occasionally, by pregnant construction, it becomes the expression of something conditional or contingent; but it does not acquire any regular use in dependent clause-making'.
41. This is known as anticipatory switch-reference. See Roberts (1997), for a typological overview of switch-reference patterns.
42. In Amele (Roberts 1987: 40) imperatives can also be used in embedded clauses.
43. For Jacaltec, see Craig (1977) and Amberber (1997c, based on Grinevald Craig p.c.); see Ikoro (1996) on Kana.
44. Imperatives are rarely used in questions. (Whitney 1891: 215, §572b) provides examples of occasional use of imperatives in questions in Sanskrit).
45. See Curnow (1997a,b) for Awa Pit; Dixon (1988: 286, 293–4) for Boumaa Fijian.
46. Also see 2.32a–b, from Yawelmani.
47. See Amha (forthcoming), for an overview of vocative forms in Omotic languages. In Indo-European languages (see e.g. Ivanov and Gamkrelidze 1984) vocative forms are often included in the paradigm of cases, despite the fact that they do not mark grammatical relations. Also see Galúcio (2001: 157), on vocative forms in Mekens, and a lengthy discussion of vocatives in Kashmiri by Wali and Koul (1997: 39).
48. A comprehensive analysis of marking an indirect—a reported, or an embedded—command is a necessary component of any typology of speech reports (see Güldemann and von Roncador 2002; Aikhenvald 2008c, and further references there).

4

Imperatives and other grammatical categories

It has been shown that person, number, and aspect can have different meanings in imperatives from what they have in other clause types. We now turn to the ways in which imperatives interact with other grammatical categories and forms.

Imperatives may—but do not have to—express fewer values for tense, aspect, and voice than declaratives. Or their categories may be rather different in nature. Few if any evidentials are as a rule marked in commands. Imperatives may also express temporal distance and location in space.

The correlations between imperatives and other categories fall into the following groups:

- CATEGORIES RELATING TO THE ADDRESSEE INCLUDING GENDER OR NOUN CLASS, NUMBER, AND PERSON (§4.1);
- CATEGORIES RELATING TO VERBAL ACTION, INCLUDING ASPECT, LOCATION IN TIME AND SPACE, MODALITY, AND INFORMATION SOURCE (§4.2);
- MARKING OF VERBAL ARGUMENTS (§4.3).

The meaning and the marking of imperative correlate with voice and transitivity of the verb. A prototypical directive speech act implies the speaker's control over the activity to be performed. As a consequence, verbs whose meanings cannot be controlled—such as verbs of state—and passive forms may not form imperatives at all. In §4.4, we look at how imperatives interact with transitivity, and with the meanings of verbs.

Imperatives interact with the form of the verb, and the scope of imperative may vary—see §4.5. Note that correlations between imperatives and grammaticalized politeness levels—such as those in Korean and Japanese—are discussed in Chapter 6, in the context of politeness and the use of honorifics in commands.

What about the correlations between imperatives and the one issuing the command? Depending on the command situation, the 'commander' can be in a higher or lower position on the social ladder vis-à-vis the addressee. The relationship between the 'commander' and the addressee can be familiar or formal. The relative status of the addressee and the 'commander' is not infrequently reflected in the special honorific forms in imperatives. We turn to these in Chapter 6, in the light of the plethora of meanings of imperatives.

The ways in which the gender of the 'commander' can be marked in an imperative are mentioned in §4.1. We have not found any other explicit expression of 'commander's' role in imperatives.

The essence of the correlations between imperatives, other grammatical categories, and semantic subgroups of verbs lies in the nature of a basic imperative meaning—a prototypical directive act. A summary is given in §4.6.

4.1 Imperatives and categories relating to addressee

The major categories of the addressee include person, gender (and nominal classification of other sorts), and number. Person distinctions are fundamental in differentiating canonical and non-canonical imperatives. Some cross-linguistic tendencies in marking various persons were formulated in Diagram 2.1.

The imperative-specific meanings of person—and additional imperative-only person values—invariably cover the inclusive term 'you and me'. This is consistent with the primacy of the addressee in the prototypical imperative schema.

The prototypical addressee of an imperative is animate; however, given an appropriate context, inanimates can also be commanded to perform activities. One says *Rain, rain, go away, come again another day.* And an impatient driver would command traffic lights: *Lights, change!* We return to this in Chapter 6. Imperative-only lexemes (or interjections) directed at non-human referents are examined in Chapter 9.

Imperatives often distinguish the addressee's gender. If gender is distinguished in the second person declarative, it may also be distinguished in the imperative. This is the case in Arabic, and in Hebrew—see Tables 2.3 and 2.4.[1] Along similar lines, in Alaaba, a Cushitic language from Ethiopia, feminine and masculine genders are distinguished in third person singular imperatives and also in declaratives (Schneider-Blum 2007: 224–5). In Kabyle, a Berber language (Vincennes and Dallet 1960: 13, 16), masculine and feminine are distinguished in plural declarative and plural imperative. There is only one gender form for the singular second person in all moods.[2]

In Cubeo, an East Tucanoan language with three genders and numerous classifiers, all of these can be used in commands (Morse and Maxwell 1999: 24–5; Cecília Brito, p.c.). In 4.1–2, commands are addressed to a man and to a woman respectively—hence masculine and feminine marking on the verb.

Cubeo

4.1 doba-xA-kɨ
sit-IMPV-MASC.SG
'Sit down!' (said to a man)

4.2 doba-xA-ko
sit-IMPV-FEM.SG
'Sit down!' (said to a woman)

In 4.3, the command is addressed to more than one person—hence the animate plural marking on the verb:

4.3 ã-Rã-Ra-xA-Rã
eat-PL.NOMZ-come-IMPV-IMPV.PL.ANIM
'Come (in order) to eat!' (said to more than one person of any sex)

Examples 4.4–5 illustrate the use of the inanimate gender and of a shape-based classifier in second person imperatives with personified agents. A mountain is classified as inanimate, and the lake as 'oblong':

4.4 ti-xA-Rõ   jɨ̃xã-RE
fall-IMPV-IMPV.INAN.SG   1excl-OBJ
'Fall on us!' (said to a mountain)

4.5 pãkã-bE-xA-bɨ
make.waves-NEG-IMPV-CL:OBLONG
'Don't make waves!' (said to a lake)

Genders in statements can be neutralized in the imperative. In Manambu, the canonical imperative has just one form for the two genders. The corresponding declarative forms distinguish two genders in the second person singular (see Table 2.23).[3] However, gender is distinguished in second person pronouns, and so a masculine and feminine addressee can be disambiguated, if required. I can say *a-war!* (IMPV-go.up) 'go up!' If I want to target a man, I would say *mən a-war!* 'you.masculine.singular go up!', and if my order is directed at a woman, I would say *ɲən a-war!* 'you.feminine.singular go up!'. (See examples 2.23–4; and also examples 2.36a–b, from Hausa.)

Genders may be distinguished in imperatives, but not in any other clause type. In Chipaya, an Uru-Chipaya language spoken in Peru (Cerrón-Palomino 2006: 148–51), of all verbal forms, masculine and feminine genders of the second person are distinguished only in imperatives. Declaratives make no such distinctions: 4.6 can refer to a man or to a woman.[4]

Chipaya

4.6   am-ki   lul-tra
      you-EMPH   eat-PRESENT.ABSOLUTE
      'You eat; you are eating' (man or woman)

Masculine and feminine genders are marked differently in canonical imperatives. 4.7a–b are used to address a man (singular addressee), or a group of men (plural addressee):

4.7a   zh-lul-a
       IMPV.SG-eat-MASC.ADDRESSEE
       'Eat (this)!' (addressed to one man)

4.7b   amtruk   lul-a
       you.pl   eat-MASC.ADDRESSEE
       'You (plural) eat (this)!' (addressed to more than one man)

The following command is addressed to a woman:

4.8   lul-um(a)
      eat-FEM.ADDRESSEE
      'Eat (this)!' (addressed to one woman)[5]

Taschelhit, a North Berber language from Morocco, distinguishes two genders in plural—but not in singular—declaratives. Canonical imperatives with plural addressee also distinguish two genders. A special feminine singular *ata* and masculine singular *a* or *awa* can be used to strengthen the imperative (Stumme 1899: 52–3). These forms are different from second singular person pronouns which distinguish masculine and feminine genders (masculine *kii, kiin*; feminine *kimi, kimin*).

Taschelhit is remarkable in yet another way. While no genders are distinguished in first person singular statements—the form *n-esker* means 'we do' (Aspinion 1953: 116–19)[6]—two genders are distinguished in second person plural: *t-eskre-m* means 'you (masculine plural) do', and *t-eskre-mt* means 'you (feminine plural) do'. There are no dual or inclusive distinctions.

TABLE 4.1 Gender and person in the imperative in Taschelhit[7]

PERSON/NUMBER/ GENDER	ENDINGS	EXAMPLE
2sg	∅	*sker!* 'do!'
1dual (inclusive)	*-aǧ*	*sker-aǧ* 'let's do (you and me, the two of us)'
1pl masculine	*-at-aǧ*	*sker-at-aǧ* 'let's do (you many and me)' (masculine)
1pl feminine	*-amt-aǧ*	*sker-amt-aǧ* 'let's do (you many and me)' (feminine)
2pl masculine	*-at*	*sker-at* 'you (masculine plural) do!'
2pl feminine	*-amt*	*sker-amt* 'you (feminine plural) do!'

In contrast, the imperative paradigm differentiates between two genders in first non-singular and in second person. There are no special imperative forms for first singular or for third person (as predicted in Diagram 2.1).

This alerts us to the fact that gender distinctions in imperatives may depend on person. Third person imperatives in Manambu distinguish two genders in the singular, just like the corresponding declaratives (Table 2.23). At present, no generalization can be made as to whether one expects more or fewer gender distinctions in non-canonical or in canonical imperatives.

If a language has multiple imperatives, only some may distinguish genders. In Koreguaje, three of the five positive imperatives distinguish masculine and feminine gender (these are the polite imperative, apprehensive imperative, and indirect imperative: see Chapter 6). In Tuyuca, special masculine and feminine forms are found only in one imperative (of eight), the 'familiar' or 'impolite'. Similarly, in Tucano only one of the eight imperatives (with a conative meaning, 'try') distinguishes two genders. In all these languages, non-imperative clauses distinguish three genders. (See Chapter 6 and Aikhenvald 2008b on multi-term imperative systems in Tucanoan languages.)

The choice of an imperative marker in Lakhota, a Siouan language, is of a different nature. The imperative is expressed by postpositional particles, according to the sex of the speaker.[8] This is one of the few instances where this language distinguishes genders.[9] The number or form of gender distinctions depends on the semantic nature of the command. Only some commands distinguish singular and plural addressees. See Table 4.2.

Amahuaca, a Panoan language from Peru (Sparing-Chavez 2008), employs vocative clitics *-pu* 'male vocative', for a male addressing another male, and *-u/-uu/-yu/-vu* 'female vocative' for all other instances—i.e. a man addressing a woman, or a woman addressing a man or another woman. If the addressee is

TABLE 4.2 Imperative particles in Lakhota[10]

SEMANTICS OF IMPERATIVE	WOMAN SPEAKING	MAN SPEAKING
Command	*na* (often omitted)	⎱ singular addressee *yo', wo'*
Permission	singular addressee *ye', we'* plural addressee *pe'*	⎰ plural addressee *po'*
Mild request (please)	singular addressee *ye'* plural addressee *pi ye'*	

plural, the marker *-can* precedes the vocative (and the male vocative *-pu* can be used to address a mixed group of men and women). That is, the form of the marker depends both on the sex of the addressee and on that of the 'commander'. There are no gender distinctions anywhere else in the grammar of the language.

We have seen that Lakhota and Amahuaca explicitly mark the gender of the 'commander' in an imperative clause.

It was shown in §3.3.2 and §2.5 that imperatives may distinguish fewer numbers than declaratives, for example, in Cavineña. The reverse also occurs: we have seen several examples of languages with a dual or inclusive (me and you) distinction in imperatives, and not in other clause types: see, for instance, the imperative paradigm in Dogon in Table 3.2. Number distinctions in imperatives and in other clause types can be the same as they are in Lavukaleve, a Papuan language from the Solomon Islands (Terrill 2003: 244). And they may also correlate with the semantic type of imperative.

Maale, an Omotic language from Ethiopia, has three canonical (addressee-oriented) imperatives which differ in the degree of politeness. The regular imperative and the polite imperative distinguish singular and plural forms—see Table 4.3. The polite imperative is built on the regular one. This agrees with the principle of iconicity—the more polite, the longer the form (see §2.1.5). The impolite imperative does not distinguish number.

TABLE 4.3 Number marking in canonical imperatives in Maale

NUMBER OF ADDRESSEE	REGULAR IMPERATIVE	POLITE IMPERATIVE	IMPOLITE IMPERATIVE
singular	Verb-*é*	Verb-*é-tera*	Verb-*ibay*
plural	Verb-*uwáte*	Verb-*uwátera*	

Similarly, in Haro, another Omotic language (Woldemariam 2007: 151–2), singular and plural forms are distinguished in the regular, non-emphatic imperative. The emphatic imperative uses just one form for both singular and non-singular addressees.

This may suggest a dependency between the illocutionary force of an imperative and the expression of number: the more brusque and strong—or 'impolite'—the command, the fewer chances there are of overtly expressing other categories, such as number. This is similar to other dependencies between grammatical categories. Aikhenvald and Dixon (1998) showed that numerous categories—including gender, number, person, aspect, and tense—are neutralized and not expressed under negation. The intuitive motivation is clear: once the clause is negated, everything else becomes irrelevant. Likewise, once the command is of exceptional strength, this strength may override the necessity to mark any further grammatical details. This is a tendency, and not a strict rule.

The presence or absence of different number forms in imperatives may correlate with other imperative-only categories. Teribe, a Chibchan language from Panama (Quesada 2000: 79–80), has a marker for an imperative with a singular addressee and another one for a plural addressee. Transitive verbs have an additional complexity: one imperative marker shows that the addressee is close to the speaker, and another one indicates that the addressee is at a distance. If spatial distance is marked, number is not. We turn to the expression of spatial distance in imperatives in the next section.

4.2 Imperatives and categories relating to verbal action

Categories relating to verbal action include aspect and time (§4.2.1–2), distance, in space and directionality (§4.2.3), information source (§4.2.4), and modalities and reality status (§4.2.5).

An aside is in order. In terms of its morphological expression, an imperative may be part of the tense–mood paradigm. This is the case in Kerek, Eskimo, and Aleut. Or it may be part of tense–aspect–mood–evidentiality system, as in Wakashan and East Tucanoan languages. Then imperatives are mutually exclusive with the categories in the same slot. In Lango (Noonan 1992), the imperative marker occurs in the mood slot, and so it cannot occur together with a mood marker. This morphological incompatibility limits the interactions between imperatives and other categories.

4.2.1 *Imperatives and aspect*

Imperatives are widely believed to be poor in aspectual distinctions compared to other clause types. Aspect is a verbal category related to the status of event (whether completed, ongoing, or having an endpoint, or not).[11] In other words, imperatives tend to have fewer aspectual forms and distinctions than non-imperatives. And, as we saw in §3.3.3, imperatives and non-imperatives may have the same aspectual forms. However, in the context of imperatives they are often reinterpreted in terms of other—imperative-specific—meanings, such as politeness.

Imperatives can have aspectual distinctions of their own, not found in non-imperatives. The most frequent imperative-only distinction is continuative versus simple (or punctual) imperative.

Mbabaram, a now extinct Australian language, has continuative aspect in the imperative only (see examples 2.54–5). No such aspect is found in declarative clauses.[12]

A further example comes from Lavukaleve. The punctual and the durative imperative are equally marked—see Table 4.4. This aspect distinction holds only for canonical imperatives. First person non-singular commands, admonitive, prohibitive, and permissive, do not make this aspectual distinction.

TABLE 4.4 Punctual and durative imperatives in Lavukaleve

PERSON/NUMBER	PUNCTUAL	DURATIVE
2sg	*-va*	*-ma*
2du	*-ila*	*-mela*
2pl	*-iva*	*-ba*

The semantic difference is illustrated in 4.9–10. In 4.9, the action of 'going inside' is 'thought of as capable of instantaneous completion'. The punctual imperative is used:

4.9   Kini   huru-va
      ACTION.PARTICLE   go.inside-PUNCTUAL.IMPV.sg
      'Go inside' (instantaneous completion is commanded)

And in 4.10, the use of the durative imperative implies that the action is 'thought of as necessarily taking some time' (p. 342):

4.10 Huru-ma
      go.inside-DURATIVE.IMPV.sg
      'Go inside!' (action will be taking some time)

When either of the two imperatives is used with the same verb, the verb acquires somewhat different meanings. In 4.11, the addressee is directed to do something that can be completed instantly. The verb *iru* with the punctual imperative means 'shut one's eye':

4.11   Iru-va
       sleep-PUNCTUAL.IMPV.sg
       'Shut your eyes!'

In 4.12, the addressee is commanded to do something which cannot be completed immediately, and will take time to complete. The verb *iru* then means 'sleep':

4.12   Iru-ma
       sleep-DURATIVE.IMPV.sg
       'Sleep!'

This is comparable to the ways in which verbs of perception ('see' and 'hear') tend to acquire controlled meanings—'look!' and 'listen!' when used in imperative constructions. We return to the correlations between imperatives and the semantics of verbs in §4.4.3.

In Lavukaleve, the choice of an imperative further correlates with the verb's semantics: punctual imperative is used with verbs whose action can be carried to completion immediately. Durative imperative is used with verbs denoting actions which would take some time to complete, or which have no endpoint. Consequently, the verb 'stay' usually occurs with durative imperative.

Verbs in declarative clauses also have a durative aspect, marked with suffixes *-nun* and *-na* (Terrill 2003: 332–4). It indicates that an action is extended through a prolonged stretch of time (and is also employed as a stylistic device in narratives, to indicate that things went on in the same way, or the same thing kept happening for a very long time). The semantics of this durative is not dissimilar from that of the durative imperative. But, in contrast to the imperative, the declarative durative does not have a punctual counterpart. Neither does it show any dependencies with the verb's semantics, in the way the durative and the punctual imperatives do in 4.11–12.

Durative, or continuative, aspects may have the same meanings in declarative and in imperative clauses. A prime example comes from Yidiñ (3.37). In Koromfe, the durative imperative involves a durative verb stem; semantically, it implies that 'the activity concerned ought to be carried out for a longer-than-usual period of time' (Rennison 1997: 37–9).[13]

We saw in §3.3.3 that imperatives and non-imperatives can have the same aspects with the same marking, and somewhat different meanings. These typically involve politeness, as in Yankunytjatjara, Russian, and Watjarri

(Douglas 1981: 230). The imperfective imperative in Supyire can be used with the same meaning as in a declarative clause—that is, to indicate that 'the desired event is expected to be durative, or incomplete in some way' (Carlson 1994: 521). They can also have overtones of politeness (see 3.35).

In other languages—such as Cayuga (Sasse 1998)—imperatives and declaratives have the same aspect distinctions. And in many languages none of the aspects expressed in non-imperative clauses can occur in commands; this is the case in Manambu, Lakhota, Oromo, Irakw, and many more.

It is not uncommon, across the world's languages, for imperatives to be able to occur with just a subset of aspectual markers used in declarative clauses. The preferred aspects involve immediacy, duration, and completion. Imperatives in English can be used in progressive and in completive forms, e.g. *Be listening to this station this time tomorrow night* (repeated from 2.109), *Be doing your homework when your parents arrive home*, and *Start the book and have it finished before you go to bed* (repeated from 2.110). Of over ten aspect markers in Tariana, only four can occur with imperatives. These are the non-completed ongoing *-daka*, as in *pi-ñha-daka* (2sg-eat-YET) 'keep eating', non-completed ongoing proximate *-sida,* as in *pi-ñha-sida* (2sg-eat-YET. PROXIMATE) 'keep eating here or straight away', completive *-niki* 'do fully', and *-pita* 'again'.[14]

It is also not uncommon for different person forms of imperatives to occur with different aspects. First person imperatives combine with the inceptive aspect marker in Ika, a Chibchan language from Colombia (Frank 1990: 88–9), while second person imperatives do not. In Tariana, only simple, zero-marked second-person-oriented imperatives can occur with aspect markers.

The category of aspect correlates with tense and time. In Boumaa Fijian, an imperative can contain three of the four tense–aspect markers. The one which does not occur with imperatives is the past tense marker.[15] This takes us to the next section.

4.2.2 *Imperatives and time*

An imperative involves telling someone what to do. For some linguists, this automatically presupposes that imperatives always refer to the future.[16] Many languages have no grammaticalized tense distinctions in imperatives: this is the case in Ndu languages, Rumanian, Sm'algyax and many others. The time reference of a command is inferred from the context, or specified with time words.

This is how Bolinger (1967: 348) sums it up: 'the present and the past cannot be acted on. The future can.' Or, as Lyons (1977: 746–7) puts it: 'We cannot rationally command or request to carry out some course of action in the past: the only tense distinctions that we might expect to find grammaticalized in the imperative, therefore, are distinctions of more immediate and more remote futurity.' In English, imperatives typically refer to 'a situation in the immediate or more remote future and are therefore incompatible with time adverbials that refer to a time period in the past or that have habitual reference: *Come yesterday, *Usually drive your car*' (Quirk et al. 1985: 828).

Indeed, as predicted by Lyons, the most frequently attested grammaticalized time reference in imperatives is that of immediate versus delayed, or future, imperative. This contrasts with a wider range of possibilities for future meanings grammaticalized in declarative clauses. The grammatical distinction of immediate and delayed, or future, imperative is widely attested in North American Indian languages (Mithun 1999: 153–4). It was first identified in Takelma by Sapir (1922: 157–8): what he referred to as 'present imperative' implies a 'more or less immediate fulfilment', while the 'command expressed by the future imperative is not carried out until some stated or implied point of time definitely removed from the immediate present'. This is not mirrored by the declarative, which has only one type of future (pp. 159–61).

A similar example comes from Fox, an Algonquian language (Dahlstrom MS: 138–40). 4.13 is a command to be carried out in the immediate future. 4.14 is a command to be carried out in the remote future.

Fox

4.13   peteki   iha·no
        back   go+2IMPV
        'Go back!'

4.14   i·ni=meko   e·šimeneki
        that=EMPH   say.thus.to.someone+2.CONJUNCT.PARTICIPLE.OBLIQUE
        išawihkani
        do.thus+2FUT.IMPV
        'Do [later on] exactly what you were told'

Just as in Takelma, declarative clauses in Fox do not distinguish between immediate and delayed future (there is just one future clitic: Dahlstrom MS: 115).[17]

Fine-grained divisions of the future found in declaratives are rarely attested in imperatives. For instance, the Western Language of the Torres Strait (Bani and Klokeid 1972) distinguishes in declaratives: 'remote future (beyond tomorrow)', 'near future (tomorrow)', and 'immediate future (today, including going on now)' (further examples are in Comrie 1985: 83–100). Tariana and the neighbouring East Tucanoan languages—including Tucano, Tuyuca, Macuna, and Barasano—distinguish 'certain' future (employed with first person only) and 'uncertain' future (employed with any person). There are no such distinctions in the imperative. Tucano does distinguish a simple imperative requiring that the action be performed immediately and a delayed imperative, urging the addressee to do something later:[18]

Tucano (West 1980: 48, 51; Aikhenvald 2008b: 203)
4.15a   ba'á-ya
         eat-IMPV
         'Eat!'

4.15b   ba'á-apa
         eat-FUTURE.IMPV
         'Eat (later)'

Immediate imperatives are often less formally marked than delayed ones—as is the case in Jarawara (4.21–2), and Koasati, a Muskogean language (Kimball 1991: 263–72). This is consistent with the principle of iconicity (§2.1.5). A simple 'root' imperative in Koasati has the force of an immediate command:

Koasati (Kimball 1991: 263)
4.16   lakáwwi-ø-DEL
        LIFT-2sg.IMPV-PHRASE.TERMINAL.MARKER
        'Lift it!'

Koasati is unusual in having two delayed imperatives: one marked with -χh meaning 'do later on' (4.17), and the other one with -χ:*hah* meaning 'do much later on' (4.18). The markers are suffixed to the simple imperative form:

4.17   am-awí:ci-ø-χh
        1sg.DAT-HELP-2sg.IMPV-DELAY
        'Help me later!'

4.18   am-hoponi-:$\acute{\chi}$:*hah*
        1sg.DAT-COOK:IMPV-LONG.DELAY
        'Cook it for me a lot later!'

In other languages—such as Tucano in 4.15a–b above—the immediate and the delayed imperatives are equally marked.[19]

A delayed imperative may have additional overtones of politeness. In Nambiquara, the immediate imperative implies an urgent command (and is called a 'strong' imperative), while the delayed imperative has no overtones of urgency (and is called 'weak') (Kroeker 2001: 30–2). In Epena Pedee, a Chocoan language from Colombia, an immediate imperative—which demands an immediate completion or cessation of an action—can be very forceful, and at times 'even rude or scolding'. In contrast, the imperative which indicates that the action should be completed some time in the future has polite overtones (Harms 1994: 129–30). In Yup'ik, an immediate imperative is not a polite way of, say, inviting a guest, while a delayed imperative is (Mithun 1999: 154).[20] This agrees with the principle of iconicity: an imperative which requires an immediate action is the brusquest and often the shortest of all.

The delayed and immediate imperatives may differ from each other in other ways. In Tubatulabal, a Uto-Aztecan language, they require different marking of grammatical relations (see 4.53–4). In Takelma (Sapir 1922: 162), number of addressee is distinguished only in the immediate imperative, but not in the 'future', or delayed imperative.

Only canonical—that is, addressee-oriented—imperatives tend to have tense distinctions. In other words, most languages with tense distinctions in second person do not have delayed imperative for first and third person imperatives.[21]

What about non-future reference in imperatives? Imperatives like *Please, be thinking about me* are 'probably intended to mean a hope that something has already started and is going on now'. As Bolinger (1967: 349) put it, 'a mother, hearing of some possible danger to her child if he is still on his way to school, might say the prayer *Please be at school already*... it can hardly be maintained that the speaker is thinking about the future if he uses words like *now* or *already*.'

That a time-frame of a command can involve present was nicely captured by David Watters (2002) in his grammar of Kham, a Tibeto-Burman language. In Kham, the immediate imperative 'addresses a current problem and elicits an immediate response'. And the non-immediate imperative gives 'ongoing applicability to the command' (Watters 2002: 309–10).

The ways imperatives are used may imply present and ongoing, rather than exclusively future, reference. In Manambu, one person would often command another one to do something they are already doing anyway: for instance, a usual reaction to someone doing a job would be to encourage them by saying *yawi a-kwur* (job IMPV-do) 'Do the work!' (Martha Pambwi, p.c.).

Having imperatives referring to past may appear nonsensical. In Bolinger's words, 'the handbooks are almost unanimous in citing *Have done* as no more than a curious relic, and on the fact of it one might imagine that a past command is impossible.' However, he goes on saying that 'imaginary situations are always possible, as when an actor-impresario in a home-made drama says *I've got it! Be born in 1898. That will make our time sequence work out*'; 'yet it ought to be possible to express "what is merely a wish" concerning a past act, if one has not yet verified whether the act has been carried out.'

We saw in §2.3 that an imperative in English can have a perfective form, as in 2.108a and 2.110. Each of such forms can be rigged to refer to the future—just as 'a guest might say on receiving a sudden invitation by telephone, *Just don't have all those good things eaten before we get there*' (Bolinger 1967: 349). But connection with the past is also possible—provided there is a situation in which 'there is a strong wish for a past action that has not been verified'. Bolinger (1967: 350) presented the following passage to several native speakers of American English:

Aline looked out of the window of the taxi which moved by inches towards the next traffic signal and the next and the next. She gave a frightened glance at her watch. Five o'clock! Neale would be leaving his office. If only she had not written that note. That stupid, reckless, incoherent note, scrawled in three minutes and left on the mantelpiece. How cowardly to confess in writing. He would never understand!

The taxi broke free of the chain of traffic and sped along the boulevard. Five-fifteen. He would be home by now.

Her lips formed an agonized wish that was a prayer: Please, Neale, <u>don't have read</u> it yet! Let me be there to explain when you do. Let me tell you what was really in my heart.

They drew up to the curb. She fumbled in her purse, gave the driver a dollar, and stepped out.

Only three of the twelve noticed the past imperative expressing Aline's desperate wish (underlined)—but no one condemned it as 'incorrect'.[22]

Example 4.19, from Syrian Arabic (Cowell 1964: 361; Palmer 1986: 112), appears to be a close approximation to a past tense imperative: the perfect form of *kāən* 'be' (*kənt* 'you were') is followed by an imperative. The meaning is 'should have':

Syrian Arabic

4.19 kənt   kōl   lamma   kənt   fəl-bēt
      you.were eat+IMP   when   you.were   in.the-house
      'You should have eaten when you were at home'

The simple past of the indirect imperative (so-called 'jussive') in Estonian can also be used with a similar overtone—that something should not have happened (but did):[23]

Estonian

4.20 <u>tulnud</u>   õhtul   õigel

come+PAST.PART=SIMPLE.PAST.OPTATIVE evening+LOC.SG right+LOC.SG

ajal   koju

time+LOC.SG   home

'(You) should have come at proper time in the evening'

Past tense imperatives are cross-linguistically rare. We can recall that past is the only tense–aspect value which cannot be expressed in imperatives in Boumaa Fijian (see §4.2.1).[24]

Not infrequently, an essentially temporal distinction—that between an 'immediate' and a 'delayed' imperative—has additional meanings relating to spatial distance. A distant imperative in Jarawara may refer to a distant time or place—see 4.21 (also 1.2). And the immediate imperative refers to 'here and now', as in 4.22 (see also 1.3):

Jarawara (Dixon 2004a: 397)

4.21 otara   noki   ti-jahi

1excl.o   wait   2sg.A-DISTAL.POS.IMPV.fem

'You (sg) wait for us (in some distant time or place)'

4.22 otara   noki   ti-na-hi

1excl.o   wait   2sg.A-AUX-IMM.POS.IMPV.fem

'You (sg) wait for us (here and now)'

This polysemy, characteristic of imperatives but not found in any other clause types, is attested in a number of languages, many from South America. In Tuyuca, the imperative marked with -*wa* describes an action to be performed later on or in a different location (Barnes 1979).[25]

This takes us to the next section.

4.2.3 *Imperatives, distance in space, and directionality*

Having special marking for distance in space is a unique property of imperative clauses which sets them apart from clauses of other types. One typical distinction is between a proximal command, for an action to be carried out close to the speaker, and a distal command, for an action to be carried out far from the speaker.

In Tariana imperatives distinguish the two degrees of spatial distance. Proximal imperative ('you, do it here' or 'you here, do it') is marked with a suffix -*si*:

Tariana (own fieldwork; also Aikhenvald 2003, 2008b)

4.23   pi-ñha-si

      2sg-eat-PROXIMAL.IMPV

      'Eat here!' (close to the speaker)

Distal imperative ('you, do it there', or 'you there, do it') is marked with the suffix -*kada*:

4.24   pi-ñha-kada

      2sg-eat-DISTAL.IMPV

      'Eat over there!' (away from where the speaker is; addressed to people outside the house)

The deictic centre of proximal and distal imperative is the speaker (not the addressee). Commands can be ambiguous: they combine reference to the distance of the action and the distance of the speaker from the addressee. This is reminiscent of Teribe (Quesada 2000: 79–80): we can recall, from §4.1, that the distal imperative is used if the addressee is far from the speaker, and proximate imperative indicates that the addressee is close.

Some languages tend to distinguish more than two degrees of spatial distance in commands. Distance in imperatives is independent of how many degrees of distance are distinguished in deictics.

Proximal imperative may have additional overtones: those of a command to be executed in the presence of the speaker (and not just in close proximity to them). In Barasano, an East Tucanoan language from Colombia, an imperative marked with -*ya* marks a command to be executed in the presence of the speaker.

Barasano (Jones and Jones 1991: 76–8)

4.25   yɨ-re   goti-ya   bɨ̃

      1sg-OBJ   tell-PRESENTIAL.PROXIMAL.IMPV   2sg

      'Tell me!'

This is comparable to the ways in which information source can be encoded in the imperatives—see §4.2.4. Distal or non-proximate imperative in Barasano requires an additional suffix -*a*-. It does not appear to have any overtones to do with the speaker being absent.

4.26   ĩ-re   goti-a-ya   bɨ̃

      3masc.sg-OBJ   tell-NON.PROX-PRES.IMPV   2sg

      'Tell him there!'

In contrast, a delayed imperative in rGyalrong (Sun 2007: 809) implies that a command 'is expected to be realized during the speaker's absence at a later time' (see example 4.47–8 in §4.2.5).

Both distant and proximate imperatives are formally marked in Barasano, Jarawara (4.21–2), and also Pemón, a Carib language from Venezuela (Armellada and Olza 1999: 9).[26] Tariana also has a formally unmarked imperative, which often refers to an order to do something straightaway; however, its exact meaning depends on the context: *pi-ñha!* (2sg-eat) 'eat!' can have a wide variety of meanings. We will see, in § 11.1.1, that this is the most archaic form in the language, and also the only one which combines with aspectual markers.

The markers of spatial distance in imperatives in Jarawara combine reference to space and to time. The delayed imperative in Tariana combines reference to distance in time and in space: it means 'do some time later or further away', and is marked with the suffix *-wa*. It is rather rare in my corpus (this may be due to its recent origin: see § 11.1.1). The two meanings can be disambiguated by context, or by using a time word as in 4.27, or a locative adverb, as in 4.28. But note that the delayed imperative never has an exclusively spatial meaning.

Tariana

4.27   desu   kuphe   pi-ñha-wa
       tomorrow   fish   2sg-eat-DELAYED.IMPV
       'Eat the fish tomorrow!'

4.28   hane-se   pi-ñha-wa
       that-LOC   2sg-eat-DELAYED.IMPV
       'Eat there (far away and later)'

Unlike delayed imperatives, distal imperatives do not appear to have overtones of politeness. We will see, in Chapter 6, that Tariana and the neighbouring East Tucanoan language have special forms for polite commands.

Another, similar kind of spatial distinction in imperatives involves 'extra-locality'—a command to perform an action in a different location. In Trio, a Carib language from Suriname (Carlin 2004: 306), the 'dislocative' suffix *-ta* marks commands to carry out an action elsewhere:

Trio

4.29   ene-ta
       look-DISLOCATIVE.IMPV
       'Look at it there!' (singular addressee)

Simple imperative is marked with the suffix *-kë* if the addressee is singular, and *-tëkë* if the addressee is plural. The marker *-tëkë* also attaches to the dislocative form, to mark plural addressee.[27] In Paumarí, an Arawá language from Brazil, the suffix -*ha* added to a simple imperative indicating that a command is to be fulfilled in a different location. Unlike all the examples above, the extralocality in Paumarí can be marked on canonical and also non-canonical, first person non-singular, imperatives (see Table 2.1 for the imperative person markers in this language).

Paumarí (Chapman and Derbyshire 1991: 220)

4.30a   a-'bai-'a-va
            1pl-eat-ASP-HORTATIVE
            'Let's eat here'

4.30b   a-'bai-ha-'a-va
            1pl-eat-DISTANCE-ASP-HORTATIVE
            'Let's go and eat (somewhere else)'

The meanings of 'extralocality' and distance are obviously linked: ordering someone to do something elsewhere typically implies 'further away' from the speaker. Unlike distal imperatives, 'extralocal' commands refer just to the location of the activity, and do not seem to make any reference to the proximity, or distance, of the addressee.

An additional semantic parameter which comes into play is that of motion and directionality. Imperatives involving motion acquire special marking in a number of Carib languages from South America. Macushi (Abbott 1991: 49–51) distinguishes three motion categories in imperatives: 'static' imperative, motion away from speaker, and motion towards speaker.[28] This distinction is made only in canonical imperatives in Macushi. This is reminiscent of how canonical imperatives have more tense and aspect distinctions than non-canonical ones.[29]

Just like for distal versus proximal imperatives, the speaker is the deictic centre. 'Static' imperative is a command which does not specify directionality—see 4.31a.

TABLE 4.5 Motion in canonical imperatives in Macushi

IMPERATIVES	NON-COLLECTIVE NUMBER (SINGULAR)	COLLECTIVE NUMBER
'Static'	-*kî*	-*tî*
Motion away from	-*ta*	-*tantî*
Motion towards	-*tane'kî*	-*tane'tî*

Macushi

4.31a   tuna   ene'-kî
         water   go-IMPV.'STATIC'.NON.COLLECTIVE
         'Bring water!'

In contrast, 4.31b–c contain imperative forms marked for motion: 'away from speaker' in 4.31b, and towards speaker in 4.31c:

4.31b   apo'   era'ma-ta
         fire   get-IMPV.MOTION.AWAY.NON.COLLECTIVE
         'Go get firewood!'

4.31c   tuna   era'ma-tane'kî
         water   get-IMPV.MOTION.TOWARDS.NON.COLLECTIVE
         'Come get the water'

The category of motion is intrinsically linked with directionality. It also correlates with distance: 'motion away from the speaker' is reminiscent of distal imperative, 'further away from the speaker'.

Languages which have directional markers on verbs usually employ them in imperatives. In Manambu, none of the aspects or tenses expressed in declaratives and interrogatives are compatible with imperatives. But imperatives have a full set of directionals which is also used in delcratives—their wealth is illustrated in 4.32.

Manambu (own fieldwork; Aikhenvald 2008a)

4.32   a-yakə-su   '(You sg, dual, plural) throw (it) upwards!'
        IMPV-throw-UPWARDS

a-yakə-sad	'(You sg, dual, plural) throw (it) downwards!'
a-yakə-saki	'(You sg, du, pl) throw (it) across away from speaker!'
a-yakə-sapar	'(You sg, du, pl) throw (it) across toward speaker!'
a-yakə-səwəl	'(You sg, du, pl) throw (it) inside or away from the Sepik River!'
a-yakə-sakw	'(You sg, du, pl) throw (it) in the outward direction!'
a-yakə-tay	'(You sg, du, pl) throw (it) sideways away from speaker!'
a-yakə-tæy	'(You sg, du, pl) throw (it) sideways toward the speaker!'
a-yakə-tay-tay	'(You sg, du, pl) throw (it) back and forth'

In Manambu, directionals can occur with canonical and with non-canonical imperatives. Only canonical imperatives in Shoshone, a Uto-Aztecan language (Dayley 1989: 48–9), take all the directional and motion suffixes (with the meanings of 'hither', 'away', and 'moving randomly'), but no tense or aspect.[30]

Once again, the speaker—that is, the one issuing the command—remains the deictic centre of motion and direction in imperatives. Directional imperatives in Papago (Zepeda 1988: 126–7) imply 'speaker requesting some movement', and in most cases this movement is towards the speaker. This centrality of the speaker comes into play in the ways imperatives interact with yet another grammatical category—that of information source.

4.2.4 *Imperatives and information source*

In about a quarter of the world's languages, the way of knowing things—or information source—is encoded in the grammar. This category is known as evidentiality (see Aikhenvald 2004, 2006c for a survey, and Aikhenvald 2008d for further details, and references).[31]

Grammaticalized evidentiality distinctions include a variety of information sources—whether the event was seen (visual evidential), or heard, smelt, or tasted (non-visual evidential), or inferred from some tangible evidence, or assumed, or learnt about by hearsay. Tariana, an Arawak language from Brazil—and many of its East Tucanoan neighbours—have all these meanings obligatorily marked on the verb, in each declarative clause. Only the reported, or secondhand, evidential occurs in commands. The other distinctions cannot be expressed.[32] The meaning of a secondhand imperative is not just 'hearsay'—it implies a command to do something on someone else's order, and is often referred to as 'imperative by proxy'. In 4.33–4, from Tariana and from Tucano, the speaker relays a command made by someone else. I did not immediately obey the command 'Come and eat here!' issued by my classificatory Tariana mother Maria. Then Jovino, another speaker of Tariana, repeated her command as 4.33, 'eat-you-were-told-to':

Tariana

4.33   pi-ñha-pida
       2sg-eat-SEC.IMPV
       'Eat (on someone else's order)!' (that is, eat-you were told to)

Tucano

4.34   ba'á-ato
       eat-SEC.IMPV
       'Eat (on someone else's order)!' (that is, eat-you were told to)[33]

Reported evidentials in commands are semantically uniform across the world's languages. The reported evidential *nganta* in Warlpiri, an Australian language, is commonly used to attribute a command to someone else other than the speaker (Laughren 1982: 140). In 4.35 the original command comes from the police—this is clear from the context.[34]

Warlpiri

4.35 Kulu-wangu   nganta-lu   nyina-ya yurrkunyu-kujaku
      fight-PRIVATIVE REPORTED-3pl   be-IMPV   police-AVERSIVE
      'Don't fight, or you will be in trouble with police (on the order of the police)'

When used in declarative clauses, a reported evidential may have epistemic extensions, to do with lack of reliability of the information relayed. This is akin to English speech reports: saying *He is a doctor* is a statement of fact. But saying *He is said to be a doctor* may have implications of 'This is what they say, but I doubt that it is so'. Such extensions have been described for many languages, including Estonian (Fernandez-Vest 1996: 171; Erelt 2002b; Metslang and Pajusalu 2002; Aikhenvald 2004). In other words, reported evidential in statements is often—though not always—a means of 'shifting' responsibility for the information and relating facts considered unreliable. The reported evidential has similar overtones in Warlpiri statements (Australian: Laughren 1982: 138). The speaker is reporting what was said by someone else—but he is not really sure:

Warlpiri

4.36 Ngaju-ku   nganta   ngulaju   yuwarli
      I-DAT   REP   that(is)   house
      'They say that house is for me' (but I don't vouch for it or am not sure)

None of these epistemic overtones are ever found in imperatives. A reported command in 4.35 does not have any overtones of 'I don't vouch for what the police said'—this is a warning that if a fight goes on, the culprits will be in trouble. That is, evidentials do not reflect speaker's attitude towards the information, or its source.

Reported evidentials in commands may have other, imperative-specific overtones. The reported evidential in Warlpiri may also attenuate an order. The sentence is then pronounced with a question intonation (Laughren 1982: 138):

4.37 Marna-lu   ma-nta,   nganta?
      spinifex-3pl   get-IMPV   REP
      'Pick up the spinifex grass, won't you?'

In Mparntwe Arrernte, the reported evidential in a command can have somewhat different overtones from those in statements (Wilkins 1989: 393). It provides softening by 'falsely indicating that the order is only being passed on through the speaker from some unnamed "commander"':[35]

Mparntwe Arrernte
4.38   Arrantherre   kwele   ntert-irr-ø-aye!
        2plS   REP   quiet-INCH-IMPV-EMPH
        'You mob are supposed to be quiet!' (lit. Someone else has said that you
        mob have to shut up!)[36]

Along similar lines, the reported evidential in Cavineña (Guillaume 2004: 182–3) is a means of 'softening' a command. This is in line with content of a typical imperative-specific meaning known as 'degree' of command (see Chapter 6).

Reported evidentials in commands often occur with canonical and non-canonical imperatives, as is the case in Tucano (Ramirez 1997; West 1980). In traditional Tariana, they used to be restricted to second person only; as a result of recent areal diffusion, they now occur with third person (see Chapter 11).

Another option is to have a special grammatical marking of information source available to the 'commander'. Maidu, an isolate from California (Shipley 1964: 51–4), has two imperatives with evidential-like distinctions. One, marked with -*pi*, is used 'when the action of the order is to be carried out in the presence of the speaker or when there is no interest in the place of the ordered action', as in 'Look! I am dancing' (Shipley 1964: 54).

The other imperative marker, -*padá*, is used 'when the ordered action is to be carried out in the absence of the speaker', as in 'when you have gotten to my house and have sat down, drink a beer' (Shipley 1964: 54). This is reminiscent of the overtone of 'presence of the speaker' in the proximal imperative in Barasano (Jones and Jones 1991: 76–8).

Meithei, a Tibeto-Burman language from India, uses the non-first-hand evidential in commands to imply that the speaker expects the order to be carried out in their absence:

Meithei (Chelliah 1997: 223)
4.39   əpəl   čá-ləm-u
        apple   eat-NON.FIRSTHAND.EVIDENTIAL-IMPV
        'Eat that apple (when I have gone)!'

The same evidential in declarative clauses marks information obtained through a non-first-hand source, usually inference based on past or present experience. The 'absential' meaning is an imperative-specific overtone of this marker. This is similar to 'absential' overtones of a postponed imperative in rGyalrong (see 4.47–8 below).

Imperatives expressing 'warning' (also known as 'apprehensive' imperatives) occasionally distinguish the information source of the speaker and of the addressee. The visual apprehensive in Tariana is a warning against something both the speaker and the addressee can see:

Tariana (Aikhenvald 2003: 384–6; own fieldwork)
4.40   pi-na   di-pasya-da
       2sg-OBJECT   3sgnf-squash-VISUAL.APPREHENSIVE
       '(Beware, a car) might squash you' (you are walking in the middle of the road and can see it)

The non-visual apprehensive is used to warn the addressee of something the addressee, or both speaker and addressee cannot see. Someone who is walking in front would say to a person behind them who they think is not cautious enough:

4.41   pi-wha-ñhina
       2sg-fall-APPREHENSIVE.NONVISUAL
       'You might fall down (you are not looking!)'

Nivkh, a highly endangered isolate from Siberia, is reported to have evidentiality in 'preventive' forms. The choice of suffixes depends on whether the speaker can directly observe the action, or whether the warning would be 'prompted not by observing some actual facts but by some previous "negative" experience' (Gruzdeva 1992: 69–70; based on Krejnović 1979: 316).[37]

That fewer evidential choices are available in commands than in statements or in questions follows from the semantic nature of the command itself. One can question the information source of a statement—'how do you know?' In contrast, a command is not intrinsically linked to an information source. This may be why comparatively few languages have any evidentials in their commands. That reported evidentials occur in commands with one uniform meaning, of relaying someone else's order, is congruent with the nature of commands as verbal orders. Other evidential meanings in commands involve the information source available to the speaker and to the addressee.

Evidentials in declarative clauses often—though far from always—have epistemic overtones, implying certainty, uncertainty, doubt, or disbelief. Importantly, these overtones are missing from the imperatives. This takes us to the next section.

4.2.5 *Imperatives, modalities, and reality status*

Imperative can occur together with a limited subset of modality markers if the morphemes are not mutually exclusive (that is, if imperative does not enter the same paradigm as mood, as it does in Wakashan, Eskimo, Samoyedic, and numerous other languages). Imperatives typically do not co-occur with markers of deontic modalities involving obligation—since obligation is part of the imperative meaning itself.

Markers of epistemic modalities—whose meanings cover doubt, possibility, probability, and the like (see Palmer 1986: 51–125, for an overview)—often cannot be used with imperatives. Modal auxiliaries in English—some of which are exponents of epistemic meanings—have no imperative forms.[38]

If they can, their meanings tend to be different. As we saw in the previous section, imperatives are often not compatible with epistemic meanings. Consequently, modal words and markers of epistemic modalities are often used to 'soften' a command.

In 4.42, from Cavineña (Guillaume 2004: 182), a second position clitic =*ni* 'maybe' is what imparts the meaning of 'do if you want to' to the command. It is also a way of making a command sound politer:

Cavineña
4.42   Ne-duju-kwe=ni   mikwana-ra
       IMPV.NSG-take-IMPV.NSG=maybe   2pl-ERG
       'You guys take it if you want!'

The 'redeployment' of a modality marker as a politeness strategy in commands is akin to using non-indicative modalities—such as conditional, subjunctive, potential, intentional, and others—in lieu of commands, as command strategies with politer or milder overtones. We return to these in Chapter 8.

Counterexpectation modality markers may have the opposite effect in commands—rather than soften commands, they make them sound more urgent and more insistent. This is the case in Cavineña:

4.43   Duju-kwe=bakwe
       take-IMPV.SG=COUNTEREXPECTATION
       'Come on! Take it!'

In Tariana, the counterexpectation marker -*pada* with imperatives means 'do something even if you do not want to'.

Modals may share their meanings in statements and in commands. This is the case for English modal-type adverb *maybe*. *Look in the university library, maybe* implies that it is possible but by no means certain that the required book will be found in this particular location. *Maybe it is in the library* has the same meaning. Along similar lines, the deontic modal particle *ge* often occurs in commands in Longgu (Hill 1997: 70), with the same meaning 'must, should'.

In languages with a grammatical category of reality status (see Elliott 2000 for an overview), irrealis forms often occur in commands. This is common in Oceanic languages—see, for instance, 2.48 from Manam.[39] We can recall that irrealis in Manam is used in a number of other meanings—including events likely to take place in the near future, counterfactual events, and habitual actions. (The exact semantic content of irrealis varies from one language to the next: see Mithun 1995.)

In other languages with a realis/irrealis distinction, this distinction does not appear in positive imperatives at all. Pendau, an Austronesian language spoken in Central Sulawesi in Indonesia (Quick 2007: 532–3) is a case in point. Irrealis forms occur in prohibitives, and also mark future, hypothetical, and customary events. Irrealis also occurs in commands in Teribe (Quesada 2000: 80). However, in Maricopa, a Yuman language, and in Caddo, a Caddoan language (Gordon 1987: 24–25; Mithun 1999: 179), all commands are cast as realis, while irrealis forms are employed in other instances of future projection.

Irrealis often has a special meaning if used in an imperative clause. In Jamul Tiipay (Miller 2001: 187, 257, 260–61), irrealis has an array of typical meanings: it expresses hypothetical and counterfactual meanings, and also occurs in purposive and apprehensive clauses ('or else': as in the second clause of 4.43). Polite imperatives are also expressed with an irrealis. A basic imperative is illustrated in 4.44; the following example contains a polite imperative:

Jamul Tiipay (Miller 2001: 257; 187)

4.44 cha'saw   me-wiich   ke-saaw   nuamaaw   me-naan   nemii-x
     food   3/2-give-PL   IMPV-eat   or.else   2-mom   get.angry-IRR
     'Eat the food they gave you, or else your mom will get angry'

4.45 nya-me-mápa-pu   me-rar-x-s
     INDEF-2-want-OBLIQUE.RELATIVE.STEM-DEM   2-do-IRR-EMPH
     'Do whatever you want (polite imperative)'[40]

Irrealis in commands may have somewhat different, imperative-specific overtones. In Tsakhur (Northeast Caucasian), the combination of an imperative with irrealis is a wish or advice, or a recommendation with respect to the past, rather than just a command.[41]

Tsakhur (Dobrushina 1999: 266)

4.46 ali=w=š-i sa dawar
3=buy=IMP-IRR one lamb
'You should buy a lamb' or 'You ought to have bought a lamb (in the past)'

And in rGyalrong, a Tibeto-Burman language with a realis/rrealis distinction, a command or a request cast in irrealis implies that it is to be realized at a later time, and in the speaker's absence. This is reminiscent of presential and absential overtones of evidentials in imperatives (§4.2.4) and also of the presential overtone of proximate imperative in Barasano (4.25). The simple imperative, not marked for reality status, implies that the speaker is going to be present when the command will be executed:

rGyalrong (Sun 2007: 809)

4.47 nə-nɐpriʔ qʰoʔ noŋme jɐ-ʃɐ
IMPV-eat.supper SEQ only.then IMPV-go
'Eat supper and then go (I will still be there)'

The irrealis implies that the actions are to be done in the speaker's absence.

4.48 nə-nɐpriʔ qʰoʔ noŋme ɐ-jɐ-tɐ-ʃɐ
IMPV-eat.supper SEQ only.then IRR_1-IRR_2-2p-go
'Eat supper and then go (during my absence)'

In some instances, only irrealis is appropriate. 4.49 was said by a father to his son, as a warning against a potentially scary experience that the 'child will undergo at a later time by himself':

4.49 ɐ-mə-nə-tə-vɐr
IRR_1-NEG-IRR_2-2p-be.afraid
'Don't be afraid (later, when I am not with you)!'[42]

This imperative-specific meaning of irrealis is not found in any other clause type in the language.

The ways in which imperatives express categories relating to verbal action are often linked to the imperative-specific meanings of force or degree of command, and politeness, distance in space and time, and information source of the speaker, and sometimes also the speaker and the addressee. We now turn to the correlations between imperatives and the marking of verbal arguments.

4.3 Imperatives and the marking of verbal arguments

In the vast majority of languages, imperatives do not have to have an overt subject—we saw examples of this in Chapter 2. Adding an overt subject to a canonical imperative in English has special stylistic implications (see §2.3). This is unlike declarative or interrogative clauses where the subject is obligatory. The motivation behind this is clear: the subject of a canonical imperative is inherent in the form (also see Davies 1986: 131–51).

Even in the absence of an overt subject, we can still identify it as such. In Koyra Chini (or Songhai), from Mali (Heath 1999: 165), the formally unrealized second person subject of an imperative controls a reflexive. This is how we know that it is the subject:[43]

Koyra Chini
4.50 bere   ni   nda   čirow!
      transform   2sgO   with   bird
      'Transform yourself (singular) into a bird'

Syntactic functions S and A can be grouped together—in accordance with tradition—as 'subject'. A number of recurrent grammatical properties link S and A in every sort of language (whether of accusative or ergative profile). One such universal property is treating S and A in the same way within an imperative construction.[44] This follows from the semantics of the imperative—the addressee is told by the speaker to be the agent—and also from the definition of subject as an NP which can be agent. (We will see, in §4.4, that verbs which imply controlled activity of their A or S are the most likely ones to be used in imperatives.)

The natural association between A and S in imperatives has been documented for languages with any type of syntactic alignment. Imperative constructions always show nominative–accusative syntax, even if other moods operate on an absolutive–ergative basis: this is the case in Sumerian, an ancient isolate from Mesopotamia (Michalowski 1980), and Päri, a Nilotic language (Andersen 1988).[45]

In addition to the universal nominative–accusative principle in imperatives, S and O can also be treated as one category in some ways, distinct from A—i.e. transitive subject is marked differently from the intransitive one. In two related languages from British Columbia, Nass-Gitskan (Rigsby 1975) and Tsimshian (Mulder 1989; Stebbins 2001), the suffix marking A on imperatives of transitive verbs can be omitted, while the suffix marking S/O is obligatory. In Nadëb, a Makú language from Brazil (Weir 1984: 121–2), S and O are unmarked, while A has to be expressed with a proclitic. These languages have an obligatory requirement that the subjects of imperatives should be expressed; the differences in the realization of A and S in imperatives are akin to different marking of imperatives depending on the verb's transitivity (see §4.4).

Many languages are similar to Tuvaluan where 'imperative formation optionally deletes subjects of intransitive or transitive verbs, but does not affect direct objects' (Besnier 2000: 34). But a few are not. In a number of Uto-Aztecan languages (such as Southern Paiute, Cahuilla, and some dialects of Hopi), the object of transitive imperatives takes the subject case (see 4.50).[46]

Cahuilla (Langacker 1977: 56)
4.51   paxa-ni-ʹ   e-ʹaš
       enter-CAUS-IMPV   your-pet(+SUBJECT.CASE)
       'Stable your horse'

Along similar lines, in Lardil, Panyjima, and other Ngayarda languages (Australian), the object of a canonical imperative, if expressed with a noun, takes nominative rather than accusative case (Dixon 1972: 135–6; Dench 1991: 204). Pronominal objects take the accusative case. This pattern may reflect an original absolutive–ergative marking. The same principle applies to the first person non-singular imperative:

Panyjima (Dench 1991: 175)
4.52   ngali   ngarna-kara-rru   mantu-muntu   martumirri
       1du.incl   eat-HORT-NOW   meat.NOM-CONJUNCTION   damper:NOM
       'Let's eat meat and damper!'[47]

We return to this in §10.1.

The form of the imperative object may interact with other grammatical meanings. In Tubatulabal, only the non-future imperative takes an object without accusative marking. See 4.53, with a non-future imperative, and 4.54, with a future imperative:

Tubatulabal (Langacker 1977: 56)
4.53   paˈagina-h   taatwa-l
       hit-IMPV   man-ABS
       'Hit the man'

4.54   paˈagina-hai   taatwa-l-a
       hit-FUT.IMPV   man-ABS-ACC
       'Hit the man after a while'

We can recall, from 3.47, that third person imperatives in Finnish take an accusative-marked object—unlike canonical imperatives whose objects appear in the nominative case.[48]

In all these instances, objects of imperatives are less formally marked than the same grammatical relation in declarative clauses. The reason is intuitively clear (see also §3.3.4). The referent of the imperative subject is typically just a second person, and there is thus hardly any need to disambiguate the subject and object of an imperative. We can recall that in Estonian and Finnish the same principle applies to the impersonal—whose subject is the impersonal generic referent 'they'.[49]

4.4 Imperatives, transitivity, and verbal semantics

A prototypical directive speech act implies the speaker's control over the activity directed to be performed. As a consequence, verbs whose meanings cannot be controlled—such as verbs of state, or passives—may hardly form imperatives. We start with the ways in which imperatives interact with transitivity classes of verbs (§4.4.1), and then turn to the ways they interact with transitivity-changing derivations (§4.4.2). Further interactions of imperatives with verbal semantics, and restrictions on forming imperatives, are addressed in §4.4.3.

4.4.1 *Imperatives and transitivity classes*

We saw in §4.3 that the subject of transitive verbs, and of intransitive verbs, is one syntactic entity in imperative (no matter whether a language is nominative-accusative or absolutive-ergative). The ways imperatives are marked can be different, depending on the verb's transitivity. This is a pervasive feature of Mayan languages from Meso-America. In Jacaltec, a transitive verb appears in its bare form without any aspect or subject marker:

Jacaltec (Craig 1977: 70)
4.55 mak   hin   an
      hit   A1   1p
      'Hit me!'

An intransitive verb marks its imperative with a suffix -*añ*:

4.56 oc-añ   pisy-añ
      enter-IMPV   sit-IMPV
      'Come in and sit down'[50]

The imperative of an intransitive verb in Tzotzil, also Mayan (Haviland 1981: 119, 217), is marked with the suffix *-an*, and that of a transitive verb contains the suffix *-o*. Unlike Jacaltec, both transitive and intransitive imperatives are formally marked:[51]

Tzotzil

4.57a   bat-an
         go-IMPV.ITR
         'Go!'

4.57b   k'el-o   li   na-e
         look-IMPV   ART   house-ENCLITIC
         'Look at the house!'

We can recall from §3.3.4 that imperative marking in Indonesian correlates with the verb's transitivity and the object's specificity (Sneddon 1996: 324). The imperative form of an intransitive verb in Indonesian has no special marker: as in many languages discussed in §2.1.1, it coincides with the bare stem:[52]

Indonesian

4.58   datang   ke sini
        come   here
        'Come here!'

A transitive verb drops the active voice prefix *meN-* if the action is performed on a specific object, as in 4.59.

4.59   lihat   foto   ini
        look.at   photo   this
        'Look at this photo!'

If there is no object, or the object is generic, the prefix is retained:

4.60   mem-baca   sekarang
        ACTIVE.VOICE-read   now
        'Read now!'

Imperatives do not affect the verb's transitivity. But verbs whose transitivity has been affected by derivations such as passive may not form imperatives as readily as other verbs. This takes us to the next section.

4.4.2 Imperatives and valency-changing derivations

Causatives and applicatives increase the number of the verb's arguments, and are among transitivizing derivations. Forming imperatives on such verbs is usually straightforward.[53] Neither are there any restrictions for imperatives on reflexives, reciprocals, and antipassives (see Dixon 1977: 280 for an example of an antipassive imperative in Yidiɲ, and Dixon 1972 for Dyirbal). This is probably due to the fact that antipassives do not involve demoting the agent.[54]

In many languages, imperatives cannot be formed on passives.[55] In Yucatec Maya, simple imperatives cannot be formed on passives. An analytic construction containing the imperative of 'go' is used instead (Hofling and Ojeda 1994: 282):

Yucatec Maya

4.61 xen   ka'   kín-s-a'-ak-ech

      go.IMPV   SUBORDORDINATOR   die-CAUS-PASSIVE-IRREAL-2sg

      'Go to be killed'

Imperatives of passives in English have been the subject of much discussion: the general consensus is that they cannot normally occur in an imperative form (cf. Dixon 1994: 132). Indeed, 4.62a–b are hardly acceptable (Takahashi 2000: 239):

4.62a *George, be taken to church by your sister!

4.62b *Be helped by Jill

However, one can devise examples where passive is quite acceptable—as are 4.63a–b:

4.63a Be checked over by a doctor, then you'll be sure there's nothing wrong

4.63b Be flattered by what he says, it'll make his day

These examples show that, for an imperative passive to be acceptable, it needs to be contextualized, i.e. accompanied by another clause, usually stating the consequences. In addition, a passive imperative sounds natural if the addressee 'can be understood to be in control of the event referred to'—being in the position to choose whether to perform or undergo it or not, as in 4.63a–b (Davies 1986: 15).

Quirk et al. (1985: 827) point out that in English passives with *be* are less common in positive than in negative directives (with the exception of fixed expressions, e.g. *Be damned*, or pseudo-passives, e.g. *Be seated*), e.g. *Don't be observed as you climb out of the window.*

Along similar lines, imperatives of passives in Japanese are rare and often problematic (Martin 1975: 961). The Japanese equivalent of 4.63a would be ungrammatical and, according to Takahashi (2000: 254), cannot be rendered acceptable through context. However, passive negative commands can be acceptable, as in 4.64:

4.64   sono   isha   ni   damas-areru   na
       the   doctor   by   taken.in.be-PASS   NEG.IMPV
       'Don't be taken in by the doctor!'

Imperatives of passives in English are widespread in advertising. 4.65 comes from a real estate agent, advertising a rather small house:

4.65   Be surprised by the size!

Imperatives of passives may have an additional function.[56] In Indonesian, an imperative of a transitive verb can be expressed with the passive. The resulting form is 'more indirect and consequently less forceful than an imperative with an active verb'.[57] And we can recall, from §2.2.1, that the first person plural imperative is rarely used in spoken Finnish, 'its function being assumed by the passive indicative': instead of saying *Menkäämme ulos* (go+IMPV+pl+1pl out), one says *Mennään ulos!* (go.PASSIVE out) 'Let's go out!' (Sulkala and Karjalainen 1992: 23).

Other verbal derivations can make a command sound milder. In Meithei, a Tibeto-Burman language from India (Chelliah 1997: 287), the benefactive 'VERB for someone other than self' and reflexive reduce the force of a command.

4.4.3 *Imperatives, transitivity, and verb classes*

A prototypical directive speech act involves a controllable action. In almost every language most transitive verbs tend to express a controllable action, while only some intransitive verbs do. Most languages of the world do not distinguish between controlled and uncontrolled varieties of S in their grammars (see Dixon 1994: 133, 71–8), and any type of S can be the potential addressee of an imperative—just like an A.

In English, an imperative can be used with just about any verb, even if the level of control is minimal or nonexistent. Given an appropriate context, sentences like *Endure it for a few days (and then I'll arrange a transfer)* or 'a whispered malevolent wish *Slip down and break your leg!*' (Dixon 1994: 132) are totally conceivable. Sadock and Zwicky (1985: 172) note that a command *Weigh 60 kilos!* sounds strange unless one can supply a specific context—for instance, a weight-loss establishment, or a fairy tale. Note that such commands may not really be directive speech acts; we will see in Chapter 7 (example 7.33) that something like *Be well on the way to going completely insane weeks beforehand* is not meant to order the address to do anything—this is part of a warning to someone doing overeating, overspending, and so on during Christmas festivities.

Unlike English, numerous languages have a restriction on using verbs which describe an uncontrolled action or a state in commands. In Onondaga (Chafe 1970: 20–21), an imperative form can only be formed on an action verb. In Tariana, stative verbs such as 'be cold', 'be sick', 'be afraid', and verbs of physical and mental states cannot form imperatives (see Aikhenvald 2001 for their verbal properties).[58] Such a restriction may not be an absolute rule: in Turkana, a Nilotic language (Dimmendaal 1983: 181), it is possible to form an imperative on a verb which refers to an uncontrolled event, e.g. 'fear' or 'die', but imperatives are less common with such verbs. They can occur in imperatives if causativized.[59]

The preference for controlled actions in imperatives may apply equally to intransitive and to transitive verbs. In Halkomelem, a Salish language from British Columbia (Galloway 1993: 308–10, 244, 247), imperatives cannot be formed on verbs whose action cannot be controlled. Such verbs can be intransitive or transitive, e.g. 'do accidentally', 'blink', 'drop (something)', or 'forget'.

If a language cannot form a simple imperative with stative verbs, a different construction may be employed instead to express a command. In Tukang Besi, only agentive verbs can form imperatives (Donohue 1999a). An imperative of the verb 'sleep' is ungrammatical:

4.66a   *Moturu!
        Sleep!

Instead, a command can be expressed by using a non-imperative form, as in 4.66b, or a serial verb construction with an agentive verb 'go' which imparts agentivity to the whole:

4.66b   Labi   'u-moturu   meana'e
        better 2sg.REALIS-sleep   now
        'You should sleep now'

4.66c   Wila   moturu
        go   sleep
        'Go and sleep!'

In Nivkh, imperatives cannot be formed with 'qualitative' verbs referring to uncontrollable actions ('be well', 'be young'); analytic constructions with the verbs 'live, be located' or 'be, become' are used instead (Gruzdeva 1992: 68, 72).

Verbs denoting uncontrollable actions can acquire the feature of 'control' when used in imperative. Verbs of perception are a case in point. In Kayardild, *marrija* typically means 'hear' in declaratives, and 'listen' in commands (where the subject's control is implied) (Evans and Wilkins 2000: 554–5). Along similar lines, the verb 'see' in statements acquires a telic meaning, 'look', in commands in Manambu, and in Tariana. The verbs meaning 'hear, listen' and 'obey' can have either of these meanings in statements in both Tariana and in Manambu. In commands, only controlled meanings are 'activated': the same verb implies 'listening' or 'obeying', but not 'hearing'.

In English, imperatives are restricted to verbs and predications which allow a dynamic interpretation, 'hence the incongruity of *Need a car, *Be old, *Sound louder' (Quirk et al. 1985: 827). Many predications defined as stative in terms of disallowing the progressive can acquire a dynamic interpretation when used in imperatives, e.g. *Know the poem by heart by the next lesson, Love your enemies*, or *Owe nobody anything*.

Among verbs which often do not allow imperative formation are copula verbs and verbs of possession (as in Harar Oromo: Owens 1985: 67; Amharic: Amberber 1997a; and in Tariana).[60] Equational copula clauses cannot form imperatives in Bukiyip Arapesh (Conrad and Wogiga 1991: 94). In Udihe, a Tungusic language (Nikolaeva and Tolskaya 2001: 263–4, 501), imperative cannot be formed on desiderative verbs, weather verbs, some modal verbs, and verbs referring to intention and psychological states.

Verbless clauses—if the language has any—typically do not form imperatives. In order to form an imperative on a verbless clause, it needs to be recast either as an intransitive clause, as in Dyirbal where they are recast as inchoatives, or as a copula clause, as in Manambu. In Udihe, the copula verb 'be' cannot form an imperative in copula constructions expressing desire, quantity, and experiential meanings (Nikolaeva and Tolskaya 2001: 264).

Most adjectives refer to states that are hardly controllable. In English, the grammatical marking of imperatives can extend to include adjectives and even nouns—one can say *Be happy!* , *Be hungry!* (perhaps meaning 'Act as if you were hungry'—Dixon 1994: 132), and *Be yourself!* But this is impossible in many other languages—including Halkomelem (Galloway 1993: 308–10), Nuuchahnulth (or Nootka: Nakayama p.c.), and Fijian.

In languages where adjectives share properties with verbs (see Dixon 2004b), forming imperatives is an additional criterion to differentiate these word classes. In Semelai and in North-East Ambae (Kruspe 2004b: 302; Hyslop 2004: 272–3), verbs occur in imperative constructions and adjectives do not. In Korean (Sohn 2004: 230), the plain-level imperative suffix *-ela/-ala* has an exclamatory function only when it occurs with an adjective.

Restrictions on imperative formation may not apply to negative imperatives in the same way as they do to positive ones. In Manambu, stative verbs
such as *rəp-* 'be enough', *warsama-* 'be angry', cannot form a canonical
imperative. They can form negative imperatives. No stative verb in Tariana
can normally have a positive imperative. A negative imperative can be formed
on verbs of quality such as 'be bad', 'be cold', but not on verbs of physical and
mental states, such as 'be unwilling', 'be lazy'. We return to the correlations
between negative imperatives and other categories in Chapter 5.

Verbs of motion—prototypically active and controllable—can differ from
other verbs in the way imperatives are formed. Motion verbs display a
number of formal idiosyncrasies in the tonal patterns of their imperatives
in Chalcatongo Mixtec (Macaulay 1996: 134–5). And we can recall, from §2.13,
that in many languages suppletive imperatives include verbs of motion.

The imperatives of verbs of motion may have more grammatical distinctions than other verbs. In Figuig (Kossmann 1997: 125–6), only the imperatives
of two irregular verbs of motion distinguish gender forms in plural. In some
languages, such as Barasano, directionality and motion are only marked in the
imperatives of motion verbs (see Jones and Jones 1991: 76–8). In the grammar
of each of these languages, this should be a reason for setting the class of
motion verbs apart from other semantic types.[61]

4.5 Imperatives and the form of the verb

Imperatives interact with the form of the verb. In Dyirbal, verbs divide into
conjugations depending on the type of final consonant. Since final consonants
are deleted in the imperative, verbal conjugations are no longer differentiated
(Dixon 1972: 110–11). In other languages—for instance, in Kiowa (Watkins
1984: 167–8)—there is no such neutralization.

Sharing mood, modality, and polarity value is a definitional property of
serial verbs (Aikhenvald 2006a). In other words, an imperative marker has the
whole serial verb as its scope. Example 4.67 comes from Eastern Kayah Li:

Eastern Kayah Li (Solnit 2006: 152)
4.67 ne   [hɛ̄   nìdā   mɛ̄]   kʌ̄   mʎ́
      2sg come listen look COMITATIVE   IMPV
      'Come, listen (and) look!'

Along similar lines, in Tariana, cohortative *ma* 'let's (do something)' and
wasã 'let's go' have the whole SVC within their scope (see Aikhenvald 2006b:
183).[62] In contrast, the scope of an imperative in a complex sentence is just one
predicate—as in Olutec, a Mixean language (Zavala 2006: 281). And in

Dolakha Newar the scope of imperative goes beyond the single clause to a sequence of clauses joined by the participial construction:[63]

Dolakha Newar (Genetti 2007: 337)
4.68 jā   na-en   yā
      rice eat-PARTICIPLE   come-IMPV
      'Eat rice and come!'

According to Genetti (2007: 337–8), such examples are 'few in connected discourse'. But, in agreement with the principle of iconicity, complex clauses with the auxiliary meaning 'give' are commonly used to soften the command 'to a request for a favor, generally for the benefit of the speaker':[64]

4.69 simā thābi ta-en   bi-u
      tree on   put-PARTICIPLE   give-IMPV
      'Put (me) on the tree'

Martin (1975: 962) decribes a similar phenomenon in Japanese, where the DOMAIN of an imperative may include sentences conjoined by the gerund or the infinitive. In a sequential construction in Mantauran Rukai, a Formosan language (Zeitoun 2007: 161), only the first verb takes the imperative suffix, and the second one is marked as subjunctive.

Numerous constraints on the ways in which imperatives can be coordinated with other clause types in English are discussed by Davies (1986: 152–60).[65] An imperative coordinated with a declarative clause is likely to get a conditional interpretation, as in 4.70.

4.70   Ask him a question and you get no answer

These 'imperative-like conditionals' (see Davies 1986: 162–203) are among non-command uses of imperatives: we return to these in Chapter 7. Some cannot be used as commands on their own. Compare 4.71a, which is perfectly acceptable, with 4.71b, which is not:

4.71a   Say any more and there'll be trouble
4.71b   *Say any more

Constraints on acceptability of imperatives in coordinate structures in English are akin to the principle formulated by Genetti (2007: 337) for Dolakha Newar: 'Imperatives do not occur with long complex sentences. Rather, imperative constructions tend to be short and succinct.' This agrees with the nature of a prototypical directive speech act.

4.6 Summary

Grammatical categories expressed in imperatives vary in their complexity. Imperatives may express more grammatical meanings than do the corresponding declaratives. They can express fewer meanings; or the meanings expressed can be different in different clause types. This applies to the CATEGORIES RELATING TO THE ADDRESSEE (§4.1), especially gender or noun class. Just a few languages have a special marking of gender of the 'commander' in imperatives but no gender distinctions in statements.

Correlations with categories relating to verbal action (§4.2) are:

(i) Imperatives generally tend to have fewer ASPECTUAL categories than do declaratives. Typical distinctions are continuative versus simple (or punctual) imperative. There is a strong tendency to distinguish these only in canonical imperatives. Unlike in declaratives, these tend to acquire imperative-specific overtones of politeness.

(ii) The most frequently attested grammaticalized time distinction in imperatives is that of immediate command ('do now!') and delayed command ('do later!')—typically distinguished for canonical imperatives only. 'Delayed' imperatives often have overtones of politeness. Imperatives do not have to always have future reference. Command forms referring to the past do exist—and uniformly have overtones of a wish for a past action to have happened.

(iii) The same imperative form may combine reference to distance in time and in space. This polysemy is hardly ever found in tense systems in declarative clauses.

(iv) 'Distance in space' is another category often found in imperatives—'do here' versus 'do there'. These may have further overtones of presence or absence of the speaker during the execution of the command. Few languages have special imperative forms depending on whether the action is to be performed in the presence or absence of the speaker, or on whether the speaker (and the addressee) can see the action or not.

(v) Imperatives may have special forms expressing motion and directionality of action. The speaker remains the deictic centre for the direction of action.

(vi) A reported (or secondhand) evidential is the most pervasive marker of information source in commands. Its meaning is uniformly that of a command by proxy—'do something that someone else (other than the speaker) told you'. Evidentials in commands never have any epistemic overtones, although their counterparts in statements often do. A reported evidential in a command may attenuate an order—something an evidential in a statement never does.

(vii) Imperatives tend not to have additional, epistemic meanings of probability or possibility. Markers of modality and of irrealis in imperatives are used to 'soften' commands, and to make them sound politer.

Categories relating to verbal action in imperatives are centered on the 'commander' as the deictic point of reference. They also tend to develop imperative-specific overtones of politeness and degree of command. We return to these in Chapter 6.

MARKING OF VERBAL ARGUMENTS in canonical imperatives may differ from that in other clauses types (§4.3), in that the subject does not have to be overtly expressed—the addressee is uniformly understood as the subject. The second argument—the object—may not be formally marked, the reason being that if the subject is just the addressee, there is no need to disambiguate the subject and the object. Imperatives universally operate on a nominative-accusative principle. The differences in marking grammatical relations in imperatives and in corresponding declaratives are rooted in the discourse-pragmatic functions and semantics, and often archaic features of imperatives (see Chapter 10).

Imperatives correlate with transitivity, and meanings, of verbs. A prototypical directive speech act implies the speaker's control over the activity. Verbs describing uncontrollable actions, states, and the like may not be able to form imperatives. Copula verbs, verb 'have', and passive forms may not have imperatives either. But passives and benefactives may develop imperative-specific meanings of politeness and indirect commands.

Imperatives may vary in their scope: a whole complex sentence may fall within the scope of imperative marked in a main clause.

Interrogatives, declaratives, and imperatives are three different moods, corresponding to different speech acts. Counterintuitive as it may seem, imperative forms do make their way into questions and into statements. These imperatives—which do not really 'command'—are part of our discussion in Chapter 7. Statements and questions can be used where one should expect a command form: we turn to these imperatives in disguise in Chapter 8.

Notes

1. The same number of gender distinctions in imperatives and declaratives are found in Amharic (Leslau 1995: 353–4; Cohen 1936: 179–81) and Dhaasanac (Tosco 2001: 14–18).

2. A similar situation obtains in a number of other Berber languages, among them Figuig, a North Berber language (Kossmann 1997: 125–6; see 2.62), Rif (Kossmann 2000: 55), Nefusi from Libya (Beguinot 1942: 43), and Tahaggart (Prasse 1973: 11–13). That a language should distinguish genders in non-singular rather than in the singular goes against Greenberg's predictions (1963: 95), formulated as Universals 37 and 45. Universal 37 reads: 'A language never has more gender categories in non-singular numbers than in the singular', and Universal 45 reads: 'If there are gender distinctions in the plural of the pronoun, there are some gender distinctions in the singular also'. A few further counterexamples are given in Plank and Schellinger (1997). See the discussion in Aikhenvald (2000: ch. 10).

   Kossmann (2001) provides a brief overview of person markers and their etymologies in some Berber languages. Siwa, the only East Berber language spoken in Egypt (Laoust 1931: 50–51), and a number of North Berber languages from Morocco such as Zemmour (Laoust 1928: 49, 53) do not distinguish genders in second person declarative or imperative.

3. In Manambu, and the related languages Iatmul, Wosera, and Boiken, gender in imperatives can be disambiguated by adding personal pronouns. Hausa (Newman 2000: 262–9) and Sidaamo (Kawachi 2007: 398, 425) also distinguish genders in second person declaratives, but not in imperatives. In Tariana, only those imperatives which can occur with the third person (the only person where feminine and non-feminine genders are distinguished) express the two genders.

4. Masculine and feminine genders are distinguished in demonstratives, and also in possessive constructions (Cerrón-Palomino 2006: 118–19).

5. We have no information about mixed groups. Likewise, there are no examples of plural imperatives with female addresses.

6. For similar examples in other Berber languages, see Kossmann (2001).

7. It appears that the masculine form can cover mixed sex referents. A similar example comes from Figuig (Kossmann 1997: 125–6). However, it appears that these forms are restricted to just two irregular verbs of motion.

8. See Boas and Deloria (1941: 111–12), for additional marking in the verb stem.

9. See Trechter (1995) for a general view of gender in declarative and imperatives particles in Lakhota, and other Siouan languages.

   It appears that certain types of imperatives tend to be associated with female speech; according to Quirk et al. (1985: 833), in English DO 'persuasive' imperatives are found more often in female than in male speech. This has nothing to do with grammatical gender.

10. Boas and Deloria (1941: 111–12). Modern Lakhota forms are briefly discussed by Ullrich (2008: 764–5).

11. See Matthews (1997), Comrie (1976), and Chung and Timberlake (1985) for a cross-linguistic analysis.

12. Perfect and imperfect distinctions in imperatives in Watjarri (Douglas 1981: 230–31) are not paralleled by those in declaratives, and can be considered

imperative-specific. Quintero (2004: 293–7) describes continuative and non-continuative imperative in Osage, a Siouan language.

13. In Kiowa (Watkins 1984: 169–70), imperfective meaning of the imperative is the same as that of the declarative: 'commands when the event is envisioned as repeated, habitual, or of some duration'. A similar example comes from Eskimo (Vaxtin 1992: 92) and Igbo, where a durative or continuative meaning and marking are the same in both clause types (Emenanjọ 1978: 190–5).

14. In Epena Pedee, a Choco language from Colombia (Harms 1994: 129), only the habitual aspect is compatible with imperatives (other aspects, such as imperfective, completive, progressive, and durative, do not occur in imperatives).

15. Along similar lines, the imperative in Babungo does not occur with past tense markers, or perfective aspect (Schaub 1985: 23–4).

16. See detailed discussion and criticisms of such statements of early generative linguists such as Postal (1964), in Bolinger (1967). For Jespersen (1940: 24.1), 'the imperative always refers to the future, often the immediate future'. Past imperatives are mentioned by Palmer (1986: 111–12). Davies (1986: 124–30) opts for considering imperatives in English as inherently 'tenseless'.

17. Most languages have fewer grammaticalized time distinctions in imperatives than in non-imperatives. Alternatively, the semantic types of future can be different in imperatives and in declaratives. Nishnaabemwin (or Ojibwe, an Algonquian language: Valentine 2001: 991–3) also distinguishes immediate and delayed imperatives (the latter 'allowing for the issue of a command to be carried out at a later time': p. 993). There are two future preverbs in non-imperative clauses: one implying volition, and the other used in contexts of consequence or obligation (pp. 772–82). Similar examples are found in other Algonquian languages, e.g. Cheyenne (Leman 1980) and Miami-Illinos (Costa 2003: 326–8); also see Mithun (1999: 172).

18. Tuyuca (Barnes 1979) has a delayed imperative, marked with the suffix *-wa*. Macuna (Smothermon et al. 1995: 62–3) has a distal imperative marked with suffix *-t*, and a future imperative marked with *-ba*. The delayed imperative in Tariana combines reference to distance in time and in space (see 4.28).

19. Immediate and delayed imperatives are both formally marked (with different affixes) in Hua (Haiman 1980: 61–3), Evenki (Nedjalkov 1997: 262–3), Yele (Henderson 1995: 35–9), Kewa (Franklin 1971: 39), and Nanai (Avrorin 1961: 135–7).

Commands with future reference may employ forms from a paradigm distinct from simple imperatives. A future imperative may come from a different paradigm: in Punjabi, the future imperative is homophonous with the infinitive (Bhatia 1993). In Huallaga Quechua, future inflection is employed for future imperatives ('do later': Weber 1996: 153). In Hixkaryana (Carib), a command with future reference involves the non-past form of the verb with the intensifier *ha* after the verb (Derbyshire 1985: 66).

20. Following a similar principle, Piapoco, a North Arawak language (Klumpp 1990), employs the distant future marker *-wa* to signal a polite imperative. In Macushi,

the future imperative is more polite and less forceful than the unmarked imperative (Abbott 1991). Similar semantic extensions have been noted for Huallaga Quechua, Evenki, and Central Alaskan Yup'ik (Eskimo-Aleut).

21. This appears to be a strong tendency, but not a rule. Yele, a Papuan language (Henderson 1995: 35–6), distinguishes first person plural delayed imperative (marked with *paa*), and second and third person (marked with *dpî*). In agreement with the iconicity principle (§2.1.5), immediate imperatives are formally unmarked; they can have all the person values. Una, also Papuan (Louwerse 1988: 36–7), has a full person paradigm for four tenses and one aspect distinctions in imperative: immediate, near deferred, regular deferred, remote deferred, and continuous. Takelma has a first person immediate imperative, but no such form for the future imperative in any of the verbal paradigms. In just one instance, in transitive verbs, the first person future imperative is 'probably expressed by simple future' (Sapir 1922: 171).

22. Many European languages have imperatives with past-in-future reference. These are often complex forms involving auxiliaries, as in French *Aie terminé quand je reviendrai* ('be done with it when I return: Wolf, Linguist List 16.11.2001). Frisian and Dutch (Wolf forthcoming) also have past tense imperatives, albeit restricted in their occurrence; they usually occur embedded in past tense narratives.

    A statement cast in the past tense may have an overtone of reproach, 'you ought to have done it in the past but failed to do it'—a past tense command of sorts. A frustrated head of department said to a member of his staff who failed to attend an important meeting, *You didn't come to the meeting*, implying 'your absence let me down'.

23. See Table 2.16 for the non-past forms of the Estonian indirect or 'mediated' imperative. See also Erelt (2002a: 115); other approaches to the place of past imperative in the Estonian paradigm are in Metslang, Mužniece, and Pajusalu 1999: 147–8; Mägiste 1976; de Sivers 1969: 76–7).

24. A past tense form may be employed as an imperative without a past tense meaning (see §2.1.2 on Amele, where the imperative forms coincide with today-past forms, and past tense forms in Russian used as imperatives of 'authority').

25. In Ika, imperatives are formed with different auxiliaries whose choice depends on whether the action is to be performed immediately at a short distance from the place of speech act or further away (see §2.2.1; Frank 1990: 86–9).

    This is similar to the ways in which demonstratives with a primarily spatial reference can be extended to refer to time. For instance, in Tariana, the distal demonstrative refers to the past, e.g. *hane-kamu* (that-year) 'past year'. The delayed imperative in Tariana can also refer to distance either in space or in time (or both)—see 4.27–8. Temporal extensions in demonstratives abound in languages with no time distinctions in imperatives, such as Irakw (Mous 1993: 90–91) and Sarcee (Cook 1984: 73–5); further examples are in Anderson and Keenan (1985).

26. Spatial distance is also distinguished in Macuna and Wanano (Aikhenvald 2008b; Waltz 1976: 46), also East Tucanoan.

27. A similar category of 'displaced' imperative is found in Panare, from the same family (Payne and Payne 1999).

28. Also see Hawkins (1998: 122–3) on Wai Wai. Imperative forms often combine with already existing directionals in a language, as in Shoshone, Barasano, Mam, Hup (Epps 2005: 960), Turkana (Dimmendaal 1983: 180), and Pero, where imperative has only nonperfective ventive ('away from speaker') aspect (Frajzyngier 1989: 88).

29. The same principle has been described for Hixkaryana (Derbyshire 1985: 195) and Trio (Carlin 2004: 307). Note that the imperatives in Trio distinguish only one motion category, ventive ('come carry out action here'), in imperatives. In Apalaí, from the same family, 'motion away' is marked in second person imperatives, and also in first person inclusive (but not in third person) (Koehn and Koehn 1986: 106–7).

30. Along similar lines, imperatives in Mam, a Mayan language (England 1983: 173–4), occur with directionals of all verbal categories.

31. Statements that evidentials are a type of mood or modality (e.g. Palmer 1986) are erroneous and unsubstantiated; see Aikhenvald (2004) and references there.

32. An overwhelming majority of languages with evidentiality systems in declarative clauses make no evidentiality distinctions in imperative clauses (examples include Sochiapan Chinantec, Samoyedic languages, Jarawara, Wakashan, and Turkic languages). None of the languages which distinguish quotative and reported evidentials in statements—such as Comanche, a Uto-Aztecan language (Charney 1993: 188–91, 217–19)—have any evidentiality in commands. A few languages have a secondhand imperative meaning 'do something on someone else's order' marked differently from evidentiality in declarative clauses. This is the case in Nganasan, Cavineña, Cora, and Lak (see references in Aikhenvald 2004). The reported enclitic -*guuq* in West Greenlandic is also used in commands on behalf of someone else (Fortescue 2003: 295–6).

33. The secondhand imperative is also found in Tuyuca (marked with -*aro*: Barnes 1979) and Wanano (-*haro*: Waltz and Waltz 1997: 40). The marking is rather uniform throughout the family; we turn to the origins and development of reported command markers in Chapter 11.

34. Similar examples are in Yankunytjatjara (Goddard 1983: 289). The original speaker can never be stated. In a few languages, including Epena Pedee, a Choco language (Harms 1994: 130, 176–8) an evidential suffix is used for commands in quoted speech.

35. The reported evidential in commands is part of the Yankunytjatjara speech etiquette: relatives who are not allowed to directly speak to each other (and are in 'avoidance' relationship) relay requests using the reported evidential. See 6.17.

36. In Shipibo-Konibo, only one of the two otherwise synonymous reportatives is used in imperatives (Valenzuela 2003: 42). The meaning is of a command on someone else's behalf.

37. Nivkh has no other evidential distinctions anywhere else in its grammar. Maidu has a three-term evidential system in declarative clauses (visual, reported, and inferred: Shipley 1964: 45). Tariana has five evidentials (Aikhenvald 2003).

   The only example of an evidential reflecting how the addressee knows what is being ordered comes from Euchee (Linn 2000: 318). This language is severely endangered, and therefore the data from it should be treated with caution: this can well be an instance of spurious language change by obsolescent speakers. Marking 'point of view of source' in commands in Mina was mentioned by Frajzyngier and Johnston (2005: 237); this may also be related to evidentiality.

38. See Jespersen (1924), Dixon (2005: 173–7); similar phenomena in Japanese are described by Alpatov (1992: 117); Also see Langacker (1977: 57–8) on modal meanings in imperatives. Quirk et al. (1985) and Huddleston (2002: 929–30) discuss the restrictions on the use of judgement words, such as *unfortunately* in imperatives in English.

39. Similar examples come from Neve'ei, an Oceanic language from Vanuatu (Musgrave 2007: 50), and also Bukawa, an Oceanic language from Morobe Province in Papua New Guinea (Eckermann 2007: 36–7); also see Lynch, Ross and Crowley (2002: 89). A partial survey of reality status in imperatives and some other directives is in Mauri and Sansò (2012).

40. Cf. Lynch, Ross, and Crowley (2002: 89): 'it is reasonable to infer that the basic Proto-Oceanic imperative was unmarked and that the irrealis was used for more courteous commands.' Irrealis marking is also associated with politeness in Alamblak, a Sepik Hill language from New Guinea (Bruce 1984; also Roberts 1990: 390; Mithun 1995: 378).

41. The same form is used in conditionals, with a counterfactual meaning. An irrealis marker with a negative imperative has a counterfactual meaning (see Chapters 5 and 7).

42. In rGyalrong, irrealis always marks third person imperatives. As expected, third person imperatives do not have distinctions to do with temporal distance.

43. Kawachi (2007) provides similar tests for Sidaamo, an East Cushitic language from Ethiopia.

44. These are discussed in Dixon (1994: 131–42) and further summarized in Aikhenvald and Dixon (2011).

45. Cavineña and Dyirbal, both ergative, group A and S together in imperatives. See also Dixon (1994: 101, 131–3). Along similar lines, in Tuvaluan (Besnier 2000: 34), 'imperative formation targets subjects of intransitive and transitive verbs as a single category'.

46. A similar pattern was described by Hill (2005: 117), for Cupeño. This phenomenon is not pan-Uto-Aztecan: in Shoshone and in Comanche, the object of transitive imperatives takes the object case.

47. The special status of imperative objects in Panyjima is matched by the special behaviour of body-part instruments and manner adverbials. In declarative clauses, these take the same case marking as the subject. But in imperative

clauses, they take the agentive suffix; this reflects the original ergative case-marking pattern in the language. More on this in Chapter 11.

48. The choice of the accusative or partitive case in questions used as a command may imply an assumption to do with politeness—see Heinämäki (1984: 167–8, 171–2), and Chapter 6.

49. Objects of imperatives may differ from objects of declaratives in other ways. Awa Pit has a special pronominal form for the first person object in imperatives, which replaces the imperative markers (Curnow 1997b: 244–5; and example 3.33a). Special object markers in imperatives have been described for Shoshone (Dayley 1989: 48–9) and Comanche (Charney 1993: 219), both Uto-Aztecan. If a language marks subject (A) and object (O) on the verb, typically fewer combinations are available in imperatives than in declarative clauses. For instance, Mara has no 3rdA to 1stO forms in imperatives (Heath 1981). In Manambu, objects of imperatives cannot be cross-referenced (reflecting an archaic pattern preserved in other languages of the Ndu family: see Chapter 11). In Indonesian, imperatives require special forms of pronominal objects: bound pronouns do not occur as objects of imperatives, and if the object is not clear from the context, a full pronoun is used (Sneddon 1996: 327). Full pronouns as objects can occur only in some non-imperative constructions (Sneddon 1996: 164–5). And see §3.3.4 on the correlations in Indonesian between the verbal stem and the specificity of the object in imperatives, which is absent from declarative clauses (Sneddon 1996: 324–5; 67–8).

50. Similar examples come from Acatec (Peñalosa 1987: 296), where the imperative is formed from the bare base stem of a transitive verb, and the suffix *-an* is added to the base stem of an intransitive verb, and Yucatec Mayan (Hofling and Ojeda 1994: 273–4). Different markers for imperatives formed on transitive and on intransitive verbs have been attested in a number of Northeast Caucasian languages of Daghestan—Godoberi (Kibrik 1996: 49), Icari Dargwa (Sumbatova and Mutalov 2003: 94–5), Bagwalal (Dobrushina 2001: 319–20), and also in Mosetén, an isolate from Bolivia (Sakel 2003).

51. Along similar lines, in Yukulta, an Australian language, imperative of transitive verbs is marked with *-ka* (e.g. *pala__ka* 'hit (that dog)!') and that of intransitive verbs with *-ṭa* or *-tʸa* on an intransitive (*tʸawiṯʸa* 'run!') (Keen 1983: 240). Similar examples are found in Kham, a Tibeto-Burman language from Nepal (Watters 2002: 309).

52. Transitivity may correlate with imperative formation in other ways. In Mangarayi, an Australian language (Merlan 1983: 9, 141–2), imperatives take the same pronominal prefixes as declarative verbs, with two exceptions: the second person singular is marked with a ∅ in imperatives of intransitive verbs and of transitive verbs with third person singular objects.

53. See Peterson (2006), Dixon (2002) on applicatives and causatives; Aikhenvald (2011) on further, non-argument-adding, effects of causative morphology. Just occasionally, the meaning of an imperative of causative may be different from that

of ordinary causation. In Nivkh (Gruzdeva 1992: 67–8), the causative suffix on an imperative verb has a permissive meaning, and 'marks the non-coreference of the listener[. . .] and the performer of the prescribed action'.

54. In Yucatec Mayan, antipassives rarely form simple imperatives A common function of the antipassive is related to discourse (as well as syntactic) operations and is linked to foregrounding the subject and backgrounding the object. That many antipassives 'do not regularly appear as imperatives' can be explained by a tendency to avoid such 'information-packed' forms (Hofling and Ojeda 1994: 280).

55. This is the case in Tariana, Colloquial Egyptian Arabic, Colloquial Welsh (King 1993), and Swahili (Ikoro 1997c: 60–61). Passives of intensive and causative stems in Hebrew do not have imperatives.

56. According to Keenan (1976: 321), in a number of Malayo-Polynesian languages, e.g. Malagasy and Maori, imperatives are frequently used in active and in non-active forms. Also see Bauer et al. (1993: 32–3), for a more detailed account of the imperatives in Maori.

57. The passive is marked with the prefix *di*-. See Sneddon (1996: 326). Using a passive in a command in Boumaa Fijian makes it less direct (Dixon 1988: 295 and p.c.). Along similar lines, passive of third person imperative ('jussive') in Amharic is a way of making a command sound polite (Amberber 1997a: 54). Such passives are often impersonal. See Givón (1993: ii. 271) on how impersonal statements are more polite than straight commands.

58. Along similar lines, in Bagvalal, verbs which refer to physical states (such as 'tremble', 'die', 'sob'), to emotional and mental states and verbs of perception typically cannot form imperatives (Dobrushina 1999: 321–2). In Arapaho (Cowell 2007) and Haida (Enrico 2003), non-volitional verbs cannot occur in imperatives.

59. Along similar lines, only non-stative verbs can occur in imperative form in Tanan, a Formosan language (Li 1973: 218). In the closely related Mantauran (Rukai), imperative can be formed on some stative verbs, while some verbs have to be 'dynamicized' or causativized in order to be be used in a command (Zeitoun 2007: 160–61).

60. In Manambu, copulas *na*- 'be (abstract states)', *tay*- 'be (of climatic states', *yas*- 'be (of physical states)', *say*- 'be (of some states, e.g. shame, pins and needles)', and *yæi*- 'be (of smells)' do not form imperatives.

61. In Chalcatongo Mixtec, motion verbs also have more aspectual stem distinctions than other verbs. Positional verbs may also form imperatives differently from others: in Teribe they take no imperative inflection, while verbs of other semantic groups do (Quesada 2000: 79–80). In Tunica (Haas 1940: 118), semelfactive forms ('do once') have a special imperative postfix.

62. The same principle applies in other languages with serial verbs: see Bruce (1988: 20) for Alamblak; Olawsky (1999) for Dagbani; Diller (2006: 165–6) for Thai; and further discussion in Dixon (2006: 339–40). See also Crowley (2002: 77) on Paamese.

63. A similar phenomenon has been described for the scope of imperatives in Haro (Woldemariam 2007: 152). This can be compared to the scope of prohibitive in English coordinate constructions such as *Don't [drink and drive]*. However, depending on intonation, *don't* can be interpreted as having scope over both verbs or over just one verb. Note that road signs *Don't drink and drive* throughout Australia uniformly imply prohibition on driving after having been drinking.

64. This is reminiscent of how Meithei, also Tibeto-Burman, employs a benefactive, to reduce the force of the command (§4.4.2).

65. Imperatives cannot be coordinated with questions: Gleitman (1965) gives *What are you doing and come here* as ungrammatical. Further discussion of constraints on coordinating imperatives with other clause types is in Lakoff (1971), Thompson (1971), and Mittwoch (1976).

5

'Don't do it': a vista of negative imperatives

Every language of the world has a way of telling someone not to do something. As Sadock and Zwicky (1985: 175) put it, 'a striking fact about imperatives is how frequently negative imperatives are handled differently from negative declaratives'. Not infrequently, they are also handled differently from the positive imperatives. We first discuss the expression of negative imperatives in §5.1. In §5.2, we turn to the expression of further grammatical categories in negative imperatives.[1] Can negative imperatives be considered a special clause type? This is addressed in the summary, in §5.3.

Commands with negative overtones do not have to be cast as prohibitives. Many languages have special forms for 'warnings', also known as 'apprehensives'. These can be roughly translated into English as 'you might fall!', or 'make sure you don't fall!'. In some languages, forms with apprehensive meanings contain an overt negator; in others, they do not: instead, warnings may assume the form of a mild prediction. Imprecatives are commands which effectively urge the addressee not to do what is being commanded, such as *Go jump in the lake* or *Go beserk on your credit cards* (see example 7.33).[2] Warnings and other semantically negative commands are discussed in Chapter 6.

5.1 Negating an imperative

An imperative can be negated similarly to a declarative. A negative imperative in English requires an obligatory *do* support followed by the negator *not*, just like the negative declarative (Davies 1986: 7)—see 5.1 and 2.106a:

5.1   Don't worry!

This applies to all verbs—including *be* and *have*, which do not require *do*-support to form their negative declaratives. Examples 5.2a and 5.2c–d are grammatical, and 5.2b and 5.2e are not:

5.2a   You are not careful what you wish for
5.2b   *You don't be careful what you wish for
5.2c   Be careful what you wish for!
5.2d   Don't be careful what you wish for!
5.2e   *Be not careful what you wish for!

The negator is often cliticized to *do*. An overt subject can be added, just as in positive imperatives (see §2.3 for a brief survey of its meanings). But, unlike positive imperatives, it follows the verb 'do' rather than preceding it (see §5.3). This is how a negative imperative in English differs from any other clause types—including declarative and positive imperative (e.g. 2.101):

5.3a   Don't you worry!
5.3b   Don't you come in here!

Non-canonical imperatives in English are negated differently: *not* is inserted after the pronoun following the marker *let:*

5.4a   Let's not worry!
5.4b   Let him not worry!

In informal speech one hears *don't* as a negator for non-canonical imperatives (Quirk et al. 1985: 831):

5.5c   Don't let's say anything about it!
5.5d   Don't let anyone fool himself that he can get away with it![3]

Negative imperatives in English are seldom followed by tags: according to Quirk et al. (1985: 831), the only operators than can occur in tags after negative imperatives are *will* and *can*, e.g. *Don't make a noise, will you?* The tag is unusual in that it has a falling intonation. This highlights the subtle ways in which negative imperatives differ from their positive counterparts, and from negative declaratives.

The negative *don't* in English is often used as a lexical item, in the meaning of 'prohibition'. The most common use is in *dos and don'ts*, an expression referring to rules or instructions of what to do and what not to. It can also be used on its own—a prime example is a collection of booklets *Don'ts for husbands, Don'ts for wives* and *Don'ts for golfers* (compiled in 1913; see Chapter 9).

Many familiar Indo-European languages use the same negative marker in imperative and in non-imperative clauses; these include French, German, and Russian. In Cupeño (Hill 2005), the same negator *qay* is used to negate either clause type; a prohibitive requires an irrealis form of the verb.

A prohibitive may involve the imperative verb form, and a special particle. In Hungarian, a prohibitive particle *ne* combines with the imperative forms to negate them—see Table 2.11 for the paradigm of the positive imperative.

Hungarian (Kenesei et al. 1998: 22)

5.6 Ne   másol-j   kulcs-ot
     NEG.IMPV copy-IMPV.2sg   key-ACC
     'Don't copy a key!' (you singular)

5.7 Ne   másol-j-unk   kulcs-ot
     NEG.IMPV copy-IMPV-1pl   key-ACC
     'Don't let's copy a key!'

The negative particle in statements and questions is *nem*. The negative and prohibitive particles in Hungarian are phonologically similar. In other languages they are not: for instance, the negative declarative marker in Maybrat, a Papuan language from Bird's Head Peninsula, is *fe* and the prohibitive is *mai* (Dol 2007: 167, 185). In Tariana, the non-imperative negation is marked with a circumfix, e.g. *ma-ni-kade* (NEG-do-NEG) '(he) does not do (it)', while the imperative negation employs an independent particle: *mhaǐda pi-ni* (NEG. IMPV 2sg-do) 'Do not do (it)!'[4]

A prohibitive can be marked by an affix different from the one used in declarative negation. In Dolakha Newar (Genetti 2007: 338), imperative verbs do not take the declarative negator *ma-*. Instead, they require the prohibitive prefix *da-* in combination with the imperative endings:

Dolakha Newar

5.8 bicaku   pir   dā-kā-u   chin
     needlessly   worry   PROH-take-IMPV   2sg.ERG
     'Don't you worry needlessly!'

Grammatical categories expressed in negative statements can be neutralized in negative commands. Declarative negative in Maale, an Omotic language from Ethiopia (Amha 2001: 119–20, 126–7, 157), is marked differently depending on tense and aspect (the suffixes are *-uwá-* 'imperfective present', *-induwá-* 'imperfective future', and *-ibá-* 'perfective aspect'). There are no tense or aspect distinctions in the negative imperative, and the marker used is quite different:

Maale

5.9 mukk-íppo
     come-NEG.IMPV.2sg
     'Don't come!' (singular addressee)

5.10   mukk-íppo-te
come-NEG.IMPV-2pl
'Don't come!' (plural addressee)

In Maale, and a few other Omotic languages (e.g. Ometo: Woldemar-iam 2007: 155–6), the number of the addressee in negative imperatives is marked in exactly the same way as in positive imperatives. And the second person singular form is less marked—this follows the same principle as that in §2.1.5 for positive commands. Unlike positive commands (see Table 4.3), negative imperatives do not have special polite forms. We return to the expression of various grammatical categories in negative imperatives in §5.2.

A negative imperative may not include an imperative marker. Negative and positive imperatives in Nadëb, a Makú language from Brazil, require the same non-indicative form of the verb; an imperative is negated with a special prohibitive particle *manih* which follows the verb, while the declarative negator *dooh* precedes the verb (Weir 1984: 193–211; 1994). Along similar lines, special prohibitive particles in Bininj Gun-wok (Evans 2003: 605) combine with the non-past form of the verb (and not with the imperative).

A negative imperative may be marked by a complex morpheme which also includes the declarative negator. In Harar Oromo, the negative imperative is formed by prefixing the declarative negator *hin-* and suffixing *-in* followed by an imperative suffix which distinguishes two numbers (see Table 2.7, and examples 2.34–5). A declarative verb is negated by prefixing *hin-* with a high tone on the first syllable of the root.

Harar Oromo (Owens 1985: 67)
5.11   hin-deem-ín-i
NEG-go-NEG.IMPV-sg
'Don't go!' (singular addressee)

The negative imperative suffix *-ti-kã-ya* in Tucano consists of the negative suffix *-ti-*, also used in non-imperative negation, the emphatic *-kã-*, and the imperative *-ya*. Neither the positive nor the negative imperative distinguish the number of the addressee:

Tucano (Ramirez 1997: 144)
5.12   apê-ya
play-IMPV
'Play!'

5.13   apê-ti-kã-ya
       play-NEG-EMPHATIC-IMPV
       'Don't play!'

The prohibitive is morphologically more complex than the corresponding declarative negative, which involves only the suffix *-ti* as an obligatory marker and is built on the positive imperative.[5]

A negative imperative may be formed with a special, prohibitive-only particle and a negative affix. In Huallaga Quechua, a command is negated with the particle *ama* (and not the declarative negator *mana)* and the negative suffix *-chu* after the imperative marker. The suffix *-chu* is used as a negator in a number of declarative clauses (Weber 1996: 101–3, 338–9). Along similar lines, the negative imperative in Amele (Roberts 1987: 40–41, 110, 226) is marked with a prohibitive particle *cain* and the negative future form of the verb.

A number of languages form a negative imperative using a prohibitive particle and a special verbal affix restricted just to prohibitives. This is the case in Dyirbal (Dixon 1972: 112):

Dyirbal
5.14   galga   wurrba-m
       PROH   talk-PROH
       'Don't talk!'

Or a negative imperative may involve a negator used in other types. In Comanche (Charney 1993: 217), a negative imperative is marked with a particle *ke-ta* consisting of a general negator *ke-* (used in other clause types) and *-ta*, an element found only in this construction. The verb is often suffixed with the 'general' aspect marker. In Vitu, an Oceanic language from West New Britain, the negative imperative requires a prohibitive negator *tawa* and has to be followed by an irrealis marker. This is unlike positive imperatives which consist just of a simple root and do not take any aspect, mood, or sequentiality markers (see 2.21).

Vitu (Van den Berg and Bachet 2006: 194)
5.15   Taua   nu   kuahi
       PROH   IRR:2sg   fear
       'Don't be afraid' (spoken to one person)

Different irrealis markers are used to distinguish singular and non-singular addressees. This is unlike positive imperatives, where the same form is used for all numbers. The non-singular addressee has to be stated with a pronoun—an option which is also available for positive imperatives (see §5.2).

5.16 Taua   miu   na   kuahi
      PROH   2pl   IRR:2pl   fear
      'Don't be afraid' (spoken to a group of people)

A negative imperative in Hausa consists of a subjunctive form of the verb accompanied by a prohibitive negator *kadà* (Newman 2000: 592–3).[6] The resulting construction is structurally similar to a statement expressing obligation. Markers of negative declaratives without prohibitive or modal force occur after an overt subject and immediately preceding the person–aspect complex; in contrast, the prohibitive occurs before the subject. The imperative form (see 2.36–7) is restricted to positive commands—prohibitives are formed in a different way, and overlap with statements. This is reminiscent of a situation whereby a non-command form is consistently deployed to express a command (see §2.1.4 on languages with no dedicated imperatives).[7]

Kwami (Leger 1994: 237–8) is another example of a language with a dedicated imperative, and an essentially non-imperative form used in commands. We can recall from 2.27 that singular and plural canonical imperatives in Kwami are each marked with a special suffix. In addition, the most frequently used singular canonical imperative forms lose their final vowel. In contrast, negative commands are expressed just with a negated subjunctive. However, to further distinguish negative commands from a negative subjunctive statement, a prohibitive particle *kàdà*—a Hausa borrowing—can be added (see Chapter 11).

Languages without a dedicated imperative form tend to also use a non-command form as a prohibitive. In Yagua, imperatives are expressed by an analytic construction containing an irrealis auxiliary, just like the future (Payne and Payne 1990: 314–15). A negative command is expressed by using a negated irrealis statement.

A prohibitive may employ a wider variety of non-command forms than an imperative. In Bunuba, an Australian language (Rumsey 2000: 92), negated future or present irrealis has a variety of meanings—including possibility, uncertainty, and also prohibition. We saw in 2.45 that positive commands are expressed using only future forms. Along similar lines, a positive command in Ngalakan (shown in 2.52) may involve a future or a present form of the verb. A negative imperative can be expressed either by a future negative or by a special 'evitative' form; either of these can also be used in statements (Merlan 1983: 101). Essentially non-command forms used in positive and in negative imperatives overlap, but only partly.

We can recall that in Navajo, a positive imperative is rendered by a variety of forms, including future tense forms (which are obligatory in force), the imperfective or progressive mode (when the act is to be carried out at once), and by the optative (when the act is to be carried out in the proximate future) (Young and Morgan 1969: 53–4). But the negative imperative employs special particles: if it is 'immediate in force', it is marked by adding the relativizing enclitic -*i* to the verb and preposing the particle *t'áadoo* 'without, don't', while the optative 'in conjunction with the particle *lágo*, "let it be not", is used to render a negative imperative in the sense of a future admonition'. The meanings and the form of the prohibitive are different from those employed for positive commands, despite a certain formal overlap.

In some languages, an imperative requires an irrealis form of the verb: we saw this in Manam (2.48–9), Teribe (§4.2.5; Quesada 2000: 80), and Vitu (5.15). But in others the realis and not the irrealis form occurs in prohibitives. This is the case in Manam:[8] the negated realis form can be used in a command—as in 5.17—and in a statement, with the meaning of obligation, as in 5.18.

Manam (Lichtenberk 1983: 418–19)

5.17 móaʔi   ʔu-péreʔ-i
      PROH   2sg.REALIS-lose-3sg.OBJ
      'Don't lose it!'

5.18 áine   bolo=bólo ʔána móaʔi i-bóad-i
      woman   unclean   food PROH   3sg.REALIS-cook-3sg.OBJ
      'An unclean (i.e. menstruating) woman must not cook food'

Prohibitives are always formally marked—independently of whether they are addressee-oriented or not. I found no examples of negative imperatives expressed exclusively via subtraction, tonal change, vowel alternations, or constituent order.[9]

We can recall, from §2.1.1–2, that imperatives are rarely expressed with analytic structures. Not so for prohibitives. In Latin, an auxiliary construction with the imperative form of the inherently negative verb *nolle* 'not want, be unwilling, refuse', followed by an infinitive, marks prohibitives, as in the famous saying by Archimedes: *noli tangere circulos meos* (not.want.2sg.IMPV touch.INF circle.ACC.PL my.ACC.PL) 'do not touch my circles!' (see 10.27). In Trio, and numerous other Carib languages, prohibitive is formed with an imperative-marked verb *e(i)* 'be' in combination with the negated form of the lexical verb: this could be translated as 'be not VERB-ing':[10]

Trio (Carlin 2004: 309)

5.19   in-eta-e-wa   eh-të
        3OBJ-listen-NON.FINITE-NEG   be-IMPV.PL
        'Don't you (plural) listen!'

In contrast, positive imperatives are formed synthetically—with numerous suffixes on the verb. A lexical negative verb with the meaning 'stop' marks imperatives in a number of languages. Lao has a dedicated imperative marker *jaal* 'don't', which is also a verb 'to abandon something, to give something up' (Enfield 2007: 216). Further similar examples are found in Heine and Kuteva (2002: 283–4). The verb *galga-l* 'leave (it)' in Dyirbal is semantically and phonologically similar to the prohibitive particle *galga* (see 5.14; Dixon 1972: 112).[11]

Along similar lines, the negative imperative in Hamer, an Omotic language from Ethiopia, is formed by using the verb *gʌrʌ* 'leave, stop' used after the dependent form of the lexical verb (perfect aspect), e.g. *kUmʌ* 'eat!', *kuman gʌrʌ* (eat+DEP stop:PERFECT) 'don't eat!' (Lydall 1976: 421, 427).

Alternatively, a negative imperative may involve using a verb form which does not have an intrinsically negative value—that is, does not have an explicit meaning of 'stopping'. In Benchnon, an Omotic language from Ethiopia, forming a negative imperative involves a converb of a lexical verb accompanied by a positive imperative of the verb *šíd* 'remain' (Rapold 2006: 259; Breeze 1990: 37).

A different kind of analytic prohibitive has been described for Warlpiri, an Australian language. The positive imperative is formed with an imperative suffix, the subject number enclitic, and the non-subject-bound pronoun (Laughren 2002: 115–16):

Warlpiri

5.20   Paka-ka=lu=jana   maliki-patu
        hit-IMPV=PL.SUBJECT=3pl.NON.SUBJECT   dog-NOM.PL
        'Hit the dogs!' (addressed to more than one person)

To express a negative command, the verb is nominalized and marked with a 'privative' case meaning 'without'; this is embedded in a matrix clause with an imperative verb, as shown in 5.21a (also see Simpson 1991: 164). The imperative verb does not combine with the negative marker *kula*: 5.21b is ungrammatical.

5.21a   Paka-rninja-wangu-rlu=lu=jana   yampi-ya
         hit-INFINITIVE-PRIVATIVE-ERG=PL.SUBJECT=PL.NON.SUBJECT   leave-IMPV
         'Don't hit them!' (lit. 'Hitting-without them leave!')

5.21b *Kula=lu=jana   paka-ka
       ?'Don't hit them?'

The analytic negative imperative in 5.21a is reminiscent of colloquial English commands like *Leave off hitting them!* Unlike 5.21a, the English expression is just one possible way of expressing a negative command, while 5.21a used to be the only option in the language.[12]

In the few languages which employ analytic structures for positive imperatives, structures of the same kind are also used for prohibitives. In Ika (see 2.13, and Frank 1990: 87–8) a special prohibitive auxiliary is used together with a negative marker on the verb:

Ika

5.22 tšoʔs-uʔ   nʌ́n
      put.down-NEG   NEG.AUX
      'Don't put it down!'

We saw, in 2.16, that imperatives in Nigerian Pidgin are formed with a subjunctive 'clause introducer' *mék* (Faraclas 1996: 24–5). The same clause structure marks negative imperatives. The negator *no* is the same as in declarative clauses:

Nigerian Pidgin

5.23 Mek   yù   no   bay   nyam!
      SUBJ you   NEG   buy   yam
      'Don't buy yams!'

And just like in positive imperatives, there is an option of omitting the second person addressee and the marker *mek* (cf. 2.18a):

5.24 No   go   tawn
      NEG   go   town
      'Don't go to town!'

Negative and positive imperatives in Nigerian Pidgin involve the same construction. Similarly, an analytic construction in positive imperatives in Boumaa Fijian is mirrored by an analytic construction in prohibitives. Negative declarative involves another analytic construction with a semi-auxiliary verb *sega* 'not' (Dixon 1988: 279) followed by the relator *ni*. A selection of positive imperatives, prohibitives, and negative declaratives are contrasted in Table 5.1. All the person–number combinations exist in positive and in negative imperatives.[13]

TABLE 5.1 Prohibitive, negative non-imperative, and positive imperative in Boumaa Fijian

	POSITIVE	NEGATIVE
DECLARATIVE	au la'o 1sgS go 'I go'	e sega [ni-au la'o]$_S$ 3sg NOT that-1sgS go 'I don't go' lit. 'That I go is not the case'
IMPERATIVE	(me+o) la'o REL+2sgS go 'Go!'	(me+o) ['ua ni la'o]$_S$ REL+2sgS don't that go 'Don't go'

The relator-cum-person complex can be omitted if the addressee is the singular 'you', in positive imperatives (see 2.15), and in prohibitives—which is why the complex is in brackets in Table 5.1.

A command to a singular addressee—the most prototypical of all—is simpler than a command to any other addressee. However, while a positive command can be reduced to just a single word—la'o! 'go!'—its negative counterpart, 'ua ni la'o 'don't go!', remains analytic. This is in no way typologically unusual: in many languages positive imperatives are expressed synthetically, i.e. with one single form, while negative imperatives are analytic, just like in Trio.

In a number of languages of Eurasia, negation is expressed using an auxiliary verb construction, with a special 'negative-only' verb. In Evenki, negative declarative and imperative constructions are formed using the same 'negative' auxiliary e-, inflected for person and number and followed by the participial form of the lexical verb. The difference between near future and delayed future is neutralized in imperatives (see Table 2.12). The near future inflection is the only one used in the negative imperative, and it does not have any temporal reference (see §5.2.2). A declarative negative clause is in 5.25:

Evenki (Nedjalkov 1997: 96, 20)
5.25 Bejumimni   homo:ty-va   e-che-n   va:-re
      hunter   bear-ACC.DEFINITE   NEG.AUX-PAST-3sg   kill-PARTICIPLE
      'The hunter didn't kill the bear'

A negative command is illustrated in 5.26:[14]

5.26 Tala   e-kel   girku-ra
      there   NEG.AUX-2sg.IMPV:NEAR.FUTURE.FORM   go-PARTICIPLE
      'Don't go there!'

Balto-Finnic languages employ different negative verbs for statements and for commands. Table 5.1 features a comparison between negative statement and negative command in Estonian (a positive verb form is given for comparison). The positive direct imperative is in Table 2.16 (the relevant part of this table is repeated here for ease of reference).

TABLE 2.16 Direct imperative in Estonian: *kirjutama* 'to write'

PERSON/NUMBER	DIRECT IMPERATIVE
1sg	—
2sg	*(sa) kirjuta*
3sg	*(ta) kirjuta-gu*
1pl	*(me) kirjuta-gem*
2pl	*(te) kirjuta-ge*
3pl	*(nad) kirjuta-gu*

Optional pronouns are given in brackets with the negative declarative which does not distinguish number and person forms.

TABLE 5.2 Negative imperatives in Estonian: *kirjutama* 'to write'

PERSON/ NUMBER	NEGATIVE IMPERATIVE	NEGATIVE DECLARATIVE	POSITIVE DECLARATIVE
1sg	—	*(ma) ei kirjuta*	*kirjuta-n*
2sg	*ära kirjuta*	*(sa) ei kirjuta*	*kirjuta-d*
3sg	*är-gu kirjuta-gu*	*(ta) ei kirjuta*	*kirjuta-b*
1pl	*är-gem kirjuta-gem*	*(me) ei kirjuta*	*kirjuta-me*
2pl	*är-ge kirjuta-ge*	*(te) ei kirjuta*	*kirjuta-te*
3pl	*är-gu kirjuta-gu*	*(nad) ei kirjuta*	*kirjuta-vad*

A remarkable feature of Estonian is full neutralization of person in negative declarative, but not in prohibitive (where only the number distinction in third person is neutralized). In the prohibitive, number and person are marked on both the prohibitive verb and the lexical verb using the same markers.

Table 5.3 features negative imperatives in Finnish. Table 2.14 (repeated here) shows positive imperative forms. In contrast to Estonian, all persons and numbers are marked on the negative declarative verb. In the prohibitive paradigm, the form of the lexical verb in the second person singular canonical imperative stands apart from others: as expected, it is the shortest and the least formally marked. The same form is used for singular and for plural number in the prohibitive.

TABLE 2.14 Imperative in Finnish: the verb *sanoa* 'to say'

PERSON/NUMBER	
1sg	—
2sg	*sano*
3sg	*sano-koon*
1pl	*sano-kaamme*
2pl	*sano-kaa*
3pl	*sano-koot*

TABLE 5.3 Negative imperatives in Finnish: *sanoa* 'to say'[15]

PERSON/ NUMBER	NEGATIVE IMPERATIVE	NEGATIVE DECLARATIVE	POSITIVE DECLARATIVE
1sg	—	*en sano*	*sano-n*
2sg	*älä sano*	*et sano*	*sano-t*
3sg	*älköön sano-ko*	*ei sano*	*sanoo*
1pl	*älkäämme sano-ko*	*emme sano*	*sano-mme*
2pl	*älkää sano-ko*	*ette sano*	*sano-tte*
3pl	*älköön sano-ko*	*eivät sano*	*sano-vat*

Prohibitive in Estonian has more person and number distinctions than the corresponding negative declarative (which has none). In Finnish, the negative imperative has fewer person–number combinations than the negative declarative. In contrast, the positive imperative in both languages has a full set of person–number combinations (except for first person singular) with no neutralization.[16] We return to prohibitives and person in §5.2.1.

We can recall that serial verbs are never used in forming positive imperatives. This restriction does not apply to prohibitives. In Warekena of Xié, a negative command is expressed by a serial verb construction consisting of the verb *-eda* 'perceive, see/hear' with person marking + the verb + *-pia* 'negative marker' (Aikhenvald 1998).

Warekena of Xié

5.27 pida   pi-yut∫ia-pia-na
      2pl+see   2pl-kill-NEG-1sg.OBJECT
      'Don't kill me'

Negative declarative in Warekena is formed with a proclitic *ya-* and a suffix *-pia*, e.g. *ya=pi-yutʃia-pia* (NEG=2sg-kill-NEG)[17] 'you do not kill', *ya=mia pi-yutʃia-pia* (NEG=PERFECTIVE 2sg-kill-NEG) 'you did not kill'. We can recall, from 3.1, that positive imperatives are structurally indistinguishable from declaratives—the only difference lies in the intonation contour.

We have now seen that a negated command may have additional morphological complexity, compared to its positive counterpart. Forming a negative imperative often involves using a periphrastic construction, or employing a form of a different, essentially non-command category. Negative imperatives may or may not share structural features with corresponding negative declaratives. That they are always more marked than corresponding positive imperatives goes together with the fact that negatives are always more marked than positives.[18]

If a negative imperative employs the same form as a corresponding negative statement, prohibitive-only particles or lexemes tend to further differentiate them. Tamambo, an Oceanic language from Vanuatu, is a case in point (Jauncey 1997: 50–51). Both positive and negative imperative have the same form as corresponding declarative clauses. The major difference lies in the intonational contours: positive and negative commands start on a higher pitch and have a distinctive sharply falling intonation. Negative commands may acquire further marking: they can be preceded by the interjection *tabu* 'forbidden'. And we saw above that Navajo, a language with no dedicated imperative forms, has special prohibitive particles.

The negative imperative follows the same principle as the positive imperative: the form addressed to a singular 'you' tends to be less formally marked—we saw this for Maale and a few other Omotic languages, for Boumaa Fijian, and for Estonian and Finnish in Tables 5.1–5.3. We now turn to the ways in which grammatical categories expressed in imperatives are realized in their negative counterparts.

5.2 Negative imperatives and other grammatical categories

In the overwhelming majority of languages, no category has more values in a negative construction than it has in its positive counterpart (Aikhenvald and Dixon 1998).[19] Estonian is a prime example of how this works. Table 5.2 shows that the language marks three persons and two numbers in the positive verb, and none of these in the negative verb. For other languages, however, this prediction is only partly true. In other words, while some categories are neutralized in prohibitives, others are not.

We envisage three options:
- (i) same categories in positive imperative and in prohibitive;
- (ii) fewer grammatical distinctions in prohibitives than in positive imperatives;
- (iii) more grammatical distinctions and possibilities in prohibitives than in positive imperatives.

We will now consider the correlations between negative imperatives and the categories considered for positive imperatives in Chapter 4: first, with categories relating to the addressee, including gender or noun class, number, and person (§5.2.1), and then those relating to verbal action, including aspect, location in time and space, modality, and information source (§5.2.2), and the marking of verbal arguments (§5.2.3). In §5.2.4, we discuss correlations with voice, transitivity, and semantics of the verb. Prohibitives display fewer restrictions than positive imperatives in their application to verbs whose semantics does not involve 'control' and 'volition' of the commander.

Can a language have more prohibitives than it has imperatives? This will be briefly addressed in §5.2.5. The prohibitive-specific categories which are linked to their illocutionary force, and correlations with politeness, are the topic of §6.4–5.

5.2.1 Negative imperatives and categories relating to addressee

The categories of the addressee cover person, gender and nominal classification, and number. In many languages, the same person–number combinations are available in negative and in positive commands—this is the case in many Indo-European languages, including English (see 5.1–4), and also Hungarian, Estonian, and Finnish.

Negative imperatives directed at the addressee 'you', and at first and third person, can form one paradigmatic set, as in Evenki (Nedjalkov 1997: 20) and in Kerek, a Chukotko-Kamchatkan language (Volodin 1992). In Kannada (Sridhar 1990: 36–7), the same negator is used for second person, first person, and third person commands. Or, just like English, the marking may be different depending on whether the negative command is addressed at 'you', 'us', or 'them'.

Along similar lines, all person–number combinations are available in Nanai (Avrorin 1961: 130). But the canonical negative imperatives are bimorphemic, while the non-canonical ones (referring to first and third person) consist of three morphemes. Note that all the persons of positive imperatives in Nanai form one paradigmatic set. We thus see that, as anticipated at the beginning of this chapter, the negative imperatives are more complex, and reveal an additional opposition between canonical and non-canonical person value absent from their positive counterpart.

Addressee-oriented imperatives in Barasano, an East Tucanoan language from Colombia, are negated with a suffix *-beti*. To emphasize the negative command in the second person, *-beti* is followed by a suffix *-koã* 'fulfilment' and then the appropriate person markers. This is the only way of negating commands in the first and third persons, and it does not have any emphatic meaning with these non-canonical persons (Jones and Jones 1991: 126–7).[20]

In Cavineña, verbs inflected with first person imperative ('hortative') or third person ('jussive') affixes are negated in the same way as verbs in statements (using the clitic =*ama*), while addressee-oriented imperatives are negated with the circumfix ø-...-*ume* for singular addressee, and *ne*-... -*ume* for plural addressee.

The second person singular imperative can be negated differently from any other form. In Italian, negating the second person singular imperative involves a negated infinitive (in bold in Table 5.4), while all forms for all other persons are negated in a straightforward way (Maiden and Robustelli 2007: 247–8).[21] That is, the distinction between canonical and non-canonical imperatives is relevant for positive and for negative commands. Just as in positive commands, second and third person forms can stand apart from those which are addressee-oriented.

A number of languages have fewer person–number distinctions in prohibitives than in positive imperatives. Many have just second person prohibitives, and have no special grammatical marking for negating a command to third or to first person. This is the case in Tariana, most East Tucanoan languages, and Urarina.[22]

The negative equivalent of a first person command in Tariana would be a future statement: to negate 'let's go' one would say 'we are not going'.

Along similar lines, prohibitive forms in Manambu only exist for second person. Positive imperatives have forms for three persons and three numbers

TABLE 5.4 Negative imperatives in Italian: *cantare* 'to sing'

Person/ Number	Positive imperative	Negative imperative
2sg	*canta!*	**non cantare!**
2pl	*cantate!*	*non cantate!*
1pl	*cantiamo!*	*non cantiamo!*
3sg	*canti!*	*non canti!*
3pl	*cantino!*	*non cantino!*

(see Table 2.23). Three prohibitives illustrated in 5.28a–c differ in their illocutionary force: from a neutral prohibition in 5.28a to a very strong and threatening one in 5.28c.

Manambu
5.28a   wukə-tukwa
        listen-PROH
        'Don't listen!'

5.28b   wukə-way
        listen-PROH.STRONG
        'Don't listen under any circumstances!'

5.28c   wukə-wayik
        listen-PROH.EXTRASTRONG
        'Don't listen no matter what (or else)!'

The prohibitives do not distinguish number of the addressee, just like the positive imperatives: see 2.23–4. If needed, a pronominal subject can be added for disambiguation.

A rarely used special form for third person prohibitive has an additional prescriptive meaning (Aikhenvald 2008a: 323–4). This form distinguishes three numbers (singular, dual, and plural), and two genders in singular:

5.29   wukə-də-ba
       listen-3masc.sg-PROH.PRESCRIPTIVE
       'He should not go; let him not go (as an obligation or duty)'

Unlike the positive imperative and second person-oriented prohibitive, such a form can be focused, yielding a structure meaning 'it is the case that he should not go'. A non-canonical prohibitive stands apart from prohibitive with a canonical, addressee-oriented meaning.[23] Just occasionally, the negative imperative has more options for expressing person than does the positive imperative. Babungo, a Bantu language (Schaub 1985: 24), can express first and third person only in negative commands.

As we saw in §5.1, a number of languages consistently employ a non-imperative form as a negative command—this can be a subjunctive, as in Hausa and Supyire, or intensive, as in Figuig.[24] These non-imperative forms are also used in statements, and have the same set of person–number distinctions as any other declarative form.

In many languages, prohibitives and imperatives have the same number distinctions—as is the case in Maale and many other Omotic languages. But the number itself can be marked in a different way. The negative imperative in Vitu requires a prohibitive negator *tawa* and has to be followed by an irrealis marker which has different forms depending on whether the addressee is singular, as in 5.15, or plural, as in 5.16. A positive imperative consists just of a simple root (see 2.21). If more than one person is addressed, a personal pronoun has to be included in a negative command. It can be included in a positive command, for disambiguation.

In Vitu, a positive imperative can optionally occur with the same irrealis marker whose form varies depending on the number of addressees, if it follows another imperative verb in a sequence of verbs, e.g. *vamule nu tani-a ni kamama* (return IRR.2sg say-3sg.OBJECT LOCATIVE.PREPOSITION:PN your. father) 'Go back and tell your dad' (van den Berg and Bachet 2006: 192). That is, prohibitive in Vitu employs a more elaborate and complex structure, also available in positive imperatives (but in a limited number of circumstances).[25] This is another example of prohibitives which are more complex than positive commands.

Prohibitives may have the same gender and noun classifier distinctions as do positive imperatives. Cubeo (see 4.1–5) distinguishes three genders in positive and in negative imperatives (Morse and Maxwell 1999: 30),[26] and Jarawara (see 5.36–7) distinguishes two. The same gender-sensitive vocative particles are used with negative and with positive imperatives in Amahuaca (Sparing-Chavez 2008). Or gender distinctions can be neutralized: we can recall, from §4.1, that genders in Chipaya are distinguished only in the imperative, but not in any other clause type or form, including prohibitive.[27]

Prohibitives with an especially strong force may correlate with the type of addressee. A normal prohibitive marked with *-tukwa* (see 5.28a) in Manambu can be jokingly addressed to a pot (if the water is not boiling fast enough), or to a piece of watermelon which is slipping off the plate. Not so with strong and extra-strong prohibitives (5.28b–c): these must have a human addressee. This requirement will be further discussed in the next chapter.

5.2.2 *Negative imperatives and categories relating to verbal action*

Categories relating to verbal action include aspect, tense, distance in space and directionality, information source, modality, and reality status. In many languages, these categories are found in positive, but not in negative, imperatives. In other words, one prohibitive form corresponds to several positive imperatives, and no aspect or tense distinctions are made.

We can recall, from Table 4.4 and examples 4.9–12, that Lavukaleve distinguishes punctual and durative positive imperatives. There is just one negative imperative, with no aspectual distinction (Terrill 2003: 336–7). Along similar lines, aspectual meanings present in positive imperatives are nonexistent in prohibitives in Koromfe, Cayuga, Kiowa, and Tariana. There is just a handful of exceptions, among them English and some other European languages. Negative and positive imperatives can be used in progressive and in completive forms. A guest might well say, upon receiving a sudden invitation by telephone, *Don't have all those good things eaten before we get there* (Bolinger 1967: 349). And a progressive imperative *Don't be checking your e-mail at eleven o'clock!* is equally possible.[28]

Similarly to Hausa, discussed in §5.1, the prohibitive in Supyire is formed using the subjunctive, in addition to the prohibitive auxiliary and the negative marker at the end of the clause (Carlson 1994: 524). A prohibitive clause can be marked for aspect—then the imperfective subjunctive auxiliary is used.

Alternatively, an aspectual form in a prohibitive construction has a different meaning from that in a positive imperative. We can recall, from 3.34a–b, that imperatives in Russian distinguish perfective and imperfective forms. The imperfective forms tend to have overtones of polite command (though the exact meaning depends on the context: see extensive discussion and examples in Shmelev 2002). Only the imperfective negative imperative has a command force. 5.30 is the only way of saying 'do not sit down'. It does not have any overtones of politeness.

Russian
5.30 Ne   sadite-sj!
      NEG   sit.IMPF+2pl.IMPV-REFLEXIVE
      'Do not sit down (imperfective)!'

The negated perfective forms of an imperative cannot be used in a purely command meaning. They only occur with an apprehensive meaning, that of 'warning', and are often accompanied by a warning 'look, look out':

5.31 Smotri-te   ne   sjadjte!
      look.IMPF-2pl.IMPV   NEG   sit.PERF+2pl.IMPV
      'Beware not to sit down (for instance, on a dirty chair)!'[29]

Along similar lines, an imperfective negative imperative in Lithuanian expresses a negative command, while its perfective counterpart is a warning (see Geniušenė 1988 for additional discussion). We return to warnings and apprehensive imperatives in Chapter 6.

A number of languages distinguish immediate versus delayed future forms in imperatives (see §4.2.2), among them Evenki, Nanai, Fox, Takelma, Tucano, Tariana, and Tuyuca. None of these have any such distinctions in negated commands (see 5.26 above). One form *ba'á-tikaya* (eat-NEG.IMPV) 'Don't eat!' in Tucano will cover the immediate imperative in 4.15a, 'eat!' and the delayed imperative in 4.15b, 'eat later!'[30]

But this is not a universal rule. Ika (Frank 1990: 87–8) distinguishes immediate and future imperatives in both positive and negative commands. So does Macuna, an East Tucanoan language from Colombia (Smothermon, Smothermon, and Frank 1995: 63). An immediate imperative is negated with the suffix *-be-* and the delayed negative imperative requires *-beha*. Examples 5.32 and 5.33 illustrate the positive and the negative immediate imperatives.

Macuna

5.32   wa-sa
       go-IMPV
       'Go!'

5.33   ba-be-sa
       eat-NEG-IMPV
       'Don't eat!'

A positive delayed imperative is in 5.34, and its negative counterpart in 5.35:[31]

5.34   ĩ-re   goti-ba
       he-OBJECT   tell-DELAYED.IMPV
       'Tell him!' (later)

5.35   busu-ri   wa-beha
       to.dawn-PARTICIPLE   go-NEG.DELAYED.IMPV
       'Don't go tomorrow!'

Tense–aspect distinctions in imperatives and in prohibitives may correlate with the illocutionary force of a command. Nambiquara (Kroeker 2001: 30–32) has a 'weak' imperative which does not imply urgency or immediate execution of a command, and a 'strong' imperative which implies that the command has to be executed immediately. The same distinctions are maintained in the negative commands.

We can recall from 4.21–2 that immediate and delayed imperatives in Jarawara combine reference to distance in time and in space: the immediate imperative refers to 'here and now' and the delayed one to 'distant time or place'. The negative imperatives have exactly the same meanings:[32]

Jarawara (Dixon 2004a: 401)

5.36 tee   kakome-rima   na
      2non.sg   be.afraid-IMM.NEG.IMPV.fem   AUX
      'Don't you be afraid!' (here and now)

Someone in the village once said, jokingly:

5.37 [Jara   fana]o   jori   ti-rijahi!
      Branco   woman   swive   2sgA-DISTAL.NEG.IMPV.fem
      'Don't you swive (copulate with) a Branco (i.e. white) woman!'

In many other languages, the imperative-specific category of distance in space is not expressed in negative imperatives. In Tariana and in Barasano, simple, non-proximate, and future imperatives are not distinguished in negative commands. All of these are replaced with a non-proximate form. Carib languages Apalaí, Hixkaryana, and Macushi (see Table 4.5) distinguish motion and non-motion forms in positive imperatives but not in prohibitives. Trio, also Carib, does not have the ventive ('come carry out action here') or the dislocative 'there' in prohibitives (Carlin 2004: 309–11).[33] Once again, this is not a strict rule: in other languages, a negative imperative can be formed on a verb containing a directional. Any of the directionals listed in 4.32, from Manambu, can be used in negative imperatives, e.g. *yakə-su-tukwa* (throw-UPWARDS-PROH.GEN) 'don't throw (it) upwards!'

In many languages, the reported evidential is the only marker of information source which occurs in positive commands. The same evidential can occur in negative commands, with the same meaning of 'order by proxy', just as in positive commands. Compare examples 5.38a–b:

Tucano

5.38a dãã   basâ-ato
       they   dance-IMPV.REP
       'May they dance!' (on someone else's order)

5.38b dãã   basâ-tikâ'-ato
       they   dance-NEG-IMPV.REP
       'May they not dance!' (on someone else's order)[34]

In Tariana, the reported evidential is hardly ever used in negative commands to second person. It is employed to relay commands to a third person. When used in clauses indicating negative consequence, it can refer to any person, just as in neighbouring Tucano (see Aikhenvald 2003: 410). We return to this in Chapter 11.

Other evidential values—visual, non-visual, or non-first-hand—can be expressed in positive commands in just a handful of languages. None of these have been attested in prohibitives.

Modality markers occur with positive imperatives, often with a meaning related to politeness, or urgency of a command. Prohibitives appear to be more restricted in that respect. For instance, the probability marker in Cavineña occurs with positive but not with negative commands. The counter-expectation marker *bakwe* has the same meaning with positive and with negative commands, making the order sound more insistent (4.43, and Antoine Guillaume, p.c.).[35] Irrealis marking in negative commands may have somewhat different meanings from those in statements, and in positive commands. We can recall that in Tsakhur, a Northeast Caucasian language, the combination of an imperative with irrealis expresses a wish, or advice (4.46). An irrealis with a negative imperative has a counterfactual meaning:

Tsakhur (Dobrushina 1999: 266)
5.39 ilj-mōš-i   sa   dawar
      PROH-3.buy.IMPF-IRR   one   lamb
      'You shouldn't have bought a lamb'

The irrealis in Semelai is used to form the familiar negative imperative of a transitive verb (Kruspe 2004a: 294, 336–8). The morpheme does not occur on intransitive negative imperatives. The prohibitive-special meaning of the irrealis marker is that of 'status' of familiarity. In other clause types, the irrealis has no such meanings. In Mosetén, an isolate from Bolivia (Sakel 2003: 154), the irrealis with a negative imperative is 'slightly more polite'. This is another example of a prohibitive-specific meaning of an irrealis.

The choice of reality status—that is, realis versus irrealis—in prohibitives can be different from that in statements, and in positive commands. In Yagua, all commands—positive and negative—involve irrealis forms. Not so in Manam—see 5.17–18 above, and further examples there discussed by Elliott (2000: 77). That realis, rather than irrealis, forms should be used in negative commands appears counterintuitive. Yet this ties in with frequently attested similarities between prohibitive and declarative clauses, which set them apart from positive commands.

Further, imperative-specific meanings and categories may be neutralized in a negative context. In Maale (Amha 2001: 157) and in Indo-Pakistani Sign Language (Zeshan 1999), politeness distinctions are neutralized in negative commands. But this is not a universal rule: both the negative and the positive imperative may have polite forms, as in Epena Pedee (Harms 1994: 130).

5.2.3 Negative imperatives and the marking of verbal arguments

In all languages, prohibitives, like positive imperatives, operate on a nominative–accusative principle. The marking of grammatical relations in imperatives and prohibitives often follows the same principle. In Estonian, the object of a positive, and of a negative, imperative appears in the nominative case (see discussion in §4.3, and also §3.3.4; Tuldava 1994: 250–51).

If prohibitives differ from positive imperatives in the ways grammatical relations are marked, they tend to share their patterns with statements. In Ponapean (Rehg 1981), Sm'algyax (Stebbins 2001), and Kana (Ikoro 1996; 1997a), the overt second person subject is always retained in prohibitives, and regularly omitted in positive commands. In Serrano, a Uto-Aztecan language (Langacker 1977: 56), the object of a positive imperative is marked with the subject case—similarly to many other Uto-Aztecan languages, such as Cahuilla (4.51). But the object of a negative imperative takes accusative marking, just as in declarative clauses:

Serrano

5.40a paa'   pɨt   paa-t
      drink   that:ABS   water-ABS
      'Drink the water'

5.40b qai=t   paa'   pɨta-i   paa-t-i
      NEG=DUB   drink   that-ACC   water-ABS-ACC
      'Don't drink the water'

Different forms of personal pronouns may occur in positive and negative imperatives. In modern French, atonic pronominal proclitics are used in negative imperatives, as in *ne me le donnez pas!* 'don't give it to me!'. Positive imperatives employ topic forms of object pronouns, as in *donnez le moi!* 'give it to me!'.

The order of clitic pronouns can be different in positive and in negative imperatives. In Italian, the clitics follow the imperative form addressed to first plural and second person; but precede the third person form, e.g. *Alza-ti subito!* 'Get up immediately (you singular)!', *Alzate-vi subito!* 'Get up immediately (you plural)!'. But in the negative imperative, the clitic may precede the verb, as in *Non ti alzare* or *Non alzar-ti!* 'Don't get up (you singular)!', and *Non vi alzate!* or *Non alzate-vi!* 'Don't get up (you plural)!' (Maiden and Robustelli 2007: 98).[36] We return to the differences in constituent order of imperatives and prohibitive constructions in §5.3.

Another, non-imperative verbal form can be co-opted in lieu of a negative imperative. In Mantauran Rukai (Zeitoun 2007: 169–70, 193–5) the negative imperative is essentially an action-state nominalization. This is why its subject is expressed with a genitive pronoun—unlike a positive imperative, whose subject is marked with a zero.

Differences in the meanings of verbal arguments in negative and in positive commands can be subtle. We saw in §4.4.1 that positive imperative forms of transitive verbs in Indonesian drop the active voice prefix *meN-* if they refer to an action performed on a specific object. If the action involves a generic referent or the verb is used intransitively, the prefix is retained. In negative imperative forms, dropping the prefix has a different effect: it affects the semantics of the command, making it 'milder', and has nothing to do with the properties of the object (Sneddon 1996: 325).

5.2.4 *Negative imperatives, transitivity, and verb classes*

Negative and positive commands often differ in how they interact with the transitivity, and the meaning, of the verb. In numerous Mayan languages, positive imperative is marked differently for transitive and for intransitive verbs—see §4.4.1. This difference is neutralized in negative imperatives—the two are negated in the same way (see Collins 1994: 375, on Mam). Restrictions on imperative formation may not apply to negative imperatives in the same way as they do to positive ones.

English has no grammatical rule excluding inherently stative verbs from imperatives. But in an imperative construction, the subject of a stative verb can acquire 'an "agentive role"—which it would not have in a corresponding declarative' (Huddleston 2002: 932). A sentence *Kim saw what time it was* describes Kim in a non-agentive role of a perceiver, while *See what time it is* implies an action, to the effect of *Find out what time it is!* or *Go and look what time it is!* Since imperatives are associated with agentivity, passive imperatives are less frequent than active ones. Positive passives with *be* 'are not often found with directive force', but 'negatives lend themselves more readily to such an interpretation' (Huddleston 2002: 933). 5.41 is perfectly acceptable, and can be interpreted as 'Don't allow yourself to be intimidated'.[37]

5.41   Don't be intimidated by those cowards!

Along similar lines, *Don't be seen!* is fine, and implies 'Avoid being seen!' There is an additional semantic requirement: a negative passive is more appropriate with a verb referring to something undesirable—as in 5.42a–b:

5.42a   Don't be hurt by what he says!
5.42b   Don't be misled by his flattery!

A positive passive imperative version of each of these, *Be hurt by what he says* or *Be misled by his flattery*, has to be contextualized in order not to be perceived as strange (bordering on ungrammatical).[38]

The same principle applies to the imperatives of English verbs which refer to uncontrollable actions or states: 5.43a is not readily acceptable, but its negative counterpart 5.43b is fine:

5.43a   ?Feel disappointed
5.43b   Don't feel disappointed

The motivation behind this is semantic: it is more natural to suggest that someone should not feel a negative emotion of disappointment than that they should feel it. Or, in Bolinger's (1967: 348) words, 'we have more occasion to command resistance than sufferance, and negative passives are correspond-ingly more frequent: *Don't be frightened (don't let yourself be frightened) by anything he says.* Most passive commands with *be* are otherwise unacceptable: *George, be taken to church by your sister.*'

In other languages, forming imperatives on passives is grammatically impossible, independently of the verb's meaning. But this does not have to apply to prohibitives. In Japanese, prohibitives—but not positive impera-tives—can be formed on passives (Takahashi 2000; and 4.64 in §4.4.2).

No stative verb in Tariana can normally have a positive imperative. A negative imperative can be formed on verbs of quality such as 'be good/well-behaved', 'be glad', 'be bad', 'be cold', 'be afraid'. Just the verbs of physical and mental states, such as 'be unwilling', 'be lazy', cannot be used in either a positive or a negative command (see Aikhenvald 2001).

In Manambu, stative verbs such as *rəp-* 'be enough', *warsama-* 'be angry' cannot form a canonical imperative. In contrast, a negative imperative is perfectly possible:

Manambu
5.44   warsama-tukwa!
        be.angry-PROH
        'Don't be angry!'

We can recall, from §4.4.3, that imperatives can be formed on stative and on dynamic verbs in Mantauran Rukai, a Formosan language (though some stative verbs have to be dynamicized: Zeitoun 2007: 160–61). Negative im-peratives are formed differently, depending on the semantic class of verb: negative imperative of dynamic verbs is formed with the circumfix *a-...-ae,* and that of stative verbs with the suffix *-ae.* The negative imperative forms are formally similar to action-state nominalizations (Zeitoun 2007: 193–5, 169). Along similar lines, the form of a positive imperative in Semelai is the same for transitive and for intransitive verbs. Negative imperatives have different forms in both (Kruspe 2004a: 333, 294).

This takes us to our next topic—languages which have more formal distinctions in prohibitives than in positive imperatives.

5.2.5 *More prohibitives than imperatives?*

Examples 5.28a–c, from Manambu, alert us to the fact that a language may have more prohibitives than positive imperatives. The neutral prohibitive can be used with just about any subject the speaker finds appropriate. The marker *tukwa* can even occur on its own, in the meaning of 'don't'. In contrast, the strong prohibitive markers -*way* and -*wayik* cannot be used on their own.

The two strong prohibitives differ from the general prohibitive in their force. This force is best explained through behavioural implications which I personally observed (see also Aikhenvald 2008a: 319–22, for a discussion of their similarities and differences). A mischievous child was told not to put a piece of clothing on, and the mother used the neutral prohibitive. The child did not pay any attention to this, and carried on doing what she was doing.

Manambu

5.45a kusu-tukwa   ñən-a-kə-l   ma:
       put.on-PROH   you.fem-LK-OBL-fem.sg   NEG
       'Do not put (this) on, it is not yours'

The mother then got really annoyed at the child's disobedience and shouted 5.45b. This means that the prohibition is something serious:

5.45b kusu-way!
       put.on-PROH.STRONG
       'Do not put (this) on!!'

On saying this, the mother is likely to get hold of something heavy to threaten to throw at the child. The child gets edgy, preparing to start running away; and she is likely to stop what she was doing. If she does not, or the parent is not satisfied with the effect, 5.45c follows—as a deafening shout:

5.45c kusu-wayik!
       put.on-PROH.EXTRASTRONG
       'Do not put (this) on!!!'

This sounds really threatening, and the child is off in a flash—she knows that the mother is well and truly mad at her, and will hit her if she does not disappear. Only the neutral prohibitive is usually contextualized, with the consequence or a reason stated. The strong prohibitives are forceful, and threatening enough in themselves. This is not to say that Manambu does not have any means of making a command equally strong. This is achieved using non-imperative clauses (or imperative strategies)—see Table 8.1 and discussion in Chapter 8.

Urarina, an isolate from Peru, also has one positive imperative, and three prohibitive forms, with different 'force' and urgency of the prohibition. Two prohibitive markers, *ɲaaui ɲe* and *nihjauria*, imply that the prohibition is absolute—as in a directive at a sermon. A weak prohibitive, marked with *kwa*, refers to weak or temporary prohibition (Olawsky 2006: 579–82).[39]

Why is this so? Is it the case that instructing people what not to do is more important than telling them what to do? Note that in addition to three special prohibitive forms, Manambu has a whole range of de facto prohibitives, used for urgent commands, warnings, prescriptions, and so on. And there are hardly any restrictions on forming prohibitives on any verb classes—in contrast to positive imperatives, which are more restricted. An argument can indeed be made that cultural constraints and prohibitions are highly important in many indigenous cultures—including Manambu. But this is mere speculation.

Distinguishing more prohibitive forms, and allowing for more flexibility in negative commands than in their positive counterparts, alerts us to the special status of prohibitives.

5.3 How prohibitives are special

Prohibitives and positive imperatives may share similar marking. Alternatively, forming a prohibitive may involve a special negator, a special verb form, or both. A prohibitive may involve using a verbal form which is not negative in itself—a subjunctive, or an infinitive. Unlike positive imperatives, prohibitives are often expressed analytically—with complex predicates involving auxiliaries, and with serial verbs. A prohibitive may involve an inherently negative verb—as Latin *nolle* 'be unwilling, refuse'—or a special prohibitive auxiliary. Or it can contain a lexical verb meaning 'stop' or 'leave'.

Imperatives and prohibitives may have the same categories. Or there may be fewer grammatical distinctions in prohibitives than in imperatives: in Maale and Indo-Pakistani Sign Language, prohibitives do not distinguish politeness. Imperative-specific aspects (durative versus continuous) tend to be neutralized in prohibitives. In contrast, imperative-specific tense—delayed versus immediate—and distance in space may or may not be expressed in prohibitives.

Prohibitives are special in a number of other ways. They can differ from positive imperatives in their intonation. The order of constituents in prohibitives and in imperatives may be different—see §5.2.3 on the order of clitics in Italian. In English, the subject of prohibitives—if present—commonly follows the verb: 5.46b is judged less common than 5.46a (Quirk et al. 1985: 830):

5.46a   Don't you open the door
5.46b   You don't open the door

The placement of the subject—if accompanied by a quantifier—may be influenced by the scope of negation (Davies 1986: 97). Example 5.47a is a 'rejection of the possibility of one of the addressee's forgetting':

5.47a   Don't one of you forget the money

5.47b presents the possibility that one of them should not forget—it is more likely to be used if the speaker expects only one of the addressees to bring money. 5.47a implies that each of them is expected to bring money:

5.47b   One of you don't forget the money

In 5.48, the position of the subject 'reflects the fact that while the first imperative is being used to reject the possibility of the addressee behaving in one way, the second presents the possibility of [their] doing something else, namely failing to turn up' (Davies 1986: 97):

5.48   Don't you be so conscientious!
        You just don't bother to turn up, if that's what you feel like doing

Constituent order in positive imperatives and in declaratives does not allow such subtle connotations to surface (but see Davies 1986: 96–8, on semantic differences between postposed and preposed subjects of the emphatic imperative with *do* which parallel these differences in constituent order in negative imperatives).

Prohibitives can thus be more elaborate than positive imperatives. They often have fewer restrictions on verb types than do imperatives. In this, they are closer to statements. So are the prohibitives in languages—like Manam—which mark prohibition with realis, and imperatives with irrealis. Many languages have no other options for negating a command addressed to first or third person but use a negated statement. This brings prohibitives and declaratives closer together.

Prohibitive-specific meanings of verbal categories may also be similar to those of positive commands, and can be associated with illocutionary force, and degrees of politeness and familiarity. Just like imperatives, prohibitives can be a special clause type in terms of categories, their meanings and marking.

How are the meanings of negative and positive imperatives similar, and how are they different? This is the topic of our next chapter.

Notes

1. Negative imperatives have another name, 'prohibitives'. The two terms are used interchangeably throughout this book. An alternative option would involve applying the term 'negative imperative' to languages where negating a command would involve using the general negative marker with an imperative. The term 'prohibitive' would be applied to languages where negating a command involves a different negator from that used in declaratives, and a different verb form or construction from the one used in imperatives. That is, English, German, French, and Russian would have a negative imperative, while Estonian, Finnish, Hungarian, and Modern Greek would have a prohibitive. This terminological approach is implicitly taken by Sadock and Zwicky (1985: 175–7), and appears in a number of grammars, e.g. Kruspe (2004a). A rarely used synonym of 'prohibitive' is 'vetative'.

   The problem with a terminological 'split' between negative imperative as a negated imperative and a prohibitive as a separate structure is that it is simplistic. It implies a binary division of languages based on surface realization of the same type of meaning. Many intermediate cases show that this oversimplification is far from helpful: see §5.1.

   Further work in the typology of prohibitives is van der Auwera and Lejeune (2005b) (based on a limited selection of languages), van der Auwera (2005, 2006b), Miestamo and van der Auwera (2007), and van Olmen and van der Auwera (2008).

2. An imprecative may have the structure of a command without a command meaning. Curses and abusive comments are often cast as commands, e.g. *Damn Lyndon Johnson* (see McCawley 1971: 6). They often do not have all the properties of an imperative; for instance, they cannot be negated, or accompanied by a tag question. We return to these in Chapters 6 and 7.

3. According to Quirk et al. (1985: 831), a more formal full form *do not* can replace *don't* in 5.1, but not in 5.4–5. See also Davies (1986: 67–98). In fixed expressions one can find *not* in canonical imperatives: *Waste not, want not* sounds archaic.

4. In the closely related Baniwa of Içana, the marking goes the other way round: a circumfix consisting of a negative prefix *ma-* and a suffix *-tsa* (also used as an emphatic marker) marks the negative imperative, e.g. *ma-aku-tsa!* (NEG-speak-NEG=EMPH) 'Do not speak!' (see also Aikhenvald 2008b). A particle *ñame* or *ña* marks non-imperative negation. The use of an emphatic marker in prohibitives is congruent with a general tendency to emphasize and reinforce any verbal negation with emphatic particles or affixes (Payne 1985: 224; see also Davies 1986: 67–98, and 5.13, from Tucano).

5. A similar structure of a negative imperative has been described for Tuyuca, also East Tucanoan (Barnes 1994) and Desano (Miller 1999: 72).

6. Along similar lines, prohibitive in Syrian Arabic is expressed by a prohibitive particle *lā* or *mā* and the verb in the subjunctive (Cowell 1964: 360); also see Holes (1990) on Gulf Arabic and Gary and Gamal-Eldin (1982: 39) on Cairene Egyptian Colloquial Arabic. The prohibitive in Hebrew involves a special imperative particle *'al* followed by the future in Modern Hebrew, or imperfective in Biblical Hebrew (see Malygina 1992, 2001; Waltke and O'Connor 1990: 660–61; Gesenius 1962). We will see in Chapter 8 that a declarative future can be used in stronger commands, with overtones of obligation. Subjunctive is also used in the negative imperative in Spanish, e.g. *canta* 'Sing (you sg)!', *no cantes* (NEG sing. SUBJ+2sg) 'Don't sing!'. Occasionally, affirmative forms of the imperative are used in popular speech in Spain (Butt and Benjamin 2004: 290). Negative imperative in Catalan (Hualde 1992: 323) is constructed with the present subjunctive.

7. We can recall from §4.2.5 that Pendau, an Austronesian language spoken in Central Sulawesi in Indonesia (Quick 2007: 532–3), has a dedicated imperative (with no difference in reality status). Irrealis forms occur in prohibitives, and also mark future, hypothetical, and customary events. Along similar lines, Aguaruna, a Jivaroan language from Peru, has dedicated forms for imperatives, but employs the apprehensive inflection for prohibitives, accompanied by person markers shared with content interrogative clauses (Overall 2008: 356).

8. Similar examples come from Teribe (Quesada 2000: 80), Terêna, an Arawak language from Brazil (Ekdahl and Butler 1979: 102; Ekdahl and Grimes 1964), Maung, an Australian language (Capell and Hinch 1970), Emmi, also Australian (Ford 1998), and numerous Campa languages from Peru (David Payne, p.c.; Michael 2008). This 'relativity of irrealis' is discussed in Mithun (1995).

9. American Sign Language could be an exception to this. According to Zeshan (1999) and Barbara Schick (p.c.), the declarative clause negator commonly occurs in negative commands. The only difference between commands and statements lies in non-manual features ('probably the same as in the positive imperative') and a headshake. Such non-manual signs are traditionally considered tantamount to prosody or intonation in spoken languages. Prohibitives may have a special intonation pattern in spoken languages: in Japanese, imperatives have a rising and prohibitives a falling intonation (Onishi 1997b; Hinds 1986: 49).

10. In Basque, negative commands involve periphrastic expressions (Saltarelli 1988). Prohibitive is expressed analytically in Hua (Haiman 1980: 173–4). In Kannada, a Dravidian language, negative imperatives are also expressed periphrastically (Sridhar 1990: 36–7), using the infinitive of the lexical verb followed by a negative imperative of *bēḍu* 'be needed' (Krishnamurti 2003: 358).

11. Similarly, in Welsh, negative commands are formed with the imperative of *peidio* 'stop' and a verbal noun (King 1993: 224–30). See §10.3.2, on how verbs grammaticalize as prohibitive markers.

12. Contemporary Warlpiri now has an additional, English-like strategy of negating a command: a negative particle *nati*, from English, accompanied by the imperative. And see Dixon (1972: 112) for a comparison between the origin of imperative in Dyirbal and the Warlpiri structure. We return to this in Chapter 11.

13. See also Churchward (1941: 22) for Standard Fijian.

14. Similar patterns have been described for related languages. The tense distinctions are also neutralized in the negative imperatives in Nanaj (which appears to have structural differences between the canonical and the non-canonical imperatives: Avrorin 1961: 129–60). In Oroč (Avrorin and Lebedeva 1968), number is marked on the participial form. See Payne (1985: 214–19) for a typological perspective on negative constructions in Tungusic and Uralic languages. Further examples from Fennic languages Udmurt, Mari, Mordva, and Samoyedic languages are in individual descriptions in Abondolo (1998c).

15. See Karlsson (1999: 168); Laanest (1975).

16. An overview of prohibitive and positive imperative paradigms in Balto-Finnic languages is in Laanest (1975); see also Abondolo (1998c).

17. A similar serial construction also involving a verb of perception was described for Piapoco, from the same subgroup of Arawak (the marker is *pika*: etymologically, *pi-* '2sg' + *-ka* 'see') (Klumpp 1990).

18. See Aikhenvald and Dixon (1998); Miestamo (2005) for negation in declarative clauses.

19. The correlations between negation and other clausal categories and the rationale behind these are discussed in Aikhenvald and Dixon (1998). There, we formulated a tentative prediction that there should not be any dependency in either direction between polarity and mood (declarative, imperative, and interrogative). This prediction appears to be confirmed by the data discussed here.

20. A similar example comes from Yimas. Prohibitives in Yimas are simpler than corresponding positive imperatives (Foley 1991: 268–76). There are two options for forming a canonical prohibitive: one by using a negative prefix and a suffix *-nt* homophonous with the present tense marker, and the other by placing *pack* 'don't' before a verb inflected for irrealis. In Yimas, the choice between having either a regular prohibitive or a complex form consisting of *pack* 'don't' and an irrealis verb form exists only for second person. First person prohibitives have just the second option.

21. We can recall, from Table 2.18, that third person subjunctive serves in lieu of the non-canonical third person imperative; the same principle applies under negation. Interestingly, the negative second person plural imperative of *credere* 'think' is frequently the subjunctive form *crediate*.

22. This appears to be the case in many more languages, e.g. Trio (Carlin 2004). But note that the fact that grammars do not mention the existence of a negated first or third person does not necessarily imply that there is no such form in the language: such forms may be rare and therefore omitted. The overwhelming majority of grammars are silent on the issue of how to say 'let's not go'.

23. The younger people's Manambu is developing a third person prohibitive formed by adding a negative suffix *-maːr-* to third person imperative. This suffix is normally used to negate focused verbal forms and subordinate clauses (the declarative main clause negator is *ma*), e.g. *wukə-kwa-d* (listen-3IMPV-masc.sg) 'May he listen; let him listen!'; *wukə-maːr-kwa-d* (listen-NEG-3IMPV-masc.sg) 'May he not listen; let him not listen!' However, traditional speakers do not accept these innovative forms.

24. See Newman 2000 (592–3) on Hausa, Carlson (1994: 524) on Supyire, and Kossmann (1997: 125, 270) on the 'positive intensive' forms used in negative commands in Figuig, a North Berber language. Aspinion (1953: 228–9) gives examples of 'subjunctive aorist' employed in negative commands in Taschelhit.

25. Along similar lines, the negative imperative form in Kana does not distinguish number of the addressee (unlike the corresponding positive command). The overt subject of a negative imperative has to be present—as a result, the number distinctions are preserved in the pronominal subject, but not in the verbal form (Ikoro 1996, 1997a).

26. I have no information about classifiers with prohibitives in Cubeo (i.e. I haven't been able to find negative counterparts for 4.4. and 4.5).

27. In Chipaya, the prohibitive is formed with the 'infinitive' form of the verb and the negative particle *ana* (Cerrón-Palomino 2006: 245). We have no information concerning the use of imperative-only gender-sensitive particles in Lakhota (Table 4.2).

28. There are no examples of prohibitive with imperfective in Yankunytjatjara and Watjarri, two Australian languages with the same aspects in declarative and positive imperative clauses. Dixon (1991: 385 and p.c.) does not exclude the possibility of using continuative imperative in prohibitives in Mbabaram and Yidiñy.

29. See also Vinogradov (1947: 598) and Bulygina and Shmelev (1997: 103), on some correlations between the control of the addressee over the situation and the apprehensive meaning, and Shmelev (2002: 278–9), on non-apprehensive uses of the negative perfective imperative in fixed expressions and under specific stylistic circumstances. Further discussion is in van der Auwera et al. (2009), Kučera (1985), Bogusławski (1985), and Benacchio (2002).

In a number of other languages, imperative tends to be formed on imperfective, rather than perfective, aspect stem (see e.g. Volodin 2001: 153 for Kerek, a Chukotko-Kamchatkan language with a perfective (resultative) versus imperfective imperative in positive, but not in negative commands).

30. Along similar lines, 'delayed' imperative in Nishnaabemwin (or Ojibwe) is restricted to only positive commands (Valentine 2001: 993).

31. Tuyuca, also East Tucanoan (Barnes 1979: 93), has a future negative imperative. We can recall from §4.2.2 that Koasati, a Muskogean language, has two delayed imperatives, 'do later on' and 'do much later on'. Both appear to be distinguished in negative commands. The continuative imperative with the overtones of politeness also has a negative counterpart (Kimball 1991: 267–9). Even, a Tungusic language closely related to Evenki (Malčukov 2001: 176–7), distinguished immediate and future imperative forms.

32. Closely related Jamamadí has the same distinctions in positive and in negative imperative as does Jarawara (R. M. W. Dixon, p.c.).

33. The same principle applies to Paumarí: there is an extralocal imperative, but no extralocal prohibitive (Chapman and Derbyshire 1991: 220–21).

34. Similar examples from Tuyuca, an East Tucanoan language, are in Barnes (1979: 90, 93).

35. The counterexpectation marker occurs only with positive commands in Tariana.

36. Along similar lines, in Spanish pronominal clitics are postposed to the positive imperative and preposed to the negative (Butt and Benjamin 2004: 291–2).

37. This reflects 'the fact that it is sometimes easier to conceive of a person's being able to avoid an experience (such as being hurt or being misled) than to imagine his ability to deliberately undergo it' (Davies 1986: 15). A similar point is formulated by Quirk et al. (1985: 827): 'passives with *be* occur chiefly in negative directives, where they generally have the meaning "Don't allow yourself to be...".'

38. Passive imperatives are more acceptable if contextualized (as we saw in 4.62a–b) and the consequences are stated. We can recall from §4.4.2 that passive imperatives in English sound natural if the addressee is in control—i.e. has a choice of undergoing the action or not (see 4.62a–b, and Davies 1986: 15). Whether forming imperatives on passives in English is a grammatical option has been a matter of concern to many scholars (see Takahashi 2000; Davies 1986: 14–15). However, most of them did not consider the semantics of the verb used in a command, concentrating on a 'syntax-only' approach. See further discussion in Lees (1964) and Stockwell et al. (1973).

39. Prohibitive constructions in Manam (Lichtenberk 1983: 419–23) appear much richer than the corresponding positive imperatives (which are the same as irrealis forms). A prohibitive-specific suffix -*tina* intensifies the prohibition. There is an additional option of using a verbal noun or a gerund in a prohibitive construction (accompanied either by a normal prohibitive marker *moaʔi* or by the form *raʔania* 'never mind'). Araona, a Tacana language from

Bolivia, has just one option for forming imperatives; there are two ways of marking a prohibition (Emkow 2006: 495–8, 513). Along similar lines, Vurës, an Oceanic language from Vanuatu (Hyslop 2003), has one positive imperative and three prohibitives, with different illocutionary force. Mosetén (Sakel 2003: 154) appears to have two types of negative imperative (and only one positive imperative).

6

Imperatives and their meanings

Imperatives, positive and negative, cover a wide range of functionally related manipulative and directive speech acts. As Whitney (1924: 215) put it, the imperative

> signifies a command or injunction—an attempt at the exercise of the speaker's will upon someone or something outside of himself [themselves—*AA*]. This, however (in Sanskrit as in other languages), is by no means always of the same force: the command slides off into a demand, an exhortation, an entreaty, an expression of earnest desire.

We start with an illustration, in §6.1.

6.1 Versatile imperative: example from English

In Huddleston's words (2002: 929), 'imperatives are characteristically used as directives', and 'a directive expresses a proposition representing a potential situation: realising or actualising that situation constitutes compliance with the directive.' A directive subsumes orders, requests, instructions, and also advice and permission, all of these reflecting different degrees of control and attitude on behalf of the 'commander'. Compliance, on the part of the addressee, involves obeying orders, acceding to requests, following advice, or doing something which is permitted. This gives us some idea about the broad spectrum of the imperative-specific meanings.[1]

In a language with just one imperative form, the imperative is—understandably—polysemous. An imperative in English can be used for an array of directive meanings. Here are some examples.[2]

(A) Orders, commands, demands
6.1a   Get out of my way!
6.1b   Keep off the grass!
6.1.c   Don't move!

(B) Requests, pleas, entreaties
6.2a Please, help me tidy up!
6.2b Kindly lower your voices
6.2c Open the door, will you?

(C) Advice, recommendations, warnings
6.3a Keep your options open!
6.3b Wait until the price is right!
6.3c Don't let yourself be too complacent!

(D) Instructions and expository directives
6.4a Insert a cassette as illustrated with its labelled side facing you
6.4b Compare these figures with those shown in Table 1 above

(E) Invitations
6.5a Come over and see my etchings
6.5b Feel free to call if you like

(F) Permission
6.6a Yes, go ahead
6.6b Take as many as you like

(G) Acceptance
6.7a Well, tell her if you want to
6.7b Take it or leave it—it's my final offer

(H) Good wishes
6.8a Enjoy your meal!
6.8b Have a good weekend!

(I) Imprecation
6.9 Go to hell!

(J) Incredulous rejection
6.10 Come on! (You don't really mean that)

(K) Self-deliberation
6.11 Let me see now (Shall I go straight home?)

The exact interpretation of imperatives in English depends on numerous factors, often hard to capture. While orders imply telling someone else what to do, requests involve asking someone to do something, with an option for the addressee not to comply (though the assumption is often that they will). The 'asking' rather than 'telling' or 'ordering' overtone is commonly signalled by additional means: *please, kindly,* an interrogative tag, or a performative parenthetical such as *I beg you.* One can think of numerous examples which would occupy middle ground between 'telling' and 'asking'—for instance, *Don't forget to buy some milk on the way home* said to a spouse can be interpreted as either. A general term for (A) and (B) suggested by Huddleston (2002: 930) is 'wilful directive': 'it is, with varying strength, my will that you comply.'

In the case of advice, recommendations, and warnings exemplified at (C), compliance is presented to the addressee as being in their interest. This 'family' of meaning also includes suggestions, which involves putting forward a possible course of action for the addressee to consider. Warnings imply that there is a potentially dangerous consequence of not complying to the directive; that is, warnings may be thought of as inherently negative.

Instructions and 'expository directives', in (D), are also non-wilful, in that compliance is in the addressee's interest and up to them. Expository directives, such as 6.4b, are commonly used—as a stylistic device—in written language. The compliance to the command is presented as something useful, serving the purpose at hand, such as comparing two sets of figures.

Invitations in (E) are similar to advice in (C): the addressee may choose whether or not to comply, and compliance is to their benefit. Unlike advice, an invitation presents you with 'what you'd like rather than what is calculated to be in your best interest' (Huddleston 2002: 931).

Permission, in (F), includes something the addressee would want to do, whereby the speaker has the authority to permit or prohibit. Giving a permission 'promotes' compliance.

Acceptance (G) is perhaps the weakest kind of directive: the implication is that compliance is not something the speaker would necessarily want, and the speaker does not have the authority or power to prevent the event from happening. Huddleston (2002: 931) notes that some instances of directives indicating 'acceptance', such as 6.7b, are 'not sharply distinct' from instances where imperatives are used in a conditional meaning, as in *Double your offer: I still won't sell.* This is an instance of imperatives which do not really command anything and whose meaning is other than purely directive.

Along similar lines, good wishes in (H) are formulaic expressions, rather than real commands. Imprecatives (I) also do not direct the addressee to do anything: an imprecation can be a curse (as in 6.9), or a mock-command urging the addressee to do the opposite of what the speaker might want.[3] Neither are (J) incredulous rejection and (K) self-deliberation really directive; rather, they can be understood as discourse formulae with a conventionalized meaning. We turn to such non-directive meanings of command forms in Chapter 7.

English employs one—imperative—verb form to express numerous meanings. Context helps disambiguate them. Additional means, including particles, parentheticals, and tags, can come to our aid (see Chapter 8).[4]

6.2 Semantic parameters in imperatives

Many of the imperative-specific directive meanings identified for English acquire formal realization in other languages. For instance, Tuyuca (Barnes 1979) has a special verbal suffix marking an invitation (6.12), another expressing permission (6.13), and another presenting a warning (6.14).

Tuyuca
6.12 Wáa-co
     go-INVITATION.IMPV
     'Let's go!'

6.13 Wáa-ma
     go-PERMISSIVE.IMPV
     'Let (me) go!'

6.14 Naa-ri
     fall-APPREHENSIVE.IMPV
     'Make sure you don't fall! You might fall (lest you fall)'

A neutral imperative expressing a straightforward order is marked with the suffix -*ya*:

6.15 Wáa-ya
     go-IMPV
     'Go!'

The range of imperatives in Tuyuca goes beyond these. There is yet another imperative urging the addressee to confirm the result, or to see for themselves:

6.16 Padeña-te
     touch-CONFIRMATIONAL.IMPV
     'Touch it (to check for yourself or to confirm)'

This is but a brief snapshot of a variety of meanings which may acquire formal realization in large imperative systems, like the one in Tuyuca and many of its East Tucanoan relatives. We will now turn to a discussion of the meanings of imperatives encoded in the grammar of the world's languages.[5]

We start with the linguistic expression of the directive meanings roughly identified in (A)–(G) above. These meanings correlate with a general feature of the STRENGTH or DEGREE of a command. The stronger the command, the stricter the requirement for the addressee's compliance, and the commander's insistence and authority. The authority itself can be institutionalized, if an order comes from a general to a soldier. Or it can be based on a societal convention, or on age, if it comes from parent to child, or from an older sibling to a younger sibling. Strength of command correlates with its illocutionary force.[6] Emphasis in imperatives is often linked to the strength of command—the more insistent the commander, the more emphasis they put on the command. Urgency of command is another parameter frequently linked to the command's strength. The grammatical marking of strength of command, and its interaction with the speaker's emotional state, are addressed in §6.3.

Strength of command, the commander's insistence and authority, and requirement for the addressee's compliance are linked with the expression of INTERPERSONAL RELATIONSHIPS in imperatives. This takes us to the issue of politeness in directive speech acts—understood as the linguistic expression of the commander's deference to the addressee.[7] Degrees of politeness can be expressed by means of honorifics, that is, 'grammatical encodings of relative social status between the participants, or between participants and persons or things referred to in the communicative event' (Brown and Levinson 1987: 276). How interpersonal relationships—including levels of politeness and honorifics—are encoded in imperatives is the topic of §6.4.1. Combination of strength of command and interpersonal relationships is the basis of imperative-specific extensions of various grammatical categories (see §6.4.2).

Further imperative-specific meanings—many of them represented in languages with numerous imperative subtypes—include various types of speech acts, consequence of performing a command, expectations that the command be performed or not, and a few others (see §6.5). A summary of the chapter is in §6.6.

Imperative forms, and constraints on their use, may vary depending on social distinctions within a society, and relevant relationships. Yankunytjatjara, an Australian language (Goddard 1983: 306–7), has a strict avoidance relationship between a man and his parents-in-law. A mother-in-law's or father-in-law's requests for food cannot be addressed directly to the son-in-law, but must be done through an intermediary. And even the intermediary's speech cannot contain a direct command; it may be relayed using the quotative particle *kunyu* without any direct command, or reference to asking:

Yankunytjatjara

6.17 mayi   kunyu   nyuntu-mpa   waputju
     food(NOM)   QUOT   2sg-GEN   father.in.law
     'Your father-in-law says food'

Imperative forms themselves may be perceived as 'too direct' or not suffi-
ciently polite. For instance, in English a polite choice is not to use an imperative. Even if accompanied by a *please*, a command *Please open the door* sounds
abrupt and rude. Other, non-imperative constructions, can be co-opted to
express additional meanings. For instance, a question *Can you open the door?*
or *Can you pass the salt?* would be always read as a request by speakers of the
language (and not as a question about the addressee's strength or capacity to
perform an action). In Brown and Levinson's (1987: 70) words, 'there is no
longer a viable alternative interpretation of the utterance except in very special
circumstances'. This is an example of a conventionalized 'command strategy',
or, using Huddleston's expression (2002: 939–42), 'non-imperative directives'.

In each instance, the degree of conventionalization varies. A statement
which encourages the addressee to perform the action could be another
option: saying *It is getting stuffy in here* (so open the door). An independent
subordinate clause—*If you could open the door*—is also a covert, mild, command. A cross-linguistic gamut of conventionalized command strategies is
the topic of Chapter 8.

6.3 Strong, weak, or neutral? Imperatives and their strength

The degree of an imperative's strength can vary, from a strict order implying
unquestionable authority and compliance to a soft and mild command
bordering on suggestion. An imperative by itself can express a neutral order.
It can be strengthened; this implies increasing the authority of the commander and/or the peremptory nature of the command, thus intensifying the
requirement that the addressee should comply. Amele employs a special
peremptory intonation contour for this purpose, both in positive and in
negative commands (Roberts 1987: 40–41), and so do many other languages.[8]

Similar effects can be achieved with segmental markers. Two particles, *no*
and *baa*, mitigate a command or a request in Ndyuka, while final *yee* and *oo*
strengthen a command (Huttar and Huttar 1994: 56–7). Udihe uses the
particle -*zA* to soften an imperative. This same particle occurs with the
forms of permissive mood—a rarely used paradigm of forms expressing
agreement or permission, and also used for polite requests (Nikolaeva and
Tolskaya 2001: 264, 270–71, 468; see also §6.5).

A marker used in other—imperative and non-imperative—contexts can serve similar purposes. Adding the affix *-niar* 'try to' to an imperative in West Greenlandic adds an element of urging or prompting to the command, suggesting an effort on the part of the addressee (Fortescue 1984: 26). In contrast, a conative imperative (meaning 'try and do') in Tariana makes a command sound more like a request or a suggestion (see §6.5, and example 6.52).

West Greenlandic derivational suffixes *-laar* 'a little' or *-tsiar* 'a bit' and *-gallar* 'a while/for the time being' have a softening effect in imperatives. This is consistent with a similar effect of *mal* 'time, once' in German (used to make a command sound milder: see 3.22). Diminutive forms and expressions meaning 'a little' often serve to lessen the force and the insistence of a request, by 'belittling' it and making it sound inconsequential (Koike 1992: 56). In Brazilian Portuguese, this effect can be achieved by attaching a diminutive suffix to a requested object, as in 6.18, or by using *um pouquinho* 'a little bit' as a softener, as in 6.19:[9]

Brazilian Portuguese

6.18 Me   dá   um   copinho   de água
     To.me   give.2sg.IMPV   ART.INDEF.masc.sg   glass+DIM   of water
     'Give me a little glass of water'

6.19 Espera   só   um   pouquinho
     Wait.2sg.IMPV   only   ART.INDEF.masc.sg   little+DIM
     'Wait just a little bit'

Similarly, in Matses, a Panoan language from Peru, and in Cavineña, a Tacana language from Bolivia the diminutive suffix on verbs is used to express politeness (Fleck forthcoming; Guillaume 2008: 683). And in Meithei, 'the force of a command can also be reduced by placing an easily attainable upper limit to the task that the addressee will have to perform in order to fulfil the conditions of the imperative'. This 'limit' can be indicated by *kharə* 'some' or *mauktə* 'just once' (Chelliah 1997: 286–7).[10] Deliberately downplaying the required activity, or limiting it to being performed just once, has an effect of mitigating the command: it then sounds less insistent, and easier to perform.

Softening a command can be achieved by a using a delimitative marker meaning 'only': in Imbabura Quechua and in Huallaga Quechua, adding the suffix *-lla* 'just, only' to the verb makes the command sound softer (Cole 1982: 31; Weber 1989: 439). This also correlates with politeness—to which we return in §6.4.

Imperatives with increased or decreased illocutionary force are expected to be more formally marked than neutral imperatives. An emphatic imperative in Haro, an Omotic language from Ethiopia (Woldemariam 2007: 152–3), expresses a stronger command than the ordinary, neutral imperative. This is marked by an emphatic *-tte* which follows the imperative marker. There are no number distinctions in emphatic imperatives (while the neutral imperative distinguishes singular and plural).

Including or omitting the overt subject may have an effect on the strength of the command, and the concomitant overtones of politeness. In Tuvaluan (Besnier 2000: 35), using an overt subject in the imperative makes it sound less peremptory and slightly more polite than if the subject is omitted:

Tuvaluan
6.20   Vau!
    'Come [here]!'

6.21   Vau   koe!
    come   you
    '[Why don't] you come [here]?'

An overt subject—second or third person—in imperatives in English (see §2.3.1) can have a wide range of functions. It may simply mark contrast, as in 6.22. Or it may have what Huddleston (2002: 926) calls 'emotive effect', with 'impatient, irritated, aggressive or hectoring' overtones, as in 6.23a–b.

6.22   You do the washing-up tonight please; Kim did it last night.
6.23a   (Just) you watch where you put your feet.
6.23b   You mind your own business.

In other examples, the overt subject implies 'soothing reassurance, encouragement, support', as in 6.24a–b:

6.24a   You just sit down and have a nice cup of tea; everything is going to be all right.
6.24b   You go back and tell him you need more time.

The exact effect depends on the context and content and also correlates with intonation and tone of voice (as mentioned in §1.2). In Huddleston's words,

what the two cases have in common is perhaps that expression of *you* emphasises the speaker's authority. In the aggressive case, the *you* emphasises that I am telling you, not asking you, to do something. In the reassuring case, I assume the position of one who is assured, one who knows best what to do.

Or, as Davies (1986: 147) put it, 'in each case the speaker is laying claim to a certain authority over his addressee'.[11]

The same grammatical technique can carry different implications in terms of force of command, depending on the person of the imperative. We recall (see Table 2.11) that imperative in Hungarian has all the person–number combinations. The force of the second person imperative can be increased by changing the position of a detachable verbal prefix (Kenesei et al. 1998: 21–2). In the neutral imperative the preverb is placed after the verb, as in 6.25.

Hungarian
6.25 Másol-j   le   egy   kulcs-ot!
       copy-IMPV.2sg PREFIX   one   key-ACC
       'Copy a key!'

If the preverb occurs as a verbal prefix (which is its usual position in declarative clauses), the imperative sounds stronger: it is understood as a threat. This is accompanied by the rising intonation, instead of the normal falling intonation in the neutral imperative:

6.26 Le-másol-j   egy   kulcs-ot!
       PREFIX-copy-IMPV.2sg   one   key-ACC
       'Copy a key or ...'

The position of the prefix in the verb of 6.26 is similar to what we find in a declarative clause. The command in 6.26 is stronger in its insistence and demand for compliance than a neutral imperative: its overtones are threatening. This is reminiscent of how declaratives can be used as strong and peremptory commands in many languages—including English: saying *You will clean the latrines* can be interpreted as a highly threatening and imposing order.[12]

In other persons in Hungarian, changing the position of the preverb transforms a command into an echo-question to a previous imperative; such a question—pronounced with a typical rise–fall pattern of a yes/no question— is understood as an offer, independently of whether the prefix appears before or after the verb. 6.27 and 6.28 are synonymous (Kenesei et al. 1998: 22):

6.27 Másol-j-ak   le   egy   kulcs-ot
       copy-IMPV-1sg   PREFIX   one   key-ACC
       '(Copy a key!) Shall I copy a key?'

6.28 Le-másol-j-ak   egy   kulcs-ot?
       PREFIX-copy-IMPV-1sg   one   key-ACC
       '(Copy a key!) Shall I copy a key?'

A similar effect can be achieved by using an emphatic marker. Babungo, a Bantu language (Schaub 1985: 23–5), employs the sentence-final emphatic particle *lôo* to increase the force of a positive or a negative command.

Hixkaryana (Derbyshire 1979: 17) uses an intensifying particle *ha* to increase force of command. The imperative-specific particle *haka* makes the command even stronger.

Additional ways of increasing or decreasing the force of a command vary from language to language. In Meithei (Chelliah 1997: 287), 'the force of a command can also be reduced with suffixes that urge the hearer to do some action for the sake of the speaker', or 'for the hearer's own sake', by using a reflexive suffix or a suffix meaning 'VERB for someone other than self'. We can recall, from 3.23, that the expression 'for me' (for the speaker) in Cantonese marks a rude, impolite command.

Increasing the force of a command can be achieved by using an attention-getting imperative. In Babungo (Schaub 1985: 24), the final emphatic particle *mǒo* is generally used to verify whether the addressee is really listening. It is used with imperative sentences if the command was made before, but was not obeyed.

The stronger the command, the more irritated the commander may sound. Tucano (Ramirez 1997: 148) and Desano (Miller 1999: 72–3) have special forms for imperatives involving 'scolding' and anger on the part of the authoritative commander. In Tucano, this would be an abrupt order from an adult to a child:

Tucano
6.29a   apê-a'sã!
         play-IMPULSIVE.IMPV
         'Play!' (an angry abrupt command)

A neutral imperative is in 6.29b:

6.29b   apê-ya!
         play-IMPV
         'Play!'

This is very much like the 'exigent' imperative in Kham: the marker *-sā:* is added to that of an immediate imperative; the meaning is that of impatience and sometimes anger (Watters 2002: 311).

The appropriate context for softening or strengthening a command depends on conventionalized interpersonal relationship: there can be one way for an adult to command a child, and another for someone to command a peer. Not surprisingly, the ways of strengthening or mitigating a command interact with politeness and conventionalized social hierarchies. Tamil (Asher

1985: 17–18) has a number of particles used to strengthen a command; their use correlates with the relationship between the addressee and the commander. Suffixes *-ṭaa* (masculine) and *-ṭii* (feminine) are used in addressing children who are one's kin or close (younger) friends, to show familiarity and affection. But when used to an addressee who is neither a relative nor a close friend, their effect is to emphasize the speaker's superior social status and often serve to display speaker's anger. There is an even stronger imperative, formed with an auxiliary verb—this indicates 'speaker's disgust or extreme impatience'.

Vocative forms which distinguish politeness also participate in the strengthening of an imperative: Kashmiri utilizes polite and impolite vocative forms (accompanied by derogatory terms) as a means of changing the strength of a command (see §6.4.1). We will further see how polite forms of imperatives soften the command in Kashmiri (see 6.40a–b in §6.4.1).

Having a special form for seeking permission is a feature of a number of languages, among them Tuyuca (6.13) and Tucano (Ramirez 1997; West 1980; see also §6.5). The use of a permissive form can also correlate with politeness and social hierarchies, as in Nkore-Kiga (Taylor 1985: 12–13): a particle granting permission is used when talking down to someone.

Lexical means of softening commands are abundant in English (see §6.1) and many other languages. The most commonly used phrase in Finnish is 'be nice and', which can be followed by an imperative (Sulkala and Karjalainen 1992: 24):

Finnish

6.30 Ole   kiltti ja   auta   minua
      be+IMPV.2sg   nice   and   help+IMPV.2sg   I.PARTITIVE
      'Please, be nice and help me!'

Indonesian (Sneddon 1996: 328–34) has an array of 'imperative softeners' which also produce polite requests.[13] Some of them are used in a similar function in other clause types. The form *ya* can occur as a sentence tag in informal statements 'to avoid the impression of marking a firm assertion'. It has the same function in imperatives—effectively drawing the listener into agreement. *Tolong*, translated as 'please', requests the addressee to do something for the speaker's benefit, while *silakan* invites them to do something for their own benefit. *Coba* has an overtone of urging. Each of these correlates with the speaker's age and status with respect to the addressee (see §6.4). And while *tolong* can only be used with a transitive verb with a specific object, other softening markers do not have such restrictions. An array of forms mark requests—from polite to very polite (see §6.4).

Further overtones to a command may be marginally related to peremptoriness and strength. In Huallaga Quechua, *maa* 'challenge' transforms a command into a challenge to carry out an action (Weber 1989: 102; see also 6.31).

Huallaga Quechua
6.31 Maa   pay-ta-raq   tapu-y
     challenge he-OBJ-yet   ask-2IMPV
     '(I challenge you to) ask him!'

A different strategy can be employed to soften or to strengthen a command. In Maori (Bauer et al. 1993: 34), a modal statement with the tense–aspect marker *me* 'obligation' is used in lieu of an imperative. How modal forms—other than imperatives—can be used for this purpose is the topic of Chapter 8.

Prohibitives may mark more degrees of strength than positive imperatives—we recall, from 5.28a–c, that this is the case in Manambu (see also §5.2.5, for examples from Urarina). The three degrees of prohibitives do not have an exact equivalent in positive commands. This, however, does not mean that Manambu lacks any means of expressing a mild, strong, or extra-strong command. To express these meanings, a plethora of strategies is employed—a summary is in Table 6.1, and examples and further discussion in Chapter 8.

TABLE 6.1 'Force' of negative and positive second person imperatives in Manambu

SEMANTICS	POSITIVE	NEGATIVE
simple command	*a*-Verb: *a-wuk* 'listen!'	Verb-*tukwa*: *wukə-tukwa* 'don't listen'
strong command	various other strategies: noun+aversive case; verb-medial form, questions, etc.	Verb-*way*: *wukə-way* 'don't dare listen'
very strong command		Verb-*wayik*: *wukə-wayik* 'don't you dare listen (or else)'

Forceful prohibitives differ from simple prohibitions in a further way: their addressee has to be a human—i.e. someone fully in control of what is not to be performed (see §5.2.2). We return in Chapter 9 to the issue of conventionalized nature of addressee in imperatives and commands.

A special verbal form can be used to make a command sound less insistent. In Manambu, a reported command is the only instance of indirect speech report (Aikhenvald 2008c). The verb is then cast in a purposive form. A direct speech report is shown in 6.32a; its indirect counterpart is in 6.32b.

Manambu

6.32a 'mən   təp-a:r   a-war'   wa-na
      you.masc village-LK+ALL IMPV-go.up say-ACT.FOC+3fem.sgBAS.VT
      'She says: 'You go upstream to the village!''

6.32b war-mən-kək   təp-a:r   wa-na
      go.up-2masc.sg-PURP village-LK+ALL say-ACT.FOC+3fem.sgBAS.VT
      'She tells (you) to go upstream to the village' (lit. She tells for you to go
      upstream to the village)

A purposive form can be used on its own. Implication is of a milder
command which does not presuppose immediate compliance—unlike the
imperative form in 6.32a:

6.33 mən   təp-a:r   war-mən-kək
      you.masc village-LK+ALL go.down-2masc.sg-PURP.DS
      '(I want) you to go upstream to the village'

This 'desubordinated' form can only be used if the speaker is the commander—the semantic property it shares with a normal imperative.

The concept of 'indirect imperative', or 'indirect command', can hardly be
considered uniform. Some grammarians treat any command with a mild illocutionary force as 'indirect' (see Sohn 1994: 49–51, on indirect expressions in
Korean). A command phrased as a recommendation can be looked upon as
'indirect', as are declarative clauses involving 'it is good that...' in Babungo
(Schaub 1985: 28–9).[14] The indirect imperative in Estonian allows us to express a
recommendation or advice from a third party (de Sivers 1969: 60–61).

A simple imperative form is often perceived as too direct, and thus threatening. A frequent option for mitigating such effect is the use of indirect
command. The direct imperative in Arapaho, an Algonquian language (Cowell 2007), is marked by using the 'imperative order'.[15] The indirect imperatives—which have their own inflectional paradigm—differ from the direct
imperatives in that the second person is not expected 'to act physically or
directly', but rather 'acts in such a way that' the action does or does not occur.
The indirect imperative can be translated as 'let (someone) do it/have someone do it'. Its uses reflect the speaker's judgement about relative social agency
and status, and play a role in constructing social identity. This is best
illustrated by a real-life example.

At a ceremony within a sweat lodge—involving a ceremonial leader, one or
more assistants to the leader, and a few more participants—everyone was seated
in a circle. Then someone else entered but there was no room for them to sit. The
leader said to his assistant using the indirect imperative: 'Let/have him sit down!'

He could have used a causative verb, 'Make him sit down', or he could have used a direct imperative form addressed to the new arrival, 'Sit down'.

The reasons why he opted for the indirect imperative are manifold. First, in a ceremonial situation, the assistant was not being called to physically make a person sit down—he was implicitly asked to have the other participants make room for the new arrival. To have used the direct imperative would have implied that the new arrival was reluctant to sit down, and needed to be told to do so. In Cowell's (2007: 50) words, 'it was neither addressee nor arrivee who was preventing the speaker's desired result from occurring, but rather conditions "in the world" partially independent of both of them'—a place had to be found for the new man. Importantly, the new arrival was a respected older man, and the assistant was younger. According to the traditional norms within Arapaho society, the younger man 'could not make' the older man sit down. The leader of the ceremony in the sweat lodge was aware of the rules:

to tell the respected elder to sit down would have been disrespectful [as] it would have implied that the elder was not committed to thinking, acting, and participating in the ceremony in a 'good way' and would have risked destroying the harmony—and thus efficacy—of the ceremony. To have told the young man to 'make' the elder sit down would have put the necessary ceremonial harmony even further in jeopardy.

In a nutshell, using an indirect command was judged to be the only way to bring about the needed result 'without showing disrespect to those involved and without disrupting the more general collective goodwill and process of the ceremony' (p. 51).

As Fowler (1982: 258) puts it: 'violence against another Arapaho damages one's spiritual state'—and consequently limits the sphere of use of direct commands. The indirect imperative in Arapaho fits in with an intricate social fabric of interpersonal relations: preserving the 'negative face' of the newly arrived elder (so that he is free of imposition) and the positive face of all participants, including the younger assistant, by not placing any of them in a socially awkward situation. The indirect imperative can thus be 'seen as a conventionalized, and socially mandated, form of deference to socially recognized authority'.

This is a relatively straightforward example of how social relationships and underlying traditions determine the use of a linguistic structure: an indirect imperative rather than a blunt command. We return to the correlations between the use of command forms and cultural stereotypes in Chapter 9.

An imperative in Tuvaluan requires a 'downtoner'—unless 'directed at small children or uttered in anger' (Besnier 2000: 35): 'An unmodified imperative is judged to be inappropriately peremptory in most interactional contexts between adults.' The adverb *laa* (also meaning 'then': p. 505) on its own makes the imperative sound more polite, and the adverb *naa* gives to a command 'a connotation of a gentle coaxing'. Strength of command thus overlaps with politeness and interpersonal relationships, and with speech acts.

A softer command may slide into a polite or humble request, and a strong order into a rude assertion of one's authority. Social conventions determine ways of saying things depending on the interlocutors' age and relative status. The applicability of different linguistic forms related to 'strength' of a command is embodied in the intricate social fabric of interpersonal relationships—the topic of our next section.

6.4 Interpersonal relationships in imperatives

In many languages, the canonical imperative with a second person singular addressee is equated with 'a direct expression of one of the most intrinsically face-threatening speech acts—commanding'. Consequently, the use of imperatives tends to be limited to circumstances of obvious authority—from an adult to a child, or someone socially superior to someone socially inferior. This could include a master and a servant, a chief and a slave, a capturer and a captive—all depending on the range of conventionalized social relationships and hierarchies.

Many languages have imperative forms differentiated for politeness—levels of politeness are encoded in the grammar and have to be marked on the verb. This is the topic of §6.4.1. Politeness and interpersonal relations can be encoded through number, or tense, or aspect of the imperative form (see §6.4.2).

6.4.1 *Honorific, polite, and familiar imperatives*

A number of languages, many of them concentrated in Asia, have special linguistic forms explicitly marking deference towards the addressee. These fully grammaticalized choices known as 'honorifics' can be expressed in imperatives.[16] They reflect social relationships between the speaker and the addressee (see Shibatani 2006 for a comprehensive overview of pragmatic functions of honorific and 'humbling' forms). Roughly speaking, an addressee-oriented honorific marks respect or deference towards the addressee, who may also be perceived as socially superior.

In Korean, honorification is grammatically marked by verbal enders (see Sohn 1994: 9–11, 41–3). Six speech levels are distinguished: plain, intimate, familiar, blunt, polite, and deferential. Each of these acquires special marking in the major clause types—declarative, interrogative, imperative, and 'propositive'—a special set of forms marking proposition to first person inclusive (you and I) (e.g. 'let's study').

Table 6.2 illustrates the marking of the six levels of honorification in these four clause types, with the verb *po* 'see':

Table 6.2 Levels of honorification in Korean

CLAUSE TYPE/SPEECH LEVEL	DECLARATIVE	INTERROGATIVE	IMPERATIVE	PROPOSITIVE
PLAIN	po-n-ta see-IND-DECL	po-ni see-Q	po-a-la see-INF-IMPV	po-ca see-PROPOS
INTIMATE	po-a see-INF			
FAMILIAR	po-ney see-DECL	po-na see-Q	po-key see-IMPV	po-sey see-PROPOS
BLUNT	po-o see-BLUNT			—
POLITE	po-a-yo see-INF-POLITE			
DEFERENTIAL	po-p-ni-ta see-ADD.HON-IND-DECL	po-p-ni-kka see-ADD.HON-IND-Q	po-si-p-si-o see-SUBJ.HON-ADD.HON-REQUEST-IMPV	po-p-si-ta see-ADD.HON-REQUEST-PROPOS
NEUTRAL	po-n-ta see-IND-DECL	po-n-unya see-IND-Q	po-la see-IMPV	po-ca see-PROPOS

The principles behind the use of speech level forms in different clause types reflect the relative status of the speaker and the addressee (including age and kinship). This is how Sohn (1994: 9-10) describes these principles (emphasis added):

The PLAIN LEVEL is used typically by any speaker to any child, to his own younger sibling, child, or grandchild regardless of age, or to one's daughter-in-law, or between intimate adult friends whose friendship started in childhood, etc. The INTIMATE LEVEL, which is also called a half-talk style, is used by a child of pre-school age to his or her family members including parents, or between close friends whose friendship began in childhood or adolescence. It may also be used to one's adult or adolescent student, or to one's son-in-law, etc. [...] The FAMILIAR LEVEL is slightly more formal than the INTIMATE LEVEL, typically used by a male adult to an adolescent such as a high school or college student or to one's son-in-law, or between two close adult friends whose friendship began in adolescence.

The remaining three levels are used only to adult hearers. The BLUNT LEVEL, which is gradually disappearing from daily usage due probably to its blunt connotation, is sometimes used by a boss to his subordinates. [...] Probably the most popular level is the polite level, which is the informal counterpart of the DEFERENTIAL LEVEL. While DEFERENTIAL LEVEL is usually used by males, the POLITE LEVEL is used widely by both males and females in daily conversations. Both the POLITE and the DEFERENTIAL LEVELS are used to a socially equal or superior person, but in general, the POLITE LEVEL is favoured between close persons. [...] In such formal occasions as oral news reports and public lectures, only the DEFERENTIAL style is used, whereas in writing for general audience, as in books, articles, and newspapers, only the PLAIN style is used.

An additional, SUPERPOLITE level is no longer used in spoken Korean, and is restricted to religious prayers, poems, and extremely formal and deferential letters (Sohn 1994: 10). No propositive form is available in the SUPERPOLITE level. According to Sohn (1994: 10), 'this may be because [...] the addressee is so vastly superior that the speaker could not propose to share an action'. The subject honorific and an addressee honorific may also be present: these reflect additional social distance between the addressee and the speaker. The same choices are available in negative commands.

The 'neutral' speech level is employed in indirect quotations. The neutral level imperative also occurs in 'such writings as exam papers [...]. In this case, the imperative illocutionary force is not a command as in a speech act but a conventionalized formal request irrespective of speech levels' (Sohn 1994: 345).

In addition, a verbal form can contain the subject- and the addressee-honorific, thus increasing deference and politeness. The deferential imperative must be accompanied by the subject honorific, as in 6.34:

Korean (Sohn 1994: 344)
6.34   ka-si-p-si-o
          go-SUBJ.HON-ADD.HON-REQUEST-IMPV
          'Please go!'

Or just the subject honorific can be present (without an accompanying addressee-honorific). The plural marker -*tul* can be optionally placed at the end of the verb form, if the addressee is plural (Sohn 1994: 42):

6.35   hayngpokha-sey-yo(-tul)
          happy-SUBJ.HON-POLITE.IMPV(-PL)
          'Be happy (everybody)'

The systems of speech levels and honorifics in Korean is among the most complex in the world. In a number of other languages, including Japanese, honorific distinctions are not made in imperatives (Hinds 1986: 47; Martin 1975: 961–6). 'Circumlocutions' are used to reflect different politeness registers—something we will return to in Chapter 8.

An example of a binary honorific system comes from Dolakha Newar (Genetti 2007: 130–31, 180–82). Honorific imperatives, and honorific pronouns, are employed if the speaker is 'considerably younger than the addressee'; they are also used 'to address deities, or others held in reverence'. Honorific imperatives are marked with the suffix -*sin*.

Non-honorific imperatives have different forms for singular and plural addressee; transitive and intransitive verbs acquire different marking. 6.36a–b illustrate non-honorific imperatives with a singular addressee for a transitive and for an intransitive verb:

Dolakha Newar
6.36a   jana   mica   ja-ŋ
           1sg.GEN   daughter   take-IMPV:TR
           'Take my daughter!' (you singular)

6.36b   chi   cõ
           2sg   stay:IMPV.INTR
           'You (singular) stay!'

Non-honorific imperatives with a plural addressee are marked in the same way, independently of whether the verb is transitive or intransitive:

6.37 chipe   thau   thau   chē   o-n
      2pl.GEN   REFL   REFL   house   go-IMPV.PL
      'Go each to your own house!'

We can recall from §2.1.2 that the exact choice of a non-honorific imperative affix depends on the verbal stem. In contrast, a honorific imperative is always marked in the same way, independently of the verb's transitivity or the number of the addressee.

6.38 thamun   boṭhā-en   bi-sin
      2pl.ERG   distribute-PARTICIPLE   give-IMPV.HON
      'You (many) distribute it for us!'

Honorific and non-honorific forms are also distinguished in negative commands. A negative non-honorific prohibitive is marked with the prefix *da-*, and distinguishes singular and plural forms. The honorific prohibitive involves the same prefix and the honorific suffix *-ku* (or *-gu*; also used as a honorific second person singular marker in the declarative past-present: Genetti 2007: 170). An example is in 6.39a–c:

6.39a da-hat
       PROH-say
       'Don't say!' (you singular)

6.39b da-hat-un
       PROH-say-PL
       'Don't say!' (you plural)

6.39c da-hat-ku
       PROH-say-HON
       'Don't say!' (you singular or plural)

In Dolakha Newar and a number of other languages, polite forms acquire an additional marking. In other languages, ordinary and polite imperatives may be equally marked. Markers of polite imperative in Koasati, a Muskogean language (Kimball 1991: 263–72), attach to the verb inflected for person; Koasati has a simple polite imperative, and a polite imperative of continuation (meaning 'please continue VERB-ing'). Tense distinctions are neutralized, and first person commands cannot be expressed in polite forms. Markers of polite imperative are mutually exclusive with other positive imperatives (which can express tense) and with negative imperative.

Alternatively, a language can have a special 'familiar', or less polite, imperative. Aguaruna, a Jivaroan language from Peru, has a familiar imperative used with family and friends. The marker *-ta* of ordinary neutral imperatives is replaced by *-ka* in the familiar one (Overall 2008: 348–9). Indo-Pakistani Sign Language has a special form for a 'rude' command implying immediate action; this type of command is usually directed at children or servants—that is, addressees with a lower status than oneself (Zeshan 1999).

Maale, an Omotic language from Ethiopia, has three imperatives which differ in degree of politeness. The regular imperative and the polite imperative distinguish singular and plural forms: see Table 4.3, repeated below. The impolite imperative does not distinguish number, but the polite imperative does.[17]

TABLE 4.3 Number marking in canonical imperatives in Maale

NUMBER OF ADDRESSEE	REGULAR IMPERATIVE	POLITE IMPERATIVE	IMPOLITE IMPERATIVE
singular	Verb-*é*	Verb-*é-tera*	Verb-*ibay*
plural	Verb-*uwáte*	Verb-*uwátera*	

Politeness distinctions in Maale interrelate with the type of speech act, and with illocutionary force. The regular, or neutral, imperative can be used for orders and to instruct someone how to perform a certain task—for instance, in describing how to get somewhere. The polite imperative has 'begging' connotations to it, and does not show strict correlations with age and status of the speaker with respect to the addressee. In contrast, the impolite imperative does: it is used 'when ordering somebody who is younger or low in status, parents to children when they are angry and most often among children when one of them acts as a boss. The impolite imperative is also used in chasing away pet animals' (Amha 2001: 126).

Large imperative systems often include polite and familiar forms. Tuyuca, an East Tucanoan language, has as many as eight positive imperative forms (Barnes 1979). These include a general or neutral imperative, and further imperative forms to do with types of speech act (invitation, permission, confirmation), a warning imperative (see 6.12–16 above), a future (or delayed) imperative, and a reported imperative. There is also a special form for familiar imperative (used to address close friends and also pets and animals). Tariana has eleven imperative forms; one of them is a polite imperative with a mild illocutionary force.

Honorifics and grammaticalized politeness are widespread in the languages of India.[18] Many of these have an impressive number of techniques to express politeness in commands. Polite, or precative, forms of the imperative in Kashmiri (Wali and Koul 1997: 40–41) imply 'request and persuasiveness': these differentiate singular and plural:

Kashmiri

6.40a   kita:b   par-ti
        book   read-POLITE.SG
        'Please read the book' (you singular)

6.40b   kita:b   pər'-tav
        book   read-POLITE.PL
        'Please read the book' (you plural)[19]

The choice of a polite form over a direct imperative correlates with the strength of an imperative. An unmarked imperative can be suffixed by politeness marker *sə:*, to 'decrease the brusqueness of the command'. The plural form of a direct imperative also marks the honorific status of the addressee: in §6.4.2 we return to this phenomenon, widely attested across the world. Repeating the imperative form correlates with the degree of politeness: while the repeated singular imperative reinforces the 'impoliteness', repetition of a plural imperative has the opposite effect: it sounds more polite. In contrast, repeating an imperative form in Tinrin (Osumi 1995: 237) gives it an overtone of urgency.

Politeness can also be encoded in vocative forms of nouns. Polite vocative forms in Kashmiri distinguish singular and plural, while impolite vocatives distinguish masculine and feminine gender, and also number of the addressee. As with the polite imperatives, 'the increase in politeness of vocatives decreases the strength of the imperative to the extent that it becomes a request' (Wali and Koul 1997: 40). Impolite vocatives may also be followed by derogatory address terms, like 'a rude or rustic person', 'copper-headed person', or terms of sexual abuse.

In Kannada, a Dravidian language (Sridhar 1990: 34–5), politeness in commands can be encoded in two ways: one option is the singular, plural, honorific, or ultra-honorific second person pronoun subject, and the other one is the use of vocatives at the end of the sentence. The vocative form can be ultra-casual, casual, informal, or polite. The polite form is appropriate in any situation, except when addressing one's close friends, younger relatives, or children: then informal or casual forms are used. The ultra-casual forms are reserved for 'back-slapping' relationships and among children; informal forms are also used in addressing servants, manual labourers, and God. The polite form is normally used when addressing elders.

In Malayalam, the 'scale of degrees of politeness or deference' in imperatives interacts with the scale of degrees of command—the more polite a command, the milder it sounds. If the addressee is lower on the social scale than the speaker, the suffixes *-ṭaa* (to a male addressee) and *-ṭii* (to a female addressee) can be added to a singular imperative (Asher and Kumari 1997: 33–4). Increased politeness can be marked on the verb with the suffix *-in*. Other (non-imperative) forms are also drawn into the system of politeness distinctions: 'at the upper end of the formality/politeness scale are forms in *-aalum* (a suffix which in other environments relates to concession).' Even more formal overtones are provided by a combination of the verb in *-aalum* 'concessive' with a third person plural reflexive pronoun, 'themselves'. A verbal form with a primary meaning of obligation doubles as a formal, polite imperative, to make a request. In other words, an array of imperative forms and command strategies are used to express imperative-specific meanings of politeness, and of force.

Degree of politeness and interpersonal relationships may be encoded through another category, rather than having an expression of their own. This is the topic of the following section.

6.4.2 *Interpersonal relationships expressed through other categories*

In many of the world's languages, plural forms correlate with politeness. In many European and some non-European languages, plural forms of verbs— and non-singular pronouns—indicate respect: a choice between a singular familiar form and a plural, polite form.[20] These forms are conventionally labelled as T- and V- forms—cf. French *tu* and *vous*, from Latin *tū* and *vōs*. In symmetrical usage—i.e. if both interlocutors use the T- forms to each other— T- forms can be seen as encoding intimacy and social closeness. V- forms (if used symmetrically) encode respect and social distance. Asymmetrical usage—i.e. one person using a T- form, and the other one using V-form— reflects power imbalance: a more powerful or authoritative interlocutor has the right to use T- and to receive V-.[21]

Why is the plural 'you' so commonly used for politeness purposes? On the one hand, addressing someone as 'you: plural' can be seen as a reflection of conventionalized indirectness, whereby the addressee is not singled out (see Lakoff 1973; Brown and Levinson 1987: 199). On the other hand, in any society where a person's social status is anchored in membership within a group, treating addressees as 'non-singular' would imply referring to 'their social standing and the backing that they derive from their groups', rather than treating them as 'relatively powerless individuals' (Brown and Levinson 1987:

199). Malagasy (Keenan and Ochs 1974: 69–74) is an instance of a combination of these two groups of motives: plural address forms are used both to avoid singling out a person, as a distancing device, and also to embed a person one addresses in the group to which they belong. The 'politeness' overtone of number is not exclusively an imperative-specific extension, but it is the one widely exploited—and conventionalized—in commands.

Another way of 'distancing' from the direct overtones of a second person addressee is using a third person form (see Brown and Levinson 1987: 200–204). In Italian and Spanish, third person forms are also used as exponents of politeness (see Clyne et al. 2003, 2004, 2006 on third person forms and politeness in some Germanic languages). The second person singular *tu*-form in Italian implies 'intimacy, familiarity, closeness between speaker and addressee' (Maiden and Robustelli 2007: 460–61), in imperatives and in other clause types. This way is also 'used (regrettably) by people who feel that they are in authority and want to stress the importance of their power (some doctors and nurses in hospitals, some policemen, etc.), or to threaten and to show contempt', as in 6.41:

Italian
6.41   Alzati e seguimi dal Commissario
        'Get up and follow me to the Commissioner'

Third person singular *Lei* implies, 'first and foremost, social distance (non-familiarity) between interlocutors'. As Maiden and Robustelli point out (2007: 461–2):

Lei, contrary to what is sometimes stated, is not an inherently 'polite' address form. It may be used even when one is being rude to one's interlocutor. But use of *tu* in circumstances where *Lei* would be expected, and no permission has been given to use *tu*, can be extremely impolite. *Lei* is generally used to strangers, regardless of their age (unless the addressee is a child), or to persons whom one regards as superior (because they are in positions of authority, or are of a significantly greater age) . . . [and] as a sign of respect towards subordinates, especially porters, cleaners, caretakers, etc, and in corner shops.

6.42   Mi dia un chiletto di vitello
        'Give me a kilo or so of veal'

The exact rules of where and how to use *tu* and where to use *Lei* are highly intricate. The same applies to German *Sie* versus *du*, French *vous* versus *tu*, Estonian *Teie* versus *sina* or *sa*,[22] and so on: each usage—and often individual or in-group attitudes to the use of such forms, in commands and in statements—are subtly different.[23]

There may be additional complications of a historical nature. In earlier stages of Italian, the second person plural pronoun *voi* was used as a singular polite address form, performing most of the functions of modern *Lei*. This usage survives in rural Tuscany, especially when talking to older people, and in some parts of southern Italy. The 'singular *voi*' may also be used by old people to address God, saints, the Virgin Mary, as in *Dio mio, aiutate-mi* 'My God, help me!'[24] But in general, such use 'produces on Italians an effect of rusticity, old-fashionedness or foreignness' (Maiden and Robustelli 2007: 463).

Using third person as a polite way of referring to the addressee is a way of making a command sound less threatening. Along similar lines, passive can be used to make a command sound politer—as is the case in Indonesian (§3.3.4).

The use of inherently polite V-forms may also have a softening effect. Second person plural verb forms serve to render the imperative 'somewhat less brusque' in Modern Greek (Joseph and Philippaki-Warburton 1987: 16). This is consistent with a general cross-linguistic tendency: the more polite the form, the less forceful the command.

Modality markers in commands can also increase or decrease the command's strength. In Sm'algyax (or Tsimshian), the uncertainty marker lowers the strength of a command (Stebbins 2001). Discourse particles can play a similar role: in Tamambo (Jauncey 1997), polite imperatives are marked with a discourse particle 'well then'. In Arapaho, an Algonquian language, two prefixes with directional meanings in non-imperative clauses have acquired imperative-specific meanings: the directional *cih-* 'towards the speaker' marks an imperative form as more emphatic, and *neh-* 'away from the speaker' indicates a stronger command (Cowell 2007: 46).

Strength of a command and politeness are typical imperative-specific extensions of tense. Evenki (Nedjalkov 1997: 18–19) distinguishes immediate and delayed commands. An immediate command has overtones of a categorical, that is, stronger, order. A delayed command usually implies a milder order, and a politer one. (There is no such option for prohibitives, since tense is not distinguished there.) In Punjabi, the future imperative has polite overtones (Bhatia 1993; also see §4.2.2, for similar examples from Yup'ik and Epena Pedee).[25]

Aspectual forms with imperatives can have similar effects. Imperfective imperatives sound polite in Yankunytjatjara, Watjarri, and Supyire (see §4.2.1). In Hup, a Makú language from Brazil, aspectual markers used with imperatives express the force of the command. The inchoative marker produces a relatively forceful directive. The telic marker can also contribute extra force to the command. And the perfective suffix is used to tone down the command, making it gentler or more polite. This is in line with the core meaning of the perfective in Hup, to indicate that the event is expected to be of short-term or limited duration. Epps (2005: 962) hypothesizes that the pragmatic extension from perfective to a politeness marker could be motivated by the fact that 'a request for a short-term, temporarily limited action is likely to represent less of an imposition on an address than a request for something more long term'. This is reminiscent of using diminutives as markers for 'softer' commands in Brazilian Portuguese (6.18–19) and in Matses.

Pendau, an Austronesian language from Sulawesi (Quick 2007: 536–8), has a variety of means for softening a command and making it sound more polite. The continuative aspectual enclitic =po can be used to 'soften the impact of a command by suggesting that there is no urgency for the task to be completed'. In contrast, using the enclitic =mo 'completive' adds to the urgency of the command, implying that the order should be carried out immediately. Using it can correlate with politeness, or with lack thereof, depending on the context: 'when used in the context of an invitation to do something for the addressee's benefit, its use can be seen as conveying politeness.' If there are no implications of any benefit for the addressee, a command with =mo would sound rude.

Correlations between an aspectual form and politeness overtones often reflect a tendency, but not a steadfast rule. Most textbooks of Russian assert that an imperfective imperative is more polite than its perfective counterpart (see 3.34a–b). However, given the right context and the right intonation, a perfective imperative can sound perfectly polite:

Russian
6.43   Pri-sjadjte   pozhalujsta
       PREVERB-sit.PERF+2pl.IMPV   please
       'Sit down please'[26]

Most languages employ an array of grammatical and lexical means to express subtle interpersonal relations and the strength of command, as appropriate for talking in different circumstances: from child to adult, from adult to child, between peers, and so on. The choice of a strategy correlates with a variety of sociolinguistic variables—among them age, sex, and educational level of the speaker. A comprehensive study of strategies for politeness and mitigating commands in Brazilian Portuguese (Koike 1992: 81–6) shows an array of such forms, used with different frequency by representatives of different social strata, and by men and women of different age groups. Honorific forms, such as Vossa Senhoria (lit. 'your Lordship') to address any dignitary or official, or Vossa Alteza, (lit. 'your Highness') to address a noble, often serve to 'soften the force of the imposition', emphasizing the 'listener's status as superior to the speaker'. Other means include using questions, or

statements in conditional forms, in lieu of commands. The pragmatic necessity for expressing subtle overtones of varied speech acts take command uses
away from imperative forms per se, so that the force of command, politeness,
and illocutionary force in general are expressed through a litany of strategies
(see Chapter 8).

Strength, or degree of command, its urgency, the necessity of compliance,
and politeness overtones correlate with further meanings which can acquire
grammatical marking in imperatives—relating to types of speech acts, consequence of the command, and more.

6.5 Types of speech acts and further meanings of imperatives

Imperatives can be used in a variety of speech acts—examples in §6.1 illustrate
the versatility of the English imperative. In many languages of the world, various
types of speech acts can be encoded as subtypes of imperatives.[27] Permissions,
suggestions, requests, and invitations are among the commonest.

Permissive forms are rather widespread throughout the world. Their meanings cover asking for permission or granting it, as in 6.13, from Tuyuca.[28] The
Amur dialect of Nivkh has a special permissive verb form used to grant
permission to the addressee, while the East Sakhalin dialect of the same
language employs imperative forms to cover this meaning. 6.44a is addressed
to one person, and 6.44b to many addressees:

Nivkh (Amur dialect: Gruzdeva 2001: 71; Krejnovič 1979: 316)
6.44a   Vi-iny-ĝa   vi-gira
        go-MOD-CONVERB.COND   go-PERM.2sg
        'If you want to go, go (I allow you to)' (a single addressee)

6.44b   Ev-d'   ha-ĝa   ev-girla
        take-FINITE   do.so-CONVERB.COND   take-PERM.2pl
        'If you want to take, take' (plural addressees)

Udihe, a Tungusic language, has a special permissive mood expressing
agreement or permission, and polite requests (Nikolaeva and Tolskaya 2001:
270–71, 468). This is described as a type of imperative by Schneider (1936: 120).
The permissive is often accompanied by the hortative particle *-ze*:[29]

Udihe
6.45   Wende-te-i-ze
        throw-PERM-2sg-HORT
        'OK, throw it'

Different forms may be perceived as having different 'strength' when used in commands and similar meanings. Lakhota (Boas and Deloria 1941: 111–12) has a separate marking for a straightforward command, a permission, and a mild request. These are marked with particles—with different forms used depending whether the speaker is a man or a woman, and the addressee singular or plural. See Table 4.2, repeated here for easy reference. If the particle *na* is omitted, the verb acquires stress on its final syllable. The form for 'mild request' also requires vowel change in the verb (Boas and Deloria 1941: 111–12).

TABLE 4.2 Imperative particles in Lakhota

SEMANTICS OF IMPERATIVE	WOMAN SPEAKING	MAN SPEAKING
Command	*na* (often omitted)	singular addressee *yo'*, *wo'* plural addressee *po'*
Permission	singular addressee *ye'*, *we'* plural addressee *pe'*	
Mild request (please)	singular addressee *ye'* plural addressee *pi ye'*	

Strength of command, type of speech act, and politeness can all be encoded in the imperative system. Deni, an Arawá language from Brazil (Koop 1980: 47–50), has a strong imperative, used only by parents to children, or older siblings to younger siblings—the expectation is that there is no option other than compliance. This imperative has overtones of immediacy. A polite imperative can be used from adult to adult or adult to child. The 'suggestive' imperative is used to express a suggestion or an invitation (this cannot be negated).

Invitations and suggestions may have a special expression, often just for first person inclusive, 'you and me'. Propositive mood in Korean is one such example (see Table 6.2). Tuyuca has a special form for an invitation to do something (6.12). A suggestive imperative in Benchnon, an Omotic language from Ethiopia (Rapold 2006: 243–4), has polite overtones. For instance, it can be used to encourage a guest to eat more:

Benchnon
6.46 m̃ʔ-ár-ā
      eat.NON.FACTUAL.STEM-NEG-2sg
      'Just help yourself!'

Formally, suggestive imperatives in Benchnon are similar to negative imperatives. In similar but not identical fashion, a negative imperative involves a
periphrastic structure reminiscent of a clause chain:

6.47   ḿʔ-ár-ā   ʃīd
       eat.NON.FACTUAL.STEM-2sg   remain
       'Don't eat!'

Many languages employ a special set of forms to express wishes, called
'optative'. They can be considered a subtype of imperative. For instance, in
Haro, an Omotic language, wishes and blessings, and also indirect commands,
are expressed with a combination of a second person imperative accompanied
by first or third person suffixes (Woldemariam 2007: 1153–4). Some grammarians employ the term 'imperative' for commands to a second person, and
'optative' for commands to oneself or to a third party. Then, optative and
imperative are said to be in a complementary distribution. In Maale, the
imperative is used for orders and instructions (see Table 4.3 in §6.4.1). The
optative is used for wishes and 'indirect' orders, especially in expressing good
wishes. A third person optative is shown in 6.48—note that despite its third
person form, the blessing is intended for the addressee:

Maale
6.48   s'oossí   maar-óngó
       God.NOM   forgive-3.OPT
       'May you get better!'

An imperative may encode overtones of consequences the addressee may
suffer depending on whether they comply with the command, or not. Santali,
a Munda language from India (Neukom 2001: 147), has a special imperative
form (called 'irrealis imperative') to 'express orders or requests that presuppose a subsequent situation'. In 6.49, *sereɲlem* cannot be used without the
following clause stating the consequence:[30]

Santali
6.49   sereɲlem   adɔ-ɲ   cala-k'-a
       sing+IRR.IMPV+2sg.SUBJ   then-1sg.SUBJ   go-MIDDLE-IND
       'Sing, then I shall go'

Santali is rather unusual in that the presupposed consequence does not
have to be negative. Many languages of the world have a special form of a
command which expresses a warning—i.e. stating a negative consequence for
non-compliance with the order. These commands are also known as apprehensives. They can be considered inherently negative; this is not to say that

they pattern in the same way as prohibitives. An apprehensive form in 6.14 from Tuyuca (Barnes 1979: 90) does not have to be accompanied by any further statement. It marks an action as undesirable. A typical function of an apprehensive is a warning against performing an unvoluntary action which could have a negative effect on them, or to an action which the actor performs intentionally but which may have an unintended negative result:[31]

Tuyuca
6.50   Juũ-ri
       burn-APPR
       'You may get burnt!' (Be careful!)

In Tucano, also East Tucanoan (Ramirez 1997: 148), the apprehensive form is accompanied by a command telling the addressee what to do, so as to avoid a potential negative consequence:

Tucano
6.51   ãyú-dó   dihatia   bɨ̃'ɨ̂-pɨ   bidî-di
       good-ADV   descend+IMPV   you-FOC   fall-APPR
       'Descend from the tree carefully, you might fall'[32]

Special apprehensive forms are not the only way of expressing negative consequence. We saw in 5.31 (§5.2.2), that in Russian and Lithuanian a negative command formed on a perfective verb has a 'warning' effect. And in many languages, 'negative consequence' is an integral part of clause linking (see Dixon 2009 for a survey).

Additional imperative forms and meanings may relate to the way of performing a commanded action. A number of languages have 'conative' imperatives, with the meaning of 'try and do'. The Tariana conative imperative (marked with a suffix -*thaɾa*) imparts additional overtones of a tentative action to the command—thus making it sound like a request, a suggestion, or even a plea:

Tariana
6.52   pi-ñha-thaɾa
       2sg-eat-CON.IMPV
       'Try and eat (please); eat it to try it out'

Such imperatives are often used within a serial verb construction which includes the verb 'try'. This further emphasizes the 'tentativeness' of the mild suggestion:[33]

6.53   pi-ñha-thaɾa   pi-wa
       2sg-eat-CON.IMPV   2sg-try
       'Please please try and eat'

This is similar to the imperative particle *gaji* 'try (to do it)' which often accompanies an imperative in Dyirbal (Dixon 1972: 116, and p.c.):

Dyirbal
6.54   gaji   ŋinda   jarrga
      CON.IMPV   you   spear:IMPV
      'You try and spear (it)!'

A malefactive imperative, 'do something to your own detriment', in Tariana is used for curses—that is, not in a strictly command meaning, e.g. *pipa-tupe* (2sg+rot-MALEF.IMPV) 'may you rot (to your detriment)'. Tucano and Wanano each have a special attention-getting imperative meaning 'hey, you, look!' (Waltz and Waltz 1997). Tuyuca has a special imperative form encouraging the addressee to check for themselves (see 6.15).

Meanings expressed in imperatives can cover an even wider range. An imperative form without any additional particle in Khezha, a Tibeto-Burman language from India (Kapfo 2005: 161, 187), is judged as neutral, and also somewhat impolite. Additional particles specify

- aspectual characteristics of the commanded activity (*ri* 'repetition of the action: that the addressee had performed the action before, and is again requested to do the same'; *e* 'gradual character of the activity'; *lo* 'accomplishment of the activity');
- urgency (*deh* 'act with no further delay'; *ley* 'order to perform action immediately, given that the addressee is delaying action');
- speech act type and interpersonal relationships (*ere* 'casual command or request');
- warning (*ley* 'apprehensive, warning against some danger');
- conative (*hi* 'try to, check and see').

There can be further variations on imperatives' meanings. Lahu has a marker for polite but firm insistence: this serves to soften the imperatives 'without detracting from their urgency' (Matisoff 1973: 377). We saw in 3.21a that the particle *dèèl* in Lao is an imperative marker which 'softens or plays down the burden of the request'. Other imperative-specific particles are semantically more complex. The particle *mèè4* states that addressee is unimpeded, implying 'do it, go ahead, I don't know why you don't, nothing's stopping you'. The particle *saa3* suggests a course of action to the addressee (implying 'do it, it will be good if you do, I know you won't do it if you don't want to'), *vaj2* asks the addressee to hurry, and *duu2* conveys a pleading tone to the imperative (Enfield 2007: 63–8).

Negative imperatives often express fewer meanings than their positive counterparts. Of the eleven imperatives in Tariana, only two occur in negative commands: such meanings as 'try and do' and politeness are not expressed. Along similar lines, the meanings of 'check for yourself', of warning, and the familiar imperative are not expressed in Tuyuca prohibitives (see §5.2). But this is not a universal rule.

An analytic prohibitive form in Trio, a Carib language from Suriname and Brazil (Carlin 2004: 309–11), is a straightforward command not to do something (see 5.19). There is a further option: a 'cessative' marked with the suffix *-ka(pi)* attached to a negated verb is a command to stop doing what the addressee is doing:

Trio
6.55   wa-kï-rï-ti-ke_mo
     NEG-1+2-do-PL-CESS_MOD
     '(Please) stop killing (hitting) me!'

This is a brief glimpse into a range of semantic nuances which could be rendered through imperatives. All of these reflect various facets and degrees of force of directive speech act, politeness and interpersonal relationships, and further aspects of commanded activities. Most of these meanings can be expressed in most languages—and if there is no imperative form at hand, another non-imperative form could be co-opted. A statement, an exclamation, or a question can be redeployed as a command. This is the topic of Chapter 8.

6.6 Summary

The meanings of imperatives are manifold. They consistently relate to the STRENGTH OF A COMMAND—encompassing commander's insistence or lack thereof, the urgency of the commanded action, and demand for the addressee's compliance. Strength of command correlates with the relative status of the commander and the addressee—whether they are equal, or one of them occupies a lower or a higher position on a social ladder. In this way, imperatives also encode INTERPERSONAL RELATIONS and POLITENESS. These can be realized through an elaborate system of honorific registers (as in Korean), or politeness forms reserved just for commands, and also vocatives and pronouns of address.

Strength of command (and the interpersonal relationships behind the ways the commands are employed) overlap with and slide into different kinds of speech acts—invitation, permission, encouragement, and the like. Various subtypes of directive speech acts can be described in terms of different 'degrees' of command: to suggest that somebody do something—or to request that something be done—is necessarily weaker and less insistent than a straightforward order 'do it!' And a humble request, or a tentative suggestion, often sounds more polite than an arrogant order. Dividing imperatives' meanings into strength, interpersonal relationship, and speech acts serves an expository purpose: it is important to keep in mind that they interact and form one cognitive package.

The complex of imperative-specific meanings—featuring speech acts, strength of command, politeness, familiarity, and other conventionalized interpersonal relations—constitutes the basis for the specific meanings of number, tense, aspect, and other categories within imperatives.

Notes

1. Imperative-specific meanings have been addressed in a variety of sources: see e.g. Hamblin (1987) and the partial discussion in Sadock and Zwicky (1985). Some authors opt for listing potential types of speech acts in which imperatives may potentially occur (e.g. Xrakovskij 1992b: 54 distinguishes command, demand, request, advice, permission; see also Davies 1986; and a colourful description of imperative meanings in Galician by Frexeiro Mato 2000). König and Siemund (2007: 314–16) classify imperatives, by their illocutionary force, into hortatives (illocutionary force: exhortations), optatives (illocutionary force: wishes), debitives (illocutionary force: obligations), rogatives (illocutionary force: petitions), and monitories (illocutionary force: warnings). Further analysis of semantic overtones of first and second person-oriented commands and their distribution is in van der Auwera et al. (2004), and van de Auwera et al. (2005a, b); see also Haverkate 1976 for subtle distinctions between orders and commands, standing orders, iterative and non-iterative commands as expressed in Spanish. The major problem in providing a general picture of the meanings of imperatives is finding common terminological ground, frequently absent from grammars, and from analytic studies. A student of imperatives often finds themself overwhelmed with different ways of referring to essentially similar things—demands and commands, petitions and requests, instructions and recommendations.

2. Based on Huddleston (2002: 929–31); see also Davies (1986), Quirk et al. (1985). Semantic descriptions of the imperative form in Biblical Hebrew (Waltke and O'Connor 1990), Arabic (Cowell 1964: 359–61), Russian (Xrakovskij and Volodin 2001), and other languages reveal similar patterns.

3. Cf. 'sarcastic' uses of imperatives in Biblical Hebrew (Waltke and O'Connor 1990: 572).

4. In Jespersen's (1924: 313–14) words, imperative is a 'will-mood in so far as its chief use is to express the will of the speaker, though only—and this is very important—in so far as it is meant to influence the behaviour of the hearer... Imperatives thus are requests and... these range from the strictest command to the humblest prayer. But we saw also that requests are very often expressed by other means than the imperative [...]—in other words, imperative and request are not convertible or coextensive terms.' See also van der Auwera (2006a).

5. This is one of two possible ways of presenting a cross-linguistic picture of the meanings of imperatives. Another option would be to outline all the imaginable options, and then see how and which of them are expressed in the world's languages. In our view this would be an unsurmountable task, given the degree of variability and unpredictability of imperative meanings in many languages (see §6.5 on Santali). Also, this essentially deductive approach runs the danger of backgrounding the facts of languages in favour of questionable hypotheses.

6. See the definition of illocutonary force by Matthews (1997: 170) as 'the force that an expression of some specific form will have when it is uttered'. 'Degree' of command is usually synonymous with 'strength' of command. Note that the category of 'degree' of command is essentially different from the category of degree, or gradability, in adjectives. Nouns and verbs can have a category of 'degree': diminutive ('a little bit'), augmentative ('a lot'), and excessive ('too much') (see Aikhenvald 2008d: 567–8 for a few other examples). Diminutives may interact with 'softening' or a request (see Brown and Levinson 1987: 109 for an example from Tamil).

7. Politeness is a semantically complex category: see Brown and Levinson (1987) for an in-depth discussion. Politeness is associated with the notion of 'face', 'the public self-image' that every member of a society wants to claim for themself. 'Face' has two related aspects: positive face, i.e. a positive image claimed by interactants, and negative face, consisting in 'the basic claim to territories'—'freedom of action and freedom from imposition' (p. 61). With this comes the differentiation between **positive politeness** oriented towards the positive face of the addressee, and **negative politeness** oriented towards satisfying the addressee's negative face: the speaker assures the addressee that they 'will not (or will only minimally) interfere with the addressee's freedom of action'. 'Hence negative politeness is characterized by self-effacement, formality and restraint' (p. 70). See also §6.4.

8. Intonation has a similar function in many other languages, including Basque (Saltarelli 1988: 28), Hixkaryana (Derbyshire 1979: 17), Hungarian (Kenesei et al. 1998: 21), Japanese (Hinds 1986: 48), Kashmiri (Wali and Koul 1997: 40–1), Kobon (Davies 1981: 23), Malayalam (Asher and Kumari 1997: 33), Rumanian (Mallinson 1986: 25), and Persian (Mahootian 1997: 27).

9. Diminutives are used in a similar function in Modern Greek, as markers of familiarity and to soften a command (Mackridge 1985: 158, and Georgios Tserdanelis, p.c.). We return to the use of honorific and 'humiliative' lexical means in Portuguese commands in §6.4.

10. In Kannada (Sridhar 1990: 38) *svalpa* 'a little' is a 'palliative device used commonly in making requests, especially in asking favors' (see example 8.11).

11. Similarly, adding a pronoun to an imperative in Tamil can also be perceived as 'aggressively rude' or as polite, depending on the context (Brown and Levinson 1987: 191, 292; based on Annamalai p.c.).

12. Similar examples come from Finnish (Sulkala and Karjalainen 1992: 24); see also Chapter 8.

13. The phrases employed to soften a command in Kashmiri (Wali and Koul 1997: 40) involve 'please/kindly', 'now what', and 'for the sake of God'. In contrast, *pelo amor de Deus* may make a command—or a plea—sound more insistent in Brazilian Portuguese. Similar examples from Rumanian are in Mallinson (1986: 25).

14. Indirect commands are often understood as reported commands embedded in complex structures with verbs of speech in a matrix clause (e.g. Nedjalkov 1997: 29–30 for Evenki; Joseph and Philippaki-Warburton 1987: 23 for Modern Greek; Hewitt 1979: 34–5 for Abkhaz; Mallinson 1986: 42 for Rumanian; Saltarelli 1988: 33–4 for Basque; see also §3.4). In some languages, such as Tuvaluan, the adverbial markers of politeness, or 'downtoners', can appear in embedded imperatives, just as in free-standing ones.

15. This is characterized by the omission of subject person markers on the verb and the absence of 'initial change' on the verb stem (i.e. absence of the lengthening of short vowels in the first syllable of the stem, and the insertion of -*Vn* when the initial vowel is long).

16. This is in line with Weinreich's (1963: 151) remark that 'the indication of the imperative seems typically to intersect with deictic categories', among them honorifics.

17. Establishing meaningful correlations between politeness and the expression of other grammatical categories is a matter for future studies, when more information is available on such correlations. For the time being, they do not amount to more than curious facts. For instance, in Maithili (Indo-Aryan: Yadav 2003: 488–9), future imperative forms are found only for second person mid-honorific and non-honorific subjects (while non-future imperative distinguishes three levels: non-honorific, mid-honorific, and honorific, in three persons).

18. See, for instance, Saxena (2002) on honorifics, politeness, and correlations with speech acts for imperatives in Kinnauri, a Tibeto-Burman language. Hindi distinguishes intimate, familiar, polite, deferred, and deferential imperatives (Shapiro 2003: 268, 277); see also Schmidt 2003: 330 on Urdu; Yadav 2003: 488 on Maithili. Bhojpuri, also Indo-Aryan (Verma 2003: 531), distinguishes non-honorific and neutral forms; and Gujarati has informal and polite forms (Cardona and Suthar 2003: 683).

19. See Wali and Koul (1997), on the nature of root alternations in the verb.

20. Along similar lines, plural verb forms in Ainu express deference; similar examples from Tagalog and Turkish are discussed by Shibatani (2006). Comrie (1975b) discusses verbal agreement with polite plurals (plural in form, but with a singular referent) in Slavic and Romance languages.

21. See Coates (2003: 33–4) for a brief overview of the pragmatics of T- and V- forms of address, with special attention to symmetrical and asymmetrical usage, and for the recent shift from status semantics to solidarity semantics of address forms, and the link to the growing informalization of the public domain; also see Fairclough (1992). Clyne et al. (2004, 2006) provide an insightful analysis of recent changes in the use of address forms in German and in Swedish. Further examples are in Brown and Levinson (1987: 198–9).

22. Capitalizing the first letter of an address term in some written traditions makes the form even politer. This issue, interesting but tangential to a study of commands, will not be discussed here.

23. See Butt and Benjamin (2004: 288–90) for a brief overview of various overtones of singular and plural imperatives in South American and Iberian varieties of Spanish.

24. How one addresses God, a saint, and other virtual beings varies from language to language: in some, as in Russian, the T-form is regularly used. The putative correlations between beliefs and address forms go beyond the realm of this study.

25. Similarly, the suffix -*qi* in West Greenlandic 'puts off the time of desired compliance to a less immediate future' and thus makes a command sound somewhat more polite (Fortescue 1984: 26).

26. See further discussion of the general meaning of aspects in Russian, and their usage in commands, in Shmelev (2002).

27. For an outline of speech acts, see Cruse (2006: 168–9), Bosco (2006), and classic work by Searle (1969, 1975, 1976). Much of the work on theory of speech acts is deductive. Here, as elsewhere, I proceed inductively, concentrating on the distinctions and meanings attested in the world's languages.

28. Similar examples come from Kulina, an Arawá language (Tiss 2004: 250–51), Yokuts, Tucano, and Desano.

29. Other person forms of the permissive also express uncertain future, and appear in questions (Nikolaeva and Tolskaya 2001: 270–72).

30. Neukom (2001: 148) points out that the 'presuppositional character' of the irrealis imperative is linked to other uses of irrealis forms in conditional clauses.

31. See Hyslop (2001: 251–3) on the apprehensive in the Lolovoli dialect of the North-East Ambae language of Vanuatu and its interactions with intentionality of the action. Similar examples are found in Aleut, Mongolian, Sikuani, and Nivkh. An alternative term is 'monitive' (see Mithun 1999: 171 for Maidu).

32. We saw in §4.2.4 that 'apprehensive' imperatives may distinguish the information source of the speaker and of the addressee. The visual apprehensive in 4.40, from Tariana, is a warning against something both the speaker and the addressee can

see. The nonvisual apprehensive in 4.41 is used to warn the addressee of something the addressee, or both speaker and addressee, cannot see. Similar distinction was found in Nivkh, a highly endangered isolate from Siberia (Gruzdeva 1992: 69–70; based on Krejnovič 1979: 316). That apprehensives have grammatical categories not attested in other command forms can be used as an argument in favour of treating them as separate systems.

33. This category in Tariana has developed as a result of calquing a similar structure from neighbouring Desano, e.g. Desano *ba-yā-ta* (eat-IMPV.try.out-LIMITATIVE) 'Eat it to try it out!' (Miller 1999: 73–4; Aikhenvald 2008b). See also Chapter 11.

7

Imperatives which do not command

Imperatives discussed this far have been presented as exponents of a directive speech act par excellence. This is often not the full story—using Whitney's (1924: 573) words, 'the imperative also sometimes signifies an assumption or concession: and occasionally, by pregnant construction, it becomes the expression of something conditional and contingent.' In other words, imperative forms do not always imply telling someone what to do. And if this is so, they are not compatible with conventional responses or reactions to commands.

An imperative in its usual function of command, order, request, or entreaty presupposes compliance. An exclamation like *Just imagine! She's getting married for the fifth time* contains an imperative form—but *imagine* is not a command to comply with. Rather, it is an attention-getting device, an expression of surprise. Neither does a speech formula like *Have a nice weekend!* presuppose compliance. And an imperative with a conditional meaning, as in *Do that again and you'll regret it*, does not have the illocutionary force of a command: the whole sentence has a conditional interpretation. What sounds like a command to do something may in fact imply the opposite. In one story, a drunk comes home late and accidentally breaks a vase. His wife, extremely annoyed, says: *That's right, break everything in the house!* If this were to be taken literally, this can be understood as a command to carry on destroying everything. But it is not—what is phrased as a directive speech act has the opposite meaning, of putting a stop to destruction.[1] Not only do the non-command uses of imperative forms have a non-command semantics: the restrictions common to imperatives may not apply to such non-prototypical uses. We discuss them throughout this chapter.

We start with non-command meanings of imperative forms in complex sentences where they convey condition or supposition, or have a concessive meaning, in §7.1.

Imperatives in speech formula, including farewells and greetings, do not represent real commands: they often just have a phatic role as tokens of speech etiquette. In §7.2, we turn to formulaic uses of imperatives, and how they occur in greetings, farewells, blessings, wishes, and curses, and also in 'mock' commands, telling the addressee to do the opposite of what would be required by common sense. Imperative forms also occur in derivations. They may develop into attention-getting devices and interjections. They can be used as major predications in narratives, and occur in questions, statements, and replies (see §7.3). A brief summary is in §7.4.

7.1 Imperatives in complex sentences

When an imperative form is included in the first clause in a complex sentence, its most common interpretation in English is as a conditional. The sentence in 7.1 is understood as 'If you ask him about his business deals he quickly changes the subject'.[2]

7.1   Ask him about his business deals and he quickly changes the subject

The conditional interpretation of the link between the two clauses derives from the implications of consequence commonly conveyed by the conjunction *and*. The first clause does not have to be positive. In 7.2 it is negative—and the form of the negative clearly shows that we are dealing with an imperative (Huddleston 2002: 937–9):

7.2   Don't make him the centre of attention and he gets in a huff

In each of these examples, the direct commanding force of an imperative is backgrounded: 7.1 is not a way of directing the addressee to ask him about his business deals. An example like 7.3 is somewhat different:

7.3   Do that again and you'll regret it

It implies that 'if you do that again, you'll regret it', and can be further interpreted as an indirect way of saying 'Don't do it again'—the opposite meaning to that of the imperative clause used on its own. The negative directive meaning results from the overtones of indesirability conveyed by the second clause—'you'll regret it'.

Command and non-command, conditional, meanings of an imperative in clause coordination can be blurred. 7.4a and 7.4b can be understood as either:[3]

7.4a   Persuade her to agree and I will be forever in your debt
7.4b   Come over around seven and then we'll be able to avoid the rush hour traffic

Constraints on the formation of imperatives do not apply to imperative forms in their conditional use (see Huddleston 2002: 938–9). 'Negatively oriented' adverbs like *ever* or *any more* do not usually occur with commanding positive imperatives: ?*Do that ever again!* and ?*Work any more!* are not grammatical. But this restriction is relaxed if an imperative expresses a condition:

7.5a   Just do that ever again and I'll brain you
7.5b   Work any more and you'll collapse

Along similar lines, commands like ?*Pay any attention to people like that!* or ?*Invent anything new!* are ungrammatical. But within a conditional structure, they are acceptable (Bolinger 1977: 162):

7.6   Pay any attention to people like that and they will never let you rest
7.7   Invent anything new and the public goes wild about you

This same imperative can occur on its own as a threat: *Just do that ever again!* An alternative will be to look upon this as an ellipsed version of 7.5a.

Imperatives of non-agentive verbs in English are not impossible, but need to be contextualized to be judged acceptable. *Feel slightly off-colour!* is not ungrammatical as a straightforward command, but may sound weird to some. But within a complex sentence with a conditional reading, this sounds fine:

7.8   Feel slightly off-colour and he thinks you are dying

Imperatives with a conditional reading can have first or third person reference, and control reflexives in a way commanding imperatives cannot. A free-standing commanding imperative can contain a reflexive co-referential with the second person subject: *Buy yourself a new outfit!* It cannot contain a reflexive co-referential with another person: ???*Buy myself a new outfit!* and ???*Buy herself a new outfit!* are ungrammatical.

But not so in complex sentences with imperatives in their conditional reading. The following examples are fully acceptable:

7.9   Buy herself a new outfit and she'll feel much more confident
7.10   Buy myself a new suit, (and) my wife raises the roof

Imperatives in their conditional uses can have a past time reference:

7.11   Express any misgivings and he accused you of disloyalty[4]

Non-canonical *let*-imperatives can only have a conditional reading with the third person, but not with first person (second person would also be acceptable):

7.12   Let anyone question what he says and he flies into a rage

According to Huddleston (2002: 939), first person inclusive *let*-imperatives are not used this way: they always retain their directive force. An example like *Let's put up the price and they'll cancel the order* cannot be used 'to convey the opposite of what is expressed in the imperative ('If we put up the price they'll cancel the order, so let's not put up the price').[5]

Imperatives may acquire conditional meanings when coordinated as a way of expressing inference, especially in the case of an undesirable consequence, as in *Go straight and you'll fall down the stairs*. This, however, does not account for the grammatical properties of imperative forms in conditional structures. Those make them into a special set which could be considered homonymous with 'commanding' imperatives.

Imperative forms with conditional meanings are not uncommon in numerous languages of Eurasia.[6] Imperative forms in Russian can express condition as part of complex sentences (Shvedova 1970: 582). This form can be accompanied by the conditional marker *by* but does not have to be. Here and further on imperative forms are in bold face.

Russian

7.13   [**Pishi**   (by)   uchenik],   uchitel'   ne   delal
        write:2sg.IMPV (COND)   pupil   teacher   NEG   do.past.masc.sg
        by   emu   zamechanij
        COND   to.him   remarks:ACC.PL
        'If the pupil had been writing, the teacher would not be making remarks to him'

This conditional imperative always appears in what looks like second person singular form, independent of the person and number of the subject. That is, the second person plural imperative *pishi-te* 'write (you plural)' cannot be used here in the conditional meaning, even if the subject is plural. This justifies Shvedova's approach to these as a special form of conditional construction (see further examples in Chung and Timberlake 1985: 248; Vinogradov 1947; Xrakovskij and Volodin 2001: 226).

While in Russian the imperative can only express a counterfactual condition, other Slavonic languages employ imperative forms for a condition of any kind (Knjazev 1988: 63). Second and third person imperatives have a conditional meaning in a number of Turkic languages. In 7.14, from Uzbek (Nasilov et al. 2001: 218–19), the third person imperative form is accompanied by a particle *-či*:

Uzbek

7.14 Qani, bizniki-ga kel-ib   **kur-sin-či,**
      well, our-DAT   come-CONV see.AUX-IMPV:3sg-PARTICLE
      ojog-i-ni   sindir-a-man
      leg-POSS:3sg-ACC   break-PRES-1sg
      'Well, let him only dare come to us, I shall break his legs'

And in Armenian (Kozintseva 2001: 266), imperatives in complex sentences without subordinating conjunctions express condition. Unlike other languages discussed so far, these clauses in Armenian always have a generic subject, and are mostly employed in proverbs:

Armenian

7.15 Erexin   bani   dir   het-e   **gna**
      child.DAT   thing.DAT   ask:IMPV:2sg with-DEFINITE   go.IMPV:2sg
      'If you ask a child to do something, you should keep an eye on it'

Imperative forms in Russian can have a concessive meaning, especially if accompanied by a conjunction meaning 'although'. 7.16 comes from a classic poem by Derzhavin (also see Xrakovskij and Volodin 2001: 242–3 for further examples):

Russian

7.16 Osel   ostanetsja   oslom,   hotja
      donkey.NOM.SG   will.remain   donkey.INSTR.SG although
      osypj   ego   zvezdami
      shower.IMPV.2sg   him   stars:INSTR.PL
      'A donkey will remain a donkey, even though you shower him (lit. shower him!) with stars'

Imperative forms in Bagwalal, a Northeast Caucasian language, can be used in concessive clauses (Dobrushina 2001: 324–6). Then, a positive imperative form is followed by a negative imperative, as illustrated in 7.17. The imperative forms are in bold.

Bagwalal

7.17 [w=e-be,   w=ē-bi-še,]   dē
     MASC=come-IMPV   MASC=come-BI.marker-PROH   I

o-š₀a

this-OBLIQUE.STEM.MASC-SUPERESSIVE

č'ihi-š   j=el-ā-l-o=j   ek'₀a

above-ELATIVE   FEM-go-MARKED.STEM.POT-FUT-PARTICIPLE-FEM   is

'Whether he comes (or) not (lit. he come, not come), I will forgive him
(everything)' (lit. will come on top of him)

Imperatives in commands in Bagwalal have a second person reference. The
same forms can refer to any person in concessive clauses. And, in addition,
imperatives in Bagwalal cannot be formed on verbs whose meaning does not
involve control. These restrictions do not apply to the concessive use of
imperative forms (which is similar to how constraints on imperative formation
in English are 'relaxed' when it comes to their use in conditional structures: see
7.8 above). Along similar lines, verbs of quality in Nivkh (Gruzdeva 2001: 68)
cannot form first or second person imperatives used as commands. But second
person singular imperatives can occur in concessive meaning:

Nivkh (Gruzdeva 2001: 77)

7.18 Tamla   čo   p'řy-ŋan   **pil-j**
     numerous   fish   come-CONV:TEMP   be.big-IMPV.2sg

     mat'ki-ja   syk   p'u-t   čo   ny-d'-yu
     be.small-IMPV.2sg   all   come.out-CONV.MANNER   fish   make-FINITE-PL

     'When a lot of fish came, whether (they are) big or whether (they are)
     small, everyone came out to process the fish'

In Uzbek and Tatar (Nasilov et al. 2001: 218), only first plural and third
person singular and plural imperatives can have a concessive meaning. 7.18 is
from Tatar:

Tatar

7.19 Ul   barýber   üz-en-čä   ešli—bar-ýbýz
     he   however   self-POSS:3sg-EQUATIVE   do—all-POSS:1sg

     karšý   **kil-ik**
     against   do-IMPV.PL

     'He will do it his own way—even if all of us are against it'

These uses are reminiscent of Whitney's (1924: 571) remark about conditional and concessive overtones of imperatives in Sanskrit. The exact meanings of imperative forms in their non-command uses in complex sentences

are often context-dependent. The forms themselves differ from imperatives in commands not just in their meanings. We have seen that constraints on forming imperatives on verbs of various semantic groups can be relaxed. And only some person forms may be able to occur in non-imperative meanings. To what extent, in each particular case, conditional and concessive uses of imperative forms in complex clauses can be treated as nascent forms of special conditional and other paradigms remains an open question.

Imperative forms can be used in complex sentences of other types. In Armenian, they can express potential consequence (in clauses with a generic actor):

Armenian (Kozintseva 2001: 266)

7.20 Ays   koɣmerum   aynk'an   šat   ē₁   [sunk] linum₂
     these   place:PL:LOC so   much   be:PRES:3sg₁,₂   mushroom
     or   t'ekuz   haruyr   takaṙ   aɣ₁   dir₂
     that   even   hundred   barrel   pickle:IMPV:2sg₁,₂
     'There are so many [mushrooms] here, that one could pickle even a hundred barrels [of them]'

Imperatives can occur embedded in clauses expressing purpose. In Dagbani, embedded imperative forms occur in indirect speech complements accompanied by the subordinator *ni*.[7]

Dagbani (Olawsky 1999: 55)

7.21a **tim'**   ma   nyu:li
      give-IMPV   me   yam
      'Give me yam!'

7.21b o   teei   ma   ni   n   **tim'**   o   nyuuli
      he   remind   me   SUB   I   give-IMPV   him   yam
      'He reminded me to give him yam'

In Tariana, prohibitives negate purposive clauses (Aikhenvald 2003: 410), as illustrated in 7.22.[8] The prohibitive marker *mhẽda* is a particle:

Tariana

7.22 diha-da-nuku   dhita-pida   dhinuɾu-se
     ARTICLE-CL:ROUND-TOP.NON.A/S   3sgnf+take-REPORTED   3sgnf+throat-LOC
     [**mhẽda-pida**   **niwhã-niki**]
     PROH-REPORTED   3sgnf+bite-COMPLETIVE
     'He put the (finger) into his throat, in such a way that he couldn't bite it off'

In a number of languages, speech reports convey the meaning of 'purpose'—that is, a purposive construction 'he gave him food to eat; literally translates as 'Having said "Eat!" he gave him food'. This is illustrated with 7.23, from Manambu (see Aikhenvald 2008c on cross-linguistic patterns of polysemy in speech reports):

Manambu

7.23 **Ak** wa-ku də-kə-k kamna:gw ata kui-d
  IMPV+eat say-COMPL.SS he-OBLIQUE-DAT food then give-3masc.
                   sgSUBJ
  'He gave him food to eat' (lit. Having said 'Eat!' he gave him food)

Imperatives may fill grammatical 'gaps' in a language. Manambu has no productive causative, but employs a number of other devices instead. One of these is a third person imperative in direct speech complements. A sentence '"May his throat be wet", he said (and) gave him water' is a functional equivalent of 'He made (or let) him drink water'.

Along similar lines, purposive constructions in Uzbek involve the verb of speech and an embedded imperative. This is illustrated in 7.24 (Nasilov et al. 2001: 215).

Uzbek

7.24 Cirk **kur-ajlik** de-b šun-ča   jul bos-di-k
  circus see-IMPV:1pl say-CONV such-EQUATIVE way press-PAST-1pl
  'To see the show in the circus, we have passed this distance' (lit. Saying 'Let us see the circus!' we have passed this distance)

These conventionalized uses of imperatives in purposive clauses are clearly connected with imperatives as exponents of directive speech acts. We now turn to further instances of conventionalized imperative forms with no command meanings implied.

7.2 Greetings, farewells, blessings, and curses: imperatives in speech formulae

In many languages of the world, imperative forms are used as tokens of politeness, in saying 'hello' and 'goodbye', and in expressions of goodwill and of annoyance. These imperative forms are tokens of speech etiquette—a kind of social glue which helps interlocutors acknowledge each other's presence. They do not command anything, and are conventionalized to varying extents. Yet using them correctly is a sine qua non for successful survival in a community.

Consider Manambu, and its plethora of speech formulae involving forms easily recognizable as imperatives. The verb 'stay' is used in the departure formula by someone preparing to leave:

Manambu

7.25 yara   **adakw**
      well   stay.IMPV
      'Stay well'

The person who is staying behind has to answer, using the imperative of the verb 'go':

7.26 yara   **ma:y**
      well   go.IMPV
      'Go well, good-bye'

If you walk along the road and pass someone, it is polite to acknowledge their presence. One way of doing it is by saying:

7.27 yara   kwa-n   **a-nay**
      well   stay-SEQ   IMPV-play
      'Staying well, play!'

If the people you encounter are obviously working, a proper thing to say is to acknowledge it by saying:

7.28 yara   kwa-n   yawi   **akur**
      well   stay-SEQ   work   IMPV+do
      'Staying well, do work'

If I sit in a house and see a passer-by, I need to acknowledge their presence. The proper thing is to use a second person imperative, encouraging them to move on in the direction they are already going. The direction is always calculated with respect to the course of the Sepik river (the major orientation point in Manambu-speaking communities). 7.29 would be used if the person's direction of movement follows the river upstream, and 7.30 if the person's direction of movement follows the river downstream.

7.29 ma:y   **a-war**
      go.IMPV   IMPV-go.up
      'Off you go upstream'

7.30 ma:y   **adi:d**
      go.IMPV   go.down.IMPV
      'Off you go downstream'

Saying 7.31 has an additional overtone of 'Go away, off you go', if trying to get rid of someone:

7.31 ma:y   a-væki
       go.IMPV   IMPV-go.across
       'Off you go across'

These pseudo-commands do not really add any information, or constitute any meaningful communication. They are purely phatic. But using them correctly makes you become part of the village life: they are the base of appropriate verbal behaviour.

Manambu is highly typical in how it employs imperative forms in greetings and farewells. In numerous languages of the world, leave-taking involves the person who is staying uttering a specification of what both parties are to do. In Tok Pisin, the one who stays behind would say:

Tok Pisin
7.32 Orait, mi stap   yu go
       'All right, I am staying, you go'

In Tzeltal (Mayan) *la?* 'come' is a response to a greeting hail; *ban* 'go' is a farewell; *naklan* 'sit down' is an offer to a visitor; and *solan* 'pass' is a trail greeting (see further examples and discussion in Brown and Levinson 1987: 99ff.). In Karajarri, an Australian language, when a person is leaving it is common to use two imperatives, *kalaya wanta* 'finish, stay'. The person who is staying behind answers *Ngawayi, kalaya yarra!* 'Yes, finish, go' (Sharp 2003a). Among the Wakasigau, a Bantu-speaking people of Southern Kenya, one greeting containing an imperative, *Bwana okaso*, 'Praise the Lord!', also serves as a mark of Christian religious 'belonging', acknowledging their 'saved' status (Milton 1982: 265).

Formulaic, conventionalized imperatives can be clearly recognizable as such. Expressions such as *Take care* or *Fare thee well* are prime examples. When an English-speaking friend says to me 'Take care' before he leaves my office he does not mean that I have to beware of some imminent danger awaiting me behind the door. Another friend who typically finishes his messages with 'Be safe' does not imply that he is leaving me in an unsafe environment. A Yiddish-speaking friend ending his message with *Sei gesund* 'Be healthy' is not expressing worries concerning my health. All these are just ways of wishing me well as a polite end to a conversation.[9]

However, formulae like *Be happy!* and *Get well!* can be felt to be genuine commands, especially if put in a command context: *Get well—that's an order! Be happy! Look on the bright side!* (Bolinger 1967: 347).

Other formulaic imperatives can only be recognized as such by a historian of the language. Most speakers of English use *Goodbye* as a departure formula, without realizing that this expression originally goes back to a contraction of a conventionalized command 'God be with you' (OED). Along similar lines, *spasibo*, the conventional way of saying 'Thank you' in Russian, is used by believers and non-believers alike: yet this form is transparently linked to a command *Spasi Bog* 'May Lord save (you)' (Isachenko 2003: 506 discusses this and numerous other examples of fossilized imperative forms in Russian greetings, warnings, and a variety of interjections).[10]

Even an expression of surprise can take the form of a command. When a respectable American-born academic sent me a brief message *Stone the crows!* this was not an incitement to throw stones at birds. Rather, it was him expressing his utmost surprise at an underperforming dean getting an appointment at a higher level of senior management.

Formulaic uses of imperative forms extend beyond rituals of greeting and departure. Requests for excuse (*Pardon me, Excuse me*), curses, and blessings are usually phrased as commands. In his highly informative and entertaining monograph, Matisoff (2000: 69) provides numerous examples of Yiddish discourse peppered with blessings and curses cast as commands. This makes Yiddish sound highly vivid and entertaining, though a trifle long-winded: 'My uncle Shloyme was—may he forgive me—something of a mooch', or 'He was in the same class as your son, may he live longer years'. The exact choice depends on speakers' linguistic creativity.

Tabooed swear words, insults, and maledictive expressions are often cast as imperatives (see Allan and Burridge 2006: 79–88 for an array of examples of verbal insults, including commands mentioning sexual activities). That an insult phrased as if it were a command is not really a command and does not share properties with an imperative form was shown by McCawley (1971: 3–4). An utterance such as *Fuck you!* contains an imperative form. But unlike an imperative *Close the door!* it cannot be embedded: while it is possible to say *I said to close the door* one can hardly say '?I said to fuck you'. A sentence like *Fuck Lyndon Johnson* is not an 'admonition to copulate with Lyndon Johnson'—rather, this is a way of 'indicating disapproval but conveying no instructions to engage in sexual relations with him' (p. 4). In other words, curses—also known as 'imprecations'—express emotional states rather than directive speech acts.[11]

RIP, 'Rest In Peace', typically written on gravestones, is another example of a speech formula containing an imperative. This usually refers to deceased people; however, this same formula can be addressed to an administrative entity which has virtually ceased to exist. Such a mock-command may turn out to be a powerful stylistic device, with a gamut of meaning overtones, including predicting future behaviours and warning about them. The following extract from the *Big Issue* 1997 (Christmas edition: AUS #36: 36–37: Börjars and Burridge 2001: 130) is meant to provide steps for making the festive season a special one (see also example 1.1). This spoofy passage identifies future actions and patterns of behaviour—all of them to be avoided, not followed. All are phrased as commands—however, none of them implies that this is what should be done. Quite the contrary: they each convey warnings, wishes, and predictions. Imperative forms are underlined.

7.33   Yule be sorry!
   1. <u>Be</u> well on the way to going completely insane weeks beforehand. <u>Act</u> like an idiot at the Christmas party. <u>Try</u> to reassure yourself that one day, some of the people you work with might consider speaking to you again.
   2. <u>Go</u> beserk on your credit card(s). <u>Get</u> yourself ridiculously in debt. <u>Take</u> every available opportunity to eat like a pig. <u>Put</u> on five kilos you will never lose.
   3. <u>Go</u> to every department store and <u>listen</u> to piped Christmas carols for hours and hours. <u>Get</u> stuck in a lift where the falalalala-la-lalala muzak doesn't stop.
   4. <u>Drive</u> to somewhere terrible for a holiday. <u>Stay</u> in three motels with plumbing that gargles and screams all night.
   5. <u>Miss</u> <u>out</u> on dinner at ten country pubs because you've arrived five minutes late and the cook's gone home (i.e. next door). <u>Break</u> <u>out</u> in acne. <u>Get</u> food poisoning.
      <u>Have</u> a great Christmas and a Happy New Year!

Mock imperatives are akin to ironic imperative uses. In Bagwalal, imperatives are often used this way—one can say about a lazy man: 'May he eat meat, give bread to father' (Dobrushina 2001). Spontaneous mock-imperatives are almost impossible to elicit. They are often a sign of speakers' annoyance, and reflect unpleasant feelings, e.g. *Tell him, if you like, I don't care* and *Go there at your own risk* (Ascoli 1978: 406). They do not presuppose agreement or disagreement.

Just once in my years of fieldwork experience in non-Western societies did I receive a mock-command from a speaker of Tariana, my classificatory sister Olivia from the Tariana community of Santa Rosa. In her opinion, I was paying far too much attention to speakers of a different dialect of Tariana, spoken in Periquitos, whom she was mocking for using occasional Tucanoan forms—such as *ba* 'evidently'. She was so annoyed with me that at one point she told me off for wanting to spoil my Tariana with the Periquitos antics, and finished her diatribe with a mock-command:

Tariana

7.34 ba **pi-a**
      ba 2sg-say
      'Say ba!' (as if you were a speaker of the Tariana of Periquitos who can't speak the language properly, and you still want to be like them)

Mock-commands can be compared to facetious advice. One can imagine a psychologist saying to a young man on how to get ahead: *Choose the right parents* (Bolinger 1967: 347).

Imperatives often form the basis of fixed expressions. In Tariana, Manambu, and Western Apache (de Reuse 2003), imperative forms are employed as attention-getting devices, and in turn-taking in story-telling. A Manambu speaker negotiating their turn in a conversation would say *Wau?* (speak+1sg.IMPV) 'Shall I talk?' (see also §2.4 on this and other person-specific meanings of imperative forms).

Further formulaic and fixed expressions involving imperatives vary across languages. In Mongolian, a negative imperative *büü med!* 'do not know!' has the sense of 'God knows'. In Portuguese, French, and Russian, a sequence of the imperative of 'go' followed by the verb 'know' or 'believe' means 'how do I know, do I know?' (French *Va savoir*, Portuguese *Vai saber*, Russian *Podi znaj* (lit. come:IMPV know:IMPV). The imperfective imperative of 'give' in Russian (*Davaj!*) is used in a meaning similar to *Come on!* in English. In the non-standard language it is used as a farewell formula.

Frequently used imperative forms develop into discourse markers. The Italian form *Guarda!* 'look!' is frequently used in discourse as a means of entitling the speaker to break into a conversation implying that they have something extremely important to say which would require immediate attention (Waltereit 2002). This form is used in situations when no 'looking', or showing, is asked for—the form has developed into a discourse marker meaning 'I have something to say that justifies an interruption'. A similar pathway could be constructed for English *Look* or *Look here*, Spanish *Mira*, or

Portuguese *Olha*: each of these forms is a powerful device of 'floor-seeking' in conversation.[12]

Along similar lines, imperatives of the verbs 'hear', 'look', and 'see' in Modern Hebrew are often used to attract listeners' attention (Malygina 2001: 284):

Modern Hebrew

7.35 **šmaa**   miška lama lanu 'otam yerak-ot?
 listen:IMPV.2sg.masc Mishka why to.us those vegetable-PL.FEM
 'Listen, Mishka, we don't need those vegetables' (lit. why to us those vegetables)

Second person imperative forms of the verbs 'go' and 'come out' used in combination with another second person imperative or a future are used as ironic commands, implying that the speaker cannot possibly perform the action:

7.36 **lex**   ta-a'amin   še-davka be-lev
 go:IMPV.2sg.masc 2sg.FUT-trust+sg.masc that-just in-heart
 yerušalayim '-mca'   'ot-ax
 Jerusalem 1sg.FUT-find   OBJ-you.fem
 'Yeah, right, trust me to meet you right in the centre of Jerusalem!' (meaning: there is no way I am going to meet you in the centre of Jerusalem)

Second person imperatives of verbs 'wait', 'look' and 'listen' are used as interjections to attract the listener's attention in a number of Turkic languages, as shown in 7.37 from Shor (Nasilov et al. 2001: 215).

Shor

7.37 **Kör,** mašýna alt-ýn-ša   kir par-dý-ŋ
 look car bottom-POSS:3sg-DAT enter go-PAST-3sg
 'Look (wait), you might get run down by the car!'

As with the English *look*, Italian *guarda*, and Hebrew *šmaa*, the listener is not expected to wait or to look anywhere—the imperative form attracts the listener's attention to potential danger.

Conventionalized imperative forms—which have lost their directive meanings—develop into interjections and discourse markers. In Jespersen's words, this use (which he terms 'imaginary imperatives') helps explain their further historical developments—'the fact that some imperatives have become prepositions or conjunctions, e.g. *When you feel that, bar accidents, the worst is over* [. . .] *I am not in the habit of beating women at any time, let alone at a lunch party* [. . .]*/ Suppose he were to come, what then?*' The forms *bar, let alone,* and *suppose* are examples of such grammaticalized imperatives; we return to this topic in Chapter 11.[13]

7.3 Imperatives in narratives, statements, questions, and replies

Imperative forms as main predicates in a narrative may refer to unexpected and spontaneous actions, without any implication whatsoever of a command. This usage of second person imperatives in Russian has been called 'dramatic imperative' by Isachenko (2003: 488–502). The dramatic imperative typically involves perfective verb forms, and may be formed on verbs referring to controllable and to uncontrollable actions:

Russian

7.38 I **prisnisj**   mne v etu
And appear.in.dream.REFL.2sg.IMPV to.me in this:ACC.SG.FEM
noch   moja   pokojnaja matushka
night+ACC.SG my+fem.sg late.fem.sg mother
'And my late mother appeared (unexpectedly) in a dream to me this night'

7.39 A sobaka menja **vozjmi** da i **ukusi**
And dog me:ACC.SG take:2sg.IMPV and EMPH bite:2sg.IMPV
'And the dog bit me all of a sudden'

The use of this form—which typically has past reference—and its status in the paradigm of Russian verbs is a bone of contention (see Isachenko 2003: 488–502; Xrakovskij and Volodin 2001: 245; Gronas 2006 for an overview of the literature). From a historical perspective, the 'dramatic imperative' is believed to have arisen as a result of a historical accident: a confusion of the homonymous second and third person singular aorist forms, and second person imperative forms of verbs ending in *-iti* (see Gronas 2006 for a reappraisal and criticism).

'Dramatic imperative' is not limited to Russian: it is productively used in Ukranian, Serbian, Croatian, Bulgarian, and Macedonian; in Czech, Slovak, and Slovene it is rare. The meaning is uniformly that of quick, unexpected action. In Macedonian and Bulgarian the 'dramatic imperative' also has overtones of iterative and intensive action. Gronas (2006: 93–8) suggests that this non-command use of imperative in Slavic languages is a reflex of preterital use of the Indo-European optative form (which gave rise to the imperative paradigm throughout Slavic languages). This use of reflexes of the

Proto-Indo-European optative has been attested in a variety of Indo-Europe-an subgroups, including Tocharian, Iranian, and Armenian (we return to this in §10.2).

Using imperative forms for unexpected and surprising actions goes beyond the Indo-European family. In Tatar, a Turkic language, the meaning of unexpected action and ensuing surprise is conveyed by a combination of a third person singular prohibitive accompanied by the interrogative particle -*me* (which does not have an interrogative meaning in this context):

Tatar (Nasilov et al. 2001: 218)

7.40 Kič   belän   färid   kil-ep   **ker-mä-sen-me**
     evening with   Farid   come-CONV enter-NEG-IMPV:3sg-INTER
     'Unexpectedly, Farid came in the evening'

In Dyirbal, an imperative can be used with a strong pragmatic effect. In 7.41, from the story of the Moon and the dew told to R. M. W. Dixon by George Watson (Nyiyija) on 22 October 1972, the Moon ensures that abso-lutely nothing happens to the grass: this strong effect is conveyed by the use of third person imperative:

Dyirbal (R. M. W. Dixon, p.c.)

7.41 baŋgul   **jabi**   balamaŋgana
     he+ERG   stop.happening:IMPV   them+ACC
     'He stopped (anything happening to) all of them (the grass)'

And in a story about why some snakes are harmless and others dangerous, also from Dyirbal, third person imperative is used, with the meaning of obligation 'had to do it' of an impatient activity: brown snakes—among the most dangerous snakes on the Australian continent—had to run away, or else they would have lost their poisonous fangs:

7.42 [jambal-maŋgan   bayi   balamaŋgan]ₛ **jiŋgali**   **yana**
     brown.snake-MANY   he   them+ACC   run:IMPV   go:IMPV
     guli   ñinay-gu
     be.wild   stay-PURP
     'All the brown snakes ran away, to become wild'

Impatience and strong assertion conspire to create a strong dramatic effect for imperative forms which no longer have any directive meaning. They always imply control of the subject. And this is reminiscent of the way in which the Russian linguist N. Nekrasov (quoted by Isachenko 2003: 498–502) described the Russian 'dramatic imperative': in sentences involving dramatic imperative, the speaker is 'in charge' of the action.

The use of imperative forms in story-telling can be of a different nature. If an indirect speech complement containing an imperative is used as a main clause, the imperative marks free indirect discourse (see Janssen and van der Wurff 1996; Güldemann and von Roncador 2002 on the notion and expression of free indirect discourse). 'Jussive' in Estonian can be used in a similar way (Erelt 2002a).

A whole narrative in Nyangumarta (Australian: Sharp 2004: 186) can consist of a series of imperatives as part of de-subordinated reported speech. 7.43 comes from a story where a dog is commanding a child to do a number of things. The verb of speech does not have to be overtly present:

Nyangumarta

7.43 Pala-ja   yapan   **ma-rra,**   yirti   **ngarta-la**   makanu,
      that-ABL   hot.stones   get-IMPV   stick   break-IMPV   long
      wika   **tili-ji-li**
      fire   flame-AFFIX-IMPV
      'And after that (he told him to) get the hot stones, a cooking stick and to break up the firewood to make a fire'

Reported discourse may develop overtones of information one does not vouch for (Aikhenvald 2004: 132–41). Hence overtones of doubt which may be associated with any verb form, including imperative used in such contexts. In Nyangumarta and Karajarri, from the Australian linguistic area (Sharp 2003a and p.c.), imperative forms can express doubt and probability. The particle *kartiny* 'doubt' occurs with a verb marked as imperative, and so do particles *wayikatu* 'maybe' and *yijakatu* 'unable':

Karajarri

7.44 Yijakatu   **kanti-ya**   pala   kurlu   marrungu
      unable   climb-IMPV   that   bad   tree
      'That old man (lit. 'bad') can't climb the tree'

The particle *janyjalku* 'yet' combines with an imperative-marked verb and the negative particle, meaning 'not yet':

7.45 Majarra   **nga-la-rna**   mayi   janyjalku
      NEG   eat-IMPV-1sg.SUBJ   vegetable.food   yet
      'I haven't eaten yet'

Imperatives may express obligation—an example from Dyirbal (R. M. W. Dixon, p.c.) is in 7.46, from a story about Minyjirral, who revives unconscious people:

Dyirbal

7.46 jañja **ŋinda-jilu**   gunga-ma
now   2sg-EMPHATIC   be.alive-make:IMPV
'Now you're the one that must cure him!'

In Turkic languages, imperative forms can convey the meaning of necessity and obligation. This typically involves a series of unwelcome and hard-to-perform actions:

Tatar (Nasilov et al. 2001: 217)

7.47 **Ešlä**   dä,   **ukÿ**   da,
work.IMPV   PARTICLE   study.IMPV   PARTICLE
bala   da   **üster**
child   PARTICLE   raise:IMPV
'You [have to] work, and study and raise kids [all at the same time]'[14]

In combination with a past tense verb, an imperative indicates that the action should have been completed prior to the moment of speech, and that the speaker regrets that it has not been completed:

7.48 Jaš   čak-ta   **ukÿ**   i-kän...
young   time-LOC   study.IMPV.2pl   be-PAST.PART
'It appears that one ought to have studied when young'

Along similar lines, in Indo-Pakistani Sign Language, imperative markers are often used in deontic meanings of 'must' and 'should' (Zeshan 1999).

Imperative forms occur in rhetorical questions, as shown in the first clause of 7.49, also from Tatar (Nasilov et al. 2001: 217):

7.49 Niček   aŋar-ga   **bar-ÿjk?**   Ul   čakÿr-ma-dÿ   či!
how   he.DAT-DAT   go-IMPV.1pl   he   invite-NEG-PAST:3sg   PARTICLE
'I wonder if we can visit him (lit.: How let's go to him?!) He did not invite (us)!'

In Kerek, and in a number of other Chukotko-Kamchatkan languages, imperatives are used in questions with future reference which do not require an immediate concrete answer (Volodin 2001: 156–7). And in Lezgian, a first person command form, called 'hortative', is used in questions one asks about oneself, questioning one's own intention:[15]

Lezgian (Haspelmath 1993: 150)

7.50 Za   wa-z   wuč   luhu-n?
1:ERG   you-DAT   what:ABS   say-HORT
'What shall I tell you?'

Imperatives in Haya, a Bantu language from Tanzania (Lehman 1977: 144), are frequent replies to questions, with no directive force implied. This is how Christina Lehman describes this use:

While the simple imperative is unambiguous, the possible imperative may possibly represent an imperative, possibly something else, e.g. the answer to a question. To illustrate, let us suppose that we call someone to come inside the house. They answer with a question corresponding to 'why should I come in?' We can answer *ó-ly-e* (2sg-eat-IMPV) meaning 'that you eat', or 'you should eat'. In English, this is most frequently rendered by the infinitive, i.e. 'to eat'. [. . .] However, the important thing is that [. . .] the construction does not have the force of an imperative, but is simply the answer to a question.

In Indo-Pakistani Sign Language, the negative imperative is used in an emphatic negative response, or in a contrastive context to refute the preceding text, along the lines of 'Don't you suppose that's true! You shouldn't think so!' (Zeshan 1999). This emphatic imperative is similar to the imperative as a 'dramatic' device—making the narration more vivid, or the negative reaction stronger.

Imperative forms can have another, quite different use. They may occur in compounds, whereby a common noun or a proper name consists of an imperative form followed by a noun, e.g. Serbo-Croatian *deri-koža* (rip:2sg-IMPV-skin) 'person who rips you off', *jebi-vetar* (copulate:2sg.IMPV-wind) 'useless person, charlatan' (Floricic 2008-b: 21), Russian *grabj-armija* (rob:2sg.IMPV-army) 'plundering army', *sorvi-golova* (tear.off:2sg.IMPV-head) 'reckless person' (Lopatin 1970: 164).[16] Such compounds appear in Italian personal names, e.g. *Bevilacqua* 'Drinkwater' (see Floricic 2008-b, for a literature survey and an argument in favour of these forms containing an imperative).[17] Formations like German *Vergiß-mein-nicht* and its English translation 'forget-me-not', German *Stell-dich-ein* (stand-you:ACC-in) 'rendezvous' (Motsch 1994: 5022), and Russian *djadja-dostanj-vorobushka* (uncle-get:2sg.IMPV-sparrow:ACC.SG) 'a very tall person' also contain imperatives in a fossilized, non-command use.

7.4 Summary

Imperatives cover more than just verbal orders: as we can recall from Chapter 6, they span wishes, hopes, advice, entreaties, requests, pleas, instructions, and so on. Any of these can be ironic. They may require compliance or they may not (Bolinger 1967: 347). Many of these meanings are not-quite-commands. But each of them reflects a directive speech act—inciting, advising, requesting, suggesting, and so on that someone else do something (or not do something, if the imperative is negative).

In this chapter we discussed different kinds of uses for imperative forms. Within complex sentences, imperatives may have conditional, concessive, and contrastive overtones. They may occur in narratives without overtones of command—but with the meaning of vivid, unexpected, important action. Or they may have modal—deontic and epistemic—meanings, which is similar to their meanings in pleas and requests: *Perhaps you could do something for me?* But in many languages non-imperative forms tend to be conventionally used in such mild, humble requests (see Chapter 8). Imperatives occur in curses, blessings, and swearing. Imperative forms can become tokens of speech etiquette and used in greetings, expression of thanks, marks of surprises without any connotation of a command. Or they may be reinterpreted as discourse markers and attention-getting devices: they may then lose their status as verbal forms altogether, and become imperatives in form only—'imaginary imperatives', in Jespersen's (1924: 315) words.

Most non-command meanings of imperatives can be linked to the imperatives' major, directive meanings which slide into modal expressions of obligation, necessity, possibility, and others. Imperatives are thus often polysemous and versatile. But in some languages, they are not versatile enough—then other forms step in to help. This is the topic of the next chapter.

Notes

1. Non-command imperatives have been described as 'pseudo-imperatives' (Ascoli 1978), 'apparent' imperatives (Bolinger 1967), or 'imaginary' imperatives (Jespersen 1924: 315).
2. See Davies (1986: 152–203), Huddleston (2002: 938–9) for further discussion. Russell (2007) provides an alternative discussion of the potential ambiguity of verbal imperative forms in conditional coordinations.
3. An imperative can be linked to a non-imperative clause expressing possible consequence through a disjunction, as in *Open the window or you'll suffer the consequences*, appears to express a straightforward command, stating the consequences of non-compliance.
4. Huddleston (2002: 938) notes that examples like 7.11 are comparatively rare, but possible. Further, similar examples of imperative forms in a conditional sense in connection with a past tense, are in Jespersen (1924: 314), e.g. *Give him time, and he was generally equal to the demands of suburban custom.* The second clause can be declarative, exclamative, or interrogative. Bolinger (1967, 1977: 134–67) offers further discussion and interpretation of conditional imperatives in English.

5. In addition to their conditional meanings, imperative-like forms in English can occur in complex sentences where they acquire concessive interpretation, e.g. *Try as you may, you won't convince them* and *Look which way they would, nothing could be seen.* Davies (1986: 219–28) provides a comprehensive discussion of their similarities with imperatives. In particular, they appear to be negated in the same way as imperatives. We will see further on in this section that in many languages of Eurasia, imperative forms can acquire concessive interpretation which can be considered a type of counterfactual conditional.

6. Jespersen (1924: 314) remarks: 'As the imperative has no particular ending in English, one might perhaps feel inclined to think that these sentences contained infinitives (though how used?) Parallel uses in other languages show us, however, clearly that they contain imperatives.' He adds examples from German, Danish, French, Latin, and Greek. In Latin, imperative forms can also express a proviso, as in *ausculta, scies* 'listen and you will know', *modo sis veni huc: invenies infortunium* 'just come over here and you'll be unlucky' (Palmer 1954: 317).

7. In Rumanian, an imperative accompanied with the subordinator *de* can occur in purposive clauses (Mallinson 1986: 73).

8. A similar phenomenon was described for Tukang Besi, where prohibitive expresses an undesirable result, i.e. a negative equivalent of 'in order to' (Donohue 1999a: 60).

9. These speech formulae, conventionalized and empty of any meaning as they may sound, appear to be very 'catchy': as the influence of English spreads across the world, some of these formulae get translated and spread as tokens of an 'upmarket' jargon. Radio announcers in Russia say now and again, at the end of their presentations, *Budjte bezopasny* 'Be safe', which raises the eyebrows of many a traditional speaker of the language (Elena Shmeleva, p.c.).

10. Along similar lines, the farewell terms *proschaj(te), prosti* are etymologically linked to the verb meaning 'forgive'; however, as Isachenko points out, the semantic link between farewell and forgiveness is lost in Modern Russian. Historically, this goes back to an old Russian custom whereby people would ask each other for forgiveness for any kind of distress they could have caused to their interlocutor, before they parted from each other.

11. Also see Tosco (2001: 280–81) on imperative forms in curses, oaths, and prayers in Dhaasanac, a Cushitic language from Ethiopia. Some languages have special 'benedictive' forms for blessings and for curses, e.g. Ladakhi (Koshal 1979: 227). Kambaata employs a sort of jussive for blessings and curses (Treis MS). Whether or not a V-form of an imperative is compatible with imprecative semantics in Russian is an open question. Some normative speakers maintain that an imprecation *Idi na huj* (lit. 'go to a penis') cannot be used with a polite plural ending *-te* (Valeria Gerlin, p.c.).

12. See Brinton (1996) on the pathways of the rise of discourse markers; and further references in Waltereit (2002).

13. Jespersen (1924: 315). Isachenko (2003: 505–7) provides a list of particles and modal words grammaticalized from imperative forms in Russian and Slovak, e.g. Russian *pustj, puskaj* 'let', and *podi* 'maybe, dare say'.

14. Similar examples abound in Russian, cf. *Vse pojdut guljatj, a ja sidi, chitaj knizhki* 'Everybody will go out, but I have to sit, read books' (lit. 'but I sit! read books!') (Gronas 2006: 98; see also Xrakovskij and Volodin 2001).

15. Questions and commands have a similar structure in Chukotko-Kamchatkan languages (see also Volodin 1976 on Itelmen). Some links between these are found in other languages. In Dime, an Omotic language from Ethiopia (Seyoum 2008: 122–3), the plural addressee in imperatives is marked with -*is*; this morpheme also occurs in content questions addressed to second person plural. In Maale, also Omotic, the impolite imperative is similar (but not identical) to the negative interrogative construction (Amha 2001: 127). However, there is an intonational difference between them. In Konso, a Cushitic language from Ethiopia (Oda, forthcoming), a 'warning' imperative contains the negative form of the future imperfective interrogative. In Haida (Enrico 2003: 131) the interrogative marker can cooccur with imperatives. An additional connection lies in the possibility of using questions as commands, with stronger or with weaker force (see, for instance, Amha 2001: 127 on this phenomenon in Amharic). We return to this in the next chapter.

16. These are said to be non-productive, and are highly lexicalized (their meaning is loosely associated with 'the action linked to the noun' following the imperative form). Such compounds are also attested in surnames and nicknames, and are more widely represented in dialects than in the literary language. Many of them may be individual creations of ingenious speakers: Emma Breger (p.c.), originally from the Odessa area, supplied me with a compound: *razdaj-beda* (give.away-trouble) 'someone who gives everything away to their own detriment'.

17. An issue for Romance languages, and also for English, is whether the verb form can be consistently analysed as an imperative, or as an indicative, or as a root form, in compounds like English *Johnny-come-lately*, French *gratte-ciel* 'sky-scraper', Portuguese *arranha-céu* 'sky-scraper', *papa-defuntos* 'undertaker' (in both literal and metaphorical sense, as in *o tarado papa-defuntos do nosso centro* 'a randy sex maniac the undertaker of our centre'), and so on. There is no such issue in Serbo-Croatian or in Russian, where the forms involved are unequivocally second person imperatives.

8

Imperatives in disguise

Versatile as they are, imperative forms are not the only way of phrasing a command, a request, or an invitation. An imperative may sound too embarrassingly imperious and imposing. An essentially non-imperative form is then co-opted, in order to 'save face' or to avoid direct confrontation, to comply with existing hierarchies, social relationships and etiquette, or to provide a more nuanced way of conveying a plethora of directive speech acts. Such 'command strategies' can be viewed as filling a gap—that is, expressing a meaning a straightforward imperative may lack.

We can recall from Chapter 6 that the English imperative spans quite a few meanings including orders, commands, demands, requests, pleas, entreaties, advice, recommendations, warnings, instructions, invitations, and good and bad wishes. A directive can be expressed through what looks like a question or a statement, with different meaning overtones and illocutionary force.[1]

Many command strategies reflect what Brown and Levinson (1987: 70) call 'conventionalized indirectness'. So, *Can you pass the salt?* would be read as a request by all native speakers. It will hardly ever be taken to be a question about the addressee's strength or capacity to perform this action. *Why don't you do some work, Norman?* is not an enquiry to an underperforming academic for a reason why he is not doing his job—it is a directive to do some work.[2]

Using a straightforward imperative often implies what Brown and Levinson (1987) call 'a face-threatening act'. Many of the imperative strategies are a way of avoiding confrontation threatening face; they can be considered as implicit, 'off-the-record' ways of handling potentially problematic situations. At the same time, many of the non-imperative directives are versatile: the same form may have polite or stern overtones, depending on context, intonation, and body language.

Non-imperative directives have a directive pragmatic function. Formally, they may share features with other clause types—declarative or interrogative. Or they can develop into minor clause types of their own (see §8.3). Non-imperative directives corroborate the principle of a mismatch between directive function and non-prototypically directive form. Likewise, imperative forms may be used in non-directive functions (as we saw in Chapter 7). Both non-imperative directives and non-directive imperatives confirm the idea of pragmatic versatility of speech act. In addition, once the directive function becomes the main one for a non-imperative directive, they provide a pool for developing new directive-only forms—and new imperative paradigms.

And we recall from §2.1.4 that numerous languages of the world—including most from the Athabascan family, and some from Indigenous Australia— have no imperative forms at all. Commands are expressed with other means, including imperfective aspect, future, and other modalities.[3] Each of these may develop into a dedicated command form, and thus give rise to a new imperative paradigm. We return to this in Chapter 10.

We now turn to recurrent techniques employed in non-imperative directives: interrogative forms (§8.1), statements (§8.2), free-standing dependent clauses (§8.3), and then nominalized forms and elliptical expressions (§8.4). At the end of §8.4, we mention other ways of framing directives without using an imperative form. Importantly, it is NOT the case that any form can be understood as a command in any language. Nor is it the case that each technique for a command strategy will have the same meaning cross-linguistically. We turn to these points in the summary in §8.5.

8.1 Interrogatives as directives

A request, an invitation, or an offer can be conveyed by what looks like a question. In English, interrogatives are used for requests; especially if 'the speaker and the addressee are not intimates' (Huddleston 2002: 939–40). A directive cast as an interrogative tends to be more polite. That is, *Can you move your car* is more polite than *Move your car*, even if accompanied by a moderating *please* or *kindly*.[4] But if the same clause is uttered with an impatient peremptory tone of voice, *Can you move your car*, it is not polite any more. Whether a request is polite or not also depends on the what is being commanded: *Can you move you car* is more easily interpretable as a polite request than something like *Can you get out of here, Norman, and stop pestering me*.

English boasts a wide variety of interrogative directives. The most frequently described ones involve (a) your—i.e. the addressee's—ability to do something; (b) your desire or willingness to do something; (c) the necessity or the obligation; and (d) the reason:

8.1a   Can you move your car   —ABILITY

8.1b   Would you like to sign here/Will you sign here   —DESIRE/WILLINGNESS

Questioning a necessity or an obligation is an alternative to a negative command:

8.1c   Must you talk so loud   —NECESSITY/OBLIGATION

If cast as a straightforward imperative, 8.1c corresponds to *Don't talk so loud*. In contrast, a question referring to a negative reason, *Why don't you...*, as in 8.1d, is in fact a positive directive:

8.1d   Why don't you come to the blackboard   —REASON

The directive in 8.1d can sound nice and friendly. In another context, however, a question *why don't you?* may have different overtones. Mr Button, from Scott Fitzgerald's short story 'The curious case of Benjamin Button', goes to the maternity ward where his wife has given birth and discovers that his son was born as an old man. He can't believe his eyes; he wants this nightmare to go away, and wants the nurse to tell him that the old man who says he is his son is lying. The desperate father says to the nurse: *Tell him he is wrong, why don't you?* He knows that she is not going to deny the horrid truth. Whether this is really a question or not is hard to know: intonation would be crucial here, something to which we have no access in the written text.

Ability questions in English 'lend themselves to indirect directions, since a likely reason for me to be interested in your ability to do something is that I want you to do it' (Huddleston 2002: 940). An ability question/request typically starts with *can you, could you, is it possible (for you), are you able, will/ would you be able*. The forms with *could/would* (called 'preterite' by Huddleston) are regarded as more polite.

Any ability question can be negated—*can't you, couldn't you* and so on. In English, negative questions add an emotive component—such as impatience: *Can't you talk a bit louder* suggests that the addressee should be able to talk louder, but for some reason is not doing so. Or they may sound more persuasive: *Couldn't you stay a bit longer?*[5]

Ability questions as mild commands and requests are common cross-linguistically, though by no means universal. Questions as requests are common in Turkish (Kornfilt 1997: 45); an interrogative request can be softened by using the abilitative affix: *sinema-ya gel-ebil-ir-mi-sin* (cinema-DAT come-ABIL-AORIST-QUESTION-2sg) 'Would you like to come to the movies?', lit. 'Are you able to come to the movies', is milder than *sinema-ya gel-ir-mi-sin*

(cinema-DAT come-AORIST-QUESTION-2sg) 'Would you come to the movies?'
Ability questions in Spanish are a conventionalized way of getting someone to
do something without imposing too much (Haverkate 1976: 225).

In Japanese, ability interrogatives are used to make requests with verbs of
giving and getting:

8.2 hon o   yonde-mora-e-masu   ka
     book OBJECT.MARKER read-get-POTENTIAL-POLITE   QUESTION
     'Can I have you read a book?'[6]

However, Hinds (1984: 183) remarks that ability questions in Japanese are
typically information-seeking requests: so, if one asks the equivalent of 'Can
you reach the pepper' in Japanese, this is understood not as a request for the
pepper, but 'rather a request for information about one's ability to reach to a
certain point'. A negative question as an invitation in Japanese is considered
more polite than its positive counterpart.[7]

Positive ability questions are not conventionalized as commands in Russian. Comrie (1984b: 281) remarks that 'if you tried it in Russian, the reaction
would be "What's this guy trying to do?"' In the colloquial language, an
ability question can be used as a peremptory command, often with an
overtone of annoyance at something that ought to have been done, but hasn't:

8.3a Ty   mozhesh   ubratj?
      you.sg   can.PRES.2sg clean.up
      'Can you clean up?' (you ought to have done so, but haven't; I am
      annoyed with you)

Negative ability questions with the verb in the conditional mood are conventionally used for polite requests:

8.3b Ne mogli   by li   vy   zakrytj okno?
      NEG can+PAST+pl COND QUESTION you.PL/POLITE close   window:ACC
      'Could you close the window?'[8]

Similarly, in Cavineña a very soft and polite request can be framed
as a polar question with potential inflection and negative particle, as 8.4
(Guillaume 2008: 186):

8.4 E-tya-u=ama=mi-ra=ekwana?
     POT-give-POT-NEG=2sg-ERG=1pl
     'Couldn't you give (a radio transmitter) to us (pl)?'

Desire/willingness questions can be seen as having a natural link with directives: in Huddleston's words (2002: 940), 'if you want or are willing to do something you are likely to comply with a request to do it. Typical formulae include *will you/would you, would you like to/care to/be so kind as to, would you mind*. The form *would* makes a request sound more tentative, less imposing and thus more polite. Interestingly, *want* with *do* is rather less polite, as in *Do you want to clear the table so that we can have lunch* is more like a demand than a mild request. Intentional forms—such as *Are you going to tidy your room?*—have an overtone of doubt as to whether you intend to do what you should do, and are thus less polite.

Questioning the desire or the ability of the addressee to carry out a request in Georgian is a way of asking somebody to do something (Harris 1984). These request-questions are pronounced with question intonation:

8.5   ginda   k̦ari   daxuro?
       you/want/it/PRES   door   you/close/it/SUBJUNC.II
       'Do you want to close the door?'

Along similar lines, a desire question in Spanish, *¿Quiere abrirme la puerta?* 'Will you open the door for me?', has the form of an interrogative, but 'the speaker's intent is not to ask a question, but to make a request' (Haverkate 1976: 225).

Necessity questions in English usually involve *must* or *have* (*need, be necessary,* and others are also possible). These directives can hardly be considered polite—a question such as *Do you have to stay here, Norman?* implies that I regard Norman staying here as undesirable; and a directive cast as a question has a negative bias. Necessity questions are thus a way of phrasing an instruction not to do something, or to stop doing it.[9]

Reason questions as directives are somewhat similar to the necessity question-directives: their polarity value is opposite to what is being requested. That is, *Why don't you move away* is a directive to move away, and *Why move away* implies 'don't move away'. In English a 'why'-question has the force of a rebuke if the verb is in the present progressive or accompanied by future *will*, as in *Why will you not open the door* or *Why don't you close the door?*, or with *Why not?* as in *Why not close the door?*

The same applies to third person subjects in desire/willingness question-directives: *Will everyone remember to sign the register* is an example. Along similar lines, a deontic directive can occur with third person, as in *Must they talk so loud?* And so can a reason question-directive, as in *Why doesn't Norman do some work for a change.* In Huddleston's words (p. 941), all these have 'indirect directive force, suggesting that you should convey the directive to whoever is to comply'.

Similar questions can be used as first person inclusive directives; they generally involve *shall we* or *why*, as in *Why don't we go now?* or *Why waste our time talking to Norman?* That is, reason questions-directives in English are conventionalized and versatile. Not so in other languages.

Georgian appears to be rather similar to English in the way questions are used for requests (see 8.5). But there is one interesting difference: 'in Georgian, it seems to be impossible to use as a request a question concerning the addressee's reasons for not carrying out an action (cf. English "Why don't you...?" "Why not...?")' (Harris 1984: 101). An example like 8.6 is not a request – though its English translation may be mistakenly interpreted as such. In Georgian, this is an 'inquiry, with an added nuance of rebuke or expression of irritation':

8.6　ķars　raṭom　ar　daxurav?
　　　door　why　NEG　you:close:it:FUT
　　　'Why aren't you closing the door?/Why won't you close the door' (an inquiry with a nuance of irritation)

Are questions used as directives still questions? The term 'whimperative'— coined by Sadock (1970)—reflects their ambiguous status. Their intonation patterns may be shared with commands. Bolinger (1982: 16–17) notes that the falling intonation on a 'why' question in a directive function 'approaches a command' (but they do not have to: we can recall that 8.5, from Georgian, is said to have question intonation). And in Sweet's (1891: 175) words,

the meaning of an imperative sentence may also be expressed by a sentence in the general interrogative form, such as *will you be quiet!* = *be quiet!* But as such sentences are uttered with a falling tone—being accordingly written with a note of exclamation—they are formally intermediate between the two classes, and may therefore be called imperative-interrogative sentences.

A question used as a directive—expressing a request or an offer, or even an order—may keep its literal meaning, and at the same time is conventionalized as a request (Searle 1975: 68–70; Morgan 1978). A useful test for whether a question-directive can be understood as a question asks how it can be responded to.

In Comrie's (1984b: 281) words (emphasis added),

it's true that 'Would you open the door' is normally going to be used as a request, perhaps even as a command. The usual response would be to carry out that request. But notice that a possible response is 'No'. If someone says 'Would you open the door'

I can say 'No, I am not going to'. I could even give you a reason. We're in a photographic darkroom and you want to go out. You say 'Would you open the door'. I can say 'No, I'm afraid, I can't at present because we are developing a film. If I open the door the light will come in and the film will be ruined'. So, particularly if I give you a reason for not carrying out your request, the reply 'no' is perfectly in order. *In some sense, there is still the residue of a question even in the literal interpretation of that structure.* Likewise, if you use the verb 'can' in a polite request, 'Can you reach me a book from that shelf?', one possible responsible answer is 'No, I'm afraid I can't. I'm not tall enough to reach it'.

The following anecdote from real life corroborates the reality of the 'residue of a question' in ability questions-directives. When he was Departmental Chair at the Australian National University, Professor R. M. W. Dixon sent a memo to faculty members, worded as follows: 'Can you come to a staff meeting from four till five p.m. on Monday' (this was followed by the agenda for the meeting). One faculty member replied: 'I can't come because I have people coming for dinner that night and I have to go home early and cook.' The memo contained a directive, but the faculty member was able to interpret it as a question about whether he could come or not. Learning from this, Dixon changed his phrasing: all future memos simply said: 'There will be a faculty meeting.' A stern directive cast as a prediction does not allow any room for misunderstandings, or for arguing. We return to statements as alternatives to commands, requests, and suchlike in §8.2.

The question overtones of question-directives are rather marginal—this is corroborated by the fact that they have to be put in context to be understood as questions: if someone says *Can you pass the salt,* and the other one says 'No, I can't', they will have to provide an explanation why—whether the salt is too far away, or it is against their convictions to pass the salt, or anything else. However, for some other question-directives, a straightforward answer would be weird, and betray lack of understanding. A French linguist was working as au pair in the States. Her English was adequate, but hardly one hundred per cent. One morning her employer said to her 'Why don't you sweep the floor today'. The linguist understood this as a reason question and explained that she was not going to sweep the floor because she was intending to do washing and ironing. This produced embarrassment—the employer did not intend her 'Why don't you . . .' as a question 'Why?', she used this as a directive: the linguist was to sweep the floor and that was it.[10]

This anecdotal evidence of misunderstanding and resulting miscommunication points towards one fact: that it is not true that everything goes and every language can use any construction to express a command or a request. Some constructions are more natural and more conventionalized than others.

Another illustrative example comes from Azeb Amha's grammar of Maale, an Omotic language from Ethiopia (Amha 2001: 127). Most speakers of Maale are proficient in Amharic, and there is a certain amount of influence of Amharic on Maale. We can recall (Table 4.3, and §6.4.1) that Maale has an impolite imperative; its form is similar to the negative interrogative. Amha remarks:

in some Ethiopian languages such as Amharic, an emphatic order is expressed by interrogative forms [...] the imperative verb *hid* (go:2masc.sg.IMPV) expresses simple order whereas a negative interrogative form, i.e. *atthedïm* 'Aren't you going?', accompanied with a special intonation expresses emphatic order. The latter kind of imperative in Amharic is understood as entailing punishment if the order is not complied with. Maale speakers interviewed were not sure of such a connection between the imperative and the interrogative,

stressing the pronunciation difference between the forms. We can conclude that the 'emphatic order' use of an interrogative in Amharic has not as yet made its way into Maale.

In many other languages, asking a question is tantamount to giving a command, but this may have to be contextualized for the question to be understood the way it is intended. A Manambu-speaking mother was annoyed at her daughter for drinking too much water in a place where there was no toilet. She tried to stop her daughter from having another glass of water by shouting:

8.7   toilet yi-k-ñina   tami akrəl   tə-na
      toilet go-FUT-2fem.sg+LK   area where be/have-ACT.FOC-3fem.sgBAS.NP
      'Where is the place for you to go to the toilet?' (meaning 'Don't drink too much!')

This is not a conventionalized command: rather, it is an ad hoc use of a rhetorical question (which does not require an answer). In the context, it had the effect of a strong command—no more water was in fact consumed.

Other kinds of questions can be conventionalized as directives. In fact, polar questions in Georgian may express a request; in 8.9 the question particle *xom* accompanied by the negation *ar* makes the request more polite than a positive question in 8.8 (Harris 1984: 98–101):

8.8   ɣvinos   momiṭan?
      wine   you:bring:me:it:FUT
      'Will you bring me (some) wine?'

8.9 ɣvinos   xom   ar   momiṭan?
     wine   QUESTION   NEG   you:bring:me:it:FUT
     'Won't you bring me (some) wine?' (politer than 8.8)

A directive interpretation is not available for every tense–aspect combination in Georgian. If a question contains a present or an imperfective form it cannot be interpreted as a request—8.10 is nothing but an information question:

8.10 ɣvino   mogakvs   čemtvis?
      wine   you:bring:it:PRES   me/for
      'Are you bringing me wine?'

Polar questions as polite requests in Kannada are always cast in future tense (Wali and Koul 1997: 44). This is another example of how a directive interpretation for what looks like an interrogative can be reserved for a limited set of forms.

Polar questions are used as polite requests in Mongolian,[11] and in Kannada. Example 8.11 (Sridhar 1990: 38) contains *svalpa* 'a little', softening a command (diminutives as command softeners were discussed in §6.3):

8.11 svalpa   majjige   koḍutti:ra:?
      a.little   buttermilk   give.NON.PAST-pl/HON-QUESTION
      'Will you give me some buttermilk?'

Using a question is a polite way of phrasing a request in Matses (Fleck forthcoming: 932).

8.12 ada   wëdëṣhka-tsia-ø
      UNCERT   dig-NON.PAST.COND-INTER:1/2
      'Would you (be willing to) dig?'

In Dom, from Chimbu Province of Papua New Guinea, interrogative-directives are a way of asking for permission, or for expressing polite requests. A mild way of asking for tobacco involves saying 'Brother, do you have tobacco?' rather than just 'Give me tobacco' (Tida 2006: 156–7). Along similar lines, a polite request in Shor (a Turkic language) may be expressed through a conjugated interrogative -*BA*- (*pe*- in 8.12) and the optative form of the verb (Nasilov et al. 2001: 212):

8.13 Sen   maɣa   sýjla-p   per-gej   pe-di-ŋ?
      you   1sg:DAT PRES.CONV   give.AUX-OPT   INTER-PAST-2sg
      'Will you please present [this] to me?'

A question can have a limited use as a directive. In Ainu (Tamura 2000: 248), interrogative sentences as ways of phrasing mild requests correspond to statements expressing approval of an action the addressee is hoping for or is requesting. That is, a way of seeking permission to accompany somebody is by saying 'Is it OK if I go with you?' Interrogatives as directives in Northern Subanen are versatile: 'depending on the situation and the voice quality of the speaker, an interrogative command can have a mitigating or an aggravating effect.' An exasperated mother rebukes the boy by using an interrogative with a directive force:[12]

8.14 Tuma kia....ʕ əndiʕ=ʕa   mə-ligu?
      why   that   NEG.IRR-2sg.ABS   ST.PAT.IRR-bathe
      'Why are you not taking a bath?'

The question words 'where', 'why', and 'when' 'suggest laziness and unreasonableness on the part of the addressee' (this is somewhat similar to 'where' in 8.7 from Manambu). The command is strong, because of the presupposition on the part of the speaker—annoyed that the child is apparently reluctant to perform the action.

We conclude that the use of questions as directives is far from universal. Some grammarians explicitly point this out—almost as a curious fact. In her analysis of the imperative in Haya (a Bantu language from Northwestern Tanzania), Lehman (1977: 148) remarks: 'There do not seem to be cases of questions with imperative force, a popular ploy in English. The elicited data indicate that questions cannot be used with indirect force in Haya, but must be taken literally. Thus, "can you pass the salt?" means just that; it is not a request that you pass the salt.'[13] And we have seen above that an interrogative directive is not always a polite or a mild alternative to a command cast in imperative form. Choosing a directive strategy is not arbitrary, and the choice is not universally predictable: the degree of conventionalization of each technique is what plays a decisive role. We return to the interactions of pragmatic functions, speech acts, and linguistic form in §8.5.

8.2 Declaratives as directives

Statements can have the pragmatic effect of a command, or a directive of any sort. In Sweet's (1891: 175) words, 'although imperative sentences are the most convenient means we have of expressing hortation, we can also express it by purely declarative sentences, such as *I beg you to come, I insist on your doing it at once.'* Performative expressions imply a direct order, request, or invitation to do something:

8.15   I order/direct/beg/implore/invite you to return her letters
8.16   Smoking is strictly prohibited

Indirect commands, instructions, and further ways of getting or enticing the addressee to do something (or not) may involve mentioning the speaker's wants or needs, or the addressee's future actions, or general necessity or obligation (Huddleston 2002: 941):

8.17a   I want/need/would like someone to hold the ladder
8.17b   You are going to/will apologise
8.17c   You must/have to/have got to come in now

In each of these cases, a directive is not particularly polite. Huddleston (2002: 941) remarks that 'politeness can be achieved [...] by combining declarative and interrogative in a doubly indirect directive' in an example like 8.18—this can be viewed as a combination of a declarative and an interrogative directive.

8.18   I wonder whether you would mind moving your car a little.

The form of the verb in a clause often contributes to a directive interpretation of a statement. We can recall, from the previous section, how only some tense forms occur in interrogative-directives, while the use of other tense forms warrants only the interrogative interpretation: thus, 8.10, from Georgian, cannot be interpreted as a request because it is cast in the present.

Future forms often have a directive force—8.17b, from English, is a stern directive expressing an obligation. Along similar lines, in Cavineña a statement marked with imperfective in its future meaning can imply a very strong order which cannot be disobeyed (Guillaume 2008: 185). The future suffix in Chemehuevi can impart a directive meaning to a clause, with an overtone of obligation, 'you are to VERB'.[14] This is similar to Navajo, where an obligation is rendered by the future tense forms (Young and Morgan 1969: 53–4).

However, it would be erroneous to believe that a directive as a future statement has the effect of a strong command in any language. Quite the opposite obtains in Jarawara: here, 'a mild command may use future modality' (Dixon 2005: 395–6). In 8.19, a Branco wants a favour from Okomobi, his Indian companion. In the narrative (told by Okomobi to R. M. W. Dixon) he uses the future form, rather than imperative: imperative is 'pragmatically direct', and the future is less so:

8.19 kobati   o-tenehe   kijo ti-na-habana   ti-ke
      Friend   1sg-scrotum:masc   rub   2sgA-AUX-FUT.fem   2sg-DECL.fem
      'Friend, could you rub it (the medicinal plant) on my balls?' (lit. you'll rub it (on) my balls (where they were bitten by an ant))

Or a speaker could use intention modality to express a mild command. When the village football team asked Dixon to take their photograph, the intention suffix was used:

8.20 Jobeto! otara tira ti-na-habone   ti-ke   [tika   makina jaa]
      name   1excO take 2sgA-AUX-INTER.fem 2sg-DECL.fem 2sgPOSS machine PERI
      'Jobeto! will you take us (i.e. our photo) (lit. you should take us) with your machine (camera)?'

In Huallaga Quechua, future tense can be used as a polite way to give a command (Weber 1989: 102, 440):

8.21 Paala-yki-ta   mana-ku-shayki
      shovel-2pers-OBJ   ask-REFL-1>2FUT
      'Could I borrow your shovel?' (lit. I will ask you for your shovel)

Along similar lines, in Nyangumarta an imperative is perceived as 'a very direct way of speaking, and often a more respectful way of issuing a command is to use the future tense' (Sharp 2004: 185).[15]

The future can be used in a command in Arapaho—and again, with different connotations from those of a future command in English:

Whereas in English use of the future tense as an imperative tends to constitute a very strong and peremptory command, emphasizing the authority of the speaker ('you *will* go to school today, young man!'), in Arapaho the use of the future often makes the utterance not really a command at all, but instead a recognition of the strong authority of the other person, who cannot be commanded, or prevented from acting, but only deferred to. (Cowell 2007: 57)

The indicative forms—future among them—occupy the lowest point in the hierarchy of command forms in Arapaho (Figure 9.8), in terms of speaker's agency and authority, with the emphatic imperative being at the highest point.

The meaning of the future in a directive may correlate with the immediacy of a required action. In Motuna, the definite future with second person expresses an urgent command, which must be fulfilled by the addressee definitely and immediately. This is consistent with its general meaning, expressing 'that an event or the inception of a state will take place immediately after the speech moment'. In contrast, the corresponding imperative expresses a general command which must be fulfilled by the addressee some time in the future (Onishi 1996: 49; 1994: 459–60). In Modern Hebrew, a future form is employed in lieu of regular imperative which is considered too harsh: future forms are considered a politer option.[16]

Statements cast in the present may have the force of strong commands or instructions: a memo to the members of a university department saying *There will be a staff meeting on Monday* excludes any potential doubt or argument. Similarly, declarative sentences in Moses Columbia Salish can have 'imperative force'; they translate as strong instructions (Mattina 1999: 13). And in Haida (Enrico 2003: 127), a command expressed with a declarative sentence with the indefinite pronoun as subject frequently has a 'chiding flavor', that is, having 'a common implication that the addressee's present behavior is deficient or wrong'.

However, these overtones are hardly universal. A declarative clause in Maori may have the force of a weak command (Bauer et al. 1993: 37 suggest that this is particularly common for female speakers). In Tuvaluan (Besnier 2000: 38), commands and suggestions can be expressed with constructions which are structurally indistinguishable from statements. Statements as 'generic' imperatives have been described for Marathi. That is, 8.22 can be understood as an instruction to read newspapers every day (Pandharipande 1997: 58).

8.22 rodz   pepar   wātslā   tar   bātmī   kalṭe
      everyday   newspaper   read.PAST-3sg.masc   then   news   understand
      'If one reads the newspaper every day then one gets/receives the news'
      (that is, you should read the newspaper every day)

In Marathi, statements in present tense can function as 'indirect suggestions by the speaker to the addressee', either with third person plural ending on the verb or cast as a passive:

8.23 kaḍak   unhāt   aśī   kāma   kelī   dzāt   nāhīt
      scorching   heat+LOC   like.this   jobs   do.PAST.3pl.n   go.pass   not.3pl
      'One should not do such jobs in (such) scorching heat' (lit. Such jobs are
      not done in such scorching heat)

We can recall, from §4.4.2, that passive and impersonal declarative forms occur in commands, with overtones of politeness.[17] In instances like the one in 8.23, the addressee is not overtly mentioned—which is a way of minimizing imposing one's will onto another person, and thus 'saving face'. Using an impersonal marker *ba-* in Haya is a means of weakening the force of a directive (Lehman 1977: 147): saying *ba-m-p' ómwóoño* (they/IMPERSONAL-me-give salt) is a polite way of asking for salt, cast as a declarative. The impersonal prefix allows one to avoid 'making any personal reference to the individual to whom one is speaking. Such a form could be used with visitors, by a prospective son-in-law to the father, to one's in-laws, and so on. Such a use is a frozen polite form conventionalized to imperative force.' Similarly, a passive statement in Korean (Sohn 1986: 274) 'usually gives a sense of distance between the speaker and the hearer due to the shading of I personalization'.[18]

This correlates with one of the strategies for avoiding face-threatening acts (Brown and Levinson 1987: 226): 'over-generalizing' involves omitting the addressee of a potentially face-threatening directive—such as *If that door is shut completely, it sticks* or *The lawn has got to be mown*. The addressee is—superficially—given the choice of deciding whether or not the general rule applies to them or not. But depending on the context, and the content, of an instruction cast in passive, the implication may be rather face-threatening: a notice saying *Pets are not allowed* or *Thongs are prohibited* is a simple statement of fact understood as a stern instruction to be followed. The addressee does not really have a choice. This illustrates the potential versatility and deceptive indirectness of non-imperatively phrased directives.[19]

Other tense forms of declarative verb can occur as directives. In Chemehuevi, a verb with a past tense marker *-vɨɨ* can be used in a command meaning, in a straightforwardly directive or a deontic 'must' meaning. Press (1979: 80–81) remarks that subjects and objects of such verbs are marked just as in an indicative clause, and that formally such verbs have nothing in common with imperatives proper. A sentence like 8.24 is ambiguous: it may either be a command or a statement about the past:[20]

8.24   kaniʃi-waʃi-vɨɨ-w
        visit-go-past-you[pl]
        'You went and visited' or 'You must go and visit'

According to one consultant, these forms differ from imperatives in that they are 'more "future" in intent, commanding something to be done after the speaker leaves', while the imperative forms are 'more immediate'. An indicative past tense form with first person plural conveys an invitation to perform an action in Tatar, Uzbek, and Shor: however, this is mostly the case with verbs of unidirectional motion or 'terminative' verbs denoting a sequence of action: in 8.25, from Uzbek, the past tense of 'go' means 'let's go':[21]

8.25 Qani,   ket-di-k   metro-ga
     well   go.away-PAST.1pl   Metro-DAT
     'Come on, let's go to the Metro station'

Along similar lines, perfective forms are commonly used in Ku Waru as strong commands or exhortations (Merlan and Rumsey 1991: 327–8; Alan Rumsey p.c.):

8.26a ola   molun
      up   be/stand-PERF-2sg
      'Stand up!!!'

8.26b pùmul
      go.PERF-1pl
      'Let's go!'

These forms are limited to second person and first person non-singular.[22]

Negation.   A declarative directive may have to include *negation*. In Maori, any negative sentence can occur as a command if the speaker has absolute authority (Bauer et al. 1993: 37).

Negative statements can be conventionally used as directives of a different kind. In Kuuk Thayorre, an Australian language from the Cape York peninsula (Gaby 2007: 494), negative statements are interpreted as polite commands, 'just like a speaker of English would use an interrogative construction to make a request, as in *Would you shut that window for me?* and offers as in *Would you like some tea?*. The statement in 8.27 implies the speaker's desire for the opposite:

8.27 nhunt   kaar   ngathun   mit   rirk-nhan
     2sgNOM   NEG   1sgDAT   work   DO-GO.AND:NON.PAST
     'Would you do some work for me?' (lit. you won't work for me)

The statement that the addressee is not going to eat, in 8.28, represents an indirect and polite offer to eat:[23]

8.28 nhunt   kaar   mungk-nhan
     2sgERG   NEG   eat-GO.AND:NON.PAST
     'Would you like something to eat?' (lit. you are not going to eat)

These examples 'should be understood in the context of a sociolinguistic setting in which direct commands and questions are dispreferred in order to protect negative face'. We can recall from Chapter 6 that 'negative face' is a cover term for as 'the basic claim to territories, personal preserve, rights to non-distraction—i.e. to freedom of action and freedom of imposition' (Brown and Levinson 1987: 61).

Cultural practices and attitudes provide additional motivation for the ways in which face-saving directives are framed. Asking questions to seek information is dispreferred in many Amazonian and Australian Aboriginal societies. Other linguistic strategies are used instead: for instance, 'triggering', that is, making a relevant statement about something the person already knows and thus volunteering information first. The knowledgeable person—who is supposed to provide the desired information—will then volunteer information if they wish to do so. This is quite unlike European-style information-seeking, typical of some researchers. As one south-east Queensland Aboriginal man commented, '[The researchers] come in with a whole lot of questions, instead of sitting down and talking' (Eades 1982: 107). Questions which may be considered intrusive and nosey are used sparingly, and hardly at all as directives.[24]

The ways in which questions and statements get redeployed to act as directives reflect the versatility of speech acts, and the continuum of their pragmatic interpretation: we return to this in the final section.

Non-indicative modalities—optative, subjunctive, conditional, potential and others—tend to be used for polite commands, invitations, requests—or instructions and prescriptions. In Whitney's (1924 (1891): §573) words, the optative in Sanskrit

appears to have as its primary office the expression of wish or desire [...]. But the expression of desire, on the one hand, passes naturally over into that of request or entreaty, so that the optative becomes a softened imperative; and, on the other hand, it comes to signify what is generally desirable or proper, what should or ought to be, and so becomes the mode of prescription.

In Punjabi (Bhatia 1993: 34), the subjunctive form conveys a suggestion or a wish, rather than a straightforward command. In Catalan (Hualde 1992: 26–7), as in many Western Romance languages, subjunctive forms preceded by the complementizer *que* 'that' are used with non-first person subjects. With second person, they have the force of an emphatic or insistent command. A command given in an imperative and not heeded can be repeated in a subjunctive:

8.29 dóna   'm   el   llibre   ara
     give.IMPV.2sg 1sg   the   book   now
     'Give me the book now!'

8.30 que   em   donguis   el   llibre, si   et   plau!
     that   1sg   give.SUBJUNC.2sg   the   book   if   2sg   please.2sg
     'Give me the book, (if you) please!'

The subjunctive accompanied by a complementizer can also be used to remind the addressee of a previous command and may have the force of a mild request, as in 8.31:

8.31 que   em   facis   això,   oi?
     that   1sg   do.SUBJUNC.2sg   that,   OK
     'Do that for me, alright?' (lit. That you may do this for me, OK?)

Free subjunctive clauses are used to express wishes—as in 8.32:

8.32 que   passis   unes   bones   festes   de   Nadal
     that   pass.SUBJUNC.2sg   some   good.fem.pl   holidays   of   Christmas
     'Have a nice Christmas vacation!' (lit. That you may have good Christmas holidays)

Along similar lines, in Modern Greek subjunctive particle *na* with an indicative verb provides a politer command than a straightforward imperative, as in 8.33:[25]

8.33 na   mu   δόsete   liɣo
     SUBJUNC.PARTICLE   me.GEN   give.2pl.NONPAST.PERF   little.neuter
     psomí
     bread.neuter
     '(Please) give me a little bread'

To make this even more polite, one could add *parakaló* 'please', literally 'I beg you', of which the clause introduced by *na* can be considered a complement clause. We return to the issue of desubordination in §8.3.

A polite request or an invitation in Uzbek can be expressed with optative modality (Nasilov et al. 2001: 211):

8.34 Men   bilan   birga   Alidžon   aka-m-ŋi
     I   with   together   Alidžon   brother-POSS:1sg-ACC
     kur-gani   bor-ib   kel-sa-iz
     see-PARTICLE   go-CONVERB   come:AUX-OPT-2pl
     'Will you please go with me to visit Alijan!'[26]

An optative in Uzbek can express 'repeated insistence to perform an immediate action' if accompanied by the particle -*či*- which indicates that politeness is not a necessary corollary of having a non-indicative form in a directive:

8.35 E   bujinbaɣ-ni   eč-sa-ŋiz-či
     well   tie-ACC   undress-OPT-2pl-PARTICLE
     'Hey, take off the tie at last (how many times do I have to tell you)!'

Subjunctive in Armenian expresses polite directives and requests. Exceptionally polite requests are cast in past subjunctive, as illustrated in 8.36 (Kozintseva 2001: 263–4):

8.36 Xndrem,..., inj   hamar   ban   nvageik'
     please,...   me   for   something   play+SUBJ.PAST:2pl
     'Please,... would you kindly play something for me'

Along similar lines, in the Majhi dialect of Punjabi, subjunctive is used for requests (Bhatia 1993: 36). Various non-indicative modalities can be deployed somewhat differently if used as directives: for instance, in Eastern Pomo requests are formed with the conditional marker, and supplications involve the desiderative modality (McLendon 1996: 530–31). In a request, a negative conditional sounds more polite than its positive counterpart.[27]

Statements cast in irrealis can have the overtones of polite commands: examples 4.44–5 from Jamul Tiipay (or Diegueño) illustrate this (also see note 40 to Chapter 4 on the association between irrealis and politeness in Oceanic languages and Papuan languages of New Guinea).[28]

Modality forms with the meaning of obligation (so-called deontic meaning) can be used in strong commands—this is the case in Marathi and Punjabi. Similarly, in Kobon (Davies 1981: 24), obligation is expressed through a special set of verb forms (different from a normal imperative), termed 'prescriptive mood':

8.37 Kale   nagɨ   lɨ-min
     2p   vine   put-PRESCRIPTIVE
     'You should tie it with vine'

Statements with modal words often have directive overtones—just as in 8.17c, from English. A deontic modal *kinəənlan* 'must' in Northern Subanen is used in instructions and prescriptions outlining what is necessary to be done (Daguman 2004: 449–50).

Tuvaluan employs the verb *tapu*, meaning 'forbidden, sacred', for negative peremptory commands (Besnier 2000: 39):

8.38 Koe koo   tapu   koe e   toe   faipati i   loto   i   te
      you INCL forbidden you NPS again speak   in inside in the
      maneapa o   te   fenua
      maneaba of the island.community
      'You mustn't speak again [publicly] in(side) the maneaba (special
      house) of the island community'

Modal meanings and directive functions can be expressed with uninflected
particles. In Cairene Egyptian Colloquial Arabic, *laazim* 'must' and *mafruud*
(ʕn) 'it is a duty that' followed by the inflected verb have a directive meaning
(Gary and Gamal-Eldin 1982: 98):

8.39 laazim tixallas   bukra
      must   you.masc.sg.finish tomorrow
      'You must finish tomorrow!'

Verbs of necessity in Finnish have a commanding effect:[29]

8.40 Sinun   täytyy   nukkua!
      you.GEN must.3sg   sleep+INF
      'You must sleep!'

Various mood and modality forms in one language can reflect different
'degrees' of the force of command. The grammatical constructions used as
directives in Marathi can be arranged in the form of the hierarchy shown in
Figure 8.1, from stronger or less polite command to a weaker and more polite
one (Pandharipande 1997: 53).

This illustrates, in a nutshell, how a plethora of modalities can be deployed
to express the nuances of directives. And we can partially predict what the
meaning of a modality form would be if employed as a directive: an optative

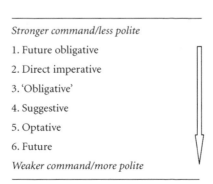

Stronger command/less polite

1. Future obligative

2. Direct imperative

3. 'Obligative'

4. Suggestive

5. Optative

6. Future

Weaker command/more polite

FIGURE 8.1 Degrees of command in Marathi

modality is likely to express a milder command than a direct imperative. However, we have seen that future forms can be used for stern commands in some languages, and for mild commands in others. The same holds for statements cast in the present. The exact semantic content and pragmatic overtones of each strategy have to be evaluated on a language-specific basis: we cannot project our insights from English onto Quechua or the other way round.

8.3 Free-standing dependent clauses as directives

Performative constructions (*I beg you to, I implore you to*, and so on) are a common way of phrasing suggestions, invitations and directives of other sorts; an example from English is in 8.15. A construction with the performative verb *okugamba* 'say' in Haya may have the effect of a polite command or a strong order, depending on the intonation (Lehman 1977: 145–7). A directive in English can be phrased as a conditional sentence: *I would be grateful to you if you could open the door.*

In many languages of the world, the performative part, or the main clause, may be ellipsed. The result is what looks like a syntactically incomplete sentence. The effects of incompleteness—result of an ellipsis—can be associated with lesser force of a command or a request as a potentially face-threatening act: 'by leaving a face-threatening act half undone' (Brown and Levinson 1987: 227). The use of subjunctive in commands often originates in such face-saving ellipsis: 8.30–33, from Catalan and from Modern Greek, illustrate how erstwhile dependent complement clauses can be used as directives on their own—as mild commands, or wishes.[30]

An *if*-clause can occur on its own, as a polite directive, usually a request. This is a feature of numerous varieties of Modern English.[31] An isolated *if*-clause in its directive function 'allows the speaker to express that he/she is not assuming the performance of the act requested of the hearer; the hearer has an option' (Stirling 1998: 281). Examples 8.41–2 come from dialogues between a doctor and a patient:

8.41   Okay if you'd like to get dressed now
8.42   ...so if you just ask the chemist to sell you a box of Gavascon

Isolated *if*-clauses are consistently used as mild and indirect directives, characterized by avoiding a face-threatening coercion of hearer's response. A corpus-based study by Stirling (1998) demonstrated that directive *if*-clauses presuppose a certain amount of social distance between the speaker and the addressee: they occur more frequently in dialogues where the speakers were unfamiliar with one another. Directive *if*-clauses occur in academic context—though they rarely get into written texts. During the plenary session of the colloquium on interrogativity (Chisholm 1984: 281), Bernard Comrie volunteered a reply to a member of the audience concerning the issue of whether *Would you open the door* is really a question:

8.43   If I could make some sort of reply to that

What is the status of such free-standing *if*-clauses? Can they be considered incomplete elliptical utterances, or should they be viewed as a minor sentence type? A number of arguments point towards the second solution. The free-standing *if*-clauses are 'prosodically complete'—that is, they have a terminal clause intonation contour rather than a contour of an incomplete utterance. If they were to be considered as elliptical, the ellipsed material should be recoverable; the construction would also be expected to be grammatically defective (see Matthews 1981: 39; Quirk et al.: 1985: 12.32–8; Stirling 1998: 289–90). But this is not the case: the 'postulated ellipsed materials'—that is, the missing main clause—cannot be easily supplied from the linguistic context. The meaning of an isolated *if*-clause is contextually unambiguous—it is understood as a directive. And in addition, an isolated *if*-clause can function as an independent clause in a complex sentence—as in 8.44:

8.44   If I can explain what is driving it, since I was at that meeting

These properties of *if*-clauses employed as directives on their own indicate that they are best analysed as a minor sentence type, a product of reanalysis of erstwhile dependent clauses as main clauses in their own right.[32]

Free-standing conditional clauses as ways of expressing requests are a feature of Modern Italian. In actual dialogue, a suggestion or a request made with a free-standing conditional is followed by a response—just as any other invitation would be expected to be:[33]

8.45   A: Se mi dice la pagina
            'If you tell me the page . . .'
        B: la pagina allora trentatre
            'The page is 33'

Free-standing conditionals as invitations have the same intonation contour as invitations or offers phrased in other ways.[34] This feature supports their status as a special—albeit hardly recognized by traditional grammarians—clause type.

Similar examples of conditionals used for requests and invitations are found in Finnish, as shown in 8.46 (Vallauri 2004: 210–11). Passive is used here for first person plural:

8.46 Jospa   sovittaisiin   vaihteeksi
     if+EMPH   make.peace.COND.PASS   for.change
     'Why don't we make peace, for a change' (lit. If we make peace for a change)

Along similar lines, free-standing conditionals in Japanese may express an offer or request. We can recall from §8.1 that Japanese utilizes numerous alternatives to a straightforward imperative, with its strongly coercive and face-threatening overtones (Vallauri 2004: 212; Martin 1975: 963–8).[35] According to Vallauri (2004: 212), free-standing conditionals in Japanese have an interrogative intonation:[36]

8.47 suwareba?
     sit+COND
     'If you sit . . .' (=please sit)

Free-standing subordinate clauses can be of other types. Desubordinated purpose clauses are a way of phrasing a command in Kayardild, Indonesian (Evans 2007) and also Yankunytjatjara. A purposive-marked subordinate clause in Yankunytjatjara is shown in 8.48, and a free-standing purposive is in 8.49 (Goddard 1985: 165–7):

8.48 ngayulu   Yami-nya   nyaku-nytja-ku   pata-ni
     1sg(NOM)   Yami-ACC   see-NOMZ-PURP   wait-PRES
     'I am waiting to see Yami'

8.49 ngayulu   ngalku-nytja-ku/kuli-nytja-ku?
     1sg(ERG)   see-NOMZ-PURP/listen-NOMZ-PURP
     'May I eat/listen?' (= will you do something so that I can eat/listen?)

In Goddard's words, '[a] purposive clause with rising intonation may constitute a complete sentence in itself'. He suggests that 'these utterances are probably best interpreted as "indirect speech acts", for they implicitly request the addressee to do something, so that the situation they depict may become possible'.

Desubordinated conditional and purpose clauses are a means of producing a milder or attenuated command or request, in agreement with a face-saving strategy formulated by Brown and Levinson (1987: 227) as 'Be incomplete, use ellipsis'. Conditional and purpose clauses contain an element of supposition,

wish, and future projection and refer to a not-yet-realized event: this deter-
mines their association with mildly wishing that something should happen
rather than demanding that it does.[37]

Not every instance of ellipsis produces the same result, nor does every
instance of desubordination. Numerous Australian languages have a
special type of dependent clause meaning 'for fear of VERB-ing'. It expresses
undesirable negative consequences to be avoided by carrying out the actions
stated in the main clause.[38] This clause type, and the verb form employed, are
labelled 'apprehensive', 'lest', or 'evitative'. An example of a 'lest' clause, from
Diyari, is in 8.50 (Austin 1981: 225). The main clause contains a command:

8.50 ŋapu-ri-ya-ayi   ŋaṯu   yiṇa   ṇanda-yaṯi
      quiet-INCH-IMPV-EMPH   1sgA   2sgO   hit-LEST
      'Be quiet or I'll hit you'

A 'lest' clause can occur on its own, with no main clause to which it is
subordinated. Then, the 'lest' suffix functions as the main verb marker. In
Austin's (1981: 229) words, 'in all the examples of this type of construction it is
clear from the context that an "understood" imperative, warning or suggestion is implicit'. Consider 8.51:

8.51 ṇulu-ka   kiṇṯala-li   yinaṇa   maṯa-yaṯi
      3sgnf.A-TOKEN   dog-ERG   2sgO   bite-LEST
      'The dog might bite you'

This 'could be said to a visitor entering one's camp as a warning that a
particular dog approaching him is ferocious and should be avoided—the
context would be clear and make it unnecessary to say "Look out!" or "Be
careful!" and so on' (Austin 1978: 229).

Conventionalized ellipsis of the main clause has different semantic effects
from what we saw for free-standing conditionals and purposives: the meaning
of the dependent clause imparts an overtone of warning to the newly arisen,
'desubordinated' command.

In Manambu, a language with extensive clause chaining, the main (final)
clause can be omitted. The dependent clause, marked with a dependent clause
suffix, can be used as a directive. Just two of over ten medial dependent clause
types in Manambu can be used on their own. Each has its own semantic
overtones and can be analysed as a new clause type 'in the making'.

Sequencing medial clauses with the verb marked with -*n* can be used to
express any sequencing relationship—be it temporal, causal, or that of a real

condition. When used on their own, they function as strong commands. A mother, fed up with her naughty child, shouted at the top of her voice:

8.52 tǝkǝr-ǝ-m   da-n!
      chair-LK-LOC   sit-SEQ
      'Sit on the chair!' (lit. Sitting on the chair!)

The intonation pattern is similar to that of an imperative, and not to that of a dependent clause (see Aikhenvald 2008a, 2009a). This is a strong and threatening command: the child either obeys or runs away. If the child persists in not doing what she is told to, the mother gets more and more annoyed, and will produce an even sterner order, using another free-standing dependent clause—but this time it is a completive clause, whose meaning is 'having VERB-ed':

8.53 tǝkǝr-ǝ-m   da-ku
      chair-LK-LOC   sit-COMPL:SS
      'Sit down on the chair immediately!' (lit. Having sat on the chair!)

Intonation-wise, these are pronounced in the same way as imperatives, except with a louder pitch. A completive clause in 8.53 does not have the rise–fall intonation typical for a completive clause in a clause chain. Its illocutionary force is comparable to German participle commands, e.g. *hingesessen!* 'sitting here!' discussed in §8.4. In my experience, children consider such commands really threatening: these are always to be obeyed (or else).[39]

What is the function of these ways for strengthening a command? We can recall, from Chapter 2 and examples 5.28a–c, that Manambu has just one dedicated imperative and three prohibitive forms. The command strategies fill what can be conceived of as a 'gap' in the system. The different degrees of strength of command corresponding to the degree of strength of prohibition are expressed through command strategies employing desubordinated clauses. Rough correspondences, with numbers of example sentences, are in Table 8.1.

TABLE 8.1 Negative commands and desubordinated clauses as command strategies in Manambu

SEMANTICS	POSITIVE	NEGATIVE
simple command	imperative, e.g. *awuk* 'listen!'	general prohibitive 'don't do it' (5.28a)
strong command	desubordinated sequencing clause (8.52)	strong prohibitive: 'don't you dare do it' (5.28b)
very strong command	desubordinated completive medial clause (8.53)	extra-strong prohibitive: don't you dare do it (or else)' (5.28c)

The effect of desubordination as a directive technique in Manambu is very different from the desubordinated conditional and purpose clauses discussed earlier in this section. This effect is akin to the effects of ellipsis and abbreviated commands and instructions in general: it produces abrupt, stern orders with no connotation of suggestion or 'indirection' of any sort.

We now turn to the pragmatic effects of verbless directives, and nominalized verbal forms in directive use.

8.4 Verbless directives, nominalized verbs, and ellipsis

Verbless directives in English are common in written notices—some examples are in 8.54:[40]

8.54a   Smoking prohibited
8.54b   No visitors beyond this point
8.54c   No smoking. No entry. Slow
8.54d   Meeting in progress

Some of these can be rephrased as positive commands: *Slow* can be recast as *Drive slowly*. Others imply prohibitions, though they do not contain an overt negator: 8.54d is an instruction not to enter the room, or not to disturb.

Verbless constructions are also commonly used in spoken language to indicate what is being ordered or asked for, e.g. *Two black coffees, please*; *Two adults, please* (as a shorthand for 'I request admission for two adults); *Single to Manchester* (booking transport) (Huddleston 2002: 942).

Adverbials on their own can have the illocutionary force of a command. The verb of motion is understood—as in 8.54 (Quirk et al. 1985: 842–3):

8.55   Forward!   On your feet!   Faster!
        Left, right!   At the double!   To the left!
        At ease!   Inside!   That way!

Several adverbials can be combined, as in *Back to base!* A noun phrase subject can be followed by an adverbial, as in *All aboard! Everybody inside!* Or a command can consist of just a noun phrase as direct object: *Backs to the wall!* ('Put your backs to the wall!'), *Hands up! Eyes down!* Alternatively, a verbless construction may consist of an adverbial and a *with*-phrase, as in *On with the show!* ('Begin or continue with show'), *Off with his head!* ('Cut off his head').

An adjective can function as directive, as in *Careful!* ('Be careful'), *Quiet!* ('Be quiet!). So can a noun, e.g. *Silence in court!* Verbless commands in Modern Hebrew may also involve nouns, or adverbials, as in *šeket!* 'Silence!',

zehirut! 'Caution! Look out!' or *day* 'Enough!'. Saying *Fora!* 'Out!' in Portuguese or *Välja!* 'Out!' in Estonian is a curt command, to be obeyed immediately.

In Northern Subanen (Daguman 2004), a curt command is an elliptical
construction that does not mention the addressee, although it implies a
second person addressee. The prohibition in 8.56 is uttered in an abrupt
manner: it does not contain a prohibitive marker, but just indicates the
undesirable state of affairs, and is thus used as a negative command.

8.56 Sasak!
     noise
     'Silence!'

Curt one-word commands can contain nouns marked for case. During my
stays in a Manambu-speaking village, I was often warned by sharp shouts:
təpa:k! (coconut+LK+DAT/AVERSIVE): this literally means 'for or for fear of
coconut', and is a warning for someone not to stand underneath a coconut
palm or to walk close to one for fear of a coconut falling on one's head. Saying
diya:k! (excrement+LK+DAT/AVERSIVE) 'for or for fear of excrement' was a
warning for someone walking on a path and not looking, for fear of stepping
onto a dog's excrement.

These elliptic commands have brusque overtones, and presuppose immediate compliance. In European languages, they are not uncommon in the
language of the military.[41]

Free-standing nominalizations, participles, and infinitives are also used as
directives. In numerous European languages, infinitives imply strong commands and proscriptions. They are frequent especially in written instructions,
as in German *den Rasen nicht betreten* '(people must) not walk on the lawn',
nicht hinauslehnen '(people must) not lean out (of a train)'; Estonian *mitte
suitsetada* 'not to smoke; smoking is forbidden'. A directive cast in the infinitive in Russian 'denotes a peremptory order, a categorical prescription and
command', and also 'expresses obligatoriness of an action, its fatal inevitability' (Vinogradov 1947: 604–5), e.g. *Uvolitj!* 'To dismiss!', *Otnesti ee von!* 'To take
her away!'[42] An infinitive in Armenian can be used as a directive only in
utterances addressed by a superior to their subordinates (Kozintseva 2001:
265–6). In Modern Hebrew, infinitive verb forms are used as curt commands,
as in 8.57:

8.57 lišon!   lišon!   'amar-ti   le-xa
     sleep:INF sleep:INF tell.PAST-1sg   to-you.masc.sg
     'Sleep! Sleep! I have told you'

They can be used in instructions issued to specific addressees or in general—8.58 is an instruction how to cook:[43]

8.58 levašel   xameš   dak-ot
     boil:INF   five   minute-pl:fem
     'Boil for five minutes [...]'

The infinitive in Italian is commonly used as a directive in 'generic instructions', especially in public notices, announcements, recipes, and so on, e.g. *spingere* (sign on a door) 'push', *tirare* (sign on a door) 'pull', *lavare prima di tagliare* 'Wash before cutting'.[44]

Infinitival directives in Turkic languages express 'categorical command to the listener'. 8.59 comes from Yakut:[45]

8.59 Cej   ih-erge!
     tea   drink-INF
     '[Come] and have tea!'

In Korean, nominal forms including free-standing nominalizations are used on formal and official occasions—in announcements, posters, and military commands:

8.60 chwulpal!
     departure
     'March!'

In 8.61, the head noun *kes* 'fact', 'that', 'thing' is preceded by an appositive adjectival clause marked with the suffix *-(u)l*.

8.61 tul-e   ka-ci   ma-l   kes
     enter-INF go-NOMZ   stop-PRES:ADJECTIVAL.CLAUSE.MARKER   that
     'No entering'

And 8.62 contains a verb nominalized with *-m*:

8.62 chwul-ip-ul   kumha-m
     exit-entrance-AC   PROHIBITIVE-NOM
     'No admission'

The exact form of infinitives varies from one language to another. Prepositional infinitives in Spanish are used as directives, and always have impositive connotations: by saying 8.62 'the speaker does not leave it to the hearer to decide' if he will execute the command (Haverkate 1976: 231).

8.63   ¡A devolverle las diez mil pesetas!
'Give him the ten thousand pesetas back!'

One cannot add a hedging particle, or a qualification such as 'whenever you want' to 8.63 (so, *¡A devolverle las diez mil pesetas cuando quieras! is ungrammatical).[46]

Free-standing nominalized forms also tend to be used as curt directives urging the addressee to act promptly. In German, 'participle commands' are restricted to a few motion and posture verbs, and are typically used if the one who is issuing an order is in a position of authority. *Hiergeblieben!* (lit. Having stayed here) 'Stay here!' can be said by a teacher to a student or by a detective to a teenage shoplifter. *Stehengeblieben!* 'Stand still!' can be said by a policeman to an offender; or by annoyed parents or teachers to a child. A parent can say to a child who is not moving quickly enough: *Jetzt aber mal schnell aufgestanden* (now but once quickly having.got.up) 'Get up quickly now!'[47]

Verbless sentences and free-standing nouns and nominalizations as directives tend to be particularly polite, and usually sound curt and stern. Their brevity correlates with the requirement for immediate compliance. This follows the principle of iconicity, that politeness mirrors social distance: the greater the politeness, the longer the message (Haiman 2003: 59). Conversely, the shorter and the more concise the message, the less polite it will be, and the more immediate the compliance to it. Ellipsis in these instances does not produce a face-saving strategy, unlike the ellipsis of the main clause resulting in desubordinated conditional or purposive clauses. On the contrary: elliptical directives are face-threatening, which is the reason why they may tend to be restricted to particular registers. They are quite appropriate in the language of the military, where insubordination is not tolerated, but not in another sort of environment conducive to more relaxed interaction.

A nominalized form as a directive can have different overtones. In Siberian Yupik Eskimo, constructions with a converb in *-lu-* can be used as polite requests.[48] A converb in *-lu-* in its typical clause-sequencing function is in 8.64:

8.64   aqumga-lu-ten   negev-u-ten
         sit-converb-2sg   get.up-intr-2sg
         '[After] sitting you got up'

Vaxtin remarks that these converbs are 'practically never used as predicates of independent action, except when the action is incomplete or contextually bound, or the sentence is unfinished'; 'this meaning of incompleteness, "imperfection" makes them appropriate for expressing the meaning of polite urging.' Example 8.65a is a straightforward command:

8.65a   itghi-ø
      come.in-IMPV.2sg
      'Come in!'

And a converbal form as a directive has overtones of polite request:

8.65b   itegh-lu-ten
      come.in-CONVERB-2sg
      'Please come in' (lit. 'Coming in!'—an incomplete, polite request)

We can recall from §3.3.3 (also see §4.2.1) that aspectual meanings of incompleteness and imperfectivity often acquire overtones of politeness in the context of imperatives. It is therefore not surprising that a converb referring to an incomplete activity should be employed as a tentative and polite request—rather than a rude and curt order. Incompleteness and ensuing ellipsis as a means of attenuation are warranted as a means of avoiding a face-threatening act—suggesting something and leaving the implicature 'hanging in the air'. Brown and Levinson (1987: 227) remark that ellipsis of this sort is 'one of the most favoured strategies for requests' in Tamil, especially if addressed to one's superior. So, 8.66 was said by a niece trying to ask her father's younger brother for an aspirin:

8.66   eenunka,   talevali . . .
      oh sir,   a headache . . .

This was a mild request, and not a demand; and gave the uncle 'an option of telling her to go and lie down, rather than dispensing a precious pill'.

We have discussed only the most common strategies. There may be further options. In English, tag interrogatives can be anchored to imperatives and declaratives as directives:

8.67a   Help yourself, will you/won't you?
8.67b   Don't tell anyone, will you?
8.67c   Let's (not) go with them, shall we?

These tags are sometimes considered elliptical or abbreviated versions of full interrogatives, *Will you help yourself?*, *Won't you help yourself?*, *Will you not tell anyone?*, *Shall we (not) go with them?* However, they are akin to interrogative-directives discussed in §8.1: as Huddleston (2002: 942) puts it, 'the indirect force of the interrogative thus matches the direct force of the imperative

FIGURE 8.2 A notice at a Sydney hotel: a pictorial command strategy

anchor'. Either a positive or a negative tag can occur with the positive imperative, but only a positive tag occurs with the negative imperative. Interrogative tags can occur with directive or predictive statements, e.g. *You will bring me a slab, won't you*, again as a mitigating device.[49]

Many other devices can be used in lieu of imperatives in directive meanings. An exclamation can be used as a direction, or instruction. Figure 8.2 shows a notice given out to guests at a hotel in Sydney. Instead of normal 'Don't disturb', the notice says *Shhhhh . . . !* on the one side, and *I am sleeping!* on the other. The pragmatic effect is a negative command—'don't disturb', or 'don't wake me up'. The form is intended to be exclamative—this is shown by an exclamation mark at the end.

Quotative markers can be used in polite requests. This is in line with content of a typical imperative-specific meaning known as 'degree' of command (see Chapter 6). To change an order to a request so as to 'mitigate assertiveness' in Korean, one uses an imperative marked with a quotative particle but without the main predicate:[50]

8.68   cal   tul-e   po-si-la-ko-yo
       well   listen-INF   try-SH-IM-QUOT-POL
       '(I request please) listen carefully'

This agrees with similar overtones of reported markers in other languages: we can recall, from §4.2.4, that the reported evidential in Cavineña is a means of 'softening' a command.[51]

Parallel statements in Marathi—whereby the first clause expresses a positive statement and the second conveys a warning—are interpreted as negative imperatives.[52] The first clause is not marked as conditional, but is interpreted as a condition:

8.69   tū   titsā   apamān   kar,   mī   punhā
        you   her   insult   do.IMPV.2sg   I   again
        tudʒhyāsī   kadhīhī   bolṇār   nāhī
        you.DAT   ever   talk.FUT   NEG
        'You insult her, and I will never talk to you again' (i.e. Don't insult her)

In their translation, these structures are similar to English examples involving an imperative expressing a condition and then a consequence, such as *Do that again and you'll regret it* (see Chapter 7). But unlike English, the Marathi structures do not contain imperative forms: their directive meaning is implicit. A similar pattern in Tuvaluan[53] involves two coordinated clauses, 'the second of which describes an undesirable situation which will take place if the situation described by the first clause takes place'. Such structures—which implicitly contain a condition—are peremptory:

8.70   Toe   tasi   te   pati   maasei,   koo   maalaia   ei   koe!
        again   one   the   word   bad   INC   doomed   Anp   you
        'One more swear word and you'll be sorry!' (lit. 'One more bad word, you'll then be doomed')

Another option for a negative directive in Tuvaluan involves a statement with the stative verb *oti* 'finished' with a nominalized verb as its subject; this verb denotes the situation which is to be stopped. A negative command like the one in 8.71 is peremptory:

8.71   Oti   te   tagi!
        finished   the   cry
        'Enough of [your] crying!'

Babungo, a Bantu language, has a special 'challenge' construction, used in order to try to influence someone to do something (marked with a particle *máa*: Schaub 1985: 24–6). One language can combine a variety of ways of phrasing a directive without relying on an imperative form. Korean has an array of strategies for framing directives with non-imperative forms. Passives, nominalized constructions (see 8.60–62 above), subordinate clauses (which translate as 'I would appreciate it if you did so and so'), and softening

FIGURE 8.3 'Don't use phones': a pictorial command strategy

FIGURE 8.4 'No smoking': a pictorial command strategy

adverbials contribute to strategies aimed at issuing indirect commands and requests and avoiding face-threatening behaviour in general.[54]

The degree of 'directness' and face-threatening—or lack thereof—of a directive correlates with a further set of not-quite-linguistic features: 'softening intonation, rhythm, soft voice, and slow speech' help make a directive sound less intrusive (see Sohn 1986: 273). In Bolinger's (1985: 106) words, intonation 'assists grammar', and 'in some instances may be indispensable to it'. Further non-linguistic features which tone down the illocutionary force of a directive include gestures, facial expressions, and other types of non-verbal behaviour—bowing, avoiding eye contact (or not).

Written instructions and warnings do not have to contain words to express a directive meaning. Figure 8.3 features a phone with a red line across. This sign can be verbalized as 'Don't use phones'. And a well-known sign with a barred cigarette (Figure 8.4) does not require an additional 'No smoking', or 'Smoking prohibited' (see 8.54a): it is self-evident. These pictorial, non-verbal directives, are part of the directives we live by—which is the topic of our next chapter.

8.5 Imperatives in disguise and versatile speech acts

Non-imperative forms can be co-opted to express directive meanings—these may be either more, or less, strong than the imperative itself. We have identified a number of recurrent techniques employed as such command strategies—which include interrogative-directives, statements cast in future, present, and past tense, or in non-indicative modalities, nominalizations, desubordinated clauses, and a few more.

It is, however, not the case that 'anything goes' in any language: a 'why'-question will be understood as a command by a native speaker of English, but not necessarily by a language learner. A future statement sounds peremptory in English, but is a polite way of framing a request in Quechua (see §8.3). Ellipsis may produce a brusque and abrupt command requiring immediate compliance—as in military orders. This agrees with the principle of iconic motivation: the longer the politer, and the shorter the ruder. But the effect of ellipsis can be different. Leaving out the main clause in conditional clauses, in English and a few other languages, results in a tentative request and a mild directive. This goes together with the principle of vagueness and tentativeness in indirect speech acts.

Competing motivations for a contextually adequate pragmatic interpreta-tion of each strategy consist in (first) getting the message through (that is, getting someone to do something) and (secondly) avoiding being too overbearing, indirect, and consequently not face-threatening.

If the main clause has been left out, the meaning of the remaining part bears a relation to what it meant originally, in the erstwhile structure. So, a 'lest'-clause will be used as a warning, and is unlikely to have the overtones of a mild request a free-standing conditional would have.

The range of statements which can be pragmatically interpreted as com-mands in an appropriate context is broad. Saying *It is cold, and the window is open* in English can be interpreted as a general statement about the state of affairs. Or this can be interpreted as a way of saying 'Close the window'. The interpretation depends on context; and a directive intent can be corroborated by the speaker's body language—for instance, an eye-gaze.[55]

The potential of such freedom of interpretation makes 'command strategies' appear an open-ended set. However, some expressions lend themselves more readily to a directive reading than others. And whether or not the addressee will interpret a statement as a directive depends on speech habits, conventions, and the ethnography of communication in a language community.[56] The role of inference in determining the pragmatic function of an utterance also depends on the overtones of imperatives themselves: we will see in the next chapter that in a society where imposition of one's will on someone else is not considered an appropriate cultural practice, imperatives are avoided and other forms are favoured instead.

That a non-imperative form can be successfully used in a directive speech act points towards a continuum between imperative (or prototypically directive), declarative, and interrogative speech acts. Figure 8.5 shows a continuum between a command in the form of an imperative in (a) and an information question in (i) (based on Givón 1989: 153–4):

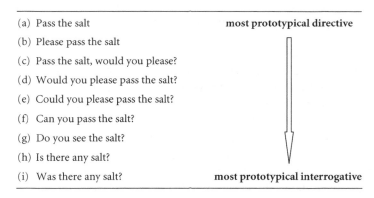

(a) Pass the salt   **most prototypical directive**

(b) Please pass the salt

(c) Pass the salt, would you please?

(d) Would you please pass the salt?

(e) Could you please pass the salt?

(f) Can you pass the salt?

(g) Do you see the salt?

(h) Is there any salt?

(i) Was there any salt?   **most prototypical interrogative**

Figure 8.5 From imperative to interrogative

Most prototypical directive has an imperative form. Any of (a)–(f) can be easily understood as directives rather than questions. Whether or not (f), (g), and (i) are perceived as directives or as questions depends on the situation, and the intonation.[57]

A comparable continuum (Figure 8.6) can be created for a relationship between imperative and declarative: (a)–(h) can be interpreted as commands, differing in their strength, politeness, and manipulative force.

While the exact order of these on the continuum is arguable—that is, whether (e) is more question-like than (d)—the overall idea is clear: we are faced with a mismatch between linguistic form and the pragmatic function of a speech act. Pragmatic functions are versatile: they may correlate with the

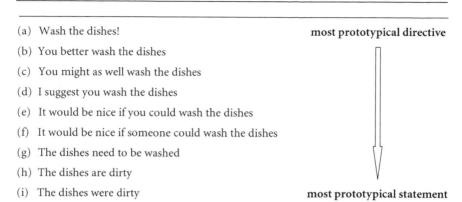

(a) Wash the dishes!   **most prototypical directive**

(b) You better wash the dishes

(c) You might as well wash the dishes

(d) I suggest you wash the dishes

(e) It would be nice if you could wash the dishes

(f) It would be nice if someone could wash the dishes

(g) The dishes need to be washed

(h) The dishes are dirty

(i) The dishes were dirty   **most prototypical statement**

FIGURE 8.6 From imperative to declarative

form, but often don't. Any linguistic form can be disguised as a command, invitation, request, or another directive act. But not every form is in a given language: imperatives and non-imperative directives come to be used in different ways in different societies.

And why do some languages use imperatives more than others? The reasons for avoiding an imperative may be rooted in the speech etiquette of culture-specific social relationships. We recall from 6.17 that in Yankunytjatjara, an Australian language (Goddard 1983: 306–7), a strict avoidance relationship between a man and his parents-in-law requires that a mother-in-law's or father-in-law's requests for food cannot be addressed directly to the son-in-law, and have to be done through an intermediary. Even the intermediary's speech cannot contain a direct command; it may be relayed using the quotative particle *kunyu* without any direct command, or reference to asking (6.17).[58]

Conventionalized non-imperative commands can be used in a directive function so frequently that they adopt this function as their own primary meaning. Non-imperative commands, and strategies, are a frequent source for developing bona fide imperative forms and parts of paradigms. We return to this in Chapter 10.

Notes

1. The issue of illocutionary force and its correlation with the form of non-imperative directives, especially interrogative, has been addressed by Givón (1984, 1989) as a continuum: see §8.5 below. See also Leech (1983: 175) for the view that illocutionary force 'must be studied in part in non-categorical, scalar terms'.

2. Conventionalized 'command strategies' are called 'non-imperative directives' by Huddleston (2002: 939–42). Another term for these is 'semantic imperative' (Press 1979: 80–81). In contrast to 'syntactic' imperatives which have an imperative form, semantic imperatives have the function, but not the form, of commands. Martin (1975: 965ff.) refers to command strategies in Japanese as 'circumlocutions'.

3. We can recall that in Navajo, 'imperative has no special form, but is rendered by the future tense forms (which are obligatory in force), the imperfective or progressive mode (when the act is to be carried out at once), and by the optative' (Young and Morgan 1969: 53–4).

4. Called 'illocutionary modifiers' by Huddleston (2002: 989).

5. Huddleston (2002: 940) notes that analytic negative forms with *can* can be ambiguous as to the scope of negation: *Can you not stand by the door* can be understood either as a positive directive with the meaning of 'Stand by the door' (then *can* is within the scope of negation, and we are dealing with a negative question conveying a positive directive) or with the meaning of 'Don't stand by the door' (and then we have a positive question conveying a negative directive).

6. See Hinds (1984: 182) and also Martin (1975: 963).

7. Along similar lines, a negative question in Estonian (especially when accompanied with conditional mood) expresses a weaker command, e.g. *Kas te ei ootaks natuke?* (QUESTION.MARK you.pl NEG wait.COND.NEG.FORM a little) 'Could you wait a little?' (Erelt 2003: 110).

8. See Xrakovskij and Volodin (2001: 207–8) for the politeness distinctions in Russian interrogative-directives.

9. Necessity questions as negative commands in Russian have a colloquial and regional overtone. A relative of a friend who was agonizing whether to carry on with an unsatisfactory marriage said to her: *Tebe eto nado?* (to.you this necessary) 'Is it necessary for you? Do you need it?' This was interpreted as an invitation to end the marriage.

10. Reason questions as directives have been described for few languages, among them Nishnaabemwin (Valentine 2001: 989), where negative interrogatives translatable as 'why don't you…' are a way of marking suggestions. Further correlations between questions and politeness are addressed in Goody (1978).

11. See Kuzmenkov (2001: 104), on this usage, and on the existing restrictions on directive interpretation of some questions but not others.

12. Daguman (2004: 453); the examples are given here in underlying form.

13. Further languages which do not employ questions as directives include Vurës, Jarawara, Tariana, Dumo, and Indo-Pakistani Sign language. The polite imperative marker in Tariana is homophonous with the present visual interrogative; this may indicate a historical connection between the two (see Aikhenvald 2008b, and Chapter 10).

14. Press (1979: 80–81). Other languages where future can be used as a strong command include Rumanian (Mallinson 1986: 28), Evenki (Nedjalkov 1997: 21), and Nishnaabemwin (or Ojibwe: Valentine 2001: 995). In West Greenlandic

(Fortescue 1984: 28), affixes 'of futurity' or of deontic modality have the force of a strong suggestion, 'you should do such and such'. And in Dom, a deontic construction meaning 'you should do such and such' involves future tense (Tida 2006: 156).

15. In Tatar, future indefinite forms can denote polite commands (Nasilov et al. 2001: 209). In Mekens (Tuparí branch of Tupí: Galúcio 2001), future is used to express an indirect command. In Nishnaabemwin (Valentine 2001: 994), a future preverb *wii* can be used in directives as a means of 'adding politeness'. Dench (2009) remarks that speakers of now extinct Martuthunira rejected the imperative inflection as 'impolite', using future instead (see 9.11).

16. For the use of future rather than imperative in positive commands in Modern Hebrew, see Sadock and Zwicky (1985: 176); Malygina (2001); see also Coffin and Bolozky (2005: 73).

17. In Sneddon's (1996: 326) words, in Indonesian a passive as a command is 'more indirect and consequently less forceful than an imperative with an active verb'.

18. The widespread character of this strategy is emphasized by Givón (1993, Vol. 2: 271), in his discussion of how impersonal statements tend to be more polite than straight commands.

19. Along similar lines, prohibitions in Indonesian are expressed as passives (using *dilarang* 'it is forbidden': Sneddon 1996: 326)—this does not make them less face-threatening.

    Another way of phrasing an instruction is by referring to conventional wisdom. Proverbs, in English as in many other languages, are used as a way of phrasing generalized advice: *A penny saved is a penny earned* can be understood, and used, as an advice—or entreaty—to be cautious with money. Brown and Levinson (1987: 226) remark that 'such generalized advice may, in context, serve as criticism; but as criticism with the weight of tradition, it is perhaps easier on face than other kinds of rule-stating'. Given the appropriate context, using a proverb can be rather pungent: a highly critical review by a prominent Australian linguist of a somewhat dubious piece of work which unfairly criticized him ended with 'People who live in glass houses shouldn't throw stones'—this was a stern piece of advice to the effect 'Don't criticize me since your work is of inferior quality'. The ending was as face-threatening as one could get: it was the context, rather than the content and the form of the proverb, that created this effect. (See Green 1975b for the ways in which proverbs are used in conversation, as instructions and advice.)

20. Nothing is known about the intonation which may be crucial for distinguishing between the two.

21. Nasilov et al. (2001: 210). The use of past tense forms as commands is reminiscent of Amele (§2.1.4), and also of Russian 'imperative of authority', described by Belikov (2001). The Russian imperative of authority homonymous with past tense forms differs from the Chemehuevi use in that it has overtones of immediacy, and also

implies that the one who is issuing a command is in charge. These forms are not restricted to motion verbs.

22. Rumsey (2003: 181) compares these to German participle commands in their illocutionary force, which brings them close to Russian imperatives of 'authority'.

23. Similar constructions as indirect directives have been described for Wari' (Everett and Kern 1997: 38).

24. In Tariana and the surrounding Tucanoan languages, information source in questions reflects the information source of the addressee (see Aikhenvald 2003: 311–19). The cultural constraints on asking too many questions, and relatively low frequency of questions in everyday interaction, can be related to restrictions on taking for granted the other person's information source (if you get it wrong, you may be accused of sorcery). This may be an additional reason why there are no questions-directives in these languages.

25. Joseph and Philippaki-Warburton (1987: 18).

26. Along similar lines, the optative construction in Dom is used for polite commands (Tida 2006: 257).

27. See also Asher and Kumari (1997: 305–10) for various modal forms in Malayalam used in a variety of directive speech acts.

28. A similar function of irrealis has been described for Wari', a Chapacura language from Brazil (Everett and Kern 1997: 37).

29. Sulkala and Karjalainen (1992: 26).

30. This is consistent with the remark by Sadock and Zwicky (1985: 193): 'Numerous languages use some typically subordinate forms, a free-standing infinitive or subjunctive, for example, as a circumlocution for the imperative.' We will see shortly that the implicatures of this desubordinating use are as versatile as most non-imperative directives. See also Lakoff (1968) on the independent subjunctive in Latin.

31. These are described for Australian English by Stirling (1998) (she also refers to their occurrence in Scottish English); see also Ford and Thompson (1986: 365), for American English, and Quirk et al. (1985: 11.38, 11.41), for British English.

32. This historical process of desubordination is not uncommon in the history of many languages and is often the source for new verbal morphology: see Aikhenvald (2004) for the development of the reported evidential in Estonian and elsewhere as a result of desubordination; and Aikhenvald (2008e) for the role of desubordination in creating modal markers out of erstwhile cases; further examples are in Evans (2007) (the term he uses is 'insubordination').

33. Vallauri (2004: 196).

34. Cresti (2000) calls this intonation type 'invito/offerta'.

35. Only two of the four conditional markers in Japanese occur as indirect commands or invitations (Hinds 1984; Hinds and Hinds 1975–6).

36. Evans (2007) mentions free-standing conditionals as means of expressing request in Spoken Mon and in Japanese. Free-standing conditionals in German also appear to be used as requests (see Stirling 1998: 280, and Buscha 1976 for isolated

translation equivalents in German). In Italian, just as in English, the meanings of a free-standing conditional are not exclusively 'directive' (see Quirk et al. 1985: 11.35, 41). Vallauri (2004: 190–95) discusses exclamatory and adversative conditionals (meaning '(But) it is not true!'), conditionals used as generic questions, and so on. The differences lie in intonation patterns.

37. See Greenberg (1986), van der Auwera (1986), König (1986), Ford and Thompson (1986), and further chapters in Traugott et al. (1986).

38. See Dixon (2009) for a cross-linguistic overview of negative consequence clause linking.

39. All these examples come from participant observation in a Manambu-speaking household with naughty children. Examples like this are next to impossible to obtain in texts (let alone in elicitation, a technique I always avoid in my own fieldwork). These phenomena have not been described for other Papuan languages of the area where Manambu is spoken; this can be the result of the data collected by the researchers.

40. Huddleston (2002: 942) analyses these as abbreviated passive performatives, e.g. *Smoking is prohibited*.

41. The special syntax of military commands—which consist of a preparatory part and the executive part with commands proper—is discussed by Sadock and Zwicky (1985: 177–8).

42. See further discussion by Xrakovskij and Birjulin (2001: 196–202), and also Isachenko (2003: 569–70).

43. Malygina (2001: 280–81). See Bolozky (1979), for an incisive analysis of Modern Hebrew command forms. Imperative particle *bevakaša* 'please' can occur with an infinitive as a directive expressing 'a request that borders on command'; *na'* 'please, let' conveys a formal request. These markers may thus tone down the stern character of infinitival commands (as also would German *bitte* in the same context), but do not turn them into mild requests or suggestions. Imperative-specific particles cannot be used in these structures in Armenian (Kozintseva 2001: 266).

44. Maiden and Robustelli (2007: 248).

45. Nasilov et al. (2001: 213).

46. See also Hualde (1992: 28) for prepositional infinitives as directives in Catalan, and Mallinson (1986: 28) for infinitives in instructions in Rumanian.

47. I am grateful to Ulrike Zeshan for these examples. She also tells me that *Hereinspaziert!* ('lit. come on in!') is a common expression 'inviting people to come in and join in some kind of (paid) display or activity, like by a circus director inviting the crowd in for the show'.

The exact usage of participle commands in German varies from speaker to speaker. Some of my German-speaking colleagues were appalled at the possibility of using participle commands with their children as being too harsh. Also see Rooryck and Postma (2007), for further analysis of participial commands.

48. Vaxtin (2001: 140).

49. Huddleston (2002: 942–3) remarks that the tag construction is 'conventionalized in that the tags correspond to only a subset of the interrogatives that can be used with indirect directive force' (see also Davies 1986: 19–28; Arbini 1969).

50. Sohn (1994: 44).

51. Guillaume (2004: 182–3).

52. Pandharipande (1997: 59).

53. Besnier (2000: 38).

54. Sohn (1986: 266–80): 'the function of indirect speech acts is to tone down utterance forces.' Many languages employ various imperative strategies to express degrees of politeness and indirectness; for instance, in Kannada and in Marathi, various degrees of politeness in imperatives are signalled by the choice of an appropriate honorific pronoun, vocative form, and also verb form.

55. Eye-gaze is a major feature of commands in Sign Languages (see Chapter 2). It is also known to play a role in spoken languages: a passive imperative in Boumaa Fijian can be 'said by the chief looking at a particular youth, who would thus indirectly be told that it was his job' to perform the command (e.g. stack the drums) (Dixon 1988: 295).

56. In addition, declaratives are not employed as directives in languages with numerous imperative forms—such as Tariana or East Tucanoan.

57. See also discussion in Ervin-Tripp (1976) and Lakoff (1972).

58. Similar avoidance relationships which warrant avoiding direct interaction of any sort, including commands, have been described for many Australian societies—such as Dyirbal and Yidiñ by Dixon (1972, 1977), Guugu Yimidhirr by Haviland (1979). Also see Basso (2007, MS) on the affinal avoidance relationships and commands in Kalapalo, a Carib language of Xingu.

9

Imperatives we live by

The English-speaking world is replete with imperative forms, used to command, entice, and invite. In *Alice in Wonderland*, the cake instructs Alice: *Eat me!* and the bottle joins in: *Drink me!* Houses in real estate advertisements beg us: *Make me your home!* The parking fee collector at the parking lot advises: *Drive safely!* A more inventive command to the same effect says *Do not drive faster than your guardian angel can fly*. A neon sign projects a mock-command: *Drink and drive—you are a bloody idiot*. Commands and instructions do not have to contain an imperative: *Drowsy drivers die* or *A power nap will save your life* could well be rephrased as *Break your drive and have a rest!*

Imperatives are particularly frequent in advertisements of all sorts, addressed to all in general and no one in particular. *Be tempted*, says a glossy magazine attempting to lure us to the pleasures of France, Italy, and Malta. *Be surprised by the size*, says a real estate advertisement, trying to sell a shabby-looking house in the north of Melbourne. *Be safe in public place* is a way of instructing people to be careful.

As we saw at the end of the previous chapter, commands may not need words. Figure 9.1 unequivocally prohibits drinking tap water; Figure 9.2 placed on the door of a university lecture room instructs us not to bring food or drink into the room. Pictorial commands and instructions vary in their sophistication and inventiveness.

Figure 9.3 is a persuasive instruction to all users of the library in James Cook University to save their work lest they lose it: it contains an imposing picture of Lord Kitchener, with his famous gesture from the posters urging Britons to enrol in the armed services at the beginning of the Great War. The instruction contains a variety of non-imperative forms: a question *Have you saved your work?* is a stern command to do so. An exclamatory sentence *Any PC and any USB can die at any moment!!!* is like a threat. The verbal part ends with an imperative: *Use multiple USBs, email, E-drive (day only)...*

The original poster exists in a variety of guises. On Figure 9.4, Kitchener is pointing his finger at the potential addressee, with a written statement *Your*

FIGURE 9.1 'Don't drink tap water': a pictorial command strategy

FIGURE 9.2 'Don't bring food or drink into the room': a pictorial command strategy

country needs you. This is a declarative clause with an obvious implication of a command: *Enrol in the army!*

Figure 9.5 explicitly addresses Britons—Kitchener is the pictorial subject who 'wants you'—that is, the Briton who happens to be looking at the poster. The next line is an explicit command, cast as an imperative *Join your country's army!* followed by the formulaic *God save the King*. A slightly different-looking Kitchener—with his general's regalia on display—conveys the same message in Figure 9.6. This is cast in a statement directly aimed at the addressee as if talking to him: *YOU are the man I want.*

These commands come from a military man and have an implication of urgency: one has no choice but to comply. The implications are conveyed by a few further non-verbal features—General Kitchener's steady eye-gaze, his

HAVE YOU SAVED
YOUR WORK?

ANY PC AND ANY USB CAN DIE
AT ANY MOMENT!!!

You must save your work in at least 2 different locations

EVERY 10 MINUTES

PLUS a third backup at the end of the day

Use multiple USBs, email, e-drive (day only)...

FIGURE 9.3 'An instruction to all users of the library in James Cook University to save their work lest they lose it': a pictorial command strategy

military attire, and the pointing gesture. In many cultures this would be considered intrusive, disturbing, and inappropriate (not the least so because finger-pointing is culturally inappropriate in many societies: see Wilkins 2003 for an account and a tentative explanation).[1]

Depending on the language and the social norms associated with it, imperatives and commands may be used in different ways, and with different frequency: this is discussed in §9.1. In §9.2 we turn to how imperatives and commands are used in context. Imperative forms interact with the lexicon—this is the topic of §9.3. Acquisition of imperatives, commanding techniques, and directive speech acts are addressed in §9.4. The last section contains a brief summary.

9.1 To use an imperative?

The English-speaking world overflows with 'do's' and 'don'ts'. The 'Good Manners' chart, issued to Queensland schools in Australia from 1898 to the 1960s,

FIGURE 9.4 'Your country needs you': a pictorial command strategy (variant 1)

contains a lengthy series of instructions—each of them phrased in the form of an imperative—for boys and girls to be courteous (and thus good, noble, useful to their country, and so on). The chart is reproduced in Figure 9.7.

Imperatives and commands in English are not restricted to humans or to animates. An administrator trying to get her photocopier to work addresses it, with an imploring intonation: *Please, be perfect! Do your job properly!* At a cricket test match between Australia and New Zealand, New Zealand supporters held out a slogan saying *Please, rain* hoping for a welcome rain which

BRITONS

"WANTS

"YOU"

JOIN YOUR COUNTRY'S ARMY!

GOD SAVE THE KING

Reproduced by permission of LONDON OPINION

FIGURE 9.5 'Your country needs you': a pictorial command strategy (variant 2)

would stop the match and allow the New Zealand team a chance of a draw. *Please, don't rain!* says a desperate gardener in times of a flood.

The same meaning can be expressed in any language (in line with Franz Boas's famous statement that anything can be said in any language),[2] but the

FIGURE 9.6 'YOU are the man I want': a pictorial command strategy (variant 3)

form such a wish may take is not necessarily imperative. Before we went on a long and exhausting expedition to Swakap from Avatip, in the remote Sepik area of New Guinea, everyone was worried that if it rained the trip would be even more difficult. A few of the members of the household exclaimed, in their native Manambu, using an irrealis form of the verb:

9.1 wa:l   akəs   ja-k-na!
     rain   IRR.NEG   fall-IRR-ACT.FOC+3fem.sgBAS.NP
     'May the rain not fall!'[3]

The ways in which imperatives are used in each individual language relate to a variety of social and interactive factors, as well as cultural conventions and constraints. These may include the relationship between the speaker and the addressee, their relative social status, the setting of the interaction, and also the existing conventions appropriate for a particular genre.

THE A.L. SERIES

"GOOD MANNERS"

BASED UPON RULES OF THE

Children's National Guild of Courtesy

COURTESY, Politeness, or Good Manners, means kindly and thoughtful consideration for others.   A Celebrated writer has said that a Boy who is Courteous and Pure is an honour to his country.   Brave and Noble men and women are always Courteous.   Three of the bravest and greatest men who ever lived – the Duke of Wellington, General Gordon and General Washington – were distinguished for their courteous behaviour.

Courteous Boys and Girls will always be careful to observe the following RULES :–

AS TO THEMSELVES	Be Honest, Truthful, and Pure. Do not use Bad Language. Keep out of Bad Company. Keep your Face and Hands clean, and your Clothes and Boots brushed and neat.
AT HOME	Help your Parents as much as you can, and do your best to please them. Be kind to your Brothers and Sisters. Do not be Selfish, but share all your Good Things.
AT SCHOOL	Be Respectful to your Teachers, and help them as much as you can; their work is very difficult and trying. Observe the School Rules. Do not "Copy," nor Cheat in any way. Do not Cut the Desks, nor Write in the Reading Books, etc. Never let another be Punished in mistake for yourself; this is Cowardly and Mean.
AT PLAY	Do not Cheat at Games. Do not Bully; only Cowards do this. Be Pleasant and not Quarrelsome. Do not Jeer at your Schoolmates, or call them by Names which they do not like.
IN THE STREET	Salute your Ministers, Teachers, and Acquaintances when you meet them; they will Salute you in return. Do not Push nor run against people. Do not Chalk on doors, walls, nor gates. Do not Throw Stones, nor destroy Property. Do not Annoy Shopkeepers by Loitering at their shop doors and windows. Do not make Slides on the pavement, nor throw Orange Peel or Banana Skins there; *dangerous accidents* often result from these practices. Do not make Fun of Old nor Crippled People, but be particularly polite to them, as well as to Strangers and Foreigners.
AT TABLE	Always Wash your Hands and Face before coming to the Table. Do not put your Knife to your Mouth. Look after Other People; do not Help yourself only. Do not be greedy. Do not Speak nor Drink with Food in your Mouth. Turn your head away from the Table and put your Hand or Handkerchief before your Mouth when you Sneeze or Cough. Do not sit with your Elbows on the Table.
EVERYWHERE	Never be Rude to *anybody*, whether older or younger, richer or poorer, than yourself. Remember to say "Please" or "Thank You"; "Yes, Sir," or "Yes, Ma'am"; "No, Sir," or "No, Ma'am." Before entering a room it is often courteous to Knock at the Door. Do not forget to close the door *quietly* after you. Always show attention to Older People and Strangers by opening the door for them, bringing what they require (hat, chair, etc.), giving up your seat to them if necessary, and in every possible way Saving them trouble. Never Interrupt when a person is speaking. Always Mind your own Business. Be Punctual. Be Tidy
REMEMBER	All these rules respecting your conduct towards others are included in the one GOLDEN RULE, "*Always do to others as you would wish them to do to you if you were in their place.*" Whenever, therefore, you are in doubt as to how you should act toward others ask yourself this question, "How should I like them to act towards me if I were in their place?" and then *Do what your conscience tells you is right.*

[COPYRIGHT]   F. J. ARNOLD & SON. LTD.. Educational Publishers. LEEDS, EDINBURGH and BELFAST.

FIGURE 9.7 'Good manners'

Despite the amazing frequency of imperatives in many genres of English,[4] the imperative enjoys a bad reputation: overusing it in face-to-face conversation creates an image of a bossy and unpleasant person. In her comparison of what she perceived as gentle and mild Arapesh culture with the harsh and rough Mundugumor, Margaret Mead (1935: 199–200) observes: 'the first lessons that a Mundugumor child learns are a series of prohibitions', and then adds: 'The people make an extraordinarily frequent use of the imperative form. When I think of a Mundugumor verb it is always the imperative form that leaps into my mind, in strong contrast to my memory of Arapesh, in which imperatives were very seldom used.' One gets an impression of a highly rigid and unfriendly environment full of prohibitions. This is what overusing imperative forms implies, for Margaret Mead as a Western scholar.

This, however, may be nothing other than projection of Margaret Mead's own—westernized—ideas about the connotations of an imperative to a society in which these connotations may not exist.[5] Mildred Larson, in her guide to translators, warns her readers against projecting one's European intuitions onto another language with different communication strategies (Larson 1998: 471):

In Africa, a friend might come and put down a couple of dishes of food on one's doorstep and say, 'Eat!'. To a person of some other culture, such as American, it might sound very harsh, and the person would feel they must obey. But, as a matter of fact, that is not the intent in the African culture. The friend has cooked supper and is simply inviting the other person to share it. That person is free to eat a full meal or just take a few mouthfuls and then say that they are satisfied. If in a text translated from an African language and culture into English, such a situation were a part of the story, the translator would not use the English imperative 'Eat!'. The translator should rather say, 'Would you like some?' or 'Help yourself, if you would like'. The words *would like* give the attitude and cultural information which was communicated by the command 'Eat!' in the African story.

Along similar lines, John Saeed (1993: 83) remarks: 'Note that, possibly as a result of the egalitarian nature of traditional Somali society, imperatives do not have the same associations of power and impoliteness as in English and are consequently much more commonly used.'[6]

The interaction of linguistic and cultural constraints may account for differences in the actual usage of imperatives. We saw in §8.2 that in many Australian Aboriginal societies asking information questions is tantamount to showing yourself as nosey and intrusive. Information is volunteered rather than directly requested—this makes communication indirect and minimally face-threatening. The same applies to commands and directive acts of all sorts. A polite request in Kuuk-Thayorre is phrased as a negative statement (8.27–8).[7]

In Nyangumarta and Karajarri, two Australian languages from Western Australia, imperatives sound brusque and abrupt (Sharp 2003a, b, 2004). If one intends to be nice and polite, other strategies will be used—we can recall from §8.2 that in Nyangumarta, a 'more respectful way of issuing a command is to use the future tense' (Sharp 2004: 185). And a Karajarri speaker might use future or potential to make their command sound not so abrupt or urgent. However, under certain circumstance using imperatives is perfectly in order. Sharp (2003a) remarks that in hunting situations Karajarri imperatives imply urgency of a command, 'and the intent of the speaker is for immediate action':

9.2   Kuwi   wanti   pirti-ngka,   karli-ya   pirti!
      meat   stay.PRES   hole-LOC   dig-IMPV   hole
      'The animal is in the hole, dig the hole!'

Imperatives are used (and expected to be followed immediately) if someone is being told to avoid a relative they are not supposed to see, or talk to, in agreement with cultural conventions. We can recall from 6.17 that in Yankunytjatjara, an Australian language (Goddard 1983: 306–7), a parent-in-law cannot directly address the son-in-law asking him for food. A request has to be done through an intermediary. This intermediary is also not allowed to use a direct way of commanding—that is, an imperative. Social and kinship relationships within a community limit the imperative usage.[8]

Nuer, a Western Nilotic language, has a specialized imperative paradigm (Crazzolàra 1933: 140). However, according to Akalu (1985: 63–4), who did an extensive first-hand anthropological study of the Nuer (especially the Nipnip group),

the Nipnip never use imperative statements in communication with each other. I have never heard any words equivalent to 'you shall'. Elder men do not give orders to young men, men do not command women, parents do not instruct children. [...]When someone is in need of help or assistance by another, his request takes the form of a petition for help [...]. In consequence, such verbal categories as obedience and disobedience seem to be absent in the language of the group. Of course, orders may be expressed not only in grammatical imperative form but also by other verbal formulations, by mimic, facial or bodily gestures. Nor did I observe any such interactions of imperative meaning among the Nipnip. In order to get to the bottom of this matter I followed especially carefully such situation in which suggestions for action are brought forward. It sometimes happens that older men propose to younger age groups that some of these should accompany them and help them in some specific enterprise such as hunting or fishing [...] or driving cattle to Gambela in order to exchange them for sorghum or tobacco. The younger age group then discusses the suggestion among themselves and they agree on which of them will participate or even all of them refrain from joining in when something enticing is in sight. Thus there is no question of a command relation in these situations. Much work is carried out without speech and it is up to each individual to decide when and how he will carry it out. Usually the pleasure of being together is so great that joint activity is a matter of course. Most of the time more attention is paid to what the elderly people are saying since they are considered to be more experienced in all matters.[9]

Akalu concludes: 'In all situations, the Nuer dislike and avoid everything that resembles superiority or directives as to how to behave.'

The Ilongot of the Philippines have a different attitude to, and consequently make different use of, commands and directives. This is how Rosaldo (1982: 204) starts her discussion of the Ilongot:

One striking feature of the Ilongot households where my husband and I lived, for close to two years in 1967–69 and again for nine months in 1974, was the salience, in daily life, of brief and undisguised directives. Although a sense of balance and reciprocity obtained in what appeared to be quite egalitarian relations among both children and adults, demands for services were so common that one quickly learned to turn to others rather than obtain desired objects by oneself. So, for example, Bayaw, who finished eating moments before his wife was heard to issue this directive: *ta denum Sawad ya, 'aika 'egkang* 'That (implying, 'over there, unconnected to you') water, Sawad c'mon, come and get up now.' And 'Insan, wanting a bit of lime in preparation for his betel chew, remained seated while he told his wife to move: *tu tangtangmu Duman, rawmu* 'This (implying, 'it is yours, is not far, alien from you') your lime container, Duman, go get it.' Duman, already occupied, did not challenge his command, but instead responded by communicating the father's words to a young daughter: *rawmud tu 'umel* 'Go get it over here, little girl.'

Throughout the traditional life of the Ilongot, commands operate 'in lines associated with age- and sex-linked social rank':

Although it is not difficult to find exceptions to the rule—men ask children directly; juniors make demands of seniors; women call on men to help with their domestic tasks, to join in garden work or hunt [. . .], women, engaged more frequently than men in daily household tasks, are both more likely to receive commands and to command their children. And children, following hierarchies of age, receive and then pass on directives from their seniors.

Again, in Rosaldo's words,

these Ilongots, who in many ways appeared more flexible and egalitarian than any people I have known, recognized and apparently enjoyed in their domestic life a hierarchy of commands blatant and (to me) unjust.

The form of commands in Ilongot correlates more with 'what Ilongots see as reasonable expectations and accounts of their objective needs than with desires to accommodate those whose relative status differs from one's own'. The shortest imperative form (incompletive aspect) is most common in directives to the young, e.g. *'ekarka* 'get going!', *pilisim* 'squeeze it (e.g. vegetables, to see if they are cooked)'. According to the Ilongots themselves, it is 'an efficient tool that wins immediate and limited responses'. Commands in the subjunctive can be used 'either to plead or to complain'. The Ilongot are aware of the difference between a straightforward imperative, such as *rawka manakdu* 'Go and fetch water!' and a more elaborate expression, e.g. *'engraw'uka enakdu* 'if only (subjunctive) you would go fetch water', pointing out that 'choice is shaped, primarily not by differential rank, but rather by the sense of speed and likelihood with which the speaker seeks compliance'. This shows that the use of commands does not directly translate into the ideas of social inequality, rank, or power. For the Ilongot, 'all people, ultimately, are "equal" or, as they put it, *'anurut* "the same"'' (Rosaldo 1982: 207).

People who generally give commands are said to have 'knowledge' and deserve 'respect'. Those who receive commands are '"lightest" and "most quick" to stir and stand: the woman who "knows" little of the world and yet takes pride in her agility around the home; the child who, still lacking "shame", appears inclined to constant movement.' The Ilongot say that a child needs commands because 'its heart lacks "knowledge" of its own. And it is through *tuydek*, or commands, that adults first shape the movements of young hearts, thus teaching youths to think of things that should be done' (p. 208).

Commands are significant for organizing the energy of the immature and the powerless, and they are also critical for a child's learning of how to behave, and of their relationships with adults. Rosaldo summarizes the social function of the commands (*tuydek*) as follows:

Tuydek, then, were seen as the exemplary act of speech. As significant in ordering domestic life as in the socialization of the young, directive utterances were, for my Ilongot friends, the very stuff of language: knowing how to speak itself was virtually identical to knowing how and when to act.

The Ilongot are aware of the special status of directive speech acts, and have a subtle classification of their types. Each has a distinct term (Rosaldo 1982: 223):

In general, Ilongots claim, 'commands' or *tuydek* should be distinguished from related acts of speech—like 'prohibitions' (*tukbur*), 'orders, warnings' (*tengteng*), 'requests' (*bēge*), 'appeals' (*'ungi'ungi*) and a variety of unclassified directives that include such things as 'awakening' (*pabengun*) and 'hurrying up' (*pekamu*). And even though they were aware of ambiguity and difficulty in discriminating among such acts as these, informants found it reasonable to assign directive utterances different directive names—and in so doing, to reflect on meanings implicated in their names for verbal deeds.

Of the three major types, *tuydek* are the commands typically received by those who are likely to 'get up' and 'move'. The typical *tuydek* call for services in which the person 'commanded' performs the action out of 'respect, or deference' towards another. The *tuydek* are concerned with finite, easily realized labour.

Requests, *bēge,* in Ilongot do not have the same connotations of a more indirect, less hierarchical variety of a command. What distinguishes a 'request' from a 'command' is the quality of the movement they evoke ('a request will only rarely involve a major movement from or interruption of the addressee's ongoing action': Rosaldo 1982: 225). A goal of a 'request' is either to secure the addressee's welfare—encouraging them to do something that will benefit them—or to get their cooperation with someone seeking help.

In contrast, *tengteng* 'order, warning' is associated with 'notions of futurity or with incompletive verbs' (p. 226). A salient feature of orders or warning of this type is 'the open-endedness of the action that they call for'. Rosaldo concludes (p. 227), that, for the Ilongot,

three culturally situated concerns emerge as necessary to a characterization of differences between directives. First, because divisions of labor in terms of sex and age are (as we have seen) conceived by Ilongots in terms of differences in 'knowledge' and capacities to 'move,' directives are distinguished in terms of their concern with interruption/movement. Second, because directives concern coordination of tasks and services in a world where hierarchy is balanced by parity, and autonomy by cooperative work, directives are distinguished in terms of hierarchical as against more mutual or reciprocal chains of service and command. And third, because directives figure centrally in the articulation of a kinship order that is experienced, most of the time, as given, and yet in fact requires repeated realization in concrete cooperative displays, directives differ with reference to the action context that a directive act evokes. In short, indigenous views of human actions and interactions—concerns for movement; for social hierarchy and cooperation; and for the temporal fragility of social bonds—prove necessary to an understanding of conventions that discriminate among directive categories that Ilongots recognize as such.

To become a competent speaker of any language one has to be able to do more than just produce grammatical sentences: without adhering 'to the complex norms of the society concerning language use in particular and personal interaction', a language learner's experience will be fraught with misunderstandings (Keenan and Ochs 1979: 114). Successful communication in Malagasy involves avoiding confrontation and associated 'shame'. Ordering and requesting is a case in point (Keenan and Ochs 1979: 153–6). Since 'giving someone an order is a confrontation experience, when such is necessary we might expect the Malagasy to have recourse to means for "softening the blow". Such is indeed the case.' So, 'an active order in Malagasy is considered a highly brusque statement and a confrontation. It is used only in situations of stress or anger, and Europeans who frequently use active imperatives in Malagasy are often misinterpreted as being much more aggressive and authoritarian than they intend to be.'

In Malagasy, a normal way of framing an order would be to 'put the verb in something other than the active voice, making the patient of the action or some circumstance of the action the subject phrase and hence the item on which attention is focused. The addressee phrase, again usually omitted, would occur as a passive agent or circumstantial agent if present. Thus the normal way to say "Wash the clothes" would be *Sasao(-nao) ny lamba* "be washed (by you) the clothes". This is consistent with polite overtones of commands which involve passive and impersonal forms (see §8.2, and example 8.23).[10]

Requests are 'often an occasion of considerable frustration on the part of the European in a Malagasy context' (Keenan and Ochs 1979: 154). Requests are not given directly,

for this would put the requestee on the spot and risk an affront to the requester if the request is denied. A normal request, even a fairly urgent one, usually takes place in stages. The requester approaches the requestee and engages him in conversation. Then he brings up the topic his request concerns but does not overtly make the request. The requestee is then free to ignore the topic and move to something else if he would prefer not to satisfy the request. He never has to confront the requester with a denial; he need not recognize the speech act as a request at all. Of course, the requester may persist and continually reintroduce a topic that concerns his needs, but if he is repeatedly ignored, he can still leave without feeling rejected, and hence shamed.

And it is also quite usual for such an indirect request to be made by someone other than the one who needs an object, or a service. A group of boys came once to Keenan and Ochs's house in the Malagasy village, and talked for about twenty minutes; then the subject of a cut foot was brought up. Eventually one of the boys in the back of the group came forward and showed his severely bleeding foot. The purpose of the visit was requesting help; but following the speech etiquette, it was not the injured boy who asked for it: his peer group performed the request on his behalf. In Keenan and Ochs's words (p. 154–5), the Malagasy requests

are indirect in two ways: They are not made explicitly, and they are often made by a third party on someone else's behalf. [...] It is important to realize here that our characterization of the Malagasy request as indirect is ethnocentric on our part. What that means is indirect relative to our norms. But for the Malagasy, performing an 'indirect' request is simply to request. To force the behaviour to be direct would make it into a social act with very different consequences. The 'indirectness' of Malagasy requests follows from the more general and pervasive norms of group, not individual responsibility and nonconfrontation.

The request behaviour of the Malagasy speakers in Madagascar is very different from what a European expects, and is easily misinterpreted: 'A European's request often seems like a confrontation to the Malagasy and this engenders hostility and lack of cooperation. And the Malagasy's request to the European often appears "devious", perhaps even dishonest.' In addition,

the European may often find himself as having been understood to have made a request where in fact none was intended. For example, on one occasion Edward [Keenan], in making idle conversation with a neighbor, happened to remark on the large pile of sweet potatoes in front of the man's house. About twenty minutes later, having returned to our own house, we were surprised to see the man's son appear with a plate of two cooked sweet potatoes! On reflection, it was clear that our casual remark was interpreted as a request by our neighbor. So in adapting to this Malagasy norm, one must learn to both listen more attentively and to understate (by European standards) one's intentions. (p. 156)

In summary, phrasing your command or request in an inappropriate form may result in a serious misunderstanding. A number of other general factors condition the ways in which requests are made in the Malagasy-speaking society:

The directness of a request will vary with the magnitude of a request and the social relations that exist between the requester and the requestee. If a request is of small magnitude, as for a piece of tobacco, it is more likely to be made, all other things being equal, in a reasonably direct way. But if the request is major, as for a bride or for sizable assistance in a bone-turning ceremony, the request will certainly be indirect. Similarly, if the two parties are *havana* (a term that covers kinsmen and close acquaintances) the request is more likely to be direct. But if one of the parties is *vahiny* (outsider, stranger, foreigner), the request is almost certain to be indirect. If one of the parties is *vahiny* and the request is minor, or if the request is major and the parties are *havana,* the degree of directness will be adjusted to suit the particular circumstances, though always falling on the indirect side by European standards.[11]

Pre-existing socially determined relationships condition the use of direct or of indirect imperative in Arapaho (Cowell 2007). We saw in §6.3 that a simple imperative in Arapaho is perceived as too direct, and thus threatening. A frequent option for mitigating such effect is using an indirect command. An indirect command is not just a face-saving device: it is a mechanism for constructing a social identity. In a situation where one person tells someone else to have their child do something, imperative is used sparingly. In Cowell's (2007: 52) words,

To use a direct causative command ('make him be quiet') when an older child is involved would imply an improper degree of immaturity—or 'craziness', as the Arapahos say—on the part of a child. Such a direct command would imply little or no agency for the child. An indirect imperative would recognize a greater degree of agency on the part of the child, and would also secondarily imply more options for the addressee in accomplishing the action, thus lessening the force and the authority and the speaker's command. In addition, correcting the child directly with a direct imperative would be rude in dismissing the authority of the parent—in Arapaho society generally, people are typically corrected by going through another, usually an older family member rather than addressing them directly. Once again, judgements about speaker, addressee, and third person are all encoded in the choice of imperative.

Importantly, however, the use of a direct or of an indirect imperative is

only partially dictated by pre-existing, clear-cut social relationships. Rather, the choice of imperative form is a way of imputing a greater degree of agency and personhood to the child. Language constructs social identity and relationships in this case, rather than simply reflecting or acknowledging it

—and this is achieved through the means of using the appropriate form of command.

A revealing example of how using an appropriate imperative may serve to shape a particular interpretation of a relationship with outsiders comes from Cowell's own fieldwork:

I am in my early forties and was working with a Gros Ventre man in his mid-thirties to translate certain texts from English to Gros Ventre based on my knowledge of Gros Ventre and Arapaho. An older Arapaho man in his sixties approached us; he knew both of us, knew that I knew Arapaho well, and knew that the younger Gros Ventre man could understand some Arapaho based on his knowledge of Gros Ventre as a second language. He asked in Arapaho what we were doing, and I replied in Arapaho that we were translating stories into Gros Ventre. The Gros Ventre man was the one writing down the texts. The older Arapaho man then said to me, using an indirect imperative, 'neyéitííhee', 'have him read it'. The reason he didn't simply tell the Gros Ventre man himself to read the material, using a direct imperative, was that he was showing respect to me as the older person, as well as the perceived 'expert' whom the younger Gros Ventre man was consulting. To have spoken directly to the Gros Ventre man would have left me out of the exchange in a way considered rude. Thus the Arapaho man went through me in addressing the younger man [...] His use of the indirect imperative was not really dictated by clear-cut social rules (given that neither I nor the other man was even Arapaho). The Arapaho man's use of the form in this case served [...] more generally to construe our relationship within Arapaho social and linguistic terms.

There is no strict correlation between social status and the choice of a grammatical form: the choice of imperative reflects negotiable relationships.[12] The way a directive act is framed reflects the speaker's attitude to the addressee and to what is to be achieved. Besides direct imperative and several indirect imperatives, Arapaho has another type of imperative, called a 'hortative' construction (which, unlike an imperative, can be used with reference to any person). The hortative construction suggests that 'the addressee's actions would be one among several possible factors responsible for accomplishing the goal', the indirect imperative 'stresses that the addressee, and only the addressee is responsible for the desired action occurring—but only indirectly' (Cowell 2007: 47). In prayers to God, the Arapaho use the indirect imperative (*hoosootíhee* 'let it rain/ make it rain'): they 'seem reluctant to "order" God to do something to a third party with a direct imperative; the indirect imperative allows one (in Arapaho) to go beyond merely hoping hortatively (*heetíh-ʔoosóótiʔ* = "let it rain"), while still maintaining a relationship of deference' (p. 57).

Potential command/request forms in Arapaho form a hierarchical scale. The mildest and the most deferential one is number 5.

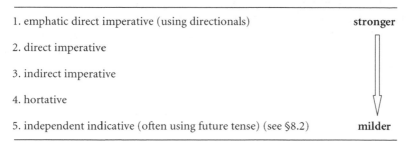

1. emphatic direct imperative (using directionals)   **stronger**

2. direct imperative

3. indirect imperative

4. hortative

5. independent indicative (often using future tense) (see §8.2)   **milder**

FIGURE 9.8 Hierarchy of commands in Arapaho

In Cowell's (2007: 57) words, 'the *general* pragmatic implications of these forms are that speaker agency and authority decline as one goes down this list. When the forms are used to an addressee who is responsible for the action of a third person, the agency and/or authority of that third person increases as one goes down the list, while that of the addressee decreases.' A future form in English can be used as a stern command, to someone who has no choice but to obey: *You will complete your assignment.* A future form in Arapaho can also be used in a directive act—but with highly deferential overtones, 'emphasizing the strong authority' of the addressee (see §8.2).

To summarize: correct and culturally appropriate usage of directive speech acts, and particularly imperative forms, is central to mastering a language and finding one's place in the society—rather than projecting one's own language norms onto the new language you are exposed to.[13] How can imperative be used in a wider context? This is our next topic.

9.2 Imperatives in context

A recently reissued series of little books entitled *Don'ts for husbands, Don'ts for wives,* and also *Don'ts for golfers* and *Don'ts for dancers* (by Blanche Ebbutt, A. & C. Black Ltd, 1913) are a treasure chest of yesteryear's conventional wisdom. Here are a couple of examples of what a good husband is never to do:

9.3   Don't expect happiness if you married for money; once she realizes it, your wife won't let you forget it.

9.4   Don't be too didactic in your home. Your wife is not to be treated as a schoolgirl to have the law laid down by you.

In each of these instances, a prohibition, or a piece of advice not to behave in a certain way, is followed by a reason why not. Figure 9.7 provides numerous examples of the same kind. It appears not enough to instruct a boy or a girl *Don't bully.* An explicit reason *only cowards do this* makes the instruction sound more persuasive.

This is a common strategy for contextualizing a command in many languages. A command in Karajarri is often accompanied by an explanation as to what could happen if it is not followed. Such an explanation can precede the imperative, as in 9.5 (Sharp 2003a):

9.5   Ranka-marta   kinyangka,   kajarri   jarri-ya-rala!
       rough-ATTR   3sg   far   become-IMPV-BEN
       'He is a rough bloke, give him room!'

Or it can follow:

9.6   Pira-la-wanungku!   Kamininy   jarri-ya-n-ku
       cover-IMPV-REFL   cold   become-ANT-2sgS-ANT
       'Cover yourself! You might get cold'

Explicitly stating the consequences of what may happen if the order is not followed is somewhat similar to parallel statements in lieu of prohibitives in Marathi (see 8.69, 'You insult her, and I will never talk to you again'). In Yidiñ, a positive or a negative imperative occurs in the main clause of a sentence with a 'lest' subordinate clause (Dixon 1977: 351–2):

9.7 giyi   djanan   maga:da,   djigurula
     PROH   stand+IMPV   outside+LOC   thunderstorm+LOC
     djiguruŋgu   bundja:ndji
     thunderstorm+ERG   hit+LEST+ABS
     'Don't stand outside, in a thunderstorm, lest a thunderbolt strike you!'

Along similar lines, in Paumarí, an imperative is often followed by a reason clause (Chapman and Derbyshire 1991: 219).

9.8 jorajora-pa'itxi   bana   tapo'ija-ra
     hurry-small   FUT:WARNING   wild.animal-OBJ
     o-noki-'i-ki-ho
     1sg-see-ASP-NONTHEME-1sg
     'Hurry a little, I have seen a jaguar'

Or it can be followed by a purpose clause, again, providing a purpose for which the command would have to be obeyed:[14]

9.9 ai   ari-hi-'iana-va,   mahija a-joi-joraki-vini
     depart 1pl-AUX-again-HORT so.that 1pl-return-quick-DEPENDENT.TRANS
     'Let's leave so that we can return quickly'[15]

Contextualizing a command may have an additional stylistic effect. According to Baranov (1988), in Russian, adding an explanatory statement makes the command milder and ensures its success, as in *Do write an article—it is not difficult for you.*

A negative command can be followed by a suggestion itself cast in imperative: 9.10, another quote from *Don'ts for husbands*, contains an advice what not to do, and followed by a suggestion what to do:

9.10 Don't expect your wife to do all the cheering up while you do all the giving way when things go wrong. Share and share alike.

Similar techniques recur in many languages across the world. In Martuthunira, from the Pilbara region of Western Australia (Dench 2009: 281), two clauses put together in sequence are in an 'alternative' relationship. A positive imperative can be followed by a negative command (what not to do instead of what is recommended that the addressee should do, in the first clause). A negative command is marked as negative future—Dench remarks that 'speakers reject the imperative inflection as impolite'.

9.11 manku-ø-rru   yirnala-a!   mir.ta   nyina-layi   nhawu-rra
     grab-IMPV-now   this:DEF-ACC   not   sit-FUT   watch-CTEMP
     yirla   thurlamanta!
     only   staring
     'Grab this fellow! Don't just sit staring!'

Alternatively, a negative command can come first, followed by a positive instruction:

9.12 mir.ta   yirra-marta   kalya-rninyji!   wurnta-l.yu   kurlany-marta!
     not   teeth-COMIT   bite-FUT   cut-IMPV   knife-COMIT
     'Don't bite it with your teeth! Cut it with a knife'

In Yidiñ, a positive command would often accompany a negative imperative: 'in addition to being told what he should not do, the addressee is also advised about what would be an appropriate course of action to undertake' (Dixon 1977: 371):

9.13 mayi   giyi   wuñḍay   ḍula?   baḍar
     vegetables+ABS PROH   stolen+ABS   dig.IMPV   leave.IMPV
     'Don't dig up vegetables that don't belong to you (literally: stolen vegetables)! Leave [them] alone!'

These strategies provide explanations or viable alternatives for commands and directive acts. They are grounded in some general principles of human behaviour. In Cialdini's (1993: 4) words, 'when we ask someone to do us a favour we will be more successful if we provide a reason'. An experiment conducted by social psychologist Ellen Langer (1989) demonstrated how this principle works. She asked a number of people waiting in line to use a library copying machine for a small favour, saying *Excuse me, I have five pages. May I use the Xerox machine because I am in a rush?* This request-cum-reason was an overwhelming success: 94 per cent of those in the queue let her skip ahead of them. But when she made the request only, saying *Excuse me, I have five pages. May I use the Xerox machine?*, only 60 per cent of those asked let her use the machine. It was providing a reason for people's compliance—using a reason clause, *because I am in a rush*—that made all the difference. The author of the experiment tried another reason clause, saying *Excuse me, I have five pages.*

May I use the Xerox machine because I have to make some copies? This also worked miracles—93 per cent of those asked let her skip the queue.[16]

The secret of the effectiveness of the request lies in the way it is structured: imperatives are powerful weapons of influence, but they have to be phrased and used in agreement with the existing conventions.[17]

Different structural types of commands may occur in different genres or contexts. In Standard Average European languages, commands are a norm in instruction manuals, recipe books and the like. Proverbs often contain commands, as in English *Scratch a Russian and find a Tartar*. Military commands in English (Sadock and Zwicky 1985: 177–8) have their own, rather special syntactic organization. Each command consists of two parts: a preparatory part telling one where to start the action followed by an executive part telling where or how to do it. The latter contains somewhat redundant information; cf. the command to place rifles on the right shoulder: *Right shoulder—arms!* In many languages, imperatives occur on their own only in abrupt informal commands, such as instructions shouted to children or animals (see McKay 2000: 301 for Ndjébbana). Imperatives are widely used in English instructions, advertisements, and rules aimed at everyone in general but without targeting or threatening a specific addressee. Once the speaker has a specific person in mind, other options come handy: we saw in Chapter 8 how non-imperative forms are used in lieu of straightforward imperatives to avoid face-threatening speech acts.[18]

There may be other preferences for the use of commands. Dixon (1977: 371) reports that Yidiñ 'uses imperatives to refer to desirable or proscribed actions, but not usually to advise on states and attitudes'. That is, the appropriate way of saying 'Don't be silly' in Yidiñ translates as 'Why are you being silly?' The following would be the appropriate Yidiñ construction 'for telling someone to behave himself':

9.14 ñundu   wañi:ngu   yaṟuñdagañ
     you.s/A   what.PURP   silly.INCH.VERBALIZER.PRES
     (lit. 'Why are you being silly?')

The consultant translated this as 'Don't be silly'.

An imperative form may have a stylistic effect: in Yankunytjatjara, the imperfective imperative may be used in a narrative relating 'a series of events which could or might happen', with a 'vivid' and 'dramatic effect' (Goddard 1983: 189, 191–2).[19] And in Nyangumarta, a narrative can consist of a series of imperatives as part of reported speech, if it describes a series of instructions

(Sharp 2003b: 186). In 9.15, a dog is commanding a child to do a number of things. The verb of speech does not have to be overtly present:

9.15 pala-ja   yapan   <u>ma-rra</u>,   yirti   <u>ngarta-la</u>   makanu,
      that-ABL   hot.stones get-IMPV   stick   break-IMPV   long
      wika <u>tili-ji-li</u>
      FIRE flame-AFF-IMPV
      'And after that (he told him) to get the hot stones, a cooking stick and
      to break up the firewood to make a fire'

Imperative forms used with a special stylistic effect are reminiscent of imperatives that 'do not command' discussed in Chapter 7. And we can recall how frequently imperative forms appear in lexicalized speech formulae—greetings, farewells, blessings, and curses—see §7.2.[20] Their command function is superseded by their formulaic use.

Imperatives may have their own, conventionalized ways of response, different from that used in answers to questions. Tariana and Baniwa of Içana both employ *haw* 'OK' (mark of agreement). Paumarí *jakaho* 'OK' implies agreement to perform a command. Paumarí has another response word, *jakana*, which implies a positive intention rather than simple agreement (Chapman and Derbyshire 1991: 220). Hixkaryana has a variety of response particles used only as reactions to second-person imperatives. Particles *hɨɨ*, *ɨɨ*, and *mm* are noncommittal or mildly positive, while *ina hami* is strongly positive.[21]

In Zargulla, an Omotic language from Ethiopia (Amha MS-b), one-word responses to calls, commands, and questions have the same plural marker -*ite* as in the imperative addressed to more than one person. 9.16a contains some of the calls (also see §9.3), and 9.16b contains the response.

9.16a yéša-ite   used to call several people or a respected person
       yéebi   used to call a single feminine person, younger or of the
                  same age or status as speaker
       yéla   used to call a single masculine person, younger or of the
                  same age or status as speaker

9.16b yé-ite   response to a call made by several people, or by a respected
                  single person
       yéé   response to a call made by person, younger or of the same
                  age or status[22]

Note that plural agreement is with the addressee, in each of these cases. So is gender agreement in 9.16a.

We now turn to further interactions between lexicon, and directives, with imperatives among them.

9.3 Imperatives and the lexicon

Directive speech acts interact with the lexicon in several ways.

FIRSTLY, a language may have special imperative-only lexemes, which stand apart from other parts of word classes. Nyangumarta (Sharp 2003b) has a number of imperative-only uninflected forms, including *kula!* 'Later! Hang on! Just a moment, wait a while!', *yakujarni!* 'Come here, come to this side!' and *yuu, yuu* 'Look out! Get away from there!'.

Ndjébbana, also Australian, has a number of uninflected single-word imperatives. The uninflected form *djóbo* 'Shoo!' is usually addressed to animals. Forms *báb* 'Sit down!', *djáddi* 'Come here!' and *kalábbuk* 'Shut up! Be quiet!' are used to children or other people with whom the speaker has a relatively close relationship. Imperative forms are used in a situation of less familiarity (McKay 2000: 300).

Directive-only words can be combined with an imperative form of the verb. Russian has a number of one-word commands, including *na!* 'take (singular addressee)', *na-te* (plural addressee) (accompanied with a gesture of giving and often with an imperative of a lexical verb: Ozhegov and Shvedova 1997), and a number of commands for shooing off non-humans, e.g. *brysj* 'shoo (to a cat)', *kysh* 'shoo (to a bird)'.

Many languages have 'let's go' and 'let's do (something)' as a one-word uninflected command, cf. Baniwa *ahʃa*; Tariana *wasã*; Jarawara *hima*; Modern Hebrew *yalla* 'let's go'; Tariana *ma* 'let's (do something)'; Tucano *te'á* 'let's go' and *mâa* 'let's do (something)'. This is similar to Moses Columbia Salish 'adhortative predicates' *húytaʔ* 'go on! come on!' and *xwús(ǝs)taʔ* 'come on, hurry up' (Mattina 1999). These may optionally be followed by a second predicate in an imperative form, as in Tucano *atia baa-ra* 'let's go, let's eat' (let's go and eat) and Moses Columbia Salish.

Uninflected imperatives may cover a wide range of meanings. In Sm'algyax (or Tsimshian: Stebbins 2000), they include *k'aha'wini* 'Not yet! Wait for me!', *laan* 'Go!', *laansm* 'Go (pl)!', *ndeh* 'Get out! Get away!', *ndo'a* 'Go on, off you go, go ahead!', *ndzu* 'Give it to me'; while Evenki has *hos'e:!* 'Leave it (alone)', *nasar'e!* 'Leave me alone!', *ma!* 'Take it!', *chivir'e:!* 'Be silent!' (Nedjalkov 1997: 21). Imperative-only lexemes can be analysed as suppletive imperatives (see §2.1.3 and below).[23]

Languages vary in how rich they are in directive-only forms. Matses (Fleck forthcoming: 536) has a system of command-only words directed at animals, typically, hunting dogs. These include whistles, the 'multifunctional long-distance interjection' *ëëë*, and four particles. The particle *kushe* 'let's go, dog/go, dog, go' is a general term for encouraging a dog while pursuing an animal,[24] or when a hunter is leaving the village to go hunting, to get the dog to follow him.

The particle *newaṣh* is used to call a dog to the hunter (getting the dog either to follow him when leaving the village or to return after having been away from the owner). This same form is also used to call dogs back to the owner when they encounter a jaguar, because the dogs might otherwise want to fight the jaguar and are likely to be injured or killed.

The particle *ëëë* is used to encourage dogs to follow a tapir, a collared peccary, or an agouti (a rodent). In Fleck's words, 'this sound is believed to travel the furthest distance in the jungle, and the hunter yells this very loudly because the dogs follow these animals far and will stop pursuing them if they don't hear their master encouraging them.' The call *ee* is used to encourage a dog to pursue a paca, a largish rodent (this is not yelled because pacas do not run far).

The particle *sh* 'Scram, dog' is used within the home to get a dog to run away 'when it is trying to steal food, going where it is not supposed to go, or hassling a visitor'. A special verb *ishka* means 'shoo away a dog'. The interjections *tdu* and *aak* are 'believed to be effective for scaring off jaguars. When a hunter sees a jaguar or senses that a jaguar is around, he may yell this to get the jaguar to run off. Also, after killing a tapir, a hunter may yell out *tdu* and/or *aak* as a precaution to keep away any jaguars that might be attracted to the kill.'

Zargulla (Amha MS-b) has a number of forms used for addressing people—that is directive-only forms used in human-to-human interaction: see, for instance, 9.16a, and 9.17.

9.17 *haʔá-ite* uttered when giving something to several people or to a respected person

haʔá when giving something to a single individual, younger or of the same age as speaker

In 9.16a (but not in 9.17), the forms agree in gender, number, and 'status' with the addressee. This is the only example of gender distinction in directive forms; the imperative itself does not differentiate genders.[25]

Zargulla is amazingly rich in directives to domestic animals—which is not all that surprising given the cultural focus on animal herding, and the variety of animals bred (which include sheep, oxen, cows, goats, and fowl). Amha (MS-b) divides the directives into 'dispersals' (telling animals to move away from a certain location) and summons (telling them to come nearer to the speaker). Summons involve repetition, lengthening of vowels, and 'what appears to be a more friendly or normal intonation'. In contrast, dispersals involve 'exaggeratedly raised voice', 'and the forms are pronounced with a higher speed'. Special forms used for oxen, cows, goats and other animals are listed in 9.18:

9.18	Animal	Summons	Dispersals
	oxen	*ʔāā* (summon for mating; can be called by name)	*wāā*
	cows	*ʔaa* (to summon, to stop/calm down when agitated)	*káis*
	goat	*miiʔo*	*ʔiššá*
	sheep	*baáʔ*	*ʔúss*
	chicken	*lúk / ɓík'*	*čúk*
	cats	*wurruu*	*kíp*
	dogs	*háč(i)*	*káč* or *kéči*

Summons for goats and sheep appear to be imitations of the noises made by the animals. Other forms are not onomatopoeic, and bear no similarity to the names of animals themselves. In contrast to domestic animals, either summon or dispersal forms are attested for some non-domesticated animals. There is only a dispersal form for birds (*cáay*)—which are considered trouble only—and only a summons form for bees which are useful (*búl búl táná bir-á*). Summoning bees involves throwing a handful of soil upwards 'so that when the soil falls back on the ground, each member of the colony would "think" that the other bees have descended and it too would descend'. The verb *birá* is a transitive verb meaning 'lead, go ahead (of speaker)', and 'it implies that the speaker and the addressee arrive at the same destination' (Amha MS-b).

Zargulla has further, rather elaborate directives for some valued animals, especially for oxen. These involve movement, direction, speed, and more:

9.19	Command to ploughing oxen to move quicker	*waáhh*
	To have oxen stop movement	*waah-á*
	To order oxen to resume movement after stopping for a while	*horó*
	To order oxen (and cows) to enter into the barn and take their places	*čér-a*

The final vowel here is the same as the singular imperative morpheme -*a* (however, it does not express number: normally a speaker would address at least two oxen). Further directives typically used include *wots-á* (lit. descend,climb. down-IMPV.SG) 'to correct an out-of-line movement of ploughing oxen ('move down!'), *kéz-a* (move.up-IMPV.SG) ('move up!'), and *ʔaats-á* (let.pass-IMPV.SG) 'directive to oxen that have reached the end of the length of the farm to return'.

Directives to cows, donkeys, and mules involve stopping movement and starting movement. The former are somewhat like summons in that they involve long vowels and repetitions. The latter are curt, pronounced with raised voice:

9.20   Directive to cows to stop movement: *ʔaaʔaa*
       Directive to donkeys to stop movement   *tooššé*
       Directive to horse or mule to stop movement   *noóč*
       Directive to donkeys to start movement   *hák'*
       Directive to horse or mule to start or continue movement   *máč'*

Similar forms are found in other Omotic languages such as Maale and Wolaitta, and also in Ethiopian Semitic and Cushitic.[26]

An elaborate system of calls to domestic animals in a Tamazight Berber-speaking community of Ayt Hadiddu was described by Bynon (1976). The Ayt Hadiddu have several varieties of domestic animal—the horse, mule, donkey, camel, cow, sheep, goat, cat, dog, and domestic fowl, all of them (except for the camel) established in North Africa at least since antiquity. For every variety of animal, there are calls which can be interpreted as 'Go!' and 'Come!'. For cat and domestic fowl—who range freely in the neighbourhood of the house or the tent—there are just these two calls. An additional call for a dog is to urge it to attack (a jackal, a thief, etc.). In the case of the seven other species, there are calls for a third command, something like 'Halt!' (although for herded animals, such as sheep and goats, the meaning may be 'Turn!'). And then there are further calls, different for each species—as Bynon (1976: 49) puts it, 'each can be said to have its own individual code'. Calls to a mule include a command to make it slow down ($ \check{s}\check{s}t(a)^n! $), make it advance when already in motion (*ušt!*), make it come to the caller (*ttzay!*), to make it get up, put itself straight, to make it advance to be tied up, to make it drink, to make it roll, to warn it before handling, and to chase it off or to make it gallop round the threshing floor. Some of these calls form masculine and feminine plural—instead of *ušt!* a masculine plural form *uštat* can be sometimes used when ploughing with two male mules, as well as a feminine plural form *uštmt!* (We can recall from §4.1 that in many Berber languages, especially in the Tamazight group, gender is only distinguished in plural and not in singular imperatives.)

Special calls to a donkey include a command to make it serve a mare; a camel can be ordered to kneel, change direction, put itself straight when blocking the way. Special calls to sheep include orders to make them turn from the direction in which they are going, to make them follow behind one, to make them dig the ground, to make the sheep leader come, and to make them lick salt. Calls can combine with imperative forms of verbs.

Calls to animals may contain unusual sounds. A retroflex velar click appears in the call to the mule to make it come. Unlike any other elements in the language, calls can be prolonged (and their duration is greater than simple gemination would be), repeated, and reduplicated. Similarly, in English, the sound made to encourage horses (the 'gee-up' click) is one of the few instances of clicks in this language.[27]

Some of these animal calls are attested throughout the North Berber-speaking area, and some cover Arabic-speaking areas of North Africa and even Spain—the areas where the same domestic animals have been bred and looked after for some thousands of years. Similarly to many imperative forms, they appear to be highly diffusible in language contact (see Chapter 10). Some of the forms recorded for Ayt Hadiddou have Arabic etymologies. For instance, *mšši!* to chase a dog away (also found among the Ait Seghrouchen, also from the Tamazight subgroup of North Berber) comes from the Maghribi Arabic *msi* 'to go, to go away, go off, leave, etc' (Bynon 1976: 59).

The areas of wealth for directive terms reflect the ecology of language, its habitat, and the activities of the people themselves: animal herders in North Africa and in Ethiopia have numerous directives to domestic animals, while the Matses, for whom hunting is a major activity, have only special forms for hunting dogs and the hunted animals. The directive terms provide us with a glimpse into the area of human to animal communication. And they are also important for tracing the origins and paths of diffusion of species and associated practices, as well as contact among speech communities.[28]

Imperative-specific words may be restricted to baby-talk. In Kambaata, *ná'a* 'Eat!' and *gá'a* 'Drink!' are used to address infants (the regular imperative forms are *ít* 'Eat!' and *ág* 'Drink!' (Treis MS).

Unanalysable prohibitive forms include Tamambo *tabu* 'forbidden! don't do it', and a special sign for 'don't do it' in Indopakistani Sign Language (which has a corresponding sign for a positive command 'do it!'). Animal directives with the meaning 'stop' (e.g. Ayt Hadiddou $u(z)^n3$ 'a command to a camel to make it stop' or $\check{s}\check{s}t(a)^n$ for a mule to make it stop, remain stationary, slow down (see §11.2) can also be considered inherently negative.

Imperatives can be accompanied with special hand signals, or other paralinguistic signals with a command function. Ndjébbana has a voiceless bilabial 'pop' sound meaning 'Stop!' and a hand signal for 'Come here!' (flat hand, palm facing down, fingers together, pointing toward addressee, four fingers bend down and back against palm in a single move: McKay 2000: 300). The deictic aspect of imperatives is reflected in the ways in which they are embodied, which is somewhat similar to demonstratives involving pointing and other gestures (see Haviland 2003; Wilkins 2003).

Imperative-only lexemes whose only function is to command the addressee are sometimes analysed as suppletive forms of canonical imperatives. We saw in §2.1.3 that suppletion is one of the means of expressing imperative, attested in numerous language families across the world.[29] Imperative-only forms of motion verbs have been documented in Berber languages of Morocco, in numerous Cushitic and Semitic languages, and also in Hausa (see 2.36–8).[30] Figuig, a North Berber language of Morocco (Kossmann 1997: 126), has the following imperative paradigm in 2.62 (repeated here):

2.62 2sg   -ø   ɣres 'slit the throat!'
      1du   -axdd   ɣers-axdd
      2pl masc   -et   ɣers-et
      2pl fem   -emt   ɣers-emt

The imperative-only form of the verb 'come' uses the suffix -*it* instead of -*et* for second person plural. Other than that, it has all the gender and number combinations of an imperative:

9.21 2sg   (a)ṛwaḥ   'come!'
      1du   (a)ṛwaḥ-axdd   'let's come!'
      2pl masc   (a)ṛwaḥ-it   'come (pl masc)!'
      2pl fem   (a)ṛwaḥ-emt   'come (pl masc)!'

Having a suppletive or an irregular imperative of a verb of motion is a common feature of many languages of Ethiopia, be they Cushitic, Omotic, or Semitic. Table 9.1 (Hayward 1979: 246) shows the irregular patterns in the verb 'come' in comparison with relatively regular forms of the equally common motion verb 'go'. Interestingly, in Eastern Oromo, Northern Somali, and Dasenech (Dhaasanac), the imperative and the non-imperative forms of 'come' are not cognate, while in Irob Saho there is a partial phonological similarity. We will see in §10.1 that the Saho form *amo* reflects a highly archaic morphological pattern lost from all modern languages except this Saho variety.

Suppletive or irregular imperative forms of motion verbs are widespread cross-linguistically. In Chalcatongo Mixtec (Macaulay 1996: 135), the verb *kii* 'come' has a suppletive imperative form (ñáʔã). Two verbs 'go' ('go to base' and 'go to neutral goal') have irregular imperatives (alongside other irregular forms too: §2.1.3; also see Macaulay 1992: 417).[31] The only irregular verb in Dyirbal is *yanu* 'go', which has an unusual imperative *yana*.[32]

Verbs of other semantic groups can also form suppletive imperatives. We saw in §2.1.3 that in Chalcatongo Mixtec they include 'bring' and 'take' (čáã (bring.IMPV) 'Bring it!', žáʔá (take.IMPV) 'Take it!'),[33] while Chrau boasts three suppletive imperatives of verb 'eat'. Quite a few verbs in Papago (Zepeda 1988: 125) have irregular imperatives: these include 'swallow', 'sing', 'take', 'say (it)', 'sit', 'eat (it)', 'give (it)', and 'run'.

This takes us to the SECOND way in which imperatives interact with the lexicon. Having suppletive or irregular forms of a verb, or a subclass of verbs, is a fact

TABLE 9.1 Irregular imperative of 'come' in some languages of Ethiopia

LANGUAGE	LANGUAGE FAMILY	'come'		'go'	
		2masc. impv	3masc.past/ perfect	2masc. impv	3masc.past/ perfect
Amharic	Semitic	*na*	*mät't'a*	*hid*	*hedä*
Gofa	Omotic	*haya*	*yeys*	*ba*	*beys*
Eastern Oromo	East Cushitic	*koottu*	*ni-ɗufe*	*deemi*	*ni-deeme*
Northern Somali		*kaalay*	*wuu yimid (yimi)*	*tag*	*wuu tegey*
Burji		*aam*	*inaa intaani*	*mari*	*inaa maranni*
Dasenech		*kari*	*he-yimi*	*si*	*he-sezi*
Irob Saho		*amo*	*yemeete*	*aduy*	*yede(y)e*

about a subset of the verbal lexicon. Consequently, if a verb, or a set of verbs forming a semantic grouping, has a special form for imperatives only, this would provide an additional criterion for their classification. In Berber and Cushitic languages with suppletive imperative forms for motion verbs, this feature would set motion verbs apart from verbs of other groups.[34] The possibility of imperative formation and command in general may correlate with lexical subclasses of verbs. We saw that imperatives of motion verbs are often irregular. Positional verbs may also form imperative in a way different from verbs of other groups. In Teribe (Quesada 2000: 79), imperative inflection is not used with positional verbs. In 9.22, an imperative of an intransitive verb 'wait' is marked with the suffix *-zong*:

9.22 ¡Kosho-zong   na!
     wait-IMPV.SG   here
     '(you sg) wait here!'

In contrast, an imperative of a positional verb 'sit' does not take the suffix, and the personal pronoun is obligatory:

9.23 ¡Pa/pāy   sük   na!
     2sg/2pl   POSITIONAL.sit   here
     'Sit/stay/be here!'

The imperative formation may thus serve as an additional criterion for classifying verbs.

A language can have lexical restrictions on forming imperatives or unusual imperative forms for some lexical subclasses. In Dhaasanac, imperatives of some verbs have culture-specific meanings. The imperative of *ʔéðeb*, lit. 'become white!', means 'become visible' and is said to an absent animal during a magical ceremony performed in order to recover lost cattle (Tosco 1999b: 93). In Manambu, the verbs 'sit' and stand' share the same suppletive imperative (see Table 2.6 in §2.1.3). Verbs which typically do not allow imperative formation include stative verbs (as in Lahu), verbs of perception (as in Russian: Bulygina and Shmelev 1997), or other verbs which imply lack of control on behalf of the speaker (see §3.8). Vocative forms (see §3.4) typically used with imperatives and commands can often be formed just on nouns with a human referent, or simply for kinship terms and, more rarely, names of high animates.

A command is typically associated with speaker's control: we saw in §4.4 that in some languages, imperatives cannot be formed on verbs which describe a non-controlled situation—one cannot order another person to be big. And if a verb of perception or emotional state appears in a command, it acquires a controlled meaning. In many Australian languages, a certain lexeme means 'hear' in a statement, but 'listen' in commands (where the subject's control is implied (Evans and Wilkins 2000: 555; R. M. W. Dixon p.c.).

The following example from Kayardild shows this:

9.24 dathina   waldarra   dathinananganda   marralda   kuwajuwaa-j,
    that   moon   that.way   ear   twist-ACTUAL
    can't   **marri-j,**   kurndumaand.   'Kiija-tha   ngijinda
    can't   hear-ACTUAL   stoops.forward   draw.near-IMPV   my
    kangka kurulu-tha   **marri-j,**   kurulu-tha   kiija-tha   bathind!'
    words properly-IMPV hear-IMPV properly-IMPV draw.near-IMPV from.west
    'That (new) moon twists his ear like this, but can't hear, he's stooping forward with his hands behind his back. "Come close and listen to my words properly, come right up close from the west!"'

That is, imperative forms may have different meanings with different sub-classes of verbs. Formation of imperatives is often a criterion for defining word classes. In various languages where adjectives share properties with verbs (see Dixon 2004b), forming imperatives is an additional criterion to differentiate these word classes. This directly relates to §4.4.3.

In addition, an imperative form may indirectly serve to categorize the referent, the addressee, or the speaker. The prototypical addressee of an imperative is usually animate; however, given an appropriate context, inanimates can also be commanded to perform activities, at least in English (see

Chapter 4). In other languages, imperatives are restricted to directive acts by humans and high animates in general.[35] That is, an imperative presupposes categorization of the addressee. And imperative-specific forms can serve to disambiguate the kind of addressee. Consider commands directed to animals. If I say in Russian *Brysj, Norman* (Shoo.to.cat Norman) 'Get away, Norman', it is obvious that I am shooing away a naughty pussycat and not an under-performing academic. We saw in §6.3 that strong prohibitives in Manambu can only be used to tell a human not to do something—that is, someone fully in control of what is not to be performed.

A **further** way in which imperatives and directive speech acts can be expected to interact with the lexicon is in how the concept of 'order' would be expressed. Most, but by no means all, languages have a lexeme meaning 'order'. Some languages have a large number of lexemes with the meaning of 'order' (as, for instance, most Indo-European languages), while tribal languages usually do not: Tucano and Tariana have only one term each: Tariana *-ira* 'order' and Tucano *dutí*, with the same meaning.[36] The term 'imperative' is widely used in the meaning of 'obligation, a must'. But how do you translate something like a Kantian imperative into non-European languages? Perhaps you don't.

Some languages which do have a dedicated paradigm for imperative do not have any verb with a specific meaning 'order'. Examples include Dyirbal and Jarawara (Dixon 1972). The concept can be expressed through the verb of speech—but this implies telling someone to do something (for instance, using the verb *gigal* 'tell to do, let do': R. M. W. Dixon p.c.).

A number of languages with no dedicated imperative do not have a lexeme 'order'. Ceʔ Wɔŋ, an Aslian language from Malaysia, has no word for 'order' or 'command': the verb ʔɔr 'instruct, tell to do something' is used. There is a special term for 'commanding supernaturally'—this refers to a command coming from a shaman, a tiger, or a youngest-born child (Kruspe 2003).

Is it the case that societies where there is no established hierarchy do not have lexical terms for ordering and commanding? It is tempting to hypothesize that commands and ordering lexicon are not used in languages spoken in egalitarian societies, which can be either nomadic hunters and gatherers (as are the Dâw (Martins 1994 and p.c.) and other Makú peoples), or slash-and-burn agricultur-alists (as is the case with various Aslian-speaking groups in Malaysia). However, some language facts go against this. Hup, a close relative of Dâw, does have a special verb meaning 'order' or 'request': *yãeh-* (this form frequently appears in verb compounds with the meaning 'order/request to do V') (Pattie Epps p.c.).[37]

9.4 How children acquire commands

The importance of the imperative in day-to-day interaction is mirrored by its appearance in child language acquisition. The high frequency of imperatives and explicit directives of other kinds in child language reflects the high frequency of such expressions in the way adults address the children. Imperatives and one-word directives are among the first to be acquired. Clancy (1985: 381) remarks, in her study of the acquisition of Japanese (involving a longitudinal study of three children):

The first stage of grammatical development in Japanese is marked by contrastive use of certain verbal inflections, usually including at least the imperative and the past tense. [...] This initial stage is typically quite early, before two years-of-age.

A striking feature of the speech of Japanese mothers to their 2-year-olds in Clancy's sample was the high frequency of explicit directives. These were often marked with -*te*, a continuative form of the verb which normally 'serves as the non-final verb form in sequences of concatenated verbs and in conjoined clauses' (Clancy 1985: 383).[38] A -*te* form followed by a verb of giving is often used to frame request. A -*te* form on its own can mark a command. This type of command was particularly frequent in mothers' speech to young children. That is, an essentially non-imperative form (or an imperative strategy) was the first form acquired by children. The 'imperative' use of -*te* is one of the earliest productive inflections acquired by children (when it is established in the command function, some children overgeneralize it as if it were a finite tense/aspect marker).

The following excerpt, from Clancy's own data (1985: 488–90), said by a mother to her 25-month-old daughter, is typical of mother's speech to 2-year-olds in her sample. Note that -*te* marks commands:

9.25 ja   sono   teeburu katazuke-te   choodai.
      well   that   table   clean-COMMAND   please
      soko ja-nai   hako no   naka ni ire-te   ki-te
      there COP+TOP-NEG box GEN inside in put-COMMAND come-COMMAND
      hako no   naka   mada ni mada mada, hako no   naka   ni
      box GEN inside in   in still   still   box   GEN inside in
      ire-te   ko-nakya.
      put-COMMAND   come-OBLIG
      mada, motto akoko no   ue katazuke-te   choodai
      still,   more   there GEN top clean-COMMAND please
      ja,   o-katazuke   shi-te
      well   cleaning   do-COMMAND

'All right, please clean up that table. Not there, put them inside that box, Inside that box, still still still, you must put them inside that box. Still, more, please clean up on top of that. All right, clean up'.

Two-year-olds were capable of recognising indirect ways of stating wishes, requests, and desires, especially since such statements were often accompanied by explicit directives (Clancy 1985: 497).

An imperative strategy appears to be acquired earlier than the imperative form by German children. During the course of their acquisition of German as a first language, children usually produce verbs with the -*en* ending, like the infinitive. This is due to the frequent use in carer speech of modals and auxiliaries which require the infinitival form of the verb, and also to the abundance of infinitival imperatives (Millis 1985: 153).

Child language acquisition of Modern Hebrew points in a similar direction. In the acquisition of Modern Hebrew, 'the initial form of verbs is quite typically in the Imperative with an instrumental kind of function, to express the child's wish to have people do things for him, or to get things done for himself' (Berman 1985: 268). Boys typically use the formally unmarked masculine form, and girls use the feminine forms marked by suffix -*i*, as in *bo!* 'come:you.masculine' versus *bó'i!* 'come:you feminine'. This reflects the carers' input into the choice of the form to be considered 'basic' by the child: a girl addressed as feminine would use the feminine form to address anyone. Infinitives show up immediately after the imperatives (the children omit the infinitive marker *li-* or *le-;* infinitives in Hebrew are not marked for gender, number, or person, e.g. *(li)shon* 'to sleep', *(la)rédet* 'to get down'). It appears that if the child wants to do something himself or herself, they will go for the infinitive, while if they want someone else to do something—look at something or give them something—they will prefer the imperative.

Berman (1985: 268) notes that infinitives as a 'command strategy' are 'overused' by children well into the third and even fourth year, as 'the most typical way of expressing requests, desires, and prohibitions'. This is not surprising, since infinitives are widely used by carers as 'a way of formulating directives more obliquely than through straightforward imperative forms'. A parent may say *lishon* 'to sleep' when telling the child to go to bed; and *lashévet* 'to sit down' is a standard instruction of nursery school teachers.

When adults address children, and when children address each other and adults, prohibition is expressed with the negative word *lo* 'no, not' plus an infinitive, instead of a normal use of *al* 'don't' plus a future-marked verb. That is, children would use *lo lingóa* 'not to touch' rather than *al tiga* 'don't touch', and *lo lakum* 'not to get up' rather than *al takumi* 'don't get up (fem)'. The reason why the infinitives are construed by adults and children alike as 'basic' in some way may be partly motivated by their formal simplicity: they require no inflection other than the prefix. The infinitives are also found in very casual and intimate interaction between adults, e.g. *nu, xevre, la-zuz kvar!* 'Well, fellows, to move' meaning 'Let's get going!'

It appears that a combination of formal simplicity, frequency in carer's speech, and overtones of familiar and indirect commands accounts for the pervasive character of imperatives and infinitives in early child language acquisition of Hebrew.

Schieffelin (1990: 93), in her study of the Kaluli people of Papua New Guinea, points out that the ways in which caretakers talk to the youngest children

are syntactically simple, drawing up on a limited number of imperatives, negative imperatives, and rhetorical questions. Rhetorical questions are employed as equivalent to negative commands: if a toddler starts putting something inedible in his or her mouth, the mother says to an older child, 'What are you eating?!—*ɛlɛmaʼ* (meaning 'Don't eat that!'), and the older sibling immediately repeats it to the toddler with the appropriate force. Older children are instructed to direct the actions of younger ones by 'using imperatives (i.e. *Mena!* 'Come') and rhetorical questions (i.e. *Oba hanaya?!* 'Where are you going?!'). (p. 92)

In Kaluli, the first verbs acquired by children include a limited number of imperatives (*hamana* 'go', *mena* 'come', *bɔba* 'look') and a number of other short forms. Children do not use uninflected verbs (Schieffelin 1985: 536). The imperative stem was used as a base and as the basic form from an early age (pp. 569–70).

Just as in Japanese, acquisition of directives and ways of framing a request is not restricted to imperative forms. A frequent request in Kaluli consists of the first person dative form of the first person pronoun *nelɔ* 'to me', and *nowɔ ne* 'some to me', two formulaic expressions. One imperative form is used only by children when whining and begging for food or for the breast, *mɔ/mo* 'give'. When not whining, children use a fuller form, *dimina* or *mina*. The reduced form is only used until the age of about 27 months (from then on only the full form is used). Kaluli children do not acquire the 'begging' form from adults— but since they have plenty of opportunity to hear other youngsters use it, they presumably acquire it 'by exposure' (p. 536).

Kaluli distinguishes between immediate and future, or delayed imperatives. These are acquired at different times. While immediate imperatives are a feature of the early language (from 25 months: 569), future imperatives are used starting at the age of 30+ months (Schieffelin 1985: 543). Note that the future imperative is not frequently used by parents when talking to children.

Similarly to mother–child interaction patterns recorded for Japanese[39] and Kaluli, imperatives and modal verbs are central in interactions with small children among the Ku Waru of the New Guinea Highlands (Rumsey 2003). In the Ku Waru data (Rumsey 2003: 180–3) 'very extensive use is made [...] of imperative and other directive forms, often repeated or paraphrased in sequence' in adult speech. These include the second person perfective regularly used as a strong directive (Merlan and Rumsey 1991: 327–8). This is replicated in the way children talk. In an excerpt from adult–child conversation, 15,3-month-old Laplin picked out just the one-word imperative form from a lengthy multi-word utterance directed at him:

9.26a Adult   kar-na   pabiyl   wa!   Kar!
              car-LOC   go.OPT.1du come+IMPV   car
              'Come, let's you and me go in the car! Car!'

9.26b Laplin wa
              come+IMPV

In Rumsey's (2003: 182) words,

that the one word he picks out to repeat from this grammatically complex utterance is the simple and potentially self-sufficient imperative verb (*wa*)—the first verb form to be learned by Ku Waru children—suggests an active intelligence at work, selectively responding to the barrage of multi-word utterances addressed to him and picking out what is most pertinent for developing a repertoire of moves enabling the reciprocal interchange of perspectives with his interlocutors.

Similarly, the large portion of verb forms used by 2-year-old learners of Catalan were the least formally marked ones—present tense and imperatives.[40]

Acquisition of imperative forms is linked to the acquisition of category of person. Correct and appropriate use of imperative is vital in socialization of a child: 'to use the imperative the child must be able to understand' that the roles of speaker and addressee are reversed (Rumsey 2003: 176).

We conclude that early acquisition of command forms, including imperatives themselves and command strategies, is related to their frequency in carers' speech and to their formal simplicity.[41] Interestingly, the more formally marked, and less frequent, future imperative forms in Kaluli are acquired later than imperative forms, which are the first ones to be used by a child. The study of the ways in which imperative specific categories are acquired by children is in its infancy, and requires further work.

Lise Menn reports that little is known about the behaviour of imperative forms and other kinds of commands in language dissolution—that is, in various types of aphasia. Formulaic and frequently used imperative commands appear to be relatively well preserved in production in agram-matic/Broca's aphasia (Lise Menn, p.c.). In narratives, direct imperatives are sometimes used instead of reported ones, and occasionally instead of declaratives (Menn 1990: 136). However, the imperative does not function as a general default form in aphasia when the speaker is unable to produce a correctly inflected form; depending on the language, the type of aphasia, and other variables, the default may be the infinitive, the first person singular, or the third person singular (Magnúsdóttir and Thráinsson 1990: 468–470; Menn and Obler 1990: 1372). Apparent comprehension of imperatives may be peculiarly disconnected from the ability to produce them (Geschwind 1975; Poeck et al. 1982). Just as in child language acquisition, robustness of imperatives in language dissolution can be considered a corollary of their relative frequency.

9.5 Imperatives to live by: a summary

Imperatives we live by are shaped by the conventions and the norms we are socialized to follow. The term 'imperative' is polysemous in many Indo-European languages. As we recall from §1.1, the English term 'imperative' in common, non-linguist usage refers to 'having the quality or property of commanding' and 'peremptory; demanding obedience, execution, action, etc.; that must be done or performed; urgent; of the nature of a duty; obligatory'. The French *impératif* is linked to 'absolute necessity' (*nécessité absolue*, as in *les impératifs de la défense nationale*), and the Portuguese *imperativo* has overtones of obligation and duty (*imperativo de honra*).[42] Just as the moral imperatives and duties can only be understood in the context of culture and history, so can the usage of the actual imperative forms. And so can the ways in which imperative forms may be conveniently rephrased to suit the language ecology and the behavioural patterns considered appropriate. The Ilongot of the Philippines, the Nuer of East Africa, and the Malagasy of Madagascar use these forms sparingly, fitting them in with general face-saving strategies and types of circumlocution for framing their requests and directive speech acts.

The semantics, and the pragmatic overtones, of the imperatives—or of any other forms—are not cross-linguistically constant. Projecting the air of authority associated with imperative in English onto other languages is fraught with danger: the fact that the Mundugumor use imperatives does not necessarily make them into a nation of authoritative bullies. As Whitney (1875: 222) put it,

in judging other languages, then, we have to try and rid ourselves of the prejudices generated by our own acquired habits of expression, and to be prepared to find other peoples making a very different selection from our own of those qualifications and relations of the more material substance of expression which they shall distinctly represent in speech.

The use of imperatives reflects the conventional hierarchies and perception of referents: we can recall that in Ilongot, imperative is used to children and women who are perceived to have energy and speed, but not too much sense or knowledge of their own. On the other hand, imperative can be deployed as a tool for defining relationships. In Arapaho, the use of a direct or of an indirect imperative is only partially dictated by pre-existing, clear-cut social relationships: the speakers choose to use an imperative or to avoid it depending on their attitudes and appreciation of each other's social status. To use or not to use an imperative is a matter of negotiation.

Uninflected imperative forms may constitute a separate word class. Formation of imperatives may be used as an additional criterion for determining subclasses of verbs. The fact that imperative forms can determine the type of addressee—whether a human or an animal—adds to the ways in which imperatives interact with the lexicon.

An imperative, or any command or request, can be accompanied by an explanation why or what for. This is a way of making the order, or request, more effective. Using an imperative form may have an additional stylistic effect. Imperatives may be preferred in some genres rather than in others. The abundance of imperative forms in instructions and advertisements in English has to do with the nature of the addressee. The 'do's' and the 'don'ts' are addressed to everyone in general and to no-one singled out in particular. That is, no one is to feel threatened by them.

Understanding and mastering directive speech acts—the ways of commanding, requesting, and so on—in a language is a key to successful communication. And using a wrong way of requesting is a sure way towards a breakdown in communication. This was shown in masterly fashion by Keenan and Ochs (1979) in relation to how to frame one's request in the Malagasy-speaking society. When children acquire their first language, commands and requests are what they hear most, and what they have to learn first, to survive and to fulfil their needs.

At the first sight, the ways in which speakers of various languages manipulate imperative and non-imperative forms in their directive functions goes against Grice's conversational maxims. The supermaxim of Quantity states:

1. Make your contribution as informative as is required (for the current purposes of the exchange).
2. Do not make your contribution more informative than is required.

The category of Relation has one single maxim, 'Be relevant'. And the category of Manner relates to '*how* what is said to be said' and subsumes 'the supermaxim "Be perspicuous'—and various maxims such as (Grice 1989: 26–7):

1. Avoid obscurity of expression.
2. Avoid ambiguity.
3. Be brief (avoid unnecessary prolixity).
4. Be orderly.

The requests and commands in Malagasy society appear (to us) obscure, ambiguous, and unnecessarily long-winded. And the fact that polite forms are often longer and less obvious to the addressee than a curt command may imply that politeness goes against communicative efficiency. In fact, this is not the case.

Communicative efficiency is based on cooperation between speakers and addressees. As Grice (1989: 26) puts it:

Our talk exchanges do not normally consist of a succession of disconnected remarks, and would not be rational if they did. They are characteristically, to some degree at least, cooperative efforts; and each participant recognizes in them, to some degree at least, a common purpose or a set of purposes, or at least a mutually accepted direction.

This 'Cooperative principle' supports the ways in which imperatives and other command forms are used and manipulated to reflect the conventions and their renegotiation in human communication, in different societies across the world. The plethora of commanding and requesting techniques in any given language reflect an ongoing struggle between striving to achieve efficient communication and the desire to save face and yet to reach the commanded, or requested result. Cooperation with the addressee is to be negotiated, so as to achieve a minor maxim 'Be polite' (Grice 1989: 28). And some non-primarily imperative forms may, over time, acquire unmistakably explicit command meanings. These are a frequent source for imperatives as separate forms, and are the topic of our next chapter.

Notes

1. See Kita (2003b) and papers in Kita (2003a) on pointing and gestures in commands.
2. Boas (1938: 132).
3. An imperative or prohibitive form can be used to address rain or another inanimate referent (see Aikhenvald 2008a: 319).

4. Imperatives are almost a must in instructions—such as those in Figure 9.7. But not necessarily so. So as not to bore their readers with endless imperatives, instructions can involve declarative clauses. A book appropriately entitled *Do's and taboos around the world* contains numerous instructions about how to behave and not to behave in every major country of the world (Axtell 1993). Each entry contains a mixture of imperatives and of statements concerning what is done and what it is polite to do. Instructions on conversation in Brazil provide an illustrative example (p. 101). The first sentence, 'Brazilians are very proud of their children and appreciate their attention to them', does not contain an overt instruction or advice cast in an imperative, 'Talk to Brazilians about their children', but this is what it implies. The next sentence contains an imperative preceded by advice stated as a declarative clause: 'Brazilian men love good jokes and love to laugh, but avoid ethnic jokes and do not discuss Argentina'. And the last sentence consists just of an imperative: 'Also avoid discussions of politics, religion, and other controversial subjects.'

5. A comprehensive study of the Mundugumor grammar and culture is still waiting to be undertaken.

6. Saeed (1999: 86) stresses again that imperative forms in Somali 'seem to carry little or no implication of power or authority'.

7. Compare self-depreciation and negative strategies as means of expression of politeness and deference in Korean, in requests and other speech acts (Kwon and Hu 2009: 96–7).

8. Josephides (2001) gives further examples of indirectness in phrasing commands and suggestions in the Kewa-speaking community in Papua New Guinea.

9. This is reminiscent of the discussion of the role of consensus rather than direct confrontation in Aboriginal societies of Central Australia (see Liberman 1985).

10. Keenan and Ochs (1979: 154) remark that 'Malagasy is in fact one of the relatively few languages in the world that has a well-developed system for forming nonactive imperatives'. See §4.4.2.

11. An additional but highly important point made here concerns 'the quality of observation' made by a fieldworker: this is bound to be 'conditioned by the role he occupies in the local social structure'. Keenan and Ochs could not have made such an insightful study of the Malagasy norms, interactions, and patterns of making requests without having become *havana* rather than remaining strangers, *vahiny*. Using their own words (1979: 157), 'had we, for example, merely lived in a town and visited different villages, we would have never been on a *havana* basis with anyone, We might have easily then mistaken the norms for interaction with *vahiny* as being the norms for everyone.' The key to reliable and successful analysis is immersion fieldwork, something to which we return in the Appendix. The lack of immersion and data collected through fleeting visits to a neighbouring township results in superficial descriptions of languages, and cannot be relied upon.

12. Also see Agha (1994: 287).

13. Using a milder imperative strategy rather than an abrupt command may correlate with a cultural requirement to contain one's anger. Among the Matsigenka Indians (Arawak) of the Peruvian jungle, men and women are expected to contain their anger and impatience as much as possible. Johnson (2003: 94) remarks that 'for a married couple, the result is that many courtesies shape the way they make their wishes known. If a man wants beer, he asks *aityo shitea* ("Is there beer?"), rather than saying *akero shitea* ("Bring me beer!"). Likewise, if a woman wants her husband to hunt, she does not command, "Go hunt!" or criticize him as a poor hunter; it is enough for her to say quietly, "There is no meat". Men and women know what is expected of them, and they generally do it without having to be told.'

14. See Dixon (2009) for a conceptual link between purpose and reason.

15. Similar contextualization of commands has been described for Warlpiri and the Western Desert language (Dixon 1972) and Indo-Pakistani Sign Language (Ulrike Zeshan p.c.), especially in emphatic commands or instructions to children.

16. Further insights into the ways in which imperatives are employed in dialogues and conversations are discussed by Lascarides and Asher (2004). The problem of intertranslatability of imperatives and mapping commands from one language onto another is especially acute in second language acquisition; see e.g. House and Kasper (1987) on various techniques employed in framing requests in a foreign language, as a component of 'interlanguage pragmatics'. Fiddick (2008) provides an insightful discussion of norms in social cooperation in the modern Western society from a psychologist's perspective.

17. In Burundi society, petitioning for gifts and favours is 'one of the most frequent and significant situations of interpersonal communication' (Albert 1972: 77). The ways in which petitions and favours are presented are highly stylized, in terms of the physical posture and speech behaviour. Requests, petitions, commands, and further directive acts are in the centre of social life, and reflect the hierarchical order of the society (see Albert 1972).

18. This is not to say that an interrogative-directive never sounds threatening. In a recent novel by Dick Francis and Felix Francis, *Dead heat* (p. 343), the main character rings up the police station: '"Can I speak to DI Turner, please?" I asked. "Can you hold", said a female voice. It wasn't so much of a question as an order.' The policewoman's directive act warranted compliance, no matter how it was phrased.

19. This is reminiscent of some uses of imperative in narratives in Russian (see, for instance, Gronas 2006); we return to this in Chapter 10.

20. And more. In Manambu, a first person imperative of the verb 'say' is a marker of interactional turn-taking.

21. The particle *ina* is a 'neutral response particle, also used after declaratives and interrogatives', while *hami* 'deduction' is an evidential particle (Derbyshire 1979: 19).

Answers to commands may contain hesitation or requests for clarification, as in Macushi (Abbott 1991: 54) and Apalaí (Koehn and Koehn 1986: 63). In Wari' (Everett and Kern 1997: 38–9), *ma'e* 'OK, all right' is a positive response to an imperative in male speech, and *ma* is its equivalent in female speech. Negative responses are expressed with semantically appropriate negative constructions. The same form can be used as a response to a question and to a command. Urubu-Kaapor has a wide variety of forms used for confirmation (as responses to either questions or commands: Kakumasu 1986: 357).

22. A positive response to a polar question contains the same plural marker: *hó-ite* 'positive response to a polar question posed by a respected person', *hóó* 'positive response to a polar question posed by a younger person'.

23. Irakw, a Cushitic language from Tanzania, is rich in irregular imperative-only forms, and expressions, e.g. *ii'ari qasaak*, lit. 'put it in the ears' (said to many) meaning 'listen' and used to start a narration (Mous 1993: 165).

24. Fleck compares this with English *sic 'em* for hunting dogs or *mush* for sled dogs.

25. This could justify considering these directive-only forms as a special word class. Zargulla—like most Omotic languages—distinguishes two genders in third person cross-referencing, but not in second person. Having gender distinctions only in imperatives (within the verbal paradigm) is infrequent, but not unheard of: see examples of Chipaya (§4.1).

26. Wolaitta also employs names and colour terms for calling cows, as special vocative terms.

27. See Abercrombie (1967: 31) and Ladefoged (1975: 118). This sound can be described as an ingressive lateral alveolar click. See Ameka (1992) for a cross-linguistic perspective on interjections.

28. Interjections and single-word directive forms are among the most highly diffusible elements (see references in Aikhenvald 2007a). An example of recent diffusion of a directive comes from my own fieldwork. The Manambu villages are plagued by European-introduced cats, miserable animals prowling everywhere and stealing whatever they can (which was a bit of a shock for me as a cat-lover). To get rid of them, I (unwittingly) shouted a few times, using a Russian interjection *brysj!* 'shoo (to a cat)'. This seems to have worked, because the cats dispersed. The speakers who saw me do it liked the idea, and started using the word. Next time when I came back to the village, I was told that to shoo a cat away, you have to say *brisj.* Directive terms are often borrowed; for instance, a command to a dog in Russian *fas!* 'Grab, take!' has its origin in German *Fass!* Bynon (1976) provides numerous examples of borrowed forms in calls to domestic animals in Ayt Hadiddou.

29. Veselinova's (2006: 141) statement that the phenomenon of suppletive imperatives is 'very stable' in the 'Afro-Asiatic phylum', and also 'common in Uralic, North Caucasian and Nilo-Saharan' has to be taken with a grain of salt because her work is based on a highly limited 'sample'. In actual fact, suppletive imperative forms are a prominent feature of Australian, Austronesian, many families of Papuan

languages, and languages of the Americas. While 'sampling' may be of certain use for preliminary hypotheses, readers and linguists alike are urged to avoid trusting pseudo-scientific conclusions based on random 'samples'. (Also note that the existence of a 'North Caucasian' grouping is by no means an accepted fact: there is no reason to believe that Northeast and Northwest Caucasian languages are related. In contrast, Afroasiatic languages form a well-established family.)

30. Laoust (1928: 51); Kossmann (1997: 126); Treis (MS). See also Ferguson (1976: 74); Hayward (1979); Tosco (2000).

31. Both these verbs have suppletive aspectual forms. The progressive stem is used as base for the imperative: compare k^wa-$noʔo$ 'go to base, go home (progressive)', $k^wá$-$noʔo$ 'go to base' (imperative); $k^wāʔā$ 'go to neutral goal' (progressive), $k^wāʔā̀$ 'go to neutral base' (imperative) (Macaulay 1996: 170; 135). There is a 'tonal component in the formation of these two imperatives—specifically, addition of a high tone to $k^wāʔā$ (and its reduced form k^wa-)' (p. 135). This alternation is imperative-specific, and not found elsewhere in the grammar.

32. This is an archaic form; we return to historical development of imperatives in §§ 10.1–2. Nunggubuyu (Australian area: Heath 1984: 343) has a defective verb 'come' which occurs only in imperative (also see Dixon 1972: 18, 116). Along similar lines, the verb *fano* 'go' has a special imperative form in Tuvaluan (Besnier 2000: 39). In Kobon, the second person singular (canonical) imperatives of the verbs of motion *ar* 'go' and *au* 'come' require additional markers: the demonstrative *u* 'there' is used with *ar*, and the vocative particle *e* is obligatory with *au* (Davies 1981: 23). ! Xun, a Khoisan language (König and Heine 2003: 8), has five imperative-only lexemes, covering the meanings of 'come', 'go', and 'leave'; some of these forms go back to archaic verbs no longer used in the modern language (see §10.2). Swahili has the following irregular imperatives: 'come': *njoo* '2sg.IMPV', *njoo-ni* '2pl.IMPV' (infinitive *ku-ja*), 'bring': *lete* '2sg.IMPV', *lete-ni* '2pl.IMPV' (infinitive *ku-leta*), 'go': *nenda* '2sg.IMPV', *nende-ni* '2pl.IMPV' (infinitive *kw-enda*), 'finish': *kwisha* '2sg.IMPV', *ishe-ni* '2pl.IMPV' (infinitive *kw-isha*), 'leave, cease': *wacha* '2sg.IMPV', *wacha-ni* '2pl.IMPV' (infinitive *ku-acha*) (Ikoro 1997c; Schadeberg 1992: 26 and p.c.). See further examples in §2.1.3.

33. The potential form of 'bring' is *kundáʔá*, and the realis form is *xindáʔá*; the potential form of 'take' is *kĩʔĩ* and the realis form is *kíʔĩ*.

34. Note that in some languages, motion verbs can be irregular throughout their paradigm. Acoma, an isolate from the American South-West, has suppletive forms for the verb 'go' in declarative and also in imperative (Maring 1967: 101–7). It thus appears to form a subclass of its own. Veselinova (2006: 141) erroneously lists Acoma as a language with suppletive imperative, on a par with Chalcatongo Mixtec and Taba which have bona fide suppletive second person imperative forms of motion verbs. See note 24 to Chapter 2, for a paradigm of 'go' in Acoma. Taba (Bowden 2001: 368) uses an imperative-only verb *mo!* 'come here!', a form perhaps related to Proto-Oceanic **mai* 'come' (see e.g. Lynch et al. 2002: 47). However, it does not always warrant an analysis as a suppletive imperative: for instance,

in Boumaa Fijian the cognate form *mai* 'come and' is a verbal modifier (Dixon 1988: 83); and in Toqabaqita (Lichtenberk 2006; 2008) *mai* is a ventive aspect marker.

35. Amha (MS-b) states this explicitly for Zargulla. Many grammarians do not state this requirement. The use of imperative can be considered on a par with other non-agreeing noun categorization devices (in the spirit of Aikhenvald 2000: 436–41).

36. It is possible to say, in Tariana, *direta-nipe* 'his ordering, his order'. And the language has a number of obligative and prescriptive modalities (apart from a score of imperative-only forms: Aikhenvald 2008b). When I asked a speaker who had graduated from a secondary school and received additional education as a nurse whether this reflects Portuguese 'imperativo', he almost snapped: *pasapeli sede-ka* 'there is no such word'.

37. It is also tempting to suggest that languages with no dedicated imperative paradigm (§2.1) would not have a verb implying 'order' or 'command'. This seems true in some cases. Willem de Reuse (p.c., 4.09.03) commented on the verbs for 'order in Western Apache':

I can't think of a monomorphemic word meaning that. The closest one can come to is: *goz'aahi* (aa mid tone and nasal, i high toned). Literal meaning is: 'that (a roundish object) which is in position somewhere'. Indeed, abstract things, such as commands, blame, songs, teachings, etc. tend to be thought of as roundish objects (-*'aa* is the classificatory verb stem for one bulky hard roundish object).

The non-literal meanings are: 'test(s), rule(s), regulation(s)'. Note that there is no distinction between 'test' and 'rule', so it's anything set down or stipulated whether as a test or as a rule. In the New Testament, one finds *bee goz'aani* (aa mid tone and nasal, i high toned) 'commandment' (e.g. 1 John 2), literally 'that which is in position somewhere with it'; I am not quite sure what *bee* 'with, by means of it' refers to here.

There is a verb these forms are derived from: *sha goz'aa* 's/he commands me' (sha is high toned), i.e. 's/he sets it (roundish object) in position for me'. There are other stems for 'to tell someone to do something', 'to send someone', but the one above is the closest one can get to the meaning of 'order' or 'command'".

However, other Athapascan languages present a different picture. Navajo has a verb 'order' (Young and Morgan 1980: 957), and so do Ahtna (Kari 1990: 563) and Slave (Keren Rice, p.c.).

38. Clancy corroborates this by an earlier study of speech by Japanese mothers to 31 2-year-olds over the course of an entire day: 22.5% of the utterances were directives.

39. For similar results of child language acqusition for American English, see a summary in Clancy (1985: 490).

40. Grinstead (2000: 125; see also Rumsey 2003: 177–8). Valdivieso (1994) presents similar conclusions concerning early acquisiton of the imperative forms in Spanish. Directives were among one-word utterances collected from children aged

23–27 months acquiring Egyptian Arabic (Omar 1973: 101). Negative imperatives appear to be acquired later, at the age of over 30 months (p. 99).

41. See also Menn (1989) on the relative frequency of imperatives in carer–child communication, compared with that in adult–adult communication.

42. *Larousse de la langue française* (1979: 937); Ferreira (1999: 311–12); Ozhegov and Shvedova (1997) mention 'moral imperative' (*nravstvennyj imperativ*).

10

Where do imperatives come from?

Dedicated command forms, positive and negative, can be preserved almost intact. Archaic in form, imperatives may also offer a glimpse into the profile of a protolanguage. This is the topic of §10.1.

Imperative forms may evolve from command strategies. Lexical items grammaticalize into imperative markers. Imperatives are often heterogeneous, in terms of their origins. In contrast to other moods, different person forms of imperatives, and even imperative forms of different verbs, may come from different sources. We turn to this in §10.2.

Negative imperatives—or prohibitives—are scarcely a mirror image of their positive 'counterparts', in their forms, and in their meanings. This is what we saw throughout Chapter 5. The sources for prohibitives—especially those which come from complex constructions—are discussed in §10.3. The final section, §10.4, features a summary of recurrent paths imperatives may follow in their historical development.

10.1 Archaic imperatives

A command addressed to a single 'you' is the most basic of imperative forms, in terms of its frequency and its formation. This is why we came to call it 'canonical'. In many languages, second person singular imperative coincides with the bare stem of the verb. Such imperative forms are often inherited, unchanged, from the protolanguage, as in many Arawak languages of South America. Archaic second person imperatives—which stand apart from other person forms in their origin—have been described for Indo-European.[1] In a similar vein, in French, 'of the Latin terminations of the imperative only the second person singular was preserved' (Pope 1934: 344).

A second person canonical imperative may require a special marker; then the marker tends to be fairly stable. The second person imperative marker -ya is preserved in all East Tucanoan languages.[2] The common Australian marker for second person imperative -ga recurs in many languages.[3]

Imperative constructions may be archaic in further ways. Imperative clauses may stand apart from clauses of other types (§4.3). In Lardil, Panyjima, and some other Ngayarda languages (Australia) the object of a canonical imperative, if expressed with a noun, takes nominative rather than accusative case (Dixon 1972: 135–6; Dench 1991: 204). That is, the object is formally unmarked. This is illustrated in 10.1 (Dench 1991: 138; a similar example is in 4.52, with a first person imperative, or 'hortative').

Panyjima
10.1 wirnta-nma   mantu   jilyantharri-ku
      cut-IMPV   meat.NOM   children-ACC
      'Cut some meat for the children'

In contrast, a direct object in a declarative or an interrogative clause has to be marked as accusative (Dench 1991: 173):

10.2 ngatha   purlpi-yayi-ku   mantu-yu   kampa-rnaanu-ku
      1sgNOM   want-INCH-PRES   meat-ACC   cook-PASSIVE.PERFECT-ACC
      'I like cooked meat'

In Dench's words, 'the special status of objects in imperative clauses is matched by the special treatment' of subjects (1991: 204). In clauses of other types, body part instruments and manner adverbials agree in case marking with the subject of the clause. But in imperatives, body part instruments, and adverbs have to be marked with the agentive suffix, 'with, by'. The agentive marking on 'left foot' in 10.3 is obligatory:

10.3 thala-nma   jina-ngku   jammpurrka-lu
      kick-IMPV   foot-AGENTIVE   left.one-AGENTIVE
      'Kick it with your left foot'

The case-marking patterns in declarative and interrogative clauses are nominative-accusative. Imperatives tell us a different story. The agentive marking on body part instruments in examples like 10.3, and the zero-marking in 10.1 (and 4.51, from Cahuilla), reflect the original ergative-absolutive pattern. This pattern can be reconstructed for Ngayrda languages; similar ergative-absolutive 'relics' occur in Martuthunira and Yinyjiparnti, close relatives of Panyjima. 'In the earlier period, nominals in O function would have been unmarked absolutive' (Dench 1991: 204)—and this only survives in archaic imperatives.[4]

Along similar lines, the nominal object of imperatives in Lardil, one of the Wellesley Islands languages, is marked with the nominative case. This same form is used to mark transitive and intransitive subjects of non-imperative sentences, suggesting that this pattern also reflects an old ergative-absolutive system (Dixon 1972: 135–6).

Suppletive imperatives may preserve archaic forms and archaic patterns. The irregular imperative *amo* 'come' in Saho, a Cushitic language from Ethiopia, reflects an old morphological pattern (a middle voice imperative singular). This has been lost from all modern languages except for this form in Saho (see §9.3 and Table 9.1; see also Hayward 1979: 252).

An imperative-only lexeme *tcí* 'come!' in !Xun is a direct descendant of the Proto-!Xun **tcí* 'to come', now surviving only in the imperative (its declarative counterpart in the modern language is *g|è*) (König and Heine 2003, and p.c., 2009).

However, not all imperative forms behave identically. The history of the best-documented languages shows that, of all the possible imperative forms, the most basic second person singular canonical imperative tends to be the most archaic.[5] Other forms often get 'co-opted' from non-imperative paradigms. As a consequence, different person forms for imperatives may differ in their origins: imperatives are often heterogeneous in their sources. And a whole imperative paradigm can be replaced with a set of forms whose original function was optative, or intentional. This takes us to the next section—the evolution of imperative forms.

10.2 How imperatives evolve

The evolution of imperatives from forms of other moods involves some common historical processes. **Reanalysis** is a historical process by which a form or a construction acquires a different structure from the one it had before, with little change to its surface form and change to its semantics.[6]

Reinterpretation (or extension) is a 'change in the surface manifestation' of a pattern 'which does not involve immediate or intrinsic modification of underlying structure' (Harris and Campbell 1995: 97).

Grammaticalization is a path from a lexical item to a grammatical morpheme (see Heine and Kuteva 2002, 2005). A typical example of grammaticalization is the verb 'finish' becoming a marker for 'completed' aspect. And we will see in §10.3 how verbs meaning 'stop' or 'leave' grammaticalize as markers of negative imperative.[7]

There appear to be cross-linguistic trends in the distribution of these mechanisms with respect to the subtypes of imperatives. Reinterpretation and reanalysis tend to affect the whole imperative set. Grammaticalization appears to be at work in developing non-canonical imperatives—that is, non-second person forms. Within multiple imperative systems, markers of terms which develop at a later stage—and whose meaning is more complex than that of an immediate order—may involve grammaticalization of erstwhile lexical items (some examples are in §11.1.1).

10.2.1 *From command strategies to command forms*

We mentioned at the end of the previous section that a second person singular canonical imperative tends to be the most basic and simple in its form, and tends to be archaic in its origin. In the history of many Indo-European languages, it stands apart from the second person plural imperative, and from other person values, simply because it preserves the original form. The other forms may come from essentially non-command forms which take on a command function. That is, the erstwhile command strategies take the place of an imperative proper.

Imperatives are often conceived as potentially face-threatening. In order to avoid this unwelcome effect, speakers employ other ways of framing directive acts. These 'imperative strategies' become conventionalized and may ultimately undergo reinterpretation as the only command forms available. This is the ultimate motivation behind reinterpreting command strategies into imperatives proper.

Pope (1934: 344) remarks that, in French, 'of the Latin terminations of the imperative only the second person singular was preserved'. In contrast, 'the second person plural was replaced by the indicative, which was also used as the optative in the first person plural'.[8]

Or the whole paradigm of the imperative may have an ultimately non-imperative source. As Jakobson (1965: 34–5) phrased it, the verb form which served as the Indo-European imperative was 'pushed out by the old optative in Proto-Slavic'.[9]

The Old Irish imperative forms with Indo-European 'secondary' personal endings 'represent older forms of the indicative' (Watkins 1963: 46–7).[10]

In his summary of the development of Indo-European mood inflection, Kuryłowicz (1964: 136) offers the following summary of sources for the verbal moods across the family:

SCHEME 10.1 Development of verbal moods in Indo-European languages

present-future → subjunctive (eventuality) $\Big\}$ imperative
past   →   optative (wish)

Individual forms may have individual histories. In Jersey Norman French, the imperative forms of the verbs *e:tr* 'be', *ave* 'have', and *save* 'know' go back to the Latin subjunctive. All other imperative forms go back to Latin imperatives (Liddicoat 1999: 167).

One of the innovations of Modern Colloquial Hebrew is the development of a new, truncated imperative based on the future as an imperative strategy. In the colloquial language, the second person future form is often used in lieu of imperative: a command cast in future sounds 'more polite' and less urgent and insistent: imperative forms 'sound too aggressive' (Bolozky 1979: 18, 2009). 10.4 is a future statement, and 10.5 is a command.

10.4 tox   šana   titragel   laze
      in   year   2masc.sg.FUT.get.used to.this
      'In a year's time, you will get used to this'

10.5 titragel   laze!
      2masc.sg.FUT.get.used   to.this
      'Get used to this!'

Only the imperative form *hitragel* would be used as a command in normative Hebrew. A further innovation sets Modern Colloquial Hebrew apart from the normative language. The future forms, used as commands, undergo vowel truncation and the loss of the personal prefix (see Bat-El 2002; Bolozky 1979).[11] Table 10.1 contrasts future, new truncated imperative, and normative imperative (Bat-El 2002: 658):

TABLE 10.1 Future, truncated imperative, and normative imperative in Modern Colloquial Hebrew

PERSON/ NUMBER/GENDER	FUTURE	TRUNCATED IMPERATIVE	NORMAL IMPERATIVE	TRANSLATION
2sg masculine	ti-ftax	ftax	ptax	'you (masc) open!'
2sg feminine	ti-ftexi	ftexi	pitxi	'you (fem) open!'

Truncated imperatives sound more informal, and somewhat more abrupt, than other ways of phrasing a command (Bolozky 1979; Ghil'ad Zuckermann, p.c.). This reflects an almost universal tendency: the shorter the command, the more brusque it sounds.

The development of this new paradigm of imperatives in the colloquial language involves reinterpretation of future as a primary command device.[12]

However, the truncated imperative is not identical with the future form. And it does not have a 'future' meaning. A new set of forms is born—based on reinterpretation and then reanalysis of an imperative strategy.

Free-standing dependent clauses can be used as directives (we saw numerous examples of this in §8.3). What looks like a syntactically incomplete sentence is a command, potentially less forceful than a straightforward imperative would be. This syntactic incompleteness has lesser force by 'leaving a face-threatening act half undone' (Brown and Levinson 1987: 227). The use of subjunctive in commands often originates in such face-saving ellipsis. Examples 8.30–33, from Catalan and from Modern Greek, show erstwhile dependent complement clauses used as directives on their own. The effect is that of mild commands and wishes rather than orders.

An erstwhile dependent clause may get to be the one and only way of expressing a command. Consider Boumaa Fijian. The imperative construction contains the relator *me* fused with the subject of the addressee: the fused form is *mo* (see Scheme 2.1, and Dixon 1988: 293–4). Examples are in 10.6 (Dixon 1988: 251) and 2.14.

10.6   mo   rai-ca   a   kuruse!
        REL+2sg   look-TR   ART   cross
        'You look at the cross!'

This is just one of the ways in which *me*, 'a highly useful relator', is deployed in the language. It also occurs in complement clauses, and can link two clauses with the sense 'in order to' or 'as a result that'. Its 'general semantic sense', that of 'should' (Dixon 1988: 284), owes its existence to the process of 'desubordination' of an erstwhile purposive clause. As Dixon (2009: 35) puts it, in Boumaa Fijian, an imperative 'could be regarded as the Focal clause of an implicit purposive linkage'.

This captures the essence of 'desubordination' as a prerequisite for reinterpreting and reanalysing a dependent clause into a new imperative paradigm. Similarly to the desubordinated *if*-clauses in English (see §8.3), the imperative *me*- clauses in Fijian are—synchronically—clauses in their own right. The 'missing' main clause cannot be easily supplied. And the imperative *me*-clauses themselves are somewhat divergent from their dependent clause lookalikes. We can recall from 2.15 that *me*-cum-person marker complex can be omitted if the addressee is second person singular. In other words, the *me*-imperative has developed a profile of its own—a sign of full grammaticalization of an erstwhile strategy for commands.

Erstwhile complement clauses can be used just for non-canonical (first and third person) imperatives. In Koromfe they contain the complementizer *ke*—see 10.22.[13]

Special, non-command functions of imperative forms may have their roots in curious historical events. The development of historical imperative in Russian is a case in point. What looks like a second person singular imperative form can be used in the meaning of an unexpected and spontaneous action in past tense.[14] It is often accompanied by an emphatic particle *i* (homophonous with the conjunction *i* 'and'):

10.7 a on i pobegi
and/but he EMPH/and run.IMPV.2sg
'And he (suddenly) ran' (lit. 'and he "you run!"')

Only second person singular imperative form is used this way; it covers all person and number values: 10.7 refers to third person singular, but any other person would be appropriate. This is quite unlike imperatives proper: second person plural is marked with *-te*, there is a first person plural form, and a variety of analytic forms are also available for first and third persons.[15] None of these are employed as 'historical imperatives'.

The origins of the 'historical' imperative have been a matter of contention. Delbrück (1893: 397) considered this use as a result of ellipsis, much in the spirit of 'desubordination' which we have just discussed. That is, a construction like the one in 10.7 would have arisen from an erstwhile sentence 'he acted as if commanded to run'.[16]

A different explanation has gained a wider acceptance. The 'historical' imperative is considered one of the few residual traces of the old aorist in Modern Russian. Its appearance is a matter of pure historical coincidence. First, second and third person singular of the old aorist and the second person singular imperative happened to coincide, in verbs whose infinitive ended in *-iti*. So, a form like *kupi* (from *kupiti* 'to buy') would mean both 'you buy!' (second person singular imperative) and 'you/(s)he bought'. Secondly, the aorist itself was in decline. As a result, the past tense semantics got transferred from the aorist to the homonymous imperative forms, before aorist was completely eliminated from the system.[17]

Gronas (2006: 91–4) comes up with another hypothesis. Historical imperative forms are attested in Ukrainian, Belorussian, Serbo-Croatian, Bulgarian, and Macedonian, with general meaning of a 'sudden, unexpected action in the past'. An additional meaning is that of repeated or intensive action, also in the past. As mentioned above, the Slavic imperative goes back to the Indo-European optative. Optative has modal meaning in many Indo-European languages, but in some it has given rise to forms with past tense meaning. Within the Iranian branch, the Avestan optative often has the meaning of a durative or intensive action in the past (Tedesco 1923). The Sogdian preterite descends from optative, and combines both modal and past tense ('preterital') meanings (see Benveniste 1951). In the Digori dialect of Ossetian, optative forms have the meaning of 'iterative past', combined with a conjunction meaning 'and'. In addition, Ironi and Digori dialects of Ossetian employ optative (accompanied with the same coordinating conjunction) to express sudden and unexpected action in the past.

This striking parallel development among Indo-European languages illustrates what Sapir (1921: 171–2) called 'parallelism in drift', that is, structural similarities between related languages, even those 'long disconnected'. It also provides support for a different account for the emergence of Russian—and Slavic—'historical' imperative. Both command-imperative and past tense 'sudden action' imperative lookalike would then come from independent reinterpretation of proto-Indo-European optative.

10.2.2 *Grammaticalization in imperatives*

Verbs may evolve into grammatical markers of imperatives. They then lose their independent status and their original lexical meaning and thus undergo grammaticalization. They may also change in how they sound—becoming shorter and snappier, as we will see below.

In most cases, grammaticalized forms come to mark just non-canonical imperatives—first person and also third person forms. Just occasionally, grammaticalized forms come to mark second person—canonical—imperatives.

MOTION VERBS are a well-attested source for imperative markers (also see Heine and Kuteva 2002). They include (i) 'come', (ii) 'go', (iii) 'leave, abandon, let'. In each case, an imperative form of the motion verb gets reinterpreted as a grammatical morpheme. We exemplify each path in turn.

(i) From 'COME' *to an imperative*   German *kommen* 'come' has evolved into *komm..!* (solidarity imperative marker), as in 10.8 and 10.9 (Heine and Kuteva 2002: 69–70):

10.8 Komm,   denk   darüber nach!
      come:2sgIMPV think:2sgIMPV about:it after
      'Come on, think about it!'

10.9 Komm,   geh   jetzt!
      come:2sgIMPV go:2sgIMPV   now
      'Come on, go now!'

This is similar to how *Come on!* in English is often used to urge an addressee to make a greater effort. The source of the grammaticalized 'hortative' marker is a second person canonical imperative.

Further examples come from Khoisan languages. In Nama (Rust 1965: 75), *haa* 'come' has grammaticalized into a 'solidarity' imperative marker *ha* 'come on!'. In !Ora (Korana), *hā* 'come' is used as a first person command marker (Meinhof 1930: 54):

10.10   hā-kham !ū
     'Let's go!'[18]

In Lezgian (Haspelmath 1993: 129, 150, 244), first person singular and plural commands are often accompanied by the sentence-initial particle *ša*, originally meaning 'come' (the form still in use as a suppletive imperative of the verb *atun* 'come'):[19]

10.11   ša   gila   čun   či   q̇armax-ri.z   kilig-in
     PARTICLE   now   WE.ABS   WE.GEN   hook-PL-DAT   look-1pHORT
     'Now let's look at our hooks'

(ii) From 'GO' to an imperative   In Rama, a Chibchan language from Nicaragua, *bang* 'go' has become a first person plural imperative suffix (Craig 1991: 476–7). As an independent verb, *bang*, with a free variant *mang*, is a suppletive imperative form of *taak* 'go'. As shown in 10.12, *bang/mang* is used as a second person imperative:

10.12   mang,   tawan   ki   yu-mang!
     go   town   to   with-go
     'Go, take it to town!'

The form *taak* is used in all other contexts (see 10.13):

10.13   i-taak-u,   tawan   ki   yu-i-taak-u
     3-go-TENSE   town   to   with-3-to-TENSE
     'He went, he took it to town'

As a suffix in its function of first person imperative marker, *-bang* no longer has any free variants, and combines with first person plural subject marker:

10.14   mwaing   yairi   s-tuk-bang
     1pl   soup   1pl-drink-1pl.IMPV
     'Let's drink our soup'

That *-bang* is now grammaticalized as an imperative suffix, with no synchronic connection with its source verb, is confirmed by the fact that it can easily combine with the verb *taak* 'go'. There is no double 'going' involved:

-bang has lost its erstwhile lexical meaning, which is what happens in grammaticalization:

10.15   ka-s-taak-bang
        RELATIONAL.PREFIX/from-1pl-go-1pl.IMPV
        'Let's go away from it'

This is just one instance of multiple grammaticalization of 'go', a ubiquitous source of new morphology in the language.

Along similar lines, the hortative verb *čóʔo* 'go' in Chalcatongo Mixtec (a Mixtecan language: Macaulay 1996: 136–7) can be used with a variety of complements (cast in potential mood), as in 10.16.

10.16   čóʔo   kee   staà
        go.HORT   eat.POTENTIAL   tortilla
        'Let's eat!'

Its straightforward meaning 'let's go' is shown in 10.17:

10.17   čóʔo
        go.HORT
        'Let's go!'

The 'hortative' itself is 'often contracted to a monosyllable'; as a result, it 'often loses the motion component of its semantic content, functioning simply as a generic hortative'. This is a prime example of how 'form and meaning covary' in grammaticalization (also known as the Parallel Reduction Hypothesis: Bybee et al. 1994: 19–21). The more grammaticalized the form, the likelier it is to undergo a process of shortening and phonological change—that is, the more remote it is from the original lexical source.[20]

(iii) From 'LEAVE, ABANDON, LET' to imperative   In Lingala, *-tíka* 'leave, let' is used as a hortative imperative auxiliary. Note that the main verb is in the subjunctive/optative mood (Heine and Kuteva 2002: 191; van Everbroek 1969: 141):

10.18   tíká   tó-kɛndɛ
        leave   1pl-go
        'Let us go!'

Hausa *bàri* 'how about; hortative marker' comes from the verb *barī* 'leave' (Cowan and Schuh 1976: 148).

The verb 'leave', which grammaticalizes into a marker of non-canonical imperative, may have a permissive, 'let' overtone.[21] The verb *let* in English, used to express non-canonical imperative—first person and third person commands—has followed a similar grammaticalization path (see an incisive discussion in Hopper and Traugott 1993: 12–14), and so has German *lassen* 'leave, let'.[22] Further examples abound. In Albanian, *lë* 'leave, let' has become a 'hortative' marker employed with both first and third persons (Buchholz et al. 1993: 273). The development of verb meaning 'leave, let' into permissive (as in German *lassen*) is discussed in Heine and Kuteva (2002: 193).

We will see, in §10.3 below, that the verb 'leave, abandon' may follow an entirely different path, grammaticalizing into a marker of prohibitive (see Dixon 1972: 112, for discussion).

What makes motion verbs a likely source for marking non-canonical imperatives? Motion verbs 'assume an interpersonal function in specific contexts' involving commands (Heine and Kuteva 2002: 193). The development of these interpersonal functions can be linked to the purposeful (or 'telic') overtones of motion verbs. Note that they often develop purposive overtones and give rise to purposive constructions, just like English *going to*, fused into *gonna* in colloquial varieties. Telicity is an important aspect of imperatives. Semantics of motion is intrinsically linked to a change of state or creating a new situation.

We can recall that Rama is among the languages where one form of the verb 'go' has fully grammaticalized into an imperative morpheme. Craig (1991: 490, note 16) explains the process in an imaginative way:

Rama is an interesting language in that its grammar encodes the fact that the intended effect of the imperative speech act is the creation of a sequence of two actions or states: a first state or action to be abandoned and moved away from and a second state or action to be embraced and moved toward [. . .] the motion verb *bang* ['go'] marks the motion toward the desired new action or state.

The metaphor of 'moving from' and 'moving toward' underlies the grammaticalization of motion verbs as exponents for commands, which have the potential of developing into dedicated imperative markers. Telic motion conspires with instigation.

In addition, 'come' has an overtone of solidarity between the speaker and the addressee, motivating the well-attested development of 'come' into a first person 'hortatory' marker. And the idea of 'moving from' lies behind another type of development for motion verbs: from 'leave, abandon' to prohibitive. This is the topic of §10.3.

Verbs of other semantic groups[23] may give rise to command markers. Verbs meaning 'GET, RECEIVE, OBTAIN' may develop into exponents of permission which can be construed as a type of command (see Chapter 6). Early Archaic

Chinese *de* 'obtain (something after making an effort)' gave rise to Late Archaic Chinese *de* 'marker of permission'.[24]

The verb 'give' in Russian has grammaticalized into a permissive marker.[25] The second person imperative form of 'give' occurs in commands directed at first and third persons. The lexical verb can occur in the form of an infinitive, or in the future form. A self-addressed 'give-2sg' form is illustrated in 10.19:

10.19   davaj   ja   pojdu   odna
        give.IMPF.2sgIMPV   I   go.FUT.1sg   alone.FEM.SG.NOM
        'Shall I go alone? Let me go alone' (lit. 'give-you.sg I will go alone')

And in 10.20, Boris Slutzkij, a well-known Russian poet, urges himself and his fellow-soldiers to get up and go. The marker, *davaj-te*, lit. 'you plural give!', is what imparts the meaning of first person inclusive imperative, 'you and me together', to the construction:

10.20   davaj-te   posle draki   pomashem   kulakami
        give.IMPF.2sgIMPV-pl   after fight.GEN.SG swing+1plFUT   fist.PL.INSTR
        'Let's swing fists after the fight!'

In these two examples, the verb 'give' has hardly any overtone of 'giving', or even 'permission'.[26] 'Give' in Russian is widely used as a grammaticalized marker of permission outside commands. The semantic path of development from 'permissive' to first and then third person commands is intuitively clear. We saw in §2.4 that permissive meaning is frequently associated with a first person command. Like English *let*, the exponent of first person command has extended to cover third person commands.[27]

In Nigerian Pidgin, the marker of imperatives is the 'subjunctive clause introducer' *mek* (Faraclas 1996: 24–5; example 2.16). This marker comes from the verb *make* 'make', which also occurs in causative serial verb constructions: *im gò mek mì go* (3SP-R make+1OP go+) 'She or he will make me go'. What is shared by *mek* as the verb 'make', *mek* as a causative marker, and *mek* as the exponent of imperative is the feature of 'control' and authority of the speaker—or the 'commander'—over the addressee, or the event to be brought about. And we saw in §4.4.1 that in some languages, verbs have to be made agentive, and the action controlled, for them to be used in imperative constructions. This correlation, between the control associated with causation and imperatives, provides motivation for the rare grammaticalization path from 'make' to be the marker of imperative in Nigerian Pidgin.

In Kusunda, a moribund isolate from Nepal, the imperative of most transitive verbs involves the verbal root and the imperative of *ə/a-* 'do, make', e.g. *pumba* 'beat', *pumba ə-go* (beat do-IMPV) 'beat (him)!' The imperative of intransitive verbs is synthetic, e.g. *ip* 'sleep', *ip-to!* 'you sleep!' (Watters et al. 2005: 91, 97–9). Optative (employed for third person command) also involves the verb 'do, make'. This is the closest analogy to the imperative in Nigerian Pidgin, and another rather unusual example of an analytically expressed imperative.[28]

10.3 Where do prohibitives come from?

Prohibitives tend to follow different development paths from their positive counterparts. Unlike canonical imperatives, even prohibitives addressed to second person often reflect new developments. Prohibitives may originate in reinterpretation and reanalysis of essentially non-command forms. Or they may follow a 'prohibitive-specific' grammaticalization path.

10.3.1 *From a 'prohibitive' strategy to a negative command*

Just like their positive counterparts, prohibitives may develop out of other forms, for which 'prohibition' comes to be their main function. Negative imperatives, or prohibitives, often differ from their positive counterparts in categories and the meaning they express. In terms of their historical development, they may follow the same path. This is the case in Slavic languages: both imperatives and prohibitives are based on the optative.

A prohibitive may be based on a different mood form than the imperative proper. Koiari, from the Highlands of New Guinea, has a special paradigm for positive imperatives. In contrast, the prohibitive is formed using obligative mood (Dutton 1996: 27–8). Or a prohibitive may be based on a non-finite form, while the positive command form preserves the inflectional markers inherited from the ancestor language.

Table 5.4 (above) contrasts negative and positive imperatives in Italian (exemplified with *cantare* 'to sing'). Here, the second person singular imperative *canta* preserves the second person singular imperative inflection. The negative imperative is a negated infinitive, *non cantare*. Just as with positive imperatives, originally non-command forms—including infinitives—undergo reinterpretation and become regular parts of imperative paradigms.

We can recall from §10.2.2 that imperatives of intransitive verbs in Kusunda are formed synthetically. Imperatives of most transitive verbs consist of the verb root followed by the imperative of 'do, make'. Prohibitives are formed in the same way. The prohibitive of *ip* 'sleep' is *n-ip-in* (2-sleep-PROH) 'don't sleep'. Prohibitive of an intransitive verb involves the prohibitive verb *ə* 'do, make' and the verb root, e.g. *unda* 'show', *unda ə-yin* (show do-PROH) 'don't show (it)'. This is an example of the same kind of (rather unusual) grammaticalization pattern, from a lexical verb 'do, make' to a command marker, shared by positive and by negative imperatives.

The development of both positive, and negative imperatives may involve desubordinated structures. In Koromfe, the positive canonical imperative consists of the verb stem. The non-canonical imperatives involve the complementizer *ke* (similarly to Boumaa Fijian *me* discussed in §10.2.2):

10.21   ke   o   gondu
         that(CONJ)   1pl   leave
         'Let's leave!' (lit. that we leave)

The prohibitive is formed using the negative complementizer *ka*, which can be roughly translated as 'lest' (Rennison 1997: 39–40):

10.22   ka   n   harɪ   mə   jʊ̃   tasgʊ
         that+NEG(CONJ)   2sg.PRONOUN   tough   1sg.PRONOUN   head   basket
         'Don't (sg) touch my hat!'

Analytic imperatives in Boumaa Fijian are similar to their negative counterparts. Both involve the 'highly useful' relator *me*—see 10.7 for a positive imperative. A negative imperative, illustrated in 10.23, includes the prohibitive particle *'ua* 'don't'. Just like the corresponding negative declarative (10.24), it contains the complementizer *ni*:

10.23   me+o   'ua   ni   la'o
         REL+2sgS   don't   that   go
         'Don't go' (lit. That you don't (be the case) that go!)

10.24   e   sega   [ni-au   la'o]
         3sg   NOT   that-1sgSUBJ   go
         'I don't go' (lit. it is not the case that I go)

In Nigerian Pidgin, the marker *mek,* which comes from 'make, do', appears in positive and in negative imperative structures—see 2.16 and 10.25 (Faraclas 1996: 26).

10.25   mek   yù   no   bay   nyam!
         IMPV   you   NEG   buy   yam
         'Don't buy yams!'

As we saw in Chapter 5, prohibitives are more often expressed analytically than their positive counterparts. In numerous instances, prohibitive markers come from grammaticalized verbs. Prohibitive markers frequently come from lexical items, and from constructions involving modal verbs.[29]

10.3.2 *Grammaticalizing a prohibitive*

Grammaticalized prohibitives may involve the negative imperative of a modal verb—typically volition or ability. Or they may involve grammaticalizing a root or a non-negative imperative form of a verb with the meaning 'stop, leave, abandon'. Further sources involve negative imperatives of verbs of perception and speech.

The last words of Archimedes are reported to have been:

10.26 Noli   turbare   circulos   meos
      not.want.2sg.IMPV disturb.INF   circle.ACC.PL   my.ACC.PL
      'Do not disturb my circles', or

10.27 Noli   tangere   circulos   meos
      not.want.2sg.IMPV touch.INF   circle.ACC.PL   my.ACC.PL
      'Don't touch my circles'

One of these was addressed to a Roman soldier who, despite being given orders not to, ended up killing the famous geometer during the conquest of Syracuse.[30]

Archimedes' words reflect one of the cross-linguistically most widely attested patterns of grammaticalization for a prohibitive construction, that of NEGATIVE VOLITION. This also highlights the discrepancy in the origins of a positive and of a negative imperative: the positive imperative is archaic, while its negative counterpart involves a transparent, and recent, grammaticalization.

It is a well-known fact that the verb 'want' and desideratives in general develop meanings to do with intention, purpose, and obligation.[31] We saw in Chapter 8 that optatives, desideratives, and constructions involving 'wanting' are often used as directives, as 'imperative strategies'. Optative forms, whose basic meaning is 'wish', can be the source for newly developed imperatives, something we mentioned earlier in this chapter for Slavic languages (and see Gronas 2006; Jakobson 1965).

The desiderative forms of the verb in Korowai, a Papuan language from the Indonesian province of Papua, are used as dedicated positive and negative command forms (van Enk and de Vries 1997: 94–5, 100–101). A desiderative second person singular form *lu-m* (enter-DESID.2sg) can mean either 'enter!', 'you want to enter', or 'you must enter'. When expressing a command meaning, the form can be optionally preceded by the modal adverb *anè*.

In its desiderative meaning, it may be optionally followed by the adverb *kholüp*. The negative imperative also coincides with the desiderative accompanied by a negative suffix and the negative adverb.[32]

Negative volition expresses the opposite—an obligation, a command, or an injunction not to do something. In colloquial English, 10.28 can well be a statement about what you might want, or not want, to do. But it is also a command, or an invitation, or an advice not to get involved with a particularly unpleasant person:

10.28   You don't want to have anything to do with Randy

'Want' in English can be used for both positive and negative commands. *Do you want to come?* can be viewed as an invitation, or a mild command. This is similar to Korowai, where both negative and positive orders involve desiderative forms. Not so in Latin: here, the inherently negative verb 'not to want' is a conventionalized—though not the only—way of expressing an order not to do something, whereas its positive equivalent is not used this way.

Along similar lines, Yimas, from the Lower Sepik family, has a special paradigm for marking imperatives. The prohibitive forms—used by younger speakers—involve 'the same form as a desiderative' and irrealis, preceded by *pack* 'don't' (Foley 1991: 275).

We saw in Chapter 8 that expressions involving 'ABILITY' are often used for suggestions and mild commands, just like English *Could you pass the salt?* And its negative counterpart—usually phrased as an ability question—can be used to stop someone from doing something, with an additional overtone of impatience or persuasiveness in *Can't you talk a bit louder?*

NEGATIVE POSSIBILITY is another well-attested path for developing prohibitives across the languages of the world (cf. Pakendorf and Schalley 2007). In Tok Pisin, a Creole language of Papua New Guinea, *no ken* (not can) is one of the conventionalized ways of producing a prohibition, as in 10.30a–b.[33] Positive commands are in 10.29a–b:

10.29a   yu   kam!
         you   come
         'Come!'

10.29b   ol   i   kam
         they   PRED   come
         'Let them come!'

10.30a yu   no   ken   kam!
        you   not   can   come
        'Don't come!'

10.30b ol   i   no   ken   kam
        they   PRED   not   can   come
        'Don't let them come!'

An imperative has the same segmental structure as a statement. Similarly, 10.30a–b can be understood as statements, 'you are not allowed to come' and 'they are not allowed to come' respectively. In each case, the intonation makes a difference.

Negative possibility is linked to NEGATIVE CONSEQUENCE. A warning against something adverse is in itself like a command not to do it. Such a statement of 'adversity' does not have to contain a marker of negation: it is inherently negative.

Such 'apprehensive' commands are a feature of numerous languages of Australia, Oceania, and Amazonia. Commands in 6.14 and 6.50, from Tuyuca, and 6.51, from Tucano (both East Tucanoan), do not have to contain a negator: the meaning of a warning itself conveys a negative overtone. An apprehensive or 'warning' imperative has developed in Tariana, an Arawak language in contact with East Tucanoan, under East Tucanoan influence— just like many other imperative categories in this language (see §11.1.1). Tariana has two forms—a visual and a non-visual apprehensive (see 4.40 and 4.41). 10.31 is a warning to someone who, according to the speaker, is not cautious enough and cannot see properly:

10.31   pi-wha-ñhina
        2sg-fall-APPREHENSIVE.NONVISUAL
        'You might fall down (you are not looking!)' (lit. 'Lest you fall down!' (be careful))

Someone who can see what's ahead will be warned with:

10.32   pi-wha-da
        2sg-fall-APPREHENSIVE.VISUAL
        'You might fall down (you can see!)' (lit. 'Lest you fall down!' (be careful))

Numerous Australian languages have a special type of dependent clause meaning 'for fear of VERB-ing'. It expresses undesirable negative consequences to be avoided by carrying out the actions stated in the main clause.

An example of a 'lest' clause, from Diyari, was in 8.50 (Austin 1981: 225). Like other dependent clauses, a 'lest' clause can undergo desubordination and come to occur on its own, with no main clause. Then, the 'lest' suffix functions as the main verb marker. A 'lest'-clause of this kind is in 10.33 (repeated from 8.51, from Austin 1981: 229), from Diyari:

10.33 ṉulu-ka   kiṇṯala-li   yinaṉa   maṯa-yaṯi
       3sgnf.a-TOKEN   dog-ERG   2sgO   bite-LEST
       'The dog might bite you'

In Austin's (1978: 229) words, this 'could be said to a visitor entering one's camp as a warning that a particular dog approaching him is ferocious and should be avoided—the context would be clear and make it unnecessary to say "Look out!" or "Be careful!" and so on.'

The idiomatic phrase in English *Lest we forget* can be interpreted as a negative command—not to forget, especially about those who sacrificed their lives for us. This is another example of a negative consequence form marking a warning, and ultimately a command.

'Warning' reflects a hypothetical situation; no wonder that English *lest* requires a subjunctive verb following it (as the OED tells us). The hypothetical mood in Wambaya, an Australian language, is used for warnings (Nordlinger 1998: 150–8). Nyangumarta uses anticipatory mood—whose major meaning is expressing something 'about to happen'—for negative consequence (Sharp 2004: 186–7):

10.34 partany   pungka-a-li
       child   fall-ANTICIPATORY-ANTICIPATORY
       'The child might fall down'

Negative consequence in itself contains an element of possibility that something might happen (see Dixon 2009, for a comprehensive survey). And indeed, forms with potential meaning can be used for negative consequences.

Voluntative-potential forms in Sakha (or Yakut, a Turkic language spoken in Siberia) are a case in point. Data from the early 20th century show that second person forms of this paradigm had an apprehensive meaning (Pakendorf and Schalley 2007: 526):

Sakha

10.35 seren   oχt-o:yo-γun
       be.careful(IMPV.2sg)   fall-VOLUNT.POT-2sg
       'be careful, (or) you might fall!'

In the present-day language, these forms have developed into prohibitives (in two of the four districts of the Sakha republic: Pakendorf and Schalley 2007: 327).[34]

In Chepang, a Tibeto-Burman language from Nepal, the indefinite future marker -*caʔ* can be used to express warning, as in 10.36 (Caughley 1982: 102). This meaning is the major one in situations where the addressee is not in control:

Chepang

10.36   naŋ   has-teʔ-caʔ
        you   vomit-CONTRARY.TO.INFORMATION.FLOW-INDEFINITE.FUTURE
        'You may be sick!'

If the verb refers to a potentially controllable action, and the addressee can be in control, an indefinite future form can be used as a negative command, not to do it. The sentence in 10.37 has two meanings: that of warning (a), and that of a command (b):

10.37   baŋ-səy   ton-teʔ-caʔ
        stone-ABL   fall-CONTRARY.TO.INFORMATION.FLOW-INDEFINITE.FUTURE
        (a) 'You may fall from (that) rock!'
        (b) 'Don't fall from (that) rock!'

And if the addressee is involved in the action and has full control, the command meaning is the only one acceptable:

10.38   jugaŋ-ma-teʔ   glyuŋh-caʔ-jə
        ever-COORD-CONTRARY.TO.INFORMATION.FLOW   go.out-INDEFINITE.
                                                  FUTURE-2du
        'Don't you two ever go out!'

We can recall the connection between imperatives and the feature of addressee having control over a commanded action. Examples in §4.4.3 showed how in some languages one cannot command another person to be something, or to be in a state which is beyond the commandee's volition or control. Chepang reflects the same principle, and clearly demonstrates a link between a warning, a negative consequence, and a negative command.

What can be conceived of as an erstwhile marker of negative consequence can develop into a prohibitive. *Nogut* (from *no good*) in Tok Pisin can be used for a warning:

10.39   Lukaut!   Nogut   yu   bagarap
        be.careful NEG.CONSEQUENCE you   be.ruined
        'Watch out! You might get hurt!' (lit. Watch out that you don't get hurt)

Or it can be used as one of the markers of negative commands:[35]

10.40   Nogut   yupela i   brukim   wanpela samting
        NEG.CONSEQUENCE you.pl PRED break.TRANS one   something
        'Don't you break anything!'

A structure with *nogut* is polysemous. This is reflected in the multiplicity of translations for 10.41 (e.g. in Mühlhäusler 1985: 165):

10.41   Nogut   yu   sindaun!
        NEG.CONSEQUENCE you   sit.down
        'Don't sit down!' (or 'You shouldn't sit down!' or 'It wouldn't be wise
        for you to sit down!')

A marker of a negative imperative may come from a grammaticalized verb, either in a root form or in the form of an imperative.

A major grammaticalization path involves STOPPING. In other words, the verb 'stop' can give rise to a prohibitive. In Welsh (Wiliam 1960: 78; King 1993: 227) the imperative forms of verb *peidio* 'cease, stop' are used as prohibitive markers (followed by a verbal noun):

10.42   paid   colli'r   arian   'na
        don't.2sg=stop.2sgIMPV   lose.the   money   that
        'Don't lose that money!'

Such a sentence does not mean 'stop doing it'—rather, it is the preferred way in the colloquial language of prohibiting someone from doing something.

Along similar lines, the verb 'stop' is used 'to negate imperatives' in Krahn, Bassa, Klao, and Sapo, Western Kru languages from Liberia and Ivory Coast. The following example is from Klao (Marchese 1986: 191). The form *bɔ* means 'stop' and also 'don't':[36]

10.43   bɔ   dɛ   di-di-dɛ
        stop   thing eat-eat-NOMZ
        'Don't eat anything!'

Negative commands with a strong overtone of 'stopping' the activity once and for all can take additional, 'cessative', marking. In Chepang, a

Tibeto-Burman language, a cessative marker *taʔ* can accompany an emphatic negative imperative: 10.44 is a way of stopping the action that had already commenced (Caughley 1982: 102–3):

10.44   taʔ   taʔ   dayh-ʔə-lə
        CESSATIVE   CESSATIVE   speak-EMPH.IMPV-NEG
        'Stop talking!'

We can recall from §6.5 that 'cessative', 'stop VERB-ing', is a semantic subtype of prohibitive (see 6.55, from Trio, a Carib language: Carlin 2004: 309–11). Conventionalizing the idea of putting a stop to an activity into a prohibition is a semantically straightforward path.

POSITIONAL verb 'stay' can develop along similar lines. In Vurës, an Oceanic language spoken in Vanuatu (Hyslop 2003), the prohibitive particle *nitog* comes from the verb *tog* 'stay' marked for third person unspecified time reference. In Mali, a Baining language from the New Britain province of Papua New Guinea, the prohibitive particle *kule* comes from the verb *kule* 'stay' (Stebbins 2003).

A MOTION VERB 'leave, abandon' may develop into a marker of negative command. The prohibitive particle *galga* in the central dialect of Dyirbal (Dixon 1972: 112; p.c. 2009) is similar in form to the transitive root *galgal* 'leave (it)'. 10.45 shows the positive command:

10.45   bala   yugu   galga   balay
        THERE.ABS.NEUTER   stick   leave   THERE
        'Leave the stick there!'

And 10.46 illustrates its negative counterpart:

10.46   bala   yugu   galga   galga-m   balay
        THERE.ABS.NEUTER   stick   PROH   leave-PROH   THERE
        'Don't leave the stick there!'

The segmental similarity of the verb 'leave' and the prohibitive marker is reminiscent of negative commands 'leave off doing it!' in some varieties of English. In Kattaŋ, an Australian language formerly spoken in New South Wales, the negative imperative particle *waɲa* is strikingly similar to the verb root *waɲa* 'leave, stop, leave off' (Dixon 1972: 112; Holmer 1966: 78; 1967: 67).

How does a verb meaning 'leave' develop into a prohibitive marker? The ultimate explanation lies in the conventions of phrasing commands, especially pervasive in Australian languages. We can recall from 9.2–9.7 (and note 15 to Chapter 9) that in many Australian languages, among them Yidiñ and

Warlpiri, a command needs to be contextualized. That is, a negative form—
what not to do—is accompanied by a positive command—what to do
instead. In Warlpiri, the proper way of speaking would be 'don't spear the
kangaroo, leave it' (lit. 'leave the kangaroo without spearing it') or 'don't
spear the kangaroo, sit' (lit. 'sit without spearing the kangaroo'). The positive
imperative accompanying a negative command typically involves verbs *yampi*
'leave it!', *ɲina* 'sit', or 'a small number of similar verbs' (Dixon 1972: 112, based
on p.c. from Ken Hale). Dixon hypothesizes that a similar situation 'prevailed
at one time in Dyirbal and Kattaŋ'. In the contemporary Dyirbal, the negative
imperative is marked by *galga* and a prohibitive inflection.

10.47 ŋinda bayi   yaɽa galga balga-m
       you   NOUN.MARKER.ABS.MASC man   PROH   hit-PROH
       'Don't you hit the man!'

Dixon (1972: 112) hypothesizes that the negative imperative may have been
originally marked just by verbal ending *-m*. And then, 'gradually, *galga* may
have become an institutionalized part of the negative imperative and moved
further forward in the sentence (nowadays it MUST precede the verb)'. As a
result of complete grammaticalization, *galga* in Dyirbal is 'an established
particle, with no verbal overtones, and is used with all verbs, including *galgal*'
'leave'.

We saw in §5.1 that in Warlpiri a negative imperative involves a complex
construction with 'leave': 'Don't hit them!' literally translates as 'Hitting-
without them leave!' (5.21a: Laughren 2002: 115–16). This reflects the same
prohibitive strategy, now completely grammaticalized: any other way of
negating a command is ungrammatical in the traditional language (cf. 5.21b).

A form meaning 'LEAVE IT, LET IT DROP, NEVER MIND' may take on a
meaning of 'don't do it!'. The ubiquitous *maski* in Tok Pisin is among the
most frequent words one hears in this language. *Maski* means 'never mind,
forget it', 'I don't care, who cares'. To say 'never mind the rain', one says *maski
ren*. *Maski long kukim kaikai* ('never mind' PREP cook.TRANS food) means
'don't bother to cook food'. In other words, this is a perfect exponent of a
linguistic 'devil-may-care' attitude. *Maski* can also be used as a conjunction
'although'. And it marks a negative command. *Maski* can be placed before or
after the subject pronoun (which is often omitted if clear from the context):

10.48 maski   yu   hambak!
       never.mind you   fool.around
       'Don't fool around!'[37]

From the synchronic perspective of Tok Pisin,[38] the development of *maski* into a marker of a negative command is similar to the development of 'leave': that is, something like 'leave doing it, forget about doing it'. Other languages of Papua New Guinea have expressions similar to *maski*. In Manambu, *ja:u* 'let it drop, forget it, don't do it' can also be interpreted as a negative command strategy. But its meaning is not exclusively negative; nor is this a verbal form (see Aikhenvald 2008a: 107–8 for its treatment as a type of adverbial expression).

A verb meaning 'SEE, LOOK' may develop into a marker of a negative command. In Warekena of Xié, an Arawak language from northwestern Brazil, a negative command is expressed with the construction: personal form of the verb *-eda* 'perceive, see/hear' + the verb+ general negator *-pia*. The verb 'to perceive' is used here as an auxiliary verb (Aikhenvald 1998):[39]

10.49 pida   pi-yutʃia-pia-na
        2sg+see   2pl-kill-NEG-1sg
        'Don't kill me!'

The positive imperative in this language is archaic, and consists just of the person marker and the verb stem: *pida* on its own would mean 'look!'.

The negated verb 'see, look' often extends to express warning—similar to English 'look out' and Latin *vide* (Löfstedt 1966: 94). An apprehensive meaning in Tatar is expressed through a combination of a main verb (in the form of a converb) and the prohibitive of *kür-* 'see':[40]

Tatar
10.50 jegýla   kür-mä!
        fall.CONV 'see'-PROH.2sg
        'Beware not to fall!' (lit. Don't see falling!)

We can thus hypothetically postulate two grammaticalization paths for 'see, look': one to warning and apprehension, and another to prohibition.

A prohibitive can develop from a VERB OF SPEECH. In Kwomtari, an isolate from Papua New Guinea (Spencer 2008: 145, 165), the prohibitive *mani* is likely to have come from *mwa nie*, from *mwa ne-ie* (no say-1subject.realis) 'I said "no"'. This form is no longer used as a verb, and does not show subject agreement. It always occurs after the final verb in the clause, and is accompanied by *kose* 'lest' before the verb:

10.51 Kose   menegu   le-te-lu   mani
        lest   thought do-3O-2subject.realis   PROH
        'Don't think of them!'

A negative imperative may involve grammaticalization of a copula construction. In a number of Northern Carib languages, the negative imperative is expressed with an analytic construction consisting of an adverbial form of the lexical verb accompanied with a copula 'be' with imperative inflection, and an additional negative adverbializer:[41]

Macushi (Abbott 1991: 52–3)

10.52   te-es-ewankono'ma-i   pra   e'-kî

NEG-DETRANS-sad-ADVERBIALIZER   NEG.ADVERBIALIZER   be-IMPV:SG

'Be not sad'

Grammaticalization of a copula construction into a prohibitive expression is reminiscent of the development of 'be, have' as modal auxiliaries with the meaning of 'obligation' (Denning 1987, and note 28 below).[42]

This concludes our brief discussion of grammaticalization paths in prohibitives. A motivation for each of these grammaticalization paths is in the semantics of the grammaticalized verb, and of the prohibition itself. We now turn to a summary of the ways in which imperatives develop.

10.4 How imperatives change: a summary

Imperative forms tend to resist change. Whitney (1924: 215) remarks that, in Sanskrit, 'of all the three modes, the imperative is the one [...] most unchanged throughout the whole history of the language'. Imperative constructions may preserve archaic patterns of marking grammatical relations. We saw in §10.1 how imperatives are the only remnant of the erstwhile ergative-absolutive system in Panyjima, Lardil, and a few other Australian languages (see also Dixon 1994: 189).

Unlike other moods, not all person forms of an imperative follow the same path. The second person canonical imperative—the most basic of all commands—tends to preserve archaic features. Non-canonical imperatives—commands to first and to third person—may come from other sources, giving rise to heterogenous sets of imperative forms.

Such innovative forms may not be limited to non-canonical imperatives. But there are no examples of canonical, and not non-canonical ones, being innovated. The less basic, non-canonical imperatives may be added to the system of grammatical command forms through grammaticalized verbs, or reinterpreting non-command forms. We are then faced with a heterogenous imperative system, whereby different person forms come from different sources.

Non-canonical imperatives may come from grammaticalized lexical items. There are hardly any clear examples of lexical forms giving rise to a whole imperative paradigm (Nigerian Pidgin and Kusunda are among the rare examples). Alternatively, the whole system of commands—the imperative paradigm—may have its origin in an essentially non-imperative set, as a result of reinterpretation of what can be conceived of as an erstwhile imperative strategy.

What stops speakers from using dedicated imperative forms? Imperatives are the most straightforward means for commanding someone to do something. They may sound imperious and authoritative. And to avoid such face-threatening acts, speakers have recourse to other, more roundabout ways, of getting addressees to do what the speaker desires (cf. Brown and Levinson 1987: 226). This avoidance is the major motivation behind employing 'imperative strategies'—the 'imperatives in disguise' discussed in Chapter 8.

Imperative strategies constitute a common source for imperative newcomers. This is when a form is employed as an alternative to a dedicated command—which sounds too harsh, i.e. too 'imperative'—and then over time 'command' becomes its major meaning.

We distinguish the following recurrent pathways of development:

  (i) the pathway of VOLITION: developing dedicated command forms out of desiderative and optative forms, whereby the semantics of 'wish' gets reinterpreted as 'command';
  (ii) the pathway of INTENTION, FUTURE, and PREDICTION, whereby future and intentional modality are reinterpreted as commands par excellence;
  (iii) the pathway of ABILITY, whereby an expression concerning being able to do something becomes a command;
  (iv) the pathway of HYPOTHESIS, SUPPOSITION, and SUGGESTION, whereby subjunctive, hypothetical, and other modal forms take on the function of command;
  (v) the pathway of DESUBORDINATION and INCOMPLETE SPEECH ACT, whereby an erstwhile purposive, complement, conditional, or another dependent clause becomes the major exponent of command.

The pathways of grammaticalization—from an independent verb, to a marker of an imperative (often just a non-canonical one)—include verbs of motion 'come', 'go', and 'leave, abandon', with an overtone of 'let'.[43]

Just like their positive counterparts, negative imperatives can develop out of non-imperative forms. The negative, and the positive forms do not have to follow the same path. Negative imperatives tend to be less archaic than the canonical positive imperative, and not infrequently involve analytic constructions. The negative imperatives in Carib languages are a product of grammaticalizing a copula construction. The positive imperative in Latin is archaic. There is also a plethora of ways of negating an imperative; some of these involve a transparent, and recent, grammaticalization of negative volition, reflected in Archimedes' last words (in 10.26–27).

In contrast to positive command forms, negative imperatives more frequently come from grammaticalization of independent verbs. All persons have the same (relatively recent) origin.

Common sources of reinterpretation and grammaticalization of prohibitives involve NEGATIVE VOLITION, NEGATIVE POSSIBILITY, and NEGATIVE CONSEQUENCE. Prohibitives develop from grammaticalized verbs meaning 'STOP', 'STAY', 'LEAVE, ABANDON'. An expression meaning 'no good, beware' can be used as a negative imperative. So can a form meaning 'don't worry, leave it, forget it'. Copulas can give rise to prohibitive constructions. Verbs meaning 'SEE, LOOK' develop into markers of warning and of negative imperative.

Why do positive and negative imperatives develop the way they do? We have seen a number of paths of development with a straightforward semantic motivation. A warning is like a negative command. A command can be replaced with a wishful optative, to sound 'nicer'. A desubordinated dependent clause can be used as a positive command, but hardly ever as a prohibition—the overtones of an incomplete speech act suggest a pathway towards a suggestion rather than stopping something from happening.

The semantic pathway for each of these developments is intuitively clear. And each of these paths may be language- or family-specific. Negative imperatives involving a copula 'be' are a feature of North Carib languages. Alternatively, the way imperatives develop may be triggered or enhanced by what is going on in a neighbouring language. This takes us to the next chapter.

Notes

1. Kuryłowicz (1964: 136–7), Lockwood (1969: 114), and Gamkrelidze and Ivanov (1984: 343). See also Costa (2003: 319–20) on the archaic character of the imperative of Miami-Illinois, an Algonquian language.
2. Aikhenvald (2008b and references there); its counterparts in West Tucanoan are Secoya -jë'ë (Johnson and Levinsohn, 1990: 48), Koreguaje -hɨʔɨ (Cook and Criswell 1993: 59), and Siona -jë'ën (Wheeler 1987: 156).
3. Dixon (2002: 213–14). However, some languages of the Australian area 'have developed in the direction of a zero imperative', 'losing the original -ga'.

4. Pronominal objects are marked with accusative case, in clauses of all types, including imperatives. This shows that the protolanguage may have exhibited a split-ergative pattern following the Nominal Hierarchy (whereby common nouns would follow an ergative–absolutive pattern, and pronouns would operate on a nominative–accusative basis).

5. We can recall from §1.2 how Watkins (1963: 44), in his classic paper on the Old Irish verb, tried to capture this special status of second person imperative: 'The imperative is by its nature an extragrammatical, extrasyntactical form, a quasi-interjection [...] incapable of combination with grammatical categories such as person and number, or syntactic categories such as negation.' Watkins' observation is mistaken in stating that imperatives do not distinguish person or number, or cannot be negated. We have seen, throughout this book, that imperatives have grammatical categories of number, gender, person, and also tense, and more in the majority of the world's languages (including Indo-European, and also Celtic). However, the intuition behind this statement reflects a valid cross-linguistic tendency for canonical imperatives to be different, and often archaic.

6. For instance, in Udi a number of verbs – which originally contained noun class agreement markers – were reanalysed as simple stems, as part of the process of losing the noun class system (Harris and Campbell 1995: 66–7). Reanalysis most often occurs together with reinterpretation (cf. Trask 2000: 274). Examples of reinterpretation without reanalysis involve 'a shift in the categorial status of a linguistic form resulting from its occurrence in ambiguous positions'. For instance, the English noun *fun* has been reinterpreted as an adjective, leading to its use in contexts like *This is a fun game* (Trask 2000: 280).

7. Grammaticalization necessarily involves reanalysis: the structure of a grammaticalized construction changes. Whether grammaticalization and reanalysis are to be considered separate mechanisms is a matter for debate (see discussion in Harris and Campbell 1995: 92).

8. Durnovo (1969: 142) notes that 1pl imperative was replaced by 1pl future in the history of Russian.

9. The Slavic imperative suffix -*ə*/-*i* originates in the Indo-European optative suffix **-i-ye-/oi* (Gronas 2006: 93; Vaillant 1930: 246).

10. And see further discussion on the role of the Proto-Indo-European 'injunctive' mood in the development of imperative forms in individual languages (Watkins 1963: 46–7). Kuryłowicz (1964: 138) mentions a number of other developments, including the replacement of imperative by optative in Gothic.

11. According to Bolozky (2009), vowel truncation in the new imperative is part of a more general process of elision of vowels *e/i* in the colloquial speech register, while the prefix loss is a feature of the new imperative.

12. Bolozky (2009) notes the frequency of these imperatives, observing that they may also coexist with the normative imperative (p. 142).The intra-speaker variation suggests that their development is still an on-going process.

13. These appear to be 'considered by speakers to originate in reported speech' (Rennison 1997: 39). The marking of the polite imperative in Awa Pit (used for suggestions and warnings) is related to the infinitive inflection and a non-future complementizer (Curnow 1997b).

    Not every clause introducer used with non-canonical imperatives is a complementizer. Third person imperatives in Koiari (Dutton 1996: 27) occur with the introducer *ene* which is not used as a complementizer (this category appears not to exist in Koiari: pp. 70–71).

14. See Gronas (2006), Daiber (2009). Isachenko (2003: 488–9) described this as a 'dramatic' imperative. See §7.3, and examples 7.38–9.

15. See e.g. Vinogradov (1947) and Xrakovskij and Volodin (2001).

16. This approach was followed by Isachenko (2003), and also Birjulin and Xrakovskij (1992: 47). A major problem lies in the fact that the idea of these constructions being elliptical goes against native speakers' intuitions. Native speakers would be expected to paraphrase an elliptical construction so as to restore the original, full sentence. This does not work for historical imperatives, which are normally paraphrased as past tense expressions accompanied with adverb 'unexpectedly, all of a sudden' (see Gronas 2006: 90, 98 for further evidence). Tentative and unlikely as it is, the hypothetical path for an imperative developing into a main clause declarative predicate can hardly be fully rejected. Daiber (2009) argues that while the narrative data appear to point towards the 'aorist' origin of the historical imperative, one can trace a believable scheme whereby an imperative form can be reinterpreted as an assertion in the past (the reverse process to that in using past tense as commands, attested in the Russian 'authoritative imperative').

17. See Shakhmatov (1925, i: 165). Problems with this historical scenario are outlined by Gronas (2006: 90–91).

18. Further, similar examples come from Baka and Ngbaka Ma'Bo, a language from the Central African Republic (Heine and Kuteva 2002: 70; Thomas 1970: 599, 601).

19. Similar particles occur in other Lezgic languages: see Magometov (1965: 277–8; 1970: 142–3); further examples are in Maisak (2005: 213–14). Blust (2009: 497–8) discusses examples of 'come' and 'go' as imperative markers, especially for first person plural and first person inclusive.

20. First person plural imperative markers *anō, ān, ānu,* or *anu* in French-based Creoles, all based on French *allons* 'let's go', constitute a further example of the same grammaticalization path (Heine and Kuteva 2002). Maisak (2005: 177–9) provides further examples of 'go' grammaticalized into a marker of first person imperative.

21. In Haitian Creole, the particle *té* 'permissive, hortative'—which can be cliticized—comes from *kité* 'let', 'allow' from French *quitter* (Hall 1953: 30, 55).

22. Estonian has developed a particle *las* 'let' (on the basis of the native verb *laskma* 'let') similar in its usage to German *lass,* from *lassen,* e.g. Estonian *las olla!,* German *lass sein!* 'let it be'. This example of parallel grammaticalization and grammatical accommodation is discussed by Metslang (2000, 2009: 61).

23. Examples of grammaticalization of verbs 'go up' and 'go down' quoted by Maisak (2005: 238, 240–41) require further study.

24. Peyraube (1999). Heine and Kuteva (2002: 147) and Bybee et al. (1994) link the development of 'get' to 'permissive' with its development into an 'abilitative', 'be able to do', as in English *get to* > 'manage to', 'be permitted to'.

25. See Xrakovskij and Volodin (2001: 120–25), Barentsen (2003), Podlesskaya (2005a, b) and further references there, on the restrictions on aspect choices in these constructions.

26. Whether or not the imperative form of 'give' with third person has overtones of seeking permission is an open question. Podlesskaya (2005a: 96) assumes that it does. This goes against the native speaker intuitions of the author, and of her consultants.

27. See Podlesskaya (2005a: 96) on the expansion of these forms in the second half of the 20th century. The form *davaj* (give.IMPF.2sg) has grammaticalized into a hortative particle meaning 'come on' used with any person. When reduplicated, *davaj-davaj* is a particle urging someone to perform a quicker action (Ozhegov and Shvedova 1997: 150). Second person commands with *davaj* (give.IMPF.2sg) or *daj* (give.PERF.2sg), as in *davaj idi* (give.IMPF.2sg go.IMPF.2sg) 'you go, let you go' or *davaj delaj shire krug* (give.PERF.2sg make.IMPF.2sg wider circle.ACC.SG) 'you make a bigger circle', are perfectly grammatical in the colloquial language (though I have not been able to find them in any of the artificially concocted corpora).

28. The marking of 'obligation'—a meaning so often deployed in imperative strategies—may develop out of verbs 'do', 'make', as in Punjabi *kar*. In Korean, *ya hada* (only in the meaning of 'do, make') expresses 'weak' obligation. Markers of obligation often develop out of grammaticalizing verbs denoting possession and existence. Verbs of possession and existence also develop into modals expressing obligation. So, Spanish *tener que*, Latin *habēre* express strong obligation. Latin *dēbēre*, Breton *dle*, and Welsh *dylai* 'owe' have a similar meaning—that of strong obligation. (See further examples, and a discussion of various motivations for grammaticalization of obligative overtones of verbs of possession, existence, need, desire, and motion, in Denning 1987.)

29. Prohibitives and imperatives do not have to develop in a way parallel to each other. Nor is it true that prohibitives always keep person inflection while imperatives do not. The example from the Italian imperative and prohibitive highlights the futility of ad hoc statements by scholars with more focus on formal approaches than on facts of languages, such as Benmamoun (2000: 113), who assumes that 'in languages where imperatives carry person agreement, a temporal inflection or a mood inflection it is more likely to be true of negative imperatives than of positive imperatives'.

30. Christy and Wells (1947: 655). This is just one of the strategies for negative command in the language. The most frequent means in the preclassical and classical period is the particle *ne* accompanied by an imperative or a subjunctive of the verb. An alternative means is *non* (a declarative negator) followed by a

present indicative (see Löfstedt 1966: 12–20 for the discussion of these, and further marking of prohibition in Latin texts of various ages). The negative volition strategy did not survive in any of the Modern Romance languages.

31. See discussion of desiderative and its intentional uses in Manambu in Aikhenvald (2008a). A partial survey of expressions of 'wanting' (based on a highly limited sample) is in Khanina (2008).

32. Another option is to use an infinitive form followed by the negative adverb (p. 102). In Chukchi (Dunn 1999: 90), intentional mood which can be used with a desiderative meaning is also used as a major way of forming commands.

33. Mühlhäusler (1985: 164–5), Dutton (1973: 111–13), author's own data.

34. See further discussion of conventionalization of 'warning' as a prohibitive in Pakendorf and Schalley (2007).

35. Mihalic (1971: 143, 30), Mühlhäusler (1985: 164–5). Other Creole languages employ different markers for 'negative consequence'; for instance, in Cape York Creole in Australia, the 'or else' meaning is marked with *bifo, bipo*, e.g. *Yupela no kaikai det bipo yu fool sik* 'Don't eat that or you'll fall sick' (Crowley and Rigsby 1979: 205).

36. In Seychelles French-based Creole, the verb *aret* 'stop' (French *arrêter*) is also used as an imperative negator (Corne 1977: 184).

37. Variants are: *yu maski hambak!* (you never.mind fool.around) 'Don't fool around!', or *maski hambak!* (never.mind fool.around) 'Don't fool around!', or *maski long hambak* (never.mind PREP fool.around). Dutton (1973: 137) remarks that *maski* can combine with *no ken*, as in *maski yu no ken hambak!*

38. The origin of *maski* is a matter of dispute. Mihalic (1971: 131) suggests that it comes from German *es macht nichts* 'it is nothing, it does not matter'. An alternative etymology involves Portuguese *más que, por más que* 'despite, although' (Don Niles p.c. 2006).

39. Along similar lines, the maker of negative imperative in Piapoco, from the same family as Warekena, is *pika*, from *pi-* '2sg' + *-ka* 'see' (Klumpp 1990: 63).

40. Nasilov et al. (2001: 194–5). In Shor, also Turkic, apprehensive is expressed with a prohibitive form of the verb and the particle *kör* 'watch out, beware!', itself a fossilized second person imperative singular of the verb *kör* 'to see'. Russian has a similar construction, lit. 'look, don't VERB' to mean 'make sure you don't VERB (or else)' (see 5.31; note that this is the only instance where perfective aspect appears in negative imperative in the language). Plungian (1988) notes a special, 'advisory' meaning for the verb 'look' in Dogon.

41. Similarly, in Trio (Carlin 2004: 309), prohibitive is based on the imperative form of copula 'be' in combination with the negated form of a lexical verb, in a non-finite nominalized form. A similar structure has been described for Hixkaryana (Derbyshire 1985: 65–6): the copula is marked with the imperative suffix and the person prefixes; the lexical verb takes the negative suffix *-hira*. No language of the Carib family, including Carib itself (Hoff 1968), expresses prohibitives through 'affirmative verb forms'.

42. Macushi has an alternative way: the verb may take a negative marker and the imperative affix, e.g. *k-es-ewankono'ma-i* (NEG-DETRANS-sad-IMPV:SG) 'Don't be sad'. The analytic construction is more polite, just as predicted by the principles of iconicity.

   In other Carib languages—such as Wai Wai (Hawkins 1998: 65)—a grammaticalized analytic construction is the only way of expressing a negative imperative.

43. The age, and the development of non-command meanings of imperative forms, has been barely touched upon in the literature. Löfstedt (1966: 94–103) notes how the non-command uses of the imperative of 'see' in Latin survive in Italian. This is an area for further investigation.

11

Imperatives in contact

Languages and dialects do not exist in a vacuum. There is always a greater or lesser degree of contact between speakers of different languages, or of different dialects of the same language. Language contact, and borrowing of forms and of patterns, provides further answers to the question 'Why do imperative forms develop the way they do?

When languages come in contact with each other, speakers tend to borrow forms and ways of saying things. The ways of phrasing commands easily spread from one language to the next. New imperatives develop under areal pressure, by means of reinterpreting, reanalysing, and grammaticalizing one's own forms. A dying language, under severe pressure from the language replacing it, may lose its command forms, and gain new ones: see §11.1. And when languages are in contact, individual command forms are borrowed: this is the topic of §11.2.

In the final section, §11.3, we ask a crucial question: what makes imperatives diffusable?

11.1 Spreading imperative patterns

We start with an illustration from one of the world's most multilingual areas—the Vaupés River Basin. A complex system of multiple imperatives is one of the features of this area.

11.1.1 *Multilingual imperatives*

If languages are in constant contact, with speakers having a good knowledge of each others' languages, one expects these languages to become similar in their grammatical structure, if not in actual forms. In a multilingual area, this is what we expect, and what we find.

The Vaupés River Basin in north-west Amazonia extends from Brazil to Colombia. The main rule of the traditional area is linguistic exogamy. This is how speakers phrase it: 'Those who speak the same language as us are our brothers, and we do not marry our sisters.' Marrying someone who speaks the same language as oneself is not done. This is tantamount to incest, and is 'what dogs do'. Language affiliation is inherited from one's father and is a badge of identity for the traditional inhabitants.[1]

Languages spoken in the area include half-a-dozen East Tucanoan languages—Tucano, Desano, Wanano, Piratapuya, Barasano and Tuyuca—and just one Arawak language, Tariana. Most dwellers of the Vaupés River Basin would be highly fluent in three or four indigenous languages, plus have a good knowledge of Portuguese, the national language of Brazil, and some also know Spanish.

Languages within the Vaupés area are in contact at all times. There are intricate rules for which language has to be used under which circumstances. So, for instance, a father's language has to be spoken when talking to father. And a mother's language is used when talking to mother. A further feature of the area is a strong aversion to borrowed forms—those that can be recognized as such. This cultural inhibition against overt borrowing is a way of keeping different languages apart. Using borrowed forms is condemned as 'language mixing'. Those who 'mix languages' are branded as 'incompetent'.[2]

As a result, the grammatical structure of these languages is gradually becoming similar. The forms remain different. This agrees with a general consensus among students of language contact—that intensive interaction within a linguistic area tends to bring about gradual convergence of language structures. Then, the conceptual categories of one language are replicated in another. Linguistic convergence does not always result in the creation of identical grammars, nor in the straightforward projection of categories from one language into the next. Languages in contact maintain their distinct typological profiles. Yet one can see the imprint of language contact—and imperatives often reflect this.

The effect of language contact is particularly obvious in Tariana, an Arawak language affected by its East Tucanoan neighbours. What helps us in this is comparison with other Arawak languages, Baniwa of Içana and Piapoco, both closely related to Tariana but spoken just outside the Vaupés River Basin, and thus free of Tucanoan impact.

Tariana has ten positive imperatives (see Aikhenvald 2003: 371–80), unlike any other Arawak language of the area. Three of these reflect changes in progress, resulting from recent formal influence of Tucano, and are treated by traditional speakers as tokens of 'language mixing', to be looked down upon.

Tariana imperatives form one paradigm: all their markers are mutually exclusive with tense and evidentiality morphemes used in declarative and interrogative clauses, and with each other.[3] In imperative clauses, the verb appears at the beginning of the clause. In contrast, in statements and questions the verb tends to occur at the end. All imperatives are negated with the particle *mhāida* 'prohibitive'. In contrast, non-imperative verbs are negated with prefix *ma-* and suffix *-kade*.

East Tucanoan languages have between eight and eleven imperative forms—that is, about as many as Tariana if we count the three imperatives 'in the making'. Imperatives in East Tucanoan languages do not take tense, evidentiality, or person markers used in declarative clauses. They distinguish fewer aspects, and if they can be negated at all, they are typically negated with a suffix employed in other clause types.

The formally unmarked simple imperative consists of the second person singular or plural, or first person plural, prefix attached to the verbal root. This is the most archaic imperative in Tariana, shared with its relatives:

11.1   pi-ñha
       2sg-eat
       'Eat!'

11.2   wa-ñha
       1pl-eat
       'Let's eat!'

This imperative is high in frequency, and is used for any order, including one to be carried out immediately. The cognates of 11.1, from Tariana, are 11.3 from Baniwa and 11.4 from Piapoco:[4]

Baniwa
11.3   pi-ihña
       2sg-eat
       'Eat!'

Piapoco
11.4   pi-yáa
       2sg-eat
       'Eat!'

This archaic imperative (see §10.1) is frequently used, and implies that the action is to be carried out immediately.

In addition, Tariana has developed a secondhand imperative, or 'imperative by proxy' (see §4.2.4). This secondhand imperative meaning 'do on someone else's order' is shared between Tariana and numerous East Tucanoan languages. Semantically identical and structurally similar constructions in Tariana and in Tucano are given at 4.33 and 4.34 (repeated here):

Tariana
11.5   pi-ñha-pida
       2sg-eat-SEC.IMPV
       'Eat (on someone else's order)!' (that is, eat-you were told to)

Tucano
11.6   ba'â-ato
       eat-SEC.IMPV
       'Eat (on someone else's order)!' (that is, eat-you were told to)

The secondhand imperatives in Tariana and in East Tucanoan languages share a variety of usages. The Tariana farewell formula *matʃa-pida* (be.good-SEC. IMPV) 'goodbye; best wishes' (lit. 'let it be good on (our) behalf') is similar to Tucano *āyu-áto* (good-SEC.IMPV), with the same meaning (see also Aikhenvald 2002: 164–5). (The verb 'be good' in Tariana is stative and does not take personal prefixes.) This is the only instance in the language where a secondhand imperative is formed on a stative verb, and is highly likely to be a loan translation of a high-frequency farewell formula.

No North Arawak language related to Tariana has a secondhand imperative. The secondhand imperative is widespread in Tucanoan languages, and the markers are cognate throughout the family—compare Tucano *-áto*, Tuyuca *-aro* (Barnes 1979), and Wanano *-haro* (Waltz and Waltz 1997: 40). They have no connection with any of the forms in declarative evidentiality-tense paradigms.[5] In contrast, the secondhand imperative marker *-pida* in Tariana occurs throughout the reported evidentiality paradigm.

In declarative clauses, the Tariana reported evidentials are *-pida* 'present reported', *-pida-ka* 'recent past reported' (consisting of *-pida* and the recent past tense marker *-ka*), and *-pida-na* 'remote past reported' (consisting of *-pida* and the remote past marker *-na*). The tense markers *-ka* and *-na* are found throughout the tense-evidentiality system, while present tense is always formally unmarked.

The present tense reported *-pida* is used to transmit information acquired almost simultaneously with the moment of speech. If someone says 11.7,

11.7   di-ñha-ka
       3sgnf-eat-REC.P.VIS
       'He is eating' (I have just seen him eat)

another participant, who cannot see the person eating, would immediately repeat this piece of information to a third party, saying 11.8:

11.8   di-ñha-pida
       3sgnf-eat-PRES.REP
       'He is eating I am told'

The present reported is used almost like a quotative evidential. During my work on Tariana place names, a young speaker would often ask his father about a name he did not know, and then repeat it, using the present reported evidential, e.g. *Piri-pani-pida* (flute-rapids-PRES.REP) '(the name is) "rapids of a flute", he has just said'.

The meaning of 'secondhand' imperative is also essentially quotative: one quotes a command by someone else, transmitting someone else's order.

Unlike Tucanoan languages and Tariana, most Arawak languages have only one reported evidential, typically used in traditional tales and in quotations. In Baniwa, the form of this reported evidential is *-pida*, cognate to Tariana *-pida*. In Baniwa, this evidential does not occur in commands.

In summary: Tariana developed a secondhand imperative marker out of its own resources, by reinterpreting the reported evidential morpheme to match a conceptual category found in East Tucanoan languages. Based on its quotative functions, it was extended to cover secondhand, or quoted, commands 'by proxy'.[6]

Tariana has also developed a proximate imperative 'do here!', marked with *-si* (4.23), a distal imperative (*-kada:* 4.24), and a delayed imperative, 'do later', *-wa:*

11.9   phima-si
       2sg+listen-PROX.IMPV
       'You listen here' (close to the speaker)

Distal imperative ('you, do it there' or 'you there, do it') is marked with the suffix *-kada* (see 4.24):

11.10   phima-kada
        2sg+listen-DISTAL.IMPV
        'Listen over there' (away from where the speaker is; addressed to people outside the house)

11.11   desu   kuphe   pi-ñha-wa
        tomorrow   fish   2sg-eat-DELAYED.IMPV
        'Eat the fish tomorrow!'

Arawak languages closely related to Tariana do not have special proximal, distal, or delayed imperatives. But a few East Tucanoan languages do. A distal imperative (with no 'proximal' counterpart) is attested in Wanano (Waltz 1976: 46) (marked with -*risa*):

Wanano

11.12 wahi wajã-risa
 fish kill-DISTAL.IMPV
 'Kill the fish' (at a distance)

Tucano has a future imperative marked with the suffix -*apa* (West 1980: 48, 51)—see 11.14. Its non-future simple imperative counterpart marked with -*ya* is in 11.13:

Tucano

11.13 ba'á-ya
 eat-IMPV
 'Eat!'

11.14 ba'á-apa
 eat-FUT.IMPV
 'Eat (later)!'

Tuyuca (Barnes 1979) has a delayed imperative, marked with the suffix -*wa* (a likely cognate to Tucano):

11.15 basa-wa
 sing-DELAYED.IMPV
 'Sing!' (some other time, later)[7]

Macuna (Smothermon et al. 1995: 62–3) has a distal imperative marked with suffix -*tẽ*, and a future imperative marked with -*ba*. But none of these languages has a proximate imperative.

The only East Tucanoan language with a threefold distinction of spatial and temporal distance in imperatives is Barasano (Jones and Jones 1991: 76–8). An imperative marked with -*ya* marks a command to be executed in the presence of the speaker:

Barasano

11.16 yʉ-re goti-ya bʉ̃
 1sg-OBJ tell-PRES.IMPV 2sg
 'Tell me!'

Distal, or non-proximate, imperative in Barasano takes an additional suffix -*a*-:

11.17 ĩ-re   goti-a-ya   bũ
       3masc.sg-OBJ   tell-NON.PROX-PRES.IMPV   2sg
       'Tell him there!'

A future imperative, marked with -*ba* (cognate to Macuna -*ba* and to Tuyuca -*wa*), indicates a command to be carried out at a considerable distance in space, or later on in time. The systems in Barasano and in Tariana are similar, but not identical. The absence of direct contact between Barasano (spoken mostly in Colombia) and Tariana makes it unlikely that one influenced the other. The similarity between the two systems is akin to Sapir's 'parallelism in drift' between languages spoken within one area.

None of the North Arawak languages in the area has any spatial or temporal distinctions in imperatives. They do have cognates for the Tariana imperative markers.

The marker of proximate imperative -*si* in Tariana is related to the general future marker -*si* in Piapoco.[8] There is no cognate morpheme in Baniwa.

The marker of delayed imperative -*wa* is cognate with Piapoco general future marker -*wa*, which can also mark purpose:

Piapoco
11.18   na-à   na-wénda-**wa**   amàca
        3pl-go   3pl-sell-FUT   hammock
        'They will go to sell hammocks'

The same morpheme has a future and a purposive meaning in Baniwa (Hohôdene dialect):

Baniwa
11.19   3i-uma-ka   3i-ihña-**wa**
        3sgnf-seek-DECL   3sgnf-eat-FUT
        'He (the vulture) is looking for (something) to eat'

The distal imperative marker -*kada* in Tariana is likely to have resulted from grammaticalization of a verbal root -*kada* (Tariana), -*kadaa* (Baniwa) meaning 'leave (something)'. This is a cross-linguistically well-attested path (see §10.2.2).

The development of proximate imperative and delayed imperative in Tariana involves reinterpretation of future morphemes. The distal imperative marker comes from a grammaticalized verbal root meaning 'leave'.

The conative imperative in Tariana meaning 'try and do it' mirrors the conative imperative meaning 'try it out' in Desano (Miller 1999: 72–4). This is a distinct imperative form, and cannot combine with any other morphemes (including other imperatives). The Desano conative imperative marker consists of the verb -*yã* 'see, try out' followed by the limiter -*ta* meaning 'exactly, just':

Desano
11.20   ba-yã-ta
         eat-IMPV+see/try.out-LIM[9]
         'Try and eat please'

The Tariana conative imperative is marked with a suffix -*thaɾa*, which has no formal similarity with the Desano form:

11.21   pi-ñha-thaɾa
         2sg-eat-CON.IMPV
         'Try and eat (please); eat it to try it out'

This suffix has no cognates in North Arawak languages. However, it is suspiciously similar to a combination of the Tucano bound verb root *tĩha*, *tiha* 'try to do, start doing' (Ramirez 1997: Vol. II, 189) and the Tariana suffix -*da* 'dubitative; politeness marker' (with a free variant -*ɾa* if preceded by a vowel: see Aikhenvald 2003).

Most East Tucanoan languages do not have phonemic aspirated consonants, and Tucano is no exception. However, Tucano does have non-phonemic aspirated stops which appear in normal to rapid speech register when a vowel gets reduced. So, vowel reduction in an unstressed syllable results in the creation of a phonetic sequence stop+*h*: as a result, one hears the demonstrative *tohó* 'that (thing), then' as *tho* (Aikhenvald 2002: 38). Similarly, -*tĩha* or -*tiha* is often heard as -*tha*. This suggests the origin of the Tariana conative imperative is a bound verb borrowed from Tucano, accompanied by the erstwhile dubitative marker of Tariana origin.

This etymology arguably involves a calque—that is, a form 'constructed by taking a word or a phrase in another language as a model and translating it morpheme by morpheme' (Trask 2000: 49). Calquing is one of the mechanisms widely used in developing new categories in language contact.

A question arises here. This suggested path of development for the conative imperative involves a loan morpheme. How is this possible in a situation like that in the Vaupés where borrowings are condemned as tokens of inappropriate language mixing?

As I have shown elsewhere (Aikhenvald 2002: 141–2, 224–8), Tariana does have a very limited number of morphemes of East Tucanoan provenance. All these morphemes are bound, fully integrated phonologically, and can be considered 'nativized'. They are no longer recognized as loans. That is, their presence does not contradict a cultural inhibition against recognizable 'language mixing'.[10]

Polite commands and suggestions in Tariana are marked with the clitic -*nha* homophonous with -*nha* 'present visual interrogative'. Polite imperatives do not have a rising intonation typical of questions, nor can other interrogative markers be used in commands:

11.22   pi-ni-nha
         2sg-do-POLITE.IMPV
         'Would you like to do (it), could you please do (it)?'

A number of East Tucanoan languages have special marking for a polite imperative. These include Tucano:[11]

11.23   weé-kãˈaˈsã
         do-POLITE.IMPV
         'Could you please do (it)?'

Developing an imperative out of an interrogative is typologically not uncommon. We saw in §8.1 that questions are often used as directives. Their overtones tend to be those of a mild suggestion. Once again, Tariana has evolved—out of its own resources—a match for polite imperatives in contact languages.

Tariana has a special first person plural imperative (or hortative) marked with -*da/-ɾa*. Functionally and formally, this morpheme is reminiscent of the Tucano hortative -*rã/-dã*:[12]

Tariana
11.24   wa-iɾa-da
         1pl-drink-HORTATIVE
         'Let's drink!'

Tucano
11.25   sĩˈri-dã
         drink-HORTATIVE
         'Let's drink!'

This same morpheme occurs in Wanano -*hiˈda* (Stenzel 2004: 331), Desano (Miller 1999: 72–3); and also in Macuna (Smothermon et al. 1995: 62).

The Tariana hortative is likely to be a recent borrowing from Tucano or from Desano, and is a feature of young people's language. Traditional speakers of Tariana are aware of the similarity between the Tariana and the Tucano morphemes, and treat the hortative as 'incorrect' Tariana 'mixed' with Tucano. This is typical of Tariana language attitudes: with the general prohibition on mixing languages viewed in terms of borrowed forms, the hortative is, not surprisingly, a marginal feature of the language.[13] The hortative can be considered an ongoing innovation rather than a completed change, in contrast to all the other imperatives discussed so far. Those are used by all speakers, and are treated as legitimate 'good' Tariana.

An additional second person imperative marked with *-ya* in Tariana has overtones of 'do it immediately':

11.26   pi-ñha-ya
         2sg-eat-IMPV
         'Eat!'

This imperative marker is strikingly similar to the imperative marker *-ya* in Tucano, Tuyuca, and Piratapuya, and its cognate *-ga* in Wanano:

Tucano
11.27   apê-ya
         play-IMPV
         'Play!'

The *-ya* imperative in Tariana is frequently used by younger speakers, and hardly ever by traditional speakers. All speakers concur that this is not 'proper Tariana'. The morpheme *-ya* in an imperative construction is condemned as a token of identifiable 'language mixing'.

This is reminiscent of the hortative in 11.24. However, Tariana *-ya* may not be an actual loan from an East Tucanoan language. Tariana has a clitic *-ya* 'emphatic' whose cognates are found in other Arawak languages. One example is Baniwa *-dza*, an emphatic clitic used in imperatives and prohibitives. In Tariana, *-ya* regularly occurs in one inherently prohibitive expression, a defective verb used as a short command:

11.28   ma:ku-ya   phia
         NEG+talk-EMPH   you
         'Shut up!'

In contrast to Arawak languages, imperatives in East Tucanoan languages are always formally marked; simple imperative suffixes include Tucano, Piratapuya, Tuyuca *-ya*, Wanano *-ga*, and Desano *-ke*.

Ma:kuya is etymologically cognate to Baniwa prohibitive *ma:ku-dza* (NEG+speak-IMPV) 'do not talk'.[14] The combination of a prefix *ma-* and a suffix -*dza* is a normal way of forming prohibitives in Baniwa; *ma:kuya* in Tariana could be either a loan from a dialect of Baniwa in which Tariana *y* corresponds to *y* (for instance, Kumandene Kurripaco) or an archaic expression.

The deployment of Tariana -*ya* as an imperative marker is an example of a semantic extension of a native morpheme under the influence of a lookalike in a contact language (this is known as grammatical accommodation: see Aikhenvald 2002, 2007a). The emphatic marker -*ya* is likely to be acquiring a new meaning as an imperative, to match the function of its East Tucanoan lookalike.[15]

Nominalizations marked with -*ri* occasionally appear in commands in Tariana, as an alternative to simple imperatives, but with a somewhat different meaning, 'make sure you do'.

11.29   pi-ñha-ri!
        2sg-eat-NOMINALIZATION
        'Eat!' (make sure you eat, lest you go hungry)

This usage is restricted to casual speech by younger people for whom Tucano is the main language of day-to-day communication. Tucano, just like most other East Tucanoan languages, has a suffix -*ri* used in commands with an overtone of warning, with the meaning of 'or else'.[16] The usage of nominalizations as commands in Tariana has in all likelihood been influenced by the -*ri* marked imperative in Tucano. That the form in 11.29 is a nominalization is corroborated by the translations given by traditional speakers of Tariana.

This is another instance of ongoing 'grammatical accommodation' which has not yet become part of the accepted grammar. Just like the -*ya* imperative, this instance of ongoing change is frowned upon by Tariana language purists, and those who are identified as users of forms like 11.29 are accused of being incompetent speakers who 'mix languages'.

Table 11.1 summarizes the mechanisms at work in the development of Tariana imperatives: reinterpretation of the language's own resources, grammaticalization of verbal roots, and grammatical accommodation—that is, extension of Tariana forms to match the meanings of lookalikes in Tucano.

The system of imperatives in Tariana is etymologically heterogeneous and multi-sourced. The markers come from different non-imperative categories, via distinct mechanisms. So do the semantic distinctions.

The Tariana multiple imperative system is only superficially reminiscent of East Tucanoan languages. There is no single East Tucanoan system which

TABLE 11.1 Multiple imperatives in Tariana: meanings, forms, mechanisms of development, and prototypes in East Tucanoan

IMPERATIVE CATEGORY	MECHANISM OF DEVELOPMENT	PROTOTYPE IN EAST TUCANOAN	ORIGIN
1. Formally unmarked simple imperative	Inherited from proto-language	None	Inherited
2. Secondhand imperative -pida 'do on someone else's order'	Reinterpretation of the proto-Tariana-Baniwa -pida 'present reported, quotative'	Secondhand imperative in Tucano and Wanano (cf. also Tuyuca)	
3. Proximate imperative -si	Reinterpretation of future marker -si	No full match: distal imperative in Wanano and Macuna; non-visual present evidential in Tucano (cf. delayed imperative in Tuyuca; distal and proximate imperative and delayed imperative in Barasano)	Contact induced: completed change
4. Distal imperative -kada	-kada 'delayed imperative', possibly grammaticalized from the verb -kada 'keep, leave'; reinterpretation of future marker -wa		
5. Delayed imperative -wa			
6. Conative -thara	Probable grammaticalization of a loan root 'try' + -da 'dubitative'	Conative imperative in Desano	
7. Polite -nha	Reinterpretation of an interrogative marker	Polite imperative in Tucano	
8*. Hortative -ra/da	Borrowed from Tucano or Desano	Same form and same meaning in Tucano, Desano, and Wanano (cf. Macuna)	Recent formal influence from Tucano; traditional speakers treat these forms as unwanted tokens of 'language mixing'; change in progress
9*. Immediate imperative -ya	Reinterpretation of emphatic -ya as a result of grammatical accommodation influenced by Tucano -ya 'imperative'	Same form and same meaning in Tucano and Piratapuya (cf. Tuyuca)	
10*. Simple imperative -ri	Reinterpretation of nominalization marker -ri as a result of grammatical accommodation influenced by the Tucano -ri 'imperative'	Same form and same meaning in Tucano (cf. Tuyuca)	

could have served as a prototype for calquing into Tariana. While some distinctions which made their way into Tariana are pervasive in East Tucanoan—for instance, the secondhand imperative—others are not. The threefold distinction between proximate, distal, and delayed imperative is unique to Tariana. Each of these distinctions may be expressed in individual East Tucanoan languages, but Tariana is unlike most other languages in the area in that it has all three in a paradigmatic opposition. The highest number of semantic analogies to the Tariana imperative distinctions are found in Tucano, Tuyuca, and Barasano, the three East Tucanoan languages with the most complex imperative systems.[17]

A language has developed a set of new semantic distinctions—to match those in the neighbour's language. This tendency to match what your neighbour says is especially strong in those languages which are in decline towards extinction.

11.1.2 Innovative imperatives: language contact and language obsolescence

In this day and age, many indigenous languages are being abandoned in favour of their more powerful neighbours. Endangered languages suffer reduction of paradigms and simplification and loss of their own features—the dangerous precursors to language shift and loss. As the obsolescent language is losing its ground, we expect it to be flooded with an influx of patterns and forms from the dominant language.

And this is what happens in many domains, including commands. A prime example comes from Nivkh, an isolate formerly spoken on Sakhalin island and in the Amur area of Russia (Gruzdeva 2000, 2007). Nivkh is currently spoken by about 75 people, and is being ousted by the national language, Russian. All speakers of Nivkh are proficient in Russian. Nivkh is losing some features and gaining some, as a result of intensive contact with the dominant language.

The imperative paradigm of traditional Nivkh is in 11.30 (Gruzdeva 2000: 126):

11.30	2sg	-ja	*Vi-ja!* 'Go (you sg)!'
	2pl	-ve	*Vi-ve!* 'Go (you pl)!'
	1du	-nate	*Vi-nate!* 'Let us (I and you.sg) go!'
	1pl	-da	*Vi-da!* 'Let us (I and you.pl) go!'
	3sg/pl	-ğaro	*Vi-ğaro!* 'Let him/her/them go!'

Imperatives in Nivkh are the only verbal forms in the language to have person marking.

As a consequence of Russian influence, the first person dual imperative form has fallen into disuse. The first person plural imperative form is being used instead—just as in Russian (see Gruzdeva 2002: 100).[18]

We saw, throughout the previous chapter, that the canonical second person imperatives tend to be stable. If an imperative is to be innovated, we expect it to be a non-canonical one. And this is what has happened in Nivkh. Contact with Russian has affected third and first person imperatives, albeit in different ways.

Traditional Nivkh did not distinguish number in third person commands. The two numbers are differentiated in the contemporary Nivkh. The erstwhile third person imperative *-ğaro* has been reinterpreted as third person singular marker. An example from Nivkh is in 11.31a. The Russian equivalent is in 11.31b. The imperative forms are in bold.

Contemporary Nivkh

11.31a	Jan	nana	oz-ba	ińk	**aj-ğaro**
	he+NOM	just	get.up-CONV:TEMP	meal:SG.NOM	cook-IMPV.3sg

'As soon as he gets up, let him cook the meal'

Russian

11.31b	kak	tol'ko	on	vstanet	**pust'**	ed-u
	as.soon.as	he:NOM		get.up.FUT:3sg	let	meal-FEM.SG.ACC
	gotovit					
	cook+PRES.3sg					

'As soon as he gets up, let him cook the meal'

To express a third person plural addressee, *-ğaro* is reduplicated, as *-ğar-ğaro*. The Russian equivalent is in 11.32b.

11.32a	In	nana	oz-ba	ińk	**aj-ğarğaro**
	they+NOM	just	get.up-CONV:TEMP	meal:SG.NOM	cook-IMPV.3sg

'As soon as they get up, let them cook the meal'

Russian

11.32b	kak tol'ko	oni	vstanut	**pust'**	ed-u
	as.soon.as	they.NOM	get.up.FUT:3pl	let	meal-FEM.SG.ACC
	gotovjat				
	cook+PRES.3pl				

'As soon as they get up, let them cook the meal'

Reduplication is a regular means for marking plurality of a lexeme in Nivkh (both traditional and contemporary). This device has been extended to express a category of number in third person command absent from the traditional Nivkh but present in the dominant Russian: 'let him cook' appears in 11.31b and 'them cook' in 11.32b.

The Russian forms are analytic. To match the Russian structures, third person imperative forms in contemporary Nivkh[19] are often accompanied by particles *p'eɤrdoχ* and *haǧaro* 'let'. Both combine with the corresponding form of the new imperative, just like Russian *pust'* 'let':

Nivkh

11.33a   Jaṇ   p'ŕy-aǧńi-ǧaj   **p'eɤrdoχ p'ry-ǧaro!**
        he+NOM come-MODAL-want-CONV:COND let   come-IMPV.3sg
        'If he wants to come, let him come!'

Russian

11.33b   Esli on   xočet   prijti,   **pust'** **prihodit!**
        if   he:NOM want.PRES.3sg come.INF let   come.PRES.3sg
        'If he wants to come, let him come!'

Nivkh

11.34a   In   p'ŕy-aǧńi-ǧaj   **p'eɤrdoχ p'ŕy-ǧarǧaro!**
        they+NOM come-MODAL-want-CONV:COND let   come-IMPV.3pl
        'If they want to come, let them come!'

Russian

11.34b   Esli oni   xotjat   prijti,   **pust'** **prihodjat!**
        if   they:NOM want.PRES.3pl come.INF let   come.PRES.3pl
        'If they want to come, let them come!'

We now turn to the new first person imperatives. Traditional Nivkh did not have first person singular imperative forms (which is consistent with the tendencies in Diagram 2.1: first person singular imperative is the least likely to occur). What could be translated as a command to oneself used to be expressed with future:

11.35 Ńi   čin   taf-toχ   t'or-i-d-ra
      I:NOM you.PL.NOM house-SG.DAT carry-FUT.FINITE-[SG]-PARTICLE
      '[Let] me take you to [your] house'

The imperative forms of the verb 'give', *t'ana* (give.IMPV.2sg) and *t'ana-ve* (give-IMPV.2pl) are used to fill the gap. The number of 'give' refers to the number of the addressees.

The construction is strikingly parallel to Russian (also see §10.2.2, on how 'give' in Russian grammaticalized as imperative marker). The imperative forms are in bold:

Contemporary Nivkh

11.36a T'ana   ń-aχ   **lu-gu-ja!**
   give:IMPV.2sg   1sg-ACC   sing-CAUS-IMPV.2sg
   'Let me sing (you.sg)!' (lit. You singular give me you singular make sing!)

Russian

11.36b Daj   (ja)   **spoju!**
   give:IMPV.2sg   (1sg:NOM)   sing.FUT.1sg
   'Let me sing (you.sg)!' (lit. You singular give I will sing!)

Contemporary Nivkh

11.37a T'ana-ve   ń-aχ   **lu-gu-ve!**
   give:IMPV.2sg-IMPV.2pl   1sg-ACC   sing-CAUS-IMPV.2pl
   'Let me sing (you.PL)!' (lit. You plural give me you plural make sing!)

Russian

11.37b Daj-te   (ja)   **spoju!**
   give:IMPV.2sg-IMPV.2pl   (1sgNOM)   sing.FUT.1sg
   'Let me sing (you.PL)!' (lit. You plural give I will sing!)

Even the constituent order is calqued, from Russian into Nivkh. The forms *t'ana* and *t'ana-ve* when used as imperatives on their own appear at the end of a clause:

11.38   Ymk-a   χasaṇ   eɣguř   **t'ana**
   mother-[SG]-VOC   scissors[-SG-NOM]   quickly   give.IMPV.2sg
   'Mother, give me the scissors quickly!'

In contrast, in 11.36–7 they occur at the beginning—just as in Russian.

The similarities between Russian and Nivkh are striking. But the parallelism is not complete. The subject of 'singing' in Nivkh 11.36a–7a occurs in the accusative case, 'me'. In Russian, only the nominative case (*ja* 1sg:NOM) is acceptable here (see also Podlesskaya 2005a).

In addition, Nivkh is adjusting its polite imperative forms to the Russian mould. The traditional language had a special polite imperative—a second person plural imperative with an additional second person plural iterative -*na*-:

11.39   Vi-na-ve!
   go-ITERATIVE.2pl-IMPV.2pl
   'Go (please) (you sg)' (polite)

Nowadays, a polite command can also be expressed with a simple second person plural imperative, without the iterative suffix, just as in Russian (11.40b):

Contemporary Nivkh
11.40a   Vi-ve!
         go-IMPV.2pl
         'Go (please) (you sg)' (polite)

Russian
11.40b   Idi-te!
         go.IMPV.2sg-IMPV.2pl
         'Go (please) (you sg)' (polite)

No forms are borrowed—but the new structures in Nivkh come to mirror those in the dominant language.

Restructuring of commands may go together with borrowing forms. We can recall, from §5.1, that the Traditional Warlpiri imperative could not be negated directly. Instead, the prohibition used to be expressed with the imperative form of 'leave' and a nominalized verb within a privative expression (meaning 'without'):

11.41   Yampi-ya=lu=jana   paka-rninja-wangu-rlu!
        leave-IMPV= PL.SUBJECT=PL.NON.SUBJECT   hit-INF-PRIV.ERG
        'Don't hit them!' (lit. Leave them hitting-without)

Contemporary Warlpiri has borrowed two negative particles from English: *nuu*, from *no*, and *nati*, from *not*. These forms occupy the initial position in a clause. And they can combine with the imperative verb form, to create a negative imperative (Laughren 2002: 116). An example is in 11.42:[20]

11.42   Nati=li=jana   maliki-patu   paka-ka!
        NEG=PL.SUBJECT=PL.NON.SUBJECT   dog-PL:NOM   hit-IMPV
        'Don't hit the dogs'

This construction is much more similar to the one in English than in the Traditional Warlpiri. But it is not a mirror image—as in the case of Russian and Nivkh. Why is this so? Warlpiri is still a vibrant and well-spoken language, the first to be learnt by hundreds of children. In contrast, Nivkh is rapidly declining, yielding to rampant dominance of Russian. There are hardly any monolingual speakers left, and every speaker of Nivkh is more proficient in Russian than in their mother tongue. No wonder Russian patterns are invading the language at a distressingly rapid rate.[21]

Negative, but not positive, imperatives in Young People's Dyirbal have been affected by the encroaching influence of English (Schmidt 1985: 66–7). We can recall from §10.3.2 that negative imperatives in Traditional Dyirbal were formed by placing a prohibitive particle before the verb and adding an inflectional suffix to the verb stem. Example 11.43 comes from the Jirrbal dialect:

11.43   galga   bani-m
        NEG.IMPV   come-NEG.IMPV
        'Don't come!'

In Young People's Dyirbal, one or both of the following changes have taken place. First, the original negative particle is replaced by the borrowed negative particle *numu*, from English *no more*. Secondly, the inflectional imperative marker is dropped; either the unmarked or the imperative form of the verb is used. All of the following variants, for 'don't come', were attested among speakers of Young People's Dyirbal. 11.44a was used by those fluent speakers who were more traditional than others (Schmidt 1985).

11.44a   *galga*   VERB-m (NEG.IMPV VERB-PROH)
11.44b   *galga*   VERB-∅ (NEG.IMPV VERB-IMPV)
11.44c   *galga*   VERB-NONFUTURE, e.g. *galga bani-ŋu* (NEG.IMPV come-NONFUTURE)
11.44d   *nomo*   VERB-m, e.g. *nomo bani-m* (NEG come-PROH)
11.44e   *nomo*   VERB-NONFUTURE, e.g. *nomo bani-ŋu* (NEG come-NONFUTURE)

Of all the innovative forms, 11.44e was the most frequently used.

Obsolescent languages are not fully acquired by the younger generation. Younger speakers tend to use less sophisticated forms, replicating the dominant languages which they know better. Complex verbal forms—including commands—tend to become simpler. Yimas, from the Lower Sepik family, has a highly complex paradigm for marking imperatives, positive and negative. The prohibitive forms—used by younger speakers—involve 'the same form as a desiderative' and irrealis, preceded by *pack* 'don't' (Foley 1991: 275). This analytic construction is reminiscent of Tok Pisin, the local lingua franca where a negator *no* or *no ken* simply precedes the verb in a prohibition.

An apparent simplification in an obsolescent language may not directly reflect the pattern in the dominant variety. East Sutherland Gaelic used to have two options for a negative imperative (Dorian 2006: 565–6). This is still preserved by the oldest speakers: they have an option of using the negative particle /(n)a/ followed by an unlenited gerund, or the negative /(x)a/ followed by lenited gerund. There is now an alternative analytic negative imperative: an invariant from *a čʰeːj*, lit. 'don't go', has become an imperative marker on its own. This has become the only way of negating a command for some younger people.

Nancy Dorian (p.c.) remarks that such imperatives, which 'translate literally as "Don't go VERB-ing"', 'sound anglicized, since American English uses this periphrasis'. But this is not found in Scottish English; moreover, it is restricted to just one out of three East Sutherland Gaelic-speaking villages. From a cross-linguistic perspective, this structure simply provides another example of grammaticalization of 'go' as an imperative marker (see §10.2.2, and especially examples from Rama, a Chibchan language). But it is probably not correct to consider this new imperative straightforwardly 'contact-induced'.[22]

We have seen how borrowed negators can occur in negative imperatives. We have not found any example of direct borrowing of an imperative marker, other than examples of grammatical accommodation of imperatives in Tariana. However, borrowed imperative forms do occur.[23]

11.2 Spreading imperative forms

Uninflected one-word commands, especially those meaning 'come on, come, go', are easily borrowed. In Rumanian, *hai* 'come on' was borrowed from Turkish. Modern Hebrew *yalla* 'let's go' is of Arabic origin.[24] The imperative form *banaga-ø* 'return!' in Jirrbal and Girramay dialects of Dyirbal is highly likely to be borrowed from Warrgamay *bana-ga* (return-IMPV) 'return!' (the form found in the Ngajan and Mamu dialects of Dyirbal is *ɲuɽba-ø* 'return!', zero-marked for imperative) (R. M. W. Dixon p.c.).

Berber and Omotic languages have a wide variety of animal calls, ordering animals to come or go, advance, sit down, stand up, and so on (see Bynon 1976, and §9.3 above). Many of these calls extend beyond just one Berber variety. For instance, the call *(s)ⁿ-hda!*, commanding a horse to slow down if in motion, or remain still if at rest, is shared by the Ayt Hadiddu, a Tamazight-speaking group of the Moroccan High Atlas, with the varieties of Rif in Algeria (Renisio 1932: 130; Bynon 1976: 19).

Some of the commands also occur in local Arabic varieties. The Ayt Hadiddou form *ṛṛa!*, a command to a donkey to advance, is shared with Ayt Seghrouchchen *ṛṛa!* (Destaing 1920: 315), Rif *arra* (Renisio 1932: 130, 332), and in Moroccan Arabic *erra!* The Ayt Hadiddou command *sabb!* to chase away a cat also occurs in Rif and Senhaja, and in Moroccan Arabic *ṣebb!* and in Spanish *zape!* The origin of this form is likely to be Berber (Bynon 1976: 59).

Some of the animal calls in Ayt Hadiddou come from Arabic verbs. The form *mšši!*, to chase a dog away, comes from the Maghribi Arabic verb *mši* 'to go away, go, go off, leave' (Classical Arabic *mašā* 'to go on foot, walk; to go').[25]

These commands are interjection-like. That they are highly spreadable from one language to the next goes together with borrowability of interjections (see Aikhenvald 2002).

A borrowed one-word command may remain uninflected in one language and take inflections in the next. The Turkish particle *hajde* 'go!' was borrowed into Bulgarian as an uninflected form. But in the closely related Serbo-Croatian it can take verbal inflection. Consider the irregular paradigm of the verb *itči* 'go' (Veselinova 2006: 145):

11.45   *ide-m*   (go-PRES.1sg)   'I go'
        id-i   (go-IMPV.2sg)   'you (singular) go!'
        id-i-te   (go-IMPV-2pl)   'you (plural) go!'
        (h)ajde   (go/come.IMPV.2sg)   'you (singular) come/go!'
        (h)ajde-te   (go/come.IMPV.2pl)   'you (plural) come/go!'

In Bulgarian, the suppletive form of 'come', *ela*, was borrowed from Modern Greek. Veselinova (2006: 146) remarks that this 'alternative suppletive form' is 'nowadays equally common, if not even more frequent than the native regular imperative of 'come'.

Modern Greek (Christiades 1980: 76)
11.46   *erx-ese*   (come-PRES.INDIC.2sg)   'you (singular) come'
        erx-ste   (come.PRES.INDIC.2pl)   'you (plural) come'
        ela   (come.IMPV.2sg)   'you (singular) come!'
        ela-te   (come.IMPV-IMPV.2pl)   'you (plural) come!'

Bulgarian
11.47   *idva-š*   (come-PRES.INDIC.2sg)   'you (singular) come'
        idva-te   (come.PRES.INDIC.2pl)   'you (plural) come'
        idva-j   (come-IMPV.2sg)   "you (singular) come!'
        idva-j-te   (come-IMPV.2pl)   'you (plural) come!'
        ela   (come.IMPV.2sg)   'you (singular) come!'
        ela-te   (come.IMPV-IMPV.2pl)   'you (plural) come!'

In a situation where borrowing forms is limited, one-word imperatives may undergo 'accommodation', adjusting to those in a contact language. The Tariana dialect of Periquitos differs from the variety spoken in Santa Rosa in the number of 'lexical accommodations', whereby Tariana words sound more similar to their counterparts in an East Tucanoan language than they are expected to. Since the preferential marriage partners of the Periquitos Tariana are the Wanano, the source of lexical accommodation is mostly Wanano. One of the most salient instances is a command—the Periquitos correspondent of Santa Rosa *wasã* 'let's go!' is *wahsã* 'come on, let's go', influenced by Wanano *bahsã* 'let's go!' (Marino and Domingo Muniz p.c.; Aikhenvald 2002: 216).

Imperative forms and imperative structures spread easily. Why so?

11.3 Why imperatives?

In intensive language contact and multilingualism, one language may evolve imperative constructions similar to those in the neighbouring languages, through grammaticalizing verbs and reinterpreting existing morphemes. Within the multilingual Vaupés River Basin, one future marker in Tariana has become reinterpreted as delayed imperative, and the other one as proximal imperative, 'do here', following the paths outlined in Chapter 10. A secondhand imperative, 'do on someone else's order', has been developed out of an erstwhile reported or quotative evidential. A conative form, 'try and do', developed out of a verb compound. As a result, the imperative categories in Tariana parallel those in East Tucanoan languages, in which Tariana speakers are fully proficient.

In a situation of intensive language contact involving Nivkh, imperatives adjust to the dominant Russian patterns. In many Aboriginal languages of Australia, negative imperatives become more like English than they were traditionally. And individual one-word imperative forms are highly borrowable.

What is it that makes the meanings associated with commands so diffusable? A major factor behind the diffusion of patterns in a situation of obligatory multilingualism is the desire to be able to say what one's neighbour can say—making 'the categories existing in the languages that are in contact mutually compatible and more readily intertranslatable' (Heine and Kuteva 2003: 561). For the coexisting systems to converge, functional, semantic, and formal matching is desirable.

Several linguistic factors facilitate diffusion of forms, and of patterns.[26]

FREQUENCY is a major facilitating factor in linguistic diffusion: the more frequent the category in one language, the likelier it is to diffuse into another. This is reminiscent of Du Bois's (1985: 363) statement: 'Grammars code best what speakers do most.' Commands are among the highest-frequency forms in Tariana conversations and narratives,

Another facilitating factor is the IMPACT A CATEGORY HAS ON CULTURAL NORMS AND BEHAVIOURIAL REQUIREMENTS. An obligatory category in a language which correlates with behavioural requirements is more susceptible to diffusion than one which does not. Such a category is also salient in terms of its frequency in texts of varied genres. The existence of obligatory evidentials presupposes a requirement for an explicit statement about how one knows things. Those who are not explicit run the danger of being treated as liars, or as incompetent. This cultural requirement may explain why evidentiality spreads so easily into contact languages, including some varieties of American Indian English (Bunte and Kendall 1981), Latin American Spanish (Laprade 1981), and Amazonian Portuguese (Aikhenvald 2002), and diffuses across linguistic areas (see Aikhenvald 2004: ch. 9). Evidentiality made its way from Carib languages into Mawayana (Carlin 2007), and from Tucanoan independently into Hup and Tariana (Epps 2005; Aikhenvald 2002). The importance of evidentiality for successful communication within the Vaupés area was undoubtedly a factor in the development of evidentiality in every clause type in Tariana—including commands.

Sharing pragmatic patterns and types of context, and subsequent diffusion of organizing discourse structures, results in common genres, idiomatic expressions, and further ways of saying things for languages in contact. Examples of borrowed interjections and speech formulae abound in the literature (see Aikhenvald 2007a; Matras 1998; Brody 1995). Commands are highly prominent in greetings and speech formulae throughout the Vaupés area. We can recall the identical structures in Tariana *matʃa-pida* (be.good-SEC.IMPV) 'goodbye; best wishes' (lit. 'let it be good on (our) behalf'), and Tucano *ãyu-áto* (good-SEC.IMPV), with the same meaning. The appearance of a reported evidential in farewell formulae is not unusual—a formula similar to that in Tucano and Tariana was documented by Fortescue (2003: 296) for West Greenlandic (*inuullua-ri-lin-nguuq* (live.well-NON.IMMEDIATE-3pl+OPTATIVE-REP) 'give my greetings to them', lit. 'may they live well non-immediately on someone else's order'). The farewell formula was calqued from Tucano into Tariana, creating an anomalous structure: secondhand, or any other imperative cannot be formed on stative verbs except in this greeting formula.

In a situation of intensive language contact, similar situations are conceptualized in similar ways and warrant similar verbal description. If one language uses serial verbs for describing a complex of subevents as one event, another language is likely to evolve a verb-sequencing construction to match this, as did Tariana (Aikhenvald 2000) and Hup, to match the Tucano 'prototype' (Epps 2007).

This brings us to a tendency to achieve word-for-word and morpheme-for-morpheme intertranslatability, enhanced by the existence of a perceivable 'gap' which facilitates diffusion. For instance, some Australian languages had no 'conventionalized counting systems,' that is, no numbers used for counting (Hale 1975: 295–6). As Aborigines came into contact with European invaders and their counting practices, this gap was filled either through borrowed forms or by exploiting native resources. Borrowing of the exclusive 1+3 pronoun *amna* into Mawayana (Arawak) from Waiwai fills an existing 'gap' in the pronominal system (see Carlin 2007).

It is likely to have been for the same reason—to express the same obligatory categories present in East Tucanoan languages—that Tariana developed a wide variety of imperative meanings which it originally lacked. Morpheme-per-morpheme loan translations from East Tucanoan languages helped maintain the iconic correspondences between Tariana and its neighbours, promoting mutual understanding and successful communication. Along similar lines, younger speakers of Nivkh have developed Russian-like ways of phrasing commands.

A final point is in order. Social changes accompany changes in the use and the ways of framing imperative constructions. Table 4.2 features imperative particles in Lakhota, a Siouan language (based on Boas and Deloria 1941; also see Ullrich 2008: 764–5). The particles vary depending on whether the speaker is a man or a woman. Lakhota speakers state that 'men say *yo* and women say *ye*'—and this holds 'as a general rule' of Lakhota behaviour for imperatives (Trechter 1995: 189). In Lakhota folk tales, 'women are represented as often opting for the entreaty *na'* (treated as 'command' *na*, often omitted: Table 4.2), 'or using an authoritative statement instead of the command form'. However, nowadays, in modern conversations 'the speaker who most often uses a command form is a woman, correcting the delivery style of her husband as she interrupts his explanation [...] to tell him to speak in Lakhota or to clarify his explanations'. This new role of a woman as a language keeper—and an authority in matters traditional—affects the sheer frequency of commands in women's speech, the way the commands are phrased, and linguistic ideology in general. Changing gender roles may in future affect the linguistic system.

Notes

1. For the full story, see Aikhenvald (2002), and (2008b) on marriage patterns and language interaction in the Vaupés area. Sorensen (1967) discusses the Colombian side of the Vaupés area where no Arawak languages are spoken.
2. See Aikhenvald (2002: 187–207) on language attitude and stereotypes in the Vaupés River Basin.

3. Stative verbs cannot form imperatives, with the exception of one instance of the secondhand imperative. In addition to the paradigm, there is also a 'malefactive' imperative which can co-occur with one imperative (secondhand), with stative verbs and—rarely—with tense-evidentiality markers.

4. Baniwa data are from Taylor (1991) and my own fieldwork, Piapoco data come from Klumpp (1990: 62).

5. See Ramirez (1997: 120–21) and Aikhenvald (2002) for the paradigms.

6. Imperatives in Tariana are not compatible with any tense markers used in declarative clauses. Using the least formally marked *-pida* as a secondhand imperative is concordant with the general lack of tense markers in Tariana imperatives.

7. Speakers of Tariana do not appear to be aware of the similarity between Tuyuca and Tariana delayed imperative *-wa* because their knowledge of Tuyuca is limited. This is in contrast to Tucano, Wanano, Piratapuya, and Desano, in which most Tariana are highly proficient (see Appendix 4 to Aikhenvald 2002).

8. Klumpp (1990: 172); Tariana *s* corresponds to Piapoco *s* before a front vowel.

9. The gloss given by Miller (1999: 74) is eat-IMPV.prove-LIM, consistent with one of the meanings of the verb *-yā*.

10. Among such morphemes are a few verbal roots which only occur with prefixes, such as Tariana *-ya-ta*, Tucano *-yaa* 'yawn, open mouth', Tariana *-wi-ña* 'whistle', Tucano *-wii* (see Aikhenvald 2002: 215–17 for some examples).

11. Ramirez (1997: i. 148).

12. Ibid. 145.

13. See Aikhenvald (2002: 213–22) on language awareness in the Vaupés area.

14. Note that *dz* in some Baniwa dialects, such as Hohôdene, regularly corresponds to Tariana *y*, e.g. Baniwa *dzawi*, Tariana *yawi* 'jaguar'.

15. This extension could be seen as an activation, or enhancement, of a tendency to use the emphatic *-ya* in commands, shared by Baniwa of Içana and Tariana. The process of activation is well attested in contact-induced change (see Aikhenvald 2007a). The development of command functions for the emphatic *-ya* in Tariana is an example of multiple motivation in language change.

16. See Ramirez (1997: Vol. I, 146–7); cf. Stenzel (2004: 390), Barnes (1979).

17. Another example of restructuring an imperative system in language contact comes from Yucuna. This North Arawak language underwent considerable restructuring under the influence of Retuarã, a Central Tucanoan language. Yucuna has a special imperative marker (homophonous with the recent past suffix) used for a command at a location away from the speaker. Contrasting examples are *pi-kuli-cha pe-'eweé* (2sg-fetch-IMPV.DIST 2sg-brother) 'Fetch your brother (he is in a different settlement)' and *pi-kulá pe-'eweé* (2sg-fetch-IMPV.DIST 2sg-brother) 'Fetch your brother' (Schauer and Schauer 2000, 2005: 314–15). This is mirrored by Retuarã 'indirect imperative' *-pe* which implies that the location is away from the speaker and that 'the person first go to the location of the event': *ōterikia bī-rēā-pe* (fruit 2sg-collect-INDIRECT.IMPV' '(Go and) collect fruit' (Strom 1992: 135–7).

18. This loss of a form which has no equivalent in the contact language is known as 'negative borrowing'.

19. From the East Sakhalin variety.

20. Gurindji, also Australian, has borrowed a negative morpheme *numu*, from a local variety of Aboriginal English *no more*. This negator is also used in negative commands, e.g. *numu ya-nta=lu* (NEG go-IMPV=PL.SUBJECT) 'Don't go!' (Laughren 2002: 128).

21. See Aikhenvald (2012) for a cross-linguistic perspective of contact-induced change in obsolescent languages which can produce highly unusual patterns of borrowing.

22. The emergence of innovative analytic imperative forms may be just a fact of language's history, not connected with obsolescence. Panare, a Northern Carib language spoken in Venezuela by over 2,000 people, has a synthetic negative imperative, formed with the prefix *k-* (first person subject-cum-second person object) and the negative imperative suffix *-(e)me*. A traditional way of saying 'don't laugh' is (Payne and Payne 1999: 133) *k-asonopi-me* (1subj.2object-laugh-NEG.IMPV) 'Don't laugh!'. Younger speakers replace this structure with an analytic one, consisting of the standard plain imperative and the general negative particle *pï*, e.g. *asonopi-kë pï* (laugh-IMPV NEG) 'Don't laugh!'.

23. Contact within a linguistic area provides support for the survival of irregular suppletive imperative forms. Irregular imperatives of the verb 'come' are an areal feature of Afroasiatic languages in Ethiopia (Ferguson 1976; Tosco 2000: 349–51; Crass 2007: 100). Some forms were listed in Table 9.1 (and see Hayward 1979, on how they preserve some archaic features). It is possible that the 'survival' of this feature among Ethiopian languages is partly due to language contact. Newman (1980: 21) reconstructs this feature as Proto-Afroasiatic. It is not found in some Chadic languages, e.g. languages of Cameroon (Zygmunt Frajzyngier p.c.) or Bole-Tangale (Schuh 1978).

24. A hybrid formation, *yàla báy* 'bye bye', in Modern Hebrew is a combination of two loans—the Arabic *yalla* and the English *bye*.

25. Bynon (1976) links the Ayt Hadiddou call to a mule *ššt(a)^n!* to make it slow down to Latin *stā*, imperative of *stō, stāre* 'stand' (Bynon 1976: 99, and references there). A Russian command *alle!* comes from French *allez!* 'go (plural)'. Some animal calls found in Berber, and in other languages, appear to be onomatopoeic in origin, e.g. *ps!* as a call to a cat (Bynon 1976: 59–60).

26. See Aikhenvald (2007a). Some of those mentioned here have been overtly identified by Heath (1978); and a few others correlate with tendencies in grammatical borrowing (e.g. Moravcsik 1978).

12

The ubiquitous imperative

Every language has a way of telling someone what to do, through directive speech acts. These subsume commands, orders, instructions, requests, suggestions, entreaties, and so on. Each of these can be expressed through a variety of means. Of these, imperatives—or imperative mood—are the dedicated grammatical device whose core meaning is that of a directive speech act, a command.

Imperatives are special. They contrast with questions, statements, and exclamations in their expression and their meaning. In Jakobson's (1971: 191) words, 'the lonely imperative' stands apart from declarative and interrogative. It most certainly does. An imperative may have its own set of forms. Several chapters of this book deal with the morphologically distinctive character of imperatives. Furthermore, other forms can be co-opted to serve primarily imperative functions, for both positive and negative commands.

We now briefly summarize our findings concerning imperatives, and how they interact with other grammatical forms. In the very last section, we turn to some further routes of investigation for imperatives and other commands across the languages of the world.

12.1 Canonical and non-canonical imperatives

For many linguists and language learners alike, 'imperative' implies a command to a second person—such as English *Get out!* And indeed, in many languages a set of special imperative forms is restricted to commands directed at 'you'. Addressee-oriented imperatives are always central to the imperative paradigms. This follows the well-established traditional approach. In Lyons's (1977: 747) words, 'it is implicit in the very notion of commanding and requesting that the command or request is addressed to the person who is expected to carry it out'. And that singular addressee forms are more basic than their non-singular counterpart follows from the fact that the singular tends to be less formally and functionally marked.

Addressee-oriented imperatives are called canonical imperatives, or imperatives in a narrow sense. In many languages, non-addressee-oriented command forms—or non-canonical imperatives—stand apart from canonical imperatives in their expression and evolution. Alternative terms are available. The term 'jussive' can be used to cover commands to third person, and 'hortative' describes commands to first person. Non-addressee-oriented imperatives share properties with each other: this is the reason to put them together, rather than using different terms for each.

Expressing an imperative.   An imperative directed at a singular addressee—the most prototypical of all—often coincides with the bare stem of the verb. Imperatives addressed to first or to third person (called here 'non-canonical' imperatives) tend to be more formally marked. Not infrequently, non-canonical imperatives are expressed analytically. In contrast, a one-word, synthetic expression is typically used for a straightforward command to the addressee.

Imperatives, both canonical and non-canonical, can be marked with:

- verbal inflection—a technique frequent in synthetic languages;
- particles—frequent in isolating and highly agglutinating languages;
- a special set of pronouns.

Imperative and person.   The idea of 'person' in imperatives is at variance with that in other clause types. 'Person' in imperatives refers to the person of the addressee, and not that of the speaker. And not all persons in the imperative behave in the same way. The canonical imperative often stands apart from the rest—a command addressed to oneself, or 'us', or 'them'. As a result, some grammarians use different terms for commands addressed to second, first, and third person. This hardly ever happens in the analysis of declarative or interrogative clauses.

The reasons why different person values for commands tend not to be subsumed under one term, 'imperative', are both formal and semantic. Second person imperatives are primarily commands. First and third person imperatives are often formed using different means than second-person imperatives, and may not form a single paradigm with them. And their meanings often go beyond just commands. See Chapter 2.

Some predictions. The most common non-canonical imperative is a first person plural inclusive—that is, the one involving the addressee plus the speaker. A special form for first person singular imperative is absent from a number of languages which have first person plural (with an inclusive reading) and third person imperative, in addition to the canonical values. Diagram 2.1 (repeated here) summarizes our expectations as to which person distinctions are likelier than others in imperative forms. That is, if a language has any type of form which qualifies as 'imperative', it will express second person in the first place.

DIAGRAM 2.1 Person distinctions in imperatives: what we expect

Non-canonical values				Canonical values
1sg and/or 1st exclusive	> 3 sg or pl	1st inclusive; non-singular	>	2p (sg, pl, or non-singular)
(a)	(b)	(c)		(d)

- If there is (b) a third person imperative, we also expect to have (c) an imperative form expressing first person non-singular, with an inclusive reading.
- And if a language has (a) an imperative for first person singular or first person exclusive, we expect it to have (b) a third person imperative and, consequently, (c) a first person non-singular one.

For instance, 11.30 shows how this hierarchy works for traditional Nivkh: Nivkh has (d), (c), (b), but no (a). Further examples are in §2.2.

The principle reflected in Diagram 2.1 is intuitively clear: imperative forms are likely to involve the addressee. They are thus expected to be directed at the addressee, or have an inclusive meaning—that is, be addressed to 'you' and 'me', not just 'me'.

Non-canonical imperatives have person-specific meaning extensions. First person commands slide into permissions and suggestions, and third person commands often express wishes rather than straightforward orders.

Expressing an imperative: further generalizations.   If a language has a special imperative form, it will cover at least the second singular addressee. No language employs a non-imperative form (say, a subjunctive or an optative) for singular addressee, or has a special paradigm just for the non-singular. This agrees with the basic character of the second singular canonical imperative. And no known language employs forms from different paradigms for singular and non-singular canonical imperative (for instance, a subjunctive form for singular, and a declarative for non-singular).

Canonical imperatives are rarely expressed with analytic forms. Not so for non-canonical imperatives, or prohibitives. We saw in Chapters 10 and 11 that canonical imperatives tend to be the most archaic of all.

Suppletive imperatives.   Canonical imperatives can have irregular or suppletive forms. Typical candidates include verbs of motion and stance (although the range of possibilities extends beyond these). The same applies to suppletive first person imperatives. In a number of languages, suppletive imperatives have a full paradigm of forms. Only languages with a suppletive singular canonical imperative also have a suppletive non-singular one, never the other way round.

Languages 'without imperatives'?   Every language has a way of expressing a directive speech act. But not every language has a dedicated set of imperatives. A form of another category—irrealis, present, imperfective, future, intentional, and some others—is then co-opted as a conventional command. This is the case in Navajo, a well-known Athapascan language, Wardaman, an Australian language, and a few others. An essentially non-imperative form can be co-opted just for non-canonical person values, or for negative imperatives. In Spanish, a positive imperative *¡come!* 'eat!' has a negated subjunctive, *¡no comas!* as its negative counterpart. (This has led some linguists to state that Spanish has no negative imperative, or that negative imperatives do not exist at all.)

Command strategies and imperatives.   Non-imperative forms used to express imperative-like meanings are called 'command strategies'.

Canonical imperatives tend to refer to the most immediate and basic of commands. They are the least formally marked, and can be perceived as too demanding, intrusive, and generally face-threatening. To avoid these potential connotations, other forms are employed to express the directive speech acts, in lieu of imperatives themselves. A command strategy may gradually become the preferred (and then perhaps the only) way of expressing a directive speech act. A new imperative paradigm comes into existence.

The ultimate motivation behind the versatility of imperative forms, and forms used in lieu of them, lies precisely in the vast semantic space of directive acts. Forms drawn into the directive 'game' may become primarily directive.

Imperatives can occur in dependent clauses. This phenomenon has only been documented for a number of languages from the Papuan area (e.g. Hua and Yagaria: see §3.4). When imperatives occur in questions, their meanings go beyond 'commanding': they may have overtones of intention: this was taken up in §7.3.

Imperatives and directives can be considered a law unto themselves: their grammatical and semantic properties set them apart from the rest of the language.

12.2 Imperatives are a law unto themselves

Recurrent features of imperatives set them apart from interrogative and declarative clause types. This was addressed in Chapter 3.

The phonology of imperatives.   Imperatives sound different from other types of clauses. They often have specific intonation patterns. Some languages have phonological processes setting imperatives apart from other clause types.

Order of constituents.   Imperative clauses may differ from questions and statements in the ways constituents are ordered. In many cases, but not everywhere, this involves putting the verb first. In languages with 'free' constituent order—determined by the pragmatics of the utterance—imperatives are likely to have a fixed order. In Romance languages, pronominal clitics occupy different places in questions and in commands. Grammatical markers—particles or affixes—may acquire meanings in imperative clauses which they do not have when used in statements and in questions.

Imperative-specific meanings of verbal categories.   The basis of meanings and extensions of meanings which are typical for imperatives lies in the nature of pragmatic and semantic overtones of imperatives in the context of directions in general: see Chapters 3, 4 and 6. Directives consistently relate to the STRENGTH OF A COMMAND—encompassing the commander's insistence or lack thereof, the urgency of the commanded action, and demand for the addressee's compliance. And this is where the relationships between the addressee and the 'commander' come into play.

Strength of command correlates with the relative status of the commander and the addressee: whether they are equal, or the addressee occupies a lower or a higher position on a social ladder. In this way, imperatives also encode INTERPERSONAL RELATIONS and POLITENESS. These can be realized through an elaborate system of honorific registers (as in Korean) or politeness forms reserved just for commands, and also vocatives and pronouns of address.

Imperative-specific meanings: strength of commands, politeness and more. Commands of different strength overlap with and slide into different kinds of speech act—invitation, permission, encouragement, and the like. The interpersonal relationships behind the ways the commands are employed also come into play: you cannot order around someone who is above you, but you can make suggestions. Various directive speech acts reflect different 'degrees' of command: to suggest that somebody do something—or to request that something be done—is necessarily weaker and less insistent than a straightforward order 'do it!' And a humble request, or a tentative suggestion, often sounds more polite than an arrogant order.

In many languages (including Brazilian Portuguese, Modern Greek, and Matses), suggesting that something be done 'a little bit' is a nicer way of getting someone to do something. The addressee is in fact really being told, or invited, to perform the action fully, and the diminutive, or an expression 'a little bit', has a softening function. This is one rather simple and straightforward example of how a form has one meaning 'a little bit' in a statement and another one in a command: softening it and making it more palatable and less threatening. An imperative-specific meaning of 'strength of command' infiltrates a diminutive form, and gives it its own imprint. In other words, the ubiquitous imperative shapes the meanings of many morphemes according to its 'mould'.

The complex of imperative-specific meanings—featuring speech acts, strength of command, politeness, familiarity, and other conventionalized interpersonal relations—forms the basis for the specific meanings of number, tense, aspect, and other categories within imperatives, addressed partly in Chapter 3, and then in Chapter 4.

Not-so-primitive imperatives. The idea that imperatives are more 'primitive' than their non-imperative counterparts is essentially flawed. We saw, in §4.1, that imperatives may have more or fewer number and person distinctions than do other clause types. Imperatives may have inclusive forms—independently of whether declaratives and interrogatives distinguish between inclusive (us: you and me) and exclusive (us: without you). In numerous instances, first person in imperatives has inclusive overtones, and thus refers to 'us, or me, with you'.

The grammar of imperatives.   Grammatical categories expressed in imperatives vary in their complexity. Imperatives may express more grammatical meanings than do the corresponding declaratives. They can express fewer meanings; or the meanings expressed may be different from those in questions and statements. This applies to the CATEGORIES RELATING TO THE ADDRESSEE (§4.1), especially gender or noun class. Some languages have a special marking of gender of the 'commander' in imperatives but hardly any gender distinctions in statements.

Aspect and tense in verbs can have different implications in imperatives and in other clause types. These meanings tend to fit into the mould of semantic features of politeness and degree of command which are characteristic of imperatives. They also correlate with the preferred aspectual meanings expressed by imperatives: imperfectivity may relate to a higher degree of politeness, and perfectivity may be just the opposite. This takes us to CORRELATIONS WITH CATEGORIES RELATING TO VERBAL ACTION (see §4.2).

It is the case that imperatives generally tend to have fewer ASPECTUAL categories than do declaratives. Typical distinctions are continuative versus simple (or punctual) imperative. There is a strong tendency to distinguish these only in canonical imperatives. Continuative imperatives tend to acquire imperative-specific overtones of politeness, and punctual imperatives may sound 'abrupt'. Once again, the command-specific overtones make aspect in imperatives into something more than just 'aspect'.

The most frequently attested grammaticalized time distinction in imperatives is that of immediate command ('do now!') and delayed command ('do later!'). This is most often distinguished for canonical imperatives only. 'Delayed' imperatives often have overtones of politeness. Imperatives do not have to always have future reference. Command forms referring to the past do exist—and uniformly have overtones of a wish for a past action to have happened. Past imperatives—rare as they are—have strong overtones of 'you should have done it'.

The same imperative form may combine reference to DISTANCE IN TIME AND IN SPACE. This polysemy is hardly ever found in tense systems in declarative clauses.

'Distance in space'—'do here' versus 'do there'—is imperative-specific. This may have further overtones of presence or absence of the speaker during the execution of the command. A few languages have special imperative forms depending on whether the action is to be performed in the presence, or in the absence of the speaker; or whether the speaker (and the addressee) can see the action or not.

Imperatives may have special forms expressing motion and directionality of action. The speaker remains the deictic centre for the direction of the action.

A reported (or secondhand) evidential is the most pervasive marker of information source in commands. Its meaning is uniformly that of a command by proxy—'do something which someone else (other than the speaker) told you'. A reported evidential in a command may have a meaning which is command-specific: to attenuate an order, having 'polite' overtones. This is something which an evidential in a statement, or in a question, never has.

Generally speaking, imperatives tend NOT TO have additional, epistemic meanings of probability or possibility. Markers of modality and of irrealis in imperatives are used to soften commands, and to make them sound politer. Evidentials in commands never have any epistemic overtones, although their counterparts in statements may do. This pushes imperatives further apart from questions or commands. That is, categories relating to verbal action in imperatives are centered on the 'commander' as the deictic point of reference: motion, direction, and spatial relationships of the addressee are defined from the commander's perspective. Categories related to verbal action—aspect, tense, reality status—develop overtones of politeness and degree of command. This is what makes them imperative-specific, and not isomorphic with what they mean in other clause types.

MARKING OF VERBAL ARGUMENTS in canonical imperatives may differ from that in other clauses types (§4.3): the subject is obvious, and thus does not have to be overtly expressed—the addressee is uniformly understood as the subject. The second argument, the object, may not be formally marked, because if the subject is only the addressee, there is no need to disambiguate the subject and the object. Imperatives tend to operate on a nominative–accusative principle. The differences in marking grammatical relations in imperatives and in corresponding declaratives are rooted in discourse-pragmatic functions and semantics, and often reflect archaic features of imperatives—also addressed in §10.1.

Verbs which form imperatives and those which do not.   Not every verb may be turned into an imperative. A prototypical directive speech act implies the speaker's control over the activity. Verbs describing uncontrollable actions, states, and the like may not be able to form imperatives. Copula verbs, verb 'have', and passive forms may not have imperatives either. But in some languages, for instance Indonesian, a passive may develop imperative-specific meanings of politeness and indirect commands. This is another example of an imperative-only meaning of a verbal form.

It is the case that in an imperative construction, the subject of a stative verb can acquire an 'agentive role'—which it would not have in a corresponding declarative. The verb 'see' in a statement describes the subject as a non-agentive role 'perceiver'. A command *See what time it is!* implies an action, to the effect of *Find out what time it is!* or *Go and look what time it is!* Command-specific overtones influence the meaning of a verb.

All this applies to canonical imperatives in the first place, and may or may not apply to non-canonical ones. Generally speaking, non-canonical imperatives may be more similar to statements than canonical ones. This is how imperatives are special, and so are prohibitives, albeit in different ways. Table 12.1 summarizes some of the general features which set imperatives apart from statements and from questions (with reference to sections where these are discussed). This is partly repeated from Table 3.3.

12.3 Commanding 'not to': how prohibitives are special

Just as every language has a way, and often more than one, of telling someone what to do, so every language has a way of doing the opposite—telling what not to do. As often happens in the linguistic literature, terminology varies. Some use 'negative imperative', others 'prohibitive'. Yet others make a conceptual distinction between the two, relating to the means of expression. The term 'prohibitive' is then restricted to instances where there is a special marker just for negative commands. The term 'negative imperative' is reserved for languages where a negator—used in clauses of other types—is also used in prohibitions. This approach is rather attractive for those who study surface expressions rather than underlying meanings. To avoid an excessive focus on the form itself, we have opted for using both 'negative imperative' and 'prohibitive' to refer to the forms employed for telling 'not to'. Generic terms—prohibitions and negative commands—are an alternative option. This is the topic of Chapter 5.

Expressing a prohibitive. Prohibitives and positive imperatives may be expressed in a similar way. Alternatively, forming a prohibitive may involve a special negator, a special verb form, or both. A prohibitive may involve using a verbal form which is not negative in itself—a subjunctive, as in Spanish, or an infinitive, as in Italian.

Unlike positive imperatives, prohibitives are often expressed analytically—with complex predicates involving auxiliaries, and with serial verbs. A prohibitive may involve an inherently negative verb—as Latin *nolle* 'be unwilling,

TABLE 12.1 How imperatives differ from other clause types: a selection of features

FEATURES	IMPERATIVES AS DISTINCT FROM OTHER CLAUSE TYPES	RELEVANT SECTIONS
Phonological properties	Distinctive intonation contour; occasionally, special phonological processes	§3.1
Order of constituents	Special order configurations (often verb first); likely to have a fixed order in languages with pragmatic-based order	§3.2
Meanings of various verbal categories	• Verbal particles may add overtones of politeness and pragmatic force to imperatives, e.g. 'a little bit' or a diminutive in a statement or question can be used as a politeness marker in a command	§3.3
	• Tendency to have inclusive overtones ('you and me') of first person imperative	§3.3
	• Imperative-specific meanings of aspects: e.g. an imperfective aspect in a command may relate to politeness	§3.3, §4.2.1
	• Typical aspectual distinctions in imperatives are continuative vs simple (or punctual), in contrast to a wider variety of options in non-imperative clauses	§4.2.1
	• Continuative aspect in imperatives has polite overtones, absent from other clause types	§4.2.1
	• A typical tense distinction in imperatives is that of immediate versus delayed command, unlike those in other clause types	§4.2.2
	• Imperatives may have special categories of distance in time and space absent from other clause types	§4.2.3
	• Reported evidentiality is the only specification typically attested in imperatives, in contrast to other clause types with numerous options	§4.2.4
	• Imperatives tend to have no epistemic extensions	§4.2.5
Restrictions on formation	• Imperatives may not be able to be formed on stative verbs or verbs which do not imply speaker's control, unlike other clause types	§4.4
Negation	• Imperatives may be negated differently from other clause types	Chapter 5

refuse'—or a special prohibitive auxiliary. Or it can contain a lexical verb meaning 'stop', or 'leave'. All these are the basis for the grammaticalization of prohibitives. And they highlight the fact that prohibitives often involve analytic forms—more often so than their positive counterparts.

Not-so-simple prohibitives. A statement that imperatives are primitive is frequent in the literature. But hardly anyone has confronted a prohibitive with a similar accusation. Why? In some languages, not-so-primitive imperatives and even-less-primitive prohibitives may have the same categories. Or there may be fewer grammatical distinctions in prohibitives than in imperatives. In Maale, an Omotic language from Ethiopia, and in Indo-Pakistani Sign Language, prohibitives do not distinguish politeness, while imperatives do. Imperative-specific aspects (durative versus continuous) tend to be neutralized in prohibitives. This is consistent with a general tendency across languages of the world: fewer meanings and categories tend to be expressed in negative than in positive clauses.

Prohibitive-specific meanings of verbal categories are similar to those of positive commands: we have strength of command, and degrees of politeness and familiarity. Just like imperatives, prohibitives can be a special clause-type in terms of categories, their meanings and marking.

In addition, prohibitives are special in a number of other ways. They can differ from positive imperatives in their intonation. The order of constituents in prohibitives and in imperatives may be different—see §5.2.3 on the order of clitics in Italian. And they can be richer in subtle meanings than positive imperatives.

An example from English illustrates this. The subject of prohibitives in English—if present at all—commonly follows the support verb *do*, something that does not happen in a positive imperative. We repeat 5.46a as 12.1 (Quirk et al. 1985: 830):

12.1   Don't you open the door

If the subject occurs with a quantifier, it can be placed either before or after the verb, with a subtle difference in meaning (Davies 1986: 97). 12.2 (repeated from 5.47a) is a 'rejection of the possibility of one of the addressee's forgetting'. The subject follows the verb. Here, each of the addresses is expected to bring money:

12.2   Don't one of you forget the money

In 12.3 (repeated from 5.47b), the subject precedes the verb. This command presents the possibility that one of them should not forget—it is more likely to be used if the speaker expects only one of the addressees to bring money.

12.3   One of you don't forget the money

This is where positive imperatives lose to their negative counterparts: they do not allow such subtleties to be expressed with simple change in constituent order (see Davies 1986: 96–8).

More on elaborate prohibitives.   Prohibitives can thus be more elaborate than positive imperatives (see also van der Auwera 2006b). They often have fewer restrictions on verb types than do imperatives. Even in English it is more natural to say *Don't be useless!* than *Be useless!* In English and many other languages, passive imperatives are less frequent than active ones (if they are allowed at all). Positive passives with *be* 'are not often found with directive force', but 'negatives lend themselves more readily to such an interpretation' (Huddleston 2002: 933). Ordering *Be intimidated!* may sound odd. *Don't be intimidated!* is perfectly acceptable, and is readily interpreted as 'Don't allow yourself to be intimidated!'

As Bolinger (1967: 348) put it, 'we have more occasion to command resistance than sufferance, and negative passives are correspondingly more frequent'. In a number of languages, prohibitives can be formed on verbs which are never used in positive commands. For instance, a stative verb such as 'be afraid' may not appear in a positive command. It can very well occur in a prohibition, 'Don't be afraid!' More imperative-specific distinctions can be made in negative than in positive imperatives, such as 'strength' of command (see §5.2.5; Tariana, Manambu, Semelai, and Rukai are among those discussed). And this is where negative imperatives are at odds with negative statements or questions. Negative statements tend to express fewer meanings than their positive counterparts: for instance, number, gender, and person are not expressed in negative statements in Tariana and Manambu (and see further examples in Aikhenvald and Dixon 1998).

Why is this so? Is it the case that instructing people what not to do is more important than telling them what to do? Does this wealth of prohibitives reflect the importance of NOT breaching the existing constraints? Or are we supposed to have more control over what we don't do than what we actually happen to do? I leave these questions to my psychologist and anthropologist colleagues to address.

Another important conclusion to draw is in the ways prohibitives appear to be closer to positive statements than they are to the positive imperatives. For example, the prohibitives in some languages—like Manam, an Oceanic languages from the Solomon Islands—are marked with the realis form of the verb, and imperatives with the irrealis. Many languages employ a negated statement as the only option for negating a command addressed to first or third person. This brings prohibitives and declaratives closer together—leaving the 'lonely' canonical imperative on its own.

Both imperatives and prohibitives are used in contexts other than directive speech acts.

12.4 Beyond directives

Imperatives—positive and negative alike—cover more than just verbal orders. They span a wide range of directive speech acts, including wishes, hopes, advice, entreaties, requests, pleas, and instructions. Any of these can be ironic. Many of these meanings are not-quite-directive. The versatile imperative forms can go way beyond these. See Chapter 7.

Within complex sentences, imperatives may have conditional, concessive, and contrastive overtones. They may occur in narratives without overtones of command—but with the meaning of vivid, unexpected, important action. Imperatives occur in curses, blessings, and swearing. Imperative forms can become tokens of speech etiquette and are used in greetings, expression of thanks, and also marks of surprise without any connotation of a command. *Tell me about it* in colloquial Australian English is not a request for information about 'it': it is an exclamation meaning something like 'I know all about it, isn't it amazing'. If I say *They have all sort of fruit jams there, guava, rosella, strawberry, you name it*, what looks like a command, *you name it*, has nothing to do with me asking you to name anything. This is more like an adverbial expression meaning 'and so on, etc', referring to various other kinds of the same thing. Similarly, *you don't say!* is not an order to be silent. It is an exclamation, an expression of surprise.

Imperative forms may be used as discourse markers and attention-getting devices. In Classical Latin, *audi!* 'you hear!' and *ausculta!* 'you listen!' were used as attention-getters, and so was *vide!* 'look, see!' (Löfstedt 1966: 92–3). Such attention-getters can keep their recognizably verbal form, as in Latin. But they may then lose their status as verbal forms altogether. This is how imperatives are ubiquitous: they go beyond their designated space, i.e. beyond directive speech acts.

12.5 Beyond imperatives

Imperative forms are not the only directives in any language. Non-imperative forms are often co-opted to express directive meanings which may be more or less strong than the imperative itself. This is the essence of imperative strategies—see Chapter 8. Languages of the world offer us an array of interrogative-directives, statements cast in future, present, and past tense, or non-indicative modalities, nominalizations, desubordinated clauses, and a few more.

A plethora of directive speech acts extends beyond imperative forms. Almost any speech act can be understood as a hidden or not-so-hidden instruction, command, or entreaty. A statement can be interpreted this way. Saying in English *The fridge is empty* can be understood as a statement about the contents of a fridge. Or it may be tantamount to asking the addressee to go food shopping straightaway. The interpretation depends on context. The speaker's body language can go together with the directive intent of such statement: a reproachful eye-gaze makes the preferred interpretation very clear. Figures 8.5 and 8.6, from Chapter 8 (repeated here), show a continuum between an imperative and an interrogative, and between an imperative and a statement.

An imperative in (a) in Figure 8.5 is the most prototypical directive. Imperatives also appear in (b)–(c). An imperative accompanied by a 'tag' in (c) makes the command milder and less abrupt. Questions—as in (d), (e), and (f)—also lend themselves to an easy interpretation as directives, and are conventionally used as such. Questions in (g) and (h) can be used to ask for salt. The question in (i) is the most prototypical information question, not easily extendable to imply a command.

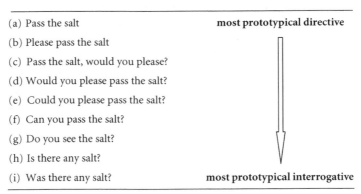

(a) Pass the salt   **most prototypical directive**

(b) Please pass the salt

(c) Pass the salt, would you please?

(d) Would you please pass the salt?

(e) Could you please pass the salt?

(f) Can you pass the salt?

(g) Do you see the salt?

(h) Is there any salt?

(i) Was there any salt?   **most prototypical interrogative**

FIGURE 8.5 From imperative to interrogative

That is, any of (d)–(f) can be easily understood as directives rather than questions. Whether or not (g), (h), and especially (i) are perceived as directives or as questions depends on the situation and the intonation.

A comparable continuum can be created for a relationship between imperative and declarative: (a)–(h) can be interpreted as commands, differing in their strength, politeness, and manipulative force—see Figure 8.6.

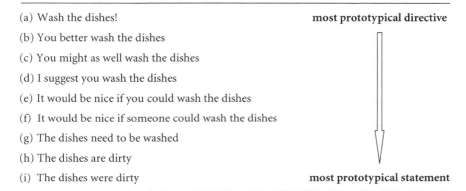

(a) Wash the dishes!   **most prototypical directive**

(b) You better wash the dishes

(c) You might as well wash the dishes

(d) I suggest you wash the dishes

(e) It would be nice if you could wash the dishes

(f) It would be nice if someone could wash the dishes

(g) The dishes need to be washed

(h) The dishes are dirty

(i) The dishes were dirty   **most prototypical statement**

FIGURE 8.6 From imperative to declarative

In each case, there is a mismatch between the linguistic form and the pragmatic function of a speech act. Pragmatic functions are versatile—they may correlate with the form, but often do not. Any linguistic form can be interpreted as a command, invitation, request, or other directive act. It is as if 'the lonely imperative' co-opts associates to fulfil its functions. This is what makes the imperative ubiquitous, and much less 'primitive' than some assume. But not every form is conventionally used as a directive in any given language: imperatives and non-imperative directives obey different principles of use in different societies.

It is not the case that 'anything goes' in any language: a 'why'-question will be understood as a command by a native speaker of English, but not necessarily by a language learner. A future statement sounds peremptory in English: *You will get Randy out of here!* is a stern command to remove the person, or the cat, in question. In contrast, in Quechua and in Arapaho, this is a nice and polite way of framing a request (see §8.3).

In Arapaho, future is used when the imperative is too peremptory and would imply the speaker had authority over the addressee (Cowell 2007). That is, future as a command strategy is used as a 'polite' equivalent of the imperative form, reflecting subtle social rules of interpersonal communication. Along similar lines, imperative in Colloquial Hebrew is somewhat rude and abrupt, and future has come to replace it, giving rise to a new imperative paradigm (Bolozky 1979).

Elliptical constructions—when one word is used instead of a whole elaborate sentence—may produce an abrupt command requiring immediate compliance, as in military orders. This agrees with the principle of iconic motivation: the longer the politer, and shorter the ruder.

But the effect of ellipsis can be different. Leaving out the main clause in conditional clauses, in English and a few other languages, results in a tentative request and a mild directive. A desubordinated *if*-clause in English is the case in point: *if you could come in* is a polite and conventionalized way of getting you to come in. And this expression no longer has the intonation pattern, and other features, of a conditional clause. A new directive clause type is on the rise (see Stirling 1998).

This goes together with the principle of vagueness and tentativeness in polite commands and requests, shared with all sorts of indirect speech acts.

Why do some languages use imperatives more eagerly than others? The reasons for avoiding an imperative may be rooted in the speech etiquette of culture-specific social relationships. In Yankunytjatjara, an Australian language (Goddard 1983: 306–7), a strict avoidance relationship between a man and his parents-in-law requires that a mother-in-law's or father-in-law's requests for food cannot be addressed directly at the son-in-law, and have to be passed through an intermediary.

Even the intermediary's speech cannot contain a direct command; it may be relayed using the quotative particle *kunyu* without any direct command, or reference to asking. This is shown in 12.4 (repeated from 6.17).

12.4 mayi   kunyu nyuntu-mpa waputju
      food(NOM)   QUOT   2sg-GEN   father.in.law
      'Your father-in-law says food'

Whether or not the addressee will interpret a statement as a directive depends on speech habits, conventions, social stereotypes, and the ethnography of communication in a language community. The role of inference in determining the pragmatic function of an utterance also depends on the overtones of imperatives themselves. In some societies, imposition of one's will on someone else is not considered an appropriate cultural practice. We then expect prototypical imperatives to be avoided and other, more roundabout forms to be favoured.

12.6 Imperatives in real life

Imperatives we live by are shaped by the conventions and the norms we are socialized to follow. Just as moral imperatives and duties can only be understood in the context of culture and history, this is also true of usage of the actual imperative forms. And of the ways in which imperative forms may be conveniently rephrased to suit the language ecology and the behavioural patterns considered appropriate. The Ilongot of the Philippines, the Nuer of East Africa, and the Malagasy of Madagascar use imperative forms sparingly, fitting them in with general face-saving strategies and types of circumlocutions for framing their requests and directive speech acts. This is the essence of Chapter 9.

In a given community, it may be a proper choice to avoid a directive speech act altogether. As Cowell (2008: 281) remarks, 'in Arapaho, it is considered rude to ask an older person if they are hungry or thirsty, thus forcing them to respond and indirectly request food or drink. Instead, food or drink are simply provided as a matter of course.' Using a future form, rather than an imperative, follows the same principle, 'by simply saying what is going to happen rather than asking for it or commanding it'.

The semantics, and the pragmatic overtones, of imperatives—or of any other forms—are not cross-linguistically uniform. Projecting the air of authority associated with imperative in English onto other languages is fraught with danger: the fact that the Mundugumor make much use of imperatives does not necessarily make them into a nation of authoritative bullies, contrary to Margaret Mead's English-based assumption (see §9.1).

The use of imperatives reflects the conventional hierarchies and perception of referents: we can recall that in Ilongot, imperative is used to children and women who are perceived to have energy and speed, but not too much sense or knowledge of their own. On the other hand, imperative can be deployed as a tool for defining relationships. In Arapaho, the use of a direct or indirect imperative is only partially dictated by pre-existing, clear-cut social relationships: the speakers choose to use an imperative or to avoid it depending on their attitudes and appreciation of each other's social status. To use or not to use an imperative is a matter of negotiation between the participants.

An imperative—or any command or request—can be accompanied by an explanation why or for what purpose something is to be done or not done. This is a way of making the order or request more effective.

Imperatives may be preferred in some genres rather than others. The abundance of imperative forms in instructions and advertisements in English has to do with the nature of the addressee. The 'do's' and the 'don'ts' are addressed to everyone in general and with no one singled out in particular. That is, no one will feel threatened by them.

Understanding and mastering directive speech acts—the ways of commanding, requesting, and so on—in a language is a key to successful communication. And using a wrong way of requesting is a sure way towards a breakdown in communication. When children acquire their first language, commands and requests are what they hear most, and what they have to learn first, to survive and to fulfil their needs.

12.7 Efficient imperatives

Imperatives and proper ways of framing and phrasing directive speech acts are central to efficient, smooth, and culturally sensitive communication. How do imperatives correlate with the conversational principles and maxims formulated by Grice?

The supermaxim of Quantity states:

1. Make your contribution as informative as is required (for the current purposes of the exchange).
2. Do not make your contribution more informative than is required.

The category of Relation has one single maxim, 'Be relevant'. And the category of Manner relates to '*how* what is said to be said' and subsumes 'the supermaxim "Be perspicuous"'—and various maxims such as (Grice 1989: 26–7):

1. Avoid obscurity of expression.
2. Avoid ambiguity.
3. Be brief (avoid unnecessary prolixity).
4. Be orderly.

Polite requests and commands in, say, Malagasy society may appear obscure, ambiguous, and unnecessary long-winded. And the fact that polite forms are often longer and less obvious to the addressee than a curt command may imply that politeness goes against communicative efficiency. In fact, this is not the case.

Communicative efficiency is based on cooperation between speakers and addressees. As Grice (1989: 26) put it:

Our talk exchanges do not normally consist of a succession of disconnected remarks, and would not be rational if they did. They are characteristically, to some degree at least, cooperative efforts; and each participant recognizes in them, to some degree at least, a common purpose or a set of purposes, or at least a mutually accepted direction.

This Cooperative Principle underlies the ways in which imperatives—and other forms employed for commands, directives, wishes, and entreaties of all sorts—are used and manipulated to reflect the conventions and their renegotiation in human communication. The plethora of commanding and requesting techniques in any given language reflect an ongoing struggle between striving to achieve efficient communication and desire to save face and yet to reach the commanded or requested result. This is touched upon in Chapter 9.

Cooperation with the addressee is to be negotiated, so as to achieve a minor maxim 'Be polite' (Grice 1989: 28). In other words, politeness is 'a major source of deviation from [. . .] rational efficiency' dictated by Grice's maxims if understood in a mechanical literal way (Brown and Levinson 1987: 95).

However, the maxims 'remain in operation at a deeper level': the speaker and the addressee are forced to correctly interpret the intended message of a hidden directive, that is, 'to do the inferential work that establishes the underlyingly intended message' and the source. In other words, a desire to maintain efficient communication lies behind the multiplicity of directives—some cast in imperatives, some not—and their avoidance or imposition.

And some non-primarily imperative forms may, over time, acquire unmistakably explicit command meanings. Imperative strategies are a source for further imperative forms, maximizing the efficiency of communication and the Cooperative Principle in each given cultural environment.

12.8 Imperatives in language history

Canonical imperatives tend to be archaic in their form, and in syntactic patterns. In Panyjima, Lardil, and a few other Australian languages, imperatives are the only remnant of the erstwhile ergative–absolutive system (further archaic features of imperative forms are discussed by Dixon 1994: 189; Watkins 1963; Kuryłowicz 1964, to name a few).

Unlike other moods, not all person forms of an imperative follow the same path of development. In contrast to second person canonical imperative—the most basic of all commands—non-canonical imperatives (commands to first and to third person) may come from different sources. The outcome is a historically heterogeneous set of imperative forms.

Such innovative forms may not be limited to non-canonical imperatives. But there are no examples of canonical—and not non-canonical imperatives—being innovated. Non-canonical forms may come from grammaticalized lexical items. There are hardly any clear examples of lexical forms giving rise to a whole imperative paradigm (Nigerian Pidgin and Kusunda are among the rare examples).

Alternatively, the whole system of commands—the imperative paradigm—may have its origin in an essentially non-imperative set, as a result of reinterpretation of what can be conceived of as an erstwhile imperative strategy. We saw in §10.2.1 how future forms became the preferred way of framing commands in Modern Colloquial Hebrew. Subsequent phonological process of syllable reduction resulted in the emergence of a new set of imperative forms, which can be traced back to future tense, but are synchronically distinct from it (see Bolozky 1979, 2009).

Imperative strategies constitute a common source for imperative newcomers. This is when a form is employed as an alternative to a dedicated command—which sounds too harsh, i.e. too 'imperative'—and then over time 'command' becomes its major meaning.

We distinguish the following recurrent pathways of development:

(i) the pathway of VOLITION: developing dedicated command forms out of desiderative and optative forms, whereby the semantics of 'wish' gets reinterpreted as 'command';

(ii) the pathway of INTENTION, FUTURE, and PREDICTION, whereby future and intentional modality are reinterpreted as commands par excellence;

(iii) the pathway of ABILITY, whereby an expression concerning being able to do something becomes a command;

(iv) the pathway of HYPOTHESIS, SUPPOSITION, and SUGGESTION, whereby subjunctive, hypothetical, and other modal forms take on the function of command;

(v) the pathway of DESUBORDINATION and INCOMPLETE SPEECH ACT, whereby an erstwhile purposive, complement, conditional, or other dependent clause becomes the major exponent of command.

The pathways of grammaticalization—from an independent verb to a marker of an imperative (often just a non-canonical one)—include verbs of motion 'COME', 'GO', and 'LEAVE, ABANDON', with an overtone of 'LET' (and see Hopper and Traugott 1993: 10–12).

Just like their positive counterparts, negative imperatives can develop out of non-imperative forms. The negative and the positive forms do not have to follow the same path. Negative imperatives tend to be less archaic than the canonical positive imperative, and not infrequently involve analytic constructions. Negative imperatives more frequently come from grammaticalization of independent verbs than do their positive counterparts. Within negative imperatives, all persons tend to have the same (relatively recent) origin.

Common sources of reinterpretation and grammaticalization of prohibitives involve NEGATIVE VOLITION, NEGATIVE POSSIBILITY, and NEGATIVE CONSEQUENCE. Prohibitives develop from grammaticalized verbs meaning 'STOP', 'STAY', 'LEAVE, ABANDON'. An expression meaning 'no good, beware' can be used as a negative imperative. So can a form meaning 'don't worry, leave it, forget it'. Copulas can give rise to prohibitive constructions. Verbs meaning 'SEE, LOOK' develop into markers of warning and of negative imperative.

Why do positive and negative imperatives develop the way they do? We have seen a number of paths of development with a straightforward semantic motivation. A warning is like a negative command. A command can be replaced with a wishful optative, to sound 'nicer'. A desubordinated dependent clause can be used as a positive command, but hardly ever as a prohibition—the overtones of an incomplete speech act suggest a pathway towards a suggestion, rather than stopping something from happening.

The semantic pathway for each of these developments is intuitively clear. And each of these paths may be specific for a language, or for a language family. Alternatively, the way imperatives develop may be triggered or enhanced by what is going on in a neighbouring language.

In intensive language contact and multilingualism, one language may evolve imperative constructions similar to those in the neighbouring languages, through grammaticalizing verbs and reinterpreting existing morphemes. This is what we saw in Chapter 11: Tariana, the only Arawak language in the multilingual Vaupés River Basin linguistic area, has developed numerous imperative forms, to mirror the distinctions obligatorily expressed in the languages from the East Tucanoan family, with which it is in constant contact. In a situation of intensive language contact involving Nivkh, imperatives adjust to the dominant Russian patterns. In many Aboriginal languages of Australia, negative imperatives become more like English than they were traditionally. And individual one-word imperative forms easily spread from one language to the next.

Imperatives are, again, ubiquitous: the meanings associated with commands easily spread across languages in contact. A major factor behind this is the desire, and the necessity, to be able to say what one's neighbour can say—making 'the categories existing in the languages that are in contact mutually compatible and more readily intertranslatable' (Heine and Kuteva

2003: 561). Frequency is a major facilitating factor in linguistic diffusion: the more frequent the category in one language, the likelier it is to diffuse into another.

Another facilitating factor here is the impact a category has on cultural norms and behavioural requirements. Knowing how to phrase commands, requests, invitations, and further ways of getting someone to do something is a key to successful communication. Obsolescent varieties are in the process of being replaced by the mainstream domineering languages. They tend to absorb 'foreign' ways of marking commands and requests, as part of the adaptation and succumbing to this pressure.

Directive speech acts—imperatives and non-imperatives we live by— occupy an important place in our day-to-day life. Phrasing a command or a request in an inappropriate way may result in breakdown of communication. Understanding and applying cultural conventions in learning the subtle over-tones of telling someone else what to do without threatening them or losing face yourself is crucial for putting Grice's Cooperative Principle into practice. For most of the world's societies, an in-depth investigation of these subtleties still awaits attention.

We now turn to the most urgent gaps in what we need to learn about imperatives, commands, and further directives, both negative and positive.

12.9 Imperatives and commands: how to know more

Throughout this book, we have focused on general trends and principles of imperatives and other ways of phrasing commands and related directive speech acts. At the present time, we have in-depth studies of these phenomena for just a smattering of languages. To fully understand the principles, more needs to be done. There is a number of in-depth studies of how the ways of framing requests and commands correlate with cultural requirements and ethnography of communication. Studies of Arapaho, Ilongot, Malagasy, and a few others are examples to follow. There are hardly any studies of this type for languages and cultures of New Guinea and South America, to name just two regions.

Imperatives are a world of their own. But there is some evidence that they may share properties with interrogatives, setting the two aside from declaratives (see examples in §3.4). The nature of similarities between non-declarative speech acts, as opposed to declaratives, is worth looking at in depth, based on facts of languages.

Social changes accompany changes in the use and the ways of framing imperative constructions. The question is: how? This is one of the urgent tasks for language analysts, grammarians and sociolinguists alike.

Child language acquisition of imperatives and commands—especially imperative strategies and conventions—also requires more in-depth studies. By and large, we lack investigations on child language acquisition in minority languages. We have hardly any information concerning how tense and aspect in imperatives are acquired, both in languages with millions of speakers and in minority languages—those that turn out to be full of intricate grammatical complexities. Schieffelin (1985) is a notable exception: her study of Kaluli, and the acquisition of immediate and delayed imperative, could be taken as a paradigm example of the work to be done.

Areal diffusion and the spread of imperatives in language contact, and their fate in language obsolescence, is another area which urgently requires further investigation.

If a language does not have a dedicated imperative paradigm, how are commands expressed? And what are command-specific extensions of morphological markers? What exactly is imperative intonation like? Only careful fieldwork-based investigation can help us understand these and further questions.

To summarize: imperatives and the ways of phrasing directives offer a fertile ground for collaborative research for scholars from all walks of linguistics—synchronic language analysts, historical linguists, typologists, sociolinguists, psycholinguists, and anthropological linguists. There is a treasure chest for projects in core areas of linguistics and cross-disciplinary studies. The most important and urgent task, however, is to pursue descriptive language analysis in the first place, combined with close attention to cultural conventions and ways of saying things. This, naturally, marginalizes artificial methods—elicitation and work with restricted corpora which fail to show the life of a real language as it is used by the speakers in their life and strife.

This book covers only a fraction of what is out there in the world of languages. The Appendix offers a resource for fieldworkers and all language analysts interested in how to know more, and how languages work, pointing towards questions to be addressed in their analysis of directive speech acts. These will provide a basis for further detailed studies of directives in languages of all sorts, including those previously undocumented or scarcely documented. And then we may hope to achieve a better understanding of the mechanisms of human cognition and communication.

Appendix
Imperatives and commands—how to know more: a checklist for fieldworkers

This checklist is included here to help linguists know more about imperatives, commands, and other directives in a language they are working on. These points to be addressed can be used by field linguists working on previously undescribed or insufficiently documented languages, and also by those who work on better-known languages, concentrating on subtle details of use which have not been accounted for before. This is by no means a questionnaire. Rather, this is a reminder of what kind of features need to be described, analysed, and illustrated, for an in-depth view of directives in a given language.

1. What to learn first, and the nature of sources

To provide a sensible analysis of imperatives, commands, and directive speech acts in general, one needs to have a pretty good idea of the overall structure of the grammar of the language as a whole. This applies to a study of any grammatical category and any semantic distinction, not just to imperatives. Without knowing what the word classes are and how they differ from each other and what properties distinguish different clause types, a study of imperatives, commands, directives, and so on is bound to be impoverished and biased.

A note on the nature of sources. If your work is based on original fieldwork, the major principle is to avoid too much straight elicitation. Ideally, the sources on the language should be mostly based on participant-observation in the speech community and on natural narratives. To understand how imperatives and commands are used under various circumstances in day-to-day life, one needs to observe the language in its spontaneous use. Gossip, casual remarks, or overheard conversations often provide many more enlightening clues than narrated stories. That is, if a language has a complex system of imperatives and commands and your grammar of it is based only on the analysis of traditional texts, some of the complexities and subtleties of expression may well be missed. The same applies to corpora—even a well-constructed corpus will not cover everything you may want to know. We have no other choice but a closed corpus for those languages which are no longer spoken. However, for a well-spoken language the attitude 'we do not need your native speakers' intuition, our corpora are good enough' constitutes a sure path to lopsided and ultimately primitive results.

Any artificial stimuli—such as video clips, especially in traditional communities—should be employed with great care, if at all. Dixon (2007) and Mithun (2007) offer further suggestions on how to do fieldwork, and to provide scientific documentation of languages. We try to understand the language as it is spoken in its own environment. As Mithun (2007) puts it, 'documenting the language as it is used for speakers in various settings from everyday conversation to formal oratory' is the priority. Let the language and the culture talk to you rather than you making them say what you want them to say!

We now turn to the checklist: which points one should not forget to address when analysing and describing imperatives and other ways of phrasing and framing commands.

2. Expressing imperatives

We start with the crucial question: how are imperatives marked? Does the language have a special paradigm for the imperative mood? What are the criteria for recognizing a form or a construction as imperative?

For instance, does the language have a special imperative inflection? If there is an imperative inflection, does it have similarities with other inflections (for instance, future or irrealis)? What morphological system does it belong to? Some languages have a mood system, with choices for interrogative, imperative, and declarative moods, and others may place imperative marking in the same system with tense-aspect and modality markers.

Does the language have special particles which mark imperatives? Are there imperative-specific forms of personal pronouns? Do imperatives differ from other clauses in their intonation? If they do, describe the intonation contours as fully as you can.

If the language does not have a set of imperative forms, which are the forms conventionally used to express commands? These could include future, irrealis, conditional, or declarative, perhaps with a command-specific intonation contour.

Are there any limitations on the subject of an imperative clause? Are second person imperatives—canonical imperatives—marked differently from imperatives with first and third person addressees (if, indeed, these are allowed)? Do all person forms of the addressee have the same meanings, or can person-specific meanings be distinguished? For instance, a command addressed at a first person may have permissive overtones, or be used as a turn-taking device. Does a command addressed to first person plural have to have an inclusive reference (us including you)? Does the generalization formulated in Diagram 2.1 apply to the language?

Does the language have suppletive imperatives? If so, what semantic fields do they cover? Can canonical and non-canonical imperatives have suppletive forms?

What further features make imperatives special in the language? In some languages, special phonological processes may apply to imperatives and to no other forms. In others, imperatives may have their own constituent order—the verb tends to come first. Do some particles or further forms have different meanings in imperatives and in statements or questions?

Chapter 2, 'Imperatives worldwide', and Chapter 3, 'How imperatives are special', provide information from a variety of languages relevant for these issues.

3. Grammatical categories of imperatives

After the major properties of imperative forms and constructions have been identified, the next step is to establish what grammatical categories imperatives have in the language.

How are grammatical categories of number, gender, tense, evidentiality, aspect, and voice expressed in imperatives? In some languages, an imperative inflection forms one system with tense–aspect choices, and so no tense or aspect specification is available in imperatives. In other languages, imperative belongs to a different system, and some aspectual meanings can be expressed, such as punctual and durative. What are the aspectual meanings expressed in imperatives in the language? Can the imperative co-occur with irrealis, future, or past tense? If so, what are the imperative-specific overtones? In some languages, imperfective aspect in imperative constructions sounds politer than perfective. Irrealis may also be a way to express a polite command. A past imperative may have overtones of 'you shouldn't have done it'.

Or perhaps imperative in the language has its own aspect contrasts not found in statements or questions, for instance, 'Keep doing it!' versus 'Do it!'

Is there a way of expressing delayed or future imperative, as opposed to that of immediate imperative? Languages with several futures in statements tend to have just one delayed imperative, but there are exceptions to this. Is the language one of these?

Does the language express distance in space in imperatives ('do here', 'do there', 'do over there')? How does distance in space in imperatives interrelate with distance in space in other categories, for instance, demonstratives?

If the language has grammaticalized expression of information source or evidentiality, it may well express some of the meanings in imperatives. A typical meaning expressed is 'reported', and it usually implies a command by proxy, 'do on someone else's behalf, or order'. Reported evidential in imperative constructions may have specific extensions to do with politeness.

Markers of modality ('maybe', 'possibly', and so on) and of reality status may occur in imperatives, albeit with imperative-specific meanings: to do with making commands sound milder or stronger, or to express politeness. Further markers—including words meaning 'a bit' and diminutives—may acquire imperative-specific extensions. It is important to provide an exhaustive account of these.

How are grammatical relations marked in imperative constructions? In some languages, the object of an imperative is marked differently from that of questions and statements.

Can the imperative be formed on any verb in the language? Does the language have different forms for imperatives of transitive and intransitive verbs? In some languages there are no imperatives of copula verbs, or of stative verbs, or of verbs referring to weather, or of passives. In others, only verbs which express controlled action can form imperatives; so, some languages have no imperative of the verb 'hear' but do have one of the verb 'listen'. Or a verb which refers to an uncontrolled action in a statement or a question is reinterpreted in a command as referring to something one can control.

How do imperatives correlate with the form of the verb? Do distinctions between verbal conjugations get neutralized in the imperative? Does imperative have scope over one complex predicate, or does every component have to be marked separately?

Can one consider imperative in the language to be more or less complex morphologically than a corresponding declarative form?

Chapter 3, 'How imperatives are special', and Chapter 4, 'Imperatives and other grammatical categories', provide information from a variety of languages relevant for these issues.

4. Negative imperatives or prohibitives

The next question is: how does polarity interact with imperative? How are negative imperatives marked? How does their marking relate to the marking of positive imperatives and that of negative declaratives? Some languages have a special prohibitive negative particle, others employ a declarative negative particle accompanying a special prohibitive form, or a plain imperative form. Can prohibitive be considered a separate clause type? Is there any special 'prohibitive' intonation?

How are categories found in declaratives and in positive imperatives expressed in prohibitives? There can be the same person distinctions as in declaratives and in positive imperatives as in prohibitives. Or the distinctions can be different. How are verbal arguments marked in prohibitives? Are there any correlations between the verb's transitivity and its use in prohibitives?

If the imperative distinguishes aspect, tense, and distance in space, does the prohibitive have the same distinctions? In some languages, such distinctions are neutralized in prohibitives. In others, prohibitives appear to be richer in forms than imperatives.

Can any verb occur in a negative imperative? In many languages—including English—it is more natural to use verbs expressing non-controlled actions in negative imperatives than in positive commands. Is this also the case in your language of study?

Is it possible to say that prohibitive in the language is more or less complex than the corresponding negative declarative? How does the prohibitive compare to positive imperative in terms of complexity?

Chapter 5, '"Don't do it": a vista of negative imperatives', provides information from a variety of languages relevant for these issues.

5. Semantics of imperatives

If the language has more than one imperative form, what are the semantic distinctions expressed? For instance, is there any special way of marking permissive, apprehensive ('lest'), or varying degrees of 'strength'?

Is politeness reflected in the imperative, and if so, how? It is always useful to try and explain conditions of the use of each form in terms of intrapersonal relations, age, social hierarchies and such-like? (This requires a substantial knowledge of the community life and relationships within it.)

Are imperatives used to express wishes, entreaties, requests, pleas, advice, recommendations, warnings, instructions, invitations, permissions, good wishes, and imprecations (see the array of meanings of the English imperatives illustrated in 6.1–11)?

What means other than imperatives are employed in the language to express meanings associated with wishes, entreaties, and the like?

Do prohibitives have the same semantic distinctions as positive imperatives? How is politeness and strength of command expressed in prohibitives (if at all)? If imperatives distinguish honorifics, do prohibitives do so too?

Do the generalizations apply both to canonical and to non-canonical imperatives?

Chapter 6, 'Imperatives and their meanings', provides information from a variety of languages relevant for these issues.

6. Non-command meanings of imperatives

Do any of the imperatives and/or prohibitives have non-command meanings? In many languages, imperatives—negative and positive—have overtones of concessives and conditionals when used in complex sentences. Imperatives of all sorts frequently occur in speech formulae, such as blessings or farewells. Imperatives are often used in imprecations. They may be a feature of a vivid narrative. An imperative may or may not be used as a reply to a question or to a command.

Are there any conventional strategies for replying to an imperative?

Do prohibitives share any non-command meanings of positive imperatives? Do they have additional meanings of their own?

Chapter 7, 'Imperatives which do not command', provides information from a variety of languages relevant for these issues.

7. Imperative strategies: imperatives in disguise

In some languages, plain imperatives sound too abrupt and rude. Non-imperative forms can then be used instead. Can any non-imperative structures be used in commands in the language of your study? What is their function, and what are their semantic and pragmatic overtones? In some languages, a future form may be used as a polite command.

Can questions be used as directives? If so, do these include both content and polar questions? Do negative questions have more or less polite overtones?

Can declarative statements be used as directives? In many languages, statements cast in future, or irrealis, or an epistemic modality ('maybe') can be used as more or less polite commands, depending on the language.

Does the language employ desubordinated clauses in lieu of imperatives, as commands, in the spirit of free *if*-clauses in English? Can nominalizations—converbs, deverbal nouns, and the like—be used as commands? What are their connotations?

Does the language employ the same types of structure for negative as for positive imperatives? What are the similarities and what are the differences?

Chapter 8, 'Imperatives in disguise', provides information from a variety of languages relevant for these issues.

8. Imperatives in real life

How is the imperative used in real-life interaction? Are imperatives more frequent in some genres than in others? Are there types of addressee to whom imperatives are used most frequently? For instance, many grammars note that abrupt, impolite, or familiar imperatives and command strategies can be appropriate when addressing children, but are avoided when addressing elders.

Does the use of imperatives correlate with existing (traditional or contemporary) social hierarchies? What are the social factors governing the use of varied command strategies with different overtones (if any)?

If the society in which the language is spoken has undergone a recent change, it is important to try and find out if the social repercussions have had any effect on the use of imperatives and other command forms. For instance, the loss of traditional hierarchies may result in the loss of some specific honorific registers and imperative structures.

Does the language have any specific imperative words? Some languages have special, interjection-like forms to encourage giving, or for driving specific animals away. How do these correlate semantically with other types of imperative (for instance, they may be more colloquial, or more impolite than other imperatives). Does the language have any additional ways of marking imperatives and commands outside the verb, e.g. with vocative forms of nouns or interjections?

Chapter 9, 'Imperatives we live by', provides information from a variety of languages relevant for these issues.

9. Where do imperatives come from?

Can you say anything about the historical origin of positive and negative imperatives? One expects canonical imperatives to be more archaic than non-canonical ones. Does this apply to your language of study? Are there any instances of grammaticalization of lexical verbs and or reanalysis of non-imperative constructions in the history of the language?

Can you say anything about imperatives and commands in (i) genetically related and/or (ii) geographically contiguous languages in contact? If there are similarities, are they due to shared genetic inheritance, areal diffusion, or independent innovation?

Chapter 10 'Where do imperatives come from?', and Chapter 11, 'Imperatives in contact', provide information from a variety of languages relevant for these issues.

Glossary of terms

This short glossary explicates the ways in which some core linguistic terms are used throughout this book within the context of problems linked to imperatives and commands. The definitions here are based, among other sources, on Matthews (1997), Dixon's glossaries (1980: 510–14; 2010: i. 331–41, ii. 442–32), and glossaries in Aikhenvald (2004: 391–4) and Aikhenvald and Dixon (2006: 333–6). If a term is polysemous, I only include the meaning in which it is used within this book. For instance, 'directive' can refer to (a) a speech act by which speakers direct and order actions by other or (b) to a directional marker. Only meaning (a) is relevant for the present volume.

Where appropriate, I give the number of a section where a particular point is discussed in detail. Complementary terms are marked as Compl. Synonyms are marked as Syn.

A   subject of a transitive verb.

ABSOLUTIVE   case inflection marking intransitive subject (S) and transitive object (O). Compl. ERGATIVE.

ACCUSATIVE   case inflection marking transitive object (O). Compl. NOMINATIVE.

ACTIVE VERB   a verb whose subject is agentive and may control the action. Compl. STATIVE VERB.

AGGLUTINATIVE   a type of language where words are easily segmentable into a sequence of morphemes, each of which typically conveys one meaning.

AGREEMENT   when two words in a syntactic construction (e.g. a noun and modifying adjective within a noun phrase) are marked for the same grammatical category. For instance, gender (an inherent category for the noun and an agreement category for the adjective).

ANALYTIC   a type of language where words realize grammatical distinctions marked by bound morphemes in synthetic languages. Compl. SYNTHETIC.

ANTIPASSIVE   valency-reducing derivation which puts the underlying A (transitive subject) argument into derived S (intransitive subject) function, and places the underlying O argument in a peripheral function (§4.4.2).

APHASIA   loss or impairment of speech as a result of brain disease or physical damage to the brain.

APPLICATIVE   valency-increasing derivation which can operate on an intransitive clause, putting the underlying S argument into A function and introducing a new O argument (which may have been in peripheral function—instrumental, comitative, beneficiary, etc.—in the underlying clause, or on a transitive verb, whereby a new O argument is co-opted from a peripheral argument, and either the underlying O assumes a peripheral function or the verb becomes ditransitive.

APPREHENSIVE   clause or a verbal form whose meaning is 'for fear that, lest (such and such thing should happen)'.

ARGUMENT, CORE   an obligatory argument for a specific verb which must be either explicitly stated or recoverable from the context.

ARGUMENT, PERIPHERAL   non-core argument, which is optional; typical non-core arguments include instrument, accompaniment, recipient, beneficiary, time, place, manner.

ASPECT   verbal category which covers composition of an event (perfective versus imperfective); sometimes also covers boundedness and completion.

ATELIC   an event which is unbounded and has no end-point. Compl. TELIC.

AUXILIARY   verb from a small closed class which accompanies another verb from an open class carrying grammatical specifications. An auxiliary (sometimes also called auxiliary verb) typically inflects for tense or aspect, instead of the verb inflecting for these categories.

AVERSIVE   case whose meaning is to refer to something for fear of which the action described by the verb should or should not take place, e.g. 'Don't go there for fear of ghosts'.

BORROWING   transfer of linguistic features of any kind from one language to another as the result of contact. (Borrowing of forms is also known as direct diffusion, and borrowing of patterns as indirect diffusion: Heath 1978; Aikhenvald 2002.)

BOUND FORM   form which cannot occur on its own but must occur attached to another form, e.g. prefix *in-* or suffix *-ing* in English. Compl. FREE FORM.

CANONICAL IMPERATIVES   imperatives with second person addressee.

CASE   a system of nominal inflection marking the syntactic function of a noun phrase in a clause.

CAUSATIVE   valency-increasing derivation introducing a causer as an A-argument.

CLASSIFIERS   a set of free or bound forms categorizing the referents of the noun in terms of their sex, shape, composition, arrangement, and so on (Aikhenvald 2006d).

CLITIC   a morpheme which cannot form a phonological word but may be able to form a grammatical word, with special phonological properties different from those of both an affix and an independent word.

COMPLEMENT CLAUSE   a special clause type whose exclusive function is to occupy the argument slot of a main verb.

CONDITIONAL   a grammatical form marking a clause expressing condition, or a clause containing a condition.

CONJUNCT/DISJUNCT   person-marking on the verb whereby first person subject in statements is expressed in the same way as second person in questions (conjunct), and all other persons are marked in a different way (disjunct). (Also used to describe cross-clausal co-reference). Syn. LOCUTOR/NON-LOCUTOR and congruent/ noncongruent.

CONSTITUENT   a word, a construction or a phrase that fills a slot in syntactic structure.

CONSTITUENT ORDER   the order in which phrasal constituents occur in a clause. This is often confused with WORD ORDER.

CONTINUOUS   an event or a process viewed as continuing over an appreciable period of time. Syn. DURATIVE.

CONVERB   a non-finite verb form marking adverbial subordination (Haspelmath 1995).

COPULA   a form (often a verb) which indicates a relationship between the copula subject and the copula complement, as the verb *be* in English *He is a plagiarist.*

COPULA CLAUSE   a clause with a relational meaning between the copula subject and the copula complement.

CORE ARGUMENT   an obligatory argument for a specific verb which must be either explicitly stated or recoverable from the context.

CORE MEANING   main and default meaning of a category or a lexical item. Syn. main meaning. Compl. EXTENSION OF MEANING.

DEBITIVE   modality indicating obligation. Syn. DEONTIC.

DECLARATIVE   a mood used in statements.

DEICTIC   category related to DEIXIS.

DEIXIS   the ways in which the reference of an element is determined with respect to speaker, addressee, or temporal and spatial setting, typically involving pointing.

DELAYED IMPERATIVE   a command 'do later'. See also DISTANCE IN TIME.

DEONTIC   form or category expressing obligation or recommendation.

DEPENDENT CLAUSE   a clause constituting a syntactic element within another clause.

DESUBORDINATION   a process whereby a subordinate clause acquires the status of a main clause. Syn. INSUBORDINATION.

DIFFUSION   is the spread of a linguistic feature within a geographical area or between languages. Diffusion can be unilateral (where A affects B) or multilateral (where A affects B in some ways and B affects A in others).

DIRECTIVE   speech act by which speakers direct and order actions by others.

DISJUNCT   opposite of conjunct; see CONJUNCT/DISJUNCT.

DISTANCE IN SPACE   an imperative-specific category with the meaning of 'do (something) here (or near the speaker/addressee)' or 'do (something) there (or far from speaker/addressee)'.

DISTANCE IN TIME   an imperative-specific category with the meaning of 'do (something) now' or 'do (something) later'. See also DELAYED IMPERATIVE; IMMEDIATE IMPERATIVE.

DURATIVE   an event or a process viewed as continuing over an appreciable period of time. Syn. CONTINUOUS.

ENCLITIC   clitic attached at the end of a phonological word.

EPISTEMIC   (a) as a philosophical term: relating to knowledge or the degree of its validation; (b) as a linguistic term: indicating necessity, probability or possibility. See also EPISTEMIC MEANINGS.

EPISTEMIC MEANINGS   meanings of (a) possibility or probability of an event or (b) the reliability of information.

EPISTEMIC MODALITY   modality associated with epistemic meanings.

ERGATIVE   case inflection marking transitive subject (A). Compl: ABSOLUTIVE.

EVIDENTIAL, EVIDENTIALITY   grammatical marking of information source. Syn. INFORMATION SOURCE.

EXCLUSIVE   non-singular first person pronoun referring to the speaker and one or more other people who do not include the addressee. Compl. INCLUSIVE.

EXTENSION OF MEANING   additional meaning of a category or a lexical item realized under particular circumstances. Compl. CORE MEANING.

FACE   the public 'self-image' that every member of a society wants to claim for themselves, associated with politeness (Brown and Levinson 1987: 61, 70). See also POSITIVE FACE; NEGATIVE FACE.

FOCUS   a grammatical mechanism for marking an element or part of a clause for prominence, or contrast, or as new information.

FORMAL MARKEDNESS   a term in a grammatical system which has zero realization— or a zero allomorph—is said to be formally unmarked.

FREE FORM   a form which can occur on its own and then constitutes a grammatical word.

FUNCTIONAL MARKEDNESS   a term in a grammatical system which is used as a generic cover term or, in underspecified context, is said to be functionally unmarked.

FUSIONAL   a type of language whose words consist of morphemes which are 'fused' together and are not segmentable.

GENDER   small closed system of agreement classes whose semantics involves sex (masculine, feminine, neuter), animacy, humanness, and rationality. Membership must be marked outside the noun itself (within the noun phrase or on the verb). Syn. NOUN CLASS. See Aikhenvald (2006d).

GERUND   a nominalized form of a verb, similar to CONVERB.

GRAMMATICAL ACCOMMODATION   involves a change in meaning of a morphological marker or a syntactic construction based on superficial segmental similarity with a marker or a construction in a different language.

GRAMMATICAL MEANING   a meaning which must be expressed in a given language (Boas 1938: 132).

GRAMMATICAL WORD   a unit within the hierarchy of grammatical units defined on grammatical criteria. See Dixon and Aikhenvald (2002).

GRAMMATICALIZATION   process whereby an item with lexical status changes into an item with grammatical status (§10.2.2; Heine and Kuteva 2002). A typical example of grammaticalization is the verb 'finish' becoming a marker for 'completed' aspect. Grammaticalization necessarily involves reanalysis (see Harris and Campbell 1995: 92).

HEARSAY   information known through verbal report. Syn. REPORTED EVIDENTIAL; SECONDHAND.

HORTATIVE   command addressed to first person. Syn. ADHORTATIVE; EXHORTATIVE.

IMMEDIATE IMPERATIVE   a command 'do immediately'. See also DISTANCE IN TIME.

IMPERATIVE   a mood used in commands.

IMPERATIVE, CANONICAL   imperatives with second person addressee.

IMPERATIVE, NON-CANONICAL   imperatives with a non-second person addressee.

IMPERATIVE STRATEGY   a form other than that of imperative mood employed as a command in lieu of the imperative mood.

IMPERFECT   an event which began in the past and is still continuing.

IMPERFECTIVE ASPECT   a verbal form used to refer to actions extending over a period of time, or continuously.

INCLUSIVE   non-singular first person pronoun referring to the speaker and one or more other people including the addressee. Compl. EXCLUSIVE.

INDIRECT SPEECH   reporting of what someone else has said by adapting deictic categories (e.g. person) to the viewpoint of the reporter. Compl. DIRECT SPEECH.

INTONATION   type of prosody realized by pitch, which generally applies to a clause or a sentence.

IRREALIS   verbal form referring to hypothetical events and/or something that has not happened. Compl. REALIS. See Elliott (2000).

ISOLATING   a type of language in which most grammatical words consist of one morpheme.

JUSSIVE   command addressed to third person.

LANGUAGE OBSOLESCENCE   a process whereby language gradually falls into disuse.

LENITION   the replacement of a sound by another sound with the same place of articulation but a weaker manner of articulation (see §11.1.2 for a lenited gerund in Scots Gaelic).

LINGUISTIC AREA   a geographically delimited area including languages from two or more language families sharing significant traits (most of which are not found in languages from these families spoken outside the area). Syn. SPRACHBUND.

LOCUTOR/NON-LOCUTOR   person-marking on the verb whereby first person subject in statements is expressed in the same way as second person in questions (conjunct), and all other persons are marked in a different way (disjunct). (Also used to describe cross-clausal co-reference). Syn. CONJUNCT/DISJUNCT and CONGRUENT/NONCONGRUENT.

MAXIMS OF CONVERSATION   a set of principles of conversation and implicatures advanced by Grice (1989). See §9.5 and §12.7.

MIRATIVE   grammatical marking of 'unprepared mind', including unexpected and also surprising information.

MODAL VERB   a verb with epistemic or deontic meaning.

MODALITY   grammatical category covering the degree of certainty of a statement (EPISTEMIC), obligation (DEONTIC), and permission. This should not be confused with MOOD.

MOOD   grammatical category expressing a speech act (e.g. statement: indicative mood; question: interrogative mood; command: imperative mood). Sometimes defined as a category which 'characterizes the actuality of the event' (Chung and Timberlake 1985: 241).

NEGATIVE FACE   a type of behaviour associated with 'the basic claim to territories'— 'freedom of action and freedom from imposition' (Brown and Levinson 1987: 61). See also POSITIVE FACE; FACE.

NOMINALIZATION   morphological derivation which forms a noun from a verb, an adjective, or a word of another word class.

NOMINATIVE   case inflection marking intransitive subject (S) and transitive subject (A). Compl. ACCUSATIVE.

NON-CANONICAL IMPERATIVE   imperatives with a non-second person addressee.

NON-VISUAL EVIDENTIAL   information source involving hearing, smelling, feeling, and sometimes also touching something.

NOUN CLASS   closed system of agreement classes whose semantics involves sex (masculine, feminine, neuter), animacy, humanness, shape, etc. Noun class membership must be marked outside the noun itself (within the noun phrase or on the verb). See Aikhenvald (2006d). Syn. GENDER.

NOUN PHRASE (NP)   a constituent which can fill an argument slot in a clause.

NUMBER   grammatical system referring to the quantity of referents, one of whose terms is singular.

OPTATIVE   a grammatical form whose main meaning is to express wishes.

PASSIVE   valency-reducing derivation which puts underlying O (direct object) argument in derived S (intransitive subject) function and places underlying A (transitive subject) argument in a peripheral function.

PERFECT   a verbal form focusing on the results of an action or process, thus relating a past event to the present. An event or a process is then viewed as completed in the past but still relevant for the present.

PERFECTIVE ASPECT   a verbal form which specifies that the event is regarded as a whole, without respect for its temporal constituency (even though it may be extended in time). Compl. IMPERFECTIVE ASPECT.

PERIPHERAL ARGUMENT   non-core argument, which is optional; typical non-core arguments include instrument, accompaniment, recipient, beneficiary, time, place, manner.

PHONOLOGICAL WORD   a unit in the hierarchy of phonological units defined on the basis of phonological criteria, typically including stress and tone. See Dixon and Aikhenvald (2002).

POLARITY   grammatical system whose terms are negative and positive.

POLYSYNTHETIC   a highly synthetic language.

POSITIVE FACE   a positive image claimed by interactants (Brown and Levinson 1987: 61, 70). Also see NEGATIVE FACE; FACE.

POTENTIAL   a grammatical form whose main meaning is to express possibility.

PRAGMATICS   meanings created by the context of use.

PROCLITIC   clitic attached at the beginning of a phonological word.

PROSODY   rhythm and intonation in speech; non-segmental features of sounds; also used to refer to a system of phonological contrasts which has scope over a sequence of segments.

PROTOLANGUAGE   putative ancestor language for a group of modern languages proved to be genetically related, with each having developed by regular changes from the protolanguage.

PUNCTUAL   an action which happens instantaneously. PUNCTUAL IMPERATIVE refers to punctual action.

REALIS   a category which encompasses real events or states, which have happened or are happening. Compl. IRREALIS. See Elliott (2000).

REALITY STATUS   a grammatical category covering REALIS and IRREALIS.

REANALYSIS   a historical process by which a morphosyntactic device comes to be assigned a different structure from that which it had, without necessarily changing its surface form and with little change to its semantics. For instance, in Udi a number of verbs—which originally contained noun class agreement markers—were reanalysed as simple stems, as part of the process of losing the noun class system (see §10.2.2; Harris and Campbell 1995: 66–7).

RECIPROCAL   a category referring to an activity in which an A argument acts on the O argument and vice versa.

REDUPLICATION   morphological process which involves repeating all or part of the root or stem of a word before, after, or in the middle of it.

REFLEXIVE   a category or a clause where underlying A and O arguments have the same reference.

REINTERPRETATION   (or extension) is a change in the surface manifestation of a pattern 'which does not involve immediate or intrinsic modification of underlying structure' (Harris and Campbell 1995: 97). Reanalysis most often occurs together with reinterpretation. Examples of reinterpretation without reanalysis involve 'a shift in the categorial status of a linguistic form resulting from its occurrence in ambiguous positions'. For instance, the English noun *fun* has been reinterpreted as an adjective, leading to its use in contexts like *This is a fun game* (§10.2.2; Trask 2000: 274, 280).

REPORTED EVIDENTIAL   a marker of information source; that is, an evidential whose main meaning is marking what has been learnt from someone else's verbal report. Syn. HEARSAY; SECONDHAND.

RESULTATIVE   a verbal form referring to the results of an action or a process.

S   subject of an intransitive verb.

SCOPE   the part of a sentence or clause with which an imperative (or a negation marker) combines in meaning (cf. Matthews 1997: 331).

SECONDHAND   (a) based on verbal report from someone who said it (as opposed to THIRDHAND); (b) same as REPORTED.

SERIAL VERB CONSTRUCTION   a single predicate consisting of two or more verbs each of which could be used as a predicate on its own. A serial verb construction refers to one event and has single mood, modality, polarity, and tense/aspect value.

SPEECH ACT   an utterance 'conceived as an act by which the speaker does something' (Matthews 1997: 349). If one says *Go away!*, one performs an act of command. If one says *Who is it?*, the act is of asking a question.

STATIVE VERB   a verb referring to a state and whose subject is not agentive and does not control the state. Compl. ACTIVE.

STRATEGY, IMPERATIVE   a form other than that of imperative mood employed as a command in lieu of the imperative mood.

SUBJUNCTIVE   a grammatical form, especially in European languages, whose major meaning is 'to mark a clause as expressing something other than a statement of what is certain' (Matthews 1997: 360).

SUBORDINATE CLAUSE   Syn. DEPENDENT CLAUSE.

SUBORDINATOR   overt marker of a subordinate clause.

SUPPLETION   a morphological process in which one form replaces another in a given context; for example English *better* is a suppletive form of *good*.

SWITCH-REFERENCE   a grammatical system whereby a marker indicates whether the subject of a dependent (medial) clause is identical or not with that of the main (final) clause.

SYNTHETIC   a language whose words consist of a large number of grammatical components. Compl. ANALYTIC.

TELIC   an event which is bounded and has an end-point. Compl. ATELIC.

TENSE   grammatical category which refers to time.

TOPIC   an argument which occurs in a succession of clauses in discourse and binds them together thematically.

VALENCY   the number of core arguments required by the verb.

VALENCY-CHANGING   derivations which may increase valency (causative, applicative) or decrease it (passive, antipassive, some varieties of reciprocal and reflexive).

VERBLESS CLAUSE   similar to a copula clause but with the predicate slot left empty. It indicates a relational meaning between the verbless clause subject and the verbless clause complement.

VISUAL EVIDENTIAL   information source involving knowledge obtained through seeing something.

WORD ORDER   the order in which words occur in a phrase, or a clause, or a sentence. Distinct from (but often confused with) CONSTITUENT ORDER.

ZERO   a term with no overt marking is said to have zero realization.

References

Abbott, M. 1991. 'Macushi', pp. 23–160 of *Handbook of Amazonian languages*, vol. 1, edited by D. C. Derbyshire and G. K. Pullum. Berlin: Mouton de Gruyter.

Abe, Isamu 1972. 'Intonational patterns of English and Japanese', pp. 337–47 of *Intonation*, edited by Dwight Bolinger. Harmondsworth: Penguin Education.

Abercrombie, David 1967. *Elements of general phonetics*. Edinburgh: Edinburgh University Press.

Abondolo, Daniel 1998a. 'Finnish', pp. 149–83 of Abondolo 1998c.

——1998b. 'Khanty', pp. 358–86 of Abondolo 1998c.

——ed. 1998c. *The Uralic languages*. London: Routledge.

Adelaar, W. F. H. 1977. *Tarma Quechua: grammar, texts, dictionary*. Lisse: De Ridder.

——1987. *Morfologia del Quechua de Pacaraos*. Lima: Universidad Nacional Mayor de San Marcos.

——2004 (with Pieter Muysken). *The languages of the Andes*. Cambridge: Cambridge University Press.

Agha, Asif 1994. 'Honorification', *Annual Review of Anthropology* 23: 277–302.

Aikhenvald, A. Y. 1990. *Sovremennyj ivrit* (Modern Hebrew). Moscow: Nauka.

——1995a. *Bare*. Munich: Lincom Europa.

——1995b. 'Person-marking and discourse in North-Arawak languages', *Studia Linguistica* 49: 152–95.

——1998. 'Warekena', pp. 225–439 of *Handbook of Amazonian languages*, vol. 4, edited by D. C. Derbyshire and G. K. Pullum. Berlin: Mouton de Gruyter.

——2000. *Classifiers: a typology of noun categorization devices*. Oxford: Oxford University Press.

——2001. 'Verb types, non-canonically marked arguments and grammatical relations: a Tariana perspective', pp. 177–99 of *Non-canonical marking of subjects and objects*, edited by A. Y. Aikhenvald, R.M.W. Dixon, and M. Onishi. Amsterdam: John Benjamins.

——2002. *Language contact in Amazonia*. Oxford: Oxford University Press.

——2003. *A grammar of Tariana, from northwest Amazonia*. Cambridge: Cambridge University Press.

——2004. *Evidentiality*. Oxford: Oxford University Press.

——2006a. 'Serial verb constructions in typological perspective', pp. 1–68 of Aikhenvald and Dixon 2006.

——2006b. 'Serial verb constructions in Tariana', pp. 178–201 of Aikhenvald and Dixon 2006.

——2006c. 'Evidentiality in grammar', pp. 320–25 of *Encyclopedia of language and linguistics*, 2nd edn, edited by Keith Brown. Oxford: Elsevier.

Aikhenvald, A. Y. 2006d. 'Classifiers and noun classes, semantics', pp. 463–70 of *Encyclopedia of language and linguistics*, 2nd edn, vol. 1, edited by Keith Brown. Elsevier: Oxford.

——2006e. 'Arawak languages', pp. 446–8 of *Encyclopedia of language and linguistics*, 2nd edn, vol. 1, edited by Keith Brown. Elsevier: Oxford.

——2007a. 'Grammars in contact: a typological perspective', pp. 1–66 of Aikhenvald and Dixon 2007.

——2007b. 'Typological dimensions in word formation', pp. 1–65 of *Language typology and syntactic description*, vol. 3, *Grammatical categories and the lexicon*, edited by Timothy Shopen. Cambridge: Cambridge University Press.

——2008a. *The Manambu language from East Sepik, Papua New Guinea*. Oxford: Oxford University Press.

——2008b. 'Multilingual imperatives: the elaboration of a category in north-west Amazonia', *International Journal of American Linguistics* 74: 189–225.

——2008c. 'Semi-direct speech: Manambu and beyond', *Language Sciences* 30: 383–422.

——2008d. 'Information source and evidentiality: what can we conclude?', *Rivista di linguistica* 2007: 1, edited by Mario Squartini, special issue on *Evidentiality between lexicon and grammar*.

——2008e. 'Versatile cases', *Journal of Linguistics* 44: 565–603.

——2009a. 'Semantics of clause linking in Manambu', pp. 118–44 of *Semantics of clause linking: a cross-linguistic typology*, edited by R. M. W. Dixon and A. Y. Aikhenvald. Oxford: Oxford University Press.

——2009b. 'Semantics and grammar in clause linking', pp. 380–402 of *Semantics of clause linking: a cross-linguistic typology*, edited by R. M. W. Dixon and A. Y. Aikhenvald. Oxford: Oxford University Press.

——2011. 'Causatives which do not cause', pp. 86–142 of Alexandra Y. Aikhenvald and R. M. W. Dixon. *Language at large. Essays in semantics and syntax*. Leiden: Brill.

——2012. 'Language contact in language obsolescence', pp. 77–109 of *Dynamics of contact-induced language change*, edited by Claudine Chamoreau and Isabelle Léglise. Berlin: Mouton de Gruyter.

——MS. 'Imperatives and other commands', position paper for 2003 Local Workshop, 'Imperatives and other commands', †RCLT.

——and R. M. W. Dixon 1998. 'Dependencies between grammatical systems', *Language* 74: 56–80.

————eds. 2006. *Serial verb constructions: a cross-linguistic typology*. Oxford: Oxford University Press.

————eds. 2007. *Grammars in contact: a cross-linguistic typology*. Oxford: Oxford University Press.

————2011. 'Explaining associations between intransitive subject (S) and transitive object (O)', pp. 143–69 of Alexandra Y. Aikhenvald and R. M. W. Dixon. *Language at large. Essays in semantics and syntax*. Leiden: Brill.

——and Tonya N. Stebbins 2007. 'Languages of New Guinea', pp. 239–66 of *Vanishing languages of the Pacific*, edited by O. Miyaoka, O. Sakiyama, and M. Krauss. Oxford: Oxford University Press.

Akalu, Aster 1985. *Beyond morals? Experiences of living the life of the Ethiopian Nuer.* Lund: Gleerup.

Akatsuka, N. 1986. 'Conditionals are discourse-based', pp. 333–51 of Traugott et al. 1986.

Albert, Ethel M. 1972. 'Culture patterning of speech behavior in Burundi', pp. 72–105 of *Directions in sociolinguistics: the ethnography of communication*, edited by John J. Gumpertz and Dell Hymes. New York: Holt, Rinehart & Winston.

Alcázar, Asier, and Mario Saltarelli, forthcoming. 'Untangling the imperative puzzle', *Papers from the 44th Regional Meeting of the Chicago Linguistics Society.*

Allan, Keith, and Kate Burridge 2006. *Forbidden words: taboo and the censoring of language.* Cambridge: Cambridge University Press.

Allan, R., P. Holmes, and T. Lundskær-Nielsen 1995. *Danish: a comprehensive grammar.* London: Routledge.

Alpatov, V. M. 1992. 'Imperativ v sovremennom japonskom jazyke', pp. 77–88 of *Tipologija imperativnykh konstrukcij* (The typology of imperative constructions), edited by V. S. Xrakovskij. St Petersburg: Nauka.

——and V. I. Podlesskaya 1995. 'Converbs in Japanese', pp. 465–85 of *Converbs in cross-linguistic perspective*, edited by M. Haspelmath and E. König. Berlin: Mouton de Gruyter.

Amberber, M. 1997a. 'A grammatical summary of Amharic', †RCLT internal document, Australian National University.

——1997b. 'A grammatical summary of Koasati', †RCLT internal document, Australian National University.

—— 1997c. 'A grammatical summary of Jacaltec.' †RCLT internal document, ANU.

Ameka, Felix 1992. 'Interjections: the universal yet neglected part of speech', *Journal of Pragmatics* 18: 101–18.

Amha, A. 2001. *The Maale language.* Leiden: CNWS.

——MS-a. 'Verbal subject-agreement and modality distinction in Zargulla'.

——MS-b. 'Directives to humans and directives to domestic animals: the imperative and some interjections in Zargulla'.

——forthcoming. 'Omotic languages'.

Andersen, T. 1988. 'Ergativity in Päri, a Nilotic OVS language', *Lingua* 75: 289–324.

Anderson, Stephen 1979. 'Verb structure', pp. 73–136 of *Aghem grammatical structure with special reference to noun classes, tense-aspect and focus marking*, edited by Larry M. Hyman. Los Angeles: Department of Linguistics, University of Southern California.

——and Edward L. Keenan 1985. 'Deixis', pp. 259–308 of *Language typology and syntactic description*, volume 2: *Grammatical categories and the lexicon*, edited by Timothy Shopen. Cambridge: Cambridge University Press.

Arbini, R. 1969. 'Tag-questions and tag-imperatives in English', *Journal of Linguistics* 5: 193–220.

Ariel, Mira 2008. *Pragmatics and grammar.* Cambridge: Cambridge University Press.

Armellada, F. C. de, and J. Olza 1999. *Gramática de la lengua Pemón (Morfosintaxis).* Caracas: Publicaciones Universidad Católica Andrés Bello.

Arvaniti, Amalia, and Maria Baltazani 2005. 'Intonational analysis and prosodic annotation of Greek spoken corpora', pp. 84–117 of *Prosodic typology: the phonology of intonation and phrasing,* edited by Sun-Ah Jun. Oxford: Oxford University Press.

Ascoli, C. 1978. 'Some pseudo-imperatives and their communicative function in English', *Folia Linguistica* 12: 405–16.

Asher, R. E. 1985. *Tamil.* London: Croom Helm.

——and T. C. Kumari 1997. *Malayalam.* London: Routledge.

Aspinion, Robert 1953. *Aprenons le bebère: initiation aux dialectes chleuhs.* Rabat: Editions Félix Moncho.

Austin, P. 1978. 'A grammar of the Diyari language of north-east South Australia'. PhD dissertation, ANU, Canberra.

——1981. *A grammar of Diyari, South Australia.* Cambridge: Cambridge University Press.

Avrorin, V. A. 1961. *Grammatika nanajskogo jazyka* (Grammar of the Nanai language), vol. 2. Moscow-Leningrad: Izdateljstvo Akademii Nauk SSSR.

——and E. P. Lebedeva 1968. 'Orochskij jazyk', pp. 191–209 of *Jazyki narodov SSSR,* vol. 5, edited by V. V. Vinogradov et al. Leningrad: Nauka.

Axtell, Roger E. 1993. *Do's and taboos around the world.* New York: John Wiley and Sons, Inc.

Baker-Shenk, Charlotte, and Dennis Cokely 2002. *American Sign language: a teacher's resource text on grammar and culture.* Washington, DC: Gallaudet University Press.

Ball, Martin J., with James Fife 1993. *The Celtic languages.* London: Routledge.

Bani, E., and T. J. Klokeid 1972. *Kala Lagau Langgus—Yagar Yagar: the Western Torres Straits language.* Dittoed report to AIAS (mimeographed).

Baranov, A. N. 1988. 'Imperative and politeness', pp. 16–17 of Birjulin et al. 1988.

Barentsen, Adrian 2003. 'O pobuditeljnykh konstrukcijakh s ispolnitelem 1-go litsa' (On exhortative constructions with the first person executor), pp. 1–33 of *Dutch contributions to the Thirteenth International Congress of Slavists: Ljubljana, August 15–21, 2003. Linguistics.* Amsterdam: Editions Rodopi B. V.

Barnes, J. 1979. 'Los imperativos en tuyuca', *Artículos en lingüística y campos afines* 6: 87–94.

——1984. 'Evidentials in the Tuyuca verb', *International Journal of American Linguistics* 50: 255–71.

——1994. 'Tuyuca', pp. 325–42 of *Typological studies in negation,* edited by P. Kahrel and R. van den Berg. Amsterdam: John Benjamins.

——1999. 'Tucano', pp. 207–26 of *The Amazonian languages,* edited by R. M. W. Dixon and A. Y. Aikhenvald. Cambridge: Cambridge University Press.

Bashir, Elena 2003. 'Dardic', pp. 818–94 of Cardona and Jain 2003.

Basso, Ellen 2007. 'The Kalapalo affinal civilty register', *Journal of Linguistic Anthropology* 17: 161–83.

——MS. 'Kalapalo imperatives'.

Bat-El, Outi 2002. 'True truncation in colloquial Hebrew imperatives', *Language* 78: 651–83.

Bauer, W. (with W. Parker and Te kareongawai Evans) 1993. *Maori*. London: Routledge.

Baum, Daniel 2006. *The imperative in the Rigveda*. Amsterdam: LOT.

Beachy, Marvin Dean 2005. *An overview of Central Dizin phonology and morphology*. Master's thesis, University of Texas at Arlington.

Beck, David 2004. *Upper Necaxa Totonac*. Munich: Lincom Europa.

Beguinot, Francesco 1942. *Il Berbero Nefûsi di Fassâto*. Rome: Instito per l'Oriente.

Belikov, V. I. 2001. 'Imperative of authority in Russian' (Avtoritarnyj imperativ v russkom jazyke), in *Abstracts for the International Congress of Researchers of the Russian language*. http://www.philol.msu.ru/~ric2001/abstract/files/morfolog.doc.

Benacchio, Rosanna 2002. 'Konkurrencia vidov, vezhlivostj, i etiket v russkom imperative' (competition of aspects, politeness, and etiquette in Russian imperative), *Russian Linguistics* 26: 149–78.

Benmamoun, Elabbas 2000. *The feature structure of functional categories: a comparative study of Arabic dialects*. Oxford: Oxford University Press.

Benveniste, Emile 1951. 'Prétérit et optatif en indo-européen', *Bulletin de le Société de Linguistique de Paris* 47: 11–20.

Berman, Ruth 1985. 'The acquisition of Hebrew', pp. 255–372 of Slobin 1985.

Besnier, Niko 2000. *Tuvaluan*. London: Routledge.

Bhat, D. N. S. 1999. *The prominence of tense, aspect and mood*. Amsterdam: John Benjamins.

Bhatia, Tej K. 1993. *Punjabi*. London: Routledge.

Binnick, Robert I. 2002–6. Project on the bibliography of tense, verbal aspect, aktionsart, and related areas: imperative mood. MS.

Birjulin, L. A., and V. S. Xrakovskij 1992. 'Imperative sentences: problems of theory', pp. 5–50 of *Tipologija imperativnykh konstrukcij* (The typology of imperative constructions), edited by V. S. Xrakovskij. St Petersburg: Nauka.

——A. V. Bondarko, and V. S. Xrakovskij, eds. 1988. *Imperative in languages of different structures: materials for the conference on 'Functional and typological trends in grammar: Imperativity'*. Leningrad: Academy of Sciences of USSR.

Bliese, Loren F. 1981. *A generative grammar of Afar*. Arlington: SIL and University of Texas at Arlington.

Bloomfield, Leonard 1933. *Language*. New York: Holt, Rinehart & Winston.

——1962. *The Menomini language*. New Haven, CT: Yale University Press.

Blust, Robert 2009. *The Austronesian languages*. Canberra: Pacific Linguistics.

Boas, Franz 1938. 'Language', pp. 124–45 of *General anthropology*, edited by Franz Boas. Boston: D. C. Heath and Company.

——and Ella Deloria 1941. *Dakota grammar*. Washington, DC: US Govt. Printing Office.

Boguslawski, Andrzej 1985. 'The problem of the negative imperative in perfective verbs revised', *Russian Linguistics* 9: 225–39.

Bolinger, Dwight 1967. 'The imperative in English', pp. 335–62 of *To honor Roman Jakobson: essays on the occasion on his seventieth birthday*. The Hague: Mouton.

——1972. 'Around the edge of language: intonation', pp. 19–29 of *Intonation*, edited by Dwight Bolinger. Harmondsworth: Penguin Education.

——1974. '*Do* imperatives', *Journal of English Linguistics* 8: 1–5.

——1977. *Meaning and form*. London: Longman.

——1982. 'Nondeclaratives from an intonational standpoint', *Papers from the parasession on declaratives*, CLS: 1–22.

——1985. *Iconicity in syntax*. Amsterdam: John Benjamins.

——1991. 'Reference and inference: inceptiveness in the Spanish preterite', pp. 319–34 of his *Essays on Spanish: words and grammar*. Newark, NJ: Juan de la Cuesta.

Bolozky, Shmuel 1979. 'On the new imperative in colloquial Hebrew', *Hebrew Annual Review* 3: 17–24.

——2009. 'Colloquial Hebrew imperatives revisited', *Language Sciences* 31: 136–43.

Borg, A., and M. Azzopardi-Alexander 1997. *Maltese*. London: Routledge.

Borgman, D. M. 1990. 'Sanuma', pp. 17–248 of *Handbook of Amazonian languages*, vol. 2, edited by D. C. Derbyshire and G. K. Pullum. Berlin: Mouton de Gruyter.

Borisova, E. G. 1988. 'Emphatic particles in imperative sentences in Russian', pp. 28–9 of Birjulin et al. 1988.

Börjars, Kersti, and Kate Burridge 2001. *Introducing English grammar*. London: Arnold.

Bosco, F. M. 2006. 'Cognitive pragmatics', pp. 546–52 of *Encyclopedia of language and linguistics*, edited by Keith Brown. Oxford: Elsevier.

Bowden, John 2001. *Taba: description of a South Halmahera language*. Canberra: Pacific Linguistics.

Breen, J. G. 1981. 'Margany and Gunya', pp. 274–393 of *Handbook of Australian languages*, vol. 2, edited by R. M. W. Dixon and Barry J. Blake. Canberra: ANU Press and Amsterdam: John Benjamins.

Breeze, Mary J. 1990. 'A sketch of the phonology and grammar of Gimira (Benchnon)', pp. 1–67 of *Omotic language studies*, edited by Richard J. Hayward. London: SOAS.

Brinton, Laurel J. 1996. *Pragmatic markers in English: grammaticalization and discourse functions*. Berlin: Mouton de Gruyter.

Brody, Jill 1995. 'Lending the "unborrowable": Spanish discourse markers in indigenous American languages', pp. 132–47 of *Spanish in four continents: studies in language contact and bilingualism*, edited by Carmen Silva-Corvalán. Washington, DC: Georgetown University Press.

Bromley, H. M. 1981. *A grammar of Lower Grand Valley Dani*. Canberra: Pacific Linguistics.

Brown, P., and S. C. Levinson 1987. *Politeness: some universals in language usage*. Cambridge: Cambridge University Press.

Brownie, John, and Marjo Brownie 2007. *Mussau grammar essentials*. Ukarumpa: SIL-PNG Academic Publications.

Bruce, Les 1984. *The Alamblak language of Papua New Guinea (East Sepik)*. Canberra: Pacific Linguistics.

——1988. 'Serialization: from syntax to lexicon', *Studies in Language* 12: 19–49.

Brüzzi, Alcionílio Alves da Silva 1967. *Observações gramaticais da língua Daxseyé ou Tucano.* Iauarete (Brasil): Centro de Pesquisas de Iauarete.

Bubenik, Vit 2003. 'Prākrits and Apabraṁśa', pp. 204–49 of Cardona and Jain 2003.

Buchholz, Oda, Wilfried Fiedler, and Gerda Uhlisch 1993. *Wörterbuch Albanisch–Deutsch.* Leipzig, Berlin and Munich: Langenscheidt Verlag Encyclopedie.

Bulygina, T. V., and A. D. Shmelev 1997. *Linguistic conceptualization of the world (on the basis of Russian grammar)* (Jazykovaja konceptualizacija mira (na materiale russkoj grammatiki)). Moscow: Jazyki russkoj kuljtury.

Bunte, Pamela A., and Martha B. Kendall 1981. 'When is an error not an error? Notes on language contact and the question of interference', *Anthropological Linguistics* 23: 1–7.

Buscha, A. 1976. 'Isolierte Nebensätze im dialogischen Text', *Deutsch als Fremdsprache* 13: 274–9.

Butt, John, and Carmen Benjamin 2004. *A new reference grammar of Modern Spanish,* 4th edn. London: Hodder Arnold.

Bybee, Joan L., William Pagliuca, and Revere D. Perkins 1994. *The evolution of grammar: tense, aspect and modality in the languages of the world.* Chicago: University of Chicago Press.

Bynon, James 1976. 'Domestic animal calling in a Berber tribe', pp. 39–65 of *Language and man: anthropological issues,* edited by William McCormack and Stephen A. Wurm. The Hague: Mouton.

Callaghan, Catherine A. 1998. 'The imperative in Proto-Utian', pp. 161–7 of *Studies in American Indian languages,* edited by Leanne Hinton and Pamela Munro. Berkeley: University of California Press.

Capell, A., and H. E. Hinch 1970. *Maung grammar, texts and vocabulary.* The Hague: Mouton.

Cardona, George. 2003. 'Sanskrit', pp. 104–60 of Cardona and Jain 2003.

——and Dhanesh Jain, eds. 2003. *The Indo-Aryan languages.* London: Routledge.

——and Babu Suthar 2003. 'Gujarati', pp. 659–97 of Cardona and Jain 2003.

Carlin, Eithne B. 2004. *A grammar of Trio, a Cariban language of Suriname.* Frankfurt am Main: Peter Lang.

——2007. 'Feeling the need: the borrowing of Cariban functional categories into Mawayana (Arawak)', pp. 313–32 of Aikhenvald and Dixon 2007.

Carlson, R. 1994. *A grammar of Supyire.* Berlin: Mouton de Gruyter.

Casad, E. 1984. 'Cora', pp. 151–459 of *Southern Uto-Aztecan grammatical sketches,* edited by R. Langacker. Dallas: SIL and University of Texas at Austin.

——1992. 'Cognition, history and Cora *yee*', *Cognitive Linguistics* 3: 151–86.

Caughley, R. C. 1982. *The syntax and morphology of the verb in Chepang.* Canberra: Pacific Linguistics.

Cerrón-Palomino, Rodolfo 2006. *El chipaya o la lengua de los hombres del agua.* Lima: Pontífica Universidad Católica del Perú, Fondo Editorial.

Chafe, Wallace L. 1970. *A semantically based sketch of Onondaga.* Supplement to *IJAL* 36.2.

Chafe, Wallace L. 1996. 'Sketch of Seneca, an Iroquoian language', pp. 551–80 of *Handbook of North American Indian languages*, vol. 17, edited by I. Goddard. Washington, DC: Smithsonian Institution.

Chapman, A. 1997. 'A grammatical summary of Thai and Lao', †RCLT internal document, Australian National University.

Chapman, S. and D. C. Derbyshire 1991. 'Paumarí', pp. 161–354 of *Handbook of Amazonian languages*, vol. 1, edited by D. C. Derbyshire and G. K. Pullum. Berlin: Mouton de Gruyter.

Charney, Jean Ormsbee 1993. *A grammar of Comanche*. Lincoln and London: University of Nebraska Press.

Chelliah, Shobhana L. 1997. *A grammar of Meithei*. Berlin: Mouton de Gruyter.

Childs, G. T. 1995. *A grammar of Kisi*. Berlin: Mouton de Gruyter.

Chisholm, William S., Jr., ed. 1984. *Interrogativity: a colloquium on the grammar, typology and pragmatics of questions in seven diverse languages*. Amsterdam: John Benjamins.

Christiades, Vasilios 1980. *201 Greek verbs fully conjugated in all the tenses*. New York: Barron.

Christy, Arthur E., and Henry W. Wells 1947. *World literature: an anthology of human experience*. Freeport, NY: Books for Libraries Press.

Chung, S., and A. Timberlake 1985. 'Tense, aspect and mood', pp. 202–58 of *Language typology and syntactic description*, vol. 3, *Grammatical categories and the lexicon*, edited by Timothy Shopen. Cambridge: Cambridge University Press.

Churchward, C. Maxwell 1941. *A new Fijian grammar*. Suva: Government Press.

Cialdini, Robert B. 1993. *Influence: the psychology of persuasion*. New York: Quill William Morrow.

Clancy, P. M. 1985. 'The acquisition of Japanese', pp. 373–524 of Slobin 1985.

Clendon, M. 2000. 'Topics in Worora grammar'. PhD dissertation, University of Adelaide.

Clyne, M., H.-L. Kretzenbacher, C. Norrby, and J. Warren 2003. 'Address in some Western European languages', *Proceedings of the 2003 Conference of the Australian Linguistics society*, http://www.newcastle.edu.au/school/lang-media/news/als2003/proceedings.html

————and D. Schüpbach 2004. 'Zur Anrede im Deutschen im internationalen Vergleich', *Sprachreport* 4: 2–7.

————C. Norrby, and D. Schüpbach 2006. 'Perceptions of variation and change in German and Swedish address', *Journal of Sociolinguistics* 10: 287–319.

Coates, Jennifer 2003. 'Address', pp. 33–4 of *International encyclopedia of linguistics*, 2nd edn, edited by William J. Frawley. Oxford: Oxford University Press.

Coffin, Edna Amir, and Shmuel Bolozky 2005. *A reference grammar of Modern Hebrew*. Cambridge: Cambridge University Press.

Cohen, Marcel 1936. *Traité de langue amharique*. Paris: Institut d'Ethnologie.

Cole, Peter 1975. 'The synchronic and diachronic status of conversational implicature', pp. 257–88 of Cole and Morgan 1975.

——1982. *Imbabura Quechua*. Amsterdam: North-Holland.

——and Jerry L. Morgan, eds. 1975 *Speech acts*. New York: Academic Press.

Collins, W. M. 1994. 'Maya-Mam', pp. 365–82 of *Typological studies in negation*, edited by P. Kahrel and R. van den Berg. Amsterdam: John Benjamins.

Comrie, Bernard 1975a. 'The antiergative: Finland's answer to Basque', in *Papers from the Eleventh Regional Meeting, Chicago Linguistic Society*, edited by R. E. Grossman, L. J. San, and T. J. Vence.

——1975b. 'Polite plurals and predicate agreement', *Language* 51: 406–18.

——1976. *Aspect*. Cambridge: Cambridge University Press.

——1984a. 'Russian', pp. 7–46 of Chisholm 1984.

——1984b. Plenary session discussion, pp. 255–87 of Chisholm 1984.

—— 1985. *Tense*. Cambridge: Cambridge University Press.

Conrad, R. J., with Kepas Wogiga 1991. *An outline of Bukiyip grammar*. Canberra: Pacific Linguistics.

Cook, D. M., and L. L. Criswell 1993. *El Idioma Koreguaje (Tucano Occidental)*. Colombia: Asociación Instituto Lingüístico de Verano.

Cook, Eng-Do 1984. *A Sarcee grammar*. Vancouver: University of British Columbia Press.

Corbett, Greville G. 2000. *Number*. Cambridge: Cambridge University Press.

——2007. 'Canonical typology, suppletion, and possible words', *Language* 83: 8–42.

Corne, Chris 1977. *Seychelles Creole grammar: elements for Indian Ocean Proto-Creole reconstruction*. Tübingen: Narr.

Costa, David 2003. *The Miami-Illinois language*. Lincoln: University of Nebraska Press.

Cowan, J. Ronayne, and Russell G. Schuh 1976. *Spoken Hausa*, part 1: *Hausa language-grammar*. Ithaca, NY: Spoken Language Services.

Cowell, Andrew 2007. 'Arapaho imperatives: indirectness, politeness and communal "face"', *Journal of Linguistic Anthropology* 17: 44–60.

——with Alonzo Moss, Sr. 2008. *The Arapaho language*. Boulder: University Press of Colorado.

Cowell, M. W. 1964. *A reference grammar of Syrian Arabic*. Washington, DC: Georgetown University Press.

Craig, C. G. 1977. *The structure of Jacaltec*. Austin: University of Texas Press.

——1991. 'Ways to go in Rama: a case study in polygrammaticalization', pp. 455–92 of *Approaches to grammaticalization*, vol. 2, edited by E. C. Traugott and B. Heine. Amsterdam: John Benjamins.

Crapo, Richley H., and Percy Aitken 1986. *Bolivian Quechua reader and grammar-dictionary*. Ann Arbor, MI: Karoma.

Crass, Joachim 2007. 'K'abeena', pp. 91–106 of *Grammatical borrowing in cross-linguistic perspective*, edited by Yaron Matras and Jeannette Sakel. Berlin: Mouton de Gruyter.

Crazzolàra, Father J. P. 1933. *Outlines of a Nuer grammar*. Vienna: Verlag der internationalen Zeitschrift 'Anthropos'.

Cresti, Emanuela 2000. *Corpus di italiano parlato*. Firenze: Accademia della Crusca.

Crowley, Terry 2002. *Serial verbs in Oceanic: a descriptive typology*. Oxford: Oxford University Press.

——and Bruce Rigsby 1979. 'Cape York Creole', pp. 153–207 of *Languages and their status*, edited by Timothy Shopen. Cambridge: Cambridge University Press.

Cruse, Alan 2006. *A glossary of semantics and pragmatics*. Edinburgh: Edinburgh University Press.

Csúcs, Sándor 1998. 'Udmurt', pp. 276–304 of Abondolo 1998c.

Curnow, T. J. 1997a. 'A grammar of Awa Pit'. PhD dissertation, ANU.

——1997b. A grammatical summary of Awa Pit. †RCLT internal document, ANU.

——2002. 'Conjunct/disjunct marking in Awa Pit', *Linguistics* 40: 611–27.

Daguman, Josephine 2004. A grammar of Northern Subanen. PhD dissertation, †RCLT, La Trobe University.

Dahlstrom, A. MS. *A grammar of Fox (Algonquian)*.

Daiber, Michael 2009. 'Metaphorical use of a Russian imperative', *Russian Linguistics* 33: 11–35.

Darbyshire, E. C. 1967. *A description of English*. London: Edward Arnold.

Dasgupta, Probal 2003. 'Bangla', pp. 351–90 of Cardona and Jain 2003.

Davidson, Alice 1975. 'Indirect speech acts and what to do with them', pp. 143–86 of Cole and Morgan 1975.

Davies, E. 1986. *The English imperative*. London: Croom Helm.

Davies, J. 1981. *Kobon*. Amsterdam: North-Holland.

Dayley, Jon P. 1989. *Tümpisa (Panamint) Shoshone grammar*. Berkeley: University of California Press.

Deibler, E. W. 1976. *Semantic relationships of Gahuku verbs*. SIL, Norman, and University of Oklahoma.

Delattre, Pierre 1972. 'The distinctive function of intonation', pp. 159–74 of *Intonation*, edited by Dwight Bolinger. Harmondsworth: Penguin Education.

Delbrück, Berthold 1893. *Vergleichende Syntax der indogermanischen Sprachen*. Strassburg: K. J. Trübner.

Dempwolff, Otto 2006. *Grammar of the Jabêm language in New Guinea*, translated and edited by J. Bradshaw and F. Czobor. Honolulu: University of Hawai'i Press.

Dench, A. 1991. 'Panyjima', pp. 125–244 of *The handbook of Australian languages*, vol. 4, edited by R.M.W. Dixon and Barry J. Blake. Melbourne: Oxford University Press.

——2009. 'The semantics of clause linking in Martuthunira', pp. 261–84 of *Semantics of clause linking: a cross-linguistic typology*, edited by R. M. W. Dixon and Alexandra Y. Aikhenvald. Oxford: Oxford University Press.

Denning, Keith 1987. 'Obligation and space: the origins of markers of obligative modality', in *Papers from the regional meeting of Chicago Linguistic Society* 23: 45–55.

Derbyshire, D. C. 1979. *Hixkaryana*. Amsterdam: North-Holland.

——1985. *Hixkaryana and linguistic typology*. Arlington: SIL and the University of Texas at Arlington.

de Reuse, Willem 2003. 'Imperatives in Western Apache'. Paper presented at a local workshop 'Imperatives and other commands', †RCLT, Melbourne.

——2006 (with the assistance of Philip Goode). *A practical grammar of the San Carlos Apache language*. Munich: Lincom Europa.

de Sivers, F. 1969. *Analyse grammaticale de l'estonien parlé*. Clermont-Ferrand: Editions G. de Bussac.

Destaing, E. 1920. *Étude sur le dialecte berbère des Ait Seghrouchen*. Paris: Leroux.

Diller, A. V. N. 2006. 'Thai serial verbs: cohesion and culture', pp. 161–77 of Aikhenvald and Dixon 2006.

Dimmendaal, G. I. 1983. *The Turkana language*. Dordrecht: Foris.

Dixon, R. M. W. 1972. *The Dyirbal language of North Quensland*. Cambridge: Cambridge University Press.

——1977. *A grammar of Yidiñ*. Cambridge: Cambridge University Press.

——1980. *The languages of Australia*. Cambridge: Cambridge University Press.

——1988. *A grammar of Boumaa Fijian*. Chicago: University of Chicago Press.

——1991. 'Mbabaram', pp. 348–402 of *Handbook of Australian languages*, vol. 4, edited by R. M. W. Dixon and Barry J. Blake. Melbourne: Oxford University Press.

——1994. *Ergativity*. Cambridge: Cambridge University Press.

——1997. *The rise and fall of languages*. Cambridge: Cambridge University Press.

——2002. *Australian languages: their nature and development*. Cambridge: Cambridge University Press.

——2004a. *A Jarawara language of southern Amazonia*. Oxford: Oxford University Press.

——2004b. 'Adjective classes in typological perspective', pp. 1–49 of Dixon and Aikhenvald 2004.

——2005. *A semantic approach to English grammar*. Oxford: Oxford University Press.

——2006. 'Serial verb constructions: conspectus and coda', pp. 338–50 of Aikhenvald and Dixon 2006.

——2007. 'Field linguistics: a minor manual', *Sprachtypologie und Universalienforschung* 60: 12–31.

——2009. 'The semantics of clause linking in typological perspective', pp. 1–54 of *The semantics of clause linking: a cross-linguistic typology*, edited by R. M. W. Dixon and Alexandra Y. Aikhenvald. Oxford: Oxford University Press.

——2010. *Basic linguistic theory*, vols. 1 and 2. Oxford: Oxford University Press.

——and Alexandra Y. Aikhenvald 2002. 'Word': a typological framework, pp. 1–41 of *Word: a cross-linguistic typology*, edited by R. M. W. Dixon and A. Y. Aikhenvald. Cambridge: Cambridge University Press.

————eds. 2004. *Adjective classes: a cross-linguistic typology*. Oxford: Oxford University Press.

Dobrushina, N. R. 1999. 'Forms of irrealis', pp. 262–8; 'Forms of imperative series', pp. 278–85 of *Elements of Tsakhur language in typological perspective*, edited by A. E. Kibrik with Ya. G. Testelec. Moscow: Nasledie.

——2001. 'Mood and modality', pp. 319–32 of *Bagwalal language: grammar, texts, vocabularies*, edited by A. E. Kibrik with K. I. Kazenin, E. A. Ljutikova, and S. G. Tatevosov. Moscow: Nasledie.

——Johan van der Auwera, and Valentin Goussev 2005. 'The optative', pp. 298–301 of *The world atlas of language structures*, edited by Martin Haspelmath et al. Oxford: Oxford University Press.

Dol, Philomena 2007. *A grammar of Maybrat, a language of the Bird's Head Peninsula, Papua Province, Indonesia*. Canberra: Pacific Linguistics.

Donohue, M. 1999a. 'A grammatical summary of Tukang Besi'. †RCLT internal document, ANU.

——1999b. *A grammar of Tukang Besi*. Berlin: Mouton de Gruyter.

Dorian, Nancy 2006. 'Negative borrowing in an indigenous language shift to the dominant national language', *International Journal of Bilingual Education and Bilingualism* 9: 557–77.

Douglas, Wilfrid H. 1981. 'Watjarri', pp. 197–272 of *Handbook of Australian languages*, vol. 2, edited by R. M. W. Dixon and Barry J. Blake. Canberra: Australian National University Press and Amsterdam: John Benjamins.

Downing, B. T. 1969. 'Vocatives and third person imperatives in English', *Papers in Linguistics* 1: 570–91.

Du Bois, J. 1985. 'Competing motivations', pp. 343–66 of *Iconicity in syntax*, edited by John Haiman. Amsterdam: John Benjamins.

Dunn, Michael 1999. 'A grammar of Chukchi'. PhD dissertation, ANU.

Durnovo, N. N. 1969. *Vvedenie v istoriju russkogo jazyka* [Introduction to the history of Russian]. Moscow: Nauka.

Dutton, T. E. 1973. *Conversational New Guinea Pidgin*. Canberra: Pacific Linguistics.

——1996. *Koiari*. Munich: Lincom Europa.

Eades, Diana 1982. '"You gotta know how to talk": ethnography of information seeking in Southeast Queensland Aboriginal Society', *Australian Journal of Linguistics* 2: 61–82. Reprinted in J. B. Pride, ed., *Cross-cultural encounters: communication and mis-communication*, Melbourne: River Seine Publications, 1985, 91–109.

Eather, B. 1990. 'A grammar of Nakkara (Central Arnhem Land coast)'. PhD dissertation, ANU.

Ebbutt, Blanche 1913. *Don'ts for husbands*. London: Black.

Eckermann, W. 2007. *A descriptive grammar of the Bukawa language of the Morobe Province of Papua New Guinea*. Canberra: Pacific Linguistics.

Ekdahl, Elizabeth M., and Nancy E. Butler 1979. *Aprenda Terêna*, vol. 1. Brasilia: Summer Institute of Linguistics.

——and Joseph E. Grimes 1964. 'Terena verb inflection', *IJAL* 30:261–8.

Elliott, J. 2000. 'Realis and irrealis: forms and concepts of the grammaticalisation of reality', *Linguistic Typology* 4: 55–90.

Emenanjo, E. Nolue 1978. *Elements of Modern Igbo grammar: a descriptive approach*. Ibadan: Oxford University Press.

Emkow, Carola 2006. 'A grammar of Araona'. PhD dissertation, La Trobe University.

Enfield, Nicholas J. 2007. *A grammar of Lao*. Berlin: Mouton de Gruyter.

England, N. 1983. *A grammar of Mam, a Mayan language*. Austin: University of Texas Press.

Enrico, John 2003. *Haida syntax*, 2 vols. Lincoln: University of Nebraska Press.

Epps, Patience 2005. 'A grammar of Hup'. PhD dissertation, University of Virginia.

——2007. 'The Vaupés melting pot: Tucanoan influence on Hup', pp. 267–89 of Aikhenvald and Dixon 2007.

Erelt, M. 2002a. 'Does Estonian have the jussive?', *Linguistica Uralica* 2: 110–17.

——2002b. 'Evidentiality in Estonian and some other languages: introductory remarks', *Linguistica Uralica* 2: 93–6.

——2003. 'Structure of the Estonian language. Syntax', pp. 93–129 of *Estonian language*, edited by Mati Erelt. Tallinn: Estonian Academy Publishers.

Ervin-Tripp, S. 1976. '"Is Sybil there?" the structure of some American English directives', *Language in Society* 5: 25–66.

Evans, Nicholas 2003. *Binij Gun-wok: a pan-dialectal grammar of Mayali, Kunwinjku and Kune*. Canberra: Pacific Linguistics.

——2007. 'Insubordination and its uses', pp. 366–431 of *Finiteness: theoretical and empirical foundations*, edited by Irina Nikolaeva. Oxford: Oxford University Press.

——and David P. Wilkins 2000. 'In the mind's ear: the semantic extensions of perception verbs in Australian languages', *Language* 76: 546–92.

Everett, D., and B. Kern 1997. *Wari'*. London: Routledge.

Fairclough, Norman 1992. *Discourse and social change*. Cambridge: Polity Press.

Faraclas, N. 1996. *Nigerian Pidgin*. London: Routledge.

Ferguson, Charles A. 1976. 'The Ethiopian language area', pp. 63–76 of *Language in Ethiopia*, edited by M. L. Bender, J. D. Bowen, R. L. Cooper, and C. A. Ferguson. London: Oxford University Press.

Fernandez-Vest, M. M. J. 1996. 'Du médiatif finno-ougrien: mode oblique en Estonien, particules en Finnois et en Same', pp. 169–82 of *L'Énonciation médiatisée*, edited by Zlatka Guentchéva. Louvain-Paris: Éditions Peeters.

Ferreira de Holanda Buarque, Aurélio 1999. *Aurélio século XXI: o dicionário da língua portuguesa*. Rio de Janeiro: Nova Fronteira.

Fiddick, Laurence 2008. 'Which norms are strong reciprocators supposed to enforce? Not all norms are psychologically the same', *International Review of Economics* 55: 77–89.

Fleck, David W. 2008. 'Coreferential fourth-person pronouns in Matses', *International Journal of American Linguistics* 74: 279–311.

——forthcoming. *A grammar of Matses*. Berlin: Mouton de Gruyter.

Floricic, Frank 2002. 'De l'impératif italien *sii* (sois!) et de l'impératif en général', *Bulletin de la Société de Linguistique de Paris* 95.1: 227–66.

——2007. 'Les impératifs italiens entre verbe et interjection', *Echo des études romanes* III-1/2: 71–92.

——forthcoming. 'La morphologie de l'impératif en italien, et plus précisément de ce qu'elle n'existe pas'.

——2008. 'The Italian verb-noun anthropolonymic compounds at the syntax/morphology interface', *Morphology* 18/2: 167–93.

Foley, W. A. 1991. *The Yimas language of New Guinea*. Stanford, CA: Stanford University Press.

Ford, C. E., and S. A. Thompson 1986. 'Conditionals in discourse: a text-based study from English', pp. 353–72 of Traugott et al. 1986.

Ford, L. 1998. 'A grammar of Emmi'. PhD dissertation, ANU.

Foris, D. P. 2001. *A Grammar of Sochiapan Chinantec*. Arlington: SIL and University of Texas at Arlington.

Fortescue, M. 1984. *West Greenlandic*. London: Routledge.

——2003. 'Evidentiality in West Greenlandic: a case of scattered coding', pp. 291–306 of *Studies in evidentiality*, edited by Alexandra Y. Aikhenvald and R. M. W. Dixon. Amsterdam: John Benjamins.

Fortuin, Egbert L. J. 2000. *Polysemy or monosemy: interpretation of the imperative and the dative-infinitive construction in Russian*. Amsterdam: Institute for Logic, Language and Computation.

Fowler, Loretta 1982. *Arapaho politics 1851–1978: symbols in crises of authority*. Lincoln: University of Nebraska Press.

Frajzyngier, Z. 1989. *A grammar of Pero*. Berlin: Dietrich Reimer Verlag.

——1993. *A grammar of Mupun*. Berlin: Dietrich Reimer Verlag.

——2001. *A grammar of Lele*. Stanford, CA: CSLI.

——2002. *A grammar of Hdi*. Berlin: Mouton de Gruyter.

——and E. Johnston 2005. *A grammar of Mina*. Berlin: Mouton de Gruyter.

Frank, Paul 1990. *Ika Syntax*. Arlington: SIL and University of Texas at Arlington.

Franklin, Karl James 1971. *A grammar of Kewa, New Guinea*. Canberra: Pacific Linguistics.

Freixeiro Mato, Xosé Ramón 2000. *Gramática da lingua Galega*. Santiago de Compostela: Edicións A Nossa Terra.

Friedman, V. A. 1997. 'One grammar, three lexicons: ideological overtones and underpinnings in the Balkan *Sprachbund*', *CLS* 33: 23–44.

Gaby, Alice 2007. 'A grammar of Kuuk Thaayorre'. PhD dissertation, University of Melbourne.

Galloway, Brent D. 1993. *A grammar of Upriver Halkomelem*. Berkeley: University of California.

Galúcio, A. V. 2001. 'The morphosyntax of Mekens (Tupi)'. PhD dissertation, University of Chicago.

Gamkrelidze, T. V., and Vyach. Vs. Ivanov 1984. *The Indo-European language and the Indoeuropeans* (Indoevropejskij jazyk i indoevropejcy). Tbilisi: Izdateljstvo Tbilisskogo Universiteta.

Gary, J. O., and S. Gamal-Eldin 1982. *Cairene Egyptian Colloquial Arabic*. Amsterdam: North-Holland.

Genetti, Carol 2007. *A grammar of Dolakha Newar*. Berlin: Mouton de Gruyter.

Geniušienė, E. Sh. 1988a. 'Vid i otricanije v imperative litovskogo jazyka', pp. 48–9 of *Imperativ v raznostrukturnyh jazykakh*. Leningrad: Nauka.

——1988b. 'Aspect and negation in the imperative of Lithuanian verbs', pp. 46–8 of Birjulin et al. 1988.

Georg, Stefan, and Alexander P. Volodin 1999. *Die itelmenische Sprache: Grammatik und Texte.* Wiesbaden: Harrasowitz.

Geschwind, N. 1975. 'The apraxias: neural mechanisms of disorders of learned movement', *American Scientist* 63: 188–95.

Gesenius, Wilhelm 1962. *Hebräische Grammatik. Mit Benutzung der von E. Kautsch bearb. 28 Aufl. von Wilhelm Geseinus' Hebräischer Grammatik verfasst von G. Bergsträsser, mit Beiträgen von M. Lidzbarski.* Hildesheim: G. Olms Verlagsbuchhandlung.

Giridhar, P. P. 1994. *Mao Naga grammar.* Mysore: Central Institute of Indian Languages.

Givón, Talmy 1980. *Ute reference grammar.* Ignacio, CO: Ute Press.

——1984. 'The speech-act continuum', pp. 245–54 of Chisholm 1984.

——1989. *Mind, code, and context: essays in pragmatics.* Hillsdale, NJ: Erlbaum.

——1993. *English grammar: a function-based introduction,* 2 vols. Amsterdam: John Benjamins.

Gleason, J. Berko, H. Goodglass, E. Green, N. Ackerman, and M. R. Hyde 1975. 'The retrieval of syntax in Broca's aphasia', *Brain and Language* 2: 451–71.

Gleitman, Lila 1965. 'Co-ordinating conjunctions in English', *Language* 41: 260–93.

Goddard, C. 1983. 'A semantically-oriented grammar of the Yankunytjatjara dialect of the Western Desert language'. PhD dissertation, ANU.

——1985. *A grammar of Yankunytjatjara.* Alice Springs: Institute for Aboriginal Development.

Golovko, E. V. 1992. 'Imperative sentences in Aleut', pp. 160–69 of *Tipologija imperativnykh konstrukcij* (The typology of imperative constructions), edited by V. S. Xrakovskij. St Petersburg: Nauka.

Goody, E., ed. 1978. *Questions and politeness: strategies in social interaction.* Cambridge: Cambridge University Press.

Gordon, Lynn 1987. *Maricopa morphology and syntax.* Berkeley: University of California Press.

Goussev, V. 2004. 'Non-specialized verbal forms in the function of imperative' (in Russian), pp. 385–415 of *Irrelis i irrealjnostj* (Irrealis and irreality), edited by J. Lander, V. Plungjan, and A. Urmanchieva. Moscow: Gnosis.

——2005. 'The typology of specialized verbal forms of imperative (Tipologiya specializirovannykh glagolj'nykh form imperativa)'. PhD dissertation, RGGU, Moscow.

Green, Georgia M. 1975a. 'How to get people to do things with words; the whimperative question', pp. 107–41 of Cole and Morgan 1975.

——1975b. 'Nonsense and reference; or, the conversational use of proverbs', in *Papers from the Eleventh Regional Meeting of the Chicago Linguistic Society*: 226–39.

Greenberg, Joseph H. 1963. 'Some universals of grammar with particular reference to the order of meaningful elements', pp. 58–90 of *Universals of language*, edited by J. H. Greenberg. Cambridge, MA: MIT Press.

Greenberg, Joseph H. 1986. 'The realis–irrealis continuum in the Classical Greek Conditional', pp. 247–64 of Traugott et al. 1986.

Grice, Paul 1989. *Studies in the way of words*. Cambridge, MA: Harvard University Press.

Grinstead, J. 2000. 'Case, inflection, and subject licensing in child Catalan and Spanish', *Journal of Child Language Acquisition* 27: 119–55.

Gronas, Mikhail 2006. 'The origin of the Russian historical imperative', *Russian Linguistics* 30: 89–101.

Gruzdeva, Ekaterina Yu 1992. 'Poveliteljnye predlozhenija v nivkhskom jazyke' (Imperative sentences in Nivkh), pp. 55–63 of *Tipologija imperativnykh konstrukcij* (The typology of imperative constructions), edited by V. S. Xrakovskij. St Petersburg: Nauka.

——2000. 'Aspects of Russian-Nivkh grammatical interference: the Nivkh imperative', pp. 121–34 of *Languages in contact*, edited by D. G. Gilbers, J. Nerbonne, and J. Schaeken. Amsterdam: Rodopi.

——2001. 'Imperative sentences in Nivkh', (translation of Gruzdeva 1992), pp. 59–77 of *Typology of imperative constructions*, edited by V. S. Xrakovskij. Munich: Lincom Europa.

——2002. 'The linguistic consequences of Nivkh language attrition', *SKY Journal of Linguistics* 15: 85–103.

——2007. 'Kompleksnoe predstavlenije jazykovykh izmenenij v uslovijakh jazykovogo sdviga (na materiale nivkhskogo jazyka)' (A systematic representation of language changes in language shift (based on Nivkh), pp. 118–212 of *Jazykovye izmenenenija v uslovijakh jazykovogo sdviga*, edited by N. B. Vaxtin. St Petersburg: Institut lingvisticheskikh issledovanij RAN.

Guillaume, Antoine 2004. 'A grammar of Cavineña, an Amazonian language from Bolivia'. PhD dissertation, La Trobe University.

——2008. *A grammar of Cavineña*. Berlin: Mouton de Gruyter.

Guirardello, R. 2000. 'A reference grammar of Trumai (Brazil)'. PhD dissertation, Rice University.

Güldemann, T., and M. von Roncador 2002. *Reported discourse: a meeting ground for different linguistic domains*. Amsterdam: John Benjamins.

Haas, Mary R. 1940. *Tunica*. New York: Augustin Publisher.

Haig, G. 1997a. 'A grammatical summary of Kurmanjî Kurdish'. †RCLT internal document, ANU.

——1997b. 'A grammatical summary of Turkish'. †RCLT internal document, ANU.

Haiman, J. 1980. *Hua: a Papuan language of the Eastern Highlands of New Guinea*. Amsterdam: Benjamins.

——1985. *Natural syntax: iconicity and erosion*. Cambridge: Cambridge University Press.

——2003. 'Iconicity', pp. 453–6 of *Encyclopedia of cognitive science*, edited by Lynn Nadel. London: Nature Publishing Group.

Hale, A. 1980. 'Person markers: finite conjunct and disjunct verb forms in Newari', pp. 95–106 of *Papers in South-East Asian linguistics*, No. 7, edited by R. L. Trail. Canberra: Pacific Linguistics.

Hale, Kenneth 1975. 'Gaps in grammar and culture', pp. 295–315 of *Linguistics and anthropology: in honour of C. F. Voegelin*, edited by M. D. Kinkade et al. Lisse: Peter de Ridder.

Hall, Robert A., Jr. 1953. *Haitian Creole: grammar, texts, vocabulary*. American Anthropologist 55, 2.2. Memoir 74.

Halliday, M. A. K. 1970. *A course in spoken English: intonation*. Oxford: Oxford University Press.

Hamblin, C. L. 1987. *Imperatives*. Oxford: Blackwell.

Hardman, M. J. 2000. *Jaqaru*. Munich: Lincom Europa.

Hargus, Sharon 2007. *Witsuwit'en grammar: phonetics, phonology, morphology*. Vancouver: University of British Columbia Press.

Harms, Philip Lee 1994. *Epena Pedee syntax*. Arlington: SIL and University of Texas at Arlington.

Harris, Alice 1984. 'Georgian', pp. 63–112 of Chisholm 1984.

——and Lyle Campbell 1995. *Historical syntax in cross-linguistic perspective*. Cambridge: Cambridge University Press.

Harris, John 1997. 'There is no imperative paradigm in Spanish', pp. 537–57 of *Issues in the phonology and morphology of the major Iberian languages*, edited by Fernando Martínez-Gil and Alfonso Morales-Front. Washington, DC: Georgetown University Press.

Harris, Martin B. 1986. 'The historical development of *si*-clauses in Romance', pp. 265–84 of Traugott et al. 1986.

——and Nigel Vincent 1988. *The Romance languages*. London: Routledge.

Haspelmath, M. 1993. *A grammar of Lezgian*. Berlin: Mouton de Gruyter.

——1995. 'The converb as a cross-linguistically valid category', pp. 1–55 of *Converbs in cross-linguistic perspective*, edited by M. Haspelmath and E. König. Berlin: Mouton de Gruyter.

Hausenberg, Anu-Reet 1998. 'Komi', pp. 305–26 of Abondolo 1998c.

Haverkate, H. 1976. 'Pragmatic and linguistic aspects of the prepositional infinitive in Spanish', *Lingua* 40: 223–45.

Haviland, John 1979. 'How to talk to your brother-in-law in Guugu Yimidhirr', pp. 161–249 of *Languages and their speakers*, edited by Timothy Shopen. Philadelphia: University of Pennsylvania Press.

——1981. *Sk'op Sotz'leb: El Tzotzil de San Lorenzo Zinacantán*. Mexico City: Universidade Autónoma de Mexico.

——2003. 'How to point in Zinacantán', pp. 243–68 of Kita 2003a.

Hawkins, J. 1998. 'Wai Wai', pp. 25–224 of *Handbook of Amazonian languages*, vol. 4, edited by D. C. Derbyshire and G. K. Pullum. Berlin: Mouton de Gruyter.

Hayward, R. J. 1979. 'Some inferences from an irregular imperative form in Saho', *Israel Oriental Studies* 9: 245–57.

Heath, Jeffrey 1978. *Linguistic diffusion in Arnhem Land.* Canberra: Australian Institute of Aboriginal Studies.

——1981. *Basic materials in Mara: grammar, texts and dictionary.* Canberra: Pacific Linguistics.

——1984. *Functional grammar of Nunggubuyu.* Canberra: Australian Institute of Aboriginal Studies.

——1999. *A grammar of Koyra Chini: the Songhay of Timbuktu.* Berlin: Mouton de Gruyter.

——2005. *A grammar of Tamachek (Tuareg of Mali).* Berlin: Mouton de Gruyter.

Heinämäki, Orvokki 1984. Aspect in Finnish, pp. 153–76 of *Aspect bound: a voyage in the realm of Germanic, Slavonic and Finno-Ugric aspectology,* edited by Casper de Groot and Hannu Tommola. Dordrecht: Foris.

Heine, Bernd, 2002. *World lexicon of grammaticalization.* Cambridge: Cambridge University Press.

——2003. 'On contact-induced grammaticalization', *Studies in Language* 27: 529–72.

——2005. *Language contact and grammatical change.* Cambridge: Cambridge University Press.

——and Tania Kuteva 2001. 'Convergence and divergence in the development of African languages', pp. 393–411 of *Areal diffusion and genetic inheritance: problems in comparative linguistics,* edited by Alexandra Y. Aikhenvald and R. M. W. Dixon. Oxford: Oxford University Press.

Helimski, Eugene 1998a. 'Nganasan', pp. 480–515 of Abondolo 1998c.

——1998b. 'Selkup', pp. 548–80 of Abondolo 1998c.

Henderson, J. 1995. *Phonology and grammar of Yele, Papua New Guinea.* Canberra: Pacific Linguistics.

Hewitt, B. G. 1979. *Abkhaz.* London: Routledge.

Hill, D. 1992. 'Longgu grammar'. PhD dissertation, ANU.

——1997. 'A grammatical summary of Longgu'. †RCLT internal document, ANU.

Hill, Jane H. 2005. *A grammar of Cupeño.* Berkeley: University of California Press.

Himmelmann, N., and J. U. Wolff 1999. *Toratán (Ratahan).* Munich: Lincom Europa.

Hinds, John 1984. 'Japanese', pp. 145–88 of Chisholm 1984.

——1986. *Japanese.* London: Croom Helm.

——and Wako Tawa Hinds 1975–6. 'Conditions on conditionals in Japanese', *Papers in Japanese Linguistics* 4: 3–12.

Hoff, B. J. 1968. *The Carib language.* The Hague: Nijhoff.

Hofling, C. A., and F. L. Ojeda 1994. 'Yucatec Maya imperatives and other manipulative language', *IJAL* 60: 272–94.

Holes, Clive 1990. *Gulf Arabic.* London: Routledge.

Holmer, N. 1966. *An attempt towards a comparative grammar of two Australian languages.* Canberra: Australian Institute of Aboriginal Studies.

——1967. *An attempt towards a comparative grammar of two Australian languages,* part 2: *Indices and vocabularies of Kattang and Thangatti.* Canberra: Australian Institute of Aboriginal Studies.

Holmes, J. 2006. 'Politeness strategies as linguistic variables', pp. 684–97 of *Encyclopedia of language and linguistics*, edited by Keith Brown. Oxford: Elsevier.

Hopper, Paul J., and Elisabeth Closs Traugott 1993. *Grammaticalization*. Cambridge: Cambridge University Press.

House, J., and G. Kasper 1987. 'Interlanguage pragmatics: requesting in a foreign language', pp. 1250–88 of *Perspectives on language in performance: studies in linguistics, literary criticism and language teaching and learning, to honour Werner Hullen on the occasion of his sixtieth birthday*, edited by M. Loerscher and R. Schultze. Tübingen: Gunter Narr Verlag.

Hualde, J. I. 1992. *Catalan*. London: Routledge.

Huddleston, R. D. 1984. *Introduction to the grammar of English*. Cambridge: Cambridge University Press.

——2002. 'Clause type and illocutionary force', pp. 851–945 of *The Cambridge grammar of the English language*, edited by Rodney Huddleston and Geoffrey K. Pullum. Cambridge: Cambridge University Press.

Huntley, M. 1982. 'Imperatives and infinitival embedded questions', in *Papers from the parasession on declaratives, CLS*: 93–106.

——1984. 'The semantics of English imperatives', *Linguistics and Philosophy* 7: 103–33.

Huttar, George L., and Mary L. Huttar 1994. *Ndyuka*. London: Routledge.

Hyman, Larry M. 1979. 'Phonology and noun structure', pp. 1–72 of *Aghem grammatical structure with special reference to noun classes, tense-aspect and focus marking*, edited by Larry M. Hyman. Southern California Occasional Papers in Linguistics 7. Department of Linguistics, University of Southern California, Los Angeles.

Hyslop, Catriona 2001. *The Lolovoli dialect of the North-East Ambae language, Vanuatu*. Canberra: Pacific Linguistics.

——2003. 'Imperatives in Vurës'. Paper presented at the local workshop 'Imperatives and commands', †RCLT, Melbourne.

——2004. 'Adjectives in North-East Ambae', pp. 263–82 of Dixon and Aikhenvald 2004.

——forthcoming. *A grammar of Vurës*.

Ikoro, Suanu M. 1996. *The Kana language*. Leiden: University of Leiden.

——1997a. 'A grammatical summary of Kana'. †RCLT internal document, ANU.

——1997b. 'A grammatical summary of Igbo'. †RCLT internal document, ANU.

——1997c. 'A grammatical summary of Swahili'. †RCLT internal document, ANU.

Ingram, Andrew J. 2003. 'Imperatives in Anamuxra'. Paper presented at the local workshop 'Imperatives and commands', †RCLT, Melbourne.

——2005. 'A grammar of Anamuxra'. PhD dissertation, University of Sydney.

——forthcoming. *A grammar of Anamuxra*. Canberra: Pacific Linguistics.

Isachenko, A. V. 2003. *Grammaticheskij stroj russkogo jazyka v sopostavlenii s slovatskim. Morflogia*. Moscow: Jazyki slavjanskoj kuljtury.

Jacob, J. A. 1968. *Introduction to Cambodian*. London: Oxford University Press.

Jaggar, P. 2001. *Grammar of Hausa*. Amsterdam: John Benjamins.

Jakobson, R. O. 1965. 'Structure of the Ukrainian and Russian imperative', reprinted as pp. 33–40 of his *Russian and Slavic grammar studies, 1931–81*, edited by Linda R. Waugh and Morris Halle. Berlin: Mouton.

——1971. 'Stroj ukrainskogo imperativa' (Organization of the Ukrainian imperative), pp. 190–97 of his *Selected writings*, vol. 2: *Word and language*. The Hague: Mouton.

——1984. 'Structure of the Russian and Ukrainian imperative', pp. 33–40 of his *Russian and Slavic grammar: studies, 1931–81*, edited by Linda R. Waugh and Morris Halle. Berlin: Mouton Publishers (translation of Jakobson 1971).

——1975. *N. S. Trubetzkoy's letters and notes*. Prepared for publication by Roman Jakobson. The Hague: Mouton.

——1995. 'Shifters and verbal categories', pp. 386–92 of his *On language*, edited by Linda R. Waugh and Monique Monville-Burston. Cambridge, MA: Harvard University Press.

Janssen, T. A. J. M., and W. van der Wurff, eds. 1996. *Reported speech: forms and functions of the verb*. Amsterdam: John Benjamins.

Jauncey, D. 1997. 'A grammar of Tamambo'. PhD dissertation, ANU.

Jespersen, O. 1924. *The philosophy of grammar*. London: George Allen & Unwin.

——1928. *A modern English grammar on historical principles*. London: George Allen & Unwin.

——1933. *Essentials of English grammar*. London: George Allen & Unwin. (Reprinted 1972.)

——1940. *A modern English grammar on historical principles*, part 5. Copenhagen: Munksgaard.

Johnson, Allen 2003. *Families of the forest: the Matsigenka Indians of the Peruvian Amazon*. Berkeley: University of California Press.

Johnson, O. E., and S. H. Levinsohn 1990. *Gramática secoya. Cuadernos Etnolingüísticos* 11. Ecuador: Instituto Lingüístico de Verano.

Johnston, Trevor, and Adam Schembri 2007. *Australian Sign Language: an introduction to sign language linguistics*. Cambridge: Cambridge University Press.

Jones, W., and P. Jones 1991. *Barasano syntax*. Arlington: SIL and University of Texas at Arlington.

Joseph, Brian D., and Irene Philippaki-Warburton 1987. *Modern Greek*. London: Routledge.

Josephides, Lisette 2001. 'Straight talk, hidden talk and modernity: shifts in discourse strategy in Highland New Guinea', pp. 218–31 of *An anthropology of indirect communication*, edited by Joy Hendry and C. W. Watson. London: Routledge.

Kakumasu, J. 1986. 'Urubu-Kaapor', pp. 326–403 of *Handbook of Amazonian languages*, vol. 1, edited by D. C. Derbyshire and G. K. Pullum. Berlin: Mouton de Gruyter.

Kangasmaa-Minn, Eva 1998. 'Mari', pp. 219–48 of Abondolo 1998c.

Kapfo, Kedutso 2005. *The ethnology of the Khezhas and the Khezha grammar*. Mysore: Central Institute of Indian Languages.

Kari, James 1990. *Ahtna Athabascan dictionary*. Fairbanks: Alaska Native Language Center, University of Alaska.

Karlsson, Fred 1999. *Finnish: an essential grammar*. London: Routledge.

Kawachi, Kazuhiro 2007. 'A grammar of Sidaama (Sidamo), a Cushitic language of Ethiopia'. PhD dissertation, SUNY, Buffalo.

Keen, S. 1983. 'Yukulta', pp. 190–304 of *Handbook of Australian languages*, vol. 3, edited by R. M. W. Dixon and Barry J. Blake. Canberra: ANU Press and Amsterdam: John Benjamins.

Keenan, E. L. 1976. 'Towards a universal definition of "subject"', pp. 303–33 of *Subject and topic*, edited by Charles Li. New York: Academic Press.

——and E. Ochs Keenan 1979. 'Becoming a competent speaker of Malagasy', pp. 113–158 of *Languages and their speakers*, edited by Timothy Shopen. Cambridge: Cambridge University Press.

Keenan, E. Ochs 1974. 'Conversation and oratory in Vakinankaratra, Madagascar'. PhD dissertation, Department of Anthropology, University of Pennsylvania.

Kenesei, I., R. M. Vago, and A. Fenyvesi 1998. *Hungarian*. London: Routledge.

Keresztes, László 1998. 'Mansi', pp. 387–427 of Abondolo 1998c.

Khanina, Olesya 2008. 'How universal is wanting?', *Studies in Languages* 32: 818–65.

Kibrik, Aleksandr E. 1977. *Structural description of Archi* (Strukturnoe opisanije archinskogo jazyla), vol. 2. Moscow: Moscow State University.

——ed. 1996. *Godoberi*. Munich: Lincom Europa.

Kimball, Geoffrey D. 1991. *Koasati grammar*. London and Lincoln: University of Nebraska Press.

King, Gareth 1993. *Modern Welsh: a comprehensive grammar*. London: Routledge.

Kita, Sotaro, ed. 2003a. *Pointing: where language, culture and cognition meet*. Hillsdale, NJ: Lawrence Erlbaum Associates.

——2003b. 'Pointing: a foundational building block of human communication', pp. 1–8 of Kita 2003a.

Klein, Harriet M. 1986. 'Styles of Toba discourse', pp. 213–35 of *Native South American discourse*, edited by Joel Sherzer and Gred Urban. Berlin: Mouton de Gruyter.

Klumpp, D. 1990. *Piapoco grammar*. Colombia: SIL.

——1995. *Vocabulario Piapoco–Español*. Santafé de Bogotá: Asociación Instituto Lingüístico de Verano.

Knjazev, Yu. P. 1988. 'Imperative in Slavic languages: an interaction of modality and temporality', pp. 62–4 of Birjulin et al. 1988.

Koehn, E., and S. Koehn 1986. 'Apalai', pp. 33–127 of *Handbook of Amazonian languages*, vol. 1, edited by D. C. Derbyshire and G. K. Pullum. Berlin: Mouton de Gruyter.

Koike, Dale April 1992. *Language and social relationship in Brazilian Portuguese*. Austin: University of Texas Press.

König, Christa, and Bernd Heine 2003. 'Imperatives in !Xun'. Paper presented at local workshop, †RCLT, Melbourne.

————forthcoming. *A grammar of !Xun*.

König, Ekkehard 1986. 'Conditionals, concessive conditionals and concessives: areas of contrast, overlap and neutralization', pp. 229–46 of Traugott et al. 1986.

König, Ekkehard and P. Siemund 2007. 'Speech act distinctions in grammar', pp. 276–324 of *Language typology and syntactic description*, vol. 1: *Clause structure*, edited by Timothy Shopen. Cambridge: Cambridge University Press.

Koop, Gordon 1980. 'Dení verb endings'. SIL.

Kornfilt, Jaklin 1997. *Turkish*. New York: Routledge.

Koshal, Sanyukta 1979. *Ladakhi grammar*. Delhi: Motilal Banarsidass.

Kossmann, Maarten 1997. *Grammaire du parler berbère de figuig*. Paris, Louvain: Éditions Peeters.

——2000. *Esquisse grammaticale du rifain oriental*. Paris, Louvain: Éditions Peeters.

——2001. 'Les désinences modales en berbère', *Rivista degli studi orientali* 74.1–4: 25–39.

Koul, Omkar N. 2003. 'Kashmiri', pp. 895–952 of Cardona and Jain 2003.

Kozintseva, N. A. 1992. 'Imperative sentences in Armenian', pp. 130–44 of *Tipologija imperativnykh konstrukcij* (The typology of imperative constructions), edited by V. S. Xrakovskij. St Petersburg: Nauka.

——1994. 'The category of evidentiality (problems of typological analysis)' (Kategorija evidentsial'nosti (problemy tipologicheskogo analiza)), *Voprosy Jazykoznanija* 3: 92–104.

——2001. 'Imperative sentences in Armenian', pp. 245–67 of Xrakovskij 2001.

Krejnovič, Eruxim A. 1979. 'Nivkhskij jazyk' (The Nivkh language), pp. 295–329 of *Jazyki Azii i Afriki: III* (Languages of Asia and Africa). Moscow: Nauka.

Krishnamurti, B. 2003. *The Dravidian languages*. Cambridge: Cambridge University Press.

Kroeker, M. 2001. 'A descriptive grammar of Nambiquara', *International Journal of American Linguistics* 67: 1–87.

Kruspe, Nicole 2003. 'Imperatives in Ceʔ Wɔŋ'. Paper presented at the local workshop 'Imperatives and commands', †RCLT, Melbourne.

——2004a. *A grammar of Semelai*. Cambridge: Cambridge University Press.

——2004b. 'Adjectives in Semelai', pp. 283–305 of Dixon and Aikhenvald 2004.

Kučera, Henry 1985. 'Aspect in negative imperatives', pp. 118–28 of *The scope of Slavic aspect*, edited by S. Michael and Alan Timberlake. Columbus, OH: Slavica.

Künnap, A. 1999. *Enets*. Munich: Lincom Europa.

Kuryłowicz, J. 1964. *The inflectional categories of Indo-European*. Heidelberg: Carl Winter Universitätsverlag.

Kuteva, Tania 2000. 'Areal grammaticalisation: the case of the Bantu-Nilotic borderland', *Folia Linguistica* 34: 267–83.

Kuzmenkov, E. A. 1992. 'Imperative sentences in Mongolian', pp. 73–76 of *Tipologija imperativnykh konstrukcij* (The typology of imperative constructions), edited by V. S. Xrakovskij. St Petersburg: Nauka.

——2001. 'Imperative verb forms in Mongolian', pp. 98–107 of Xrakovskij 2001.

Kuznetsova, A. I., E. A. Xelimsky, and E. V. Grushkina 1980. *Ocherki po seljkupskomu jazyku: Tazovskij dialekt* (Essays on the Selkup language: Taz dialect), vol. 1. Moscow: Izdateljstvo Moskovskogo Universiteta.

Kwon, Suhyun, and Seungwan Hu 2009. 'On politeness: cross-cultural differences', *KLing. Korea University Working Papers in Linguistics* 3: 79–101.

Laanest, A. 1975. *Sissejuhatus läänemeresoome keeltesse* (Introduction to Balto-Finnic languages). Tallinn: Eesti NSV Teaduste Akadeemia, Keele ja Kirjanduse Instituut.

——1982. *Einführung in die ostseefinnischen Sprachen.* Hamburg: Buske.

Ladefoged, Peter 1975. *A course in phonetics.* New York: Harcourt Brace Jovanovich.

Lakoff, George 1984. 'Performative subordinate clauses', in *Proceedings of the Tenth International Meeting of the Berkeley Linguistics Society,* 472–80.

Lakoff, Robin 1968. *Abstract syntax and Latin complementation.* Cambridge, MA: MIT Press.

——1971. 'If's, and's and but's about conjunction', pp. 115–49 of *Studies in linguistic semantics,* edited by Charles J. Fillmore and D. T. Langedoen. New York: Holt, Rinehart & Winston.

——1972. 'Language in context', *Language* 48: 907–27.

——1973. 'The logic of politeness; or minding your p's and q's', *Papers from the Ninth Regional Meeting of the Chicago Linguistic Society,* 292–305.

Lambrecht, Knut 1994. *Information structure and sentence form: topic, focus, and the mental representation of discourse referents.* Cambridge: Cambridge University Press.

Langacker, R. 1977. *An overview of Uto-Aztecan grammar: studies in Uto-Axtecan grammar,* vol. 1. Arlington: SIL and University of Texas at Arlington.

Langdon, Margaret 1970. *A grammar of Diegueño: the Mesa Grande dialect.* Berkeley: University of California Press.

Langer, E. J. 1989. 'Minding matters: the consequences of mindlessness-mindfullness', *Advances in Experimental Social Psychology* 22: 137–73.

Laoust, E. 1928. *Cours de berbère marocain: dialectes du Maroc Central.* Paris: Librarie orientaliste Paul Geuthner.

——1931. *Siwa: son parler.* Publications de l'Institut des Hautes-études Marocaines. Tome XXII. Paris: Leroux.

Laprade, R. A. 1981. 'Some cases of Aymara influence on La Paz Spanish', pp. 207–27 of *The Aymara language in its social and cultural context: a collection of essays on aspects of Aymara language and culture,* edited by M. J. Hardman. Gainesville: University Presses of Florida.

Larousse de la langue française: lexis. 1979. Paris: Larousse.

Larson, Mildred L. 1998. *A guide to cross-language equivalence,* 2nd edn. Lanham, MD: University Press of America.

Lascarides, A., and N. Asher 2004. 'Imperatives in dialogue', pp. 1–17 of *Semantics and pragmatics of dialogue for the new millennium,* edited by P. Kuehnlein, H. Rieser, and H. Zeevat. Amsterdam: John Benjamins.

Laughren, Mary 1982. 'A preliminary description of propositional particles in Warlpiri', pp. 129–63 of *Papers in Warlpiri grammar: in memory of Lothar Jagst,* edited by S. Swartz. *Work papers of SIL-AAB,* series A, vol. 6. Darwin: Summer Institute of Linguistics.

Laughren, Mary 2002. 'Syntactic constraints in a "Free Word Order" language', pp. 83–130 of *Language universals and variation*, edited by Mengistu Amberber and Peter Collins. London: Prager.

Laycock, D. 1965. *The Ndu language family (Sepik District, New Guinea)*. Canberra: Linguistic Circle of Canberra Publications.

Leech, Geoffrey 1983. *Principles of pragmatics*. London: Longman.

——and Jan Svartvik 1975. *Communicative grammar of English*. London: Longman.

Lees, Robert B. 1964. 'On passives and imperatives in English', *Gengu Kankyu* 46: 28–41.

Leger, R. 1994. *Eine Grammatik der Kwami-Sprache (Nordostnigeria)*. Cologne: Rüdiger Köppe Verlag.

Lehman, Christina 1977. 'Imperatives', pp. 143–8 of *Haya grammatical structure*, edited by E. R. Byarushengo, A. Duranti, and L. M. Hyman. Los Angeles: University of Southern California.

Leman, Wayne 1980. *A reference grammar of the Cheyenne language*. Greeley: Museum of Anthropology, University of Northern Colorado.

Leslau, Wolf 1995. *Reference grammar of Amharic*. Wiesbaden: Harrassowitz.

Levenston, E. A. 1969. 'Imperative structures in English', *Linguistics* 50: 39–43.

Li, C., and S. Thompson 1981. *Mandarin Chinese: a functional reference grammar*. Berkeley: University of California Press.

Li, Paul. 1973. *Rukai structure*. Taipei: Institute of History and Philology, Academia Sinica.

Liberman, Kenneth 1985. *Understanding interaction in central Australia: an ethnomethodological study of Australian Aboriginal people*. Boston: Routledge & Kegan Paul.

Lichtenberk, F. 1983. *A grammar of Manam*. Honolulu: University of Hawai'i Press.

——2006. 'Serial verb constructions in Toqabaqita', pp. 254–72 of *Serial verb constructions: a cross-linguistic typology*, edited by Alexandra Y. Aikhenvald and R. M. W. Dixon. Oxford: Oxford University Press.

——2008. *A grammar of Toqabaqita*. Berlin: Mouton de Gruyter.

Liddicoat, A. 1999. 'Questions in Romance languages'. Workshop on questions, ANU.

Linn, M. 2000. 'A grammar of Euchee (Yuchi)'. PhD dissertation, University of Kansas.

Lockwood, W. B. 1969. *Indo-European Philology*. London: Hutchinson.

Löfstedt, Leena 1966. *Les expressions du commandement et de la défense en latin et leur survie dans les langues romanes*. Helsinki: Société Néophilologique.

Long Yaohong and Zheng Guoqiao 1998. *The Dong language in Guizhou Province, China*. Arlington: SIL and University of Texas at Arlington.

Lopatin, 1970. 'Slovoobrazovanie imen suschestviteljnykh' (Word formation of nouns), pp. 46–176 of *Grammatika sovremennogo russkogo literaturnogo jazyka*, edited by N. Ju. Shvedova. Moscow: Nauka.

Louwerse, John 1988. *The morphosyntax of Una in relation to discourse structure: a descriptive analysis*. Canberra: Pacific Linguistics.

Lydall, Jean 1976. 'Hamer', pp. 393–438 of *The non-Semitic languages of Ethiopia*, edited by M. L. Bender. East Lansing: African Studies Center, Michigan State University.

Lynch, John, Malcolm Ross, and Terry Crowley 2002. *The Oceanic languages*. London: Routledge.

Lyons, John 1977. *Semantics*, vol. 2. Cambridge: Cambridge University Press.

Lytkin, V. I. 1966. 'Komi-permjackij jazyk' (The Komi-Permiak language), pp. 300–315 of *Jazyki narodov SSSR*, vol. 3. Moscow-Leningrad: Nauka.

Macaulay, Donald 1992. *The Celtic languages*. Cambridge: Cambridge University Press.

Macaulay, Monica 1982. 'Verbs of motion and arrival in Mixtec', pp. 404–16 of *Proceedings of the Eighth Annual Meeting of the Berkeley Linguistics Society*.

——1996. *A grammar of Chalcatongo Mixtec*. Berkeley: University of California Press.

Mackridge, Peter 1985. *The modern Greek language*. Oxford: Clarendon Press.

Mägiste, J. 1976. 'Viron imperatiivin preteriti', *Virittäjä* 48–51.

Magnúsdóttir, S., and H. Thráinsson 1990. 'Agrammatism in Icelandic', pp. 443–543 of Menn and Obler 1990a.

Magometov, A. A. 1965. *Tabasaranskij jazyk*. Tbilisi: Mecniereba.

——1970. *Aguljskij jazyk*. Tbilisi: Mecniereba.

Mahootian, S. 1997. *Persian*. London: Routledge.

Maiden, Martin, and Cecilia Robustelli 2007. *A reference grammar of modern Italian*, 2nd edn. London: Arnold.

Maisak, T. A. 2005. *Tipologia grammatikalizacii konstrukcij s glagolami dvizhenija i glagolami pozicii*. Moscow: Jazyki slavjanskikh kultur.

Malčukov, Andrej L. 2001. 'Imperative constructions in Even', pp. 159–80 of *Typology of imperative constructions*, edited by V. S. Xrakovskij. Munich: Lincom Europa.

Mallinson, G. 1986. *Rumanian*. London: Croom Helm.

Malygina, L. V. 1992. 'Imperative sentences in Modern Hebrew', pp. 144–51 of *Tipologija imperativnykh konstrukcij* (The typology of imperative constructions), edited by V. S. Xrakovskij. St Petersburg: Nauka.

——2001. 'Imperative sentences in Modern Hebrew', pp. 268–86 of Xrakovskij 2001.

Marchese, Lynell 1986. *Tense and aspect and the development of auxiliaries in Kru languages*. Arlington: SIL and University of Texas at Arlington.

Maring, Joel 1967. 'Grammar of Acoma Keresan'. PhD dissertation, Indiana University.

Marmion, Douglas Edric 1996. 'A description of the morphology of Wajarri'. Honours thesis, University of New England.

Martin, Samuel E. 1975. *A reference grammar of Japanese*. Tokyo: Charles E. Tuttle. Company.

Martins, Silvana A. 1994. *Análise da morfosintaxe da língua Dâw (Maku-Kamã) e sua classificação tipológica*. MA thesis, Florianópolis, Brazil.

——2005. *Fonologia e gramática Dâw*. Amsterdam: LOT.

——and Valteir Martins 1999. 'Makú', pp. 251–68 of *The Amazonian languages*, edited by R. M. W. Dixon and Alexandra Aikhenvald. Cambridge: Cambridge University Press.

Maslova, E. S. 1988. 'On the structure of the imperative paradigm in the language of Kolyma Jukaghirs', pp. 78–80 of Birjulin et al. 1988.

Matisoff, James A. 1973. *The grammar of Lahu*. Berkeley: University of California Press.

Matisoff, James A. 2000. *Blessings, curses, hopes and fears: psycho-ostensive expressions in Yiddish*. Stanford, CA: Stanford University Press.

Matras, Y. 1998. 'Utterance modifiers and universals of grammatical borrowing', *Linguistics* 36: 281–331.

——2002. *Romani: a linguistic introduction*. Cambridge: Cambridge University Press.

Matthews, P. H. 1981. *Syntax*. Cambridge: Cambridge University Press.

——1997. *Concise dictionary of linguistics*. Oxford: Oxford University Press.

Matthews, Stephen, and Virginia Yip 1994. *Cantonese: a comprehensive grammar*. London: Routledge.

Mattina, N. 1999. 'Moses-Columbia imperatives and Interior Salish', *Anthropological Linguistics* 41: 1–27.

Mauri, Caterina, and Andrea Sansò 2012. 'The reality status of directives and its coding across languages', *Language Sciences* 34, 2: 147–70.

McCawley, James D. (Quang Phuc Dong) 1971. 'English sentences without overt grammatical subject', pp. 3–10 of *Studies out in left field: defamatory essays presented to James D. McCawley*, edited by Arnold M. Zwicky, Peter H. Salus, Robert I. Binnck, and Anthony L. Vanek. Edmonton Alberta: Linguistic Research.

MacDonald, L. 1990. *A grammar of Tauya*. Berlin: Mouton de Gruyter.

McGregor, W. 1990. *A functional grammar of Gooniyandi*. Amsterdam: John Benjamins.

——1994. 'The grammar of reported speech in Gooniyandi'. *Australian Journal of Linguistics* 14: 63–92.

McKay, Graham R. 1975. 'Rembarrnga, a language of Central Arnhem Land'. PhD dissertation, ANU.

——2000. 'Ndjébbana', pp. 155–354 of *The handbook of Australian languages*, vol. 5, edited by R. M. W. Dixon and Barry J. Blake. Melbourne: Oxford University Press.

McLellan, M. 1992. 'A study of the Wangurri language'. PhD dissertation, Macquarie University.

McLendon, S. 1996. 'Sketch of Eastern Pomo, a Pomoan language', pp. 507–50 of *Handbook of North American Indian languages*, vol. 17, edited by I. Goddard. Washington, DC: Smithsonian Institution.

Mead, M. 1935. *Sex and temperament in three primitive societies*. New York: Morrow.

Meinhof, Carl 1930. *Der Koranadialekt des Hottentottischen*. Berlin: Reimer.

Mel'čuk, Igor A. 1994. 'Suppletion: towards a logical analysis of the concept', *Studies in Language* 18: 339–410.

——2000. 'Suppletion', pp. 510–22 of *Morfologie/Morphology: Ein internationales Handbuch zur Flexion und Wortbildung/An international handbook on inflection and word formation*, vol. 1, edited by Geert Booij, Christian Lehmann, and Joachim Mugdan. Berlin: Mouton de Gruyter.

Melnar, L. R. 2004. *Caddo verb morphology*. Lincoln: Nebraska University Press.

Menn, L. 1989. 'Some people who don't talk right: universal and particular in child language, aphasia, and language obsolescence', pp. 335–45 of *Investigating obsolescence: studies in language contraction and death*, edited by Nancy Dorian. Cambridge: Cambridge University Press.

——1990. 'Agrammatism in English: two case studies', pp. 117–78 of Menn and Obler 1990a.

——and L. K. Obler, eds. 1990a. *Agrammatic aphasia: a cross-language narrative sourcebook.* Amsterdam: John Benjamins.

——————1990b. 'Cross-language data and theories of agrammatism', pp. 1369–89 of Menn and Obler 1990a.

Merlan, Francesca 1983. *Ngalakan grammar, texts and vocabulary.* Canberra: Pacific Linguistics.

——1994. *A grammar of Wardaman: a language of the Northern Territory of Australia.* Berlin: Mouton de Gruyter.

——and Alan Rumsey 1991. *Ku Waru: language and segmentary politics in in the Western Nebilyer Valley, Papua New Guinea.* Cambridge: Cambridge University Press.

Metslang, H. 2000. 'Reflections on development of a particle in Estonian', pp. 59–86 of *Estonian: typological studies*, vol. 4, edited by Mati Erelt. Tartu: Tartu University Press.

——2009. 'Estonian grammar between Finnic and SAE: some comparisons', *Sprachtypologie und Universalienforschung* 62: 49–71.

——L. Muižniece, and K. Pajusalu 1999. 'Past participle finitization in Estonian and Latvian', *Estonian: typological studies* 3 (Tartu Ülikooli eesti keele õppetooli toimetised 11): 128–57.

——and K. Pajusalu 2002. 'Evidentiality in South Estonian', *Linguistica Uralica* 2: 98–109.

Metzger, R. G. 1998. 'The morpheme *KA-* of Carapana (Tucanoan)', *SIL Electronic Working Papers* 1998–003.

Michael, Lev David 2008. 'Nanti evidential practices: language, knowledge, and social action in an Amazonian society'. PhD dissertation, University of Austin, Texas.

Michalowski, P. 1980. 'Sumerian as an ergative language', *Journal of Cuneiform Studies* 32: 86–103.

Miestamo, Matti 2005. *Standard negation: the negation of declarative verbal main clause in a typological perspective.* Berlin: Mouton de Gruyter.

——and Johan van der Auwera 2007. 'Negative declaratives and negative imperatives: similarities and differences', pp. 59–78 of *Linguistics festival, May 2006, Bremen*, edited by Andreas Ammann. Bochum: Brockmeyer.

Mihalic, F. 1971. *The Jacaranda dictionary and grammar of Melanesian Pidigin.* Milton: Jacaranda Press.

Mikushev, R. A. 1988. 'Towards the question of the imperative paradigm in Komi', pp. 81–3 of Birjulin et al. 1988.

Miller, A. 2001. *A grammar of Jamul Tiipay.* Berlin: Mouton de Gruyter.

Miller, M. 1999. *Desano grammar.* Arlington: SIL and University of Texas at Arlington.

Miller, W. 1996. 'A sketch of Shoshone, a Uto-Aztecan language', pp. 639–720 of *Handbook of North American Indian languages*, vol. 17, edited by I. Goddard. Washington, DC: Smithsonian Institution.

Millis, Anne E. 1985. 'The acquisition of German', pp. 141–254 of Slobin 1985.

Millward, C. 1971. *Imperative constructions in Old English*. The Hague: Mouton.

Milton, Kay 1982. 'Meaning and context: the interpretation of greetings in Kasigau', pp. 261–77 of *Semantic anthropology*, edited by David Parkin. London: Academic Press.

Mitchell, T. F. 1962. *Colloquial Arabic: the living language of Egypt*. London: English Universities Press.

Mithun, Marianne 1995. 'On the relativity of irreality', pp. 367–88 of *Modality in grammar and discourse*, edited by Barbara Fox and P. J. Hopper. Amsterdam: John Benjamins.

——1999. *The languages of Native North America*. Cambridge: Cambridge University Press.

——2007. 'What is a language? Documentation for diverse and evolving audiences', *Sprachtypologie und Universalienforschung* 60: 42–55.

Mittwoch, Anita 1976. 'Grammar and illocutionary force', *Lingua* 40: 21–42.

Moravcsik, E. 1978. 'Language contact', pp. 93–123 of *Universals of human languages*, vol. 1, edited by Joseph H. Greenberg, Charles A. Ferguson, and Edith A. Moravcsik. Stanford, CA: Stanford University Press.

Morgan, J. L. 1978. 'Two types of convention in indirect speech acts', pp. 261–80 of *Syntax and Semantics. Volume 9. Pragmatics*, edited by Peter Cole. New York: Academic Press.

Morphy, F. 1983. 'Djapu, a Yolngu dialect', pp. 1–88 of *Handbook of Australian languages*, vol. 3, edited by R. M. W. Dixon and Barry J. Blake. Canberra: ANU Press and Amsterdam: John Benjamins.

Morse, Nancy L., and Michael B. Maxwell 1999. *Cubeo grammar*. Arlington: SIL and University of Texas at Arlington.

Mortensen, C. A. 1999. *A reference grammar of Northern Embera languages*. Arlington: SIL and University of Texas at Arlington.

Motsch, W. 1994. 'Word-formation: compounding', pp. 5021–4 of *The encyclopedia of language and linguistics*, edited by R. E. Asher and J. M. Y. Simpson, vol. 9. Oxford: Pergamon.

Mous, M. 1993. *A grammar of Irakw*. Hamburg: Buske.

——2003. 'Nen', pp. 283–306 of *The Bantu languages*, edited by Derek Nurse and Gérard Philippson. London: Routledge.

——forthcoming. *A grammar of Alagwa*.

Moutafakis, Nicholas J. 1975. *Imperatives and their logics*. New Delhi: Sterling Publishers PVT Ltd.

Mühlhäusler, P. 1985. 'Internal development of Tok Pisin', pp. 75–166 of *Handbook of Tok Pisin (New Guinea Pidgin)*, edited by S. A. Wurm and P. Mühlhäusler. Canberra: Pacific Linguistics.

Mulder, Jean 1989. 'Syntactic ergativity in Coast Tsimshian (Sm'algyax)', *Studies in Language* 13: 405–35.

Musgrave, Jill 2007. *A grammar of Neve'ei, Vanuatu*. Canberra: Pacific Linguistics.

Myhill, J. 1998. 'A study of imperative usage in Biblical Hebrew and in English', *Studies in Language* 22: 391–443.

Nakayama, Toshihide 2001. *Nuuchahnulth (Nootka) morphosyntax*. Berkeley: University of California Press.

Narrog, Heiko 2005. 'On defining modality again', *Language Sciences* 27: 165–92.

Nash, D. G. 1980. *Topics in Warlpiri grammar*. New York: Garland.

Nasilov, D. M., X. F. Isxakova, Sh. S. Safarov, and I. A. Nevskaya 1992. 'Imperative sentences in Turkic languages', pp. 106–19 of *Tipologija imperativnykh konstrukcij* (The typology of imperative constructions), edited by V. S. Xrakovskij. St Petersburg: Nauka.

————————(2001) 'Imperative sentences in Turkic languages', pp. 181–220 of Xrakovskij 2001.

Nedjalkov, I. 1997. *Evenki*. London: Routledge.

Neukom, L. 2001. *Santali*. Munich: Lincom Europa.

Newman, Paul 1980. *The classification of Chadic within Afroasiatic*. Leiden: Leiden University Press.

——2000. *The Hausa language: an encyclopedic reference grammar*. New Haven, CT: Yale University Press.

Newman, S. 1944. *Yokuts language of California*. New York: Viking Fund Publications in Anthropology no. 2.

——1996. 'Sketch of the Zuni language', pp. 483–506 of *Handbook of North American Indian languages*, vol. 17, edited by I. Goddard. Washington, DC: Smithsonian Institution.

Nikolaeva, Irina, and Maria Tolskaya 2001. *A grammar of Udihe*. Berlin: Mouton de Gruyter.

Noonan, M. 1992. *A grammar of Lango*. Berlin: Mouton de Gruyter.

Nordlinger, Rachel 1998. *A grammar of Wambaya*. Canberra: Pacific Linguistics.

Nuyts, Jan 2006. 'Overview and linguistic issues', pp. 1–26 of *The expression of modality*, edited by William Frawley. Berlin: Mouton de Gruyter.

Oberg, S. Gy. 1999. 'Requests in Akan discourse', *Anthropological Linguistics* 41: 230–51.

Oda, Ongaye, forthcoming. 'A grammar of Konso'. PhD dissertation, University of Leiden.

Okell, J. 1969. *A reference grammar of Colloquial Burmese*. London: Oxford University Press.

Olawsky, K. 1999. *Aspects of Dagbani grammar—with special emphasis on phonology and morphology*. Munich: Lincom Europa.

——2006. *A grammar of Urarina*. Berlin: Mouton de Gruyter.

Omar, Margaret K. 1973. *The acquisition of Egyptian Arabic as a native language*. The Hague: Mouton.

Onishi, M. 1994. 'A grammar of Motuna (Bougainville, Papua New Guinea)'. PhD dissertation, ANU.

Onishi, M. 1996. 'A grammatical summary of Motuna'. †RCLT internal document, ANU.

——1997a. 'A grammatical summary of Ainu'. †RCLT internal document, ANU.

——1997b. 'A grammatical summary of Japanese'. †RCLT internal document, ANU.

——1997c. 'A grammatical summary of Bengali'. †RCLT internal document, ANU.

——2001. 'Introduction: non-canonically marked subjects and objects: parameters and properties', pp. 1–52 of *Non-canonical marking of subjects and objects,* edited by Alexandra Y. Aikhenvald, R. M. W. Dixon, and M. Onishi. Amsterdam: Benjamins.

Osborne, C. R. 1974. *The Tiwi language.* Canberra: Australian Institute of Aboriginal Studies.

Osumi, Midori 1995. *Tinrin grammar.* Honolulu: University of Hawai'i Press.

Oswalt, Robert Louis 1961. 'A Kashaya grammar (Southwestern Pomo)'. PhD dissertation, University of California.

Overall, Simon E. 2008. 'A grammar of Aguaruna'. PhD dissertation, La Trobe University.

Owens, J. 1985. *A grammar of Harar Oromo (Northeastern Ethiopia).* Hamburg: Helmut Buske Verlag.

Ozhegov, S. I., and N. Y. Shvedova 1997. *Explanatory dictionary of Russian (Tolkovyj slovarj russkogo jazyka).* Moscow: RAN.

Pakendorf, Brigitte, and Ewa Schalley 2007. 'From possibility to prohibition: a rare grammaticalization pathway', *Linguistic Typology* 11: 515–40.

Palmer, F. R. 1986. *Mood and modality.* Cambridge: Cambridge University Press.

Palmer, Leonard Robert 1954. *The Latin language.* London : Faber & Faber.

Pandharipande, R. 1997. *Marathi.* London: Routledge.

Parker, Gary John 1969. *Ayacucho Quechua grammar and dictionary.* The Hague: Mouton.

Patz, E. 1991. 'Djabugay', pp. 245–347 of *Handbook of Australian languages,* vol. 4, edited by R. M. W. Dixon and Barry J. Blake. Melbourne: Oxford University Press.

Payne, Doris L., and Thomas E. Payne 1990. 'Yagua', pp. 249–474 of *Handbook of Amazonian languages,* vol. 2, edited by D. C. Derbyshire and G. K. Pullum. Berlin: Mouton de Gruyter.

Payne, John R. 1985. 'Negation', pp. 197–242 of *Language typology and syntactic description,* vol. 1: *Clause structure,* edited by Timothy Shopen. Cambridge: Cambridge University Press.

Payne, Thomas E., and Doris L. Payne 1999. 'A grammatical summary of Panare'. †RCLT internal document, ANU.

Pearson, Greg, and René van den Berg 2008. *Lote grammar sketch.* Ukarumpa: SIL.

Peñalosa, Fernando 1987. 'Major syntactic structures of Acatec (dialect of San Miguel Acatán)', *IJAL* 281–310.

Peterson, David 2006. *Applicative constructions.* Oxford: Oxford University Press.

Peyraube, Alain 1999. 'On the modal auxiliaries of possibility in Classical Chinese', pp. 27–52 of *Selected papers from the Fifth International Conference in Chinese Linguistics.* Taipei: Crane.

Pizziconi, B. 2006. 'Politeness', pp. 679–84 of *Encyclopedia of language and linguistics*, edited by Keith Brown. Oxford: Elsevier.

Plank, F. 1991. *Paradigms: the economy of inflection*. Berlin: Mouton de Gruyter.

——and W. Schellinger 1997. 'The uneven distribution of genders over numbers: Greenberg Nos. 37 and 45', *Linguistic Typology* 1: 53–101.

Plungian, V. A. 1988. 'The verb "look" in imperative constructions in Dogon', pp. 101–2 of Birjulin et al. 1988.

——1995. *Dogon*. Munich: Lincom Europa.

Podlesskaya, Vera 2005a. 'Russkie glagoly *datj/davatj:* ot pramykh upotreblenij k grammatikalizovannym', *Voprosy jazykoznanija* 2: 89–103.

——2005b. '"Give"-verbs as permissive auxiliaries in Russian', *Language Typology and Universals* 58.1: 124–38.

Poeck K., G. Lehmkuhl, and K. Willmes 1982. 'Axial movements in ideomotor apraxia', *Journal of Neurology, Neurosurgery, and Psychiatry* 45: 1125–9.

Pope, M. K. 1934. *From Latin to Modern French with especial consideration of Anglo-Norman*. Manchester: Manchester University Press.

Popjes J., and J. Popjes 1986. 'Canela-Krahô', pp. 128–99 of *Handbook of Amazonian languages*, vol. 1, edited by D. C. Derbyshire and G. K. Pullum. Berlin: Mouton de Gruyter.

Poppe, Nikolaus 1951. *Khalkha Mongolische Grammatik mit Bibliographie, Sprachproben und Glossar*. Wiesbaden: Franz Steiner Verlag.

Posner, R. 1996. *The Romance languages*. Cambridge: Cambridge University Press.

Postal, Paul 1964. 'Underlying and superficial linguistic structure', *Harvard Educational Review* 34: 246–66.

Potsdam, E. 1998. *Syntactic issues in the English imperative*. London: Taylor & Francis.

Prasse, Karl-G. 1973. *Manuel de grammaire touaregue (tăhăggart)*, vols. 6 and 7. Copenhagen: Akademisk Forlag.

Press, Margaret 1979. *Chemehuevi: a grammar and lexicon*. Berkeley: University of California Press.

Pustet, R. 2001. 'A grammatical summary of Lakhota'. †RCLT internal document, La Trobe University.

Queixalos, F. 2000. *Syntaxe Sikuani (Colombie)*. Louvain: Peeters.

Quesada, J. Diego 2000. *A grammar of Teribe*. Munich: Lincom Europa.

Quick, Phil 2007. *A grammar of the Pendau language of Central Sulawesi, Indonesia*. Canberra: Pacific Linguistics.

Quintero, Carolyn 2004. *Osage grammar*. Lincoln: University of Nebraska Press.

Quirk, R., S. Greenbaum, G. Leech, and J. Svartvik 1972. *A grammar of contemporary English*. London: Longman.

————1985. *A comprehensive grammar of the English language*. London: Longman.

Ramirez, H. 1992. *Le Bahuana, une nouvelle langue de la famille Arawak*. Paris: Chantiers Amerindia. Supplement 1 au n°. 17 *d'Amerindia*, Paris.

——1994. *Le parler Yanomami des Xamatauteri*. Paris.

Ramirez, H. 1997. *A fala Tukano dos Yepâ-masa*, vol. 1: *Gramática*; vol. 2: *Dicionário*; vol. 3: *Método de aprendizagem*. Manaus: Inspetoria Salesiana Misionária da Amazônia.

Rapold, Christian J. 2006. 'Towards a grammar of Benchnon'. PhD dissertation, University of Leiden.

Reh, Mechthild 1985. *Die Krongo-Sprache (Nìino Mó-dì)*. *Beschreibung, Texte, Wörterverzeichnis*. Berlin: Reimer.

Rehg, K. (with D. C. Sohl) 1981. *Ponapean reference grammar*. Honolulu: University of Hawai'i Press.

Renck, G. L. 1975. *A grammar of Yagaria*. Canberra: Pacific Linguistics.

Renisio, A. 1932. *Étude sur le dialectes berbères des Beni Iznassen, du Rif et des Senhaja de Sraïr*. Paris: Leroux.

Rennison, J. 1997. *Koromfe*. London: Routledge.

Ribeiro, Eduardo Rivail 2006. 'Macro-Jê'. pp. 665–9 of *Concise Encyclopedia of Languages of the World*, edited by Keith Brown and Sarah Ogilvie. Oxford: Elsevier.

Riccardi, Theodore 2003. 'Nepali', pp. 538–80 of Cardona and Jain 2003.

Rice, K. 1989. *A grammar of Slave*. Berlin: Mouton de Gruyter.

Riese, Timothy 1998. 'Permian', pp. 249–75 of Abondolo 1998c.

Rigsby, Bruce 1975. 'Nass-Gitskan: an analytic ergative syntax', *IJAL* 41: 346–54.

——and N. Rude 1996. 'Sketch of Sahaptin, a Sahaptian language', pp. 666–92 of *Handbook of North American Indian languages*, vol. 17, edited by I. Goddard. Washington, DC: Smithsonian Institution.

Roberts, J. 1987. *Amele*. London: Routledge.

——1990. 'Modality in Amele and other Papuan languages', *Journal of Linguistics* 26: 363–401.

——1997. 'Switch-reference in Papua New Guinea: a preliminary survey', pp. 101–241 of *Papers in Papuan linguistics* 3. Canberra: Pacific Linguistics.

Robins, R. H. 1938. *The Yurok language: grammar, texts, lexicon*. Berkeley: University of California Press.

Robinson, L. W., and J. Armagost 1990. *Comanche dictionary and grammar*. Arlington: SIL and University of Texas at Arlington.

Rodrigues, Aryon D. 2006. 'Macro-Jê', pp. 165–206 of *The Amazonian languages*, edited by R. M. W. Dixon and Alexandra Y. Aikhenvald. Cambridge: Cambridge University Press.

Rood, David, and Allan R. Taylor 1996. 'Lakhota', pp. 440–82 of *Handbook of North American Indian languages*, vol. 17, edited by I. Goddard. Washington, DC: Smithsonian Institution.

Rooryck, Johan, and Gertjan Postma 2007. 'On participial imperatives', pp. 297–322 of van der Wurff 2007a.

Rosaldo, M. Z. 1982. 'The things we do with words: Ilongot speech acts and speech act theory in philosophy', *Language in Society* 11: 203–37.

Rowan, O., and E. Burgess 1979. *Parecis grammar*. Brasilia: SIL.

Rubino, C. 1998. 'A grammatical summary of Ilocano'. †RCLT internal document, ANU.

Rumsey, Alan 2000. 'Bunuba', pp. 34–152 of *Handbook of Australian languages*, vol. 5, edited by R. M. W. Dixon and Barry J. Blake. Melbourne: Oxford University Press.

——2003. 'Language, desire, and the ontogenesis of intersubjectivity', *Language and Communication* 23: 169–87.

Russell, Benjamin 2007. 'Imperatives in conditional conjunction', *Natural Language Semantics* 15: 131–66.

Rust, F. 1965. *Praktische Namagrammatik*. Cape Town: Balkema.

Sadock, J. 1970. 'Whimperatives', pp. 223–38 of *Studies presented to R. B. Lees by his students*. Edmonton, Alberta: Linguistic Research.

——1974. *Toward a linguistic theory of speech acts*. New York: Academic Press.

——2004. 'Speech acts', pp. 53–73 of *Handbook of pragmatics*, edited by L. Horn and G. Ward. Oxford: Blackwell.

——and A. Zwicky 1985. 'Speech act distinctions in syntax', pp. 155–96 of *Language typology and syntactic description*, vol. 1, *Clause structure* edited by Timothy Shopen. Cambridge: Cambridge University Press.

Saeed, J. I. 1993. *Somali reference grammar*. Kensington: Dunwoody Press.

——1999. *Somali*. Amsterdam: John Benjamins.

Sakel, Jeannette 2003. 'A grammar of Mosetén'. PhD dissertation, University of Nijmegen.

——2004. *A grammar of Mosetén*. Berlin: Mouton de Gruyter.

Salminen, Tapani 1998. 'Nenets', pp. 516–47 of Abondolo 1998c.

Saltarelli, M. 1988. *Basque*. London: Croom Helm.

Sammallahti, Pekka 1998. 'Saamic', pp. 43–95 of *The Uralic languages*, edited by Daniel Abondolo. London: Routledge.

Sandler, Wendy 1999. 'Cliticization and prosodic words in a sign language', pp. 223–54 of *Studies on the phonological word*, edited by Alan T. Hall and Ursula Kleinherz. Amsterdam: John Benjamins.

Sapir, E. 1921. *Language*. New York: Harcourt, Brace & World.

——1922. 'The Takelma language of southwestern Oregon', *HAIL* 2: 1–296.

Sasse, H. J. 1998. 'A grammatical summary of Cayuga'. †RCLT internal document, ANU.

Saul, Janice E., and Nancy F. Wilson 1980. *Nung grammar*. Arlington: SIL and University of Texas at Arlington.

Saxena, Anju 2002. 'Request and command in Kinnauri: the pragmatics of translating politeness', *Linguistics of Tibeto-Burman Area* 25: 185–93.

Saxton, D. 1982. 'Papago', pp. 93–266 of *Studies in Uto-Axtecan grammar*, vol. 3. Arlington: SIL and University of Texas at Arlington.

Schachter, P., and F. T. Otanes 1972. *Tagalog reference grammar*. Berkeley: University of California Press.

Schadeberg, Thilo C. 1992. *A sketch of Swahili morphology*. Cologne: Köppe.

Schalley, Ewa. 2008. 'Imperatives: A typological approach'. PhD dissertation, Universiteit Antwerpen.

Schalley Ewa, and Johan van der Auwera 2005. 'On synthetic and analytic imperatives in Slavic', *Slavica Gandensia*, 32: 153–181.

Schaub, Willi 1985. *Babungo*. London: Croom Helm.

Schauer, Stanley, and Junia Schauer 1978. 'Una gramática del Yucuna', *Artigos en lingüística e campos afines* 5: 1–52.

———2000. 'El yucuna', pp. 515–32 of *Lenguas indígenas de Colombia: una visión descriptiva*, edited by M. S. González de Pérez and M. L. Rodríguez de Montes. Santafé de Bogotá: Instituto Caro y Cuervo.

———2005. *Meke kemakánaka puráka'aloji. Wapura'akó chu, eyá karíwana chu. Diccionario bilingüe yukuna-español español-yukuna*. Bogotá: Editorial Fundación para el Desarrollo de los Pueblos Marginados.

Schieffelin, Bambi 1985. 'The acquisition of Kaluli', pp. 525–93 of Slobin 1985.

———1990. *The give and the take of everyday life: language socialization of Kaluli children*. Cambridge: Cambridge University Press.

Schmerling, Susan F. 1974. 'Contrastive stress and semantic relations', pp. 608–16 of *Papers from the Tenth Regional Meeting of the Chicago Linguistic Society*, edited by M. W. LaGaly et al.

———1975. 'Imperative subject deletion and some related matters', *Linguistic Inquiry* 6: 501–11.

———1980. 'On the syntax and semantics of English imperatives', MS, Department of Linguistics, University of Texas at Austin.

———1982. 'How imperatives are special, and how they aren't', pp. 202–18 of *Papers from the parasession on nondeclaratives*. CLS.

Schmidt, Annette 1985. *Young people's Dyirbal: an example of language death from Australia*. Cambridge: Cambridge University Press.

Schmidt, Ruth Laila 2003. 'Urdu', pp. 286–350 of Cardona and Jain 2003.

Schneider, Evgenij 1936. *Kratkij udegejsko-russkij slovar'* (A concise Udihe-Russian dictionary). Moscow, Leningrad: Uchpedgiz.

Schneider-Blum, Gertrud 2007. *A grammar of Alaaba, a Highland East Cushitic language of Ethiopia*. Cologne: Rüdiger Köppe.

Schöttelndryer, B. 1980. 'Person markers in Sherpa', pp. 125–30 of *Papers in South-East Asian linguistics*, edited by R. L. Trail. Canberra: Pacific Linguistics.

Schuh, Russell G. 1978. *Bole-Tangale languages of the Bauchi area (Northern Nigeria)*. Berlin: Reimer.

Scotton, C., and H. Owsley 1982. 'What about powerful questions?', pp. 219–27 of *CLS* 1982.

Searle, J. R. 1969. *Speech acts: an essay in the philosophy of language*. Cambridge: Cambridge University Press.

———1975. 'Indirect speech acts', pp. 59–82 of Cole and Morgan 1975.

———1976. 'A classification of illocutionary acts', *Language in Society* 5: 1–23.

———1979. *Expression and meaning: studies in the theory of speech acts*. Cambridge: Cambridge University Press.

———1999. *Mind, language and society: philosophy in the real world*. New York: Basic Books.

Seki, L. 2000. *Gramática da língua Kamaiurá*. Campinas: Editora da Unicamp.

Serzisko, F., MS. 'A grammatical summary of Ik (Kuliak)'. †RCLT internal document, La Trobe University.

Seyoum, Mulugeta 2008. *A grammar of Dime*. Amsterdam: LOT.

Shackle, Christopher 2003. 'Panjabi', pp. 581–621 of Cardona and Jain 2003.

Shakhmatov, A. A. 1925. *Sintaksis russkogo yazyka* (Syntax of Russian). Leningrad: Izdateljstvo Akademii nauk SSSR.

Shapiro, Michael C. 2003. 'Hindi', pp. 250–85 of Cardona and Jain 2003.

Sharp, J. 2003a. 'Imperatives and commands in Karajarri'. Paper presented at the workshop 'Imperatives and commands', †RCLT, La Trobe University.

——2003b. 'Imperatives and commands in Nyangumarta'. Paper presented at the workshop 'Imperatives and commands', †RCLT, La Trobe University.

——2004. *A grammar of Nyangumarta*. Canberra: Pacific Linguistics.

Sherwood, David Fairchild 1986. *Maliseet-Passamaquoddy verb morphology*. Canadian Ethnology Service, Paper No 105.

Shetter, William Z. 1994. *Dutch: an essential grammar*. London: Routledge.

Shibatani, M. 2006. 'Honorifics', pp. 381–90 of *Encyclopedia of language and linguistics*, edited by Keith Brown. Oxford: Elsevier.

Shipley, William F. 1964. *Maidu grammar*. University of California Publications in Linguistics 41.

Shmelev, D. N. 2002. *Selected works on Russian* (Izbrannye trudy po russkomu jazyku). Moscow: Jazyki russkoj kuljtury.

Shvedova, N. Ju. 1970. 'Prostoe predlozhenie' (Simple sentence), pp. 541–651 of *Grammatika sovremennogo russkogo literaturnogo jazyka*, edited by N. Ju. Shvedova. Moscow: Nauka.

Siewierska, Anna 2004. *Person*. Cambridge: Cambridge University Press.

Simoncsics, Péter 1998. 'Kamassian', pp. 580–601 of Abondolo 1998c.

Simpson, Jane 1991. *Warlpiri morpho-syntax: a lexicalist approach*. Dordrecht: Kluwer Academic.

Slobin, Dan Isaac, ed. 1985. *The cross-linguistic study of language acquisition*, vol. 1: *The data*, edited by D. Slobin. Hillsdale, NJ: Lawrence Erlbaum Associates.

Smith, I., and S. Johnson 2000. 'Kugu Nganhcara', pp. 355–489 of *The handbook of Australian languages*, vol. 5, edited by R. M. W. Dixon and Barry J. Blake. Melbourne: Oxford University Press.

Smothermon, J. R., and J. H. Smothermon (with P. S. Frank) 1995. *Bosquejo del Macuna: aspectos de la cultura material de los macunas; Fonología; Gramática*. Bogotá: Instituto Lingüístico de Verano.

Sneddon, J. N. 1996. *Indonesian reference grammar*. Brisbane: Allen & Unwin.

Sohn, H.-M. 1986. *Linguistic expeditions*. Seoul: Hanshin.

——1994. *Korean*. London: Routledge.

——1999. *The Korean language*. Cambridge: Cambridge University Press.

——2004. 'The adjective class in Korean', pp. 223–41 of Dixon and Aikhenvald 2004.

Solnit, David B. 2006. 'Verb serialization in Eastern Kayah Li', pp. 146–59 of Aikhenvald and Dixon 2006.

Sorensen, A. P., Jr. 1967. 'Multilingualism in the Northwest Amazon', *American Anthropologist* 69: 670–84. Reprinted as pp. 78–93 of *Sociolinguistics*, edited by J. B. Pride and J. Holmes. Harmondsworth: Penguin, 1972.

Sparing-Chavez, Margarethe 2008. *Materials on Amahuaca*. Dallas: SIL.

Spencer, Katharine 2008. 'Kwomtari grammar essentials', pp. 53–77 of *Kwomtari phonology and grammar essentials*, edited by Murray Hornsberger, Carol Hornsberger, and Ian Tupper. Ukarumpa: SIL/PNG Academic Publications.

Sridhar, S. N. 1990. *Kannada*. London: Routledge.

Stebbins, Tonya N. 2001. 'A grammatical summary of Sm'algyax'. †RCLT internal document, La Trobe University.

——2003. 'Imperatives and commands in Mali'. Local workshop 'Imperatives and other commands'. †RCLT.

Stegnij, V. A. 1992. 'Imperative sentences in Klamath', pp. 64–72 of *Tipologija imperativnykh konstrukcij* (The typology of imperative constructions), edited by V. S. Xrakovskij. St Petersburg: Nauka.

Stenzel, K. S. 2004. 'A reference grammar of Wanano'. PhD dissertation. University of Colorado.

Stirling, L. 1998. 'Isolated *if*-clauses in Australian English', pp. 273–94 of *The clause in English: in honour of Rodney Huddleston*, edited by P. Collins and D. Lee. Amsterdam: John Benjamins.

Stockwell, Robert. P., Paul Schachter, and Barbara Partee 1973. *The major syntactic structures of English*. New York: Holt, Rinehart & Winston.

Strom, Clay 1992. *Retuarã syntax*. Arlington: SIL and University of Texas at Arlington.

Stumme, Hans 1899. *Handbuch des Schilhischen von Tazerwalt. Grammatik—Lesestücke—Gespräche—Glossar*. Leipzig: J. C. Hinrichs'sche Buchhandlung.

Sulkala, H., and M. Karjalainen 1992. *Finnish*. London: Routledge.

Sumbatova, Nina B., and Rasul O. Mutalov 2003. *A grammar of Icari Dargwa*. Munich: Lincom Europa.

Sumbuk, Kenneth M. 1999. 'Morphosyntax of Sare'. PhD dissertation, University of Waikato.

Sun, Jackson 2007. 'The irrealis category in rGyalrong', *Language and Linguistics* 3: 797–819.

Sweet, H. 1891. *A new English grammar, logical and historical*. Oxford: Clarendon Press.

Takahashi, Hidemitsu 1994. 'English imperatives and speaker commitment', *Language Sciences* 16: 371–85.

——2000. 'English imperatives and passives', pp. 239–58 of *Constructions in cognitive linguistics*, edited by Ad Foolen and Frederike van der Leek. Amsterdam: John Benjamins.

——2005. 'Imperatives in subordinate clauses', *Annual Report on Cultural Science* 117: 45–87.

——2008. 'Imperatives in concessive clauses: compatibility between constructions', *e-Language*.

Tamura, Suzuko 2000. *The Ainu language*. Tokyo: Sanseido.

Taylor, Charles 1985. *Nkore-Kiga*. London: Croom Helm.

Taylor, Gerald 1991. *Introdução à língua Baniwa do Içana*. Campinas: Editora da Unicamp.

Tedesco, P. 1923. 'a-Stämme und aya-Stämme in Iranischen', *Zeitschrift für Indologie und Iranistik* 2: 281–316.

Tepljashina, T. I., and V. I. Lytkin 1976. 'Permskie jazyki' (Permic languages), pp. 97–228 of *Osnovy finno-ugorskogo jazykoznanija: Marijskij, permskie i ugorskie jazyki* (Foundations of Finno-Ugric linguistics: Mari, Permic and Ugric languages). Moscow: Nauka.

Tereschenko, N. M. 1966. 'The Enets language' (Enetskij jazyk), pp. 438–57 of *Jazyki narodov SSSR*, vol. 3. Moscow-Leningrad: Nauka.

——1973. *Syntax of Samoyede languages (Sintaksis samodijskih jazykov)*. Leningrad: Nauka.

——1979. *Nganasanskij jazyk* (The Nganasan Language). Leningrad: Nauka.

Terrill, A. 2003. *A grammar of Lavukaleve*. Berlin: Mouton de Gruyter.

Thiesen, W. 1996. *Gramática del idioma Bora*. Pucallpa: Instituto Lingüístico de Verano.

Thomas, D. D. 1971. *Chrau grammar*. Honolulu: University of Hawai'i Press.

Thomas, Jacqueline M. C. 1970. *Contes, proverbes, devinettes ou énigmes, chants et prières Ngbaka-Ma-Bo (République Centrafricaine)*. Paris: Klincksieck.

Thompson, L. C. 1965. *A Vietnamese grammar*. Seattle: University of Washington Press.

Thompson, Sandra A. 1971. 'The deep structure of relative clauses', pp. 79–94 of *Studies in linguistic semantics*, edited by Charles J. Fillmore and D. T. Langedoen. New York: Holt, Rinehart & Winston.

Tida, Syuntarô 2006. 'A grammar of the Dom language, a Papuan language of Papua New Guinea'. PhD dissertation, University of Kyoto.

Tiss, Frank 2004. *Gramática da Língua Madiha (Kulina)*. São Leopoldo (RS): Oikos.

Tosco, M. 1999a. 'A grammatical summary of Somali'. †RCLT internal document, ANU.

——1999b. 'A grammatical summary of Dhaasanac'. †RCLT internal document, ANU.

——2000. 'Is there an "Ethiopian Linguistic area"?', *Anthropological Linguistics* 42: 329–65.

——2001. *The Dhaasanac language*. Cologne: Rüdiger Köppe.

Trask, R. L. 2000. *The dictionary of historical and comparative linguistics*. Edinburgh: Edinburgh University Press.

Traugott, E. C., A. ter Meulen, J. S. Reilly, and C. A. Ferguson, eds. 1986. *On conditionals*. Cambridge: Cambridge University Press.

Trechter, Sara 1995. 'The pragmatic functions of gender deixis in Lakhota'. PhD dissertation, University of Kansas.

Treis, Yvonne, MS. 'Zur Grammatik des Befehlens, Wünschens, Segnens und Verfluchens im Kambaata (Kuschitisch)'.

Trubetskoy, N. S. 1975. *N. S. Trubetzkoy's letters and notes*, ed. Roman Jakobson. The Hague: Mouton.

Trudgill, P. 2004. *New dialect formation: the inevitability of colonial Englishes.* Oxford: Oxford University Press.

Tsitsipis, L. D. 1998. *A linguistic anthropology of praxis and language shift: Arvanítika (Albanian) and Greek in Contact.* Oxford: Clarendon Press.

Tuldava, J. 1994. *Estonian textbook.* Bloomington: Indiana University.

Ullrich, Jan 2008. *New Lakota dictionary.* Bloomington, IN: Lakota Language Consortium.

Vaillant, A. 1930. 'L'impératif-optatif du slave', *Slavia* 9: 241–56.

Valdivieso, Pilar Gallo 1994. 'Adquisiciones gramaticales en torno al imperativo: lo que se apriende dando "órdenes"', pp. 47–58 of *La adquisición de la lengua española*, by Susana López Ornat, Almudena Fernández, Pilar Gallo, and Sonia Mariscal. Madrid: Siglo Ventiuno de España.

Valentine, J. Randolph 2001. *Nishnaabemwin Reference grammar.* Toronto: University of Toronto Press.

Valenzuela, P. 2003. 'Evidentiality in Shipibo-Konibo, with a comparative overview of the category in Panoan', pp. 33–62 of *Studies in evidentiality*, edited by Alexandra Y. Aikhenvald and R. M. W. Dixon. Amsterdam: John Benjamins.

Vallauri, E. L. 2004. 'Grammaticalization of syntactic incompleteness: free conditionals in Italian and other languages', *SKY Journal of Linguistics* 17: 189–215.

van den Berg, René, and Peter Bachet 2006. *Vitu grammar sketch.* Ukarumpa: SIL.

van der Auwera, Johan 1986. 'Conditionals and speech acts', pp. 107–214 of Traugott et al. 1986.

——2005. 'Prohibitives: why two thirds of the world's languages are unlike Dutch', pp. 25–30 of *Proceedings of the Fifteenth Amsterdam Colloquium*, December 19–21, 2005, edited by Paul Dekker. Amsterdam: University of Amsterdam.

——2006a. 'Imperatives', pp. 565–7 of *Encyclopedia of language and linguistics*, 2nd edn, edited by Keith Brown. Oxford: Elsevier.

——2006b. 'Why languages prefer prohibitives', *Journal of Foreign Languages* 1: 1–25.

——Nina Dobrushina, and Valentin Goussev, 2004. 'A semantic map for imperative-hortatives', pp. 44–66 of *Contrastive analysis in language: identifying linguistic units of comparison*, edited by Dominique Willems, Bart Defrancq, Timothy Colleman, and Dirk Noël. Basingstoke: Palgrave Macmillan.

—— —— ——2005. 'Imperative-hortative systems', pp. 294–7 of *The world atlas of language structures*, edited by Martin Haspelmath, M. Dryer, D. Gil, and B. Comrie. Oxford: Oxford University Press.

——Ludo Lejeune, with Umarani Passuwany and Valentin Goussev 2005a. 'The morphological imperative', pp. 286–9 of *The world atlas of language structures*, edited by M. Haspelmath, M. Dryer, D. Gil, and B. Comrie. Oxford: Oxford University Press.

—— ——with Valentin Goussev 2005b. 'The prohibitive', pp. 290–93 of *The world atlas of language structures*, edited by M. Haspelmath, M. Dryer, D. Gil, and B. Comrie. Oxford: Oxford University Press.

——Andrej Malchukov, and Ewa Schalley, 2009. 'Thoughts on (im)perfective imperatives', pp. 93–106 of *Form and Function in Language Research. Papers in*

Honour of Christian Lehmann, edited by Johannes Helmbrecht et al. Berlin: Mouton de Gruyter.

——and Taeymans, Martine 2004. '**Let's**, in English and in Dutch', pp. 239–47 of *An international master of syntax and semantics: papers presented to Aimo Seppänen on the occasion of his 75th birthday*, edited by Gunnar Bergh. Göteborg: Universitas Gothoburgensis.

van der Wurff, Wim, ed. 2007a. *Imperative clauses in generative grammar: studies in honour of Frits Beuksema*. Amsterdam: John Benjamins.

——2007b. 'Imperative clauses in generative grammar: an introduction', pp. 1–94 of van der Wurff 2007a.

van Driem, G. 1993. *A grammar of Dumi*. Berlin: Mouton de Gruyter.

van Enk, Gerrit J., and Lourens de Vries 1997. *The Korowai of Irian Jaya: their language in its cultural context*. New York: Oxford University Press.

van Everbroek, R. 1969. *Grammaire et exercices lingala*. Anvers-Leopoldville: Standaard-Boekhandel.

van Marle, Jaap 2003. 'Paradigms', p. 239 of *International encyclopedia of linguistics*, 2nd edn, vol. 3, edited by William J. Frawley. Oxford: Oxford University Press.

van Olmen, Daniël, and Johan van der Auwera 2008. '**Ne chante pas**, ou, tout simplement, **Arrête**? Sur la fréquence des constructions prohibitives rétrospectives', pp. 225–33 of *Linguista sum: mélanges offerts à Marc Dominicy à l'occasion de son soixantième anniversaire*, edited by Emmanuelle Danblon et al. Paris: Harmattan.

Vaxtin, N. B. 1992. 'Imperative sentences in Eskimo', pp. 89–98 of *Tipologija imperativnykh konstrukcij* (The typology of imperative constructions), edited by V. S. Xrakovskij. St Petersburg: Nauka.

——2001. 'Imperative sentences in Asiatic Eskimo', pp. 129–44 of Xrakovskij 2001.

Veerman-Leichsenring, Annette 1991. 'Gramatica del popoloca de metzontla (con vocabulario y textos)'. PhD dissertation, University of Amsterdam.

Verma, Manindra K. 2003. 'Bhojpuri', pp. 515–37 of Cardona and Jain 2003.

Verma, Sheela 2003. 'Magahi', pp. 498–514 of Cardona and Jain 2003.

Verstraete, Jean-Christophe 2005. 'Two types of coordination in clause combining', *Lingua* 115: 611–26.

Veselinova, Ljuba N. 2003. 'Suppletion in verb paradigms'. PhD dissertation, University of Stockholm.

——2006. *Suppletion in verb paradigms*. Amsterdam: John Benjamins.

Vidal, A., and H. E. Manelis Klein 1998. 'Irrealis in Pilagá and Toba? Syntactic versus pragmatic coding', *Anthropological Linguistics* 40: 175–97.

Viitso, T.-R. 1998a. 'Fennic', pp. 115–48 of *Uralic languages*, edited by D. Abondolo. London: Routledge.

——1998b. 'Estonian', pp. 115–48 of Abondolo 1998c.

——2003. 'Structure of the Estonian language', pp. 9–92 of *Estonian language*, edited by Mati Erelt. Tallinn: Estonian Academy Publishers.

Vincennes, Louis de, and J. M. Dallet 1960. *Initiation à la langue berbère (Kabylie)*, vol. 1: *Grammaire*. Fort-National: Ficher de documentation berbère.

Vinogradov, V. V. 1947. *Russkij Jazyk* (The Russian language). Moscow: Uchpedgiz.

Volodin, A. P. 1976. *Itel'menskij jazyk* (The Itelmen language). Leningrad: Nauka.

——1992. 'Imperative sentences in Kerek', pp. 98–106 of *Tipologija imperativnykh konstrukcij* (The typology of imperative constructions), edited by V. S. Xrakovskij. St Petersburg: Nauka.

——2001. 'Imperative in Kerek', pp. 145–58 of *Typology of imperative constructions*, edited by V. S. Xrakovskij. Munich: Lincom Europa (translation of Volodin 1992).

Wali, K., and O. N. Koul 1997. *Kashmiri*. London: Routledge.

Waltereit, Richard 2002. 'Imperatives, interruption in conversation, and the rise of discourse markers: a study of Italian *guarda*', *Linguistics* 40: 987–1010.

Waltke, Bruce K., and M. O'Connor 1990. *An introduction to Biblical Hebrew syntax*. Winona Lake, IN: Eisenbrauns.

Waltz, Nathan 1976. *Hablemos el guanano: una gramamtca pedagogica del guanano*. Bogotá: Instituto Lingüístico de Verano.

——2000. 'El Wanano', pp. 453–67 of *Lenguas indígenas de Colombia: una visión descriptiva*, edited by M. S. González de Pérez and M. L. Rodríguez de Montes. Santafé de Bogotá: Instituto Caro y Cuervo.

——and Carolyn Waltz 1997. *El agua, la roca y el humo: estudios sobre la cultura wanana del Vaupés*. Santafé de Bogotá: Instituto Lingüístico de Verano.

Wang Jun and Zheng Guoqiao 1993. *An outline grammar of Mulao*. Canberra: National Thai Studies Centre, ANU.

Watkins, Calvert 1963. 'Preliminaries to a historical and comparative analysis of the syntax of the Old Irish verb', *Celtica* 6: 1–49.

——2001. 'An Indo-European linguistic area and its characteristics: ancient Anatolia. Areal diffusion as a challenge to the comparative method?', pp. 44–63 of *Areal diffusion and genetic inheritance: problems in comparative linguistics*, edited by Alexandra Y. Aikhenvald and R. M. W. Dixon. Oxford: Oxford University Press.

Watkins, Laurel J. 1984. *A grammar of Kiowa*. Lincoln: Nebraska University Press.

Watkins, T. Arwyn 1993. 'Welsh', pp. 289–348 of *The Celtic languages*, edited by Martin J. Ball with James Fife. London: Routledge.

Watters, D. 2002. *Grammar of Kham*. Cambridge: Cambridge University Press.

——(with the participation of Yogendra P. Yadava, Madhav P. Pokharel, and Balaram Prasain) 2005. *Notes on Kusunda grammar (a language isolate of Nepal)*. Kathmandu: National Foundation for the Development of Indigenous Nationalities.

Watts, R. 2003. *Politeness*. Cambridge: Cambridge University Press.

Weber, D. J. 1989. *A grammar of Huallaga (Huánuco) Quechua*. Berkeley: University of California Press.

——1996. *Una gramática del quechua del Huallaga (Huánuco)*. Lima: Instituto Lingüístico de Verano.

——and W. Thiesen, forthcoming. *A grammar of Bora*.

Weinreich, Uriel 1963. 'On the semantic structure of language', pp. 142–216 of *Universals of language*, edited by Joseph H. Greenberg. Cambridge, MA: MIT Press.

Weir, E. M. H. 1984. 'A negação e outros tópicos da gramática Nadëb'. MA thesis. Universidade Estadual de Campinas, Brazil.

——1994. 'Nadëb', pp. 291–324 of *Typological studies in negation*, edited by P. Kahrel and R. Van Den Berg. Amsterdam: John Benjamins.

Welch, Bettie, and Birdie West 2000. 'El tucano', pp. 419–33 of *Lenguas indígenas de Colombia: una visión descriptiva*, edited by M. S. González de Pérez and M. L. Rodríguez de Montes. Santafé de Bogotá: Instituto Caro y Cuervo.

Wendel, T. D. 1993. 'A preliminary grammar of Hanga Hundi'. MA thesis, University of Texas at Arlington.

Werner, H. 1997. *Die kettische Sprache*. Wiesbaden: Harrassowitz.

West, Birdie 1980. *Gramática popular del Tucano*. Santafé de Bogotá: Instituto Lingüístico de Verano.

Whaley, L. J. 1997. *Introduction to typology: the unity and diversity of language*. London: Sage.

Wheeler, A. 1987. *Gantëya Bain: el pueblo siona del río Putumayo, Colombia*, vol. 1: *Etnología, gramática, textos*. Santafé de Bogotá: Instituto Lingüístico de Verano.

Whitney, William Dwight 1875. *The life and growth of language: an outline of linguistic science*. London: Henry S. King.

——1924 (1891). *Sanskrit grammar*. Leipzig: Breitkopf & Härtel.

Wierzbicka, Anna 2003. *Cross-cultural pragmatics: the semantics of human interaction*. Berlin: Mouton de Gruyter.

Wiliam, Urien 1960. *A short Welsh grammar*. Llandybie: Llyfrau'r Dryw.

Wilkins, David P. 1989. 'Mparntwe Arrente (Aranda): studies in the structure and semantics of grammar'. PhD dissertation, ANU.

——2003. 'Why pointing with the index finger is not a universal (in sociocultural and semiotic terms)', pp. 171–215 of *Pointing: where language, culture, and cognition meet*, edited by Sotaro Kita. Mahwah, NJ: Lawrence Erlbaum Associates.

Wilson, Peter J. 1982. *Una descripción preliminar de la gramática del Achagua (Arawak)*. Bogotá: Asociación Instituto Lingüístico de Verano.

Wistrand Robinson, L., and J. Armagost 1990. *Comanche dictionary and grammar*. Arlington: SIL and University of Texas at Arlington.

Woldemariam, Hirut 2007. 'The grammar of Haro with comparative notes on the Ometo Linguistics group'. PhD dissertation, Addis Ababa University.

Wolf, H., forthcoming. 'Past tense imperatives' ('Imperatieven in de verleden tijd').

Wolfart, H. C. 1996. 'Sketch of Cree, an Algonquian language', pp. 390–439 of *Handbook of North American Indian languages*, vol. 17, edited by I. Goddard. Washington, DC: Smithsonian Institution.

Woodbury, A. C. 1986. 'Interactions of tense and evidentiality: a study of Sherpa and English', pp. 188–202 of *Evidentiality: the linguistic coding of epistemology*, edited by W. L. Chafe and J. Nichols. Norwood, NJ: Ablex.

Xrakovskij, V. S., ed. 1992a. *Tipologija imperativnykh konstrukcij* (The typology of imperative constructions). St Petersburg: Nauka.

——1992b. 'Typological questionnaire for the description of imperative constructions', pp. 50–54 of Xrakovskij 1992a.

——ed. 2001. *Typology of imperative constructions*. Munich: Lincom Europa.

——and A. P. Volodin 2001. *Semantika russkogo imperativa*. Moscow: URSS.

Yadav, Ramawatar 2003. 'Maithili', pp. 477–97 of Cardona and Jain 2003.

Young, Robert W., and William Morgan 1969. *The Navaho language: the elements of Navaho grammar with a dictionary in two parts containing basic vocabularies of Navaho and English*. Education Division, United States Indian Service.

————1980. *The Navajo language: a grammar and colloquial dictionary*. Albuquerque: University of New Mexico.

Zaicz, Gabor 1998. 'Mordva', pp. 184–218 of Abondolo 1998c.

Zavala, Roberto 2006. 'Serial verbs in Olutec (Mixean)', pp. 273–300 of Aikhenvald and Dixon 2006.

Zeitoun, Elizabeth 2007. *A grammar of Mantauran (Rukai)*. Taipei: Institute of Linguistics, Academia Sinica.

Zepeda, Ofelia 1988. *A Papago grammar*. Tucson: University of Arizona Press.

Zeshan, U. 1999. 'A grammatical summary of IPSL'. †RCLT internal document, ANU.

——2000. 'A grammatical summary of American Sign Language'. †RCLT internal document, La Trobe University.

——2004. 'Interrogative constructions in signed languages: crosslinguistic perspectives', *Language* 80: 7–39.

Zuber, R. 1983. *Non-declarative sentences*. Amsterdam: John Benjamins.

Index of authors

Index of languages, linguistic families and areas

Note that the genetic affiliation of each language is shown in parentheses after the language name. For example, Estonian (Balto-Finnic, Finno-Ugric, Uralic) indicates that the Estonian language belongs to the Balto-Finnic subgroup of the Finno-Ugric branch of the Uralic family. Only established subgroupings, concerning which there is consensus, are given. Papuan and Australian are given as areal indications, not as genetic families.

Index of subjects

Note that entries in the glossary and in the fieldworker's guide do not appear in this index.